Windows Server® 2012

Hyper-V® Installation and Configuration Guide

Windows Server® 2012

Hyper-V® Installation and Configuration Guide

Aidan Finn

Patrick Lownds

Michel Luescher

Damian Flynn

SYBEX®

A Wiley Brand

Acquisitions Editor: Mariann Barsolo

Development Editor: David Clark

Technical Editor: Hans Vredevoort

Production Editor: Eric Charbonneau

Copy Editor: Sharon Wilkey

Editorial Manager: Pete Gaughan

Production Manager: Tim Tate

Vice President and Executive Group Publisher: Richard Swadley

Vice President and Publisher: Neil Edde

Book Designers: Judy Fung and Maureen Forys, Happenstance Type-O-Rama

Compositor: Cody Gates, Happenstance Type-O-Rama

Proofreader: Rebecca Rider

Indexer: Ted Laux

Project Coordinator, Cover: Katherine Crocker

Cover Designer: Ryan Sneed

Cover Image: © Michael Knight / iStockphoto

Copyright © 2013 by John Wiley & Sons, Inc., Indianapolis, Indiana

Published simultaneously in Canada

ISBN: 978-1-118-48649-8
ISBN: 978-1-118-67701-8 (ebk.)
ISBN: 978-1-118-65143-8 (ebk.)
ISBN: 978-1-118-65149-0 (ebk.)

For general information on our other products and services or to obtain technical support, please contact our Customer Care Department within the U.S. at (877) 762-2974, outside the U.S. at (317) 572-3993 or fax (317) 572-4002.

Wiley publishes in a variety of print and electronic formats and by print-on-demand. Some material included with standard print versions of this book may not be included in e-books or in print-on-demand. If this book refers to media such as a CD or DVD that is not included in the version you purchased, you may download this material at http://booksupport.wiley.com. For more information about Wiley products, visit www.wiley.com.

Library of Congress Control Number: 2012956397

Dear Reader,

Thank you for choosing *Windows Server 2012 Hyper-V Installation and Configuration Guide*. This book is part of a family of premium-quality Sybex books, all of which are written by outstanding authors who combine practical experience with a gift for teaching.

Sybex was founded in 1976. More than 30 years later, we're still committed to producing consistently exceptional books. With each of our titles, we're working hard to set a new standard for the industry. From the paper we print on to the authors we work with, our goal is to bring you the best books available.

I hope you see all that reflected in these pages. I'd be very interested to hear your comments and get your feedback on how we're doing. Feel free to let me know what you think about this or any other Sybex book by sending me an email at nedde@wiley.com. If you think you've found a technical error in this book, please visit http://sybex.custhelp.com. Customer feedback is critical to our efforts at Sybex.

Best regards,

Neil Edde
Vice President and Publisher
Sybex, an Imprint of Wiley

To my family and friends, who have made this possible by helping and supporting me over the years.
—Aidan Finn

I would like to dedicate this book to my family, friends, colleagues, and most of all to my wife, Lisa, and our precious children.
—Patrick Lownds

For my family, friends, and colleagues who have been supporting and inspiring me all the time.
—Michel Luescher

This book is dedicated to my brilliant and beautiful wife, Breege. She has been my inspiration, my motivation, and my rock.
—Damian Flynn

Acknowledgments

When I first thought about writing this book back in 2011, I thought it might be something that I could do alone over a short period. But then we started to learn how much had changed in Windows Server 2012, and how much bigger Hyper-V had become. I knew that I would need a team of experts to work with on this project. Patrick Lownds, Michel Luescher, Damian Flynn, and Hans Vredevoort were the best people for the job. Luckily, they were willing to sign up for the months of hard work that would be required to learn this new version of Windows Server 2012 and Hyper-V, do the research, annoy the Microsoft project managers, and reach out to other members of the community. Thank you to my coauthors, Patrick, Michel, and Damian, for the hard work that you have done over the past few months; I have learned a lot from each of you during this endeavor. When it came to picking a technical reviewer, there was one unanimous choice, and that was Hans, a respected expert in Hyper-V and System Center. Hans' name might not be on the cover, but his input can be found in every chapter. Thank you (again) Hans, for taking the time to minimize our mistakes.

Patrick, Damian, and Hans are Microsoft Most Valuable Professionals (MVPs) like myself. The MVP program is a network of experts in various technologies. There are many benefits to achieving this award from Microsoft, but one of the best is the opportunity to meet those experts. Many of these people helped with this project and you'll see just some of their names in these acknowledgments.

Starting to write a book on a product that is still being developed is quite a challenge. There is little documentation, and the target keeps moving. Many people helped me during this endeavor. Who would think that a person who barely passed lower-grade English when he finished school could go on to have his name on the covers of five technical books? Mark Minasi (MVP) is the man I have to thank (or is it blame?) for getting me into writing books. Mark once again was there to help when I needed some information on BitLocker. Jeff Wouters, a consultant in the Netherlands, loves a PowerShell challenge. Jeff got a nice challenge when a PowerShell "noob" asked for help. Thanks to Jeff, I figured out some things and was able to give the reader some better real-world solutions to common problems. If you're searching for information on Windows Server 2012 storage, there's a good chance that you will come across Didier Van Hoye (aka Workinghardinit). Didier is a fellow Virtual Machine (Hyper-V) MVP and has been there to answer quick or complex questions. Brian Ehlert (MVP) is an important contributor on the TechNet Hyper-V forum and is an interesting person to talk to for alternative points of view. Brian helped me see the forest for the trees a number of times. We have a great Hyper-V MVP community in Europe; Carsten Rachfahl found some functionality that we weren't aware of and helped us understand it. A new guy on the MVP scene is Thomas Maurer, and his blog posts were useful in understanding some features.

Thanks to the MVP program, we gain access to some of the people who make the products we work with and write about. Numerous Microsoft program managers answered questions or explained features to me. Ben Armstrong (aka the Virtual PC Guy) leads the way in Virtual Machine expertise, has answered many questions for us as a group, provides great information on his blog, and has been a huge resource for us. Thanks too to Senthil Rajaram for doing his best to explain 4K sector support to me; any mistakes here are mine! Charley Wen, John Howard, and Don Stanwyck all helped me come to grips with the massive amount of change in Windows Server networking. Joydeep Buragohain also provided me with great information on

Windows Server Backup. We Hyper-V folks rely on Failover Clustering, and we also had great help from their program managers, with Rob Hindman and Elden Christensen leading the way. Thanks to all for your patience, and I hope I have reproduced your information correctly.

I would also like to thank MicroWarehouse, my employer, for the flexibility to allow me to work on projects like this book. The opportunity that I have to learn and to share in my job is quite unique. I work with some of the best customer-focused experts around, and I've learned quite a bit from them.

Of course, the book wouldn't be possible at all without the Sybex team. This book kept growing, and there was a lot more work than originally estimated. Pete Gaughan, the acquisitions and developmental editor, David Clark, Eric Charbonneau, and a whole team of editors made this possible. In particular, I want to pay special thanks to Mariann Barsolo, who believed in this project from day 1, and made a huge effort to get things moving.

My family are the ones who made everything possible. Thank you to my mom, dad, and sister for the encouragement and help, in good times and bad. From the first moment, I was encouraged to learn, to question why and how, to think independently, and to eventually become a pain in the backside for some! Without my family, I would not be writing these acknowledgments.

—*Aidan Finn*

Third time lucky! It takes personal commitment and dedication to write a book, but it takes a lot of support as well. It would not be possible without help from family, friends, and colleagues. I would like to thank my wife, Lisa, for helping to keep everything together, and my children for being especially patient. A special thanks to the editors at Sybex for taking on this book project and for making the dream a reality; my coauthors, Aidan, Damian, and Michel; plus our technical reviewer, Hans. Finally, I would like to thank a number of people for helping me along the way: Ben Armstrong, Patrick Lang, Rob Hindman, Mallikarjun Chadalapaka, Subhasish Bhattacharya, Jose Barreto, and Allison Hope.

—*Patrick Lownds*

I never thought that I would write a book, as I'm not a big fan of reading books. But when Aidan and Patrick asked me in early 2012 if I would think about providing a few chapters on a Windows Server 2012 Hyper-V book, I couldn't resist. Working with this excellent team of knowledgeable experts was a great experience that I didn't want to miss, and it was also an honor to be part of it. Thank you guys for this great opportunity!

It was quite a challenge writing a book on a product that is still under development. Therefore, I would like to express my special thanks to the great people who took time out from their busy schedules to share their experience, discuss features, or give me very good advice for this book. A big thank you goes to the following people: Nigel Cain, Paul Despe, Ronny Frehner, Florian Frommherz, Michael Gray, Asaf Kuper, Thomas Roettinger, Cristian Edwards Sabathe, Jian Yan, and Joel Yoker.

Hans Vredevoort deserves a very special thanks for all the great feedback provided and the interesting discussions we had. Of course I also would like to thank the Sybex team for their support and patience. Even though I squirmed when I received your status mails telling me I missed another deadline, you helped me keep pushing to make this all happen.

And last but certainly not least, thanks a lot, Carmen, for supporting me with all my crazy ideas and projects. This all wouldn't be possible without you.

—*Michel Luescher*

During the process of writing my first book, I promised myself that I would never do it again. So, what changed? As the project progressed, and the products continued to be revised through their release milestones, somewhere along the path to publishing the challenge of writing also changed to become enjoyable. When Aidan then suggested the idea for this book while we were walking around Seattle one cold night in February, I was surprised to hear myself agreeing to the idea and feeling the excitement of being involved! It was not many weeks after that when we had the pleasure of meeting our representative from Sybex in Las Vegas to sell the plan; thanks to Aidan we were on a roll.

Collecting, selecting, and validating all the details that goes into the chapters of a technical book clearly requires a lot of input from many different people, especially respected experts and co-authors, Aidan, Patrick, and Michel, with whom it has been an honor working alongside. Our technical editor, Hans, deserves a very special consideration. It was his job to read our work in its earliest format, dissect our content to ensure its accuracy, and create labs to reproduce our implementation guides and recommendations. This was no minor achievement, yet he continued to excel at finding and squashing the bugs, and forcing us to rethink all the time. Thank you Hans.

In addition, a very special thanks to my work colleagues at Lionbridge, especially Oyvind, Steve, Benny, and the "Corp IT" Team for supporting and encouraging me, and my infamous "Lab." I would also like to acknowledge the fantastic team at Microsoft, who has, over the years, put up with my "constructive" criticism (of products) and helped me out of many complex road blocks, especially Pat Fetty, Nigel Cain, and Travis Wright. The reality is that there are many people who helped along the way, too many to list individually; I offer my sincere appreciation to you all.

I would like to thank my amazing wife for always providing direction to my life; my parents for their enduring support and encouragement; my family—immediate, extended, and acquired by marriage! Their constant support and belief in me are the best gifts they could ever give.

—*Damian Flynn*

About the Authors

Aidan Finn, MVP, has been working in IT since 1996. He is employed as the Technical Sales Lead by MicroWarehouse, a distributor (and Microsoft Value Added Distributor) in Dublin, Ireland. In this role, he works with Microsoft partners in the Republic of Ireland and Northern Ireland, evangelizing Microsoft products such as Windows Server, Hyper-V, Windows client operating systems, Microsoft System Center, and cloud computing. Previously, Aidan worked as a consultant and administrator for the likes of Amdahl DMR, Fujitsu, Barclays, and Hypo Real Estate Bank International, where he dealt with large and complex IT infrastructures. Aidan has worked in the server hosting and outsourcing industry in Ireland, where he focused on server management, including VMware VI3, Hyper-V, and System Center.

Aidan was given the Microsoft Most Valuable Professional (MVP) award in 2008 in the Configuration Manager expertise. He switched to the Virtual Machine expertise in 2009 and has been renewed annually since then. Aidan has worked closely with Microsoft in Ireland and the United Kingdom, including presentations, road shows, online content, podcasts, and launch events. He has also worked in the community around the world, presenting at conferences and participating in podcasts.

When Aidan isn't at work, he's out and about with camera in hand, lying in a ditch, wading through a bog, or sitting in a hide, trying to be a wildlife photographer. Aidan was the lead author of *Mastering Hyper-V Deployment* (Sybex, 2010). He is one of the contributing authors of *Microsoft Private Cloud Computing* (Sybex, 2012), *Mastering Windows Server 2008 R2* (Sybex, 2009), and *Mastering Windows 7 Deployment* (Sybex, 2011).

Aidan runs a blog at www.aidanfinn.com, where he covers Windows Server, Hyper-V, System Center, desktop management, and associated technologies. Aidan is also on Twitter as @joe_elway.

Patrick Lownds is a senior solution architect at Hewlett Packard's TS Consulting, EMEA in the Data Center Consulting practice and is based out of London. Patrick is a current Virtual Machine Most Valuable Professional (MVP) and a Microsoft Virtual Technology Solution Professional (v-TSP). Patrick has worked in the IT industry since 1988 and has worked with a number of technologies, including Windows Server Hyper-V and System Center.

In his current role, he works mainly with the most recent versions of Windows Server and System Center and has participated in both the Windows Server 2012 and System Center 2012 SP1 Technology Adoption Programs.

Patrick has also contributed to *Mastering Hyper-V Deployment* (Sybex 2010) and *Microsoft Private Cloud Computing* (Sybex, 2012). He blogs and tweets in his spare time and can be found on Twitter as @patricklownds.

Michel Luescher is a senior consultant in the Consulting Services division at Microsoft Switzerland. Primarily, Michel is focused on datacenter architectures and works with Microsoft's enterprise customers. In this role, he works mainly with the latest versions of Windows Server and System Center to build datacenter solutions, also known as the Microsoft private cloud. He joined Microsoft in January 2009 and has since been working very closely with the different divisions and communities, including several product groups at Microsoft. Michel has worked with Windows Server 2012 since the first release back in September 2011 and is involved in various rapid deployment programs (RDPs) and technology adoption programs (TAPs), helping Microsoft customers with the early adoption of the pre-released software.

Michel is a well-known virtualization and datacenter specialist and regularly presents at events. On his blog at www.server-talk.eu, Michel writes about Microsoft virtualization and private cloud. On Twitter you will find him as @michelluescher.

Damian Flynn, Cloud and Datacenter Management MVP, is an infrastructure architect at Lionbridge Technology, a Microsoft Gold Certified Partner. Damian, based in Ireland, is responsible for incubating new projects, architecting business infrastructure and services, and sharing knowledge, while leveraging his continuous active participation in multiple Microsoft TAPs with over 18 years IT experience. He blogs at www.damianflynn.com and tweets from time to time as @damian_flynn. He has published numerous technical articles, coauthored *Microsoft Private Cloud Computing* (Sybex, 2012), presented at various conferences including Microsoft TechEd, and contributes code on CodePlex.

Contents at a Glance

Contents

Introduction

Windows Server 2012 Hyper-V brings something new to the market. Microsoft marketing materials claim that this release goes "beyond virtualization." That might seem like hyperbole at first, but take some time to look at how you can change the way IT works by building a private, public, or hybrid cloud with Hyper-V as the engine of the compute cluster. Then you'll understand how much work Microsoft put into this release.

The original release of Hyper-V was the butt of many jokes in the IT industry. The second release, Windows Server 2008 R2, brought respectability to Hyper-V, and combined with the System Center suite, was a unique offering. It was clear that Microsoft was focusing on service, not servers, recognizing what businesses value, and empowering IT staff to focus on engineering rather than on monotonous mouse-click engineering. Then came the Windows Server 2012 announcements at the Build conference in Anaheim, California, in 2011. Even Microsoft's rivals were staggered by the scale of the improvements, choosing to believe that the final release would include just a fraction of them.

We now know that Microsoft took an entire year after the release of Windows Server 2008 R2 to talk to customers, gather requirements and desires, and plan the new release. They listened; pain points such as the lack of supported NIC teaming were added, difficulties with backup in Hyper-V clusters were fixed, and little niggles that caused administration annoyance had their corners rounded. More important, Microsoft had a vision: Windows Server 2012 would be "built from the cloud up" (another line from Microsoft's marketing). This is the first hypervisor designed to be used in a cloud rather than trying to build wrappers around something that focuses on servers first. Many features were added and improved to enable a business to deploy a private cloud, or a service provider to build a flexible, secure, and measured multi-tenant public cloud. Much of this release is ready to go now, but Microsoft built for the future too, with support for emerging technologies and scalability that is not yet achievable in the real world.

Usually with a Microsoft release, you'll hear headlines that make you think that the product is designed just for massive enterprises with hundreds of thousands of employees. Windows Server 2012 Hyper-V includes features that honestly are intended for the upper end of the market, but some of the headline features, such as SMB3.0 storage or Hyper-V Replica, were designed to deal with the complexities that small/medium enterprises have to deal with too.

This book is intended to be your reference for all things Windows Server 2012 Hyper-V. The book was written by three MVPs and a Microsoft consultant who give you their insight on this product. Every chapter aims to give you as much information as possible. Starting from the basics, each chapter will bring you through concepts, showing you how to use and configure features, and lead you to the most complex designs. Most chapters include scenarios that show you how to use Windows Server 2012 Hyper-V in production, in customer sites or your own.

PowerShell was added in Windows Server 2012, and you'll find lots of PowerShell examples in this book. This was a deliberate strategy. Most IT pros who have not used PowerShell are scared of this administration and scripting language, because it is different from how they normally work. Pardon the pun, but it is powerful, enabling simple tasks to be completed more quickly, and enabling complex tasks (such as building a cluster) to be done with a mouse click. You don't need to be a programmer to get to a point where you use PowerShell. None of this book's authors are programmers, and we use the language to make our jobs easier. If you read this book, you will find yourself wanting to use and understand the examples, and hopefully you'll start writing and sharing some scripts of your own.

The book starts with the basics, such as explaining why virtualization exists. It then moves through the foundations of Hyper-V that are common to small or large enterprises; gets into the fun, deep, technical complexities; and returns to common solutions once again, such as disaster recovery, backup, and virtual desktop infrastructure.

Who Should Read This Book

We are making certain assumptions regarding the reader here. You are

◆ Experienced in working with IT

◆ Familiar with terminology such as VLAN, LAN, and so on

◆ Comfortable with installing Windows Server

This book is not intended to be read by a person starting out in the IT industry. You should be comfortable with the basics of server administration and engineering concepts.

The intended audience includes administrators, engineers, and consultants who are working, or starting to work, with virtualization. If you are a Hyper-V veteran, you should know that this release includes more new functionality than was in previous releases combined. If you have experience with another virtualization product, don't assume that your knowledge transfers directly across; every hypervisor does things differently, and Windows Server 2012 Hyper-V includes functionality not yet seen in any of its rivals.

You don't have to work for a Fortune 500 company to get value from this book. Let's face it; that would be a rather small market for a publisher to sell to! This book is aimed at people working in all parts of the market. Whether you are a field engineer providing managed services to small businesses or an architect working for a huge corporation, we have something for you here. We'll teach you the theory and then show you different ways to apply that knowledge.

What's Inside

Here is a glance at what's in each chapter:

Chapter 1: Introducing Windows Server 2012 Hyper-V presents you with the newest version of Microsoft's hypervisor. The chapter starts with a brief history of the evolution of IT, up to the present with virtualization, and introduces you to where businesses are going with cloud computing. The chapter also deals with the thorny issues of licensing Windows Server 2012 and licensing for various virtualization scenarios.

Chapter 2: Deploying Hyper-V Hosts is where you will learn how to get Hyper-V up and running. This is the starting point for all deployments, large or small. The chapter also covers the host settings of Hyper-V.

Chapter 3: Managing Virtual Machines is a long chapter where you will learn how to deploy and configure virtual machines by using the wizards and PowerShell. This chapter also discusses how Dynamic Memory works in Windows Server 2012 and the all new and bigger Live Migration.

Chapter 4: Networking is the chapter that discusses how to connect the services in your virtual machines to a network. The chapter starts with the basics, such as how to create virtual switches, and understanding extensibility, and moves on to more-advanced topics such as supporting hardware offloads/enhancements, Quality of Service (QoS), and converged fabric design. This is also the chapter where you will find NIC teaming.

Chapter 5: Cloud Computing is a logical extension of the Networking chapter, building on many of the concepts there to create clouds. You will learn about private VLANs (PVLANs), network virtualization, resource pools, and resource metering, which will give you all the components to start building the computer cluster of your very own cloud.

Chapter 6: Microsoft iSCSI Software Target will be a popular subject for many readers. Windows Server 2012 has a built-in iSCSI target, allowing you to provide storage over the known and trusted storage protocol. Whether you are a small business that wants iSCSI storage on a budget, or you are building a lab where you need to simulate a SAN, this chapter will give you the material you need.

Chapter 7: Using File Servers Storing your virtual machines on file shares is now supported. This is made possible thanks to technologies such as SMB Multichannel and SMB Direct, which, when combined, can match or even beat legacy storage protocols. You'll learn how to use this new tier of storage, as well as how to build the new scalable and continuously available Scale-Out File Server architecture.

Chapter 8: Building Hyper-V Clusters gives you the knowledge of how to build highly available Hyper-V virtualization or cloud infrastructures. You'll learn about the architecture, the roles of the networks, and best practices for building these clusters. Other subjects include host maintenance and Cluster-Aware Updating.

Chapter 9: Virtual SAN Storage and Guest Clustering reminds us that high availability is not limited to just hosts. The reason we have IT is to have services, and those services often require high availability. This chapter shows you how to build guest clusters, as well as how to take advantage of the new ability to virtualize Fibre Channel SANs.

Chapter 10: Backup and Recovery covers this critical task for IT in any business. Virtualization should make this easier. This chapter discusses how the Volume Shadow Copy Service (VSS) works with Hyper-V virtual machines, and how Windows Server 2012 has improved to support better backup of highly available virtual machines, as well as virtual machines that are stored on SMB3 file shares. This chapter also shows you how small businesses and lab environments can use Windows Server Backup to back up running virtual machines with application consistency.

Chapter 11: Disaster Recovery has great value to businesses. Being able to keep the business operating in the face of a disaster is something that all IT pros and businesses know should be done, but often has proven to be too difficult or expensive. This chapter discusses the theory of disaster recovery (DR) and business continuity planning (BCP), and how Hyper-V can make this achievable.

Chapter 12: Hyper-V Replica is a feature that has gotten a lot of attention since it was first announced; this is built-in disaster recovery replication that is designed to scale for large clouds and to deal with the complexities of the small business. This chapter explains how Hyper-V Replica works, how to deploy it, how to survive a disaster, and how to get your business back to a production site afterward.

Chapter 13: Using Hyper-V for Virtual Desktop Infrastructure gives you a free and scalable solution. Here you will learn how to engineer Hyper-V in this scenario and see how to deal with the unique demands of virtual machines that replace PCs instead of servers.

How to Contact the Authors

We welcome feedback from you about this book or about books you'd like to see from us in the future.

Aidan Finn can be reached by writing to blog@aidanfinn.com. For more information about his work, visit his website at www.aidanfinn.com. You can also follow Aidan on Twitter at @joe_elway.

Patrick Lownds can be contacted via email at Patrick_Lownds@hotmail.com, you can also follow him on Twitter at @PatrickLownds.

Michel can be contacted by mail at michel@server-talk.eu, on Twitter at @michelluescher. And for more information, read his blog at www.server-talk.eu.

Damian Flynn can be reached via email at hyperv@damianflynn.com, you can follow him on Twitter at @damian_flynn, and you can read his technology blog at www.damianflynn.com.

Sybex strives to keep you supplied with the latest tools and information you need for your work. Please check their website at www.sybex.com/go/winserver2012hypervguide, where we'll post additional content and updates that supplement this book should the need arise.

Part 1

The Basics

## Chapter 1

Introducing Windows Server 2012 Hyper-V

One thing has remained constant in IT since the invention of the computer: change. Our industry has moved from highly centralized mainframes with distributed terminals, through distributed servers and PCs, and is moving back to a highly centralized model based on virtualization technologies such as Hyper-V. In this chapter, you will look at the shift that has been happening and will learn what has started to happen with cloud computing. That will lead you to Windows Server 2012 Hyper-V.

With the high level and business stuff out of the way, you'll move on to technology, looking at the requirements for Hyper-V, the scalability, and the supported guest operating systems.

You cannot successfully design, implement, manage, or troubleshoot Hyper-V without understanding the underlying architecture. This will help with understanding why you need to install or update some special software in virtual machines, why some features of virtual machines perform better than others, and why some advanced technologies such as Single-Root I/O Virtualization exist.

One subject that all techies love to hate is licensing, but it's an important subject. Correctly licensing virtualization means that you keep the company legal, but it also can save the organization money. Licensing is like a sand dune, constantly changing and moving, but in this chapter you'll look at how it works, no matter what virtualization platform you use.

We cannot pretend that VMware, the company that had uncontested domination of the virtualization market, does not exist. So this chapter presents a quick comparison of their solution and Microsoft's products. This chapter also gives those who are experienced with VMware a quick introduction to Hyper-V.

We wrap up the chapter by talking about some other important things for you to learn. The most important step of the entire project is the assessment; it's almost impossible to be successful without correct sizing and planning. Microsoft makes this possible via the free Microsoft Assessment and Planning Toolkit. One of the most important new features in Windows Server 2012 is PowerShell. This might not be a PowerShell book, but you will see a lot of PowerShell in these pages. We introduce you to PowerShell, explain why you will want to learn it, and show you how to get started.

In this chapter, you'll learn about

◆ Virtualization and cloud computing

◆ Hyper-V architecture, requirements, and supported guest operating systems

◆ Sizing a Hyper-V project and using PowerShell

Virtualization and Cloud Computing

You have to understand where you have come from in order to know where you are going. In this section, you are going to look at how the IT world started in the mainframe era and is now moving toward cloud computing. You'll also learn why this is relevant to Windows Server 2012 Hyper-V.

Computing of the Past: Client/Server

How computing has been done has changed—and in some ways, almost gone full circle—over the past few decades. Huge and expensive mainframes dominated the early days, providing a highly contended compute resource that a relatively small number of people used from dumb terminals. Those mainframes were a single and very expensive point of failure. Their inflexibility and cost became their downfall when the era of client/server computing started.

Cheap PCs that eventually settled mostly on the Windows operating system replaced the green-screen terminal. This gave users a more powerful device that enabled them to run many tasks locally. The lower cost and distributed computing power also enabled every office worker to use a PC, and PCs appeared in lots of unusual places in various forms, such as a touch-screen device on a factory floor, a handheld device that could be sterilized in a hospital, or a toughened and secure laptop in a military forward operating base.

The lower cost of servers allowed a few things to happen. Mainframes require lots of change control and are inflexible because of the risk of mistakes impacting all business operations. A server, or group of servers, typically runs a single application. That meant that a business could be more flexible. Need a new application? Get a new server. Need to upgrade that application? Go ahead, after the prerequisites are there on the server. Servers started to appear in huge numbers, and not just in a central computer room or datacenter. We now had server sprawl across the entire network.

In the mid-1990s, a company called Citrix Systems made famous a technology that went through many names over the years. Whether you called it WinFrame, MetaFrame, or XenApp, we saw the start of a return to the centralized computing environment. Many businesses struggled with managing PCs that were scattered around the WAN/Internet. There were also server applications that preferred the end user to be local, but those users might be located around the city, the country, or even around the world. Citrix introduced server-based computing, whereby users used a software client on a PC or terminal to log in to a shared server to get their own desktop, just as they would on a local PC. The Citrix server or farm was located in a central datacenter beside the application servers. End-user performance for those applications was improved. This technology simplified administration in some ways while complicating it in others (user settings, peripheral devices, and rich content transmission continue to be issues to this day). Over the years, server processor power improved, memory density increased on the motherboard, and more users could log in to a single Citrix server. Meanwhile, using a symbiotic relationship with Citrix, Microsoft introduced us to Terminal Services, which became Remote Desktop Services in Windows Server 2008.

Server-based computing was all the rage in the late 1990s. Many of those end-of-year predictions told us that the era of the PC was dead, and we'd all be logging into Terminal Servers or something similar in the year 2000, assuming that the Y2K (year 2000 programming bug) didn't end the world. Strangely, the world ignored these experts and continued to use the PC because of the local compute power that was more economical, more available, more flexible, and had fewer compatibility issues than datacenter compute power.

Back in the server world, we also started to see several kinds of reactions to server sprawl. Network appliance vendors created technologies to move servers back into a central datacenter, while retaining client software performance and meeting end-user expectations, by enabling better remote working and consolidation. Operating systems and applications also tried to enable centralization. Client/server computing was a reaction to the extreme centralization of the mainframe, but here the industry was fighting to get back to those heady days. Why? There were two big problems:

◆ There was a lot of duplication with almost identical servers in every branch office, and this increased administrative effort and costs.

◆ There aren't that many good server administrators, and remote servers were often poorly managed.

Every application required at least one operating system (OS) installation. Every OS required one server. Every server was slow to purchase and install, consumed rack space and power, generated heat (which required more power to cool), and was inflexible (a server hardware failure could disable an application). Making things worse, those administrators with adequate monitoring saw that their servers were hugely underutilized, barely using their CPUs, RAM, disk speed, and network bandwidth. This was an expensive way to continue providing IT services, especially when IT is not a profit-making cost center in most businesses.

Computing of the Recent Past: Virtualization

The stage was set for the return of another old-school concept. Some mainframes and high-end servers had the ability to run multiple operating systems simultaneously by sharing processor power. Virtualization is a technology whereby software will simulate the hardware of individual computers on a single computer (the host). Each of these simulated computers is called a *virtual machine* (also known as a *VM* or *guest*). Each virtual machine has a simulated hardware specification with an allocation of processor, storage, memory, and network that are consumed from the host. The host runs either a few or many virtual machines, and each virtual machine consumes a share of the resources.

A virtual machine is created instead of deploying a physical server. The virtual machine has its own guest OS that is completely isolated from the host. The virtual machine has its own MAC address(es) on the network. The guest OS has its own IPv4 and/or IPv6 address(es). The virtual machine is isolated from the host, having its own security boundary. The only things making it different from the physical server alternative are that it is a simulated machine that cannot be touched, and that it shares the host's resources with other virtual machines.

HOST RESOURCES ARE FINITE

Despite virtualization being around for over a decade, and being a mainstream technology that is considered a CV/résumé must-have, many people still don't understand that a host has finite resources. One unfortunate misunderstanding is the belief that virtual machines will extract processor, memory, network bandwidth, storage capacity/bandwidth out of some parallel under-utilized universe.

In reality, every virtual machine consumes capacity from its host. If a virtual machine is using 500 GB of storage, it is taking 500 GB of storage from the host. If a virtual machine is going to use 75 percent of a six-core processor, that machine is going to take that processor resource from the host. Each virtual machine is competing with every other virtual machine for host resources. It is important to understand this, to size hosts adequately for their virtual machines, and to implement management systems that will load-balance virtual machines across hosts.

There are two types of virtualization software for machine virtualization, shown in Figure 1.1:

Type 1 Also known as a *hypervisor*, a Type 1 virtualization solution runs directly on the hardware.

Type 2 A Type 2 virtualization solution is installed on an operating system and relies on that operating system to function.

VMware's ESX (and then ESXi, a component of vSphere) is a Type 1 virtualization product. Microsoft's virtual server virtualization solution, Virtual Server, was a Type 2 product, and was installed on top of Windows Server 2003 and Windows Server 2003 R2. Type 2 virtualization did have some limited deployment but was limited in scale and performance and was dependent on its host operating system. Type 1 hypervisors have gone on to be widely deployed because of their superior scalability, performance, and stability. Microsoft released Hyper-V with Windows Server 2008. Hyper-V is a true Type 1 product, even though you do install Windows Server first to enable it.

FIGURE 1.1
Comparing
Type 1 and Type 2
virtualization

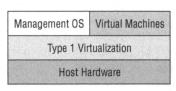
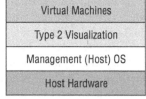

The early goal of virtualization was to take all of those underutilized servers and run them as virtual machines on fewer hosts. This would reduce the costs of purchasing, rack space, power, licensing, and cooling. Back in 2007, an ideal goal was to have 10 virtual machines on every host. Few would have considered running database servers, or heavy-duty or critical workloads, on virtual machines. Virtualization was just for lightweight and/or low-importance applications.

The IT world began to get a better understanding of virtualization and started to take advantage of some of its traits. A virtual machine is usually just a collection of files. Simulated hard disks are files that contain a file system, operating system, application installations, and data. Machine configurations are just a few small files. Files are easy to back up. Files are easy to replicate. Files are easy to move. Virtual machines are usually just a few files, and that makes them relatively easy to move from host to host, either with no downtime or as an automated reaction to host failure. Virtualization had much more to offer than cost reduction. It could increase flexibility, and that meant the business had to pay attention to this potential asset:

◆ Virtual machines can be rapidly deployed as a reaction to requests from the business.

◆ Services can have previously impossible levels of availability despite preventative maintenance, failure, or resource contention.

◆ Backup of machines can be made easier because virtual machines are just files (usually).

◆ Business continuity, or disaster recovery, should be a business issue and not just an IT one; virtualization can make replication of services and data easier than traditional servers because a few files are easier to replicate than a physical installation.

Intel and AMD improved processor power and core densities. Memory manufacturers made bigger DIMMs. Server manufacturers recognized that virtualization was now the norm, and servers should be designed to be hosts instead of following the traditional model of one server equals one OS. Servers also could have more compute power and more memory. Networks started the jump from 1 GbE to 10 GbE. And all this means that hosts could run much more than just 10 lightweight virtual machines.

Businesses want all the benefits of virtualization, particularly flexibility, for all their services. They want to dispense with physical server installations and run as many virtual machines as possible on fewer hosts. This means that hosts are bigger, virtualization is more capable, the 10:1 ratio is considered ancient, and bigger and critical workloads are running as virtual machines when the host hardware and virtualization can live up to the requirements of the services.

Virtualization wasn't just for the server. Technologies such as Remote Desktop Services had proven that a remote user could get a good experience while logging in to a desktop on a server. One of the challenges with that kind of server-based computing was that users were logging in to a shared server, where they ran applications that were provided by the IT department. A failure on a single server could impact dozens of users. Change control procedures could delay responses to requests for help. What some businesses wanted was the isolation and flexibility of the PC combined with the centralization of Remote Desktop Services. This was made possible with virtual desktop infrastructure (VDI). The remote connection client, installed on terminal or PC, connected to a broker when the user started work. The broker would forward the user's connection to a waiting virtual machine (on a host in the datacenter) where they would log in. This virtual machine wasn't running a server guest OS; it was running a desktop OS such as Windows Vista or Windows 7, and that guest OS had all of the user's required applications installed on it. Each user had their own virtual machine and their own independent working environment.

The end-of-year predictions from the analysts declared it the year of VDI, for about five years running. Each year was to be the end of the PC as we switched over to VDI. Some businesses did make a switch, but they tended to be smaller. In reality, the PC continues to dominate, with Remote Desktop Services (now often running as virtual machines) and VDI playing roles to solve specific problems for some users or offices.

Computing of the Present: Cloud Computing

We could argue quite successfully that the smartphone and the tablet computer changed how businesses view IT. Users, managers, and directors bought devices for themselves and learned that they could install apps on their new toys without involving the IT department, which always has something more important to do and is often perceived as slowing business responsiveness to threats and opportunities. OK, IT still has a place; someone has to build services, integrate them, manage networks, guarantee levels of service, secure the environment, and implement regulatory compliance.

What if the business could deploy services in some similar fashion to the app on the smartphone? When we say *the business*, we mean application developers, testers, and managers; no one expects the accountant who struggles with their username every Monday to deploy a complex IT service. With this self-service, the business could deploy services when they need them. This is where cloud computing becomes relevant.

Cloud computing is a term that started to become well-known in 2007. The cloud can confuse, and even scare, those who are unfamiliar with it. Most consider cloud computing to mean outsourcing, a term that sends shivers down the spine of any employee. This is just one way that *the cloud* can be used. The National Institute of Standards and Technology (NIST), an agency of the United States Department of Commerce, published The NIST Definition of Cloud Computing (http://csrc.nist.gov/publications/nistpubs/800-145/SP800-145.pdf) that has become generally accepted and is recommended reading.

There are several traits of a cloud:

Self-Service Users can deploy the service when they need it without an intervention by IT.

Broad Network Access There is a wide range of network connectivity for the service.

Resource Pooling There is a centralized and reusable collection of compute power and resources.

Rapid Elasticity There is ample compute power and resources available if more is required, enabling the user to consume resources as required with no long-term commitment.

Measured Service Resource utilization can be measured, and the information can be used for reporting or cross-charging.

Nothing in the traits of a cloud says that cloud computing is outsourcing. In reality, outsourcing is just one deployment model of possible clouds, each of which must have all of the traits of a cloud:

Public A public cloud is one that is run by a service provider in its own facility. The resources are shared by the tenants (customers).

Private A private cloud comes in two forms. It could be a cloud that is run by a service provider but is dedicated to a single customer. Or a private cloud could be one that is run internally by an organization, with absolutely no outsourcing. The private cloud is the ultimate in server centralization.

Hybrid This is where there is a connection between a private cloud and a public cloud, and the user can choose the best location for the new service, which could even be to span both clouds.

Community In a community cloud, numerous organizations work together to combine their compute resources. This will be a rare deployment in private enterprise, but could be useful in collaborative research environments.

Microsoft's Windows Azure and Office 365, Amazon Elastic Compute Cloud (EC2), Google Docs, Salesforce, and even Facebook are all variations of a public cloud. Microsoft also has a private cloud solution that is based on server virtualization (see *Microsoft Private Cloud Computing*, Sybex 2012). These are all very different service models that fall into one of three categories:

Software as a Service   A customer can subscribe to a Software as a Service (SaaS) product instead of deploying a service in their datacenter. This gives them rapid access to a new application. Office 365 and Salesforce are examples of SaaS.

Platform as a Service   A developer can deploy a database and/or application on a Platform as a Service (PaaS) instead of on a server or a virtual machine's guest OS. This removes the need to manage a guest OS. Facebook is a PaaS for game developers, and Windows Azure offers PaaS.

Infrastructure as a Service   Infrastructure as a Service (IaaS) provides machine virtualization through one of the deployment models and complying with the traits of a cloud. This offers a familiar working environment with maximized flexibility and mobility between clouds.

Windows Server 2012 Hyper-V can be used to create the compute resources of an IaaS cloud of any deployment type that complies with the traits of a cloud. To complete the solution, you will have to use System Center 2012 with Service Pack 1, which can also include VMware vSphere and Citrix XenServer as compute resources in the cloud.

Cloud computing has emerged as the preferred way to deploy services in an infrastructure, particularly for medium to large enterprises. This is because those organizations usually have different teams or divisions for managing infrastructure and applications, and the self-service nature of a cloud empowers the application developers or managers to deploy new services as required, while the IT staff manage, improve, and secure the infrastructure.

The cloud might not be for everyone. If the same team is responsible for infrastructure and applications, self-service makes no sense! What they need is automation. Small to medium enterprises may like some aspects of cloud computing such as self-service or resource metering, but the entire solution might be a bit much for the scale of their infrastructure.

Windows Server 2012: Beyond Virtualization

Microsoft was late to the machine virtualization competition when they released Hyper-V with Windows Server 2008. Subsequent versions of Hyper-V were released with Windows Server 2008 R2 and Service Pack 1 for Windows Server 2008 R2. After that, Microsoft spent a year talking to customers (hosting companies, corporations, industry experts, and so on) and planning the next version of Windows. Microsoft wasn't satisfied with having a competitive or even the best virtualization product. Microsoft wanted to take Hyper-V beyond virtualization—and to steal their marketing tag line, they built Windows Server 2012 "from the cloud up."

Microsoft has arguably more experience at running mission-critical and huge clouds than any organization. Hotmail (since the mid-1990s) and Office 365 are SaaS public clouds. Azure started out as a PaaS public cloud but has started to include IaaS as well. Microsoft has been doing cloud computing longer, bigger, and across more services than anyone else. They understood cloud computing a decade before the term was invented. And that gave Microsoft a unique advantage when redesigning Hyper-V to be their strategic foundation of the Microsoft cloud (public, private, and hybrid).

Several strategic areas were targeted with the release of Windows Server 2012 and the newest version of Hyper-V:

Automation   A cloud requires automation. Microsoft built their scripting and administration language, PowerShell, into Windows Server 2012. The operating system has over 2,500 cmdlets (pronounced *command-lets*) that manage Windows Server functionality. There are over 160 PowerShell cmdlets for Hyper-V.

Using PowerShell, an administrator can quickly make a configuration to lots of virtual machines. An engineer can put together a script to deploy complex networking on a host. A consultant can write a script to build a cluster. A cloud can use PowerShell to automate complex tasks that enable self-service deployment or configuration.

Networking   One of the traits of a cloud is broad network access. This can mean many things to many people. It appears that Microsoft started with a blank sheet with Windows Server 2012 and redeveloped networking for the cloud. Performance was increased, availability was boosted with built-in NIC teaming, the limit of VLAN scalability in the datacenter was eliminated by introducing network virtualization and software-defined networking, partner extensibility was added to the heart of Hyper-V networking, and the boundary of subnets for service mobility was removed.

Storage   It became clear to Microsoft that customers and service providers were struggling with storage. It was difficult to manage (a problem for self-service), it was expensive (a major problem for service providers), and customers wanted to make the most of their existing investments.

Some of the advances in networking enabled Microsoft to introduce the file server as a new, supported, economical, scalable, and continuously available platform for storing virtual machines. Industry standards were added to support management of storage and to increase the performance of storage.

Worker Mobility   It's one thing to have great services, but they are pretty useless if users cannot access them the way that users want to. Previous releases introduced some new features to Windows Server, but Microsoft didn't rest.

Direct Access is Microsoft's seamless VPN alternative that is not used that much. In Windows Server 2012, the deployment of Direct Access was simplified (to a few mouse clicks in Server Manager), the requirements were reduced (you no longer need IPv6 in the datacenter or Forefront User Access Gateway), and performance was increased at the client end in Windows 8 Enterprise.

Microsoft's VDI solution in Windows Server 2008 R2 was mind-boggling, with many moving pieces in the puzzle. Microsoft simplified the architecture of their VDI to be a scenario wizard in Server Manager. The Remote Desktop Protocol (RDP), the protocol used to connect users to remote desktops such as VDI virtual machines, was improved so much that Microsoft had to rename it RemoteFX. Microsoft has tackled the challenges of peripherals being used on the client, streaming rich media, and quality of service over long-distance connections such as WANs and the Internet.

The Cloud   Pretty much every improvement made in Windows Server 2012 Hyper-V plays a role in a public, private, or hybrid cloud. A number of cloud-specific technologies were put in place specifically for cloud deployments, such as Resource Metering. This new feature records the resource utilization of individual virtual machines, giving you one of the NIST traits of a cloud.

We could argue that in the past Microsoft's Hyper-V competed with VMware's ESXi on a price verus required functionality basis. If you license your virtual machines correctly (and that means legally and in the most economical way), Hyper-V is free. Microsoft's enterprise management, automation, and cloud package, System Center, was Microsoft's differentiator, providing an all-in-one, deeply integrated, end-to-end deployment, management, and service-delivery package. The release of Windows Server 2012 Hyper-V is different. This is a release of Hyper-V that is more scalable than the competition, is more flexible than the competition, and does things that the competition cannot do (at the time of writing this book). Being able to compete both on price and functionality and being designed to be a cloud compute resource makes Hyper-V very interesting for the small and medium enterprise (SME), the large enterprise, and the service provider.

Windows Server 2012 Hyper-V

In this section, you will start to look at the technical aspects of Windows Server 2012 Hyper-V.

The Technical Requirements of Hyper-V

The technology requirements of Windows Server 2012 Hyper-V are pretty simple:

Windows Server 2012 Logo   To get support from Microsoft, you should ensure that your hardware (including optional components) have been successfully Windows Server 2012 logo tested. You can check with the manufacturer and on the Microsoft Hardware Compatibility List (HCL) for Windows Server (www.windowsservercatalog.com).

If you're just going to be testing, the logo isn't a requirement but will be helpful. There is a very strong chance that if your machine will run Windows Server 2008 x64 or Windows Vista (this includes PCs and laptops), it will run Windows Server 2012. You should check with the hardware manufacturer for support.

64-Bit Processor   Microsoft is releasing only 64-bit versions of Windows Server, and Hyper-V requires an x64 processor.

32-BIT AND 64-BIT GUEST OPERATING SYSTEMS

You can run both x86 and x64 guest operating systems in Hyper-V virtual machines.

CPU-Assisted Virtualization   The processor must support CPU-assisted virtualization, and this feature must be turned on in the settings of the host machine. Intel refers to this as VT-x, and AMD calls it AMD-V.

Data Execution Prevention   In a buffer overrun attack, a hacker writes an instruction into data memory with the deliberate intention of getting the processor to execute malicious code. With Data Execution Protection (DEP) enabled, memory with data is tagged so that it can never be executed by the processor. This prevents the attack from succeeding. DEP must be available in the server's BIOS and must be enabled in the host machine's settings for Hyper-V to install or start up. This protects the inner workings of Hyper-V from malicious attacks by someone who has logged in to a virtual machine on the host. Intel refers to DEP as the XD bit (Execute Disable bit), and AMD calls it the NX bit (No Execute bit). See your hardware manufacturer's documentation for more information. Every server from a major manufacturer should have this support. Usually issues occur only on consumer-grade PCs and laptops.

SECOND LEVEL ADDRESS TRANSLATION

There was some confusion when Microsoft announced that the desktop version of Windows, Windows 8 (Pro and Enterprise editions), would support Client Hyper-V. This is the same Hyper-V as on Windows Server 2012, but without server functionality such as clustering, Live Migration, NIC teaming, and so on.

Windows 8 Client Hyper-V is great for administrators who want to use a virtual machine for their administrative functions with a different user account, consultants who want a portable demo environment, or testers/developers who want a local or mobile lab.

Client Hyper-V has all of the same requirements as Windows Server 2012—plus one more, and that's what caused the aforementioned confusion. Second Level Address Translation (SLAT) is required on a Windows 8 computer to enable Hyper-V. SLAT is a processor feature that allows Hyper-V to offload the mapping of virtual machine memory to the host's physical memory. This reduces the pressure on the host's processor and improves virtual machine memory performance. Intel refers to SLAT as Extended Page Tables (EPT), and AMD refers to it as Rapid Virtualization Indexing (RVI), which was previously known as Nested Page Tables (NPT). Outside the server space, SLAT is a relatively new feature. For example, Intel Core Duo processors don't have EPT, but Core i processors (i5 and so on) do support it.

Windows Server 2012 Hyper-V does not require SLAT, despite what some misinformed bloggers might state. Having host processors with SLAT does greatly improve the performance of memory-intensive workloads such as SQL Server or Remote Desktop Services session hosts. Note that SLAT has been around in server processors for quite a while—for example, in Intel Xeon X5500 and later.

The Architecture of Hyper-V

Understanding the architecture of Hyper-V is of great value when you are trying to troubleshoot problems or figure out why or how Microsoft accomplishes certain things.

Figure 1.2 shows the architecture of Hyper-V. A common misunderstanding is that Hyper-V is a Type 2 virtualization product. This is because you must install Windows Server 2012 (and the required drivers) to enable Hyper-V, and some people mistakenly believe that Hyper-V must therefore run on top of the operating system. When you enable Hyper-V, the host will reboot twice. During this process, Hyper-V is slipped underneath the Windows Server 2012 installation to run on the hardware at ring –1 on the processor. At this point, the Windows Server installation becomes known as the *Management OS*. Older terms such as *parent* or *root partition* are no longer used for the Management OS. The kernel of the Management OS is running at ring 0 on the host's processor.

FIGURE 1.2
The architecture
of Hyper-V

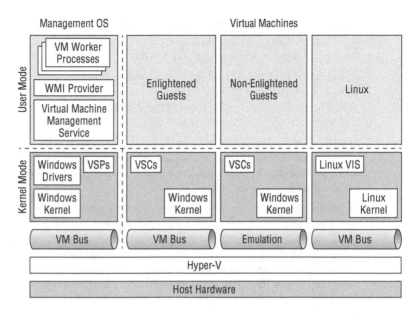

In user mode, you can find the Virtual Machine Management Service (VMMS). This process, called VMMS.EXE, can be found in Control Panel ➢ Services as Hyper-V Virtual Machine Management. This is the service that manages Hyper-V on this host. The Hyper-V-VMMS logs in Event Viewer are a great place to start troubleshooting a problem on a host. A Windows Management Instrumentation (WMI) provider provides a gateway to the VMMS; this is used by tools such as Hyper-V Manager and agents such as those used by System Center.

There is one worker process for every virtual machine that is running on the host. This worker process is used to manage the virtual machine. When you perform Live Migration on a virtual machine, this is managed by the worker process of that virtual machine. If you enable Dynamic Memory for a virtual machine, the worker process is involved in allocating memory to the virtual machine.

And this leads us to the virtual machines. There are three kinds of virtual machines in the world of Hyper-V:

Enlightened Windows Guests This is a virtual machine with a Windows guest OS that has the Hyper-V integration components installed. The Hyper-V integration components are like drivers. They make the guest OS that is installed in a virtual machine aware that it is running in a Hyper-V virtual machine. The integration components add driver support for virtual devices that Hyper-V can offer, such as the SCSI controller (with support for hot add/removal of storage) or the synthetic network adapter. Additional functionality can also be made possible with the installation of integration components, such as Dynamic Memory for supported guest operating systems.

The integration components are referred to as virtualization service clients (VSCs), which Microsoft documentation also calls virtual service clients and virtualization service consumers. VSCs in the virtual machines (in kernel mode) cooperate with virtualization service providers (VSPs) in kernel mode in the Management OS. This pairing is made possible by a communications channel called the VMBus. There is one VMBus channel for every virtual machine that is running. The VMBus is protected by DEP. This means that if an attacker does successfully gain control of the guest OS of a virtual machine, that attacker cannot send instructions to the Management OS via the VMBus to perform a buffer overrun attack.

Enlightened guests are capable of some additional management functions. You can initiate a clean shutdown of a guest OS from a management tool such as the Hyper-V Manager console. This will initiate a shutdown of the guest OS from inside the virtual machine instead of crudely turning the virtual machine off.

Another feature is Key Value Pairs (KVPs). A KVP allows the guest OS to share information with the Management OS. For example, a heartbeat will let the Management OS know that a virtual machine's guest OS is running. A KVP might even return information such as the guest OS's version or computer name.

Emulated Guests   Some organizations need to run the legacy operating systems Windows NT and Windows 2000 Server to keep old applications operating. They might want to upgrade the version of Windows Server but can't because the application vendor has gone out of business. This can be a major problem, because you cannot get hardware to support these operating systems. This means that these installations are potentially great candidates to run as virtual machines where hardware support won't be an issue because the hardware is abstracted by Hyper-V.

The Hyper-V integration components can be installed only in supported guest operating systems. Microsoft does not support legacy operating systems such as Windows NT and Windows 2000 Server. This does not prevent you from running those legacy operating systems in Hyper-V virtual machines. The integration components won't be installed, so we refer to these virtual machines as being emulated. There are no VSCs in these virtual machines. That means there is no support for the virtual SCSI controller, the synthetic network adapter, or Dynamic Memory.

Emulated devices in these virtual machines require extra context switches on the host processor to move between kernel and user mode. This reduces the performance of the virtual machine compared to the potential performance of an equivalent enlightened virtual machine. This is not ideal, but it does allow for legacy operating systems to run as virtual machines on hardware that is still supported by the manufacturer (replacement parts are still available).

Enlightened Linux Guests   Years after the first release of Hyper-V, there are still people who say that Hyper-V does not support Linux being installed in virtual machines. This is untrue; several Linux distributions and versions are supported as guest operating systems by Microsoft.

Linux can be enlightened, much like Windows, by Linux Integration Services. Microsoft has developed these integration services to offer almost all of the same functionality for Linux virtual machines, with some exceptions being Dynamic Memory and support for Volume Shadow Copy Service (a Windows service used for application-consistent backups). There is support for multiple processors, the virtual SCSI controller, clean shutdown, guest OS clock synchronization from the host (KVP), and heartbeat (KVP).

At the time of this writing, the latest version of Linux Integration Services was 3.4. You should use your favorite search engine to check whether that's the latest version, and keep it updated to ensure the best performance and feature availability.

For Microsoft, the word *support* is important. Some companies use the word *support* to say that something works. For Microsoft to support something means that they need to be able to do engineering or have a relationship with another company that can do that engineering. Microsoft supports several Linux distributions and versions. However, Linux Integration Services works very well in a wide range of Linux distributions without support from Microsoft.

Microsoft did something very interesting with Linux Integration Services. The Hyper-V Linux Integration Services are built into the Linux kernel in version 3.3 and later. That means that any Linux distribution/edition that has Linux kernel v3.3 or later has Linux Integration Services for Hyper-V already installed.

Maximum Scalability

One of the goals of virtualization is to increase the density of virtual machines that are running on a host. For larger organizations, this can mean that they have fewer hosts. This reduces space consumption, and the costs incurred by power, cooling, licensing, rack space, support, and so on. Hardware capabilities have increased significantly in recent years, and Moore's law would have us believe that this will only continue. Microsoft did a lot of engineering to increase the maximum specifications of a Windows Server 2012 Hyper-V host, as you can see in Table 1.1.

A logical processor is a thread of execution. A 10-core processor that doesn't have Hyper-Threading available or enabled has 10 threads of execution and therefore has 10 logical processors. If you were to enable Hyper-Threading on that processor, you would have 20 threads (10 cores, each with two threads) or logical processors. A single Windows Server 2012 Hyper-V host can support up to 320 logical processors. That could be configured as follows:

◆ Sixteen 10-core processors with Hyper-Threading enabled

◆ Thirty-two 10-core processors with no Hyper-Threading

MY LOGICAL PROCESSORS ARE MISSING!

If you are lucky enough to have a host with more than 64 logical processors, you might panic if you start Task Manager in the Management OS and can see only 64 logical processors. This is because the Management OS can see a maximum of 64 logical processors. All of the logical processors in the host are available to the virtual machines on that host, so don't worry.

This isn't a problem for the Management OS either. If your Management OS needs to use 64 logical processors, then you have a problem. The Management OS should be nothing but a Management OS for Hyper-V. Don't make it a domain controller, don't install SQL Server, don't turn it into a Remote Desktop Services session host; Microsoft's support services won't like it. Instead, install those applications in virtual machines that are running on the host.

A single host can also have up to 4 TB of RAM. A single host can also support up to 1,024 running virtual machines, and up to 2,048 virtual processors in virtual machines. That is a lot of memory and compute power that you can allocate.

For almost everyone, these numbers are pretty crazy. Most of us will not see a server of this scale in the next few years. But never say never; who wants to be remembered for saying something like 640 KB of RAM will always be enough for people! These numbers do have a real impact. If you make the decision to deploy Windows Server 2012 Hyper-V, then you know that it will scale, probably more than your hosts will ever need to.

TABLE 1.1:   Maximum host scalability

ITEM	MAXIMUM NUMBER
Logical processors per host	320
Physical RAM in a single host	4 TB
Running virtual machines on a single host	1,024
Virtual processors running on a single host	2,048

Does this mean that you should run your entire business on a few gigantic hosts? No; there is a trade-off. You should try to consolidate and reduce your host numbers, but balance this with the risk of having too many eggs in one basket. Failover clusters, if deployed, will give us high availability, but they give us minimized downtime and not zero downtime in the event of host failure.

Prior to the release of Windows Server 2012, a Hyper-V virtual machine was limited to four virtual processors and 64 GB RAM, assuming that the host had four logical processors and 64 GB RAM to provide. That did limit the sorts of workloads that you could run as virtual machines, and left organizations with some applications running physical servers for performance reasons.

Windows Server 2012 aims to make it possible to virtualize as many workloads as possible. To accomplish this, Microsoft has hugely increased the maximum specifications of a virtual machine, as shown in Table 1.2. A virtual machine can now scale out to 64 virtual CPUs and 1 TB RAM. That should make it possible for just about every workload to run in a virtual machine on Windows Server 2012, assuming that the guest OS supports this scalability (it varies). Now the "we didn't virtualize it because it was too resource hungry" excuse cannot be used. Size your hosts (including networking and storage) correctly, virtualize the workloads, and take advantage of the hardware abstraction and flexibility that Hyper-V can provide.

TABLE 1.2:   Maximum virtual machine scalability

ITEM	MAXIMUM NUMBER
Virtual processors per virtual machine	64
Maximum RAM per virtual machine	1 TB

An example of a massive workload is online transaction processing (OLTP), a database service that runs at the back end of a massive web application. Microsoft has blogged about the results of a test comparing a virtual machine that has 64 virtual CPUs with an equivalent physical installation (`http://blogs.technet.com/b/server-cloud/archive/2012/11/08/windows-server-2012-hyper-v-delivers-on-scalability-and-performance-for-virtualized-enterprise-applications.aspx`). With a database supporting 75,000 simulated customers in a stock broker scenario, the virtual machine had nearly 94 percent of the transaction-processing capacity of the physical alternative. That is impressive, because it enables an organization to virtualize these workloads onto fewer physical servers (hosts) and obtain the benefits of virtualization such as cost reduction, better flexibility, easier backup, and more-reliable disaster recovery. In addition, migrating the workloads will be much easier when the hardware becomes obsolete.

Failover Clustering gives us high availability, a feature that caters for unplanned host failure. The virtual machines on the host will stop because the host has stopped, but they will automatically fail over to another host in the same cluster and start up without any human intervention. Some further improvements even allow you to order this process to reflect application or server dependencies. Microsoft has increased the scalability of a cluster of Hyper-V hosts. Table 1.3 shows the cluster scalability of Windows Server 2012 Hyper-V.

A Windows Server 2012 Hyper-V cluster can have 64 nodes (what a physical server is called in a cluster). The cluster may also scale out to contain 8,000 highly available virtual machines.

Note that you must always stay within the limits of a single host while scaling out the cluster, and vice versa. For example, you could have eight hosts, each running 1,000 virtual machines. You cannot scale that cluster out any more because you have reached the virtual machines/cluster limit of 8,000.

This increase to 64 nodes and 8,000 virtual machines enables very large infrastructures, such as those in a public cloud (hosting companies) or huge enterprises, to have fewer clusters and therefore have fewer units of administration. A cluster can start small, and whenever monitoring detects that resource contention is approaching, operators can keep adding hosts, and administrators can add them to the storage and cluster.

TABLE 1.3:   Maximum virtual machine scalability

ITEM	MAXIMUM NUMBER
Maximum hosts in a single cluster	64
Maximum number of virtual machines in a single cluster	8,000

BEWARE OF OLDER INFORMATION

Microsoft started making announcements about the scalability of Windows Server 2012 (previously Windows Server 8) in 2011. The figures increased with every public test release, right up to the announcement of general availability in August 2012. You might find many old blog posts and documents containing information that has become obsolete.

Supported Guest Operating Systems

We could consume several pages of text in this book telling you which guest operating systems are supported by Microsoft. But that would be foolish. The list of guest operating systems is fluid, changing (increasing) over time—particularly in the case of the supported Linux guest operating systems, which has gone from including just SUSE Linux Enterprise Server to all of the commonly used distributions. The latest version (at the time of this writing) could be found at http://technet.microsoft.com/library/hh831531.

In the case of Windows Server 2008 R2 Hyper-V, we found that the list of supported guest operating systems on TechNet was not updated to match the actual list of guest operating systems that Microsoft supported. The updated list was published on the TechNet Wiki site.

There are some things to note:

Integration Components/Services   The latest version of the Window Hyper-V integration components, as they were at the time, were included in Windows 8 and Windows Server 2012. The integration components for Windows guest operating systems get updated from time to time, sometimes by service packs and sometimes by hotfixes. You might need to update the integration components in the guest OS to the latest version. Note that a Windows update released in November 2012 required an upgrade of the integration components of virtual machines with a guest OS of either Windows 8 or Window Server 2012.

Maximum Number of Virtual Processors   A virtual machine will have from 1 to 64 virtual processors. Each virtual processor gives the virtual machine access to a logical processor on the host for increased parallel processing. Some guest operating systems support a smaller number of virtual processors. In the past, some have deliberately exceeded the maximum number of virtual processors for a given guest OS and have usually experienced guest OS crashes very quickly. Remember, these are referred to as maximum supported numbers for a reason; don't expect help from Microsoft other than "reduce the number of virtual processors to a supported number."

CONVERTING MACHINES TO HYPER-V VIRTUAL MACHINES

Be careful if you are converting a physical machine with lots of cores that is running a legacy operating system. The conversion tool will probably create a virtual processor for every core, and the resulting number of virtual processors might exceed the maximum number of virtual processors for the guest OS.

Linux Is Supported   Microsoft does support the major distributions of Linux as guest operating systems on Windows Server 2012 Hyper-V.

Licensing Windows Server 2012 in Virtualization

Stop! Don't turn the page to the next topic! The natural reaction of a techie is to tune out when the topic of licensing is brought up, but the techie plays an important role in getting licensing right, because some technical input is required. Get it right, and not only do you stay legal, but you also save money, and that's more budget for doing more cool things. That should be a good enough reason to keep reading.

ALWAYS ASK A QUALIFIED EXPERT FOR LICENSING ADVICE

This book does not provide licensing expertise. The information contained within this section is intended to introduce you to the topic of Windows Server licensing in virtualization. If you need advice about a specific scenario you are working on, you should contact your reseller (if you are a small/medium customer), your Large Account Reseller (if you are a large customer), or your distributor (if you are a reseller).

The information in this section is subject to change, so you should always check to see that you have the latest information.

Common Misunderstandings in Licensing

People commonly get a few things wrong in terms of licensing Windows Server virtual machines. Here are the corrections to the most common misconceptions:

There Is No Such Thing as Hyper-V Licensing   Some people think that you have to buy licensing for Hyper-V. Actually, there is no Hyper-V licensing. Large Account Resellers (LARs), distributors, and Microsoft all make exactly $0 from Hyper-V. We can question why Microsoft has made so much effort with Hyper-V, but it is probably to protect the presence of the Windows Server brand in the datacenter and to encourage more System Center sales.

Microsoft licenses Windows Server for virtualization. You will purchase the same Windows Server licensing no matter what virtualization product you install on the host.

You Never Assign Licenses to Virtual Machines   Some organizations have gotten into a habit of purchasing one copy of Windows Server for every virtual machine that is created with that guest OS. In their heads, these people think that they have assigned a license to the virtual machine. In fact, according to the licensing rules of Windows Server, they have assigned the license to the host and taken advantage of the virtualization benefits of Windows Server to license the virtual machine.

Licensing Is Mobile but Only under Certain Conditions   There are two general types of Windows Server license that you can purchase. An original equipment manufacturer (OEM) license (www.microsoft.com/oem/en/licensing/sblicensing) is tied to a physical machine when you purchase it. The license cannot be reassigned to another server. That license dies when the server is disposed of. That's why OEM licenses are the least expensive way to license Window Server. You can add mobility to an OEM license by attaching Software Assurance (www.microsoft.com/Licensing/software-assurance/Default.aspx), which enables you to move the license (as well as a number of other benefits). Then, if you dispose of the physical machine originally attached to the OEM license, the license can survive.

A volume license, or VL (www.microsoft.com/licensing/), is one that is bought as part of a Microsoft licensing contract such as Open, Open Value Subscription, Select, or Enterprise Agreement. These programs provide easier licensing management through a portal, and easier operating system deployment through a single-product Multiple Activation Key (MAK) or automated product activation using Key Management Services (KMS), as well as other benefits that a licensing expert can brief you on. A volume license that is assigned to a physical machine can be moved to another physical machine, but cannot be moved again for 90 days.

MSDN, TECHNET, AND SPLA LICENSING

MSDN (http://msdn.microsoft.com/subscriptions/cc150618.aspx) subscriptions are intended to give the licensed person rights to use Microsoft software to design, develop, test, or demonstrate his or her programs on any number of devices.

A TechNet (http://technet.microsoft.com/subscriptions/ms772427.aspx) subscription is intended to give IT pros easy access to Microsoft software for evaluation purposes only.

MSDN and TechNet licensing cannot be used for production systems. This is a mistake that is commonly made by Microsoft partners; those partners can get cheap access to Microsoft software for internal production usage through the Partner Action Pack (https://partner.microsoft.com/40016455) or free access by achieving one or more partner competencies (www.microsoft.com/partner/licensingcalculator/default.aspx).

We do not cover Microsoft's licensing program for hosting companies in this chapter. Services Provider License Agreement (SPLA) is a fluid program in which the only constant is change. SPLA has some unique rules that are very strange when compared to other production licensing programs. Check with your SPLA LAR or distributor for details on virtualization licensing.

Windows Server 2012 Licensing

The licensing for Windows Server had remained relatively unchanged for many years. Microsoft decided to simplify the licensing and align it with that of System Center with the release of Windows Server 2012.

In the past, there were three core editions (nothing to do with the Core Installation type) of Windows Server:

Standard was intended for basic physical servers or small businesses.

Enterprise was used for physical workload high availability (Failover Clustering) and light virtualization.

Datacenter was to be used in dense virtualization.

Table 1.4 compares these three core editions of Windows Server before Windows Server 2012. Some notes about the table's details:

The Indicated Cost The costs shown are Open NL, the most expensive Microsoft volume licensing program, and were correct at the time of writing this book. The U.S. dollar price is used for easy comparison.

Licensing Basis The Standard and Enterprise editions were licensed per server. The Datacenter edition was licensed per processor, and you had to purchase at least two Datacenter licenses, even if the host had only one processor.

Features and Scalability All of the features and scalability of Windows Server were included in the Enterprise and Datacenter editions. The Standard edition supported a smaller number of processors and less RAM and did not have all of the features such as Failover Clustering and Live Migration.

Virtualization Rights A Virtual Operating System Environment (VOSE) is a licensing term for a guest OS, the OS that you install in a virtual machine. You license physical machines for Windows Server. You license virtual machines based on the virtualization rights of the host.

For example, if you purchased VMware vSphere for a host, and wanted to run four virtual machines that would have Windows Server as their guest OS, you would have licensed the host for Windows Server Enterprise and used the host's virtualization rights. This kept the licensing simpler (you license a single host instead of multiple servers) and it was cheaper (one copy of Enterprise at $2,358 was $546 cheaper than four copies of Standard at $726 each). The customer had the choice of installing Windows Server Enterprise on the host too, but they were using VMware vSphere, which was an additional cost, so vSphere was installed on the host instead of Window Server, and Windows Server was installed in the four virtual machines.

TABLE 1.4: Core Windows Server 2008 R2 editions

EDITION	LICENSE BASED ON	FEATURES	SCALABILITY	VIRTUALIZATION RIGHTS	COST
Standard	Per server	Limited	Limited	One free VOSE	$726
Enterprise	Per server	All	All	Four free VOSEs	$2,358
Datacenter	Per processor, minimum of two licenses per server	All	All	Unlimited free VOSEs	$4,809

Note that the indicated Datacenter cost is for two licenses.

PER PROCESSOR IS PER SOCKET IN MICROSOFT LICENSING

In Microsoft licensing, when you see the phrase *per processor*, it means *per socket*. It does not mean that you license each core or logical processor within a CPU. For example, a server with two 10-core processors has two processors or sockets. This server would be licensed for two processors.

Microsoft decided to simplify Windows Server licensing with the release of Windows Server 2012, as you can see in Table 1.5. There are a number of changes:

Windows Server 2012 Standard Edition The Standard edition of Windows Server 2012 now has all of the same features and scalability of the Datacenter edition. The only difference is the number of free VOSEs, or free installations of Windows Server, that are deployed on a licensed host.

Windows Server 2012 Standard has gone from one free guest OS installation of Windows Server to two.

The price of Windows Server 2012 did increase slightly, but this comes with the ability to create a Failover Cluster, and with double the number of VOSEs.

You now have to count physical processors (sockets, not cores or logical processors) when licensing a server for Windows Server 2012. The Standard license covers two processors or sockets. If a server will have four processors, you must purchase two copies of Windows Server 2012 Standard for it; there is no double-install or need to enter two product keys because this is simply an accounting operation.

Windows Server 2012 Standard is now the edition intended for use in light virtualization with optional high availability, such as a large host with a few virtual machines, a host in a small business, or for physical application clusters.

There Is No Enterprise Edition of Windows Server 2012   You can no longer purchase an Enterprise edition of Windows Server. There were two reasons to have the Enterprise edition in the past. The first was to take advantage of features (such as Failover Clustering) or scalability (processors and memory) that the Standard edition did not have. Windows Server 2012 Standard now has those features and scalability at a fraction of the cost of the Enterprise edition.

The other reason was light virtualization. The Enterprise edition entitled you to four free VOSEs on a licensed host. Now if you want four free guest OS installations of Windows Server 2012 Standard, you can purchase two copies of Windows Server 2012 Standard for that host. This stacks the virtualization rights (two copies, each with two free VOSEs) and gives you the same solution. The Enterprise edition of Windows Server 2008 R2 was $2,358, which made each VOSE cost $589.50. Two copies of Windows Server 2012 Standard will cost $1,764, which means each VOSE will cost $441, saving you $148.50 per guest OS installation. You read that right: You can pay less for a Microsoft solution! This will be especially good news for those folks who use a subscription-based volume licensing scheme such as Open Value Subscription.

Windows Server 2012 Datacenter Edition   The Datacenter edition has gone from being a per-single-processor license with a minimum purchase of two per host, to a per-processor license that covers two processors.

TABLE 1.5:   Core Windows Server 2012 editions

EDITION	LICENSE BASED ON	FEATURES	SCALABILITY	VIRTUALIZATION RIGHTS	COST
Standard	Per processor, each license covers two processors	All	All	Two free VOSEs	$882
Datacenter	Per processor, each license covers two processors	All	All	Unlimited free VOSEs	$4,809

VOSEs GUEST OS INSTALLATIONS

The free virtualization rights of Windows Server enable you to install Windows Server (not the desktop OS) on the host that you are licensing. This includes downgrade rights; for example, you can purchase Windows Server 2012 for a host and deploy Windows Server 2008 R2 virtual machines on it.

The VOSE rights are nontransferrable. This means that if you license a host, you cannot use its VOSE rights on another host. You must license that host for the maximum possible number of virtual machines that will run Windows Server, even if those virtual machines are on that host for just 1 second.

The free virtualization rights are not a feature limit; they simply limit how many virtual machines you can install Windows Server into. For example, you could license a host with a single Windows Server 2012 Standard edition, and legitimately deploy 500 Linux virtual machines on it. How you license your Linux guest operating systems is between your employer/customer and the Linux publishers.

The unlimited virtualization rights of the Datacenter edition really are unlimited. There is no "fair usage" clause. Microsoft really is encouraging you to create as many virtual machines on a licensed host as your host and virtualization solution can support.

Hyper-V Server 2012

As usual, Microsoft has released a version of Windows Server that is dedicated to being used as a Hyper-V host. Hyper-V Server 2012 has all of the same Hyper-V and Failover Clustering features and functionality as the Standard and Datacenter editions of Windows Server 2012. There are some major differences:

Virtualization Rights   There are no free virtualization rights for installing Windows Server as a guest OS with Hyper-V Server 2012. At first, you might think that this makes Hyper-V Server 2012 seem pretty useless, but that is not the case. There are a number of uses for this free product:

- A customer might have licensed their Hyper-V hosts using Windows Server 2008 R2 and have no Software Assurance (a benefit of which is free upgrades) or budget to afford new licensing. They can upgrade the hosts to Hyper-V Server 2012 to take advantage of the new features while continuing to use their Windows Server 2008 R2 licensing for their virtual machines' guest operating systems.

- A student might want to use Hyper-V Server on a machine to run virtual machines with time-limited trial editions to learn Microsoft's products and pass certification exams.

- A company might want to designate one or more hosts to run only virtual machines with Linux guest operating systems.

- The virtualization rights of Windows Server would be irrelevant to a VDI deployment, so Hyper-V Server would be suitable for the host.

Administration   Hyper-V Server 2012 does not have a GUI; it is very similar to a Core installation of Windows Server 2012. You are given a basic text wizard to configure the host, but Hyper-V Server 2012 is supposed to be remotely managed and configured using PowerShell, the Remote Server Administration Toolkit (RSAT) for Windows Server 2012 for Windows 8, or enterprise management suites such as System Center 2012 with Service Pack 1.

Virtualization Scenarios

This section describes a few common virtualization scenarios to demonstrate how to use Windows Server 2012 licensing.

SINGLE HOST WITH LIGHT VIRTUALIZATION

You have a host with a single processor. You want to deploy three virtual machines on this host. One of the virtual machines will run Windows Server 2012, a second will run Windows Server 2008, and a third will run CentOS 6.3 (a Linux distribution).

This host can be licensed with a single copy of Windows Server 2012. The Linux distribution is irrelevant to Windows licensing, and there is no licensing cost to creating virtual machines. You simply license the host for the number of virtual machines that will run Windows Server. There will be two virtual machines with Windows Server as their guest OS. Windows Server 2012 Standard edition will cover two VOSEs, including downgrade rights for the guest operating systems.

What would happen if you wanted to have four 8-core processors with Hyper-Threading into that host? That's 64 logical processors. In that case, you will not need 32 copies of Windows Server 2012 Standard; you have four processors, and you'll need two copies of Windows Server 2012 Standard.

Maybe you want to have a host with six virtual machines running Windows Server. If that's the case, you don't need to spend $5,292 on six copies of Windows Server 2012 Standard. You can stack virtualization rights by assigning three copies of Windows Server Standard to the host, each giving you two VOSEs, and resulting in a total of six VOSEs. This will cost $2,646; licensing per host will save you money.

WHAT WILL YOU DO WITH THESE SAVINGS?

As you might guess, Microsoft has a few suggestions on how to spend the money that you save by efficiently licensing your Windows Server virtual machines.

The first way to spend your budget is to buy System Center for each of your hosts to improve your end-to-end management and build a Microsoft public or private cloud. There are three ways to do that:

◆ Buy the System Center Server Management License (SML), licensing all of the System Center components the exact same way as Windows Server 2012.

◆ For anyone buying fewer than 25 hosts, you can purchase the Core Infrastructure Suite (CIS). This comes in Standard or Datacenter editions, and includes both Windows Server and the System Center SML for a host and virtual machines on the host, at a small discount.

◆ If you are buying 25 or more hosts, you can purchase Enrollment for Core Infrastructure (ECI). ECI has identical licensing to CIS but is intended for larger enterprises and has a much bigger discount.

An alternative is to attach Software Assurance (SA) to your host licensing if the license program doesn't already include it. This add-on will entitle you to upgrade your hosts or virtual machines to a newer version of Windows Server when it is released, as well as including other benefits. Many might question the worth of SA, but it does offer some value. Imagine a time in a couple of years when you acquire a new server application that requires Windows Server "vNext." If your hosts don't have Software Assurance, you'll either have to get a new host or a new physical server, or acquire entirely new licensing for the hosts.

Software Assurance has another benefit called Cold Backups for Offsite Recovery. If you replicate virtual machines with a Windows Server guest OS to a disaster recovery (DR) site, those replica virtual machines in the DR site require Windows Server licenses, even if they are powered off. You could use Hyper-V Server 2012 for the DR site (reducing your costs) and take advantage of this benefit. In this case, you would spend less money on SA than you would spend on Windows Server licensing for the DR site hosts and have access to the many other SA benefits.

Single Host with Dense Virtualization

Imagine that you have a host with two processors, and you want to run 12 virtual machines on it with Windows Server as their guest OS. You could legally license this host with six copies of Windows Server Standard, costing $5,292.

Although that option would be legal, it would not be the most cost-effective way to license the host and virtual machines. Instead, you can buy a single copy of Windows Server 2012 Datacenter edition, costing $4,809. This will save you $483 and gives you the flexibility to deploy as many Windows Server virtual machines as your host and virtualization platform will allow.

What if you were going to license a host that has 16 10-core processors with Hyper-Threading enabled (320 logical processors), has 4 TB of RAM, and will run 1,024 virtual machines? This host has 16 processors and therefore will require eight copies of Windows Server 2012 Datacenter edition. This will cost $38,472. That might seem wildly expensive, but it's a lot less than the $451,584 that 512 copies of Windows Server 2012 Standard would cost to license 1,024 VOSEs. If only we all had to work with this size of host and had this problem!

A Small Virtualization Cluster

In this example, we have a small, two-node virtualization cluster with a total of eight virtual machines. Each host will have one or two processors. This is a pretty common deployment in the SME space.

The wrong licensing solution would be as follows: You assume that you could get away with placing four virtual machines on each host. You would purchase two copies of Windows Server 2012 Standard for each host (a total of four licenses) to cover four VOSEs on each host. This should cover any temporary host maintenance or failover scenarios. This solution is not legitimate because it breaks the mobility rules of Windows Server licensing; moving or failing over the four virtual machines from host A to host B would require a license move. OEM licenses cannot move, and volume licenses can move only once every 90 days.

To license this two-node cluster correctly, you need to license each host for the maximum number of virtual machines that could reside on the hosts, even for 1 second. There are eight virtual machines, and therefore you need to license each host for up to eight virtual machines—that is, four copies of Windows Server Standard per host, with a total of eight copies of Window Server Standard for the cluster.

When consulted, a licensing expert should ask whether this company will be planning growth in the near future. If this could result in the company having 12 or more virtual machines, the customer should purchase one Windows Server 2012 Datacenter edition per host. This will be less expensive than stacking copies of Windows Server 2012 Standard edition and will give the customer the flexibility to deploy as many virtual machines as needed without having to purchase additional Windows Server licensing.

By the way, this is very similar to licensing nonclustered hosts that allow virtual machines to move between them with Live Migration.

HYPER-V LICENSING IS FREE

We have not mentioned Hyper-V since we started talking about licensing and mentioned that there is no such thing as Hyper-V licensing. You license your hosts for the number of virtual machines that will license Windows Server. If you've read the facts and studied the examples, you'll see that the following are true:

◆ Licensing virtual machines is much cheaper than licensing physical servers.

◆ There is no cost to installing Windows Server 2012 on a host. This is effectively free because you've paid for the virtual machines with per-host licensing and you have the right to install your host-assigned license on the host if you choose to.

If you don't choose Hyper-V as your virtualization platform, odds are that you'll go with vSphere. You will be licensing your Windows Server virtual machines as documented previously, no matter what virtualization you'll use. You could have elected to use the host licensing to install Windows Server on the host and enable Hyper-V, but instead, you'll have elected to spend a lot more money on an alternative virtualization solution. We'll leave the rest of the VMware vs. Microsoft debate to social media and marketing people. However, we do need to talk a little bit more about VMware.

VMware

Even the most ardent Hyper-V fan has to give VMware a lot of credit. Machine virtualization was driven by VMware, and they have forced Microsoft to create an excellent virtualization solution in Windows Server 2012 Hyper-V. The credible and competitive Windows Server 2012

Hyper-V also forced VMware to reverse an unpopular licensing change and to introduce previously unannounced features in vSphere 5.1.

Migrating from VMware

It is possible to convert VMware virtual machines into virtual machines that you can run on Windows Server 2012 Hyper-V. This is known as virtual-to-virtual (V2V) conversion. There are several ways to accomplish this:

Microsoft Virtual Machine Converter Accelerator   Accelerators are free products that are released by Microsoft to assist you with specific administration tasks. The Microsoft Virtual Machine Converter (MVMC) Solution Accelerator (`http://technet.microsoft.com/library/hh967435.aspx`) converts VMware virtual machines into Windows Server 2012 Hyper-V virtual machines. It supports vSphere 4.0, 4.1, and 5.0 hosts that are managed by vCenter 4.1 or 5.0. This tool is tiny (just over 4 MB) and will not only convert the virtual machine but will also remove the VMware tools and install the Hyper-V integration components. It is limited to supporting Windows 7, Windows Vista, Windows Server 2008 R2, Windows Server 2008, Windows Server 2003 R2 with SP2, and Windows Server 2003 with SP2 guest operating systems.

System Center 2012 with Service Pack 1   System Center Virtual Machine Manager (VMM) has the ability to take control of vSphere installations and convert VMware virtual machines into Hyper-V virtual machines. The solution by itself is not as powerful as the MVMC. However, MVMC can be run using PowerShell. This means that you can use MVMC as part of a bigger solution, such as a System Center Orchestrator run book that could be used in a repeated, automated, and audited fashion to convert lots of virtual machines in a larger project.

Third-Party Solutions   You could use a third-party solution, such as the free V2V Easy Converter by 5nine (`www.5nine.com/vmware-hyper-v-v2v-conversion-free.aspx`). The 5nine solution has a nice feature: It supports guests that run Windows as well as Ubuntu and CentOS, two of the most common free Linux server distributions.

Virtual Machine Migration Toolkit   The Virtual Machine Migration Toolkit (VMMT) is a program that is the result of a partnership between Microsoft and Veeam Software, and is available only to specially selected Microsoft partners in a few countries. This solution uses Microsoft and Veeam products to automate the conversion of lots (perhaps thousands) of vSphere virtual machines into Hyper-V virtual machines.

Transferring Skills to Hyper-V

Although there are many similarities between ESXi or vSphere and Hyper-V, there are also many differences. There is no right way. VMware chose to do things one way, and Microsoft had the opportunity to observe and to do some things very differently. This can cause a learning curve for VMware product veterans who are trying to adapt to Hyper-V.

The biggest difference between the two platforms is the hypervisor architecture. VMware's hypervisor is referred to as a *monolithic hypervisor*. This Type 1 virtualization is bigger than Hyper-V and contains the drivers. This means that VMware writes the drivers and has a smaller HCL, even though this still includes the typical tier 1 servers that you will likely purchase.

You've already seen that Hyper-V places the drivers in kernel mode in the Management OS. This Type 1 virtualization is known as a *paravirtualized hypervisor*.

vSphere uses a file system called the Virtual Machine File System (VMFS). VMware allows you to extend VMFS volumes by using extents, but they do not recommend it unless you have no other choice (http://blogs.vmware.com/vsphere/2012/02/vmfs-extents-are-they-bad-or-simply-misunderstood.html). Meanwhile, Microsoft uses NTFS (with a new file system called ReFS being added) and has no such concerns with extending a file system. VMware uses the file system to orchestrate itself in a cluster. Microsoft uses a host in the cluster to orchestrate Cluster Shared Volumes (CSVs) because they found that it could give much better performance/scalability.

Some things are quite similar. VMware has Raw Device Mapping, and Hyper-V has pass-through disks. These features present raw LUNs on your physical storage directly to virtual machines. The paid-for versions of vSphere include high availability (HA) to create host clusters. All versions of Windows Server 2012 Hyper-V, including Hyper-V Server 2012, include Failover Clustering to give you HA. The non-free versions of vSphere include vMotion, a feature to move virtual machines from one host to another with no downtime to service functionality. Hyper-V includes Live Migration, a similar feature that supports a wide range of virtual machine mobility between hosts.

You cannot assume that one hypervisor is implemented the same way as another. Lots of little details are different on both platforms. Unfortunately, VMware veterans too often assume that they can implement Hyper-V without learning how the Microsoft solution works. The result is an unhappy employer or customer who has to engage with an actual Hyper-V expert to undo the damage and rescue the Hyper-V farm. That same rule can probably be safely applied to Hyper-V engineers assuming that they can deploy vSphere. If you are a VMware expert and you are reading this book to learn, we strongly recommend that you don't skip any pages or sections. You never know which little nugget of information could be the difference between being an IT hero or a villain.

Other Essential Knowledge

This section highlights a few other topics that we strongly recommend that you learn more about.

Microsoft Assessment and Planning Toolkit

Microsoft released and has continued to improve the Microsoft Assessment and Planning Toolkit (MAP) to help engineers and consultants get off to a good start with their deployment projects. MAP (http://technet.microsoft.com/library/bb977556.aspx) is a free tool that is used to scan and assess an existing environment. In the context of planning a Hyper-V project, it will do the following:

◆ Discover physical and virtual machines (including Hyper-V, vSphere, and ESXi)

◆ Use this data to identify the machines that could possibly be converted into Hyper-V virtual machines (candidates)

◆ Gather resource utilization data of the virtual machine candidates over a predetermined time frame

◆ Enter the specifications of possible hosts and storage

◆ Use the gathered performance data to estimate how many hosts will be required to run your virtual machine candidates

◆ Generate a spreadsheet with lots of detailed information and a report in Microsoft Word format that can be used as the basis of a project proposal

MAP is free. It requires only a short amount of time for installation, minimal effort for configuring resource monitoring, and no time at all for entering various host specifications to size a solution. This scientific approach is much better than sticking a proverbial wet finger in the wind to guesstimate the required number of hosts and their specifications.

SIZING A CLOUD

A veteran of the hosting industry can tell you that you cannot use traditional sizing techniques to size a cloud. That is because you have no existing workloads to convert into Hyper-V virtual machines or to assess. A cloud features self-service, so the service provider (the IT department in the case of a private cloud) has no idea what will be deployed on the cloud in the future.

The approach that some hosting companies use is to identify a number of different host and storage technologies, specifications, and their costs. The costs of owning (networking, rack space, licensing, power, high availability, disaster recovery, systems management, cooling, and so on) are determined, and these are used to calculate the cost to the customer of the service. For example, a megabyte of RAM might cost a certain amount per month. Find a sweet spot between minimized cost and maximum level of service, and you have yourself a possible architecture.

A public cloud service provider will usually need to be very price competitive, while dealing with the highest levels of security for its tenants. The providers, like those operating a private cloud, might want to consider different tiers of hosts and storage, with some offering cheaper service at reduced cost and availability, while others offer better performance and availability but at a higher cost. Public clouds might lean toward the lower-cost option while private clouds might focus more on availability, but this should be dictated by the strategy decision makers.

PowerShell

As you get further into this book, you might start to wonder whether you accidentally picked a PowerShell book instead of a Hyper-V one. Microsoft gave us a lot of power in PowerShell. You can rapidly deploy change to lots of virtual machines with a single line of code, or you can automate complex tasks with a script. You will see lots of examples of this throughout the rest of this book.

Although some might have believed that PowerShell was being widely used, this was not actually the case. Most people simply never had a reason or the time to invest in PowerShell. Now they might hear that PowerShell is all over Windows Server 2012 and Hyper-V, and they might wonder if it is too hard to learn. The reality is that Microsoft makes it quite easy to pick up some PowerShell administration and scripting skills.

PowerShell is made up of cmdlets. Each cmdlet does some action to something. The naming of cmdlets reflects this:

```
Verb-Noun
```

Here is an example:

```
Get-Help
```

That's the cmdlet that will provide you with help in PowerShell. You can use this to get help on another cmdlet. For example, you can start PowerShell and type in the following:

```
Get-Help Get-Command
```

Get-Command is used to get information on a PowerShell cmdlet. You can get examples of how to use it by running the following:

```
Get-Help Get-Command -Examples
```

Armed with the knowledge that the results of that instruction will give, you are now able to list all of the Hyper-V PowerShell module cmdlets:

```
Get-Command -Module Hyper-V
```

There are a number of ways that you can run PowerShell:

PowerShell Window   This is like a command prompt, and is the best way to quickly make simple changes using single cmdlets.

Scripting Using Notepad   You can write a script (saved as a .PS1 file). This script runs lines in sequence and can include programming structures and decision making.

Third-Party Scripting Tools   Some excellent scripting tools have been released to help administrators write and manage their PowerShell scripts. These tools can offer better script debugging and management functionality than you will get in Windows Server 2012.

You don't need to spend any money to get a PowerShell scripting tool. Windows Server 2012 includes the Integrated Scripting Environment (ISE), a very nice tool for PowerShell beginners and veterans (see Figure 1.3).

There are two ways to type PowerShell in ISE. You can open one or more scripting windows. Unlike with Notepad, each line is numbered. This is useful if you run a long script, it reports an error, and that error is on line 36. You can scroll straight to line 36 in ISE, but you have to slowly count to line 36 in Notepad.

ISE also features a PowerShell window. There is a good reason for using this window. As you type, you will notice that ISE includes the ability to suggest or auto-complete your cmdlets. Type New- in ISE and you'll see it offer you every possibility to complete your cmdlet. This is a nice way to discover cmdlets. If you type New-VM followed by a space and a hyphen, you'll see that ISE can suggest ways to use the cmdlet.

The Commands pane on the right can be used to search for cmdlets. When you find one, you can click a button called Show Details. This can reveal the different ways (if available) to use a cmdlet and the flags/parameters that can be used, with the mandatory ones being highlighted with an asterisk. You can select and complete the parameters in the Command pane and then click Run to run the configured cmdlet or click Insert to add it to the PowerShell window.

FIGURE 1.3
The Integrated
Scripting
Environment

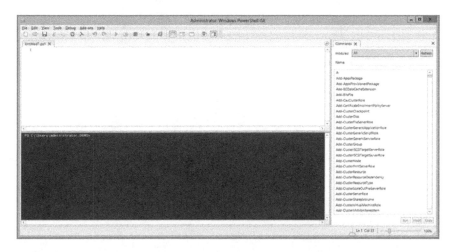

Other nice features in ISE include the ability to debug a script (troubleshooting by pausing a running script to inspect the code and variables) by using the options in the Debug menu, or use Start Snippets in the Edit menu to discover PowerShell snippets.

PowerShell might take some effort to learn at first, but you will quickly learn the value of it. A simple script can save you lots of time in the long term. Scripts can give you consistent results when run repeatedly. For example, a consultant can use a single script on lots of customer sites to standardize configurations and achieve the same high levels of deployment.

And here's your best reason to learn PowerShell: The most powerful features of Hyper-V are revealed and enabled only by PowerShell. You'll see many examples of this as you progress through this book.

You will never be the first person to look for help on PowerShell. There are plenty of places to find help or solutions; just go to your favorite search engine and start there. Here are a few other resources:

Scripting with Windows PowerShell Videos `http://technet.microsoft.com/ scriptcenter/powershell.aspx`

This is the first of five videos teaching the basics of PowerShell scripting.

The Script Center `http://technet.microsoft.com/scriptcenter/default`

This Microsoft site has lots of example solutions.

PowerShell for Beginners `http://social.technet.microsoft.com/wiki/contents/ articles/4307.powershell-for-beginners-en-us.aspx`

This is a collection of resources on the Microsoft TechNet Wiki.

## Chapter 2

Deploying Hyper-V

Virtualization brings many benefits to your business, such as increasing its flexibility, increasing its availability, and improving its cost-efficiency. You may already know that Hyper-V is strong in terms of cost, but what about features and functions? With all the improvements in Windows Server 2012 Hyper-V, organizations can leverage an operating system that has been built for cloud computing.

In this chapter, you'll learn about

- What needs to be prepared for a Hyper-V deployment
- How to install and configure Hyper-V
- How to leverage some of the new features
- How a Hyper-V host can be migrated

Preparing a Hyper-V Deployment

This first section is all about preparing for a new Hyper-V deployment. The focus is on understanding the requirements and decisions you will have to make. This preparation should be done before you start the installation. It's probably better to take a "few more minutes" to think about your environment and the deployment before you insert the DVD (or ISO image) and start with the installation.

Design and Architecture

Server virtualization is a key enabler of Infrastructure as a Service (IaaS) by decoupling architecture layers such as the hardware from the operating system, the application from the operating system, and so on. The Hyper-V role in Windows Server 2012 and Hyper-V Server 2012 provides software infrastructure and basic management tools that can be used to create and manage a virtualized server computing environment. Leveraging Hyper-V, the resources exposed to users will be virtualized instances of operating systems.

Microsoft's virtualization platform is built on the Windows Server ecosystem and can benefit from this broad partner ecosystem in the area of hardware and also software solutions. Therefore, the design patterns are written in a product-agnostic approach.

CONSIDERATIONS FOR SMALL DEPLOYMENTS

A stand-alone host server architecture is mainly considered for small deployments, such as branch offices. In these cases, Hyper-V consists of a single host running Windows Server 2012 with the Hyper-V role enabled to run a number of virtual machine guests. This model, shown in Figure 2.1, provides server consolidation but does not provide high availability. Therefore, it also does not require expensive, shared storage. In the best case, the "Management OS," also called the management or parent partition, will be dedicated to the virtualization server role only. But of course this might not work for all scenarios. For example, local backup software is required, which should be one of the few exceptions.

FIGURE 2.1
Small deployments

Stand-Alone Hyper-V Host(s)

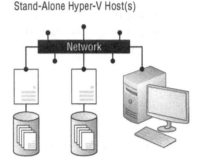

In this design, the host server is a single point of failure. The architecture requires a "save state" or "power off" of the virtual machine guests if the host server needs maintenance or rebooting. This pattern is appropriate for test and development environments as well as small branch offices, where the limitations regarding availability are acceptable.

A great solution for branch offices with limited hardware or disaster recovery requirements is the Hyper-V Replica functionality, which replicates the virtual machine to another Hyper-V host. Hyper-V Replica tracks the write operations on the primary virtual machine and replicates these changes to the replica server efficiently over a WAN. The network connection between the two servers uses HTTP or HTTPS and supports both integrated and certificate-based authentication. This service might also be offered by a service provider for a disaster recovery datacenter.

CONSIDERATIONS FOR MEDIUM AND LARGE DEPLOYMENTS

The architecture suggested for medium deployments is usually based on Windows Server 2012 Hyper-V and Failover Clustering. This model, shown in Figure 2.2, provides server consolidation as well as high availability for the virtual machines. The management partition is dedicated to the virtualization server role only. Minimizing the server roles in the root partition has additional benefits such as reducing the attack surface and the frequency of updates, which are covered later in this chapter in more detail. Using Failover Clustering requires shared storage, which can be Fibre Channel, iSCSI—or new in Windows Server 2012, Server Message Block 3 (SMB3). Chapter 7, "Using File Servers," goes into more detail on how SMB3 works. Chapter 6, "The Microsoft iSCSI Software Target," details the Microsoft iSCSI Software Target in Windows Server 2012.

FIGURE 2.2
Medium and large
deployments

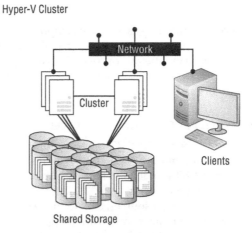

As mentioned before, for high availability, the Hyper-V hosts will be configured as a failover cluster that provides automatic failover of resources to other hosts as well as the use of virtual machine mobility capabilities like Live Migration. Compared to the stand-alone model, these hosts should be utilized only to the level that they will still be able to take one host failure without impact.

Migration of virtual machines can be performed without any downtime across all cluster nodes by leveraging Live Migration. However, identical hardware specifications (for example, processors and memory) are required for all involved Hyper-V hosts. Usually, virtual machines are stored on shared storage configured for Cluster Shared Volumes (CSV), which offers the benefit of a single namespace used by several resources at the same time. If an outage is detected, the failover cluster will automatically fail over and restart all failed cluster resources (in this case, virtual machines) on the remaining Hyper-V nodes. Chapter 8 "Building Hyper-V Clusters," goes into more detail on how a Hyper-V failover cluster works.

Medium and large deployments should be managed by the Microsoft System Center 2012 SP1 suite, which offers these components:

◆ App Controller, for virtual machine deployment and management

◆ Configuration Manager, for deployment

◆ Data Protection Manager, for backup

◆ Operations Manager, for monitoring

◆ Orchestrator, for automation

◆ Service Manager, for service and process management

◆ Virtual Machine Manager, for fabric and VM management

We do not cover the System Center because it is beyond the scope of this book. *Microsoft Private Cloud Computing* by Aidan Finn, Hans Vredevoort, Patrick Lownds, and Damian Flynn (Sybex, 2012) covers System Center 2012; even though the book does not cover Windows Server 2012, it's a great read on the possible concepts.

Hardware

The host server architecture is a critical component of a virtualized infrastructure and a key variable in its consolidation ratio and cost analysis. The ability of a Hyper-V host to handle the workload of a large number of consolidation candidates increases the consolidation ratio and helps provide the desired cost benefit. Some aspects that should be taken into consideration are presented in this section.

CONSIDERATIONS FOR COMPUTING RESOURCES

As with Windows Server 2008 R2, the server operating system is available only as a 64-bit version. No 32-bit editions of the operating system are provided. However, 32-bit applications will run on the 64-bit Windows Server 2012 operating system. Therefore, 64-bit processors are required for running Hyper-V.

For more computing resources, look for processors with higher frequency and multiple cores. Don't expect a perfect linear scale with multiple cores. The scaling factor can even be less when Hyper-Threading is enabled, because Hyper-Threading relies on sharing resources on the same physical core. The general recommendation is to have Hyper-Threading enabled, as long as the supported logical processors (LPs) are not exceeded. Finally, don't underestimate the L2 or L3 processor cache, which often plays a bigger role than the frequency.

NOTE Do not compare processor specifications, especially frequency, across manufacturers or even across different generations of processors from the same manufacturer. The comparison in many cases is a misleading indicator of speed and performance.

In addition to a 64-bit processor, Hyper-V requires processors that support the features shown in Table 2.1.

TABLE 2.1: CPU requirements

PROCESSOR TECHNOLOGY	AMD	INTEL
Processor architecture	64-bit	64-bit
Hardware virtualization	AMD-V	Intel VT
Hardware Execute Disable	No eXecute (NX) bit	eXecute Disable (XD) bit
Optional: Second Level Address Translation (SLAT)	Rapid Virtualization Indexing (RVI)	Extended Page Tables (EPT)

Various tools can help identify the capabilities of a processor. A well-known tool is CPU-Z, which is available for free from CPUID (www.cpuid.com). In addition, AMD has the Virtualization Technology and Microsoft Hyper-V System Compatibility Check Utility, and Intel has the Processor Identification Utility.

WMI can be used to identify whether DEP is available:
use `wmic OS Get DataExecutionPrevention_Available`, where `true` means DEP is enabled.

Hyper-V also supports Second Level Address Translation (SLAT). The reduction in processor and memory overhead associated with SLAT improves scalability with respect to the number of virtual machines that can be concurrently executed on a Hyper-V host. In addition, the Windows hypervisor processor overhead drops from about 10 percent to about 2 percent and reduces memory overhead by about 1 MB for each virtual machine.

Virtualization is always related to discussions about performance. We might assume it's all about high performance, but you will have noticed that many servers are tuned specifically for "green IT." Newer generations of processors are generally more energy efficient, and they may expose more power states to the operating system for power management, which enables better power management.

Out of the box, most of the servers are configured for optimal power usage. This means that servers are running with a lower CPU core speed by default. Depending on the workload hosted on a host, you might need to adjust this configuration to get the full processor performance, especially if you face performance issues. The most effective way to solve this is to change the BIOS setting to a mode similar to Maximum Performance (see Figure 2.3); this varies from vendor to vendor.

FIGURE 2.3
BIOS Power Profile
settings

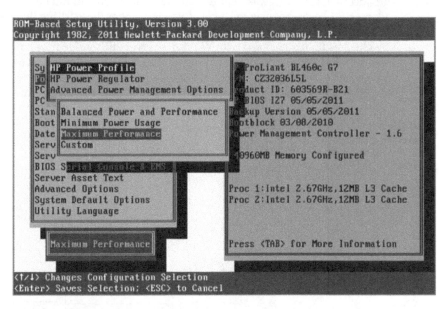

HP has an interesting white paper, "Configuring and Tuning HP ProLiant Servers for Low-Latency Applications," which might be helpful when choosing the right configuration:

```
http://h20000.www2.hp.com/bc/docs/support/SupportManual/c01804533/c01804533
.pdf?jumpid=reg_R1002_USEN
```

CONSIDERATIONS FOR STORAGE

With Windows Server 2012, you have the option to choose from among various storage architectures. In the past, the choice was mainly between local and shared storage, and whether SAS, iSCSI, or Fibre Channel should be used. With Windows Server 2012, the discussion around storage has become a bit more complex. Before making any decision, you should consider SMB3 as a new option for storing virtual machines. Chapter 7 goes into more detail on what such a solution would look like.

When it comes to Hyper-V storage sizing, high input/output operations per second (IOPS) and low latency are more critical than maximum sustained throughput. Keep in mind that you might end up with much more (free) disk space than needed to get the number of IOPS required. During the selection of drives, this translates into selecting those that have the highest rotational speed and lowest latency possible and choosing when to use SSD or flash-based disks for extreme performance.

CONSIDERATIONS FOR NETWORKING

Back in Windows Server 2008 R2, different networks were required for Hyper-V and Failover Clustering to function properly. This usually ended up with hosts having six or more 1 Gb network adapters. To get high availability or to load-balance the load, third-party software from Broadcom, HP, or Intel was required. At that time, Microsoft did not support teaming of network adapters. If you're not new to Hyper-V, you remember these "difficult days," when we had to get all these different driver and software versions installed and configured to make Hyper-V work.

This has finally changed with Windows Server 2012, as we now have built-in Windows NIC teaming. But it's not just about making your network adapter highly available. The idea behind leveraging a converged fabric is to get more out of your network. Now, as 10 GbE connections are getting more popular, this can make a big difference, as shown in Figure 2.4.

FIGURE 2.4
Converged fabric

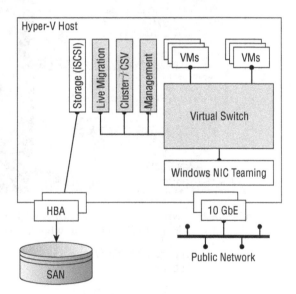

As you can see in Figure 2.4, instead of having 6 + 1 Gb network adapters, we would start with just two 10 Gb network adapters and create one network team out of it. As Windows Server 2012 now also has the option of configuring serious Quality of Service (QoS) settings, we will use the "Allow Management Operating System to share this Network Adapter" option. This will create a virtual network adapter for the Management OS. It will be possible to create more than one virtual network adapter, which makes this a very flexible design and allows the two 10 GbE adapters to be used for different workloads in a dynamic way. You will read more about this later in this chapter.

Operating System

The hypervisor from Microsoft is part of the operating system. As often is the case with Microsoft, there are some decisions around licensing that should be considered before starting. This section covers the most important answers to the questions an administrator might have surrounding Windows Server 2012 licensing in a Hyper-V context.

WINDOWS SERVER EDITION

The license model changed in Windows Server 2012, as shown in Table 2.2. No worries—we won't start a license-selling pitch here. But there are some important changes that also have a (positive) impact on server operators and administrators. With Windows Server 2012, it will be easier than ever to determine the right edition for a deployment.

From Windows Server 2008 onward, using a Datacenter edition license allows you to install an unlimited number of guests (virtual guest machines) running Windows Server. This makes the Datacenter edition very attractive for highly virtualized environments where it provides a cloud-level scale with lower cost. On the other hand, the Standard edition now offers the same enterprise-class features as the Datacenter edition. Yes, this means there are no technical differences or limitations anymore.

TABLE 2.2: Windows Server licensing

EDITION	FEATURES	LICENSING MODEL
Datacenter	Full Windows Server with unlimited virtual instances	Processor + CAL
Standard	Full Windows Server with two virtual instances as a maximum	Processor + CAL
Hyper-V Server	Server Core with Hyper-V only, with no virtual instances	Free

Consider using the Datacenter edition whenever possible when virtualizing at a high scale, which also allows for a high level of flexibility. Check the Microsoft Product Use Rights (PUR) from this website for additional information:

`www.microsoft.com/licensing/about-licensing/product-licensing.aspx`

FULL OR CORE INSTALLATION MODE

When installing Windows Server, you have the option to choose between Server Core (a command-line-based installation) and Server with a Graphical User Interface (GUI), formerly also known as

Full Installation. Server Core still includes only services and features needed to support common infrastructure roles, such as domain controllers, DNS servers, and also Hyper-V. This kind of installation has the following characteristics:

◆ A smaller attack surface

◆ Less required disk space

◆ Less required servicing

With Windows Server 2012, Server Core has become the standard installation option highlighted in the Windows Setup routine. It is the recommended installation mode by Microsoft, unless there is a particular need for the GUI to be present. When installing a new server, you can choose between the Standard and Datacenter edition, and for each there is the option for Server Core or Server with a GUI. The main differences between the installation modes are summarized in Table 2.3.

TABLE 2.3:   Windows Server installation modes

	SERVER CORE	**MINIMAL SHELL**	**GUI MODE**
Footprint	~4 GB less than GUI mode	~300 MB less than GUI mode	~10 GB
Server Manager	N/A	N/A	Available
MMC	N/A	Available	Available
Windows PowerShell	Available	Available	Available

Consider also an intermediate state. You can start using a Server with a GUI installation so you can use the graphical tools to configure the server. When the configuration is finished and you're happy with the result, you can remove the GUI at any time. This particular option is new to Windows Server 2012 and is clearly a big advantage for inexperienced administrators or those new to the Server Core installation mode. Turning off the GUI later gives them the aforementioned benefits whenever they are ready to say goodbye to the GUI.

In addition to the Server Core and Server with a GUI installation modes, Windows Server 2012 can also be configured in a third mode called Minimal Server Interface. This interface is very similar to the GUI installation except that the following components are not installed:

◆ Windows Explorer

◆ Internet Explorer

◆ Start screen

◆ Desktop

The Minimal Server Interface mode contains Server Manager, the Microsoft Management Console (MMC), and a subset of Control Panel items that are not available with the Server Core installation mode. However, Minimal Server Interface mode is not available when you install Windows Server 2012, but it can be configured using Server Manager or Windows PowerShell, which you will look at later in this chapter.

KNOWING THE LIMITS

With the release of Windows Server 2012, Microsoft attempted to say that the sky is not the limit. The updated limits on host and guest maximums are simply outstanding. Take a quick look at Table 2.4 to understand the differences between Hyper-V in Windows Server 2008 R2 and in Windows Server 2012.

TABLE 2.4:   Hyper-V limits

RESOURCE	WINDOWS SERVER 2008 R2	WINDOWS SERVER 2012
Host—logical processors	64	320
Host—physical memory	1 TB	4 TB
Host—v-procs per host	512	2,048
Host cluster—nodes	16	64
Host cluster—virtual machines	1,000	4,000
VM—max v-procs per VM	4	64
VM—max memory per VM	64 GB	1 TB
VM—max virtual disk size	2 TB	64 TB
VM—max VHD size	2 TB	64 TB with VHDX

As you can read in the table, Hyper-V can provide up to 1 TB of memory per virtual machine. This is a huge leap forward. Just keep in mind that the guest operating system has to support that much memory as well. Operating systems such as Windows Server 2008 and 2008 R2 Standard edition support only up to 32 GB of memory. Have a look at the Microsoft TechNet article on "Memory Limits" for details on the different Windows guests:

```
http://msdn.microsoft.com/en-us/library/windows/desktop/aa366778(v=vs.85).aspx
```

Don't Forget the Documentation

Before you start with the Hyper-V installation, consider preparing a configuration document as well as a checklist like the one in Figure 2.5. They should include all decisions and explanations as to why, for example, the Server Core installation mode has or hasn't been used. Also document all important steps to make sure all hosts are configured the same way, even when someone else is doing it. The success of the installation is not only about technical "clicks." The planning is also important.

FIGURE 2.5
Hyper-V deployment checklist

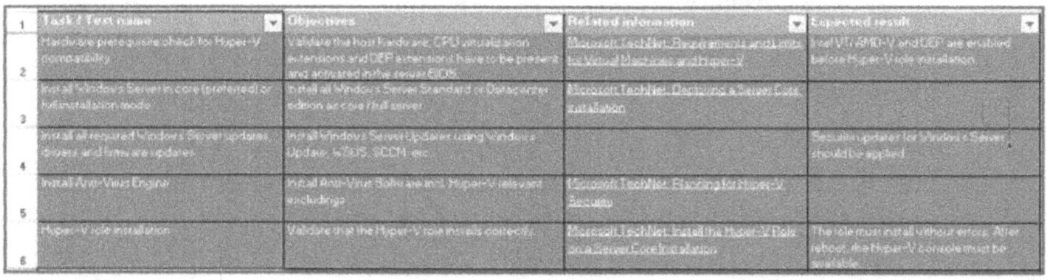

The following are some steps you may want to include in your Hyper-V checklist:

◆ Upgrade your hardware to the latest firmware/BIOS.

◆ Install Windows Server 2012 (Server with a GUI).

◆ Install all required drivers.

◆ Install and configure MPIO.

◆ Install and configure Windows NIC teaming.

◆ Configure Regional settings as well as Date and Time settings.

◆ Check the paging file.

◆ Configure network adapters.

◆ Change the computer name.

◆ Join the Computer to the domain.

◆ Enable Remote Desktop.

◆ Install the latest Windows updates.

◆ Install the Hyper-V role.

◆ Install antivirus software.

◆ Install management agents for monitoring, backup, and so on.

Of course, these tasks can be automated by using operating system deployment tools such as System Center, PowerShell scripts, and group policies. Nevertheless, documentation or a checklist about who is doing what will still be helpful.

Windows PowerShell

Windows PowerShell is not new, but it's becoming more and more critical for deployments and server configurations, especially for mass deployments. PowerShell could also be compared to the famous Swiss army knife, which helped MacGyver in many cases. In other words, if a functionality isn't working as required, PowerShell might be able to make it work.

Also consider this: PowerShell is also very handy for documentation. Only the cmdlet and its result need to be documented, so pages of printed screens are no longer required. This can save a lot of time and also ensures that the configuration is done as documented, because simply copying and pasting cmdlets should always bring about the same result.

Building the First Hyper-V Host

Starting with a stand-alone host is probably the best approach if you are new to Hyper-V, because this deployment is very straightforward. It also helps you to more quickly understand how Hyper-V works—and how to evolve building a bigger Hyper-V farm.

Preparing Windows Server

Because Hyper-V is a role of Windows Server, the first requirement is to have a freshly installed operating system. This task is not different from installing a new Windows Server used for Active Directory or a file server, for example. There are no Hyper-V-specific options available. Unless you use the free Hyper-V Server, the Hyper-V role is also not enabled by default, even when you use the Datacenter edition (see Figure 2.6).

FIGURE 2.6
Windows Server
installation

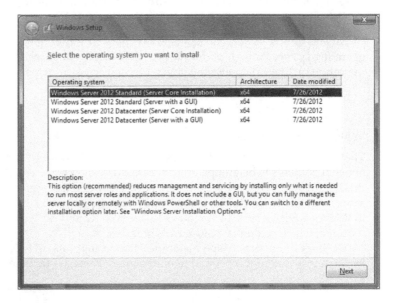

As mentioned earlier in this chapter, Server Core installation mode is preferred for a Hyper-V deployment. However, you might want to start with the Server with a GUI mode and then switch to the Server Core mode after you've completed all the configuration.

In general, we recommend configuring just the bare minimum of the operating system. Then directly proceed with the Hyper-V role installation and finish the advanced configuration later. To proceed, the host should be configured as follows:

1. Install all required drivers.

2. Configure network adapters for the management network.

3. Enable Remote Desktop for remote administration.

4. Change the computer name.

5. Check Regional settings as well as Date and Time settings.

6. Add the computer to the domain.

7. Install the latest Windows updates.

8. Install relevant Hyper-V and Failover Clustering hotfixes.

9. Add additional storage for virtual machine placement.

NOTE Microsoft System Center 2012 Configuration Manager and Virtual Machine Manager offer options for an automated and for a Hyper-V-optimized bare-metal deployment (BMD) to reduce manual interaction. The BMD from Virtual Machine Manager is based on booting from VHD, as opposed to the OS deployment in Configuration Manager.

For end-to-end power management, as explained earlier in this chapter, also configure the operating system for high-performance. This can be done using the control panel, or the following command, which applies the high performance power schema:

```
powercfg /S 8c5e7fda-e8bf-4a96-9a85-a6e23a8c635c
```

Windows NIC Teaming

The built-in teaming in Windows Server 2012, called *Windows NIC teaming*, enables multiple network adapters to be grouped into a team. Also known as *load balancing and failover (LBFO)*, this feature helps ensure the network's availability and the aggregation of network bandwidth across multiple network adapters, without requiring any third-party software. This is new to Windows Server 2012. In Windows Server 2008 R2 and earlier, vendor driver support was required, which could have caused lots of issues.

The built-in network adapter teaming solution supports up to 32 network adapters and even works across different types and manufacturers. There are three teaming modes:

- Static Teaming
- Switch-Independent
- Link Aggregation Control Protocol (LACP)

NIC teaming in Windows Server 2012 supports a Hyper-V-optimized traffic distribution method called Hyper-V Port, as shown in Figure 2.7. This method allows the switch to determine whether specific source MAC addresses are on only one connected network adapter. The switch will then balance the load on multiple links, based on the destination MAC address for the virtual machine. In combination with the virtual machine queue (VMq), there is a particular benefit. However, this method is limited to a single virtual machine on a single network adapter.

FIGURE 2.7
Windows NIC
teaming

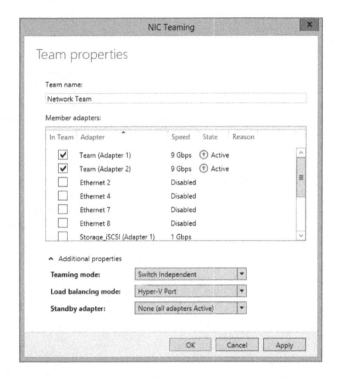

This network adapter teaming can be enabled from Server Manager or by using Windows PowerShell. In the following example, we create a new network team called Network Team with the members Ethernet 3 and Ethernet 4. There is no need to install a feature, because all components are available by default.

1. In Server Manager, click Local Server.

2. At the Properties section, click Disabled next to Network Adapter Teaming. The NIC Teaming window opens.

3. In the Teams section, click Tasks ➢ New Team.

4. Specify the Team Name (in this example, Network Team). Select from the Member Adapter the two network adapters (in this example, Ethernet 3 and Ethernet 4) and click OK.

5. Depending on the network design, configure the Additional Properties such as Teaming mode and Load Balancing mode. Click OK to create the network team.

The network team creation process may take several minutes, during which time the connection to the server might be lost. As soon as the network connection has been restored, click Refresh Now in the NIC Teaming window to verify the configuration.

The new network adapter teaming can also be created easily by using PowerShell:

```
New-NetLbfoTeam -Name "Network Team" -TeamMembers "Ethernet 3", "Ethernet 4"
-TeamingMode SwitchIndependent -LoadBalancingAlgorithm HyperVPort
```

Chapter 4, "Networking," goes into more detail on how Windows NIC teaming works.

PAGING FILE

When you install Windows Server, the default setting for the page file is configured to Automatically Manage Paging File Size For All Drives. Hyper-V hosts often are loaded with lots of memory. Therefore, in previous versions of Windows Server, the operating system created a huge file for the virtual memory. But there is no advantage to Hyper-V having such a huge paging file. Keep in mind that the physical memory is allocated to the virtual machines and not used by the management OS.

As mentioned earlier in this chapter, no other software should be installed on the Hyper-V host, besides the management and backup agents. If this is the case, the general recommendation is to leave this setting at the default. There are no official statements indicating that the virtual memory settings need to be changed for Windows Server 2012 Hyper-V.

But there are always cases where this does not apply. What should be done when the virtual memory does allocate too much disk space? The paging file configuration can be done in the computer properties under Advanced—Performance Options, as shown in Figure 2.8.

FIGURE 2.8
Paging file
configuration

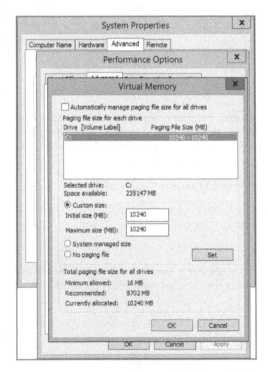

If the Hyper-V host has been installed with the Server Core installation mode, this UI will not be available. So we will use a script that can be run at the command prompt:

```
$Pagefile = Get-WmiObject Win32_ComputerSystem
$Pagefile.AutomaticManagedPagefile = $false
$Pagefile.Put()
$NewPagefile = gwmi -query "select * from Win32_PageFileSetting where name='C:\\
pagefile.sys'"
$NewPagefile.InitialSize = [int]"10240"
$NewPagefile.MaximumSize = [int]"10240"
$NewPagefile.Put()
```

A general good rule of thumb is to have a page file of between 4 GB and 6 GB. We usually don't configure more than 10 GB. But again, only change the size of the paging file when the default value is not optimal configured automatically.

NOTE There is one thing you need to keep in mind when it comes to troubleshooting. When the page file is configured with a lower value than the physical memory, the memory dump might be incomplete when the system crashes. A support engineer might require a full memory dump for an analysis of the problem. If necessary, you can temporarily set the page file to a higher number just for collecting the memory dump.

Installing the Hyper-V Role

At this stage, Windows Server has been installed and configured with the basic settings. The easiest way to install Hyper-V now is by using Server Manager, which opens by default when logging on to a newly installed server. The Add Roles And Features wizard simplifies the installation process and takes care of all role dependencies:

1. In Server Manager, click Manage ➢ Add Roles And Features.

2. Verify the Destination Server on the Before You Begin page and click Next to proceed.

3. On the Installation Type page, select Role-Based Or Feature-Based Installation and click Next to proceed.

4. From the Server Selection page, select the server from the Server Pool and then click Next.

5. Select Hyper-V from the Server Roles page and click Next.

6. The Hyper-V Management Tools are automatically selected on the Feature page. Click Next to proceed.

7. The Create Virtual Switches, Virtual Machine Migration, and Default Stores pages allow you to configure the host defaults. If you want to use your own virtual switch name, wait until after you install the role to create the switch. Click Next to proceed.

8. On the Confirmation page, select Restart The Destination Server Automatically If Required and click Install.

As a part of the installation, if the option has been selected, the server will reboot automatically. Verify that the installation is finished by checking Server Manager again. The Virtual Switches, Virtual Machine Migration, and Default Stores are part of the post-installation configuration that you'll explore in the next chapter. Note that for the Hyper-V installation as well as its advanced configuration, PowerShell is a good companion on your way to mass-deploying virtualization. The sooner you explore these options, the earlier you can benefit from automated (unified) installation for multiple hosts.

As mentioned before, another way to install and configure the Hyper-V role is to leverage PowerShell. This is required on hosts installed as Server Core. The following is a ready-to-fire PowerShell command, which will work on Server Core but also on Server with a GUI:

```
Install-WindowsFeature Hyper-V -IncludeManagementTools -Restart
```

Unlike when using the Add Roles And Features wizard from Server Manager, PowerShell does not include the management tools and snap-ins. To include these management tools, simply add the -IncludeManagementTools parameter to the cmdlet. On Server Core, the management tools and snap-ins cannot be run, unless you change to the minimal-shell option.

NOTE In Windows Server 2012, OCLIST.exe has been removed from the operating systems. Instead, the following options can be used to manage the roles and features:

- ◆ DISM.exe
- ◆ Install-WindowsFeature
- ◆ Get-WindowsFeature
- ◆ Uninstall-WindowsFeature

SOFTWARE AND TOOLS ON THE HYPER-V HOST

The parent partition should be dedicated to only the Hyper-V role, exclusively, without being shared with other roles such as Active Directory. Don't even bother messing with it. Additional roles can negatively affect the performance of the server and its workload. This includes both "roles" as defined in Server Manager as well as additional software and services from third-party vendors. Minimizing the roles installed in the parent partition also keeps the attack surface low and reduces the frequency of updates required to keep the machine up-to-date. Administrators should carefully consider what software they plan to install in the parent partition. A small part of the storage role is already configured by default, which does not affect this recommendation.

Of course, a Hyper-V host needs to be monitored and protected. Therefore, management agents from the Microsoft System Center suite (or equivalent) are OK to be installed. However, don't install other System Center components, such as the management server itself, on your Hyper-V hosts.

NOTE One thing to consider with the Server Core installation mode is that the lack of having a graphical user interface can prevent administrators from having tools and software installed in the parent partition. The lack of a GUI will also scare off everyone not familiar with Server Core—not a strong argument, but something to consider if you are fighting the notion of "multipurpose" servers in your organization.

Configuring the Hyper-V Host

Configuring the Hyper-V host is probably one of the most important steps for your Hyper-V deployment. If you have to deploy multiple hosts, you will soon appreciate the power of PowerShell automation vs. clicking your way through installation and configuration. PowerShell is the right tool for the job, and therefore the following sections outline the equivalent PowerShell command of performing the task discussed.

DEFAULT STORES

With the previous version of Hyper-V, many customers ran into the problem that the operating system could run out of disk space, rendering Windows Server unbootable or terribly slow. The reason was that, by default, virtual machines were created on the system drive. The Hyper-V installation process in Windows Server 2012 now finally includes the option to initially change the default stores for the virtual machine and its virtual hard disks (see Table 2.5).

TABLE 2.5: Hyper-V default path

STORES	DEFAULT PATH
Virtual hard disk files	`C:\Users\Public\Documents\Hyper-V\ Virtual Hard Disks`
Virtual machine configuration file	`C:\ProgramData\Microsoft\Windows\ Hyper-V`

The setting can of course be changed after the installation by using the Hyper-V Manager. Select your Hyper-V host, open Hyper-V Settings, as shown in Figure 2.9, and update the path for Virtual Hard Disks as well as the path for Virtual Machines.

FIGURE 2.9
Hyper-V default
store settings

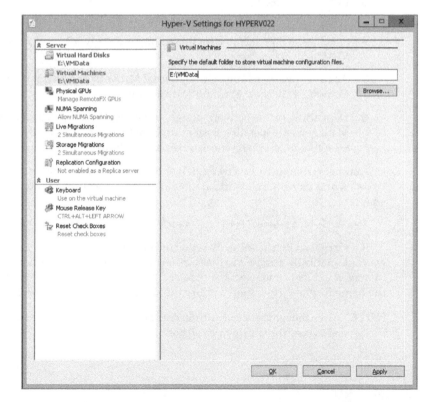

Another option is to use PowerShell to configure the default stores:

```
Set-VMHost -VirtualMachinePath "E:\VMData" -VirtualHardDiskPath "E:\VMData"
```

VIRTUAL SWITCH

Virtual machines require a virtual switch for any kind of communication. Most common is the external switch, which is connected to a physical network adapter to access a physical network. Windows Server 2012 supports Single-Root I/O Virtualization (SR-IOV) and different switch extensions, which we'll explain in a later chapter in detail.

Less popular are the internal virtual network, in which the communication is limited between the host and virtual machines, and the private virtual network, in which only the virtual machines on the same host can communicate with each other. Keep in mind that both switch types are not very useful in a cluster.

If no virtual switch has been created during the Hyper-V role installation, a new virtual switch can now be created, as shown in Figure 2.10. In the following example, we create a new virtual switch called Public Network with the corresponding network adapter Ethernet 2:

1. In the Server Manager, click Tools and select Hyper-V Manager. Verify that the desired host is added to the console.

2. Select the Virtual Switch Manager from the Actions pane on the right.

3. By default, New Virtual Network Switch is already selected, so just select the desired switch type (example: External). Click Create Virtual Switch.

4. Specify the Switch Name (in this example, Public Network). The Default Name is "New Virtual Switch".

5. As the connection type, select External Network and assign the network adapter (in this example, Ethernet 3) from the drop-down list.

6. Depending on the network design and network adapter capabilities, select the "Allow Management Operating System to share this Network Adapter" check box, as well as the SR-IOV and VLAN ID check boxes. Click OK to create the virtual switch.

Another option is to use PowerShell to configure a new virtual switch with the name Public Network and using the network adapter Ethernet 3 (you will probably use the teamed network adapter for this):

```
New-VMSwitch -Name "Public Network" -NetAdapterName "Ethernet 3"
```

If a virtual switch has already been created during the Hyper-V role installation, a name was automatically assigned to that virtual switch. To modify this name, just open the Hyper-V Management tools and select the required host. Then open Virtual Switch Manager and update the name for the virtual switch or use the PowerShell cmdlet to do so.

NOTE Even though the failover cluster does not require identical switch names, it's still recommended to keep the same logic on all hosts.

FIGURE 2.10
Create a new Hyper-
V virtual switch.

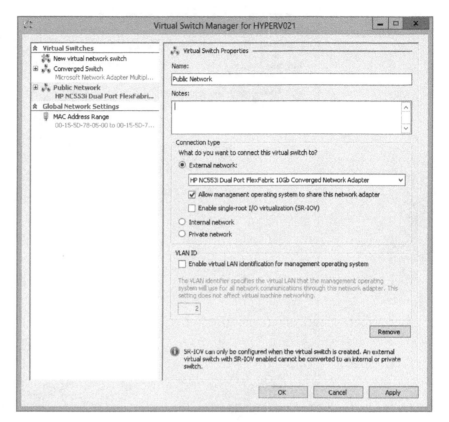

MAC ADDRESS RANGE

Hyper-V allows a virtual machine to be created with a static or dynamic MAC address. By default, Hyper-V assigns a dynamic MAC address from its MAC address pool to the virtual machines. If required, the Hyper-V administrator can also configure or assign a fixed MAC address to a virtual machine.

All Hyper-V MAC address ranges start with the same three octets (00-15-5d), which have been registered by Microsoft. The next two octets are generated by using the last two octets from the IP address of the first network adapter, converted to hexadecimal. This would give 256 different addresses when using 00 as the MinimumMacAddress and FF as the MaximumMacAddress.

If the number of addresses is not enough or there are duplicate MAC address pools for whatever reason, the setting can be changed using the Virtual Switch Manager from the Hyper-V Manager, as shown in Figure 2.11.

FIGURE 2.11
Hyper-V MAC pool

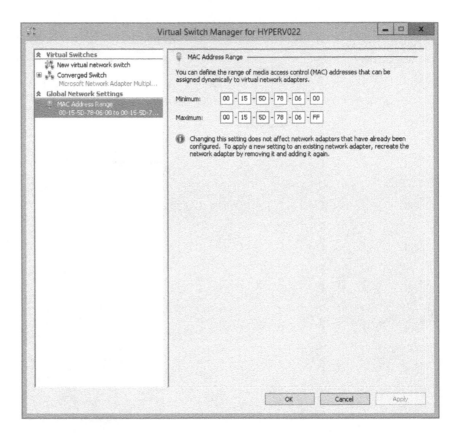

With PowerShell, the Set-VMHost command can be used to change this setting:

```
Set-VMHost -MacAddressMinimum "00-15-5D-78-80-00" `
-MacAddressMaximum "00-15-5D-78-8F-FF"
```

The preceding example would also increase the MAC address pool from 256 to 4,096 possible MAC addresses. It defines the valid MAC range from 80-00 to 8F-FF, allowing 16 × 256 addresses to be used, or 4,096. This change should be done before virtual machines or internal networks adapters are created to make use of the pool.

NOTE   The MAC address pool is stored in the Registry under HKLM\SOFTWARE\Microsoft\ Windows NT\CurrentVersion\Virtualization. Even when you use sysprep to prepare the image for further deployment on the machine, these values are not reset and you would need to remove them before running SYSPREP.exe.

THE CONVERGED NETWORK

To achieve the design of the converged network introduced at the beginning of this chapter, we will have to create a virtual switch. For this exercise, we call it Public Network and will use the Network Team created just a few pages ago. We then create virtual adapters for the management and cluster networks explained in Table 2.6.

TABLE 2.6:   Hyper-V networks

NETWORK	ADAPTER NAME	QOS	TYPE
Management	vEthernet (Management)	5	Public
Cluster / CSV	vEthernet (Cluster)	20	Private
Live Migration	vEthernet (Migration)	30	Private
Virtual Machines	External Public	10	Public

This option is available only by using PowerShell. The first command creates the virtual switch:

```
New-VMSwitch -Name "External Public" -MinimumBandwidthMode Weight `
-NetAdapterName "Network Team"
```

We then rename the virtual port, which has been created automatically for the parent partition:

```
Rename-VMNetworkAdapter -ManagementOS -Name "External Public" `
-NewName "Management"
```

To create additional virtual ports for the parent partition, just use this command:

```
Add-VMNetworkAdapter -ManagementOS -Name "Cluster" -SwitchName "External Public"
Add-VMNetworkAdapter -ManagementOS -Name "Migration" `
-SwitchName "External Public"
```

If required, configure the VLAN tagging for the virtual ports:

```
Set-VMNetworkAdapterVlan -ManagementOS -VMNetworkAdapterName "Management" `
-Access -VlanId "100"
```

Before you can configure the IP addresses, the Bandwidth Weight has to be configured. Run this command for all virtual network adapters:

```
Set-VMNetworkAdapter -ManagementOS -Name "Management" -MinimumBandwidthWeight "5"
Set-VMNetworkAdapter -ManagementOS -Name "Cluster" -MinimumBandwidthWeight "20"
Set-VMNetworkAdapter -ManagementOS -Name "Migration" -MinimumBandwidthWeight "30"
```

And run the following for the virtual network switch:

```
Set-VMSwitch "Public External" -DefaultFlowMinimumBandwidthWeight "10"
```

To avoid any errors and to simplify the configuration, you might want to disable all disconnected or unused network adapters. You can disable these in the Network Connections window in the Control Panel, or use PowerShell to disable all network adapters with the status Disconnected:

```
Get-NetAdapter -Physical | Where-Object {$_.Status -eq "Disconnected"} | `
Disable-NetAdapter }
```

Chapter 4 goes into more detail on how a converged network works.

Providing Security

As you can imagine, security is important, especially in a highly virtualized environment. Because Hyper-V is based on Windows Server, the existing processes and tools for delegation, antivirus protection, firewalling, and so on can be applied very well with some minor adaptations. Additional tasks include protecting the facility, having a backup and disaster recovery plan in place, developing update plans, and much more will be required to operate a datacenter securely.

DELEGATION

Granting just a limited group access to a hypervisor (or even a standard server) is a general practice in most enterprises. This leads to the question, what options do we have to securely delegate access to Hyper-V for other engineers?

Hyper-V in Windows Server 2012 makes it much easier as it comes with a built-in group called Hyper-V Administrators. But instead of adding an engineer to this group, you might consider using an Active Directory group to centrally manage access to all of your Hyper-V hosts. Consider this example: John Doe is a member of the Active Directory global group called GlobalHyperVAdmin. This global group is a member of the local group on each Hyper-V host called Hyper-V Administrators. By using Group Policy Preferences, this configuration could even be automated.

For more-advanced permission management, the Authorization Manager (AZMAN.msc) could be used:

1. Open the Authorization Manager by typing AZMAN.msc from the Start menu or a command prompt.

2. Right-click Authorization Manager and click Open Authorization Store.

3. Select the InitialStore.xml file, which is located under C:\ProgramData\Microsoft\Windows\Hyper-V\. Click OK to proceed.

4. Expand Hyper-V Services—Definitions, right-click Task Definition, and select New Task Definition.

5. A new window pops up in which you specify the name and description of the new task definition—for example, Read-Only Activities.

6. Click Add. Then switch to the Operations tab to select the operations you want to add. In this example, select all tasks starting with *View*.

7. Right-click Role Definitions and select New Role Definition.

8. A new window pops up, in which you specify the name and description of the new role—for example, Read-Only Administrator.

9. Click Add. Then switch to the Tasks tab to select the previously created task definition (in this example, Read-Only Activities). Click OK.

To assign the definitions to a role, you have to do the following:

1. Expand Hyper-V Services, right-click Role Assignments, and select New Role Assignment.

2. A new window pops up in which you can select the previously created role definition (in this example, Read-Only Administrator). Click OK.

3. The role has now been added. Right-click it and select Assign Users And Groups with the desired source—for example, Active Directory.

As mentioned before, it's recommended that you offload the delegation to Active Directory groups to have it centrally managed rather than have to configure every host individually.

NOTE As soon as System Center Virtual Machine Manager (VMM) is used for managing Hyper-V, any authorization needs to be configured from the VMM console. Manually performed delegation using Authorization Manager (AZMAN.msc) will automatically be replaced by VMM.

WINDOWS UPDATES

The standard process would be to install the latest updates from the official channel Windows Update by using either a direct connection or the company's internal provider like Microsoft's Windows Server Update Services (WSUS). But not all relevant updates are published to Windows Updates as some updates are required only under certain circumstances. A hotfix is intended to correct only the problem that is described in its article and you should only apply the hotfix if you have seen the described symptoms.

Microsoft's knowledge base is a good resource to use to find these hotfixes, as well as the blogs from the authors of this book, of course. Microsoft recently published article 2784261 with recommended hotfixes and updates for failover clustering. This will be an important article for every engineer who builds or supports Windows Server 2012 Hyper-V failover clusters. Often these hotfixes are not provided by Windows Updates and have to be downloaded and installed manually.

A simple PowerShell one-liner to install all patches from a directory could look like the following:

```
gci | foreach {iex ("wusa " + $_.name + " /quiet /norestart | out-null")}
```

ANTIVIRUS SOFTWARE

Although the use of antivirus software provides additional security, Hyper-V requires special configuration—for instance, certain services and files have to be excluded to avoid problems later. There have been several discussions on the Internet (blogs and communities) about whether a Hyper-V host really needs to have an antivirus scanner installed; we would say it depends on the situation and the environment. Usually a datacenter has a high level of security for external-facing communication. But what happens with internal "guests"? Because Hyper-V probably will host critical workloads, it's important to make this service as secure as possible. You may want to ask yourself some of the following questions to help you determine the best security options:

- By using a network plug-in (for example, a meeting room), do guest devices get only limited network access?

- Do you have any other kind of security in your datacenter/network, such as IPsec?

- Are you using Server Core installation mode for the Hyper-V hosts?

- Do you restrict Internet access for the Hyper-V hosts?

- Is the Windows Firewall enabled on the Hyper-V hosts?

If you have answered no to most of these questions, you really have to think about how to make the hosts more secure. Ultimately, controlling the host means having full control over the virtual machines—all of them. Although the same does not apply the other way around (you can control a virtual machine but can't get hold of the host), this is vital to remember when designing security for a Hyper-V host.

But as we have said, just installing antivirus software on a Hyper-V host doesn't solve the entire problem; it may even generate new ones. In the past, virtual machines disappeared from the Hyper-V Manager or couldn't be started anymore after such an installation. Therefore, the Virtual Machine Management Service (VMMS.exe) and VM worker process (VMWP.exe) have to be excluded from the scanner. Also exclude the directories that contain the virtual machine configuration and virtual hard disk files from active scanning.

NOTE We highly recommend that you check the Microsoft knowledge base for recommendations and correct configurations. Also the Microsoft Support KB article 961804 is not yet updated for Windows Server 2012. Do not assume that your product will work on Windows Server 2012 just because it did on Windows Server 2008 R2.

Managing Hyper-V

The main management tool for working with Hyper-V has been the MMC for Hyper-V, Failover Cluster Manager, or VMM. With Windows Server 2012, Hyper-V finally gets full PowerShell support, which provides access to not only all the functionality available in the GUI, but also the functionality not exposed through the GUI.

NOTE VMM is a great alternative for managing multiple Hyper-V hosts. However, SCVMM is beyond the scope of this book. You might want to consider evaluating the System Center 2012 SP1 suite.

TABLE 2.7:   Changes to the Hyper-V Management Console

HYPER-V HOST	VIRTUAL MACHINES
New, Virtual Machine (existing)	Connect (existing)
New, Virtual Hard Disk (existing)	Settings (improved)
New, Floppy Disk (existing)	Turn Off (existing)
Import Virtual Machine (improved)	Shut Down… (existing)
Hyper-V Settings (improved)	Save (existing)
Virtual Switch Manager (improved)	Pause (existing)
Virtual SAN Manager (new)	Reset (existing)
Edit Disk… (existing)	Snapshot (existing)
Inspect Disk (existing)	Move… (new)
Stop Service (existing)	Rename… (existing)
Remove Server (existing)	Enable Replication… (new)

Hyper-V Management Console

The Hyper-V Manager uses the classic MMC approach, with the Actions pane on the right-hand side displaying the available actions. The options available to configure Hyper-V hosts and virtual machines are outlined in Table 2.7.

To manage a Hyper-V host from a client machine, the Remote Server Administration Toolkit (RSAT) has to be installed. It was released shortly after Windows Server 2012 became generally available and can be downloaded directly from Microsoft:

```
www.microsoft.com/en-us/download/details.aspx?id=28972
```

Hyper-V PowerShell

PowerShell isn't new to Windows, but in Windows Server 2012, the new version 3 of PowerShell can be used to manage all major roles and features, including Hyper-V. There are more than a whopping 2,500 new PowerShell cmdlets spread across the operating system to manage nearly all aspects of Windows.

To get a list of the new Hyper-V cmdlets, you can use the `Get-Command -Module Hyper-V` command in PowerShell. You can always get detailed help within PowerShell, including a list of parameters for a specific cmdlet, by using the `Get-Help` cmdlet. For instance, if you want help creating a new virtual machine, you can use the following PowerShell command: `Get-Help New-VM`.

PowerShell 3 also introduces a new cmdlet called `Show-Command` that opens a GUI leveraging the PowerShell ISE. This capability makes it easy to understand the options and the syntax of a cmdlet. The syntax of `New-VM`, for example, can be displayed by typing **Show-Command New-VM** in a PowerShell console, which opens the dialog box shown in Figure 2.12.

FIGURE 2.12
Show-Command
New-VM

NOTE In PowerShell 3.0 the Server Manager cmdlet module does not have to be imported before running the cmdlets anymore. The module is automatically imported the first time a cmdlet is used. Also, Windows PowerShell cmdlets are not case-sensitive.

The best way to learn PowerShell is to start with some easy, yet real-world scenarios, such as creating a new virtual machine. Which parameters are important when creating a new VM? Here are some examples:

- VM name (-Name)
- Location for VM config files (-Path)
- Amount for startup memory (-MemoryStartupBytes)
- Location for virtual hard disk (-NewVHDPath)
- Size for virtual hard disk (-NewVHDSizeBytes)
- Network connection (-SwitchName)

If you don't know the parameters, check the New Virtual Machine Wizard. These parameters would look like the following:

```
New-VM -Name "MyFirstVM" -Path "E:\VMData\" -MemoryStartupBytes 512MB `
-NewVHDPath "E:\VMData\MyFirstVM\MyFirstVM_disk_1.vhdx" -NewVHDSizeBytes 40GB `
-SwitchName "External Public"
```

You can check the details of the newly created virtual machine by running the Get-VM command. Use the pipe option to display all details of this machine: Get-VM | fl *. By default, the virtual machine will be created with a single processor and static memory. As a next step, the virtual machine needs to be configured for Dynamic Memory and 2 processors. This can be done as follows:

```
Set-VM -Name "MyFirstVM" -ProcessorCount "2" -DynamicMemory `
-MemoryMaximumBytes "4294967296"
```

Because the virtual hard disk is empty, you might need to attach an ISO image to start the installation by configuring the VM's DVD drive:

```
Set-VMDvdDrive -VMName "MyFirstVM" -Path "C:\ISOs\WINDOWSSERVER.ISO"
```

Finally, let's start the virtual machine:

```
Start-VM -Name "MyFirstVM"
```

A mistake that often happens is that ISO images become mounted forever. With a simple query, these virtual machines can be identified. If needed, the problem could even be fixed in the same way. The following example makes a query for vmgues, which is needed to update Integration Services:

```
Get-VM | Get-VMDvdDrive | Where-Object {$_.DvdMediaType -ne 'None' `
-and ($_.Path -like 'C:\Windows\system32\vmguest.iso')}
```

As you can see, the new Hyper-V PowerShell modules are straightforward. However, this is just the top of the iceberg. As you might imagine, there is much more PowerShell can do for you.

NOTE   We like to keep and store PowerShell commands in a Microsoft OneNote file, which we can easily reuse later and have the option to share with others. You might also want to maintain a central store or documentation on a file share for team-wide usage.

Server Core

As in the previous version, Server Core comes with a limited configuration menu called Server Configuration (SCONFIG.cmd), shown in Figure 2.13. On Hyper-V Server, this menu is started automatically. In Server Core installation mode, however, this has to be launched explicitly. This tool helps with the most recent configuration tasks, such as changing the computer name, configuring the IP address, or joining the computer to the domain.

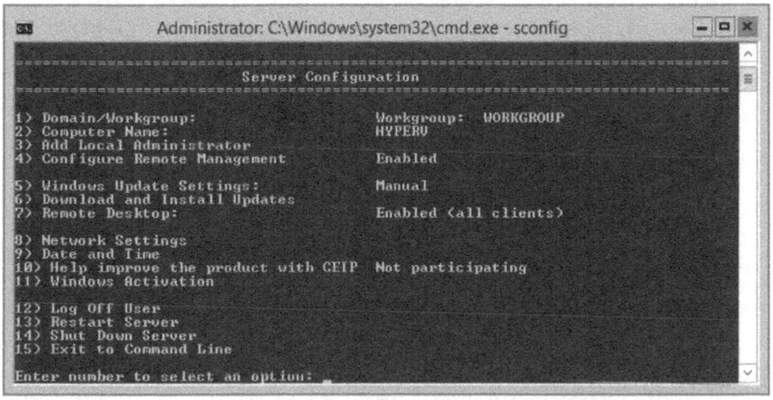

FIGURE 2.13
Server Core Server configuration menu (SCONFIG.cmd)

In Windows Server 2008 and Windows Server 2008 R2, you could not switch between Server Core and Full Installation modes. The only way to change the mode was to reinstall the entire operating system. Starting with Windows Server 2012, you have the flexibility to switch between Server Core and Server with a GUI modes. However, you still have to be aware of one small thing: when changing the installation mode after the server is set up, one reboot is required to complete the process. But, compared to what had to be done in the past, you should find this acceptable. After all, switching modes is not a day-to-day action. If it is, you should reconsider your architecture.

CONVERTING FROM GUI TO SERVER CORE

The scenario where you deploy a server with a GUI and then remove the GUI management tools and desktop shell to convert the server to Server Core installation mode will probably also be the most common and probably also the scenario in which you can also benefit the most from the easy installation using the GUI and having a secure platform when transforming to Server Core.

You can easily do this via Server Manager by using the Remove Roles And Features wizard to help you:

1. In the Server Manager, click Manage and select Remove Roles And Features.

2. On the Before You Begin page, verify the Destination Server and then click Next.

3. From the Server Selection page, select the server from the Server Pool and then click Next.

4. Leave the Server Roles page as is and click Next.

5. From the Feature page, deselect the User Interface And Infrastructure check box and con-firm the removal of the Windows PowerShell ISE. Click Next.

6. On the Confirmation page, select Restart The Destination Server Automatically If Required and then click Remove.

As a part of the removal, the server reboots automatically. You can choose to manually reboot the system, but the process is not completed until you've rebooted the server. Some graphical management tools, such as the PowerShell ISE, will be removed as part of this process.

Another way is to use this PowerShell command:

```
Uninstall-WindowsFeature Server-Gui-Mgmt-Infra,Server-Gui-Shell –Restart
```

Whereas in previous versions of Windows Server a role or feature was just disabled, the binary files can now be removed completely from the operating system to conserve disk space and reduce the attack surface even further. To completely remove a role or feature, use the -Remove option with the Uninstall-WindowsFeature cmdlet:

```
Uninstall-WindowsFeature Server-Gui-Mgmt-Infra,Server-Gui-Shell –Remove –Restart
```

The component would then have the status Removed in Server Manager and Disabled With Payload Removed in DISM.exe. The host needs access to an installation source to add the role or feature back to the operating system.

Although converting to Server Core mode is a very good choice for the Hyper-V hosts for performance, security, and patching reasons, consider maintaining a single "emergency" man-agement host that still runs with the GUI (in case you need to make an emergency change). Otherwise, the preceding PowerShell makes a perfect last statement in any provisioning script that you have running to deploy your Hyper-V hosts.

CONVERTING FROM SERVER CORE TO GUI

The second scenario is to install the GUI to a server configured as Server Core. As explained earlier, you also have the option of having a Minimal Server Interface instead of using the full Server with a GUI mode. The Minimal Server Interface mode can be installed by using the fol-lowing PowerShell cmdlet:

```
Install-WindowsFeature Server-Gui-Mgmt-Infra –Restart
```

If the Minimal Server Interface would be not enough, the full Server with a GUI mode can be installed using this PowerShell cmdlet:

```
Install-WindowsFeature Server-Gui-Shell –Restart
```

Of course, the server GUI can also be installed directly in almost one step by using the fol-lowing PowerShell cmdlet:

```
Install-WindowsFeature Server-Gui-Mgmt-Infra,Server-Gui-Shell –Restart
```

NOTE   After adding the GUI, make sure all management consoles are working as expected. If for example the Hyper-V Manager doesn't work, simply re-install the RSAT component using Server Manager.

If the host doesn't have access to Windows Update, the process will fail. However, the installation can be done using the original `INSTALL.wim` image as the source to complete the process:

1. Create a folder where `INSTALL.wim` will be mounted by running the following command:

   ```
   mkdir C:\MountDir
   ```

2. Determine the index number for the server (such as the index number for `SERVERDATCENTER`) by using this command:

   ```
   dism /Get-WimInfo /WimFile:<YourDrive>:sources\install.wim
   ```

3. Then mount the WIM file to the folder created before by using the following command:

   ```
   dism /Mount-Wim /WimFile:<YourDrive>:\sources\install.wim `
   /Index:<YourIndexNumber> /MountDir:C:\MountDir /ReadOnly
   ```

4. Start PowerShell and run the `Install-WindowsFeature` cmdlet:

   ```
   Install-WindowsFeature Server-Gui-Mgmt-Infra,Server-Gui-Shell –Restart `
   –Source C:\MountDir\Windows\WinSxS
   ```

Don't forget to unmount the WIM image after the task has been completed:

```
dism /Unmount-Wim /MountDir:C:\MountDir /Discard
```

Without access to the original source file used to mount the WIM, the unmount process will fail with the error message "The device is not ready."

Upgrading Hyper-V

Windows Server 2012 was announced on September 4, 2012, and from then on, all these great features became available to everyone. If you're still using Hyper-V on Windows Server 2008 R2 or even Windows Server 2008, you probably are planning to upgrade your own hosts to the latest version.

You have various options for the update. Usually, we discourage upgrading operating systems in-place to avoid potential problems. You may also want to change or adopt some of the new features that require a design change anyway, in which case a reinstallation often is the easier and less painful approach.

If you want (or have to) upgrade Hyper-V by using the in-place method, a detailed guide is available on Microsoft TechNet:

```
http://technet.microsoft.com/en-us/library/jj134246
```

For users with Hyper-V R2 clusters, the Cluster Migration Wizard in Failover Cluster Manager or Virtual Machine Manager 2012 SP1 can help.

Performing In-Place Migration

In-place migration is considered by many administrators as a first option, because it's an easy way to migrate the current environment to a new platform (in this case, Windows Server 2012). But as mentioned earlier, this method also carries some risks.

First you have to make sure that all installed roles, features, applications, and configurations are compatible with the new operating system. This process is actually very straightforward, because the Windows Server installation routine provides a special option called Upgrade: Install Windows And Keep Files, Settings And Applications when it detects a previous Windows installation. A Compatibility Report is also created and saved on the desktop, so you could use that for later reference in solving any compatibility issues.

But, be warned! Before you start with an in-place migration, you should make sure to have a full backup of your Hyper-V host in case something breaks during the upgrade. This would also be your ticket back to Windows Server 2008 (R2) in case of any compatibility issues.

Using the Windows Server Migration Tools

The Windows Server Migration Tools allow administrators to easily migrate their roles and features with an optimized amount of effort from servers running an older version of Windows Server to Windows Server 2012. These migration tools are based on PowerShell and must be installed on both the destination and the source server.

For Hyper-V, the migration tools can be configured to migrate the following components:

- Hyper-V settings (automated)
- Virtual network adapter settings (automated)
- Virtual machine queue (VMQ) settings (automated)
- External virtual networks (partially automated)
- Virtual machines (automated)
- Customized remote administration settings (manual)

The Windows Server Migration tool is installed first on the destination server by using PowerShell:

```
Install-WindowsFeature Migration –ComputerName <computer_name>
```

After creating a deployment folder on the destination server, the source server can be registered by using SmigDeploy.exe. A very detailed migration guide for Hyper-V is available on Microsoft TechNet. We don't discuss this migration because it is beyond the scope of this book.

```
http://technet.microsoft.com/en-us/library/jj574113
```

Exporting and Importing Virtual Machines

One of the changes in Windows Server 2012 that we like very much is the new Import Virtual Machine wizard, shown in Figure 2.14. The goal in Windows Server 2012 was to help prevent configuration problems by completing an import successfully in the past. If you worked with Hyper-V on Windows Server 2008 or 2008 R2, you know what I'm talking about. As mentioned, this process has changed in Windows Server 2012, as the import wizard now validates the configuration of virtual machine files when they are imported to identify potential problems before importing them.

In addition, Windows Server 2012 has a built-in ability to fix potential problems when moving/importing virtual machines on a host. Rather than just disconnecting the virtual network adapter or virtual hard disk if the component is not available, as happened in the past, the wizard will now prompt for new input.

FIGURE 2.14
Import Virtual
Machine wizard

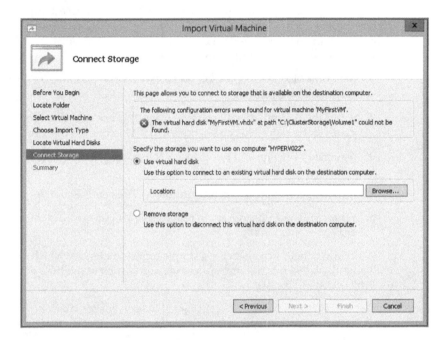

Another great enhancement in Windows Server 2012 Hyper-V is the capability to import virtual machines that haven't been exported before. In other words, we just need to have the virtual machine configuration file (XML) and the virtual hard disk (VHD or VHDX) and we can easily import the machine with the exact same configuration. This also enables you to just copy the files from one host to another and then initiate the import process.

This is another great opportunity to leverage the new PowerShell cmdlets. This command registers the virtual machine in-place without copying the data to a new location:

```
Import-VM -Path "E:\VMData\MyFirstVM\Virtual Machines\0E8B9B51-2DED-4676-AFB6-
A1B10DB3F331.xml"
```

If the process fails, an incompatibility report can be created. This helps identify the cause of a problem—for example, that the virtual switch is not available.

```
$VMReport = Compare-VM -Path "E:\VMData\MyFirstVM\Virtual Machines\0E8B9B51-2DED-
4676-AFB6-A1B10DB3F331.xml"
```

To display the report, run the following command:

```
$VMReport.Incompatibilities | Format-Table -AutoSize
```

If the virtual switch was the cause, you can fix this by adding new commands after the pipe:

```
$VMReport.Incompatibilities | Disconnect-VMNetworkAdapter
```

Upgrading Integration Services

After upgrading to Windows Server 2012 and moving all virtual machines to the new host, one important post-activity is often forgotten. The virtual machines need to be updated with the latest drivers or so-called Integration Services. This is a simple setup that has to be run on every virtual machine that is not running Windows Server 2012 or Windows 8. (These have the new drivers built in and don't have to be updated.)

To achieve this, simply follow these steps:

1. In Server Manager, click Tools and select Hyper-V Manager. Verify that the desired host is added to the console.

2. Select the desired virtual machine from the view and click Connect from the Actions pane on the right. This opens the Virtual Machine Connection.

3. Navigate to Action and select Insert Integration Services Setup Disk, which mounts the ISO image to the virtual machine.

4. Run the setup to upgrade Integration Services and reboot the virtual machine if required.

5. When finished, don't forget to remove the ISO image after the upgrade (C:\Windows\system32\vmguest.iso).

With PowerShell, we can create a simple report to identify which virtual machines are not using the latest Integration Services version (which at the time of this writing is version 6.2.9200.16433):

```
Get-VM | Where-Object {$_.IntegrationServicesVersion -ne "6.2.9200.16433"} `
| Format-Table -Property Name, State, IntegrationServicesVersion, ComputerName `
-AutoSize
```

New in Windows Server 2012, the setup will detect whether the current version is already installed and block the installation. In the previous version, the setup was done anyway—which wasn't that smart.

Be aware that an update of Integration Services also might be required after installing, as outlined in Table 2.8.

TABLE 2.8:   Hyper-V Integration Services

HYPER-V VERSION	INTEGRATION SERVICES VERSION
WS2012 RTM	6.2.9200.16384
WS2012 RTM + KB2770917	6.2.9200.16433

Real World Solutions

Here are a few problems and solutions that you might encounter when installing a new Windows Server 2012 Hyper-V.

CHALLENGE

You have been asked to install a few Hyper-V hosts, but your deployment tool of choice is not yet ready? And of course the idea is to have all hosts configured identically.

SOLUTION

This solution is going to use a PowerShell script and a XML file containing all required information. The script will take care on the install the required roles and features as well as configure the Hyper-V role. The script of course would have to get tuned and adopted to work in your environment. Please note there is no error handling or logging added.

The XML file could look like the following:

```xml
<?xml version="1.0" encoding="utf-8"?>
<Config>
  <Host>
    <Computer Name="HYPERV21" Domain="server-talk.eu" WinSysLocal="en-US" />
    <VMHost VirtualMachinePath="C:\VMs" VirtualHardDiskPath="C:\VMs"
MacAddressMinimum="00-15-5D-78-21-00" MacAddressMaximum="00-15-5D-78-21-FF" />
  </Host>
  <Network>
    <Teaming Name="Network Team" TeamMember1="00-17-A4-77-00-2B" TeamMember2="00-
17-A4-77-00-2D"/>
    <VirtualSwitch Name="Public Network" BW="10" NetVirtDriver="true" />
  </Network>
  <NetworkAdapter>
  <PubMgmt Name="Public_Mgmt" IP="192.168.1.21" SubnetPrefix="24"
Gateway="192.168.1.1" DNS1="192.168.1.101" DNS2="192.168.1.102" VLAN="" BW="5" />
    <PrivMigration Name="Private_Migration" IP="10.10.10.21" SubnetPrefix="24"
VLAN="" BW="30" />
    <PrivCluster Name="Private_Cluster" IP="10.10.11.21" SubnetPrefix="24" VLAN=""
BW="20" />
    <General DisableDisconnected="true" />
    </NetworkAdapter>
</Config>
```

Where the PowerShell script would look like this:

```
# -----------------------------------------------------------------------------
---------------------
# Declare and define global variables
# -----------------------------------------------------------------------------
---------------------
# Get XML Information
[XML]$ConfigXML = Get-Content ".\HostConfigFile.xml"
```

```
# Host OS Settings
$strComputerName = $ConfigXML.Config.Host.Computer.Name
$strComputerDomain = $ConfigXML.Config.Host.Computer.Domain
$strComputerWinSysLocal = $ConfigXML.Config.Host.Computer.WinSysLocal


# Hyper-V Settings (VM Host)
$strVirtualMachinePath = $ConfigXML.Config.Host.VMHost.VirtualMachinePath
$strVirtualHardDiskPath = $ConfigXML.Config.Host.VMHost.VirtualHardDiskPath
$strMacAddressMinimum = $ConfigXML.Config.Host.VMHost.MacAddressMinimum
$strMacAddressMaximum = $ConfigXML.Config.Host.VMHost.MacAddressMaximum


# Network Settings
$strNetworkTeamName = $ConfigXML.Config.Network.Teaming.Name
$strNetworkTeamMember1 = $ConfigXML.Config.Network.Teaming.TeamMember1
$strNetworkTeamMember2 = $ConfigXML.Config.Network.Teaming.TeamMember2
$strVirtualSwitchName = $ConfigXML.Config.Network.VirtualSwitch.Name
$strVirtualSwitchBW = $ConfigXML.Config.Network.VirtualSwitch.BW
$strNetVirtDriver = $ConfigXML.Config.Network.VirtualSwitch.NetVirtDriver


# Network Adapter Configuration
$strNICNamePubMgmt = $ConfigXML.Config.NetworkAdapter.PubMgmt.Name
$strNICPubMgmtIP = $ConfigXML.Config.NetworkAdapter.PubMgmt.IP
$strNICPubMgmtSubnet = $ConfigXML.Config.NetworkAdapter.PubMgmt.SubnetPrefix
$strNICPubMgmtGW = $ConfigXML.Config.NetworkAdapter.PubMgmt.Gateway
$strNICPubMgmtDNS1 = $ConfigXML.Config.NetworkAdapter.PubMgmt.DNS1
$strNICPubMgmtDNS2 = $ConfigXML.Config.NetworkAdapter.PubMgmt.DNS2
$strNICPubMgmtVLAN = $ConfigXML.Config.NetworkAdapter.PubMgmt.VLAN
$strNICPubMgmtBW = $ConfigXML.Config.NetworkAdapter.PubMgmt.BW
$strNICNamePrivMigration = $ConfigXML.Config.NetworkAdapter.PrivMigration.Name
$strNICPrivMigrationIP = $ConfigXML.Config.NetworkAdapter.PrivMigration.IP
$strNICPrivMigrationSubnet = $ConfigXML.Config.NetworkAdapter.PrivMigration.
SubnetPrefix
$strNICPrivMigrationVLAN = $ConfigXML.Config.NetworkAdapter.PrivMigration.VLAN
$strNICPrivMigrationBW = $ConfigXML.Config.NetworkAdapter.PrivMigration.BW
$strNICNamePrivCluster = $ConfigXML.Config.NetworkAdapter.PrivCluster.Name
$strNICPrivClusterIP = $ConfigXML.Config.NetworkAdapter.PrivCluster.IP
$strNICPrivClusterSubnet = $ConfigXML.Config.NetworkAdapter.PrivCluster.
SubnetPrefix
$strNICPrivClusterVLAN = $ConfigXML.Config.NetworkAdapter.PrivCluster.VLAN
$strNICPrivClusterBW = $ConfigXML.Config.NetworkAdapter.PrivCluster.BW
$strNICDisconnected = $ConfigXML.Config.NetworkAdapter.General.
DisableDisconnected


# Configure Operating System
# ------------------------------------------------------------------------------
----------------------
```

```
Write-Output 'Renaming computer'
Rename-Computer -NewName $strComputerName


Write-Output 'Joining domain'
Add-Computer -DomainName $strComputerDomain


Write-Output 'Changing Windows system local language'
Import-Module International
Set-WinSystemLocale -SystemLocale $strComputerWinSysLocal



# Install Hyper-V
# ------------------------------------------------------------------------------
---------------------
Write-Output 'Installing Multipath-IO Feature'
Add-WindowsFeature Multipath-IO
Write-Output 'Installing Failover Cluster Feature'
Add-WindowsFeature Failover-Clustering -IncludeManagementTools
Write-Output 'Installing Hyper-V Role'
Add-WindowsFeature Hyper-V -IncludeManagementTools -Restart



# Configure Classic Network
# ------------------------------------------------------------------------------
---------------------
Write-Output 'Creating network team'
Get-NetAdapter -Physical | Where-Object {$_.MacAddress -eq
$strNetworkTeamMember1} | Rename-NetAdapter -NewName "Converged Team (Adapter 1)"
Get-NetAdapter -Physical | Where-Object {$_.MacAddress -eq
$strNetworkTeamMember2} | Rename-NetAdapter -NewName "Converged Team (Adapter 2)"
$strNetworkTeamMembers = Get-NetAdapter -Physical | Where-Object {$_.Name -like
"Converged Team (Adapter *" }
New-NetLbfoTeam -Name $strNetworkTeamName -TeamMembers $strNetworkTeamMembers.
Name -TeamingMode SwitchIndependent -LoadBalancingAlgorithm TransportPorts


If ($strNICDisconnected -eq "true") {
  Write-Output 'Disabling disconnected network adapters'
  Get-NetAdapter -Physical | Where-Object {$_.Status -eq "Disconnected" } |
Disable-NetAdapter }


Write-Output 'Creating a new virtual Switch with one default virtual port for
parent partition'
New-VMSwitch -Name $strVirtualSwitchName -MinimumBandwidthMode weight
-NetAdapterName $strNetworkTeamName
```

```
Write-Output 'Renaming the virtual port for the parent partition'
Rename-VMNetworkAdapter -ManagementOS -Name $strVirtualSwitchName -NewName
$strNICNamePubMgmt


Write-Output 'Creating addional virtual ports for the parent partition'
Add-VMNetworkAdapter -ManagementOS -Name $strNICNamePrivMigration -SwitchName
$strVirtualSwitchName
Add-VMNetworkAdapter -ManagementOS -Name $strNICNamePrivCluster -SwitchName
$strVirtualSwitchName


Write-Output 'Assigning the default Virtual Port to a VLAN'
Set-VMNetworkAdapterVlan -ManagementOS -VMNetworkAdapterName $strNICNamePubMgmt
-Access -VlanId $strNICPubMgmtVLAN
Set-VMNetworkAdapterVlan -ManagementOS -VMNetworkAdapterName
$strNICNamePrivMigration -Access -VlanId $strNICPrivMigrationVLAN
Set-VMNetworkAdapterVlan -ManagementOS -VMNetworkAdapterName
$strNICNamePrivCluster -Access -VlanId $strNICPrivClusterVLAN


Write-Output 'Assigning IPv4 addresses to virtual ports in parent partition'
New-NetIPAddress -IPAddress $strNICPubMgmtIP -InterfaceAlias "vEthernet
($strNICNamePubMgmt)" -PrefixLength $strNICPubMgmtSubnet -DefaultGateway
$strNICPubMgmtGW
New-NetIPAddress -IPAddress $strNICPrivMigrationIP -InterfaceAlias "vEthernet
($strNICNamePrivMigration)" -PrefixLength $strNICPrivMigrationSubnet
New-NetIPAddress -IPAddress $strNICPrivClusterIP -InterfaceAlias "vEthernet
($strNICNamePrivCluster)" -PrefixLength $strNICPrivClusterSubnet


Write-Output 'Assigning DNS Server for virtual ports in parent partition'
Set-DnsClientServerAddress -InterfaceAlias "vEthernet ($strNICNamePubMgmt)"
-ServerAddresses $strNICPubMgmtDNS1, $strNICPubMgmtDNS2


Write-Output 'Disable DNS registration for private network adapters'
$strVNICNamingPrivMigration = "vEthernet (" + $strNICNamePrivMigration + ")"
Set-DnsClient -InterfaceAlias $strVNICNamingPrivMigration
-RegisterThisConnectionsAddress $false
$strVNICNamingPrivCluster = "vEthernet (" + $strNICNamePrivCluster + ")"
Set-DnsClient -InterfaceAlias $strVNICNamingPrivCluster
-RegisterThisConnectionsAddress $false


Write-Output 'Assigning Minimum Bandwidth to ports'
Set-VMNetworkAdapter -ManagementOS -Name $strNICNamePubMgmt
-MinimumBandwidthWeight $strNICPubMgmtBW
Set-VMNetworkAdapter -ManagementOS -Name $strNICNamePrivMigration
-MinimumBandwidthWeight $strNICPrivMigrationBW
```

```
Set-VMNetworkAdapter -ManagementOS -Name $strNICNamePrivCluster
-MinimumBandwidthWeight $strNICPrivClusterBW
Set-VMSwitch $strVirtualSwitchName -DefaultFlowMinimumBandwidthWeight
$strVirtualSwitchBW


If ($strNetVirtDriver -eq "true") {
  Write-Output 'Enabling Windows Network Virtualization Filter Driver'
  Enable-NetAdapterBinding -Name $strNetworkTeamName -ComponentID ms_netwnv
}



# Configure Hyper-V
# --------------------------------------------------------------------------
---------------------
Write-Output 'Configuring Hyper-V Role'
Import-Module Hyper-V
Set-VMHost -VirtualMachinePath $strVirtualHardDiskPath -VirtualHardDiskPath
$strVirtualMachinePath
Set-VMHost -MacAddressMinimum $strMacAddressMinimum  -MacAddressMaximum
$strMacAddressMaximum



# Finish Installation / Configuration
# --------------------------------------------------------------------------
---------------------
Write-Output 'Please restart computer to finish configuration'
#Restart-Computer
```

You don't like typing? Check my blog (www.server-talk.eu) for a downloadable version of this script.

CHALLENGE

You've installed a new Windows Server 2012 Hyper-V host and everything seemed to work fine, but then some issues with the storage appeared? As an example, an error in a clustered Hyper-V environment could be "Element not found (0x80070490)" when failover a clustered disk.

SOLUTION

Have you checked if all hardware (and software) is certified for Windows Server 2012? Always make sure the host bus adapters (HBA) and especially the storage itself are using the latest firmware and driver and are listed in the Windows Server Catalog.

www.windowsservercatalog.com

CHALLENGE

The installation of Windows Server 2012 stops with the error message "Windows cannot install required files. The file may be corrupt or missing. Make sure all files required for installation are available, and restart the installation. Error code: 0×80070570". The only option is to confirm the error message, which then cancels the installation process.

SOLUTION

This kind of problem occurs with corrupt installation media, for example ISO-Images which is the default media provided by Microsoft. Always make sure the MD5 or SHA1 value is correct compared to the one provided in the download portal. The download tool with the least failures would be the "Microsoft File Transfer Manager" or Akamai.

```
http://transfers.ds.microsoft.com/
```

## Chapter 3

Managing Virtual Machines

The purpose of Hyper-V is to allow us to create and run virtual machines that will run business services. This chapter focuses on the subject of virtual machine management. You will start by looking at the processes of creating virtual machines. You will then learn how to manage the settings of virtual machines, starting with some of the basics and then delving deeper with subjects such as Dynamic Memory.

A virtual machine with no operating system or application is pretty useless. In the next part of the chapter, you will look at installing operating systems, including Windows and Linux, and deploying many virtual machines. Then you will read about the often overlooked subject of application compatibility with virtualization.

With some virtual machines running, you are ready to start learning about and trying operational tasks such as Live Migration, snapshots, and virtual machine placement.

In this chapter, you'll learn about

◆ Creating and configuring virtual machines

◆ Deploying virtual machines

◆ Using virtual machine operations such as Live Migration

◆ Installing operating systems and applications

Creating Virtual Machines

The first thing anyone wants to do after creating a virtualization host is to create some virtual machines to test the technology. In Chapter 1, "Introducing Windows Server 2012 Hyper-V," you learned that a virtual machine is an abstraction of hardware, creating an independent simulated machine. This virtual machine has a configuration that mimics a hardware specification, providing controlled access to resources on the host server such as processor, memory, storage, and network. This virtual machine will have its own operating system, network presence, and security boundary, just like a physical machine such as a PC or a server. The subject of this section is the creation of these virtual machines. There are two ways you can do this: you can create virtual machines by using a wizard or by using PowerShell.

Create a Virtual Machine by Using the New Virtual Machine Wizard

The New Virtual Machine Wizard can be started in one of two ways, depending on whether the host you are working with is clustered (see Chapter 8, "Building Hyper-V Clusters").

If you are creating a non–highly available (HA) virtual machine, such as one on a nonclustered host or one that will be on a clustered host but not HA, then you can create the virtual machine in Hyper-V Manager by selecting the host and clicking New ➤ Virtual Machine in the Actions pane. The New Virtual Machine Wizard appears.

HIGHLY AVAILABLE VIRTUAL MACHINE

An HA virtual machine is one that is created on a cluster of Hyper-V hosts. The virtual machine will automatically fail over and boot up on another host if the current host should stop operating. This is the primary function of a cluster of hosts (see Chapter 8).

If you want to create an HA virtual machine, you can do this in Failover Cluster Manager. Navigate into Roles in the cluster of choice, and click Virtual Machines ➤ New Virtual Machine. This opens a dialog box where you select the host in the cluster that the virtual machine will be created on. After that, the New Virtual Machine Wizard starts. This is the same wizard that you can start in Hyper-V Manager. The only difference is that it will add the virtual machine as an HA role on the cluster.

The first screen, Specify Name And Location, shown in Figure 3.1, asks you to name the virtual machine. The name does not have to be unique, but it is highly recommended that it is. Hyper-V will use a GUID to uniquely identify the virtual machine under the covers; more on that later. You might think that the virtual machine name should be forced to be unique. However, Windows Server 2012 is a cloud operating system that was designed to be multi-tenant, and you never know what name a customer will use for their virtual machine. For internal deployments, it is a best practice to use unique virtual machine names, and preferably name the virtual machines after the desired computer name of the guest operating system that will be installed.

The Specify Name And Location screen includes an option to specify a path to store the virtual machine's files. This is not selected by default, and Hyper-V will store the virtual machine's files and virtual hard disks in the storage paths that are defined in the host's settings. A side effect of this default choice is that it will create a very flat file structure that is difficult to manage. A folder, named after the GUID of the virtual machine, will be created to store the virtual machine's configuration files. The virtual hard disk(s) of the virtual machine will be stored in the root of the folder that is specified in the host settings, and not in a subfolder for the virtual machine. The virtual hard disk is named after the virtual machine (for example, New Virtual Machine.VHDX). You cannot have two identically named files in the same folder, and this will cause a failure in the creation process.

To avoid this confusion and to keep virtual machine files nicely organized, it is strongly recommended that you select the option to Store The Virtual Machine In A Different Location. By choosing this option, the wizard will create a subfolder named after the virtual machine in the path of your choosing. All of the virtual machine's files will be stored in this subfolder, making them easy to find and manage.

FIGURE 3.1
Specify the new virtual machine's name and location.

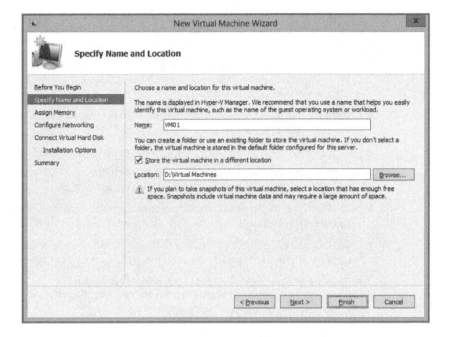

The most commonly used storage design places all of a virtual machine's files in a subfolder for that virtual machine.

Both camps of virtual machine storage agree on one thing: the default storage settings for virtual machines and virtual hard disks on a Hyper-V host are unsuitable for just about any purpose. By default, these locations are as follows:

◆ Virtual hard disks are created at `C:\Users\Public\Documents\Hyper-V\Virtual Hard Disks`

◆ Virtual machine files are stored at `C:\ProgramData\Microsoft\Windows\Hyper-V`

You can override these locations when creating a virtual machine or virtual hard disks. However, you might want to change these settings to something like these:

◆ `D:\Virtual Machines`: Virtual machines should usually be stored on a dedicated LUN on a nonclustered host.

◆ `C:\ClusterStorage`: This is where the clustered storage (Cluster Shared Volumes) of a Hyper-V cluster is mounted—for example, `C:\ClusterStorage\Volume1`.

You can change these default storage locations by opening Hyper-V Manager, connecting to the relevant host, clicking the Hyper-V Settings action, browsing to Virtual Hard Disks And Virtual Machines, and changing the shown storage paths.

If you clicked Finish, the New Virtual Machine Wizard would use the default options for the remaining settings and create the new virtual machine. You can click Next to continue the wizard to the Assign Memory screen, shown in Figure 3.2, and customize the virtual machine.

The Startup Memory setting defines how much of the host's memory will be immediately allocated to the virtual machine when the virtual machine starts up.

Hyper-V has a memory optimization feature called Dynamic Memory that you will learn about in much greater detail when you look at configuring virtual machines later in this chapter. With Dynamic Memory enabled, a virtual machine will boot up with its assigned amount of Startup Memory. After that, pressure for more memory in the virtual machine will cause the host to allocate more physical RAM to the virtual machine; and when the virtual machine is idle, the RAM will be removed via a process called *ballooning*. Not all guest operating systems (Linux, for example) and not all applications (the Exchange Mailbox role, for example) support Dynamic Memory.

If you are not using Dynamic Memory, specify how much RAM will be allocated to the virtual machine by entering the amount in megabytes in Startup Memory. The virtual machine will instantly consume this entire amount of RAM from the host when the virtual machine starts.

If you are using Dynamic Memory, you can select the Use Dynamic Memory For This Virtual Machine check box. Startup Memory should be, at the very least, the minimum amount of RAM to boot the desired guest OS of the new virtual machine. A more conservative approach is to set Startup Memory to an amount that is enough to start (not to run optimally, because the virtual machine will request more RAM) the services or applications in the virtual machine, such as 1,024 MB for a SQL Server virtual machine.

FIGURE 3.2
Configure the new virtual machine's memory.

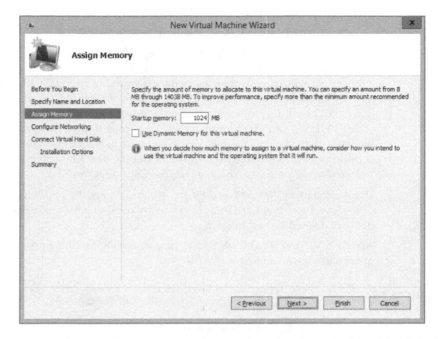

The new virtual machine will have one virtual network adapter (or virtual NIC) by default. The Configure Networking screen allows you to configure which virtual switch the virtual machine will be connected to, if at all.

Chapter 4, "Networking," will teach you about networking Hyper-V hosts and virtual machines. But right now, you should know that a virtual switch can connect a virtual machine's virtual network adapter(s) to a physical network (with or without a VLAN), to other virtual machines, and to the management OS of the host itself.

The default setting of Connection is Not Connected, which isolates the virtual NIC from all networks, including the Management OS of the host. You should change this, if required, to connect the virtual NIC to a virtual switch. Note that you can change this later, configure VLAN filtering, and add additional virtual NICs to a virtual machine.

VIRTUAL HARD DISKS

Although you can connect a virtual machine directly to a LUN on a host or a SAN, this is rarely chosen. Virtual hard disks are files, stored on a formatted LUN, that simulate a hard disk. A virtual machine that uses a virtual hard disk will read and write inside that file. The benefit of this type of virtual storage is that it's abstracted from the underlying physical LUN. Files are easy to create (and great for self-service), easy to extend, easy to back up and replicate, easy to move, and easy to delete. There is no hardware integration (the only dependency is a formatted LUN that the host can access), so this simplifies ownership of virtual hard disks. None of these benefits apply to raw LUNs, known as pass-through disks in Hyper-V.

The subject of virtual hard disks (types, formats, and management) will be covered in much more detail when you look at configuring virtual machines.

The Connect Virtual Hard Disk screen, shown in Figure 3.3, allows us to configure virtualized storage for a virtual machine. You have three options:

Create A Virtual Hard Disk Here you specify the name, location, and size of the virtual hard disk. The default size is 127 GB. The type of disk being created is a dynamic (the file starts small and grows over time as data is stored in it) VHDX file. Windows Server 2008 and Windows Server 2008 R2 offer only a type of virtual hard disk called VHD. Windows Server 2012 still supports that format, but now offers a faster and more scalable format called VHDX. The VHD format, which dates back to pre-Microsoft virtualization days in the 1990s, scales out to 2,040 GB. VHDX can scale to a maximum supported size of 64 TB, which is the maximum supported size of NTFS and the new file system called ReFS (assuming you want to back it up using Volume Shadow Copy Service).

Use An Existing Virtual Hard Disk You can choose this option if you have already created or deployed a virtual hard disk, or if you are reusing one from a restored backup or an accidentally deleted virtual machine.

Attach A Virtual Hard Disk Later You would choose this option if the previous two options are not suitable.

FIGURE 3.3
Configure a new virtual machine's storage.

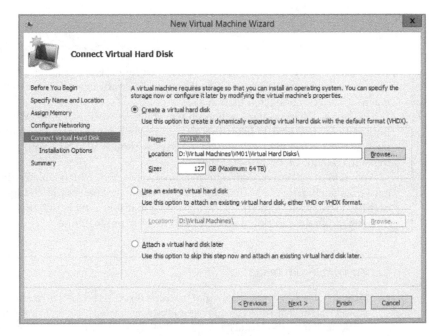

Many organizations have a policy to never use dynamic virtual hard disks for performance and maintenance reasons. You'll learn why later in this chapter. They will choose to either deploy fixed virtual hard disks in advance or to attach one after creating the virtual machine. Anyone that is happy with dynamic virtual hard disks can choose the option to create one in the Connect Virtual Hard Disk screen.

At this point, you can finish the wizard, and a new virtual machine will be created with the name, placement, and configuration of your choosing.

Hyper-V uses GUIDs to uniquely identify virtual machines rather than their names, just as Windows uses security identifiers (SIDs) to track users, computers, and groups. One way you can retrieve the GUID of a virtual machine is to look at its files:

1. Browse to the folder where the virtual machine was created.

2. In there you will find a folder called Virtual Machines. Look for an XML file. The name of the file is the GUID of the virtual machine.

Create a Virtual Machine by Using PowerShell

The PowerShell alternative to the New Virtual Machine Wizard is New-VM. You can find more about this cmdlet by running Get-Help New-VM, Get-Help New-VM, or by browsing to http://technet.microsoft.com/library/hh848537.aspx.

You can mimic the actions of the New Virtual Machine Wizard by running this:

```
New-VM -Name VM02 -Path "D:\Virtual Machines" -MemoryStartupBytes 1024MB
```

This single line of code does the following:

1. Creates a new virtual machine called VM02

2. Places it in a subfolder called VM02 in D:\Virtual Machines

3. Assigns the virtual machine 1 GB of startup memory (You could use 1GB instead of the 1,024 MB that is shown in the example.)

The New-VM cmdlet does not enable or configure Dynamic Memory. You will see how to do that later in the chapter.

The default action of this cmdlet is to create a virtual machine with no virtual hard disk, allowing you to attach one to the virtual machine at a later point. You can override this by using some additional flags when running New-VM:

Create A Virtual Hard Disk Using NewVHDPath and NewVHDSizeBytes will create a new virtual hard disk (dynamic VHDX) of the size that you specify and at the location you specify. The following example creates a 60 GB VHDX file in the same folder as the virtual machine:

```
$VMName = "VM02"
$VMPath = "D:\Virtual Machines"
New-VM -Name $VMName -MemoryStartupBytes 1024MB -Path $VMPath -NewVHDPath `
"$VMPath\$VMName\Disk0.VHDX" -NewVHDSizeBytes 60GB
```

Use An Existing Virtual Hard Disk If you already have deployed a virtual hard disk or created one of your preferred configuration, you can configure the new virtual machine to attach that disk as its boot device:

```
New-VM "VM02" -MemoryStartupBytes 1024MB -Path "D:\Virtual Machines" -VHDPath `
"D:\Virtual Machines\VM02\Disk0.VHDX"
```

When the virtual machine is created, you can find the GUID by running the following:

```
(Get-VM VM02).VMId
```

Now you know how to perform the most basic of operations used to create a virtual machine. Let's look at why you probably will want to be able to do more-advanced configurations, and how to do them.

Designing Virtual Machines

How often had engineers purchased new physical servers straight from a catalog or website without customizing them? It was very rare; each application had requirements and recommended configurations, and every organization had its own way of specializing and managing hardware. The same holds true for virtual machines. In this section, you are going to look at how to design and configure a virtual machine to suit the needs of the guest operating system, the application that will be installed, and your management system.

Virtual Machine Maximums

One of the goals of server virtualization is to replace all physical servers with virtual machines. Machine virtualization is not a new technology, but many computer rooms and datacenters have succeeded with converting only a relatively small percentage of servers into virtual machines. This can be for a number of reasons:

Budget, Politics, or Project Scope   Some virtualization projects run out of money and stop after converting some physical servers into virtual machines. Unfortunately, some project failures are less logical, as the projects simply stop after reaching a certain point, either because of organizational politics or simply because the bureaucracy says that the project has been completed, even though maybe 60 percent or more of physical servers may still be left operational.

Lack of Compatibility   Not all servers are virtualization candidates; some are ruled out because of their lack of compatibility with virtualization. For example, a server that is deeply integrated into physical communications might have physical interfaces that cannot be virtualized. Some servers might be running operating systems that are not supported by the hypervisor; for example, Hyper-V does not support Unix. And some applications do not support Hyper-V; for example, Oracle supports only its software on Oracle's own virtualization products. Even VMware fans have to consider Microsoft SQL Server a better alternative than Oracle!

Scalability   A virtual machine can support only so many virtual CPUs (logical processors). This limits the number of cores that a virtual machine has access to, therefore limiting the compute power and the number of simultaneously running threads (check the System ➢ Processor Queue Length metric in Performance Monitor in the guest OS).

Windows Server 2008 R2 Hyper-V virtual machines were limited to four virtual CPUs—that's just four logical processors. This placed sever limitations on what applications could be virtualized in larger datacenters. Windows Server 2008 R2 Hyper-V virtual machines were also limited to 64 GB RAM. Although this wasn't as crippling as the number of virtual CPUs, it did prevent larger workloads, such as online transaction processing (OLTP) or data warehouses from being virtualized.

LOGICAL PROCESSORS

A *logical processor* is a thread of execution on a host. A 10-core processor with no Hyper-Threading has 10 logical processors. If a host had one of these processors, you could run virtual machines with up to 10 virtual CPUs, with each virtual CPU running on a different logical processor at the same time.

A 10-core processor with Hyper-Threading enabled has 20 logical processors. A host with one of these processors can have virtual machines with up to 20 virtual CPUs, with each one running simultaneously on a different logical processor.

Enabling Hyper-Threading on Intel Xeon 5500 or later processors can boost processor performance of heavy virtual workloads, such as SQL Server. Doubling the number of logical processors does not double the compute power, but it can add a smaller percentage of compute power.

A host is limited to 320 logical processors. This is the equivalent of 16 10-core processors with Hyper-Threading enabled.

One of the goals of Windows Server 2012 was to enable any application that required more processor or memory to be installed in a Hyper-V virtual machine. As a result, Hyper-V now supports the following:

Up to 64 Virtual CPUs per Virtual Machine   This assumes that the host has 64 or more logical processors and that the guest operating system supports this configuration.

Up to 1 TB RAM per Virtual Machine   This is possible if the host has 1 TB to allocate to the virtual machine and the guest operating system supports this much memory.

This increased level of support should ensure that processor and memory scalability are almost never a concern when considering the installation of applications into virtual machines if the host hardware is specified appropriately.

GIANT VIRTUAL MACHINES

An organization will not normally plan to deploy lots of these gigantic virtual machines on a single host. Each logical processor may in fact be dedicated to a virtual CPU. A Windows Server 2012 or Hyper-V Server 2012 host can have 320 logical processors and up to 4 TB of RAM. Therefore, an organization might deploy two or four such virtual machines on a very large host. The benefits of doing this are the same as always with virtualization: flexibility, agility, reduced purchase and ownership costs, ease of backup, simpler DR replication, and so on.

Other virtual machine maximums include the following:

IDE Controllers   A virtual machine must boot from a disk attached to IDE Controller 0 in a virtual machine. This controller can have two devices. There is also an IDE Controller 1, which can also have two devices; the virtual DVD drive is one of these by default.

> **WHY BOOTING FROM IDE DOESN'T CAUSE A PROBLEM**
>
> Those who are unfamiliar with Hyper-V might be shocked to see that Hyper-V virtual machines boot from a virtual IDE controller. This has nothing to do with hardware and does not require a physical IDE controller. The virtual device does not have a performance impact, as Ben Armstrong (Hyper-V Senior Program Manager Lead with Microsoft) explains on his blog at `http://blogs .msdn.com/b/virtual_pc_guy/archive/2009/12/01/why-hyper-v-cannot-boot-off-of-scsi-disks-and-why-you-should-not-care.aspx`.

SCSI Controllers A SCSI controller can be attached to 64 pass-through disks (raw LUNs that are accessed directly by a virtual machine) or virtual hard disks. A virtual machine can have up to four SCSI controllers. That means a virtual machine can be attached to 256 virtual SCSI disks. A VHDX virtual hard disk can be up to 64 TB. And that means a virtual machine can have up to 16,384 TB of virtual storage.

Note that the SCSI controller requires that the guest operating system of the virtual machine has the Hyper-V integration components installed for the device driver to work.

There is a positive side effect of adding more virtual processors and SCSI controllers that is new in Windows Server 2012. Historically, a virtual machine had one storage channel. Now, a virtual machine gets one storage channel for every 16 virtual processors and per SCSI controller. Each device now has a queue depth of 256, instead of the previous limit, which was 256 per virtual machine. The handling of storage I/O is now distributed across all virtual processors instead of being bound to just a single one.

Network Adapters You can attach up to eight network adapters, also known as *synthetic network adapters*, in a virtual machine. A synthetic network adapter, shown as `Network Adapter` in virtual machine settings, is the best type of virtual NIC to use because it requires fewer host processor and context switches to transmit packets through a virtual switch.

The synthetic network adapter requires the Hyper-V integration components to be installed in the guest operating system of the virtual machine.

There is one network adapter in a virtual machine when you create it.

Legacy Network Adapters You can have up to four legacy network adapters in a virtual machine. The legacy network adapter is a less efficient virtual NIC that does not require the Hyper-V integration components to be installed in the guest OS. Therefore, this type of virtual network adapter could be used with older operating systems such as Windows NT 4 or Windows 2000 Server. Legacy network adapters cannot take advantage of any hardware offloads to accelerate virtual machine communications.

The synthetic network adapter does not support PXE booting, which is usually used for OS deployment solutions such as Windows Deployment Services (WDS) or System Center Configuration Manager. It is rare that virtual machines will be deployed using OS deployment mechanisms such as these in production environments. However, OS deployment experts love to use virtualization for creating and testing OS images. In that case, you can use a legacy network adapter in the virtual machine because it does support PXE booting.

VIRTUAL MACHINE BIOS

If you edit the settings of a Hyper-V virtual machine, you will see the following boot order:

1. CD
2. IDE
3. Legacy network adapter
4. Floppy

You can change the order of these devices by selecting one and clicking Move Up or Move Down. There is also a Num Lock check box to enable Num Lock in the virtual machine.

Fibre Channel Adapters   You can have up to four Virtual Fibre Channel adapters in a virtual machine. You can learn more about this topic in Chapter 9, "Virtual SAN Storage and Guest Clustering."

The maximums of a virtual machine should not be considered as a goal. Microsoft recommends that you always allocate only enough resources to a virtual machine for its guest operating system and application(s) to be able to perform as required. For example, granting a virtual machine 32 virtual CPUs when it requires only 4 will waste physical processor capacity on the host. When that virtual machine is getting a quantum (a slice of time on the host processors), it will occupy 32 logical processors. That will waste the 28 occupied but unused logical processors that could have been used by other virtual machines.

The advice for sizing a virtual machine is the same as it would be for a physical server: grant only those resources that are required by the workload.

Note that you cannot hot-add resources to a running virtual machine—with two exceptions:

◆ You can add a disk to a SCSI controller while the virtual machine is running.

◆ You can increase Maximum or decrease Minimum RAM in a Dynamic Memory–enabled virtual machine's settings while it is running.

You also can change the virtual switch connection of a virtual machine's network cards. This is not quite hot, because there will be a brief moment of disconnection, and you might need to change the IP address(es) in the guest OS.

Auto-Start and Auto-Stop Actions

There are various ways to configure virtual machines to respond when their host is shut down or starts up.

AUTOMATIC START ACTIONS

There are three possible start actions you can set for a virtual machine when the host that it is placed on boots up. You can find these options under Automatic Start Action in the settings of the virtual machine:

Nothing   The virtual machine will not start up.

Automatically Start If It Was Running When The Service Stopped   The virtual machine will be automatically started if it was running when the host stopped. This is the default option, and generally the one that is most used.

Always Start This Virtual Machine Automatically   The host will start the virtual machine whether it was running or not prior to the host stopping.

Both of the automatic start actions allow you to define a Startup Delay. This value (in seconds) dictates how long the virtual machine will wait after the Management OS is running to start. The purpose of this Startup Delay is to prevent all virtual machines from starting at the same time and creating processor/storage/memory contention.

You can use PowerShell to configure this setting. The following example configures all virtual machines with a name starting with VM0 to start if they were running when the host stopped and delays the virtual machines' start up by 5 minutes:

```
Set-VM VM0* -AutomaticStartAction StartIfRunning -AutomaticStartDelay 300
```

AUTOMATIC STOP ACTIONS

There are three ways to deal with virtual machines if the host they are running on is shut down. You can find these settings under Automatic Stop Action in a virtual machine's settings:

Save The Virtual Machine   This default setting configures all virtual machines to save their current state to a VSV file that is stored in the Virtual Machines subfolder where the virtual machine is stored. After this, the virtual machine stops running. When you start up the virtual machine, it reads the saved state and then continues to execute as if it had never stopped. A placeholder BIN file that is slightly larger than the memory size of the virtual machine is stored in this subfolder while the virtual machine is running. This reserves enough disk space to write the save state. Hyper-V will maintain this BIN file only if you choose this option.

Turn Off The Virtual Machine   This setting causes the virtual machine to be powered off when the host shuts down. This is like hitting the power button on a computer and is normally going to be the least used setting. It can be useful for guest OSs that refuse to shut down (and therefore prevent the host from shutting down), or you might use it if you need to quickly shut down a host without waiting for virtual machines.

Shut Down The Guest Operating System   This option cleanly shuts down the virtual machine via the guest OS integration components (required) before shutting down the host. You might choose this option if you do not want to save virtual machines to a saved state or if you do not want BIN files to consume disk space.

You can configure the Automatic Stop Actions via PowerShell. This instruction configures all virtual machines on a host to shut down when the host shuts down:

```
Set-VM * -AutomaticStopAction -ShutDown
```

Dynamic Memory

Service Pack 1 for Windows Server 2008 R2 added the Dynamic Memory feature to Hyper-V to optimize how host memory was allocated to virtual machines by the Management OS. Dynamic Memory has been improved in Windows Server 2012 Hyper-V.

INTRODUCING DYNAMIC MEMORY

Several host resources can limit the number of virtual machines that can be placed on, or run on, a host or cluster of hosts:

Processor A host has only so much compute power, and each running virtual machine consumes some of this. The amount varies, depending on the demands of the guest OS and installed applications.

Processors have scaled out immensely in the past few years, and the host's CPU is rarely the bottleneck on virtual machine-to-host density.

Storage Storage space is finite and will be consumed by a virtual machine. The physical disks have a limit on storage input/output operations per second (IOPS), and the connection to the disks will have limited bandwidth. The more demanding the virtual machines, the more IOPS and bandwidth will be used.

Careful consideration must be given when analyzing the requirements of virtual machines and planning host storage. Some applications can be very demanding of IOPS and storage connectivity, such as virtual desktop infrastructure (VDI) and OLTP. However, the emergence of SSD, caching technology, and faster networking mitigate this limitation.

Network Virtual machines connect to the physical network via one or more network connections on the host. It is rare, but possible, for virtual machines to require more bandwidth than is available on a host. Windows Server 2012 includes NIC teaming, so you can aggregate bandwidth by adding more NICs to a single logical host connection. (See Chapter 4 for more information.)

Memory Virtual machines consume RAM from a host. The most widely encountered bottleneck in the growth of virtual machine-to-host density is not processor, storage, or networking; it is the finite amount of RAM in a host that each virtual machine is consuming a piece of.

In the recent past, we have seen hardware manufacturers release servers on which every spare square centimeter seems to have a DIMM slot. In addition, increasingly large ECC memory is hitting the market (one very large DIMM costs more than several smaller ones that provide the same amount of memory). It makes sense economically over three years to put as much RAM into a single host as possible. Practical limits (such as balancing the risk of host loss and convincing a financial controller to pay more now for bigger hosts to reduce later costs of ownership) can force you into purchasing more less densely populated hosts that will cost more to own and operate over the same timeframe.

Without Dynamic Memory enabled in a virtual machine, the virtual machine must be given a large amount of RAM. For example, a SQL server might need 8 GB of Startup Memory. The virtual machine will consume all of that 8 GB, even if it is not required by the guest OS and application. That would be rather wasteful.

Microsoft introduced Dynamic Memory to accomplish several things:

- It optimizes the allocation of RAM to virtual machines. Dynamic Memory gives enabled virtual machines a startup amount of memory, allowing them to expand up to a maximum amount of memory when required, and retrieves the memory back from the virtual machine when it is no longer required.

- Dynamic Memory simplifies memory sizing. Administrators often added up the sum requirements of an application and OS, and installed RAM into a server, only to find it barely being used. Removing the RAM was difficult (because of downtime, ownership issues, and the risk that the RAM might be rarely required), so the capacity was wasted. The same holds true for virtual machines. Because Dynamic Memory allocates only what the virtual machine requires, administrators know that RAM will not be wasted on inaccurately sized virtual machines.

- Self-service and cloud computing are enabled by Dynamic Memory. Customers, as compared to administrators, are less skilled at sizing their virtual machines. Customers can start small and grow big, taking advantage of the elastic trait of a cloud. If Resource Metering is enabled (Chapter 5, "Cloud Computing"), customers will be charged for only what they use.

How Dynamic Memory Works

To understand Dynamic Memory, you must first understand the settings that are used to enable and configure it, per virtual machine. You can configure Dynamic Memory for a virtual machine in Hyper-V Manager by selecting the virtual machine, clicking Settings in the Actions pane, and clicking Memory in the left navigation pane of the settings window. The settings, shown in Figure 3.4, are as follows:

Startup RAM   You already met this setting when you were creating a virtual machine. This is the amount of memory that is allocated to a virtual machine when it starts up, whether you enable Dynamic Memory or not.

If you do not want to enable Dynamic Memory, specify (in megabytes) how much memory the virtual machine will require. All of this memory will be allocated from the host's pool of RAM to the virtual machine when the virtual machine starts up. The virtual machine will fail to start if this memory cannot be completely assigned to the virtual machine.

If you do want to enable Dynamic Memory, set this to the amount of RAM that will successfully start the guest operating system (required) and start its services/applications at a basic level (optional, but often recommended).

Enable Dynamic Memory   You will enable Dynamic Memory for this virtual machine by selecting this check box. This can be done only when a virtual machine is turned off, so it's best done at the time of virtual machine creation or during a maintenance window. Selecting this check box will enable the remaining memory settings to be configured.

FIGURE 3.4
Configuring the memory of a virtual machine

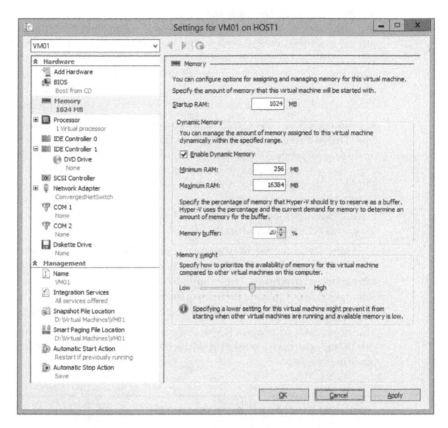

Maximum RAM   The Maximum RAM setting controls the amount of memory that the virtual machine can consume. The maximum setting is 1,048,576 MB or 1 TB, which is the maximum amount of RAM that can be allocated to a virtual machine. Note that a virtual machine can never be allocated more RAM than is available on a host.

You can increase the value of Maximum RAM while a virtual machine is running. This means that a service will not require downtime to give it more memory.

Memory Buffer   This is an additional amount of memory that is allocated to a virtual machine. The default value of 20 percent is usually changed only when required. If a virtual machine requires 1,000 MB of RAM, for example, Dynamic Memory will allocate 1,200 MB of RAM to the virtual machine. The buffer is used in two ways. It is available as spare memory to the guest OS should it have an instant need for more memory that Dynamic Memory cannot respond to quickly enough. (Note that Dynamic Memory is quick, but a host might have a shortage of unallocated RAM.) The buffer is usually not wasted by a guest OS; Windows will use the additional memory as a file cache. Note that SQL Server will never use this RAM for file caching, so we generally set the buffer of SQL Server virtual machines to its lowest value of 5 percent. The maximum value is 2000 percent.

Memory Weight Dynamic Memory uses the Memory Weight (also known as Priority) value to determine how to divide up host memory when there is contention—that is, when several virtual machines are asking for all of the remaining host RAM. Memory weight is a sliding value from low (0) to high (100). A virtual machine with a higher Memory Weight is capable of making a better case for a share of the remaining memory on a contended host than a virtual machine with a lower Memory Weight. This value is usually left in the middle (50) and changed only for virtual machines with higher or lower service-level agreements.

Minimum RAM Microsoft did a considerable amount of engineering (referred to as MinWin) in Windows 8 and Windows Server 2012 to reduce the overall footprint of these operating systems. Although they still require 512 MB to boot up (just like their predecessors), the new operating systems can consume much less memory when they are left idle. This is particularly true in VDI and hosting environments, where many virtual machines can be left unused for months. Startup RAM would have to be 512 MB (minimum) to start the virtual machines, but Minimum RAM allows us to define an amount of memory that is lower (as low as 8 MB) than the Startup RAM.

This new Dynamic Memory setting allows idle virtual machines to use less memory than they booted up with. The unused memory is returned to the host and can be used by more-active virtual machines. This could also be combined with System Center Virtual Machine Manager Power Optimization to squeeze virtual machines down to few hosts during idle periods so that unused hosts could be powered off (and powered up again when required).

You can reduce Minimum RAM while a virtual machine is running. This means that you can better optimize a workload while monitoring the actual RAM usage as the virtual machine is idle.

SECOND LEVEL ADDRESS TRANSLATION

Microsoft added support for Second Level Address Translation (SLAT) in Windows Server 2008 R2 Hyper-V. SLAT takes advantage of dedication functions in Intel EPT–capable and AMD NPT/RVI processors to offload the mapping of physical to virtual memory. SLAT can boost the performance of memory-intensive workloads such as databases (Exchange or SQL Server) and Remote Desktop Services (RDS) by around 20 percent.

You do not need to configure anything to use SLAT; you just need a capable processor. SLAT-capable processors are not required for Windows Server 2012 Hyper-V, but they are recommended. Server processors have been coming with SLAT support for several years.

Windows 8 Client Hyper-V does require a SLAT-capable processor. This is for performance reasons. Desktop and laptop processors, such as Intel Core (i3, i5, and i7), have come with this support only in recent years.

You can also configure these settings in a virtual machine by using `Set-VMMemory`. PowerShell uses Priority instead of Memory Weight. Note that you can use MB or GB instead of entering the true byte value of the memory setting.

```
Set-VMMemory VM01 -StartupBytes 1GB -DynamicMemoryEnabled $True -MinimumBytes `
256MB -MaximumBytes 16GB -Buffer 5 -Priority 100
```

Now it's time to see how Dynamic Memory puts these settings to use. Figure 3.5 shows a sequence of events during which memory is assigned to and removed from a virtual machine. The VM worker process (`VMWP.EXE` in the Management OS of the host) of each virtual machine with Dynamic Memory enabled is responsible for managing Dynamic Memory for that machine. There is a connection between the worker process and the Dynamic Memory Virtual Service Client (DMVSC) through the VMBus. (DMVSC is one of the Hyper-V integration components installed in the guest OS of the virtual machine.)

FIGURE 3.5
Dynamic Memory scenarios

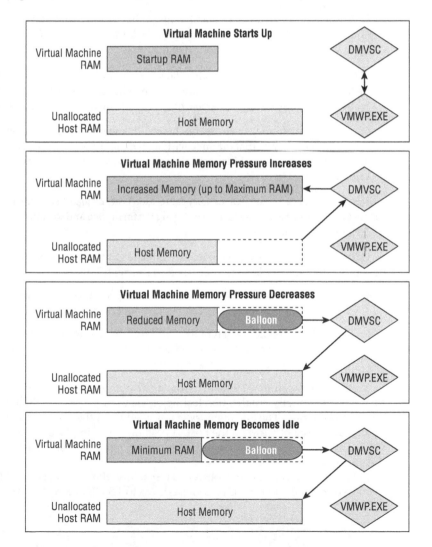

A virtual machine must be allocated with its Startup RAM for it to be able to boot up. That amount of memory is removed from the host and assigned to the virtual machine. There is a tiny, variable overhead for managing this memory (a few megabytes), whether Dynamic Memory is enabled or not.

Say that the Startup RAM setting is 1 GB, and the Maximum RAM setting is 16 GB. If you logged into the guest OS of the virtual machine, you would see that its memory (via Task Manager or Performance Monitor) is actually 1 GB and not the 16 GB that you might have expected. This is because the virtual machine has booted up with 1 GB, and the guest OS has not yet been given 16 GB of RAM by Dynamic Memory.

The memory pressure in the virtual machine might increase. This will be detected by the Management OS. Memory can be allocated to the virtual machine as long as there is unallocated memory on the host. A rapid and specially developed Plug and Play process is used to inject memory into the virtual machine. Remember that the Memory Buffer will be allocated as a percentage of the assinged RAM.

In this example, the virtual machine might have gone from Startup RAM of 1 GB and expanded up to 3 GB. Now if you looked at Task Manager or Performance Monitor in the guest OS, you would see that the memory size was 3 GB.

NOTE Hyper-V will do its best to fairly allocate memory to virtual machines if there is not enough RAM left for all of their demands. An algorithm will take the Memory Weight (Priority) and the memory pressure of each virtual machine to divide up the remaining memory.

Sometimes a high-priority virtual machine with low memory pressure might get less memory than a low-priority virtual machine with high memory pressure, or vice versa. As memory is allocated to a virtual machine, its pressure changes, and this affects how further memory is allocated by the algorithm.

System Center can preempt a memory contention issue by load-balancing virtual machines across hosts with more available resources, using Performance and Resource Optimization (PRO) or Dynamic Optimization.

If the pressure in the virtual machine subsides and memory becomes idle, that memory will be removed by the DMVSC and returned to the host. This happens in one of two ways:

◆ Other virtual machines have high memory pressure, and memory is contended on the host. Hyper-V will immediately remove idle memory from virtual machines.

◆ There is no contention. Hyper-V will leave the memory in the virtual machine for several minutes, just in case it is required again. This will save some CPU cycles. The memory will eventually be removed if it is still idle.

You cannot just remove memory from a running machine, physical or virtual. Dynamic Memory, like other virtualization technologies, uses a process called ballooning, as noted earlier in this chapter. The idle memory is removed from the virtual machine and returned to the unallocated pool of RAM on the host. A balloon is put in place of the removed memory in the virtual machine. This gives the illusion that the memory is still there, but it is not available to the guest OS.

Let's return to our example of a virtual machine that has Startup RAM of 1 GB and has increased to 3 GB. Now it has ballooned down to 1.5 GB of RAM. If you check the memory in the guest OS of the virtual machine, you will see that it is still 3 GB. Remember that you can never remove memory from a running machine; the balloon has fooled the guest OS into believing that it still has its high-water mark of RAM. The memory amount can increase, but it will not go down while the guest OS is running. The value will reset when the virtual machine's guest OS starts up again.

MONITORING DYNAMIC MEMORY

These are the only accurate ways to track memory allocation on a Hyper-V host without using Dynamic Memory–aware systems management solutions:

Hyper-V Manager　The Assigned Memory column for the virtual machines shows the amount of memory allocated to each virtual machine including the Memory Buffer.

Management OS Performance Monitor　The Hyper-V Dynamic Memory counters (Balancer, Integration Service, and VM) give you lots of information about Dynamic Memory on a host, such as what memory has been assigned, how much is guest visible, and what is the current pressure.

If the virtual machine becomes busy again and pressure increases, Hyper-V will detect this. Memory will be allocated to the virtual machine and deflate the balloon a little at a time.

If a virtual machine becomes idle, the pressure for memory will be very low. This will enable the DMVSC to return memory to the host. If the Minimum RAM value is lower than the Startup RAM value, Dynamic Memory will continue to remove idle memory and reduce the virtual machine to a value lower than what it booted up with. This will minimize the resource consumption of the idle virtual machine and free up memory for more-active virtual machines.

How does this affect our example virtual machine?

◆	It booted up with 1 GB.

◆	It increased to 3 GB.

◆	It ballooned down to 1.5 GB.

Now the virtual machine might become idle and balloon further down, as far as its Minimum RAM value of 256 MB. Logging into the guest OS and checking the memory will still show us 3 GB (the previous high-water mark). Hyper-V Manager might show the virtual machine using 308 MB RAM (256 MB plus the Memory Buffer of 20 percent). At this point, we have saved 921 MB (1,229 MB, the Startup RAM plus Memory Buffer, minus 308 MB), which can be made available to other virtual machines.

A host can never assign more memory than it has. That means that the total sum of memory being used by virtual machines cannot exceed the amount of memory that is on the host—don't forget that the Management OS will use a small amount of memory too. This means that we do not overcommit memory with Dynamic Memory.

In Hyper-V, there is no shared-paging or memory overcommitment as is found in other virtualization platforms. With shared paging, a hypervisor performs a single instance process of memory management. If two virtual machines have a common page of memory, it is stored once in the host's physical RAM. This option is usually one of the first that you are told to turn off by other vendors when you open a support call. Shared paging at the hypervisor layer might also have problems if a guest operating system does this process internally to reduce its own memory footprint.

In memory overcommitment, a hypervisor lies to a virtual machine about the RAM that it has been assigned. With such a hypervisor, a virtual machine might be assigned 1 GB RAM at bootup, but the guest OS believes it has 16 GB RAM to use. If the guest OS tries to use it and the hypervisor does not have the physical RAM to allocate, then the hypervisor has to lie. This lie is accomplished by using second-level paging to simulate RAM; a host paging file blindly pages RAM for the virtual machine with no visibility over page usage or priority. This will hugely reduce memory performance, and requires additional (very fast) disk space on the host for the second-level paging file.

Microsoft did look at these approaches and saw the drawbacks on supportability, performance, and stability. This is why Dynamic Memory does not overcommit memory; service performance is more important than virtual machine density.

SMART PAGING

Imagine that you have lots of idle virtual machines with Dynamic Memory Minimum RAM configured. Each of these virtual machines is on a host and has ballooned to below its Startup RAM as in Figure 3.6. The host's RAM is completely filled with virtual machines. Now one of three scenarios happens:

- The host reboots, thus requiring virtual machines (if configured to automatically start) to boot up with their Startup RAM.

- One or more virtual machines reboot, each requiring its Startup RAM.

- One or more virtual machines reset, and each one requires its Startup RAM.

FIGURE 3.6
Virtual machines, on using Minimum RAM, have filled a host.

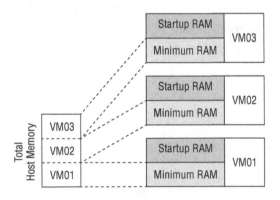

The problem is that the host RAM was already full of virtual machines, and these once idle virtual machines now need more memory than they had before—the sum of the Startup RAM values is higher than the sum of the Minimum RAM values. The host has a responsibility to get the virtual machines back up and running.

This is actually a rare, and theoretical, circumstance. Someone or something has deliberately squeezed a large number of idle virtual machines onto a host until the RAM was contended. Realistically, there will be only a few virtual machines that have ballooned down below their Startup RAM. A host might have failed in a densely populated Hyper-V cluster, causing virtual machines to be failed over to this host. System Center Power Optimization might have been used too aggressively to move virtual machines onto fewer hosts, and shut down the idle hosts, and a patching window may have caused virtual machines to reboot.

A well-sized implementation would have prevented these issues. Failover Clustering will use the "best available" host (the one with the most RAM) to fail over each virtual machine. Always ensure that you have enough host capacity in a cluster to handle a failover scenario if performance is more important to you than budget when sizing high availability. Don't be too ambitious with System Center Power Optimization; always leave room for at least one (or more in bigger environments) failover host and be aware of automated patching windows.

A management system such as System Center will also intervene, where possible, to load-balance and move virtual machines (with no downtime) to more-suitable hosts. All of these techniques should make this Minimum RAM vs. Startup RAM contention issue a rare event. But even then, Hyper-V has to successfully give these virtual machines enough memory for their Startup RAM to get them running again.

Smart Paging is a process whereby a Smart Paging file is temporarily created to simulate memory for a virtual machine when one of the three preceding scenarios occurs and the host does not have enough memory to start up previously running virtual machines that must be auto-started. This is not second-level paging; Smart Paging exists only to enable virtual machines to start up and return to their idle state, so they can balloon back down to their previous amount of memory, below their Startup RAM. Eventually this does occur, and the Smart Paging file will be removed. If a virtual machine continues to use a Smart Paging file, alerts in Event Viewer will inform you. This would be indicative of overly aggressive placement of virtual machines on this host.

There is not a single Smart Paging file for the host. Instead, each virtual machine that requires Smart Paging will have its own Smart Paging file. You can see the default storage location (where the virtual machine is stored) in the virtual machine settings under Smart Paging File Location. You can retrieve this path by using the following PowerShell command:

```
(Get-VM VM01).SmartPagingPath
```

You can change the path (while the virtual machine is powered off) by running this:

```
Set-VM VM01 -SmartPagingFilePath "D:\SmartPaging"
```

OTHER DYNAMIC-MEMORY SIDE EFFECTS

There are two other side effects of increasing and decreasing memory in a virtual machine.

The Save State BIN File

A virtual machine can be configured to automatically save its state when a host shuts down. The state of the virtual machine's processors and memory is written to a VSV file in the Virtual

Machines subfolder where the virtual machine's configuration is stored. If the virtual machine is configured to save its state when the host shuts down, Hyper-V will maintain a BIN file. This placeholder file is a few megabytes larger than the amount of memory currently assigned to the virtual machine. It ensures that the virtual machine will always have disk space to write its save state to.

The BIN file will increase and decrease in size to roughly match the memory that is allocated to the virtual machine. You should account for this when sizing your storage. This can be quite a surprise for administrators who are creating virtual machines with very large memories. You can remove this BIN file by changing the virtual machine to use one of the alternative Automatic Stop Actions in the virtual machine settings in the GUI or via PowerShell:

```
Set-VM VM01 -AutomaticStopAction ShutDown
```

The Guest OS Paging File

If the guest OS of the virtual machine is set to automatically manage the paging file, you might see it increase in size as memory is allocated to the virtual machine. This won't be an issue with relatively small amounts of increase, but it would be a problem if a virtual machine was expanding from 512 MB to 64 GB of RAM. The paging file could attempt to fill the drive that it is on, thus depriving you of storage and reducing the optimal size of the paging file. Here are two suggestions:

◆ Ensure that the paging file disk has sufficient space for growth.

◆ Manually configure the guest OS paging file for virtual machines that are configured to have massive potential growth.

DYNAMIC MEMORY STRATEGIES AND CONSIDERATIONS

There are many ways to configure Dynamic Memory. You might have a one-size-fits-all approach to all virtual machines that might be suitable for a cloud. You might perform a very granular configuration per virtual machine on a private, non-cloud environment in which IT is directly involved with the management of everything.

Self-Service and Startup RAM

Say you run a cloud with self-service. Your customers, internal or external, can use a portal to deploy their own virtual machines from a library of templates, all of which are managed by your organization. Your virtual machine templates are set up with Dynamic Memory enabled. Every virtual machine will boot up with a Startup RAM of 512 MB and maybe grow to a Maximum RAM of 4 GB, 8 GB, or more. And there's the problem.

Just about every application (at least from Microsoft) that you install requires a SQL Server database. SQL Server will refuse to install if the prerequisites check finds less than 1 GB RAM in the guest OS of the virtual machine. The virtual machine has had no need to increase the RAM beyond 1 GB, and the installer fails. You can be guaranteed lots of calls from customers looking for help. A few of those help desk calls will be from angry people who claim that they are paying for 4 GB RAM or more and that you're trying to con them. You could ask them to temporarily spike their memory (run MSPAINT.EXE and set the image size to 10,000 by 10,000 pixels), but that won't calm the customers down.

Alternatively, you can try different configurations with your virtual machine templates and prevent the issue from happening at all.

You could set the virtual machine to have a Startup RAM that is the most common minimum prerequisite for an installation. 1 GB is the minimum amount of memory required by SQL Server 2012. You could combine this with Minimum RAM set to 256 MB. Any new virtual machine will quickly balloon down from 1 GB until SQL Server or a similarly demanding application is installed. Any unused virtual machine will have only a very small footprint on the host.

Some public cloud operators are concerned that Dynamic Memory shows the guest OS administrator only the high-water mark of memory allocation since the guest OS last booted up. In that case, the Startup RAM could be set to match the Maximum RAM. This will require a lot of memory to be available to start the virtual machine. Once the virtual machine is running, it can balloon down to a much lower Minimum RAM. The downside to this approach is that you are almost guaranteeing Smart Paging activity if lots of virtual machines need to start up at the same time and there is no other host to load-balance to.

Using Maximum RAM

Here are three possible approaches, using names not created by Microsoft, to setting the Maximum RAM of a virtual machine:

Elastic   This approach uses the default maximum RAM of 1 TB. A virtual machine will take what it can from the host, up to this amount. This is a very cloud purist approach, as customers can take what they need and pay for it later using Resource Metering. But the elastic approach has a few major problems.

Customers might use the resources, but will they pay for them? Legal contracts can mean much less than you might think in the real world of business relationships. How long might it take to get a customer to pay if you have to follow up with debt collection or legal actions?

The other issue is more common; there are a lot of bad business applications out there, and memory leaks happen. If a memory leak happens in a virtual machine with a massive Maximum RAM setting, then that bad application will keep eating host memory until it either hits the maximum or consumes all that the host has to offer.

Cloud computing is already difficult enough to size with the unpredictable nature of future workloads that you can't predict. The elastic approach makes this even worse because the memory usage for virtual machines has no limits other than the total host capacity.

Realistic   This is the opposite of the elastic approach. Administrators will create virtual machines and templates with smaller amounts of Maximum RAM. Virtual workloads are monitored, and the Maximum RAM setting can be increased as required. This increase could be automated, but that's going to be subject to the same flaws as the elastic maximum memory approach.

The realistic approach requires monitoring and alerting of virtual machines so that an administrator can increase the Maximum RAM of those machines (without downtime). Each increase would be small, only enabling what memory assignment the virtual machine requires during genuine peak usage.

Although this completely optimizes memory allocation and solves the problems of the elastic approach, it does require some human effort, which has an operational cost of its own.

Optimistic   Some organizations have a policy of allocating a reasonably large amount of memory to all machines (PC or server) so that there is no restriction on performance and administrator intervention is minimized. The thought is that memory is often a bottleneck on performance, and memory is cheaper than administrator time and reduced service levels for the business. In other words, being a memory scrooge is false economics.

The optimistic Dynamic Memory approach is a balance between being elastic and being realistic. Virtual machines are created with a reasonably generous amount of Maximum RAM. The virtual machines should still be monitored, but the amount of alerts and human intervention should be much lower. There is some risk of the problems of the elastic approach, but the amount of RAM is much lower, and so the problems should be fewer and contained.

Using Minimum RAM

We have to consider the potential impact of Smart Paging when using Minimum RAM. Aggressive usage of this useful feature on hosts that cannot be load-balanced (for example, by System Center) will lead to Smart Paging when these hosts are overloaded. Here are some things to consider:

◆   Do not manually overload non-load-balanced hosts with virtual machines.

◆   When designing hosts, always leave enough hosts to deal with host failure. For example, a 64-node Hyper-V cluster probably needs several (N+4 maybe), and not just one (N+1), failover host.

◆   When using System Center Power Optimization, keep in mind that virtual machines will probably patch at night, when you have squeezed the virtual machines down to fewer hosts. Always leave enough host capacity powered up for System Center to load-balance the virtual machines as they power up. For example, you might shut down six of ten hosts and barely squeeze the virtual machines onto the remaining four hosts. That will cause Smart Paging during reboot/resets. Instead, shut down just five hosts and still reduce your power costs by 50 percent at night while avoiding Smart Paging.

HOST MEMORY RESERVE

There is a single pool of RAM on a host. From this pool, the Management OS consumes RAM for itself, and Dynamic Memory assigns memory to virtual machines. Without any controls, high-pressure virtual machines could consume the entire RAM from the host, and leave the Management OS without the ability to get any more memory. This could cause the Management OS to freeze (the virtual machines would still continue to operate) until the virtual machines balloon down.

Hyper-V has a control to prevent this from happening. The Host Memory Reserve is used by the Management OS to reserve host RAM for itself so that Dynamic Memory cannot claim it.

The formula for calculating this value has not been made public at the time of this writing. What we do know is that the setting is calculated much more conservatively than it was in Windows Server 2008 R2 with Service Pack 1. This means that a host will reserve slightly more memory for itself than it would have before. A Management OS requires at least 512 MB to start but usually requires around 2 GB RAM to run optimally.

The setting (amount of MB to be reserved specified in REG_DWORD `MemoryReserve` at `HKLM\SOFTWARE\Microsoft\Windows NT\CurrentVersion\Virtualization`) should not be tampered with and should be left to be managed by Hyper-V, unless you are instructed otherwise by Microsoft support.

Processors

You can configure the virtual CPUs of a virtual machine by editing the settings of the virtual machine and clicking Processor. Note that Processor can expand, to reveal further settings called Compatibility and NUMA.

PROCESSOR SETTINGS

A virtual machine can have from 1 to 64 virtual processors. The number of virtual processors cannot exceed the number of logical processors in the host. Keep this in mind if you plan to move the virtual machine around different hosts by using Live Migration. Although you can configure the number of virtual CPUs in uneven numbers, this is not recommended. You can configure the number of virtual CPUs by using the Number Of Virtual Processors setting (which has a default of 1), as shown in Figure 3.7.

The Resource Control options allow you to customize how the virtual CPUs of this virtual machine access the physical logical processors that they will run on. There are three settings:

Virtual Machine Reserve (Percentage)   Each virtual CPU will run on a host's logical processor, taking up a share of its time. Using this setting, you can guarantee a minimum amount of time on the processor for this virtual machine. This is a percentage value from 0 (the default—nothing guaranteed) to 100 (only this virtual machine will use the logical processors it runs on). It defines how much of a logical processor a single processor of this virtual machine will consume.

The overall reservation of host processor for this virtual machine will be displayed in Percent Of Total System Resources. For example, a virtual machine with two virtual CPUs with a reserve of 50 percent, on a host with four logical processors, will be guaranteed a minimum of 25 percent of all processor capacity: $100/[(2 \times 50\%) \times 4]\%$.

Typically this setting is not used, but it can be useful for some processor-heavy applications, such as SharePoint, that should be guaranteed some cores on the host without having to contend with other lightweight virtual machines.

Virtual Machine Limit (Percentage)   This rarely used setting can be used to cap the logical processor utilization of the virtual CPUs. Just as with Virtual Machine Reserve, this setting is per virtual processor, and the total host processor limit will be calculated for you and displayed in Percent Of Total System Resources.

Relative Weight   This is a weight value of between 0 and 10,000 that defaults to 100. This is used by Hyper-V to decide which virtual machines will get access to logical processors when there is processor contention. A virtual machine with a higher Relative Weight will get more time on the host's logical processors.

FIGURE 3.7
Configuring virtual processors in a virtual machine

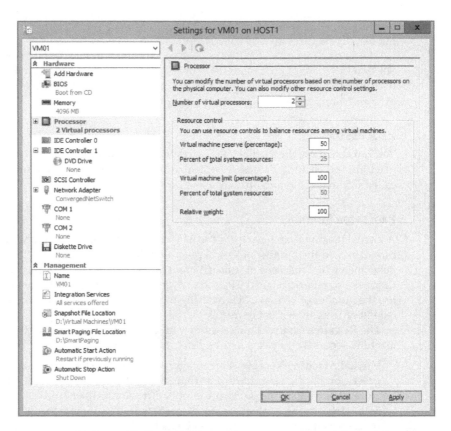

Set-VMProcessor is the PowerShell cmdlet for configuring virtual machine CPUs. You can mimic the Processor settings in Hyper-V Manager by running this:

```
Set-VMProcessor VM01 -Count 4 -Reserve 100 -Maximum 100 -RelativeWeight 1000
```

COMPATIBILITY

There is just a single setting in the GUI called Migrate To A Physical Computer With A Different Processor Version. With this setting enabled, you can use Hyper-V Live Migration to move a virtual machine to hosts with different versions of processor from the same manufacturer. For example, you could move a running virtual machine from a host with Intel E5 processors to a host with Intel Xeon 5500 processors with no impact on service availability.

This setting is off by default. This is because it reduces the physical processor functionality that the virtual machine can use. Basically, the virtual machine is reduced to the lowest set of processor features made by that manufacturer (Intel or AMD). This is quite a price to pay for Live Migration across hosts of different ages. You can avoid this in one of two ways:

Buy the Newest Processor You Can Afford   When you install a new farm of Hyper-V hosts, you should purchase the latest processor that you can afford. If you require new hosts in 12 months, you still have a small chance of being able to buy the hosts with the same processor.

Start New Host or Cluster Footprints   Larger environments might start entirely new host footprints with no intention of regularly live-migrating virtual machines between the newer hosts (or cluster) and the older hosts (or cluster). This is not advice that you can give to a small/medium enterprise and should be reserved for larger organizations.

If you have no choice, and you must support Live Migration between different generations of processor from the same manufacturer, you must enable the Migrate To A Physical Computer With A Different Processor Version setting. You can also do this with PowerShell:

```
Set-VMProcessor * -CompatibilityForMigrationEnabled $True
```

Hyper-V veterans might notice that one compatibility setting of the past (and for the past) is missing. Older operating systems such as Windows NT 4 Server require the virtual CPUs to run with compatibility for older operating systems enabled. Otherwise, these historic operating systems cannot be installed. You still have the setting, but it can be reached only via PowerShell; this shows you how often Microsoft expects people to use it!

```
Set-VMProcessor VM02 -CompatibilityForOlderOperatingSystemsEnabled $True
```

NUMA

Non-Uniform Memory Access (NUMA) is a hardware architecture driven by the way that physical processors access memory on the motherboard of servers.

What is NUMA?

A large processor, one with many cores, may be designed by the manufacturer to divide itself up to enable parallel direct connections to different banks of memory, as shown in Figure 3.8. This example shows an 8-core processor that has been divided into two NUMA nodes. Cores 0–3 are in NUMA Node 0 and have direct access to one set of memory. Cores 4–7 are in NUMA Node 1 and have direct access to another set of memory.

If a process that is running on cores in NUMA Node 0 requests memory, a NUMA-aware operating system or hypervisor will do its best to assign RAM from NUMA Node 0. This is because there is a direct connection to the memory in that same node. If there is not enough memory available in NUMA Node 0 to meet the request, then something called *NUMA node spanning* will occur, and the operating system or hypervisor will assign RAM from another NUMA node, such as NUMA Node 1. The process that is running in NUMA Node 0 has indirect access to the memory in NUMA Node 1 via the cores in NUMA Node 1. This indirect access will slow the performance of the process.

FIGURE 3.8
A NUMA architecture

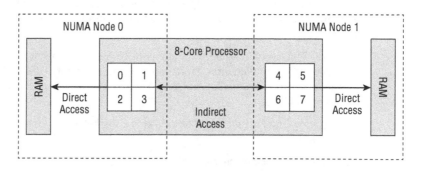

NUMA is not unique to Hyper-V. This hardware architecture is one that operating systems (Windows and Linux) and hypervisors (Hyper-V and ESXi), and even some applications (such as IIS 8, SQL Server, and Oracle) have to deal with.

The example in Figure 3.8 is a simple one. Imagine that you have two of those 8-core processors, or maybe ten 16-core processors. You could have a lot of NUMA nodes. The truth is, there is no rule for NUMA architecture and sizing. It depends on the processor that you have and the memory placement/sizing on your motherboard. You could search for information for your processor, but the quickest solution might be to discover what your hardware actually has:

- CoreInfo by Microsoft SysInternals (`http://technet.microsoft.com/sysinternals/cc835722.aspx`) can dump your NUMA architecture when run with the `-N` flag.

- You can run the `Get-VMHostNumaNode` PowerShell cmdlet to see the architecture and sizes of the NUMA nodes.

- The NUMA Node Memory counters in Performance Monitor show the memory size and utilization of your NUMA nodes.

Hyper-V and NUMA

Hyper-V is NUMA aware. When a virtual machine runs in a NUMA node, Hyper-V will do its best to allocate memory to that virtual machine from the same NUMA node to minimize NUMA node spanning.

Dynamic Memory can cause a virtual machine to span NUMA nodes. Refer to Figure 3.8. Imagine that both NUMA nodes have 16 GB of RAM. A virtual machine, VM01, is running in NUMA Node 0 and has been allocated 10 GB of RAM from the direct access memory. Now memory pressure grows in the virtual machine, and Dynamic Memory needs to assign more RAM. There is no more free RAM left in NUMA Node 0, so Dynamic Memory needs to assign indirect access memory from another NUMA node.

You might want to prevent this from occurring. You can do this via Hyper-V Manager:

1. Select the host and click Hyper-V Settings in the Actions pane.

2. Open the NUMA Spanning settings.

3. Clear the Allow Virtual Machines To Span Physical NUMA Nodes check box (enabled by default).

Changing the NUMA spanning setting requires you to restart the Virtual Machine Management Service (VMMS, which runs in user mode in the management OS). You can do this as follows:

4. Open Services (Computer Management or Administrative Tools), find a service called Hyper-V Virtual Machine Management, and restart it. This will not power off your virtual machines; remember that they are running on top of the hypervisor, just as the management OS is.

You can view the current NUMA node spanning setting by running the following PowerShell snippet:

```
(Get-VMHost).NumaSpanningEnabled
```

To disable NUMA spanning on the host and restart the VMMS, you can run the following piece of PowerShell:

```
Set-VMHost -NumaSpanningEnabled $false
Restart-Service "Hyper-V Virtual Machine Management"
```

NUMA was not a big deal with Windows Server 2008 R2 Hyper-V; it was something that was dealt with under the hood. We were restricted to a maximum of four virtual CPUs per virtual machine, so NUMA node spanning was uncommon. But Windows Server 2012 Hyper-V supports up to 64 virtual CPUs and 1 TB RAM in a single virtual machine; there is no doubt that a larger virtual machine (even six or eight virtual CPUs, depending on the host hardware) will span NUMA nodes. And that could have caused a problem if Microsoft had not anticipated it.

Windows Server 2012 Hyper-V reveals the NUMA node architecture that a virtual machine resides on to the guest OS (Windows or Linux) of the virtual machine when it starts up. This allows the guest OS to schedule processes on virtual CPUs and assign memory to processes while respecting the NUMA nodes that it is running on. This means we get the most efficient connections at the virtual layer, and therefore the physical layer, between processors and memory. And this is how Microsoft can scale virtual machines out to 64 virtual processors and 1 TB RAM without making compromises.

NUMA AND LINUX

Linux might be NUMA aware, but it does not scale out very well. Once a Linux operating system, on any physical or virtual installation, scales about seven processors or 30 GB RAM, then you must set numa=off in the GRUB boot.cfg. This will reduce the performance of memory and the services running in that Linux machine. In the case of Linux, it would be better to scale out the number of virtual machines working in parallel if the application is architected to allow this, rather than scaling up the specification of the virtual machines.

There is one remaining consideration with NUMA and larger virtual machines that span NUMA nodes. The NUMA architecture that the guest operating system is using cannot be changed until it powers off. What happens when the running virtual machine is moved (via Live Migration) to another host with a smaller NUMA node architecture? The answer is that the guest operating system will be using invalid virtual NUMA nodes that are not aligned to the physical NUMA structure of the host, and the performance of the services provided by the virtual machine will suffer.

Ideally, you will always live-migrate virtual machines only between identical hosts, and any new hosts will be in different server footprints. And just as with processor compatibility, this can be an unrealistic ambition.

Figure 3.9 shows the NUMA settings of a virtual machine, which you can find by editing the settings of a virtual machine and browsing to Processor ➢ NUMA. The Configuration area shows the current NUMA configuration of the virtual machine. This example shows two virtual processors that reside on a single socket (physical processor) in a single NUMA node.

FIGURE 3.9
Two virtual
processors that
reside on a single
socket (physical
processor) in a
single NUMA node

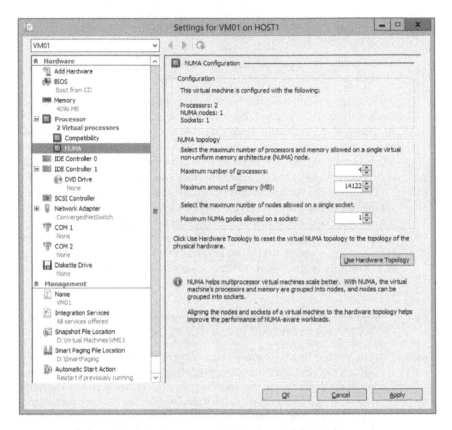

The NUMA Topology area allows you to customize the virtual NUMA node. This should be sized to match the smallest NUMA node on the hosts that your virtual machine can be moved to via Live Migration. This can be tricky to do, so Microsoft made it easy:

1. Move the virtual machine to the host with the smallest NUMA nodes.

2. Shut down the virtual machine.

3. Open the NUMA settings of the virtual machine.

4. Click the Use Hardware Topology button to complete the NUMA settings for the virtual machine.

We could not find a PowerShell alternative at the time of this writing.

Virtual Storage

A virtual machine needs somewhere to install its operating system and applications, and somewhere to store its data. This section describes the storage of Hyper-V virtual machines.

THE STORAGE FORMATS

You can use three disk formats in Hyper-V: pass-through disks, VHD format, and VHDX format.

Pass-Through Disks

A raw LUN, known as a pass-through disk, can be assigned to a virtual machine. There are two reasons to do this:

◆ Getting nearly 100 percent of the potential speed of the RAW disk is not enough. Pass-through disks are often used in lab environments to perform tests at the very fastest possible speed.

◆ You need to create guest clusters that can share a LUN, where using virtual or file server storage is not an option.

Perform the following to attach a pass-through disk to a virtual machine:

1. Create a LUN in the underlying physical storage.

2. Ensure that the LUN is visible in Disk Management on the host. Do not bring the LUN online on the host.

3. Edit the settings of the virtual machine and browse to the controller that you want to add the disk to.

4. Select Hard Drive and click Add.

5. Change Controller and Location as required to select the controller of choice and a free channel.

6. Select the Physical Hard Disk radio button and select the raw disk that you want to connect to the virtual machine. Note that the name, such as Disk 2, will match the label in Disk Management.

Using PowerShell you can use Get-Disk to identify the LUN (disk number). You can attach this LUN as a pass-through disk to the virtual machine by running Add-VMHardDiskDrive.

```
Add-VMHardDiskDrive VM02 -ControllerType SCSI -ControllerNumber 0 `
-ControllerLocation 0 -DiskNumber 2
```

Pass-through disks are the least flexible and most expensive to own type of storage that can be used. They cannot be moved; they require traditional backup; they require application- or storage-based DR replication; and they do not lend themselves to self-service creation/administration in a cloud.

Virtual hard disks are the alternative to pass-through disks. Virtual hard disks are just files that simulate disks. Because they are software, they are easy to manage, and they do lend themselves to thin provisioning, self-service in a cloud, and easy administration. Virtual hard disks are easy to back up (they are just files), easy to replicate to DR sites, and easy to move. And most important, virtual hard disks can run at nearly the speed of the underlying physical storage.

VHD Format

The VHD format has been around since the 1990s, when it was created by Connectix, a company that Microsoft acquired and whose technology became the foundation of Microsoft's machine virtualization. The VHD disk format has been supported by Microsoft Virtual Server and by Hyper-V since Windows Server 2008. VHD has a major limitation—which wasn't considered a limitation just a few years ago: VHD cannot scale beyond 2,040 GB (just under 2 TB).

VHDX Format

Windows Server 2012 adds a new disk format called VHDX that can scale out to 64 TB, which is also the maximum LUN size supported by NTFS and ReFS. The VHDX format also has the following features:

◆ It allows application developers to use VHDX as a container and store metadata in the file.

◆ VHDX maintains an internal log (within the file) to maintain consistency of the contained data. For example, it should prevent data corruption during power outages.

◆ VHDX (on IDE or SCSI virtual controllers) supports UNMAP to allow Windows 7 SP1 and Windows Server SP1 and later guest OSs to inform supporting underlying storage to reclaim space that used to contain data for thin provisioning (useful for dynamic VHDX—dynamically expanding disks will be explained later in the chapter). This requires the integration components to be installed in the guest OS. The unused space is reclaimed when the volume is defragged or when you run `Optimize-Volume -DriveLetter <X> -ReTrim`. Note that pass-through disks attached to Virtual Fibre Channel or SCSI controllers also can support Unmap.

OTHER USES FOR VIRTUAL HARD DISKS

The virtual hard disk is one of the two datacenter container file types used by Microsoft. Windows Imaging File Format (WIM) files are used in operating system deployment. For example, you'll find some WIM files in the Windows Server 2012 installation media: one called `boot.wim` boots up the installation routine (a boot image), and `install.wim` contains the operating system image that will be deployed to the machine.

Virtual hard disks are used for virtualization to store virtual machine data, but they are also used for a few other things.

A computer can be configured to boot from a virtual hard disk instead of an operating system on a traditional NTFS-formatted LUN. This is referred to as a Native VHD or boot from VHD. Note that the use of the term *VHD* in this case comes from a time when the VHD format was the only kind of virtual hard disk, and sometimes VHD is used as a general term to include VHD and VHDX. You can boot from either VHD or VHDX files when using Windows Server 2012 or Windows 8 boot loaders.

A virtual hard disk can also be used when Windows Server Backup (WSB) is backing up computers (see Chapter 10, "Backup and Recovery"). The backup data is stored in a virtual hard disk. Windows Server 2012 uses VHDX by default for the backup media; VHDX can scale out to 64 TB and can support backing up of larger volumes than the VHD format, which is limited to 2,040 GB.

DISK SECTOR ALIGNMENT

Alignment is a process whereby files are constructed in block sizes that match the way that they are physically stored on disks. Hard disks have used 512-byte sectors up to now. That means that data is read from and written to the disk in 512-byte chunks. Therefore, pretty much every operating system, hypervisor, and file type has been designed to be aligned for 512-byte sectors; for example, the VHD format is designed to be read and written in 512-byte chunks.

However, a change has been occurring in the storage business. Disks have started to adopt larger 4K-sector sizes. This allows the disks to get bigger and maintain performance. The storage industry gives us two kinds of 4K disk:

Native 4K Disks This disk format requires an operating system and files that are aligned to and support 4K sectors without any assistance or emulation. The disk reads and writes 4K chunks of data so the physical sector size of the disk is 4K. The operating system will read and write 4K chunks of data so the logical sector size of the disk is 4K.

512-Byte Emulation (512e) Disks The storage industry is providing 4K disks with firmware that emulates a 512-byte disk. When an operating system requests a 512-byte sector, the disk will read in 4K and extract the requested 512 bytes. The real concern is with the performance of the emulated write operation known as read-modify-write (RMW). The operating system will send 512 bytes down to the disk to write. The disk must spin to read the 4K sector that contains that 512 bytes, read the sector, inject the 512 bytes into the 4K of data, and write the 4K. RMW requires disk activity that 4K-aligned files do not need, and therefore is much slower. Microsoft believes (http://technet.microsoft.com/library/hh831459) RMW speeds could be between 30 percent and 80 percent slower than nonemulated writes. In this case, the physical sector size is 4K, but the logical sector size is 512 bytes.

Windows Server 2012 supports native 4K disks (http://msdn.microsoft.com/library/windows/desktop/hh848035(v=vs.85).aspx). You can install Windows Server 2012 on a native 4K disk and use it as a Hyper-V host. Windows Server 2012 will read and write 4K at a time without any emulation.

The structure of a VHD file that is created on a Windows Server 2012 host is padded so that it is aligned to 4K. Microsoft has also included an RMW process in VHD to allow it to be stored on native 4K disks. Note that you will need to convert VHDs that are created or used on hosts previous to Windows Server 2012 or Hyper-V Server 2012. This is because they lose the enhancement that aligns the disk to 4K and allows native 4K storage.

Microsoft is the first virtualization manufacturer to produce a virtual hard disk format (VHDX) that is designed to allow native 4K alignment without RMW. This means that VHDX is the best storage option on 512-byte-sector disks (scalability and data consistency), on 512e disks, and on 4K disks (performance). The VHD is retained on Windows Server 2012 for backward compatibility. A best practice is to convert VHD files into the VHDX format if you do not require support for legacy versions of Hyper-V.

WINDOWS 8 CLIENT HYPER-V AND VHDX

The VHDX format and 4K matching capability of VHDX are also supported by Windows 8 Client Hyper-V, giving you offline portability between virtualization in the datacenter and virtualization on the client device.

THE TYPES OF VIRTUAL HARD DISK

There are three types of virtual hard disk: fixed size, dynamically expanding, and differencing. The three types are available if you choose either VHD or VHDX as your format.

Fixed-Size Virtual Hard Disk

When you create a fixed virtual hard disk of a certain size, a virtual hard disk is created that is that size on the physical storage. For example, if you create a 100 GB fixed VHDX, a 100 GB VHDX file is created.

The creation process for a fixed virtual hard disk can take some time. This is because each block of the VHDX is zeroed out to obscure whatever data may have been stored on the underlying file system.

Fixed virtual hard disks are the fastest of the virtual hard disk types, and are often recommended for read-intensive applications such as SQL Server or Exchange.

However, many virtual machines use only a small percentage of their virtual storage space. Any empty space is wasted, because the virtual hard disk file is fully utilizing the underlying physical storage (preventing SAN thin provisioning from having an effect). You could deploy small fixed virtual hard disks, monitor for free space alerts, and expand the virtual hard disks as required. However, this requires effort and the virtual hard disk to be offline (usually requiring the virtual machine to be powered off too).

OFFLOADED DATA TRANSFER

Windows Server 2012 has added support for using Offloaded Data Transfer (ODX) with ODX-capable SANs. ODX was originally intended to speed up the copying of files between servers on the same SAN. Without ODX, the source server reads the file from a LUN on the SAN and sends it to the destination server, which then writes the file to another LUN on the same SAN. With ODX, the servers and SAN exchange secure tokens, and the SAN copies the file from one LUN to another without all of the latent traffic. This can be advantageous for the deployment of virtual machines to SAN-attached hosts from a library that is stored on the SAN; this will be very helpful for a self-service cloud.

The creation of fixed virtual hard disks is also accelerated by ODX. Some Hyper-V customers refused to adopt the fixed type because it was slow to create, even though it offered the best performance. ODX greatly reduces the time to create fixed virtual hard disks and should resolve this issue.

Dynamically Expanding Virtual Hard Disk

The dynamically expanding (often shortened to *dynamic*) type of virtual hard disk starts out as a very small file of just a few megabytes and grows to the size specified at the time of creation. For example, you could create a 127 GB dynamic VHDX. The file will be 4 MB in size until you start to add data to it. The file will gradually grow to 127 GB as you add data.

The dynamic virtual hard disk has spawned a lot of debate over the years in the Hyper-V community. There are those who claim that the dynamic type is just as fast as the fixed virtual hard disk, and there are those who say otherwise. In Windows Server 2008 R2, Microsoft increased the block size in a dynamic VHD from 512 KB to 2 MB. This meant that the dynamic VHD would grow more quickly. The growth rate was increased again with dynamic VHDX in Windows Server 2012.

However, real-world experience shows that write speed is not the big concern with the dynamic type. Imagine you have lots of dynamic virtual hard disks stored on the same physical volume. They all grow simultaneously in random patterns. Over time, they fragment, and this fragmentation scatters the VHDX all over the volume. Anecdotal evidence points out that the read performance of the VHDX files will suffer greatly, and this will reduce the performance of intensive read operations such as database queries. This could reduce the performance of interactive applications to below service-level agreement levels. Fixed virtual hard disks offer superior read performance over time in a production environment.

The benefit of the dynamic virtual hard disk is that it does consume only the space required by the contained data plus a few additional megabytes. This can reduce the costs of purchase and ownership of physical storage and enable the usage of SAN thin provisioning. Dynamic virtual hard disks are very useful for those who need to minimize spending and in lab environments but are not concerned with the loss in read performance.

IT'S NOT JUST A CHOICE OF ONE OR THE OTHER

If you are concerned just about performance, the fixed type of virtual hard disk would seem to be the correct way to go. But can you deploy fixed virtual hard disks quickly enough in your cloud? Can you accelerate the creation or copy of a 100 GB fixed virtual hard disk using ODX? What if you do not have ODX because you are using SMB 3 storage?

Some organizations have adopted a hybrid model. In this situation, virtual machines are configured to boot using dynamic virtual hard disks attached to IDE Controller 0 and Location 0. This means that a large virtual hard disk takes up a small amount of space in a template library and takes a shorter amount of time to deploy than a fixed-size alternative.

Any data will be stored in fixed virtual hard disks that are attached to the SCSI controller(s) of the virtual machine. Storing data in this way will ensure that the data virtual hard disk will be less prone to fragmentation. This also isolates the data, making the configuration and management of the virtual machine and its guest OS/data more flexible.

Using multiple types of virtual hard disk does come at a cost; it increases the complexity of deployment and maintenance.

Differencing Virtual Hard Disk

The differencing type is used when you need to be able to rapidly provision one or more virtual machines and you need to:

◆ Do it quickly

◆ Use as little storage space as possible

When you create a differencing virtual hard disk, you must point it at a parent virtual hard disk that already has data in it. The differencing disk will start out very small with no data. A virtual machine will use the differencing disk as follows:

◆ Data older than the differencing disk is read from the parent disk.

◆ Any new data that must be stored is written to the differencing disk, causing it to grow over time.

◆ Any data newer than the differencing disk is read from the differencing disk.

The traits of differencing disks make them very useful for pooled VDI virtual machines (the sort that are created when a user logs in and deleted when they log out) and virtual machines used for software testing. A virtual machine is prepared with an operating system and generalized using Sysprep (if the guest OS is Windows) with an automated configuration answer file. The virtual machine is destroyed, and the hard disk is retained and stored in a fast shared location that the host(s) can access. This virtual hard disk will be the parent disk. New virtual machines are created with differencing virtual hard disks that point to the generalized virtual hard disk as their parent. This means that new virtual machines are created almost instantly and only require the guest OS to start up and be customized by the answer file.

Differencing disks are the slowest of all the virtual hard disk types. Differencing disks will also grow over time. Imagine deploying applications, security patches, service packs, and hotfixes to virtual machines that use differencing disks. Eventually they will grow to be bigger than the original parent disk, and they will run slower than the alternative dynamic or fixed types.

A common problem is that people assume that they can mess with the parent disk. For example, they try to expand it or replace it with a newer version with an updated guest OS. This will break the link between the parent and the differencing disks.

It is for these reasons that differencing disks should not be used for any virtual machine that will be retained for more than a few hours or days, such as a production server.

VIRTUAL HARD DISK MANAGEMENT

You will use the same tools to create VHD and VHDX formats, and VHDX will be the default format.

Creating Virtual Hard Disks

You can create virtual hard disks in several ways, including these:

◆ The New Virtual Machine Wizard will create a dynamic VHDX file as the boot disk for a new virtual machine. We have already covered this earlier in the chapter.

◆ Disk Manager can be used to create virtual hard disks. We do not cover this method in this book.

◆ You can click New ➤ Hard Disk in the Actions pane in Hyper-V Manager to start the New Virtual Hard Disk Wizard. This will create a new virtual hard disk in a location of your choosing that you can later attach to a virtual machine.

◆ You can edit the storage controller settings of a virtual machine, click Add to add a new Hard Drive, and click New to start the New Virtual Hard Disk Wizard. This will add the new virtual hard disk (stored in your preferred location) and attach it to the controller with the Location (channel) of your choosing.

◆ You can use the New-VHD PowerShell cmdlet.

The New Virtual Hard Disk wizard will step you through the decision-making process of creating a new virtual hard disk:

1. The Choose Disk Format option enables you to select either VHD or VHDX (selected by default).

2. You are asked which type of virtual hard disk to use (dynamic is selected by default) in the Choose Disk Type screen.

3. Specify Name And Location asks you to enter the filename of the virtual hard disk and the folder to store the file in.

4. The Configure Disk screen asks you to specify how the virtual hard disk will be created.

If you are creating a differencing virtual hard disk, you are simply asked to enter the path and filename of the desired parent disk.

If you are creating a dynamic or fixed virtual hard disk, the screen is different. If you want a new empty virtual hard disk, you enter the desired size of the disk. Alternatively, you can create a new virtual hard disk that is made using the contents of a LUN that is attached to the server or from another virtual hard disk. These options can be used in a few ways, including the following:

◆ You want to convert a pass-through disk or a LUN into a virtual hard disk. This might be useful for people who used pass-through disks in past versions of Hyper-V and who now want to convert them to VHDX files that are more flexible and equally as scalable.

◆ You would like to convert an existing virtual hard disk into a Windows Server 2012 virtual hard disk. This could be useful if you have used a VHD on an older (Windows Server 2008 or Windows Server 2008 R2) version of Hyper-V and want to convert it into one that is padded for better performance on 512e physical disks.

Using the PowerShell alternative can be a bit quicker than stepping through the New Virtual Hard Disk Wizard, especially if you need to create lots of virtual machines or virtual hard disks. The following example creates a 100 GB fixed VHDX:

```
New-VHD -Path "D:\Virtual Machines\parent.vhdx" -Fixed -SizeBytes 100GB
```

The next example creates a differencing VHDX that uses the first VHDX as its parent:

```
New-VHD -Path "D:\Virtual Machines\VM01\differencing.vhdx" -ParentPath `
"D:\Virtual Machines\parent.vhdx"
```

If you want to create VHDX files that are optimized for 512e or 4K disks, you must use the New-VHD PowerShell cmdlet. There are two ways to configure a VHDX to get the best performance and to get operating system compatibility:

Physical Sector Size   You can optimize the file structure of a VHDX to match the sector size of the physical storage that it is stored on. This will affect performance of the VHDX, the guest OS storage, and the guest application(s). Remember that a virtual machine's storage might be moved from one storage platform to another.

Logical Sector Size   A VHDX has sector sizes that are seen by the guest OS and application(s). You can configure a VHDX to have a specific sector size to optimize the performance of your guest operating system and application(s). Remember that some operating systems or applications might not support 4K sectors.

Creating VHDX files with a sector size that doesn't match the physical storage will greatly reduce your storage performance. Therefore, it is recommended that you match the physical sector size of VHDX files with the type of physical disks that you are using. For example, a 4K guest OS should use VHDXs with 4K logical and physical sector sizes if the disk is 4K. However, a non-4K-capable guest OS should use VHDXs with a 512-byte logical sector size and a 4K physical sector size to get RMW and the best compatibility possible when stored on a 4K disk. Table 3.1 shows how to match the physical sector size of the VHDX with the physical disk to get the best performance.

TABLE 3.1: Physical disk vs. VHDX physical sector size

PHYSICAL DISK TYPE	VHDX PHYSICAL SECTOR SIZE
512-byte	512, 512e, 4K (no difference in performance)
512e	4K, 512e, 512 (decreasing order of performance)
4K	4K, 512e (decreasing order of performance)

The following example creates a VHDX with 4K logical and physical sector sizes:

```
New-VHD -Path "D:\Virtual Machines\VM02\test.vhdx" -Dynamic -SizeBytes 100GB `
-LogicalSectorSizeBytes 4096 -PhysicalSectorSizeBytes 4096
```

The guest OS and application(s) must support 4K sectors if you choose 4K logical and physical sector sizes for the VHDX. The next example creates a VHDX file that matches the 4K sector of the physical storage but uses 512-byte logical sectors:

```
New-VHD -Path "D:\Virtual Machines\VM02\test.vhdx" -Dynamic -SizeBytes 100GB `
-LogicalSectorSizeBytes 512 -PhysicalSectorSizeBytes 4096
```

REFS AND HYPER-V

The Resilient File System (ReFS) is Microsoft's "next generation" file system, offering greater levels of availability and scalability than NTFS (see http://msdn.microsoft.com/library/windows/desktop/hh848060(v=vs.85).aspx). ReFS currently has limited support in Windows Server 2012, but it is envisioned to be a successor to NTFS, which has been around since the early 1990s.

ReFS can be used on nonclustered volumes to store virtual machines. However, you must disable the ReFS Integrity Streams (the automated file system checksums) if you want to be able to store VHD or VHDX files on the volume.

Attaching Virtual Hard Disks

In Hyper-V Manager, you can edit the settings of a virtual machine, browse to the controller of choice, select the Location (channel), click Add, and browse to or enter the path to the desired virtual hard disk.

Alternatively, you can use the `Add-VMHardDiskDrive` PowerShell cmdlet. This example adds an existing (fixed) VHDX file to the boot location of the IDE 0 controller of a virtual machine called VM01:

```
Add-VMHardDiskDrive VM01 -ControllerType IDE -ControllerNumber 0 `
-ControllerLocation 0 -Path `
"D:\Virtual Machines\VM01\Virtual Hard Disks\VM01.vhdx"
```

You could instead attach a virtual hard disk to a SCSI controller in the virtual machine:

```
Add-VMHardDiskDrive VM01 -ControllerType SCSI -ControllerNumber 0 `
-ControllerLocation 0 -Path `
"D:\Virtual Machines\VM01\Virtual Hard Disks\VM01.vhdx"
```

Modifying Virtual Hard Disks

You will probably want to view the settings of a virtual hard disk before you modify it. You can do this in a few ways, including these:

- Browse to an attached VHD in the setting of a virtual machine and click Inspect.

- Run the Inspect task in the Actions pane of Hyper-V Manager and browse to the virtual hard disk.

- Run `Get-VHD` with the path to the virtual hard disk.

The Edit Virtual Hard Disk Wizard will step you through the possible actions for modifying a virtual hard disk. Note that the virtual hard disk must be offline (usually requiring an attached virtual machine to be offline) to modify it. There are two ways to access it in Hyper-V Manager:

- Click Edit Disk in the Actions pane of Hyper-V Manager and browse to the virtual hard disk.

- Browse to the desired virtual hard disk in the settings of a virtual machine and click Edit.

The Choose Action screen will present the possible actions, depending on whether the virtual hard disk is of fixed, dynamic, or differencing type:

- Dynamic and differencing virtual hard disks can be compacted to reduce their storage utilization.

- You can convert from one type to another, such as dynamic to fixed.

- Virtual hard disks can be expanded.

- Differencing disks can be merged with their parent to create a single virtual hard disk with all of the data.

The wizard will vary depending on the action that is chosen:

Compact   This action compacts the size of the virtual hard disk on the physical storage and requires no further information from you.

The `Optimize-VHD` (`http://technet.microsoft.com/library/hh848458.aspx`) cmdlet also performs this action.

Convert   Using this action, you can create a copy of the virtual hard disk of the desired format and type in the location of your choice. The time required depends on the storage speed, storage connection, and the size of the virtual hard disk. Creating a fixed virtual hard disk without ODX support might take some time.

A new virtual hard disk of the desired type and format is created. It is up to you to replace and/or delete the original virtual hard disk.

You can use `Convert-VHD` (`http://technet.microsoft.com/library/hh848454.aspx`) to switch between virtual hard disk formats and types by using PowerShell:

```
Convert-VHD "D:\Virtual Machines\VM01\Disk.vhd" -Destinationpath "D:\Virtual
Machines\VM01\Disk.vhdx"
```

Expand   This action allows you to increase the size of a virtual hard disk. This operation would be near instant for a dynamic disk, very quick for a fixed disk with ODX support, and potentially slow for a fixed disk with no ODX support.

Performing an expand action is like adding a disk to a RAID array. You will need to log in to the guest OS and use its disk management tools to modify the file system. For example, you could use Disk Management if the guest OS was Windows, and expand the volume to fill the newly available disk space in the virtual hard disk.

PowerShell lets you expand or shrink a virtual hard disk by using `Resize-VHD` (`http://technet.microsoft.com/library/hh848535.aspx`). Don't make any assumptions; make sure that the guest OS and file system in the virtual hard disk support the shrink action before you use it (tested backups are recommended!).

Merge   The merge action updates the parent disk of a selected differencing virtual hard disk with the latest version of the sum of their contents. There are two options. The first allows you to modify the original parent disk. The second option allows you to create a new fixed or dynamic virtual hard disk.

Do not use this action to update the parent virtual hard disk if it is being used by other differencing disks.

You can also use the `Merge-VHD` PowerShell cmdlet (`http://technet.microsoft.com/library/hh848581.aspx`) to perform this action.

`Set-VHD` (`http://technet.microsoft.com/library/hh848561.aspx`) is also available in PowerShell to change the physical sector size of a virtual hard disk or to change the parent of a differencing disk.

Removing and Deleting Virtual Hard Disks

You can remove virtual hard disks from a virtual machine. Virtual hard disks that are attached to IDE controllers can be removed only when the virtual machine is not running. SCSI-attached virtual hard disks can be removed from a running virtual machine, but you should make sure that no services or users are accessing the data on them first.

You can remove a virtual hard disk from a virtual machine in Hyper-V Manager by editing the settings of the virtual machine, browsing to the controller, selecting the disk, and clicking Remove. You can use PowerShell to remove a virtual hard disk. This example will remove the first virtual hard disk from the first SCSI controller, even with a running virtual machine:

```
Remove-VMHardDiskDrive VM01 -ControllerType SCSI -ControllerNumber 0 `
-ControllerLocation 0
```

Removing a virtual hard disk from a virtual machine will not delete it. You can use Windows Explorer, the Del command, or the Remove-Item PowerShell cmdlet to delete the virtual hard disk file.

THE VIRTUAL MACHINE FILES

A virtual machine is made up of several files:

Virtual Machine XML File   This is stored in the Virtual Machines subfolder and describes the virtual machine. It is named after the unique ID (GUID) of the virtual machine.

BIN File   This is the snapshot placeholder.

VSV File   This is a saved state file.

VHD/VHDX Files   These are the two types of virtual hard disk.

AVHD/AVHDX Files   These are snapshots, and there is one for each virtual hard disk.

Smart Paging File   Hyper-V temporarily creates this file when Smart Paging is required.

Hyper-V Replica Log   This file exists when you enable replication of a virtual machine (see Chapter 12, "Hyper-V Replica").

Remember that a virtual machine can also use raw LUNs if you choose to use pass-through disks.

Network Adapters

Virtual machines can have one or more virtual network adapters that are connected to a virtual switch. You can learn much more about this topic, and the advanced configuration of virtual network adapters, in Chapter 4.

ADDING NETWORK ADAPTERS

You can add, remove, and configure virtual network adapters in a virtual machine's settings in Hyper-V Manager. To add a virtual network adapter, you can open Add Hardware, select either a (synthetic) Network Adapter or a Legacy Network Adapter, and click Add. You can use the Add-VMNetworkAdapter cmdlet to add network adapters by using PowerShell. The following example adds a (synthetic) network adapter without any customization:

```
Add-VMNetworkAdapter VM01
```

You can also add a legacy network adapter. `Add-VMNetworkAdapter` does allow you to do some configuration of the new virtual network adapter. This example creates a legacy network adapter and connects it to a virtual switch:

```
Add-VMNetworkAdapter VM01 -IsLegacy $True -SwitchName ConvergedNetSwitch
```

CONFIGURING VIRTUAL NETWORK ADAPTERS

You can configure the settings of a virtual network adapter in Hyper-V Manager by browsing to it in the virtual machine's settings, as shown in Figure 3.10. The basic settings of the virtual network adapter are as follows:

FIGURE 3.10
Network Adapter settings in a virtual machine

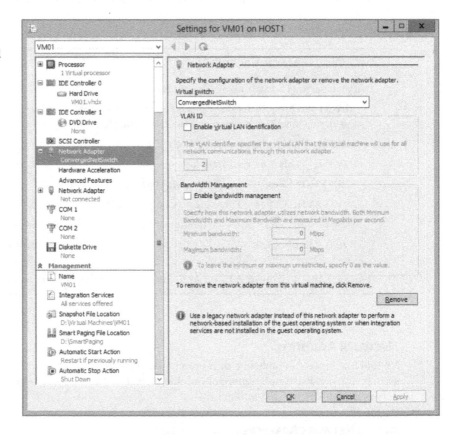

Virtual Switch The name of the virtual switch that the virtual machine is connected to. Note that the virtual machine will expect to find an identically named virtual switch if you move it from one host to another via Live Migration.

Enable Virtual LAN Identification   Enabling this allows a virtual network adapter to filter VLAN traffic for a specific VLAN ID. This means that the virtual network adapter will be able to communicate on the VLAN. It can communicate only with other VLANs via routing on the physical network.

The VLAN Identifier   This is where you enter the VLAN ID or tag for the required VLAN. This setting is grayed out unless you select the Enable Virtual LAN Identification check box.

Bandwidth Management   Windows Server 2012 has built-in network Quality of Service (QoS). This allows you to guarantee a minimum or maximum amount of bandwidth for a virtual machine. The PowerShell alternative is much more powerful than this GUI option.

Remove Button   This can be used to remove the virtual network adapter.

All of these settings are covered in great detail in Chapter 4. The Hardware Acceleration settings are also covered in that chapter.

The Advanced Features settings, shown in Figure 3.11, allow you to further configure a virtual network adapter.

FIGURE 3.11
Advanced Features
settings of a virtual
network adapter

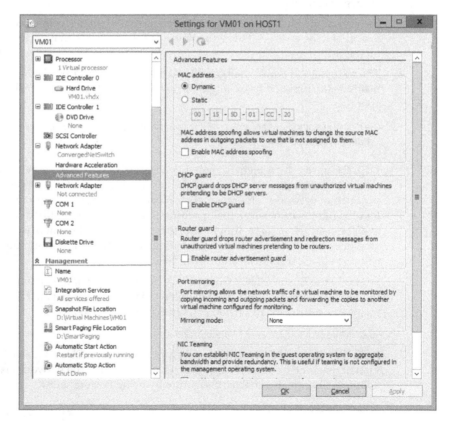

The main Advanced Features settings are as follows:

MAC Address   By default, a virtual machine uses a dynamically created MAC address. You'll find that a virtual machine has an unpredictable MAC address that is generated from a pool. Each host has a pool of possible MAC addresses, which you can find in Hyper-V Manager by clicking Virtual Switch Manager in Actions and then clicking MAC Address Range. You can enable dynamic MAC addresses as follows:

```
Set-VMNetworkAdapter VM01 -DynamicMacAddress
```

Dynamic MAC addresses may cause problems for some virtual machines. Linux can bind IP address configurations to MAC addresses rather than network adapters; this can cause Linux guest OSs to go offline after Live Migration when they change a MAC address. Some applications or network services may require static MAC addresses.

You can enter a static MAC address by selecting Static rather than Dynamic and entering a valid MAC address. You will have to generate a valid MAC address. Note that System Center Virtual Machine Manager simplifies this process by supplying a static MAC address from a managed central pool.

Some services, such as Windows Network Load Balancing, might require MAC Address Spoofing to be enabled. This will allow a virtual network adapter to change MAC addresses on the fly.

The next piece of PowerShell configures a static MAC address for the mentioned virtual machine (assuming it has a single virtual network adapter), and enables MAC address spoofing:

```
Set-VMNetworkAdapter VM01 -StaticMacAddress "00165D01CC01" `
-MacAddressSpoofing On
```

DHCP Guard   A problem for network administrators occurs when authorized server administrators build unauthorized (Windows or Linux) DHCP servers and place them on production networks. This is a real problem in self-service clouds; invalid addresses can be handed out to customer virtual machines, can break their ability to communicate, and can even be a security risk by influencing the routing of traffic. There is nothing you can do to stop guest OS administrators from configuring DHCP servers, but there is something you can do to block them from answering DHCP requests.

Selecting the Enable DHCP Guard check box will prevent the virtual machine from answering DHCP clients via this virtual network adapter. This is not enabled by default. You can script this setting for all virtual machines by using PowerShell:

```
Set-VMNetworkAdapter * -DhcpGuard On
```

Router Guard   The Router Guard feature is similar to DHCP Guard, but it prevents the virtual machine from sending out router redirection to the network via this virtual network adapter. You can also enable this feature by using PowerShell:

```
Set-VMNetworkAdapter * -RouterGuard On
```

FOR THE SECURITY CONSCIOUS

Environments that require network security, such as public clouds (hosting companies), will want DHCP Guard and Router Guard to be turned on by default. Strangely, Microsoft left these two security features disabled by default.

If you are using a virtual machine deployment solution such as System Center Virtual Machine Manager, you can enable the settings by default in your virtual machine templates. Alternatively, you could write a script that is scheduled to run on a regular basis. The script would do the following:

1. Enable DHCP Guard and Router Guard on all virtual machines

2. Disable the feature on just those required virtual machines, such as virtualized DHCP servers

Only Hyper-V administrators have access to the settings of a virtual machine. That means that guest OS administrators won't have access to your virtual machine settings (including network and security configuration) unless you delegate it to them.

Port Mirroring You can enable Port Mirroring to do network traffic analysis for a virtual machine from another virtual machine. This can be useful in a cloud or a change-controlled environment (pharmaceutical industry) for which you need to do diagnostics but cannot install analysis tools on production systems in a timely manner.

The concept is that you change the Mirroring Mode from None (the default setting) to Source on the virtual network adapter that you want to monitor. On another virtual machine, the one with the diagnostics tools, you set the Mirroring Mode of the virtual network adapter to Destination. Now the incoming and outgoing packets on the source virtual network adapter are copied to the destination virtual network adapter.

You can enable Port Mirroring by using PowerShell:

```
Set-VMNetworkAdapter VM01 -PortMirroring Source
Set-VMNetworkAdapter VM02 -PortMirroring Destination
```

Here's the quickest way to disable Port Mirroring:

```
Set-VMNetworkAdapter * -PortMirroring None
```

Note that the source and destination virtual network adapters must be on the same virtual switch (and therefore the same host).

NIC Teaming Windows Server 2012 is the first version of Windows Server that includes and supports NIC teaming (only the Microsoft version). There is much more on this subject in Chapter 4. You must select the Enable This Network Adapter To Be Part Of A Team In The Guest Operating System check box if you want to enable a virtual machine to create a NIC team from its virtual NICs (limited to two virtual NICs per guest OS team). This setting has nothing to do with NIC teaming in the host's Management OS.

```
Set-VMNetworkAdapter VM01 -AllowTeaming On
```

HARDWARE ACCELERATION FEATURES

Features such as Virtual Machine Queuing and IPsec Task Offloading are enabled by default in a virtual network card. This does not mean that they are used; it means only that a virtual machine can use these features if they are present and enabled on the host. You would disable features only if you need to explicitly turn them off—for example, if you have been advised to do so by Microsoft Support.

USING INTEGRATION SERVICES

In Chapter 1, you learned about the role of integration components or services. A number of services allow the host and virtual machine to have a limited amount of interaction with each other. You can enable (they are on by default) or disable these features by opening a virtual machine's settings and browsing to Integration Services. There you will find the following:

Operating System Shutdown   This is used to cleanly initiate a shutdown of the guest OS and virtual machine from the host or a management tool.

Time Synchronization   The virtual machine's clock will be synchronized with that of the host. Typically, you leave this enabled unless you are told otherwise by Microsoft Support or it causes guest OS clock issues.

Data Exchange   This is a feature that uses Key Value Pairs (KVPs) to allow the host to get limited but useful information from the guest OS, and vice versa. Some information can be requested from the host by the guest OS (HostExchangeItems), some can be requested from the guest OS by the host (GuestExchangeItems), and some information is automatically shared by the guest OS with the host (GuestIntrinsicExchangeItems).

Heartbeat   This is used to detect whether the integration components/services are running, and therefore whether the guest OS is running.

Backup (Volume Snapshot)   Volume Shadow Copy Services (VSS) can be used on the host to get an application-consistent backup of a virtual machine, including the guest OS and VSS-capable applications (SQL Server, Exchange, and so on) if the guest OS is supported by Hyper-V and supports VSS (Linux does not have VSS support).

Typically, these features are left enabled because they are very useful. You should not disable them unless you have a valid reason. Remember that the integration components/services must be installed in the guest OS (and kept up-to-date) for this functionality to work correctly.

> **MORE ON KVPS**
>
> Ben Armstrong (a Microsoft senior program manager lead of Hyper-V) shared a very nice PowerShell script (which still works on Windows Server 2012) on his blog (http://blogs .msdn.com/b/virtual_pc_guy/archive/2008/11/18/hyper-v-script-looking-at-kvp-guestintrinsicexchangeitems.aspx). If you run the PowerShell script, it will ask you for a host to connect to and a virtual machine on that host. The script will then display the GuestIntrinsicExchangeItems. You can also add a line to display the GuestExchangeItems.
>
> Another Microsoft program manager, Taylor Brown, has written and shared updated scripts to add or read KVPs (http://blogs.msdn.com/b/taylorb/archive/2012/12/05/customizing-the-key-value-pair-kvp-integration-component.aspx).
>
> The amount of information that the guest OS shares with the host varies depending on the guest OS. Windows guests certainly share more information, including Windows version, edition, service pack, build number, and the IPv4 and IPv6 addresses of the guest OS.

Performing Virtual Machine Operations

This section presents how to enable, configure, and perform common and critical virtual machine operations.

Adding and Removing Virtual Hardware

Adding and removing virtual hardware to and from a virtual machine is a basic but important task for building a virtual machine that is suitable for its role in the network.

Adding virtual hardware to a virtual machine requires that the virtual machine is not running. You can edit the settings of the virtual machine in Hyper-V Manager (Failover Cluster Manager if the virtual machine is on a clustered host), and click Add Hardware. You can add several kinds of virtual devices to a virtual machine. Table 3.2 shows the available devices you can add and the PowerShell alternatives.

TABLE 3.2: Virtual hardware you can add to virtual machines

VIRTUAL HARDWARE	EXAMPLE POWERSHELL ALTERNATIVE
SCSI controller	Add-VMScsiController VM01
Network adapter	Add-VMNetworkAdapter VM01
Legacy network adapter	Add-VMNetworkAdapter VM01 -IsLegacy $True
Fibre Channel adapter	Add-VMFibreChannelHba VM01 -SanName VirtSan1
RemoteFX 3D adapter	Add-VMRemoteFx3dVideoAdapter VM01

Two things that you should note:

◆ You cannot add a Virtual Fibre Channel adapter without first adding a virtual SAN to connect the adapter to a physical host bus adapter (HBA). See Chapter 9 to learn more about this topic.

◆ You cannot add a RemoteFX 3D adapter (for enhanced remote desktop graphics) without first adding the Remote Desktop Virtualization Host role service to the Management OS of the host that that the virtual machine is placed on.

Each of the Add- cmdlets has an equivalent Remove- cmdlet to remove it from the virtual machine.

Working with Snapshots

When talking about snapshots in the context of virtual machines, we are actually talking about the ability to capture the state and configuration of a virtual machine as it was at a point in time. You can use the virtual machine after the snapshot, change its virtual hardware and settings, and upgrade the guest OS and/or applications. All this is undone if you apply the snapshot.

How Snapshots Work Under the Covers

Figure 3.12 shows a virtual machine as it progresses through various states of having no snapshots, through having numerous snapshots, and then having the snapshots deleted and merged.

Before we proceed, you should refresh your knowledge of the differencing type of virtual hard disk. This is because Hyper-V uses a special kind of differencing disk that is called an *advanced virtual hard disk*, historically referred to as an *AVHD file*.

At the top-left of Figure 3.12, you can see a virtual machine that is reading from and writing to a virtual hard disk in a standard way. This changes when a snapshot of the virtual machine is created, as shown at the top-right of the figure:

1. An AVHD file is created, using the original virtual hard disk as a parent.

   If there is more than one virtual hard disk, an AVHD will be created for each virtual hard disk.

   We have two formats of virtual hard disk in Windows Server 2012, and we have two kinds of AVHD files to match. Any VHD type virtual hard disk will get an AVHD format AVHD file with an .AVHD file extension. Any VHDX type virtual hard disk will get a VHDX format AVHD file with an .AVHDX file extension; this is because the AVHDX file needs to match the traits and features of the VHDX file. It can be confusing at first because AVHD is used as a general term to include both the AVHD and the AVHDX formats.

2. The virtual machine switches to using the AVHD file as its virtual hard disk. All data from before the snapshot is read from the virtual hard disk. All modifications are written to the AVHD file. All data that is newer than the snapshot is read from the AVHD file.

   The performance of the virtual machine has been degraded at this point. The AVHD file will grow as new data is written to it. This consumes physical storage space in addition to the virtual hard disks. This can cause quite a surprise when an old snapshot fills a

LUN and Hyper-V has to pause all of the virtual machines that are stored on that LUN to protect them from corruption (for example, storage controller write caches might contain committed writes, but they cannot flush to disk).

3. A second snapshot of the virtual machine is created. This creates a second AVHD file, which uses the first AVHD as its parent. Now the virtual machine starts to use the second AVHD file as its virtual hard disk. All modifications are written to the second AVHD file, and the virtual machine will read data from the virtual hard disk and both the AVHDs, depending on when the data was created.

Now the performance of the virtual machine really starts to degrade. Hyper-V can retain up to 50 snapshots of an individual virtual machine. This is not a goal; it is a maximum. In fact, some would say you're probably acting very carelessly if you are keeping 50 snapshots of any virtual machine!

An administrator who wants to send a virtual machine back in time will apply the snapshot. This undoes any settings changes that were made to the virtual machine since the snapshot (such as increasing the memory). When applying a snapshot, you can choose to erase all data since the snapshot was created, or to create another new snapshot.

You can create nonlinear trees of snapshots if you want, with various configurations of the virtual machine over time. This is probably a really bad thing to do to any production or virtual machine of any value outside a lab.

4. Eventually the administrator will delete one or more of the snapshots. (An entire tree or branch can be selected.) Hyper-V will delete the snapshots from the console, and perform a live merge of the AVHDs, eventually storing the latest version of the sum of the data in the original virtual hard disk.

FIGURE 3.12
Virtual machine
snapshots in action

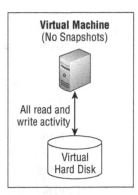
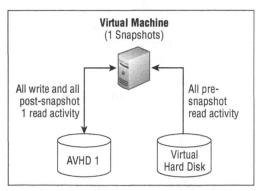

Live snapshot merging—a feature much desired by customers and by Microsoft's support group—arrived in Windows Server 2012 Hyper-V. This means that you do not need to shut down a virtual machine on Windows Server 2012 Hyper-V for the merge of the AVHD files into the original virtual hard disks to occur, as was required on older versions of Hyper-V.

Note that a dynamic virtual hard disk will grow before the AVHD files are deleted. This can be an issue if AVHDs have filled a hard disk. This will not be a problem for fixed virtual hard disks because they are already at the maximum size and no additional growth is required. If you have a disk space issue that prevents a snapshot merge, you will need to move the virtual machine to a volume that has more free space or erase other files to allow the required growth (the maximum required space will be the maximum size of the dynamic virtual hard disk).

SNAPSHOTS, CHECKPOINTS, AND CONFUSION!

There are lots of kinds of snapshots. The snapshot that we are discussing in this chapter is a virtual machine snapshot. Think of it as a photograph that captures a virtual machine as it was at the time the snapshot was created. You can use this snapshot to return the virtual machine back to that state.

This has nothing to do with NTFS volume snapshots, VSS backup snapshots, or even SAN snapshots. Unfortunately, *snapshot* is an overused label, but the term is commonly used by the major virtualization vendors to describe this functionality.

To add to the confusion, you are going to see the word *checkpoint* also being used by Microsoft in relation to snapshots. System Center actually refers to a snapshot as a checkpoint of a virtual machine. And just to make your head spin just that little bit more, the folks behind PowerShell for Hyper-V decided to use *checkpoint* as a verb: you will checkpoint a virtual machine to create a snapshot!

MISADVENTURES IN SNAPSHOTTING

Before you look at using snapshots, we should talk about the dangers of them. A very large percentage of support calls are related to people assuming things about snapshots that just aren't true. For example:

◆ An administrator assumes that you can replace the parent virtual hard disk with one that is larger or has the latest service pack, and that won't break the link with the AVHD. Wrong!

◆ Someone (it's always "someone") assumes that you can delete that great big AVHD file that's wasting disk space when all the virtual machines go into a paused state because the volume is full. Wrong!

◆ A person assumes that a virtual machine snapshot is the same as the type of snapshot used in backups, and therefore keeping 50 snapshots of a virtual machine is a superb free backup solution for the small/medium business. Wrong!

◆ People assume that snapshots are supported. They're sort of wrong. Yes, Hyper-V does support snapshots, but not all products that you'll install in your guest OSs will. You need to do your research on those applications first.

The list goes on and on, and the lowest common denominator is that someone assumes something about snapshots. If you are going to assume knowledge about snapshots, then assume that you need to do some research, ask someone more experienced, and learn some hard facts. Unfortunately this warning has had to be rather blunt; being polite has not worked very well in the past.

PASS-THROUGH DISKS MAY NOT APPLY

Pass-through disks are simple LUNs and must follow the rules of physical disks. They cannot take advantage of the many virtualization features that virtual hard disks can, such as these:

◆ Simpler backup performed by the host

◆ Easy expansion

◆ Migration from one location to another

◆ Virtual machine snapshots

The pass-through disk is the least flexible and most feature-poor type of disk that you can use in any machine virtualization solution. If you need the best performance, the most scalability, and the most flexible and cloud-friendly storage, then you should use fixed VHDX virtual hard disks, preferably with ODX-capable storage.

MANAGING SNAPSHOTS

With the warnings out of the way, let's move on to looking at how to use snapshots. Creating a snapshot of a virtual machine is rather simple:

1. Open Hyper-V Manager.

2. Select the virtual machine.

3. Click Snapshot in the Actions pane.

   A snapshot is created. It appears in the Snapshots pane in the middle of the Hyper-V Manager console.

4. Optionally, rename the snapshot to something descriptive.

You have a snapshot. You can do the same thing with PowerShell. Checkpoint-VM creates a snapshot of a virtual machine. You can optionally name the snapshot:

```
Checkpoint-VM VM01 -SnapshotName "Snapshot of clean install done on `
Wednesday 31st October"
```

You can rename a snapshot at any time either in Hyper-V Manager or by using Rename-VMSnapshot.

After using the virtual machine, you might wish to restore it to the state it was in at the time of the snapshot. You can do this in Hyper-V Manager by right-clicking the desired snapshot and clicking Apply. You have three choices:

◆ Cancel does nothing.

◆ Apply discards all changes since the snapshot and returns the virtual machine to the state it was in at that time.

◆ Take Snapshot And Apply takes a snapshot first, so you do not lose the current state of the virtual machine. Then the old snapshot will be applied to restore the virtual machine to that state.

The following is the PowerShell way to apply (restore) a virtual machine snapshot without being prompted. If you want the Take Snapshot And Apply action, you need to first run Checkpoint-VM.

```
Restore-VMSnapshot -VMname VM01 "Snapshot of clean install done on `
Wednesday 31st October" -Confirm:$False
```

Where is the snapshot file created? The AVHD file is always created at the same location as the parent virtual hard disk. An XML file that describes the snapshot is also created in the subfolder Snapshots. By default, that subfolder can be found where the virtual machine XML file is stored. You can control this setting by editing the properties of the virtual machine and changing the path that is set in Snapshot File Location. This is the SnapshotFileLocation property of the virtual machine:

```
PS C:\ > Get-VM VM01 | FL *snapshot*


SnapshotFileLocation : D:\Virtual Machines\VM01
ParentSnapshotId     : 97ec2aae-2f73-45fa-b813-151b2d82e2da
ParentSnapshotName   : Snapshot of clean install done on Wednesday 31st October
```

You'll notice in this example that you can also see which snapshot the virtual machine is currently using. You can do the same in Hyper-V Manager by looking for a green arrow called Now. Figure 3.13 shows a tree of snapshots. You can see the Now arrow, which has a dotted line from the bottom snapshot. This means that the bottom snapshot was the last one created/applied.

FIGURE 3.13
A tree of snapshots

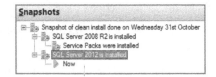

Get-VMSnapshot also shows you the hierarchy of snapshots for a virtual machine:

```
PS C:\ > Get-VMSnapshot VM01
```

VMNAME	NAME	SNAPSHOTTYPE	CREATIONTIME	PARENTSNAPSHOTNAME
VM01	Snapshot of clean install done on Wednesday 31st October	Standard	31/10/2012 20:08:49	
VM01	SQL Server 2008 R2 is installed	Standard	31/10/2012 20:20:01	Snapshot of clean install done on Wednesday 31st October
VM01	Service Packs were installed	Standard	31/10/2012 20:32:17	SQL Server 2008 R2 is installed
VM01	SQL Server 2012 is installed	Standard	31/10/2012 20:33:05	Snapshot of clean install done on Wednesday 31st October

You can right-click a snapshot and select one of two actions to delete:

Delete Snapshot   This deletes the snapshot in question. Hyper-V will automatically merge the required AVHD(s) without the need to shut down the virtual machine.

Delete Snapshot Subtree   The current snapshot, and any snapshot that is a child of it (or grandchild, or lower), will be deleted with all the necessary live merges being done automatically for you.

Be aware that performing a lot of merges at the same time could cause a spike in storage activity. To remove a snapshot, you can run Remove-VMSnapshot. Adding -IncludeAllChildSnapshots deletes all the child snapshots.

```
Remove-VMSnapshot VM01 "Snapshot of clean install done on Wednesday `
31st October" -IncludeAllChildSnapshots
```

The status of the virtual machine will immediately change to indicate that a merge is in progress and will show the progress as a percentage. This could be near instant if the snapshot has little or no contained data.

WHEN TO USE SNAPSHOTS?

If snapshots are so dangerous, should you never use them? You can use snapshots as long as the following hold true:

- You understand how virtual machine snapshots work.
- You don't make assumptions.
- You understand the risks.
- Any applications that are running in the virtual machine support snapshots.
- You do not keep the snapshots for very long, because they do keep growing and performance can degrade over time.

Some features of Hyper-V actually use Hyper-V snapshots. You will see snapshots in the DR site if you use certain features of Hyper-V Replica (see Chapter 12).

Snapshots really come in handy for anyone who needs to repeat certain actions over and over with virtual machines. They can perform some action, undo the changes, and repeat. Examples include the following:

- OS deployment consultants who need to repeatedly run Sysprep and capture an operating system image
- Software deployment packagers/testers
- People who are testing software that's been developed
- Consultants who need a repeatable demo lab
- Trainers who want a classroom that they can rapidly reset

Using Live Migration

One of the biggest reasons that organizations have chosen to deploy server virtualization is to get better flexibility and agility for their infrastructure and their services. Virtualization abstracts servers from their hardware by changing the machines into files and memory. Files are easy to move, memory can be copied, and that's where Live Migration comes in. Once upon a time, Microsoft's Quick Migration was made fun of. Live Migration is what makes Windows Server 2012 Hyper-V the most flexible and agile virtualization product on the market.

THE BRIEF HISTORY OF LIVE MIGRATION

Windows Server 2008 Hyper-V did not have Live Migration (known as vMotion in the vSphere world). Instead, Microsoft offered up Quick Migration. It would allow us to move virtual machines from one clustered host to another in the same cluster with some downtime:

1. The virtual machine would be placed into a saved state.

2. The SAN LUN that the virtual machine was stored on was failed over to the destination host.

3. The virtual machine was started up from its saved state.

Writing and reading the saved state was dependent on storage connection speed and disk performance. The disk failover might take a second or two. A large virtual machine could be offline for several minutes. This could not compete with vMotion's apparent zero downtime migration of virtual machines, and Quick Migration could not be used for production systems during business hours without affecting the targets of service-level agreements.

Windows Server 2008 R2 brought Live Migration to Hyper-V. Live Migration could move a virtual machine from one Hyper-V host in a cluster to another host in that cluster with no downtime to service availability, achieving the same results as vMotion. There were some limitations:

◆ We could perform only one Live Migration at a time on a host.

◆ Live Migration could not take full advantage of 10 GbE or faster networking.

◆ Hyper-V had no zero-downtime mechanism for moving virtual machine files and virtual hard disks.

◆ Live Migration, like vMotion at the time, was constrained within the cluster. Studies (such as the Great Big Hyper-V Survey of 2011) showed that one-third of Hyper-V customers ran nonclustered hosts only, and another third ran a mixture of clustered and nonclustered hosts. A significant number of customers with Hyper-V clusters had several small/medium clusters.

CHANGES TO LIVE MIGRATION IN WINDOWS SERVER 2012

There are several changes to Live Migration in Windows Server 2012:

Live Storage Migration You can relocate the files and virtual hard disk(s) of a running virtual machine with no loss of service availability. Files can be moved to a single location or scattered across various folders/volumes. The latter could be useful to support Microsoft's Cloud Fast Track reference architecture.

Live Migration Does Not Require a Cluster   You can use Live Migration to move running virtual machines between clustered hosts, nonclustered hosts, and between clustered and nonclustered hosts.

Support for Virtual Machines Stored on Shared Folders   You can use Live Migration on virtual machines that are stored on Windows Server 2012 file shares. This includes HA virtual machines in a Hyper-V cluster and non-HA virtual machines on nonclustered hosts. The latter enable Live Migration of virtual machines between nonclustered hosts without moving their storage.

Shared-Nothing Live Migration   Live Migration does not require shared storage, such as SAN or a shared folder, to live-migrate virtual machines between hosts. That means that we can move virtual machines and their storage between nonclustered hosts, between hosts in different clusters, and between clustered and nonclustered hosts. Note that you should remove the virtual machine from the cluster (no downtime required) to perform Live Migration on it from a clustered host to any other host.

Better Usage of Available Bandwidth   Windows Server 2012 can make much better usage of large-capacity networks, such as 10 GbE, or 56 Gbps InfiniBand. Live Migration copies and synchronizes the memory of running virtual machines over the network (ideally a dedicated network). This means that you can drain a large host (up to 4 TB of RAM) more quickly than before.

Unlimited Simultaneous Live Migrations   Windows Server 2008 R2 Hyper-V could perform only one simultaneous Live Migration at a time between two hosts. Windows Server 2012 can combine this with support for higher-capacity links to perform more Live Migrations at once. This can be very useful when performing planned (patching) or unplanned (hardware repair) host maintenance. Microsoft does not place an arbitrary limit on the number of simultaneous Live Migrations. Instead, you are limited by the processor (System Interrupts, as seen in Task Manager in the Management OS) and the capacity of the Live Migration network. Not enforcing a limit means that large organizations can take full advantage of datacenter networks such as InfiniBand.

At the time of this writing, Windows Server 2012 Hyper-V offered more mobility for virtual machines than any other hypervisor, including vSphere 5.1. You can even use Live Migration to move virtual machines between different network footprints with different address schemes, using Network Virtualization to maintain service availability to abstract the IP address(es) of the virtual machine.

The requirements of Live Migration are as follows:

Forest Membership   The source and destination host should be in the same Active Directory forest.

Common Version of Hyper-V   Both the source and destination host must be running either Hyper-V Server 2012 or Windows Server 2012 Hyper-V.

Common Host CPU Instruction Set   The physical processors on the source and destination hosts must be from the same manufacturer. If they are different editions of processor, such as E5 and X5500, then Migrate To A Physical Computer With A Different Processor Version must be enabled in the processor compatibility settings of the virtual machine.

Live Migration Network   There must be at least 1 Gbps of bandwidth between the source and destination hosts. The more bandwidth you have, the quicker you can move your virtual machines.

Traditionally, a dedicated NIC or NIC team was used for Live Migration. You can still do this in Windows Server 2012. Alternatively, you can use the concepts of QoS and converged fabrics (see Chapter 4) with large-bandwidth NICs and/or an aggregation of NICs in a team.

We now can define Live Migration as the movement of virtual machines, their files, and/or their storage, without any loss in availability for the services that they provide.

The performance of Live Migration of virtual machines has been improved in Windows Server 2012 Hyper-V. Live Migration of a running virtual machine copies/synchronizes the memory and processes of a running virtual machine from one host to another. This allows the running virtual machine to change hosts with no downtime to its services. Live Migration, performed by the virtual machine's VM worker process (VMWP.EXE) in the Management OS, works as follows:

1. An administrator or management system instructs a virtual machine to be moved from Host1 to Host2 by using Live Migration.

2. The configuration (the hardware specification) of the virtual machine is copied to and initialized on Host2. Host2 must be able to support the dependencies, such as connected virtual SANs or virtual switches, or the Live Migration will abort.

    It is during this step that a dynamic MAC address would be allocated to the virtual machine from the pool on the destination host. Remember that Linux guests will need a static MAC address to keep their IP configuration online.

3. The memory of the running virtual machine is broken up into pages. The memory is copied over the Live Migration network. Hyper-V tracks changes to the memory pages. Any copied page is marked as clean.

4. The virtual machine is running, so some pages will be modified. These pages are marked as dirty and must be synchronized.

5. Live Migration will perform up to 10 synchronizations or iterations to copy any dirty memory pages to the destination host. Each synchronized page is marked as clean.

6. Eventually, either all pages are clean, only a small amount of memory is left, or 10 iterations have been completed. The synchronization process will stop.

7. The virtual machine is now paused on Host1.

    Our definition of Live Migration has been carefully worded to say that it is the movement of virtual machines without interruption of service availability. We have not said that the virtual machine won't be offline. Live Migration, vMotion, and similar migration solutions all feature some downtime. This downtime can even be several seconds long. This is why you sometimes will see a dropped packet or two when using Ping to test vMotion or Live Migration. Ping is based on the Internet Control Message Protocol (ICMP) and is designed to detect latency. Most business applications (Outlook/Exchange, SQL Server, and so on) are based on TCP, and TCP is designed to allow for latency. This means that TCP-based applications will notice reduced performance for services in a virtual machine that is being moved by vMotion or Live Migration, but they will not detect a service outage.

8. The remaining state of the virtual machine is copied over the network to the copy of the virtual machine on the destination host.

9. The virtual machine is un-paused on Host2.

10. After a successful start on Host2, the virtual machine is removed from Host1.

The part of Live Migration that Microsoft tuned in Windows Server 2012 to is the first copy of the memory pages. The process used to blindly start at the first page and work through to the last one. This ignored the fact that some parts of memory are more active than others, and this meant that more iterations were required. Windows Server 2012 Live Migration prioritizes memory based on activity: the least active pages are copied first, and the most active pages are copied last. This means that there is less risk of change since the last copy and less need for more iteration.

THE COMMITMENTS OF LIVE MIGRATION

Microsoft has made two commitments when it comes to Live Migration:

NO NEW FEATURES THAT PREVENT LIVE MIGRATION

Microsoft will not introduce any new features in Hyper-V that will prevent or not support Live Migration. This has meant that some features such as Virtual Fibre Channel adapters and Single-Root I/O Virtualization have required some ingenuity that other virtualization vendors have not considered.

A VIRTUAL MACHINE WILL ALWAYS REMAIN RUNNING

Live Migration never burns its bridges; a virtual machine will always remain running if there is a problem during the process of Live Migration. This means that the source copy is not removed until the virtual machine is successfully activated using the destination copy.

STORAGE LIVE MIGRATION

Storage Live Migration is a process whereby the files and/or virtual hard disks of a virtual machine can be moved from one location to another with no loss of services provided by the virtual machine. These are some reasons to use Storage Live Migration:

◆ We can move the storage of a virtual machine to higher or lower tiers of storage in a cloud to reflect seasonal usage patterns. This could even be made possible via a self-service portal without involving administrators.

◆ A virtual machine can be moved if we run out of disk space.

◆ We can relocate virtual machines when migrating between older and newer storage systems.

◆ Storage Live Migration is also used by Shared-Nothing Live Migration.

The process of Storage Live Migration works as follows:

1. You instruct Live Migration to move the files of a virtual machine.

2. The files start to copy from the source location to the destination location.

3. Hyper-V starts to send block modifications for the virtual hard disk(s) to both the source and destination virtual hard disks during the copy process. This process, referred to as *IO mirroring*, will ensure that the source and destination virtual hard disks are in sync when the copy is completed.

4. The copy completes. The virtual machine will attempt to use the destination copy of the file(s). If this is successful, the source copy of the file(s) are removed. If the switch is unsuccessful, the virtual machine will continue to use the source copy, the administrator will be alerted, and the destination files will be removed.

Select the virtual machine and click the Move action to perform a Storage Live Migration in Hyper-V Manager. This will start the Move (or Live Migration) Wizard. The first screen asks you to choose the move type. Move The Virtual Machine is a machine Live Migration, which you will look at soon. The second option, Move The Virtual Machine's Storage, is the option for Storage Live Migration.

Figure 3.14 shows the Choose Options For Moving Storage screen.

FIGURE 3.14
The options for moving virtual machine storage

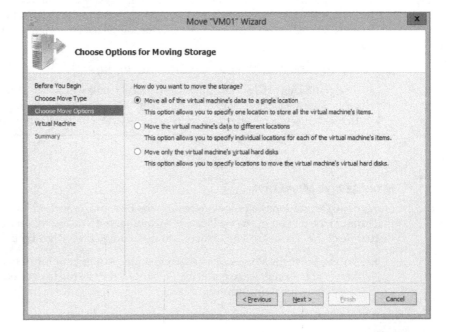

Here you are asked how you want to move the virtual machine's storage:

Move All Of The Virtual Machine's Data To A Single Location   This option moves all of the virtual machine's files—including the configuration XML, the snapshots, the Smart Paging file, and the virtual hard disks—to a single folder. You will be asked to enter a single destination location for all of the virtual machine's files.

Move The Virtual Machine's Data To Different Locations   Choosing this option enables you to place all of the virtual machine's files in different folders and even on different volumes. You can choose which of the virtual hard disks and other virtual machine file types to move (see Figure 3.15). The wizard asks you to enter a location for each selected file/file type.

FIGURE 3.15
Moving virtual machine files to different locations

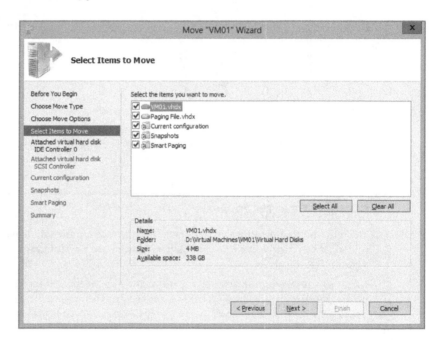

Move Only The Virtual Machine's Virtual Hard Disks   With this option, only the virtual hard disks are moved. You can choose which virtual hard disks to move (see Figure 3.16). If you select multiple virtual hard disks, you are asked for a destination location for each file.

PowerShell gives you the ability to move virtual machine storage without using the wizard. This is quicker if you know what you are doing, and it enables automation and movement of many virtual machines via a script. The following example moves a virtual machine to a single folder. Note that the destination folder(s) are created for you if they do not exist.

```
Move-VMStorage VM01 -DestinationStoragePath 'C:\Virtual Machines\VM01'
```

FIGURE 3.16
Selecting a virtual
hard disk to move

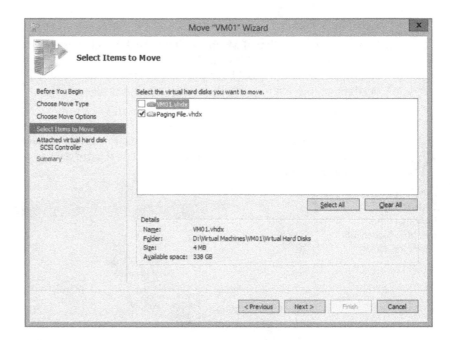

> ## Cleaning Up After Yourself
>
> You will find that moving a virtual machine's storage around will leave behind lots of empty folders. If you dislike this messy behavior, you can use a scripted solution to clean up the file system after the move.
>
> Niklas Åkerlund wrote and shared a script that will perform a Storage Live Migration and clean up the empty folders that are left behind. You can find this script at http://vniklas.djungeln .se/2012/09/26/in-windows-hyper-v-2012-move-vmstorage-leaves-folders-behind/

Using Move-VMStorage to move multiple files is more complicated. The cmdlet uses a hash table to specify the source and destination virtual hard disks, as you can see with this example:

```
Move-VMStorage VM01 -VirtualMachinePath "D:\Virtual Machines\VM01" `
-SnapshotFilePath "E:\VM Snapshots\VM01" `
-SmartPagingFilePath "F:\VM Smart Paging\VM01" `
-VHDs @(@{"SourceFilePath" = "C:\Virtual Machines\VM01\Virtual Hard `
Disks\VM01.vhdx"; `
"DestinationFilePath" = "G:\VM Storage1\VM01\VM01.vhdx"}, `
@{"SourceFilePath" = "C:\Virtual Machines\VM01\Virtual Hard `
Disks\Paging File.vhdx"; "DestinationFilePath" = `
"H:\VM Storage2\VM01\Paging File.vhdx"})
```

If you want to move just a single VHD, you can use the following piece of PowerShell:

```
Move-VMStorage VM01 -VHDs @(@{"SourceFilePath" = `
" D:\Virtual Machines\VM01\Virtual Hard Disks\VM01.vhdx"; `
"DestinationFilePath" = `
"E:\Virtual Machines\VM01\Virtual Hard Disks\VM01.vhdx"})
```

A normal (machine) Live Migration is the sort of task that can be performed quite frequently. The only resource consumption is bandwidth on a dedicated Live Migration network. That means administrators can move virtual machines at will, and management systems can use Live Migration for load balancing, without impacting the performance of services. Storage Live Migration increases IOPS on the underlying physical storage. For example, if you were to move a virtual machine from one folder to another on the same physical disk spindles, you would temporarily do the following:

♦ Double the disk usage of the file(s) during the move until the source copy of the file(s) was removed

♦ Double the IOPS of the file(s) during the move

Storage Live Migration is not something that you should be doing as frequently as machine Live Migration. It is a planned move, in response to a particular storage demand.

By default, a host can perform two simultaneous Storage Live Migrations at once. This is configured in the host settings under Storage Migrations. You can also configure this via PowerShell:

```
Set-VMHost -MaximumStorageMigrations 4
```

Enabling Virtual Machine Live Migration

When you enable Hyper-V on a host, you are asked whether you want to enable and configure Live Migration. You can do this or skip it, and later change the Live Migration configuration in the host settings (see Figure 3.17).

LIVE MIGRATION BETWEEN HOSTS IN A CLUSTER

You do not need to enable Live Migration or configure authentication on clustered Hyper-V hosts if you are going to perform Live Migration only between hosts in the same cluster. All that is required is to select one or more Live Migration networks and set their order of preference.

You can use Live Migration to move virtual machines from/to a cluster. This requires that you configure Live Migration on the source/destination hosts. If the virtual machine is HA, you can remove it from the cluster and perform Live Migration to the other cluster or nonclustered host. If the virtual machine is moved to a cluster, you can then make it HA. This can all be done without any downtime to the services provided by the virtual machines.

You can enable or disable inbound and outbound Live Migration on a host by selecting or clearing the Enable Incoming And Outgoing Live Migrations check box. Selecting the check box will enable the remaining settings on the screen.

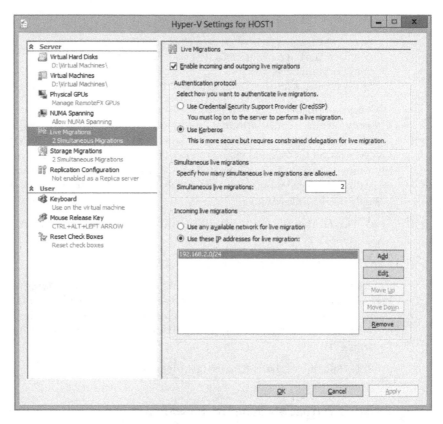

FIGURE 3.17
Live Migration
host settings

The Authentication Protocol settings are used to control how the hosts participating in Live Migration will authenticate against each other. They also impact how you can manage Live Migration. You have two options; one is simple to set up but limited, and the other requires a bit more work but is more administrator friendly:

Use Credential Security Support Provider (CredSSP)   CredSSP authentication is the simplest of the two authentication options because it requires you only to enable authentication. No further work is required. However, you must log in to the source host (the console or via Remote Desktop) and run Hyper-V Manager or PowerShell from there to perform the Live Migration. The Live Migration will fail with a security fault if you try to perform the Live Migration from another machine such as your PC or the destination host. This is a gotcha for those new to Windows Server 2012 Live Migration.

Use Kerberos   If you want to be able to perform Live Migration from anywhere, such as your PC, the destination host, or a management system, then you need to enable Kerberos. The configuration does not stop there, because you will need to enable Kerberos-constrained delegation in the computer object of every Hyper-V host that will be involved in virtual machine Live Migration. You will look at how to do constrained delegation later in this chapter.

The Simultaneous Live Migrations setting sets the maximum number of possible Live Migrations that can be done at the same time on this host. Live Migration will use the lowest value of this setting on a source and destination host. For example, if Host1 is set to 20 and Host2 is set to 5, then a maximum of five simultaneous Live Migrations will be possible between these two hosts.

The Simultaneous Live Migrations value is a maximum, and not an objective. Live Migration consumes processor from the hosts involved; this is visible as System Interrupts in Task Manager in the Management OS. Performing too many simultaneous Live Migrations could starve virtual machines of processor access, and the Live Migration network could become a bottleneck. Hyper-V will protect you from yourself; Live Migration will perform as many simultaneous Live Migrations as you allow, but it will restrict the number so it will not impact the performance of virtual machines on the participating hosts.

WHAT IS THE RIGHT AMOUNT OF SIMULTANEOUS LIVE MIGRATIONS?

This is going to change from one company to another, from one network to another, and from one host specification to another. There is no one right answer.

The best advice we can give is that you perform a series of tests to determine which limit gives you the best results. Try to live-migrate one virtual machine at a time. Then try two, five, ten, fifteen, twenty, and so on. Time how long it takes, monitor resource utilization of the hosts, and check whether Live Migration is allowing the number that you are trying. Find the sweet spot and use that as your limit for that host.

The final setting is Incoming Live Migrations. By default, any network in the host can be used for incoming Live Migration on the host. You should change this to a dedicated network or one where you have applied QoS rules; Live Migration will consume as much bandwidth as it can and this could impact other services on the host, such as virtual machine communications or host monitoring. Typically, you will configure one or more dedicated networks by selecting Use The IP Addresses For Live Migration, clicking Add, and entering the network address (such as 192.168.2.0/24) for the desired network. You can enter more than one network and set their preference using the Move Up and Move Down buttons.

KERBEROS-CONSTRAINED DELEGATION FOR LIVE MIGRATION

To use Kerberos authentication, which enables management of Live Migration from any domain member by an authorized administrator (or system), you will need to configure constrained delegation in Active Directory in the computer objects of the Hyper-V hosts that will participate in the migrations. You will be delegating two service types:

- CIFS is used to access the storage of the virtual machine via a shared folder. It is used to access storage during a Storage Live Migration or a Shared-Nothing Live Migration, or to access a virtual machine's files on a file server.

- Microsoft Virtual System Migration Service (MVSMS) is used to perform the Live Migration of the virtual machine between hosts.

There are two possible designs for Live Migration–constrained delegation:

Live Migration with SMB 3 Shared Storage In this case, the nonclustered hosts are using a common file share(s) that they both have full control rights to. The virtual machines that will be migrated are stored on this file share(s). Kerberos-constrained delegation will be enabled as follows in the Active Directory computer object of each Hyper-V host, as shown in Figure 3.18:

1. Delegate all other possible Live Migration hosts for MVSMS.

2. Delegate the file server(s) for CIFS.

FIGURE 3.18
Enabling Kerberos-constrained delega-tion with file shares

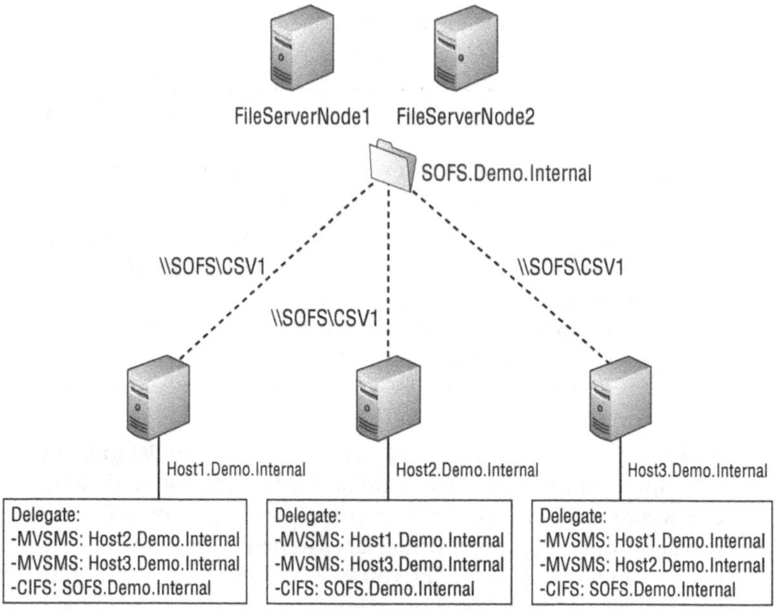

Shared-Nothing Live Migration This is the migration type used to move virtual machines between nonclustered hosts with no common file shares (maybe using direct-attached or internal storage), or hosts that are not in the same cluster (including between a clustered host and a nonclustered host). In this case, you will set up constrained delegation in the Active Directory computer object of each involved host. You will delegate all other possible Live Migration hosts for the following (as shown in Figure 3.19):

1. MVSMS

2. CIFS

FIGURE 3.19
Enabling Kerberos-
constrained
delegation for
Shared-Nothing
Live Migration

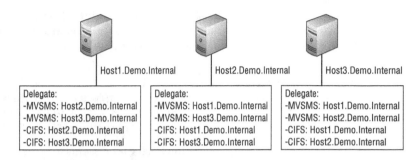

There are two ways to enable constrained delegation. The first is to use Active Directory Users And Computers with the Advanced view turned on:

1. Edit the properties of the host's computer object and navigate to the Delegation tab.

2. Select the Trust This Computer For Delegation To Specified Services Only option.

3. Ensure that the Use Kerberos Only suboption is selected.

4. Click Add to open the Add Services window.

5. Click Users And Computers and enter the name(s) of the other host(s) and/or file server(s) and then click OK.

6. You are returned to Add Services. Select the machine(s) and the necessary protocol(s). For example, if you are using a file share on FileServer1, you would select the CIFS service type for FileServer1. Use the Ctrl key to make multiple selections. Click OK when you have finished.

7. Review the changes in the computer object properties, as shown in Figure 3.20.

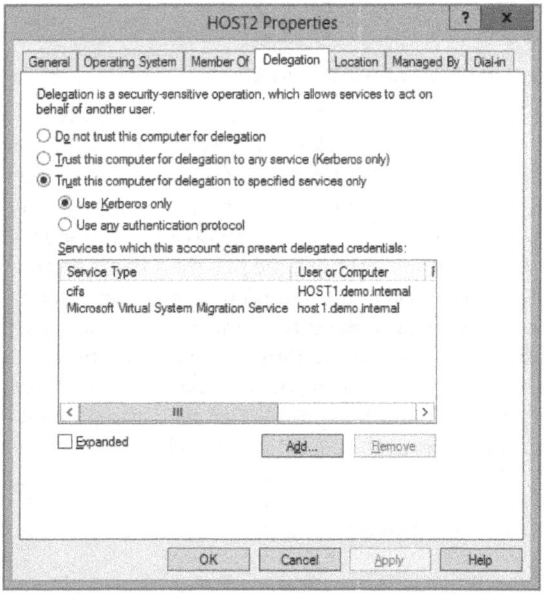

FIGURE 3.20
Configured
Kerberos-
constrained
delegation

That was all a bit mouse intensive and could be painful to implement in a large environment. The PowerShell alternative would make for a nice function in a script. This snippet configures Host1 with Kerberos Constrained Delegation for Host2:

```
$HostName = "Host2"
$HostFQDN = "$HostName.demo.internal"
Get-ADComputer Host1| Set-ADObject -Add @{"msDS-AllowedToDelegateTo" `
"Microsoft Virtual System Migration Service/$HostFQDN", "Microsoft Virtual `
System Migration Service/$HostName", "cifs/$HostFQDN", "cifs/$HostName"}
```

The final step in enabling constrained delegation seems to be never shared or discussed: you need to reboot each Hyper-V host that had its computer object edited. In the case of nonclustered hosts, the best time to do this is before you have created or placed virtual machines on the host. Otherwise, you have to wait for a maintenance window. You can live-migrate virtual machines off a clustered host without any service impact to perform the host reboot.

Now your nonclustered hosts (or hosts in different clusters) are ready to perform Kerberos-authenticated Live Migration, managed by an authorized administrator, from any domain member machine.

CONSTRAINED DELEGATION AND FILE SHARE LIBRARIES

You might have encountered Kerberos-constrained delegation before, when working with Hyper-V or System Center Virtual Machine Manager. Without delegation, a virtual machine cannot mount ISO files that are accessed via a file share. The process for enabling CIFS delegation for the file server on each host has been documented by Microsoft at http://technet.microsoft.com/library/ee340124.aspx. Remember, the hosts must be rebooted after updating their computer objects.

SHARED-NOTHING LIVE MIGRATION

Shared-Nothing Live Migration takes (machine) Live Migration and Storage Live Migration and joins them into a single task sequence. The goal is to move a virtual machine, including its files, from one host to another host with no impact on service availability.

Storage Live Migration will move the virtual machine files while the virtual machine is running on the source host. The Storage Live Migration task will be the first 50 percent of the progress bar. As with most things, the progress bar is an indication of task sequence progress and not of time to completion. An automatically created/removed temporary file share is created on the destination host so the virtual machine can still access its storage.

After the storage is moved, the virtual machine will live-migrate, copying and synchronizing its memory, before switching over to the destination host.

It might not sound like much after everything you have read, but Share-Nothing Live Migration will be a very useful tool for Hyper-V administrators.

PERFORMING LIVE MIGRATIONS

You will once again use the Move action to move a virtual machine via Live Migration:

1. Select the Move The Virtual Machine option in the Move Wizard.

2. Enter the name of the computer in the Specify Destination Computer screen. You need to enter a fully qualified domain name for hosts that are in different domains in the Active Directory forest.

3. Figure 3.21 shows the Choose Move Options screen.

FIGURE 3.21
Choose the Live Migration options.

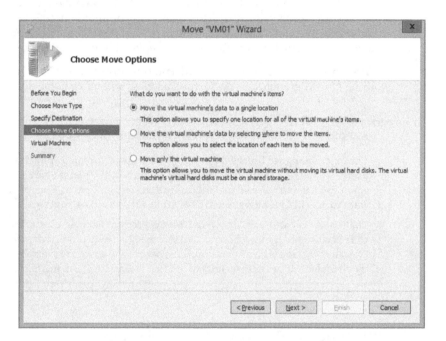

There are three ways you can move a virtual machine:

Move The Virtual Machine's Data To A Single Location   This performs a Shared-Nothing Live Migration and stores the files in a single folder of your choosing on the destination host. You will need to create a folder if you want to place the virtual machine into it.

Move The Virtual Machine's Data By Selecting Where To Move The Items   This is also a Shared-Nothing Live Migration, but it allows you to place the virtual hard disks and the other file types of the virtual machine into specific folders/volumes.

There are three ways that the files can be moved:

◆ Hyper-V will do an automated file placement using the paths specified in the destination host's settings.

◆ You can select locations for each of the virtual hard disks, and the remaining files are placed according to the destination host's settings.

◆ You can select a location for each virtual hard disk and each of the other file types.

Move Only The Virtual Machine   This is the option you will choose to perform a Live Migration of the virtual machine if its files are stored on a file share(s) that the source and destination hosts have full control rights to. The virtual machine will live-migrate over the Live Migration network to the destination host. The virtual machine will continue to use its files on the file share without moving them.

Choosing this option with a virtual machine that is stored on direct-attached or internal storage will result in an error. This is because you should have selected one of the other two options to perform a Shared-Nothing Live Migration. You will be prompted whether to either discard the virtual machine's storage or replace it with an alternative virtual hard disk(s).

After this, you just finish the wizard, entering any storage paths if prompted for Shared-Nothing Live Migration, and the virtual machine will move to the destination host.

REPORTS OF QUICK MIGRATION'S DEATH ARE PREMATURE

The much-maligned Quick Migration is still present in Windows Server 2012 Hyper-V. It can be useful when trying to troubleshoot Live Migration or Cluster Shared Volume issues. It's used when you need to move virtual machines and you don't have 1 Gbps of bandwidth, or you don't want to use the Live Migration bandwidth to move a virtual machine.

That latter scenario is used by Windows Server 2012 Failover Clustering. By default, when you pause a clustered Hyper-V host, any virtual machine with low priority will be moved using Quick Migration instead of Live Migration. Most people will choose to override this action for low priority virtual machines so that Quick Migration is never used when a host is paused.

Importing and Exporting Virtual Machines

Sometimes you cannot live-migrate a virtual machine to another host. For example, maybe you need to move a virtual machine by using an out-of-band method such as a USB drive, upload it to a cloud, or move a virtual machine's files from a Windows Server 2008 R2 host to a new Windows Server 2012 host. The import and export mechanisms allow you to do this. Exporting a virtual machine puts the files of the virtual machine into an organized state so they can be transported to another host. The other host can import those files to bring the virtual machine back online.

WHAT'S NEW WITH EXPORT AND IMPORT?

Many people faced a common problem when importing a virtual machine in past versions of Hyper-V if the import host was not configured identically to the destination host. Say a virtual machine was connected to a virtual network called External1 on Host1. The virtual machine was exported and transported to Host2, where there was a virtual network called Network1. The virtual machine would import, but the virtual network card would not be connected to any virtual network, and there was nothing to tell you that. If the import found a problem, it would simply remove the offending part of the virtual machine that caused the issue.

A Windows Server 2012 Hyper-V import that finds an incompatibility with the virtual machine will report the issue and offer you the opportunity to fix it before completing the import.

Another issue was that a virtual machine had to be exported to be imported. This could cause a problem if you didn't have an opportunity to export the virtual machine—for example, the original host had a sudden hardware failure and you were trying to rescue the virtual machines on another host. It was possible to build an export by hand, or to create a virtual machine and attach the virtual hard disks. But this is not something you want to do when you're in a rush, or when there are lots of virtual machines to get working.

Windows Server 2012 Hyper-V offers a new import option that will import a nonexported virtual machine. It will scan the files that you present for the virtual machine's XML configuration file, scan it for the configuration, and bring the virtual machine back online.

EXPORTING VIRTUAL MACHINES

You can export a virtual machine in Hyper-V Manager by doing the following when the virtual machine is not running:

1. Select the virtual machine and then select the Export action. This opens the Export Virtual Machine window.

2. Enter the path where you want the virtual machine to be exported.

You can also accomplish this by using PowerShell:

```
Export-VM VM01 -Path "C:\Exports"
```

The virtual machine is exported as a copy. The original virtual machine is left in place. You can remove the original virtual machine if you need to.

IMPORTING VIRTUAL MACHINES

You can import a virtual machine in Hyper-V Manager by clicking the Import Virtual Machine action:

1. Browse to the folder containing the virtual machine.

2. Choose the virtual machine you want to import in the Select Virtual Machine screen.

3. Choose one of the three actions in the Choose Import Type screen:

    Register The Virtual Machine In-Place This option loads the virtual machine in Hyper-V without moving it. The unique ID of the virtual machine will be reused. This option is appropriate if you are rescuing a nonexported virtual machine.

    Restore The Virtual Machine If you choose this option, you will restore the virtual machine, reusing the unique ID, to a location of your choosing. It is suitable for use if you have transported an exported virtual machine on removable storage.

    You will have the option to specify alternative locations for the virtual machine configuration file, the snapshots, and the smart paging file. You can skip that option, and the files will be stored with the virtual hard disks, which you must choose a location for.

Copy The Virtual Machine   This option creates a copy of an exported virtual machine. Each copy, stored in a location of your choosing, will have a unique ID.

Just as with the restore option, you can optionally choose a location for each of the file types, or you can choose to store them with the virtual hard disk which must be given a location.

The Import-VM cmdlet (http://technet.microsoft.com/library/hh848495.aspx) will allow you to import virtual machines using PowerShell. This option could be very quick for rescuing virtual machines. The following script gets the path and filename of the nonexported virtual machine, uses it to register the virtual machine in place, and then starts the virtual machine for you.

```
$VMXML = Get-Item "D:\Virtual Machines\VM01\Virtual Machines\*.xml"
$VMName = Import-VM -Register -Path $VMXML.FullName
Start-VM $VMName.Name
```

TESTING THE IMPORT/REGISTER OPTION

Consultants might want to demonstrate the new ability to register a virtual machine. To do this, you need a virtual machine with all of its files. Deleting a virtual machine from Hyper-V Manager will delete the files, so that's out of the question.

You can back up a virtual machine and restore it to an alternative location. Alternatively, you can shut down a virtual machine, stop the VMMS (which unlocks the virtual machine's configuration file), copy the entire virtual machine to another location, and restart the VMMS.

Installing Operating Systems and Applications

You are ready to start installing guest operating systems now that you know how to build virtual machines.

Installing Operating Systems

The list of supported guest operating systems is fluid. Rather than put the list in print and see it become obsolete in a matter of months, we would instead forward you to the official listing on the TechNet site at http://technet.microsoft.com/library/hh831531. You will find Windows Server, Linux, and client operating systems on this list. Other information that you will find includes the following:

◆   What the maximum supported number of virtual CPUs in a VM is for the guest OS

◆   Where to get the latest version of integration components for the guest OS

Installing an operating system in a virtual machine is not that different from doing it in a physical machine:

1. Insert the installation media (mount an ISO by editing the virtual machine settings, or by using Set-VMDvdDrive).

2. Power up the virtual machine (click the Start action in Hyper-V Manager or use `Start-VM`).

3. Get console, keyboard, and mouse access to the virtual machine via the Virtual Machine Connection window (select the virtual machine in Hyper-V Manager and click the Connect action).

4. Install the guest OS in the virtual machine.

After the guest is installed, you should always attempt to install the latest version of the integration components. For Windows guest OSs, open the Action menu in the Virtual Machine Connection window, and select Insert Integration Services Setup Disk. This will force the virtual DVD drive to mount the integration components' installation ISO (`C:\Windows\System32\VMGuest.ISO` in the Management OS). Normally you are prompted whether to run the setup file. If not, you can start it manually. The setup will not continue if it detects that a current version of the integration components is already installed.

INTEGRATION COMPONENTS MAINTENANCE

The integration components that are provided or installed in a guest OS should be kept up to date. Sometimes the updates provide security fixes, sometimes they introduce new functionality, and sometimes they fix bugs. You can run a script to query the version of the integration components, as shown by Didier Van Hoye in a blog post (`http://workinghardinit.wordpress.com/2012/12/07/checking-host-integration-services-version-on-all-nodes-of-a-windows-server-2012-hyper-v-cluster-with-powershell`), to determine which virtual machines require an update. You might do this update manually, you could use PowerShell's ability to do remote execution, or you could use System Center to automate this update for you. System Center options include

◆ Performing the update manually from Virtual Machine Manager

◆ Using an Orchestrator runbook to automate the update and reboot of the virtual machines

◆ Publishing the integration components installer as an application, and requiring this application to install on a collection of virtual machines at a date and time of your choosing

---

If you are installing Linux, you should use the version of Linux Integration Services that is mentioned on the TechNet page.

GUEST OS INFORMATION WILL AGE

In the past, we found that the content on TechNet might not be well maintained over time. Instead, members of the community and Microsoft staff created and maintained a TechNet Wiki page with the latest information on supported Guest OSs and integration components. No such page existed at the time of writing this book. Use your favorite search engine to check for the existence of such a page.

Using Virtual Machine Templates

Just as with physical machines, there are several methods that you could use to deploy new virtual machines:

Build Each One by Hand   You can create a new virtual machine, and install the operating system by hand. This is the slowest of all methods and will always be your starting point to get your first virtual machine.

Use Traditional OS Deployment Techniques   You could use Sysprep to generalize the guest OS (Windows only) of a virtual machine and use an operating system deployment solution (such as Windows Deployment Services, Microsoft Deployment Toolkit, System Center Configuration Manager, or others) to capture an image of the virtual machine. This step of the process is commonly used by OS deployment engineers for the creation of an image for physical machine deployment.

You then could create new virtual machines by hand and deploy the guest operating system over the network. The virtual machine would temporarily require a legacy network adapter to boot on the network using PXE.

Even this option is pretty slow compared to the alternatives that virtualization enable.

Create a Library File Share of Virtual Hard Disks   Once again, you build a virtual machine and generalize the guest OS. But instead of capturing the image, you shut down the virtual machine, and copy the virtual hard disk to a file share (a library). This library will also contain ISOs that can be mounted by virtual machines. This is the type of technique that System Center Virtual Machine Manager makes easy for you, but you can do it by hand if you do not have it.

You can create a new virtual machine and copy the generalized virtual hard disk to the required location. Attach the virtual hard disk to IDE Controller 0 and Location 0, and then start the virtual machine. The guest OS will be specialized for the new instance, and a new virtual machine is online in minutes.

SOME HANDY WINDOWS SERVER 2012 TIPS

Windows Server 2012 includes file system de-duplication for at-rest files (http://blogs.technet .com/b/filecab/archive/2012/05/21/introduction-to-data-deduplication-in- windows-server-2012.aspx). You can use this to greatly reduce the disk space utilization of a library of ISOs and virtual hard disks.

Another trick is to use Server Manager to enable roles and features in a virtual hard disk (Windows Server 2012 guest OS only) before you deploy it. This could save you some time and enable you to deploy different kinds of virtual machines from just a single virtual hard disk.

Import Copies Of Virtual Machines   This is a variation of the library approach. Create and generalize (Windows guest OS only) the template virtual machine. Shut down the virtual machine and export it. Move the export folder to the file share.

Whenever you need a new virtual machine, import the virtual machine by using the copy option to create a new virtual machine with a unique ID.

Designing Virtual Machines for Applications

In some ways, virtual machines are no different from physical servers. One of these ways is that you should always check a software vendor's requirements before acquiring or building a machine to run their software, be it an operating system or an application. Unfortunately, this is something that many overlook. For example:

♦ It was only with the release of Service Pack 1 for Exchange 2010 that the Exchange product group supported highly available Mailbox servers on a virtualization cluster (VMware, XenServer, or Hyper-V).

♦ Microsoft never supported the restoration from backup or snapshot of a domain controller that was installed in a virtual machine before Windows Server 2012.

♦ The Exchange Mailbox role cannot use and does not support Dynamic Memory.

♦ Before the 2012 release, only the Enterprise and Datacenter editions of SQL Server could use Dynamic Memory in a virtual machine.

♦ The SharePoint product group recommends setting the Virtual Machine Reserve of SharePoint virtual machines to 100 percent so they don't have to share logical processors with other virtual machines.

WINDOWS SERVER 2012 VIRTUAL DOMAIN CONTROLLERS

A Windows Server 2012 domain controller can be restored from backup or from a snapshot if it is running on a Windows Server 2012 Hyper-V host in a Windows Server 2012 functional-level forest. In fact, we can even clone Windows Server 2012 domain controllers by copying the virtual machine. This is thanks to a new feature called GenerationID. You can learn more at www.microsoft.com/download/details.aspx?id=30707.

Therefore, we strongly urge you to always check the vendors of your operating system and software to get their support statements and recommendations. You can find guidance for Microsoft's server products at http://support.microsoft.com/kb/957006.

Performance Monitoring of Guest Operating Systems

A common mistake is to rely on the performance metrics that a guest operating system gathers. Some of them are useful (such as memory utilization and queue lengths), but others are unreliable (such as CPU metrics). Hyper-V adds counters and objects that you can track by using Performance Monitor in the Management OS of the host. These are the only true metrics that you can rely on for virtual machines. For example, you should use the Hyper-V Hypervisor Virtual Processor metrics to get an accurate measure of CPU utilization by a virtual machine.

Real World Solutions

Here are some virtual machine management problems you might encounter and their possible solutions.

Replacing Virtual Switches

CHALLENGE

You have been told that some network engineering will be taking place, and you must move every virtual machine that is on a virtual switch called External1 to a different virtual switch called External2. This sounds simple until you find that there are more than 400 virtual machines connected to External1 on the host that you manage. How will you complete this task as quickly as possible?

SOLUTION

A common problem is the need to make a simple change—but to lots of virtual machines. Using the GUI is out of the question because it is too slow. This is where PowerShell can prove its value. This one line of code will make the required change to the over 400 virtual machines:

```
Get-VMNetworkAdapter * | Where-Object {$_.SwitchName -Eq "External1"} | `
Connect-VMNetworkAdapter -SwitchName "External2"
```

The code does the following:

- Gets all virtual network adapters
- Filters them for only those that connect to a virtual switch called External1
- Connects those remaining virtual network adapters to External2

Performing Simultaneous Live Migration

CHALLENGE

Your monitoring system has detected a hardware fault on a nonclustered Hyper-V host. There are 200 virtual machines running on the host. All of the virtual machines are stored on a file share, and your hosts are all configured for Kerberos-constrained delegation. Live Migration is configured, and you can do up to 20 simultaneous Live Migrations. You need to drain the host of virtual machines as quickly as possible. How will you do this?

SOLUTION

If the host was clustered, you could take advantage of a Failover Clustering feature called Live Migration Queuing. This would allow you to pause the host. This puts the host into maintenance mode and forces the host to transfer the virtual machines to other hosts in the cluster. However, this host is not clustered, and you do not want to manually start Live Migration of each virtual machine because it will take too long.

The following code uses a PowerShell V3 concept called *workflows* to perform up to five (limited by Windows Workflow Foundation) simultaneous tasks:

```
Workflow Invoke-ParallelLiveMigrate
{
Param
    (
    # Param1 List
    [string[]]
    $VMList,

    # Param2 The host you are live migrating from
    $SourceHost,

    # Param3 The host you are live migrating to
    $DestinationHost
    )


ForEach -Parallel ($VM in $VMList)
    {
    Move-VM -ComputerName $SourceHost -Name $VM -DestinationHost $DestinationHost
    }
}


#The script starts here. First we define the two hosts:
$FromHost = "Host2"
$ToHost = "Host1"


$VMList = Get-VM -ComputerName $FromHost
if ($VMList -ne $Null)
    {
    Invoke-ParallelLiveMigrate -VMList $VMList.Name $FromHost $ToHost
    }
else
    {
    Write-Output "There is nothing to move"
    }
```

The code does the following:

1. Gets a listing of every virtual machine on Host2 (the source host).

2. Sends the list of virtual machines, the name of the source host, and the name of the destination host to a workflow called Invoke-ParallelLiveMigrate.

3. The workflow live-migrates all of the virtual machines to Host1 by using a loop. The loop allows up to five simultaneous Live Migrations. The loop will continue until all of the virtual machines have been moved off of Host2.

> ## OVERCOMING THE LIMITS OF WINDOWS WORKFLOW FOUNDATION
>
> A PowerShell workflow is enabled by Windows Workflow Foundation (WF). WF limits a workflow to five parallel threads of execution, and this cannot be expanded. This limits the preceding PowerShell example to five simultaneous Live Migrations.
>
> Jeff Wouters, a PowerShell wizard in the Netherlands, wrote a blog post (http://jeffwouters .nl/index.php/2012/11/powershell-workflow-foreach-parallel-limited-to- 5-parallel-threads/) on how to overcome this limit by using a feature of PowerShell called ScriptBlock.

Rapid Virtual Machine Creation

CHALLENGE

You manage the Hyper-V infrastructure for a software development company. They use Hyper-V virtual machines to test new builds of their software every day. They need new virtual machines for each set of tests. The process that has been used up to now requires too much manual intervention and is too slow. You have been asked to create a better solution that will feature automation, will be flexible, and will allow software developers/testers to vary the specification of each virtual machine.

SOLUTION

The solution is to combine many of the solutions that are featured in this chapter in a PowerShell script. The script reads in a comma-separated values (CSV) file that can be created in Microsoft Excel. The header row lists a set of defined headers for columns. Each column configures a specific setting in a virtual machine. Each additional row specifies a virtual machine. Each line of the CSV file is read in and used to create a virtual machine according to that specification.

To speed up the creation of virtual machines, the script enables virtual machines to be created by using differencing disks. These differencing virtual hard disks point to selected parent virtual hard disks. This enables the testing infrastructure to deploy lots of virtual machines from a range of template virtual hard disks in a very speedy fashion. Virtual machines can be quickly destroyed and re-created.

Other settings such as Dynamic Memory, processor counts, and high availability are also available. The design of the CSV file is described in the script. This script and the CSV file design can be customized to suit the needs of any organization.

```
# Instructions
##############
#
# This script will read a comma-separated values (CSV) file to create VMs.
# The CSV file is specified in $CSVPath. A log file is created by this script.
# This log file is specified in $LogPath.
#
```

```
# The script expects to see a CSV file with a header row that specifies the
# column names (variables).
# Each row after that will define a new VM to create.  The variables are as
# follows:
#
# VMName: The name of the new VM to create
# VMPath: Where to create the VM's files
# DiskType: Differencing, Fixed, or Dynamic (the default). No value = Dynamic.
# DiffParent: Used when DiskType = Dynamic. Specifies the parent for the
# differencing disk
# DiskSize: Used if DiskType = Fixed or Dynamic (or blank). Size in GB for the
# new VHDX
# ProcessorCount: How many vCPUs the VM will have
# StartupRAM: Amount in MB that the VM will boot up with (Dynamic Memory or not)
# DynamicMemory: Yes or No (default). Do you enable DM or not?
# MinRAM: Amount in MB for Minimum RAM if DM is enabled.
# MaxRAM: Amount in MB for Maximum RAM if DM is enabled.
# MemPriority: 0-100 value if for Memory Weight DM is enabled
# MemBuffer: 5-2000 value for Memory Buffer is DM is enabled
# StaticMAC: Any non-Null value will be used as a MAC address. No error
# detection.
# AddToCluster: The new VM will be added to the specified cluster if not blank.
# Start: If set to Yes, then the VM will be started up.


# Clear the screen
cls


$CSVPath = "\\demo-sofs1\CSV1\VMs.txt"
$LogPath = "C:\Scripts\VMsLog.txt"


# Remove the log file
Remove-Item -Path $LogPath -ErrorAction SilentlyContinue


Import-Csv $CSVPath | ForEach-Object {


# Construct some paths
$Path = $_.VMPath
$VMName = $_.VMName
$VHDPath = "$Path\$VMName"


Add-Content $LogPath "Beginning: Creating $VMName."
```

```
# Only create the virtual machine if it does not already exist
if ((Get-VM $VMName -ErrorAction SilentlyContinue))
    {
    Add-Content $LogPath "FAIL: $VMName already existed."
    }
else
    {

    # Create a new folder for the VM if it does not already exist
    if (!(Test-Path $VHDPath))
        {
        New-Item -Path $VHDPath -ItemType "Directory"
        }

    # Create a new folder for the VHD if it does not already exist
    if (!(Test-Path "$VHDPath\Virtual Hard Disks"))
        {
        $VhdDir = New-Item -Path "$VHDPath\Virtual Hard Disks" -ItemType `
        "Directory"
        }

    # Create the VHD if it does not already exist
    $NewVHD = "$VhdDir\$VMName-Disk0.vhd"
    if (!(Test-Path $NewVHD))
        {
        # Have to set these variables because $_.Variables are not available
        # inside the switch.
        $ParentDisk = $_.DiffParent
        $DiskSize = [int64]$_.DiskSize * 1073741824
        switch ($_.DiskType)
            {
            'Differencing' {New-VHD -Differencing -Path $NewVHD -ParentPath `
            $ParentDisk}
            'Fixed' {New-VHD -Fixed -Path $NewVHD -SizeBytes $DiskSize}
            Default {New-VHD -Dynamic -Path $NewVHD -SizeBytes $DiskSize}
            }
        if (Test-Path $NewVHD)
            {
            Add-Content $LogPath "  Progress: $NewVHD was created."
            }
            else
            {
            Add-Content $LogPath "  Error: $NewVHD was not created."
            }
        }
        else
        {
```

```
        Add-Content $LogPath "  Progress: $NewVHD already existed"
        }


# Create the VM
New-VM -Name $_.VMName -Path $Path -SwitchName ConvergedNetSwitch -VHDPath `
$NewVHD -MemoryStartupBytes ([int64]$_.StartupRam * 1MB)


# Is the VM there and should we continue?
if ((Get-VM $VMName -ErrorAction SilentlyContinue))
    {
    Add-Content $LogPath "  Progress: The VM was created."


    # Configure the processors
    Set-VMProcessor $_.VMName -Count $_.ProcessorCount -ErrorAction `
    SilentlyContinue
    If ((Get-VMProcessor $_.VMName).count -eq $_.ProcessorCount)
        {
        Add-Content $LogPath "  Progress: Configured processor count."
        }
        else
        {
        Add-Content $LogPath "  ERROR: Processor count was not configured."
        }


    # Configure Dynamic Memory if required
    If ($_.DynamicMemory -Eq "Yes")
        {
        Set-VMMemory -VMName $_.VMName -DynamicMemoryEnabled $True `
        -MaximumBytes ([int64]$_.MaxRAM * 1MB) -MinimumBytes ([int64]$_. `
        MinRAM * 1MB) -Priority $_.MemPriority -Buffer $_.MemBuffer
        If ((Get-VMMemory $_.VMName).DynamicMemoryEnabled -eq $True)
            {
            Add-Content $LogPath "  Progress: Dynamic Memory was set."
            }
            else
            {
            Add-Content $LogPath "  ERROR: Dynamic Memory was not set."
            }
        }


    # Is a static MAC Address required?
    If ($_.StaticMAC -ne $NULL)
```

```
        {
        Set-VMNetworkAdapter $_.VMName -StaticMacAddress $_.StaticMAC `
        -ErrorAction SilentlyContinue
        If ((Get-VMNetworkAdapter $_.VMName).MacAddress -eq $_.StaticMAC)
            {
            Add-Content $LogPath "  Progress: Static MAC address set."
            }
            else
            {
            Add-Content $LogPath "  ERROR: Static MAC address was not set."
            }
        }


    Add the VM to the cluster?
        $ClusterName = $_.AddToCluster
        If ($ClusterName -ne $NULL)
        {
        If (Add-ClusterVirtualMachineRole -Cluster $_.AddToCluster -VMName `
        $_.VMName -ErrorAction SilentlyContinue)
            {
            Add-Content $LogPath "  Progress: Added VM to $ClusterName `
            cluster."
            }
            else
            {
            Add-Content $LogPath "  ERROR: Did not add VM to $ClusterName `
            cluster."
            }
        }


    # Start the VM?
        If ($_.Start -eq "Yes")
        {
        Start-VM $_.VMName -ErrorAction SilentlyContinue
        If ((Get-VM $_.VMName).State -eq "Running")
            {
            Add-Content $LogPath "  Progress: Started the VM."
            }
            else
            {
            Add-Content $LogPath "  ERROR: Did not start the VM."
            }
        }
```

```
# End of "Is the VM there and should we continue?"
Add-Content $LogPath "Success: $VMName was created."
}
else
{
Add-Content $LogPath "FAIL: $VMName was created."
}


    }
}
```

Part 2

Advanced Networking and Cloud Computing

Chapter 4

Networking

Some of the biggest improvements in Windows Server 2012 Hyper-V are related to networking. The relatively simple virtual network of the past has been replaced by a more feature-rich, manageable layer 2 and an extensible virtual switch. There were cheers when Microsoft announced the introduction of built-in NIC teaming, something that has been requested by users of Microsoft server virtualization since it first emerged. This chapter discusses how to create and configure NIC teaming and the new Hyper-V extensible virtual switch.

The performance of Hyper-V storage and virtualized workloads depends heavily on networking. Simply adding more capacity to network connections is not enough, and in some cases can cause adverse results. Microsoft added support for a number of hardware features that accelerate and offload network processing. These additions allow high-capacity network links to be used, and otherwise processor-intensive functions to be offloaded to network hardware, while improving application performance. This chapter covers these offloads and how to configure them.

A new host networking architecture called *converged fabrics* has also been added in Windows Server 2012. With converged fabrics, we can use fewer network cards and fewer network switch ports, thus reducing the cost and complexity of networking. And an interesting side result is easier host deployment and automation. Converged fabrics use all the features discussed in this chapter, plus the new Quality of Service functionality for guaranteeing a minimum level of service.

In this chapter, you'll learn about

- ◆ The Hyper-V extensible virtual switch and NIC teaming

- ◆ Networking hardware enhancements in Windows Server 2012 Hyper-V

- ◆ Quality of Service and converged fabrics

Basic Hyper-V Networking

Networking is a huge subject in Windows Server 2012 Hyper-V. We are going to start with the basics, moving through some new features that can be difficult to understand at first, and building your knowledge up in layers, before you go on to the more-complex topics in Chapter 5, "Cloud Computing," Chapter 7, "Using File Servers," and Chapter 8, "Building Hyper-V Clusters." We recommend that you read through each subject, even if you are experienced in networking or Hyper-V. At the very least, this will serve as a refresher, but you might find that you learn something that will be important to later topics.

In this section, you will look at the basics of Hyper-V networking that are required to connect your virtual machines to a network. You will be introduced to the new Hyper-V virtual switch before looking at the greatly anticipated NIC teaming feature.

Using the Hyper-V Extensible Virtual Switch

In the past, Hyper-V had a relatively simple virtual device in the host called a *virtual network* to connect virtual machines to networks. The virtual network has been replaced by something much more exciting (for nerds who get excited by this sort of thing) and powerful: the virtual switch. This is a central piece in Microsoft's Windows Server 2012 cloud operating system strategy. Users of previous versions of Hyper-V will still create the new virtual switch the same way that they created the virtual network, and the same types are still used. However, it won't be long until the power of the switch becomes evident.

Understanding the Virtual Network Interface Controller

In Chapter 3, "Managing Virtual Machines," you saw that virtual machines could have one or more virtual network interface controllers (NICs) in their configuration to allow the virtual machines to connect to a network. Virtual NICs are not confined to just virtual machines; the management OS can also have virtual NICs. This might be a little difficult to understand at first. Where does this NIC reside? What does it connect to? It resides in the management OS, and it appears in Network Connections just like a physical NIC. Like every virtual NIC in virtual machines, the management OS virtual NICs connect to a virtual switch. You will see a few ways to create and use virtual NICs as you proceed through this chapter.

Introducing the Virtual Switch

The virtual switch performs the same basic task as a physical server. A physical switch connects the NICs of physical servers to a network, providing each connection with its own isolated source-to-destination connection. A network administrator might route that network or might make it an isolated network. There are three kinds of virtual switch, and each kind will connect the virtual NICs of virtual machines to a different kind of network:

External Virtual Switch　The role of the external virtual switch, shown in Figure 4.1, is to connect virtual NICs to a physical network. Each virtual NIC is connected to a single virtual switch. The switch is connected to a physical network. This connects the virtual NICs to the physical network.

The virtual NICs participate on a LAN, just like the NICs in a physical machine do. Each virtual NIC has its own MAC or Ethernet address, and each network stack has its own IPv4 and/or IPv6 address. Each virtual NIC is completely separate from all of the other virtual NICs and from the NICs that are used by the management OS in the host itself. For example, the Windows Firewall in the management OS has nothing to do with the networking of the virtual machines in the host, and vice versa.

FIGURE 4.1
An external virtual
switch

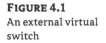

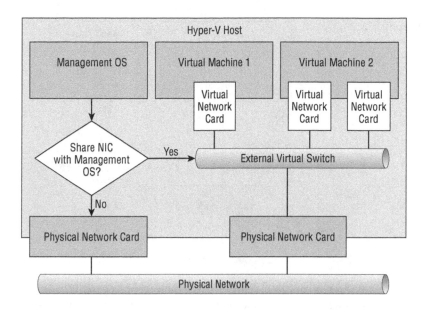

FIGURE 4.1
An external virtual
switch

You can have more than one external virtual switch in a host. For example, if you want two external switches, you will need two connections to a physical network. Thanks to the many innovative features of Hyper-V in Windows Server 2012, you do not need more than one virtual switch to support multiple networks, as you will learn in this chapter and in Chapter 5.

Traditionally, an administrator wanted to isolate the network connection of the management OS from that of the virtual machines, so it had its own physical network connection. However, when there were a limited number of physical NICs in the host, the management OS could share the physical network connection that was used by the virtual switch. Doing this creates a virtual NIC in the management OS that is connected to the external virtual switch. This management OS virtual NIC appears in Network Connections with a name of vEthernet (<Name Of Switch>) and a device name of Hyper-V Virtual Ethernet Adapter. The management OS virtual NIC needs to be configured (settings and/or protocols) just as a physical NIC would require.

The Hyper-V administrator can choose between connecting the management OS to the virtual switch or directly to a physical NIC—if the administrator is not considering something else called converged fabrics, which you will read about later in the chapter.

Private Virtual Switch   Figure 4.2 shows a private virtual switch. This type of virtual switch has no connections to either the management OS or the physical network; it is completely isolated, and therefore any virtual NICs that are connected to a private virtual switch are isolated too.

FIGURE 4.2
A private virtual
switch

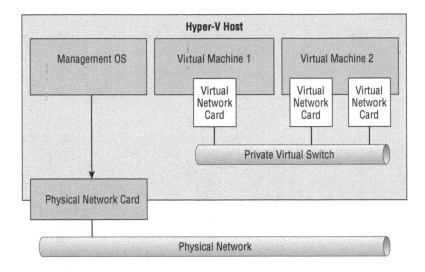

In past versions of Hyper-V, the private virtual switch was often used to secure sensitive workloads that should not be open to contact by the physical network or other virtual machines. One virtual machine running a firewall service could have two virtual NICs: one connected to an external switch, and another connected to the private network where the sensitive workload was connected. The firewall would then control and route access to the private network.

Virtual switches (of any type) are not distributed. This means that a virtual machine connected to a private network on Host1 cannot communicate with a virtual machine connected to a similarly named private network on Host2. This could cause issues if the cooperating virtual machines were migrated to different hosts. This could be avoided by adding some complexity, such as new isolated VLANs on the physical network or rules to keep virtual machines together. However, as you will see in Chapter 5, there are new techniques we can use instead of private networks, such as Port ACLs (access control lists) or third-party solutions, that can isolate our workloads without the use of private virtual switches.

Internal Virtual Switch The internal virtual switch isolates connected virtual NICs from the physical network, but it connects the management OS by using a virtual NIC, as you can see in Figure 4.3.

As with the private virtual switch, you do have to take care to keep virtual machines on this switch together on the same host. Otherwise, the machines will not be able to reach each other across the network. While the internal type of the virtual switch has a place in a lab environment, it has little use in production systems, thanks to the new cloud networking functionality in Windows Server 2012 that can achieve the same results, but with the flexibility of being able to move virtual machines between different hosts. (Chapter 5 provides more details.)

FIGURE 4.3
Internal virtual
switch

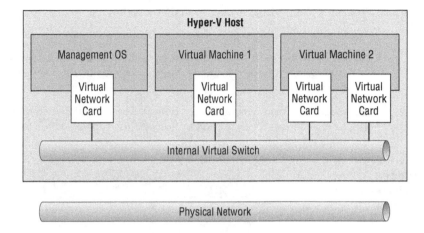

CREATING VIRTUAL SWITCHES

If you want to create a virtual switch for basic functionality, you can do this in the Hyper-V
Manager console. Under Actions, you will see an option for Virtual Switch Manager. Clicking
that option opens the Virtual Switch Manager for the selected host, as shown in Figure 4.4.

FIGURE 4.4
The Virtual Switch
Manager

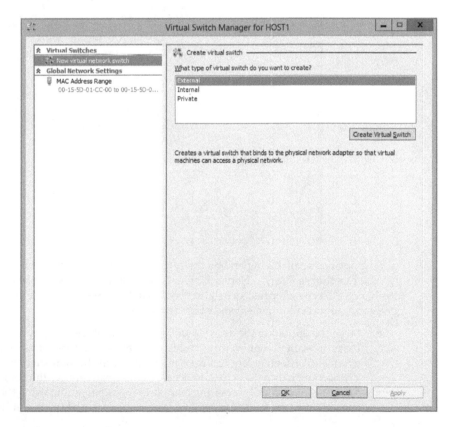

To create a new virtual switch, you do the following:

1. On the left side of the screen, under Virtual Switches, select New Virtual Network Switch.

2. On the right-hand side of the screen, under Create Virtual Switch, choose the type of virtual switch you want to create. You can change this type in a moment or after you create the switch.

3. Click the Create Virtual Switch button. The Virtual Switch Manager window changes to reveal more configuration options for the type of switch that you have selected (see Figure 4.5).

FIGURE 4.5
Configure the new virtual switch.

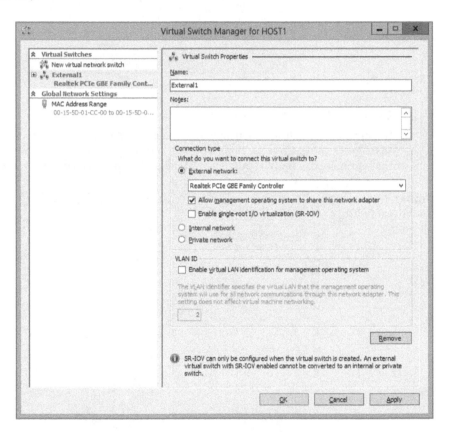

The options available depend on the type of virtual switch that you have decided to create. You can choose External Network (with further options), Internal Network, or Private Network to change the type of virtual switch that you want to create. The choice of External Network has one configuration requirement and offers two options:

◆ From the options in the drop-down list box, you choose the physical network adapter that you want to connect the virtual switch to. Only connections that are unused will be available. Unfortunately, this does not give you the human-friendly name of the network connection; it uses the actual device name. You can retrieve the device name of the desired network connection by opening Network Connections and using the details view or by running the Get-NetAdapter | Format-Table -Autosize PowerShell cmdlets.

MEANINGFUL NETWORK NAMES

The way that Windows names the network connections has been an annoyance for administrators for a long time. Local Area Connection, Local Area Connection 1, and so on, or Ethernet, Ethernet 1, and so on, as the names appear in Windows Server 2012, have nothing to do with the names or the orders of the devices on the physical hardware. One workaround has been to plug in the network cables one at a time, and rename the network in Network Connections with a more meaningful name such as Management OS or External1.

Some manufacturers are choosing to store the NIC names from the back of the server chassis in the BIOS (PCI-SIG Engineering Change Notice, or ECN). Windows Server 2012 has a new feature called Consistent Device Naming (CDN) that can detect those BIOS-stored names of the network devices and use them to name the network connections for you. This makes life much easier for operators and administrators. With CDN, you just need to know what switch port is connected to what NIC port on the back of the server and, in theory, the network names will have a corresponding name, making server or host network configuration much easier.

♦ The Allow Management Operating System To Share This Network Adapter option is selected by default if you have chosen to create an External Network. You should clear this check box if you want to physically isolate the management OS networking on a different network. In the past, Hyper-V engineers typically wanted to isolate the management OS from virtual machine traffic and so have cleared this option.

Single-Root I/O Virtualization (SR-IOV) is a new feature in Windows Server 2012 Hyper-V that allows virtual NICs to run with less latency than usual if you have the required hardware. You'll learn more about this feature later in the chapter. It is not selected by default and should be selected only if you are absolutely certain that you do want to enable SR-IOV; this will require some understanding of this advanced feature. Note that this option can be selected only when you create the switch, and it cannot be changed without deleting and re-creating the switch.

A SHORTCUT TO NETWORK CONNECTIONS

How much administrative or engineering effort is wasted navigating through Control Panel or Server Manager to get to Network Connections? There is a quicker route: just run NCPA.CPL.

If you choose either of the following configurations for the virtual switch, a management OS virtual NIC will be created and connected to the virtual switch:

♦ An external virtual switch that is shared with the management OS

♦ An internal virtual switch

If you did choose one of these configurations, you can configure the management OS virtual network with a VLAN ID. This will isolate the traffic at the virtual and physical switch level, and will require some work by the physical network administrators to trunk the connected switch ports to support VLANs. Choosing this option does not place the virtual switch on the VLAN; it places only the management OS virtual NIC on that VLAN.

When you create a virtual switch, you might get a warning that the creation process may disconnect anyone using services on the management OS. For example, creating an external virtual switch via Remote Desktop will disconnect your session if you select the Remote Desktop NIC to be the connection point for an external switch.

You can return to Virtual Switch Manager to modify a switch (except for the SR-IOV setting) or to even delete it.

ALWAYS HAVE A BACKDOOR TO THE HOST

Virtualization hosts, such as Hyper-V hosts, are extremely valuable resources because they can support numerous servers. From a business's point of view, those multiple services enable the organization to operate. Configuring networking from a remote location, such as a remote office or your desk on another floor, can have risks. If you make a mistake with the network configuration, you can disconnect the host, the virtual machines, and your own ability to use Remote Desktop to fix the problem quickly.

Therefore, we strongly urge you to consider having a secured backdoor to get remote KVM access to your hosts such as Dell's DRAC or HP's iLO. Some solutions offer SSL and Active Directory integrated authentication so only authorized administrators can gain remote access. This can be coupled with physical network remote access and firewall policies where security is a concern. If you make a mistake while remotely configuring networking on the host, you can use the KVM console to log into the server, fix the issue, and quickly return to normal service without having to travel to the computer room or request local operator assistance.

You can use New-VMSwitch to create a virtual switch, which is disconnected from the management OS by using PowerShell:

```
New-VMSwitch "External1" -NetAdapterName "Ethernet" -AllowManagementOS 0
```

That snippet creates an external virtual switch by default. You can change the type by adding the -SwitchType flag and choosing from External, Internal, or Private:

```
New-VMSwitch "Internal1" -SwitchType Internal
```

This creates a new virtual switch that virtual machines can be connected to. The management OS will also get a new virtual NIC called vEthernet (Internal1) that will require an IP configuration. Here is how you can configure IPv4 for this virtual NIC:

```
NewNetIPAddress -InterfaceAlias "vEthernet (Internal1)" -IPAddress 10.0.15.1
-PrefixLength 24 -Default Gateway 10.0.15.254Set-DnsClientServerAddress
-InterfaceAlias "vEthernet (Internal1)" -ServerAddresses 10.0.15.21, 10.0.15.22
```

Get-VMSwitch can be used to retrieve a virtual switch. Set-VMSwitch can be used to configure a virtual switch. For example, you can quickly reconfigure a virtual switch to use a different physical connection by using this line of PowerShell:

```
Set-VMSwitch "External1" -NetAdapterName "Ethernet 3"
```

You could always change your mind about not sharing the virtual switch's network connection with the management OS:

```
Set-VMSwitch "External1" AllowManagementOS 1
```

Here's an example of the power of PowerShell; you can quickly move all the virtual NICs that are connected to one virtual switch to another virtual switch in one line of code instead of dozens, hundreds, or even thousands of mouse clicks:

```
Get-VMNetworkAdapter * | Where-Object {$_.SwitchName -EQ "Private1"} | `
Connect-VMNetworkAdapter -SwitchName "External1"
```

The first piece of the code retrieves all the virtual NICs on the host, before filtering them down to just the ones connected to the Private1 virtual switch. The remaining virtual NICs are then changed so they connect to the External1 virtual switch instead.

By default, all newly created virtual NICs have a dynamically assigned MAC or Ethernet address. Each MAC address is assigned from a pool of addresses that are defined in the Virtual Switch Manager screen, as you can see in Figure 4.6. You can alter this range of MAC addresses if required by the network administrator. Note that this will not affect the in-use MAC addresses of any virtual NIC that is currently in operation on the host at the time of the change.

FIGURE 4.6
The MAC address range for this host

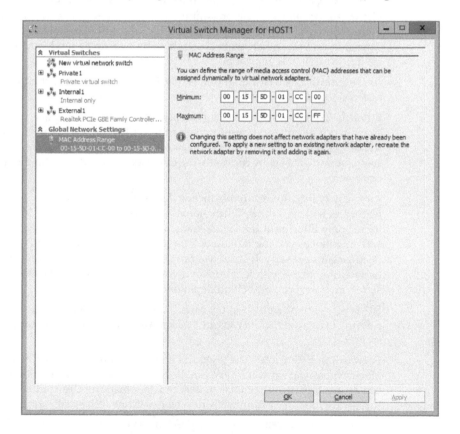

You have learned the basics of configuring a virtual switch. Now it's time to see why it's called the *extensible* virtual switch.

ADDING VIRTUAL SWITCH EXTENSIBILITY

By itself, the Hyper-V virtual switch is a powerful network appliance, but it can be given more functionality by installing third-party extensions. Each of these extensions adds functionality to the Hyper-V virtual switch instead of replacing it. The extensions are certified Network Driver Interface Specification (NDIS) filter drivers or Windows Filtering Platform (WFP) filters/drivers.

As you can see in Figure 4.7, three types of extensions can be added to a Hyper-V extensible virtual switch:

Capturing Extension   The role of the NDIS filter capturing extension is to monitor network traffic as it passes through the virtual switch. It may not alter this traffic. The extension may report back to a central monitoring service or application to allow administration.

In the legacy physical datacenter, network administrators would use data from network appliances to analyze problems between two computers. Those tools are useless when the two computers in question are running on the same host and the traffic never leaves the virtual switch and never gets near the physical network. This extension type offers network, virtualization, and application administrators the tools that can analyze communications within the virtual switch itself. The monitoring solution is agile because the virtual switch extension provides a hardware abstraction; there is no dependency on having certain physical hardware that is supported by a network monitoring solution.

At the time of this writing, InMon is offering a beta version of their capture filter solution called sFlow Agent for Windows Server 2012 Hyper-V.

Filtering Extension   The filtering extension can inspect (doing everything a capturing extension can do), modify, and insert packets in the virtual switch. It can also drop packets or prevent packet delivery to one or more destinations. As you can see in Figure 4.7, the filtering extension sees inbound data before the capturing extension, and it sees outbound data after the capturing extension.

As you may have guessed, this means that certified third-party filter extensions can add feature-rich virtual firewall functionality to the Hyper-V extensible virtual switch. The ability to apply filtering at the virtual-switch layer means that the dependency on physical firewall appliances and the misuse of VLANs for virtual machine and service network isolation is no longer necessary. Instead, we can use flatter networks and leverage software-defined networking (SDN) with less human involvement, and this makes Windows Server 2012 more suited for enterprise and cloud deployment.

5nine Software offers a solution, called Agentless Security Manager for Hyper-V, that has a filtering extension that has advanced firewall functionality from within the Hyper-V virtual switch.

Forwarding Extension   The third and final extension type is the forwarding extension. This all-encompassing extension type can do everything that the forwarding and filtering extensions can do. But forwarding extensions also can do something else: they can make the Hyper-V virtual switch look like a completely different switch to third-party administration software.

The forwarding extension is the first extension to see incoming data and the last extension to see outgoing data.

At the time of this writing, there are two known solutions in this space. Cisco has the Nexus 1000V, described as a distributed virtual switching platform that extends Cisco functionality into the Hyper-V extensible virtual switch. It can be managed using the same Cisco command tools that are used to configure the physical network. NEC offers a solution called ProgrammableFlow for Hyper-V that promises to give you software-defined networking (see Chapter 5), security, and easier administration for cloud computing.

You can install multiple forwarding extensions on a host, but only a single forwarding extension can be enabled in each specific virtual switch. This is because the forwarding extension creates a lot of change that will be very specific to the solution at hand.

FIGURE 4.7
The architecture of
the Hyper-V exten-
sible virtual switch

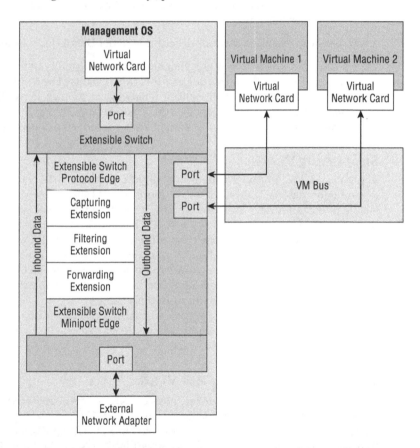

You will have to refer to the vendors of the third-party extensions for specific guidance and instructions for their solutions. However, you can perform the following operations in the Virtual Switch Manager:

◆ Enable and disable extensions.

◆ Reorder extensions within their own type. For example, you cannot make a monitoring extension see inbound data before a filtering extension sees it.

To perform these operations on a virtual switch, you follow these steps:

1. Open Virtual Switch Manager.

2. Click the expand button on the relevant virtual switch to expand its properties.

3. Click Extensions.

Here you can do the following:

◆ Select (to enable) or deselect (to disable) the check boxes beside an extension.

◆ Select an extension and click Move Up or Move Down to reorder the extension within its own extension type.

◆ Select an extension to see its description under Details for Selected Extensions.

The small amount of text in this chapter on the extensibility of the Hyper-V virtual switch might mislead you on the importance of this functionality. The features, security, flexibility, and the extension of SDN into the physical network make the extensibility of the virtual switch extremely important. In fact, it's one of the headline-making features of Windows Server 2012 that make it a true cloud operating system and is described extensively in Chapter 5.

Supporting VLANs

The virtual LAN (VLAN) is a method of dividing a physical LAN into multiple subnets for a number of reasons. VLANs can create more address space, control broadcast domains, and isolate traffic. They have been used (many say misused) to create security boundaries that are routed and filtered by firewalls. Each VLAN has an ID, or tag, that is used to dynamically associate a device with that VLAN so it can communicate only on the VLAN.

We can support VLANs in Hyper-V in many ways, some of which you will read about in Chapter 5. You have already seen how to associate a management OS virtual NIC with a VLAN when the management OS shares a physical connection with an external virtual switch. We will cover additional basic VLAN solutions in this chapter.

The typical request is to have a single virtual switch that can support many virtual machines connected to many VLANs. In reality, what is being requested is to have many virtual NICs connected to many VLANs; you'll soon see why.

CONFIGURING PHYSICAL ISOLATION OF VLANS

A very crude approach is to have one physical NIC for every required VLAN. You can see this in Figure 4.8. In this example, you have two VLANs, 101 and 102. A port is configured on the switch for each VLAN. Each port is connected to a physical NIC on the host. An external virtual switch is created for each of the VLANs/physical NICs. And the virtual NICs of the virtual machines are connected to the associated VLANs/virtual switches.

FIGURE 4.8
Physical isolation
for each VLAN

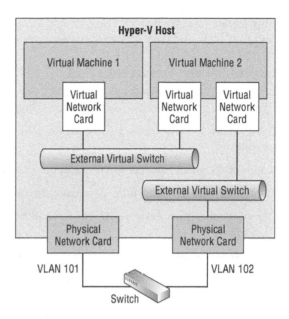

This is not a good solution. It might be OK for a lab or the smallest of installations, but it is not flexible, it is not scalable, and it will require lots of NICs if you have lots of VLANs (and double the number if you require NIC teaming).

ISOLATION OF LAN TRAFFIC FROM INTERNET CONNECTIONS

Although the Hyper-V virtual switch securely isolates traffic, it is always desirable to physically isolate LAN traffic from Internet traffic. This isolation protects against distributed denial-of-service (DDoS) attacks that are sustained, artificially creating exceptional levels of traffic designed to crash appliances, hardware, or services. Physically isolating LAN services from Internet services means that the LAN services can remain available to internal users while the DDoS attack is underway.

The ideal is that the physical isolation is done at the host level, with Internet services having their own hosts on a physically isolated network infrastructure. But small and medium businesses don't have that luxury; they must use some level of shared infrastructure. They can have Internet-facing virtual machines (virtual NICs) operational on one external virtual switch (and physical connection), and internal services running on another external virtual switch (and physical connection), as previously shown in Figure 4.8. And once again, the ideal is to physically isolate the routing and switching to ensure that the DDoS attack does not affect the physical infrastructure for internal services.

The only scalable approach to VLANs is to deal with them at the software layer. There are many ways to do that, and the next two options are some of those that you can use.

ASSIGNING VLAN IDs TO VIRTUAL NICs

With this approach, you create a single external virtual switch and then configure the VLAN ID of each virtual NIC to link it to the required VLAN. The benefits are as follows:

◆ The solution is software based, so it can be automated or orchestrated for self-service cloud computing.

◆ Scalability is not an issue because the approach is software based.

◆ The solution requires very little infrastructure configuration.

◆ The solution is secure because only the virtualization administrator can configure the VLAN ID.

Figure 4.9 shows the solution. The network administrator creates the required VLANs and sets up a trunk port in the switch. The physical NIC in the host is connected to the trunk port. An external virtual switch is created, as usual, and connected to the physical NIC. Virtual machines are created, as usual, and their NICs are connected to the single virtual switch, even though lots of virtual machines are going to be connected to lots of VLANs. The trick here is that the virtualization administrator (or the orchestration software) assigns each virtual NIC to a specific VLAN. The trunk is passed into the virtual switch, and this allows the virtual NIC to be bound to and communicate on the assigned VLAN and only the assigned VLAN.

Note that if you trunk the switch port, every virtual NIC that is assigned to the switch port must be assigned a VLAN ID to communicate.

FIGURE 4.9
Using virtual NICs
to assign VLAN IDs

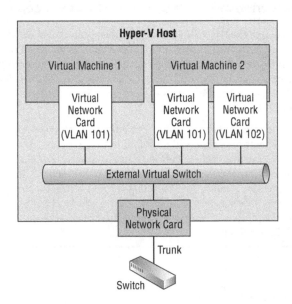

You can configure the VLAN ID of a virtual NIC as follows:

1. Open the settings of the virtual machine.

2. Click the required virtual network adapter.

3. Select the Enable Virtual LAN Identification check box and enter the required VLAN ID.

You can change virtual NIC VLANs while a virtual machine is running. You can also change the VLAN ID of a virtual network by using PowerShell:

```
Set-VMNetworkAdapterVLAN -VMName "Virtual Machine 1" -Access -VLANID 101
```

This is a simple scenario; Virtual Machine 1 has only a single virtual NIC, so we can just target the virtual machine to assign the VLAN to that virtual NIC. The virtual NIC is configured in access mode (a simple assignment) to tag only traffic for VLAN 101.

What if we had to assign a VLAN to a virtual machine with more than one virtual NIC, such as Virtual Machine 2, previously seen in Figure 4.9? Set-VMNetworkAdapter allows us to specify the name of a specific virtual NIC. That's a problem, because the name of each virtual NIC in the virtual machine settings is the rather anonymous Network Adapter, no matter how many virtual NICs the virtual machine has. So which one do you configure? First, you could run the following to get the virtual NICs of the virtual machine:

```
$NICS = Get-VMNetworkAdapter -VMName "Virtual Machine 2"
```

The results of the query are stored as an array in the $NICS variable. An *array* is a programming construct that contains more than one value. Each result is stored in the array and is indexed from 0 to N. In this case, Virtual Machine 2 has two virtual NICs. That's two entries in the array, with the first being indexed as [0] and the second indexed as [1]. We know that we want to configure the second virtual NIC to be in VLAN 102:

```
Set-VMNetworkAdapterVLAN -VMName "Virtual Machine 2" -VMNetworkAdapter `
$NICS[1].Name -Access -VLANID 102
```

If you want, you can flatten the entire solution down to a single, difficult-to-read line, in the traditional PowerShell way:

```
Set-VMNetworkAdapterVLAN -VMName "Virtual Machine 2" -VMNetworkAdapter `
{Get-VMNetworkAdapter -VMName "Virtual Machine 2"}[1].Name -Access `
-VLANID 102
```

USING A VIRTUAL SWITCH VLAN TRUNK

Another approach to dealing with VLANs is to simply pass the VLAN trunk up through the virtual switch port and into the virtual NIC of the virtual machine. In the example in Figure 4.10, the virtual NIC of Virtual Machine 1 will be configured in access mode to connect to a single VLAN. The virtual NIC of Virtual Machine 2 will be configured in trunk mode to allow VLANs that are specified by the Hyper-V or cloud administrator.

FIGURE 4.10
Trunk mode for a
virtual NIC

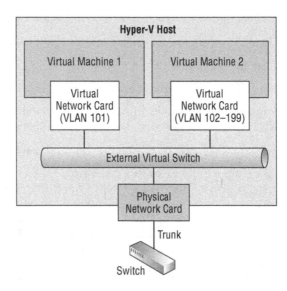

There is a certain level of trust being placed on the administrator of the guest operating system in a virtual machine that is granted trunk mode access to VLANs. The guest OS administrator should know the following:

◆ How to configure VLANs in the guest OS

◆ What traffic to send over what VLAN

◆ Not to misuse this delegated right

There is a certain amount of control that the Hyper-V or cloud administrator retains. Only specified VLANs will be trunked, so the guest OS administrator can successfully tag traffic for only the delegated VLANs.

Creating a trunked virtual switch port through to a virtual NIC is an advanced feature that should be rarely used, and it does not have a place in the GUI. You can configure trunk mode to the virtual NIC by using PowerShell only:

```
Set-VMNetworkAdapterVLAN -VMName "Virtual Machine 2" -Trunk -AllowedVLANList `
102-199 -NativeVLANID 102
```

The cmdlet has configured the virtual switch's port for `Virtual Machine 2` to be trunked for VLANs 102 to 199. A required safety measure is to specify a fallback VLAN in case the guest OS administrator fails to set VLAN IDs within the guest OS. In this example, the fallback VLAN is 102.

In this example, only one virtual NIC is in the virtual machine; you can target specific virtual NICs by using the method that was shown in the previous section. You can query the results of your VLAN engineering as follows:

```
PS C:\> Get-VMNetworkAdapterVLAN


VMName                VMNetworkAdapterName Mode    VlanList
------                -------------------- ----    --------
VirtualMachine1       Network Adapter      Access  101
VirtualMachine2       Network Adapter      Trunk   102,102-199
```

This is where we're going to leave VLANs for now, but we will make a quick return during the coverage of NIC teaming.

Supporting NIC Teaming

If you ever delivered presentations on or sold Hyper-V implementations before Windows Server 2012, you were guaranteed one question: is there built-in NIC teaming? Finally, the answer is yes—and it is completely supported for Hyper-V and Failover Clustering.

NIC teaming, also known as *NIC bonding* or *load balancing and failover (LBFO)* for NICs, was not supported by Microsoft in the past. Third parties such as server manufacturers offered NIC teaming software. But this software made huge changes to how Windows and Hyper-V networking worked, and Microsoft never supported these solutions in any way on their operating systems or for virtualization. Microsoft Support has a policy that could require customers to re-create a problem without third-party NIC teaming to prove that the add-on is not the cause of a problem.

But now Windows Server 2012 includes a NIC teaming solution. We no longer need to use third-party NIC teaming software, although hardware vendors might continue to offer it with the promise of additional features, albeit with the price of losing support from Microsoft.

If you have used NIC teaming in the past, you might be tempted to skip ahead in the chapter. Instead, we urge you to read this section of the book because it might prevent you from making some mistakes that are caused by common misunderstandings of how NIC teaming works. You will also require the knowledge in this section when you start to look at enabling Receive-Side Scaling (RSS - for SMB Multichannel) and Dynamic Virtual Machine Queue (DVMQ).

UNDERSTANDING NIC TEAMING

In NIC teaming, we group NICs together to act as a single unit, much as we use RAID to group disks. This results in the following:

Load Balancing   When we have two or more NICs, we can distribute and balance the network traffic across each NIC in a team. This is sometimes referred to as *NIC or link aggregation*, but those terms can mislead those who are not knowledgeable about NIC teaming. Although a NIC team does aggregate NICs, you don't just get a 20 GbE pipe when you team together two 10 GbE NICs. Instead, you get the ability to distribute traffic across two 10 GbE NICs, and how that distribution works depends on how you configure the team, and that decision depends on various factors that you will soon be familiar with.

Failover   Services that are important to the business usually have a service-level agreement (SLA) indicating that they must be available (not just operational) to the customer (or the end user) a certain percentage of the time. With features such as fault-tolerant storage and highly available Hyper-V hosts, we can protect the SLA from the operational point of view, but networking affects the availability of the service; a single faulty switch can bring down the entire service.

By using failover in NIC teaming, we put in more than one NIC to cover the eventuality that something will fail in the networking stack. In Figure 4.11, there are two NICs in the NIC team. The Hyper-V virtual switch is connected to the team instead of to a physical NIC. That means that all virtual NICs have two paths in to and out of the physical network. Both physical NICs are connected to different switches (possibly in a stack, or one logical switch configuration), and each switch has two paths to the upstream network. In this configuration, 50 percent of the entire physical network, from the NICs to the upstream network, could fail, and the virtual machines would still remain operational via one path or another through the vertical stack.

It is this high availability that is so desired for dense enterprise-level virtualization, where so many eggs (virtual machines or services) are placed in one basket (host).

FIGURE 4.11
NIC teaming with highly available networking

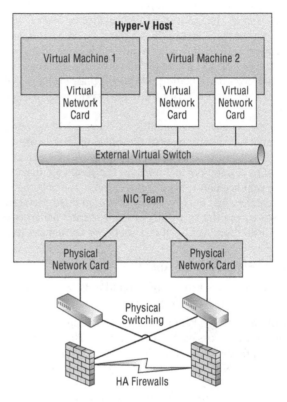

Together, these two functions are known as *LBFO*. Typically, NIC teaming might add more functionality, support VLANs, and require some configuration depending on the environment and intended usage.

Using Windows Sever 2012 NIC Teaming

The NIC teaming in Windows Server 2012 gives us LBFO as you would expect. You can see the basic concept of a NIC team in Figure 4.12. A Windows Server 2012 NIC team is made up of 1 to 32 physical NICs, also known as *team members*. The interesting thing is that these NICs can be not only any model, but also from any manufacturer. The only requirement is that the team member NICs have passed the Windows Hardware Quality Labs (WHQL) test—that is, they are on the Windows Server 2012 Hardware Compatibility List (HCL), which can be found at www.windowsservercatalog.com. The team members can even be of different speeds, but this is not recommended because the team will run at the lowest common denominator speed.

The ability to combine NICs from different manufacturers offers another kind of fault tolerance. It is not unheard of for there to be a NIC driver or firmware that is unstable. A true mission-critical environment, such as air traffic control or a stock market, might combine NICs from two manufacturers just in case one driver or firmware fails. If that happens, the other NIC brand or model should continue to operate (if there wasn't a blue screen of death), and the services on that server would continue to be available.

A NIC team has at least one team interface, also known as a *team NIC* or *tNIC*. Each team interface appears in Network Connections. You will configure the protocol settings of the team interface rather than those of the team members. The team members become physical communication channels for the team interfaces.

FIGURE 4.12
Components of a
NIC team

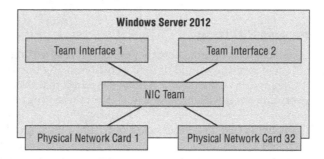

There are some important points regarding team interfaces:

The First Team Interface and Default Mode   The first team interface is in a mode known as Default mode: all traffic is passed through from the NIC team to the team interface. You can configure and then assign a VLAN ID to the original team interface, putting it in VLAN mode.

Additional Team Interfaces   You can have more than one team interface. Any additional team members that you create must be in VLAN mode (have an assigned VLAN ID). All traffic tagged for that VLAN will go to that team interface. This traffic will no longer travel to the original team interface that is in Default mode.

This is useful if you are doing nonvirtual NIC networking and want to support more than one VLAN connection on a single NIC team.

The Black Hole   If traffic for a VLAN cannot find a team interface with the associated VLAN ID or a team interface in Default mode, that traffic is sent to a black hole by the team.

External Virtual Switches and NIC Teaming   You can configure a Hyper-V external virtual switch to use the team interface of a NIC team as the connection to the physical network, as shown previously in Figure 4.11.

In this case, Microsoft will support this configuration only if there is just one team interface on the NIC team and it is used for just the external virtual switch. In other words, the NIC team will be dedicated to just this single external virtual switch. This team interface must be in Default mode, and not assigned a VLAN ID in this scenario. All VLAN filtering will be done at the virtual NIC or guest OS levels.

NIC teaming enables us to give our hosts and virtual machines higher levels of availability in case of an outage. We can use one or more NIC teams for the management OS and associated network connections (possibly using additional team interfaces), and we can use another NIC team to connect the external virtual switch to the physical network.

NIC TEAMING AND WI-FI NICS

You cannot team Wi-Fi NICs.

CONFIGURING NIC TEAMS

If you asked administrators how they configured the settings of their NIC teams in the past, most of them probably would (if they were honest) say that they just took the default options; the NIC team just worked. Some might even admit that they looked at the list of options, figured that everything was working anyway, and left the settings as is—it is best not to mess with these things.

The reality is that their success resulted from a lot of blind luck. It is only when you start to place a massive load (the kind that dense virtualization can create) or you purchase 10 GbE networking and want to see how much of it you can consume, that you soon realize that there must be more to NIC teaming, because the default options are not giving you the results that you were expecting. And there is more to it than accepting the defaults:

◆ What sort of switching environment do you have? That affects how the switch ports that are connected to the team members will know that this is a team.

◆ What kind of workload are you putting on the NIC team? This will determine how outbound traffic is distributed across the team and how inbound traffic is handled by the switches.

◆ How will your NIC team configuration impact the usage of advanced NIC hardware features?

The first choice you have to make is related to the kinds of switching in the physical network that the NIC team is connected to:

Switch-Independent Teaming   A NIC team configured for Switch-Independent Teaming is probably connected to multiple independent switches, but it can be used where there is just a single switch. The switches connected to this type of NIC team have no participation in the functionality of the team and require no manual or automated configuration.

Normally, all team members are active and share the burden if one of them fails. The Switch-Independent Teaming option has one odd feature that you can use: you can configure one of the team members to be a hot standby NIC that will be idle until a team member fails. The usefulness of this feature might be limited to troubleshooting; if you suspect a driver, NIC team configuration, or switch issue is being caused by the NIC team load balancing in a two-member NIC team, you could set one of the team members to be a hot standby (without breaking the team) to see whether that resolves the issue.

Switch-Dependent Teaming As the name suggests, with this kind of NIC team, there is a dependence on the switches having some kind of configuration. In Switch-Dependent Teaming, all of the switch ports that the NIC team is connected to must be a part of a single switch or logical switch—for example, a stacked switch made up of multiple appliances.

There are two ways to configure Switch-Dependent Teaming, depending on the physical switching environment.

The first is *Static Teaming*, also called *Generic Teaming* (see IEEE 802.3ad draft v1 for more information). This configuration requires the server administrator to configure the team, the network administrator to configure the switch ports, and for the cabling to be highly managed. Being static, it is not a very flexible solution in a dynamic cloud environment.

The second approach is Link Aggregation Control Protocol (LACP) or Dynamic Teaming (see IEEE 802.3ad-2000 for more information). LACP is a layer 2 control protocol that can be used to automatically detect, configure, and manage, as one logical link, multiple physical links between two adjacent LACP-enabled devices. An LACP-enabled NIC team will reach out to LACP-enabled switches to inform the devices of the NIC team's presence and team members. This allows for quicker and easier deployment and configuration with less human involvement, which is more cloud-friendly.

The second choice you have to make regarding the configuration of a NIC team is how to distribute the traffic across the team. There are two options:

Hyper-V Port This approach is usually, but not always, the option that you will select when creating a team for a virtual switch. Each virtual NIC that is transmitting through the NIC team is assigned (automatically by the NIC team) a team member (a physical NIC) for outbound and inbound communications. This means that if you have a team made up of 32 1-GbE team members, one virtual NIC will always be able to transmit at a maximum of only 1 GbE, depending on how much the bandwidth is being shared or throttled. At first this might seem like an illogical choice; more bandwidth is always better, right? Not always.

The reason that virtualization first was adopted was that applications were using only a small percentage of the resources that were available to them in legacy physical server installations. This included processor, memory, storage, and network bandwidth. Most workloads do not require huge amounts of bandwidth and will work just fine with a share of a single NIC. Hyper-V Port is suitable when dense hosts are deployed, with many more virtual NICs (such as those in virtual machines) than there are physical NICs (team members) in the NIC team.

Hyper-V Port is also required if we decide to turn on a feature called Dynamic Virtual Machine Queue (DVMQ) that improves network performance for virtual NICs. DVMQ is an offload that binds the MAC address of a virtual NIC to a queue on a specific physical NIC (team member). When the physical network sends traffic to a virtual NIC, it needs to know which team member to target. Hyper-V Port gives some level of dependency; the physical network knows which team member to target with traffic addressed for a specific virtual NIC so that DVMQ can optimize the flow of traffic. Without this binding, the physical network would hit random or all team members, and DVMQ would have been all but useless.

Note that when a team is configured for Hyper-V Port load distribution but is not used by a Hyper-V virtual switch, that team will always transmit on only a single team member.

Don't make the mistake of thinking that Hyper-V Port doesn't give you link aggregation. It does, but it's a bigger-picture thing, where the sum of your virtual NICs share the total bandwidth with team member failover. You just need to remember that each virtual NIC can use only one team member at a time for network transmissions.

Address Hashing The Address Hashing option hashes the addressing of outbound packets and uses the results to distribute the packets across the members of the NIC team. With this configuration, traffic from a single source can have access to the total bandwidth of the NIC team. How that traffic is distributed depends on how the hashing algorithm performs. There are three types of data that Address Hashing load distribution can automatically choose from:

◆ 4-tuple hash: This method hashes TCP/UDP ports and it is the most granular data offering the best results. It cannot be used for non-TCP or non-UDP traffic and it cannot be used for encrypted data, such as IPsec, that hides the TCP/UDP ports.

◆ 2-tuple hash: Address hashing will use the source and destination IP addresses from the packets.

◆ Source and destination MAC addresses: This is used if the traffic is not IP based.

There are four basic types of NIC teams based on the configuration of switch dependency and load distribution. Notes on each configuration are shown in Table 4.1.

TABLE 4.1:   NIC team configurations

	HYPER-V PORT	**ADDRESS HASHING**
Switch-Independent	Each virtual NIC sends and receives on the same team member.	Sends across all team members and receives on just one team member NIC.
	Best used when:	Best used when:
	• The number of virtual NICs greatly exceeds the number of team members.	• Switch diversity is important.
	• You want to use DVMQ.	• You need to have a standby team member.
	• You do not need any one virtual machine to exceed the bandwidth of a single team member.	• You have heavy outbound but light inbound services, such as web servers.
Switch-Dependent	Each virtual NIC sends on a single team member. Inbound traffic is subject to the (physical) switch's load distribution algorithm.	Outbound traffic is sent across all team members. Inbound traffic is sent across all team members, based on how the (physical) switch is configured.
	Best used when:	Best used when:
	• You want to use LACP.	• Switch diversity is important.
	• You do not need any one virtual machine to exceed the bandwidth of a single team member.	• You want maximum bandwidth availability for each connection.

You might be thinking that there is more to NIC teaming than you previously believed. Don't think that this is Microsoft just making NIC teaming complex. It's not that at all; go have a look at any NIC teaming software or manuals that you have been using before Windows Server 2012 and you'll soon see that these options are not all that unique. Most of us have never really had to deal with large-capacity networking before, so we've never really had an opportunity to see how a misconfigured team with the default options can underperform. Our advice is to take some time reading through the options, maybe reviewing it a few times, before moving forward. You might even want to take note of what page this guidance is on so you can quickly return to it in the future.

LEARN MORE ABOUT WINDOWS SERVER 2012 NIC TEAMING

Jose Barreto and Don Stanwyck of Microsoft presented on the subjects of NIC Teaming and Server Message Block (SMB — the file server protocol) Multichannel at the TechEd North America 2012 conference. You can find the video recording and the slides of this presentation (WSV314) at the following site:

```
http://channel9.msdn.com/Events/TechEd/NorthAmerica/2012/WSV314
```

CREATING NIC TEAMING IN VIRTUAL MACHINES

Are you wondering who in their right mind would want to create a NIC team in a virtual machine? In some scenarios, it is required—for example, when virtual NICs use Single-Root IO Virtualization (SR-IOV). When SR-IOV is enabled on a host, all connections to the physical NIC bypass much of the management OS, including NIC teaming. That means a virtual switch (and therefore all the connecting virtual machines) that is enabled for SR-IOV does not have network-path fault tolerance. We can solve that by providing two SR-IOV NICs in the host, each with its own virtual switch, and by putting two virtual NICs in each required virtual machine, and then by enabling NIC teaming in the virtual machine. You can see this scenario in Figure 4.13.

FIGURE 4.13
Enabling NIC teaming in a virtual machine for SR-IOV

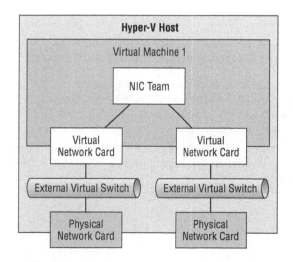

Windows Server 2012 NIC teaming is not available for legacy operating systems, so you will need to use Windows Server 2012 as the guest OS for this architecture.

The process for creating the team inside the virtual machine will be the same as it is for a physical server. However, you must configure each virtual NIC that will be a team member in the virtual machine to allow NIC teaming. There are two ways to do this, both of which are available to only the Hyper-V administrator or cloud management system.

In Hyper-V Manager, you can do the following:

1. Open the settings of the virtual machine.

2. Expand the first virtual NIC that will be a team member and browse to Advanced Features.

3. Select the check box labeled Enable This Network Adapter To Be Part Of A Team In The Guest Operating System.

4. Repeat this configuration change for each virtual NIC that will be a team member in the guest operating system.

Alternatively, you can use PowerShell. The first example configures all virtual NICs to allow NIC teaming:

```
Set-VMNetworkAdapter -VMName "Virtual Machine 1" -AllowTeaming On
```

If a virtual machine has many virtual NICs and you want to target this setting change, you could run this code snippet that uses an array to capture and configure the virtual NICs:

```
$VNICS = Get-VMNetworkAdapter -VMName "Virtual Machine 1"
Set-VMNetworkAdapter -VMNetworkAdapter $VNICS[0] -AllowTeaming On
Set-VMNetworkAdapter -VMNetworkAdapter $VNICS[1] -AllowTeaming On
```

Now these NICs are configured to support NIC teaming in the guest OS.

How will you configure switch dependency and load distribution in a guest OS NIC team? There is no choice to make; you will find that you can use only Switch-Independent teaming with Address Hashing inside a guest OS. A guest OS NIC team can be created with lots of virtual NICs, but Microsoft will support only the solution with two team members (virtual NICs in the team).

DON'T GO CRAZY WITH GUEST OS NIC TEAMING

You should not do something just because you can, and guest OS NIC teaming is a perfect example. Your usage of this solution should be very limited. For example, say you are enabling SR-IOV for some virtual machines, and their workloads need network-path fault tolerance—or you're a consultant with limited resources who needs to demonstrate the technology.

If your scenario doesn't require NIC teaming in the guest OS, continue with the simpler, and more cloud friendly design in which a virtual NIC connects to a virtual switch that is connected to a NIC team.

CREATING AND CONFIGURING NIC TEAMS

After you have determined your NIC team design, you can create one. You can do this by using the GUI or PowerShell. In the GUI, you can get to the NIC Teaming utility in one of two ways, opening the window shown in Figure 4.14:

◆ Launch LBFOADMIN.EXE.

◆ Open Server Manager, browse to Local Server, and click the hyperlink beside NIC Teaming (which will be set to either Disabled or Enabled, depending on whether there is a NIC team).

FIGURE 4.14
The NIC Teaming console

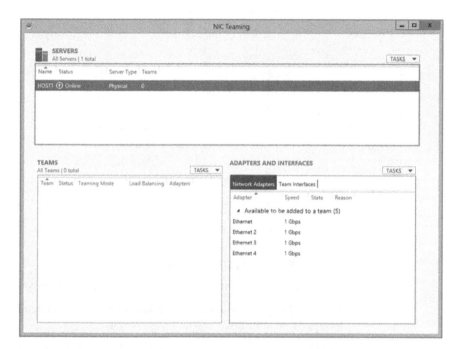

The Network Adapters view under Adapters And Interfaces shows the NICs that are installed in the machine as well as their speed and current team membership status. You can create a new team in two ways. The first is to select each NIC, expand Tasks under Adapters And Interfaces, and select Add To New Team. This opens the New Team window (Figure 4.15) with the NICs already preselected. The second method is to click Tasks under Teams and select New Team. This opens the New Team window with no NICs preselected. Now you will configure the team:

1. Select or modify the selection of NICs that will be team members.

2. Name the team. This will be the name of the first team interface and how the team interface will appear in Network Connections.

FIGURE 4.15
Creating a new
NIC team

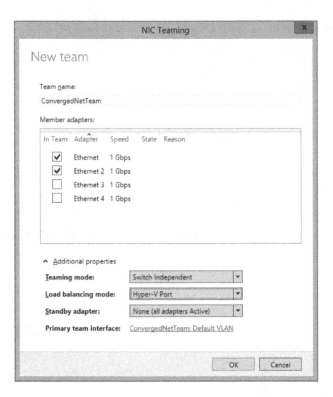

3. Expand Additional Properties to configure the NIC team.

   You configure the NIC team by using three drop-down list boxes:

   ◆ Teaming Mode: Choose from Static Teaming (Switch-Dependent), Switch-Independent, and LACP (Switch-Dependent).

   ◆ Load Balancing Mode: The options are Address Hash and Hyper-V Port.

   ◆ Standby Adapter: This is available only in Switch-Independent teaming mode. You select which team member will be the hot standby if another member fails.

   If you are creating a NIC team for a Hyper-V Switch, you are finished and can click OK. However, if your intention is to bind this team interface to a VLAN, continue to step 4.

4. You can click the hyperlink beside Primary Team Interface to open the New Team Interface window. Here you can choose to leave the Team Interface in Default mode (accepting packets tagged for all VLANs, except those tagged for other Team Interfaces on the NIC team). Or you can bind the new Team Interface to a VLAN by selecting Specific VLAN and entering the VLAN ID.

   Your new team will be created when you click OK. The team will appear under Teams. The NICs will be shown as team members in Network Adapters under Adapters And Interfaces. The new NIC team will also appear as a Microsoft Network Adapter Multiplexor Driver in Network Connections using the NIC team name as the connection name.

You can also create a team by using PowerShell. The following example creates it in LACP Switch-Dependent mode, with Hyper-V Port load distribution, using two selected NICs. If every NIC was to be in the team, you could replace the names of the NICs with the * wildcard.

```
New-NetLBFOTeam -Name "ConvergedNetTeam" -TeamMembers "Ethernet", "Ethernet `
2" -TeamingMode LACP -LoadBalancingAlgorithm HyperVPort -Confirm:$false
```

The -Confirm:$false flag and value instruct this cmdlet not to ask for confirmation. You can use this option with a cmdlet if there is no -Force flag. The -LoadBalancingAlgorithm flag requires some special attention. If not selected, it defaults to Address Hash. But if you want to specify a load-balancing algorithm, the cmdlet demands that you know precisely which kind of load distribution you require for your NIC team. It's not just a matter of Hyper-V Port vs. Address Hashing, as in the GUI. The cmdlet breaks down the Address Hashing options into its four possible hashing methods:

◆ HyperVPort: The Hyper-V Port load distribution method.

◆ IPAddresses: 2-tuple hash but requires IP.

◆ MacAddresses: The least efficient but does not depend on IP.

◆ TransportPorts: 4-tuple hash is the most efficient but requires visibility of destination TCP/UDP ports.

If you want to keep it simple and duplicate what is in the GUI, do one of the following:

◆ Do not use the flag if you want generic Address Hashing.

◆ Use the flag and specify HyperVPort.

If this is a NIC team for normal server communications (in other words, not for a Hyper-V virtual switch), you can configure the protocols and IP addressing of the team interface in Network Connections. Do not configure the protocol settings of the team members. The only selected protocol in the team members should be Microsoft Network Adapter Multiplexor Protocol.

You can always return to the NIC Teaming console to modify or delete teams, and you can do the same in PowerShell by using Set-NetLBFOTeam and Remove-NetLBFOTeam. The full list of LBFO PowerShell cmdlets and their documentation can be found at http://technet.microsoft.com/library/jj130849.aspx.

The status of the team members is shown in Adapters And Interfaces, and the health of the team is in Teams. You can also retrieve team status information by using Get-NetLBFOTeam.

If a team or team members are immediately unhealthy after the creation of the team, double-check both the NIC team and the switch configurations. For example, an LACP team will be immediately unhealthy if the switches are incompatible; the NIC team will have a fault and the team members will change their state to Faulted: LACP Negotiation. You can also find status information for NIC teaming in Event Viewer at Application And Services Logs ➢ Microsoft ➢ Windows ➢ MsLbfoProvider ➢ Operational. Strangely, important issues such as a NIC being disabled create Information-level entries instead of Warning or Critical ones.

After your team is ready, you should test it for the LBFO functionality:

◆ Put outbound and inbound loads through the NIC team to determine the maximum throughput.

◆ Test the failover by removing a cable and/or disabling a NIC one at a time.

CREATING AND CONFIGURING TEAM INTERFACES

If your NIC team is not going to be used to connect a Hyper-V virtual switch to the physical network, you can add more team interfaces to the team. Each additional team interface will be in VLAN mode, binding it to a specific VLAN. This will allow the server in question to connect to multiple VLANs or subnets without the expense or complexity of adding more physical connections.

You can use the NIC Teaming console to add a team interface:

1. Select the team you are adding the team interface to in Teams.

2. Browse to Team Interfaces in Adapters And Interfaces.

3. Select Tasks and click Add Interface. This opens the New Team Interface window.

4. Name the new interface. It is a good idea to include something descriptive such as the purpose or VLAN ID in the name.

5. You can have a maximum of only one team interface in Default mode. Specify the VLAN ID for this VLAN mode team interface in Specific VLAN.

A new team interface is created when you click OK, and the team interface name will appear in Network Connections. You can then configure the protocols of this new connection.

The PowerShell alternative for creating a team interface (or team NIC) is as follows:

```
Add-NetLBFOTeamNIC -Team "ConvergedNetTeam" -Name "ConvergedNetTeam - VLAN `
102" -VLANID 102 -Confirm:$false
```

If the original team interface is not going to be used to connect a Hyper-V virtual switch, you can switch it from Default mode to VLAN mode by editing it in the GUI, or by running PowerShell:

```
Set-NetLBFOTeamNIC -Team ConvergedNetTeam -Name "ConvergedNetTeam" -VLANID 101
```

You should be aware that changing the team interface to use a different VLAN will change its name from `ConvergedNetTeam` to `ConvergedNetTeam - VLAN 101`.

If you view the team interfaces in the NIC Teaming console or run `Get-NetLBFOTeamNIC`, you will see that one of the team interfaces is the primary team interface. This is the original team interface.

CONNECTING A HYPER-V SWITCH TO THE NIC TEAM

You can create a new virtual switch or change a virtual switch to use the NIC team. You can do this in Virtual Switch Manager by using these steps:

1. Get the device name (from Network Connections or `Get-NetAdapter | FL Name, InterfaceDescription`).

2. Create or edit an external virtual switch that will not be used for SR-IOV (remember that NIC teaming in the management OS and SR-IOV are incompatible).

3. Change the External Network to select the device that is the team interface for the NIC team.

It's a little easier in PowerShell because you can use the team interface name instead of the device name (`InterfaceDescription`). Here is how to modify an existing external virtual switch to use the team interface of a new NIC team:

```
Set-VMSwitch -Name External1 -NetAdapterName ConvergedNetTeam
```

Now you know how to create, and importantly, design NIC teams to suit your workloads. Don't go rushing off yet to create lots of NIC teams. First you're going to want to learn how to take advantage of some powerful hardware features in Windows Server 2012 Hyper-V, and then you'll get to read how you might need only one or two NIC teams in places where you might have used four or more in the past.

Networking Hardware Enhancements

Windows Server 2012 Hyper-V can do quite a lot with the most basic of networking hardware. But at some point, you will need to leverage hardware features to scale up hosts more, to accelerate performance, to reduce latency, and to conserve host resources for the applications in the virtual machines. Network hardware can offer several enhancements that provide this functionality. In this section, you are going to look at those features that can greatly improve how Hyper-V works.

Single-Root I/O Virtualization

Hyper-V has always used software to connect virtual machines to the physical network. Software can never be as efficient as hardware. SR-IOV is a hardware solution based on PCI-SIG I/O Virtualization (IOV) specifications that is designed to replace the role of software in virtual machine connectivity.

Introducing SR-IOV

Before we proceed, let's wander down memory lane to see how Hyper-V network traffic travels in to virtual machines from the physical network, and vice versa. Figure 4.16 shows how traffic passes between Hyper-V virtual machines and the physical network. It's quite the S-shaped journey that each packet takes, flipping between kernel mode and user mode and back again. It's actually not that bad; the vast majority of applications function very well with this architecture.

FIGURE 4.16
The normal flow of virtual machine network traffic

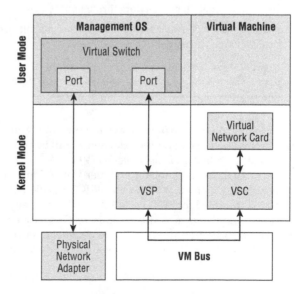

However, as good as they are, the software operations of copying data from one place to another eventually reach a scalability limit. The path of the traffic causes a slight latency. SR-IOV is a hardware feature that reduces the role of software in the networking link between virtual machines and the physical network. It can offer the following:

- Scalability for the future

- Reduced network latency for virtualized workloads

- Increased throughput

- Lower host resource utilization

- Increased levels of security

READ LOTS MORE ABOUT SR-IOV AND HYPER-V

John Howard, a Microsoft program manager who worked on SR-IOV in Windows Server 2012, wrote a series of eight blog posts about SR-IOV. Each post is very detailed, explaining why SR-IOV exists, how it works, and how to configure it in Windows Server 2012 Hyper-V. You can find the first of this series here:

    http://blogs.technet.com/b/jhoward/archive/2012/03/12/everything-you-wanted-to-
    know-about-sr-iov-in-hyper-v-part-1.aspx

In another blog post, Bob Combs from the Windows Networking team said that Microsoft had the following improvements in their testing:

- Up to 50 percent lower CPU utilization

- Up to 50 percent lower network latency

- Up to 30 percent higher network throughput

All of that leads to being able to run more virtual machines on a host and improved application performance. You can read that blog post here:

    http://blogs.technet.com/b/privatecloud/archive/2012/05/14/increased-network-
    performance-using-sr-iov-in-windows-server-2012.aspx

With SR-IOV, you move from what was shown in Figure 4.16 to what is shown in Figure 4.17. You can immediately see that network latency will be reduced and that we are relying on a new hardware feature called a *Virtual Function (VF)*.

When a virtual NIC is enabled for Hyper-V, it no longer connects to the virtual switch. It instead connects directly to a VF on the SR-IOV-enabled physical NIC. A VF is a lightweight PCIe function designed for SR-IOV. A NIC may have many VFs, as many as 256 depending on the hardware, and this means you could have 256 virtual NICs connecting directly to the physical NIC via their VFs. VFs are designed to channel data and have no configuration options. VFs are not unique to Hyper-V, and yes, they are a secure feature.

FIGURE 4.17
A logical view of
SR-IOV-enabled
networking

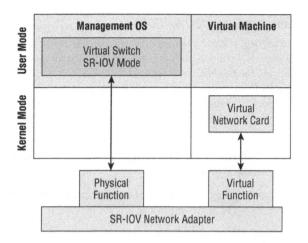

This raises an important question. A major reason that people adopted virtualization was flexibility. We have removed some of the abstraction that Hyper-V offers by connecting a virtual NIC to a VF in a physical NIC. Will this affect Live Migration? The answer is that it won't. Microsoft has a policy that no new features can be added to Hyper-V if they prevent Live Migration, and SR-IOV with all its hardware integration is no exception.

If you open Device Manager in the guest OS of an SR-IOV-enabled virtual machine, you will see something very interesting. Each virtual NIC will have two devices:

◆ The driver for the VF

◆ The standard Microsoft Hyper-V network adapter from the Hyper-V Integration Components

When you perform Live Migration on an SR-IOV-enabled virtual machine, it will switch the virtual NIC(s) from the VF device to the Microsoft Hyper-V network adapter without changing IP addresses or dropping packets. This returns the virtual machine to the hardware abstraction that Live Migration requires. When Live Migration is complete, the virtual NIC(s) will switch back to a VF device if an available one is found on the host.

There are several points to note about SR-IOV:

◆ The server motherboard, the BIOS, and the NIC must all support SR-IOV. The processor must also support Second Level Address Translation (SLAT — this is almost guaranteed on supporting hardware), which is known as Intel EPT or AMD NPT/RVI (see Chapter 1, "Introducing Windows Server 2012 Hyper-V").

◆ A new driver model was required for SR-IOV, so the NIC vendor must supply a suitable driver.

◆ SR-IOV bypasses the networking stack in the management OS, so you cannot do teaming of the SR-IOV-enabled physical NICs. See the previous information on how to perform NIC teaming in the guest OS.

◆ Do not enable any policies, such as QoS, on the SR-IOV virtual switch.

◆ As was stated earlier when we covered the creation of virtual switches, you can enable SR-IOV only when making a new external virtual switch; it cannot be turned on afterward.

ENABLING AND CONFIGURING SR-IOV

As with all of the hardware enhancements discussed in this chapter, the first place you should always start is with the documentation of the hardware vendor to see if they have any specific instructions for the NIC settings or for the BIOS.

You will then create an external virtual switch that is connected to the physical NIC that will provide the VFs. Select the Enable Single-Root I/O Virtualization (SR-IOV) check box when creating the virtual switch. If you forget to do this, you will need to remove and re-create the virtual switch. The PowerShell for creating the virtual switch with SR-IOV enabled is as follows:

```
New-VMSwitch -Name "ExternalSRIOV1" -EnableIOV $True -NetAdapterName "Ethernet `
3" -AllowManagementOS 0
```

Remember to create two virtual switches, each connected to an SR-IOV-enabled NIC, if you want to enable NIC teaming in the guest OS of your SR-IOV-enabled virtual machines:

```
New-VMSwitch -Name "ExternalSRIOV2" -EnableIOV $True -NetAdapterName "Ethernet `
4" -AllowManagementOS 0
```

Running `Get-VMSwitch | FL *IOV*` will return the SR-IOV configuration for your physical NICs. The results will include the following:

- `IovEnabled`: Is SR-IOV enabled on this NIC?

- `IovVirtualFunctionCount`: The number of VFs on this physical NIC.

- `IovVirtualFunctionsInUse`: The number of VFs being used.

- `IovQueuePairCount`: There is generally one queue pair required per VF. However, some hardware vendors might support RSS with the VF, and this might increase the consumption of queue pairs. This counter shows the total count of queue pairs on the NIC.

- `IovQueuePairsInUse`: The number of queue pairs that are in use.

- `IovSupport`: A true or false value indicating whether your hardware supports SR-IOV.

- `IovSupportReasons`: Is there an issue with SR-IOV? A status of {OK} is desired.

You can have up to eight SR-IOV-enabled virtual NICs in a virtual machine. You can enable SR-IOV in the virtual NICs in the GUI by following these steps:

1. Open the virtual machine's settings, browse to the virtual NIC, expand it, and select Hardware Acceleration.

2. Select the check box labeled Enable SR-IOV.

3. Repeat for each required virtual NIC in the virtual machine.

Enable SR-IOV is actually a setting called `IOVWeight`. The name implies that you can use a weight-based model to allocate bandwidth on the SR-IOV-enabled NIC. Not so fast! `IOVWeight` has a very simple function in Windows Server 2012: when it is 0, the virtual NIC is SR-IOV disabled; and when it has a value of 1 to 100, SR-IOV is enabled. You can enable all virtual NICs in a virtual machine for SR-IOV by using the following PowerShell example:

```
Get-VM "Virtual Machine 1" | Set-VMNetworkAdapter -IovWeight 1
```

TROUBLESHOOTING SR-IOV

You have already seen `IovSupportReasons` in action. You can also get at this value by running `(Get-VMHost).IOVSupportReasons`. `Get-NetAdapterSRIOV` will return information on any supported SR-IOV physical NICs, and `Get-NetAdapterSRIOVVF` will return the settings of available virtual functions.

If you are still having problems with SR-IOV even after double-checking all the settings, you need to look at the hardware. Check the documentation from the NIC and server hardware vendors to make sure that there are no additional settings; the BIOS might need configurations in several places. You should also check that you have the latest firmware installed. Finally, you might need to open a support call with your hardware vendor.

Receive-Side Scaling

Receive-Side Scaling (RSS) plays an important role in Microsoft's Windows Server 2012 strategy, enabling something called SMB Multichannel on high-capacity NICs. (You will read about this in Chapter 7.)

INTRODUCING RSS

When packets arrive in a NIC to be processed, the NIC has always relied on a single core in the processor. As servers and their workloads have grown, this single-core solution has become a bottleneck. The introduction of 10 GbE networking followed by RDMA over Converged Ethernet (RoCE)—at up to 40 Gbps for Ethernet and 56 Gbps for InfiniBand—compounds this problem. A single core can never offer enough processing capacity to process packets as they arrive.

RSS is a feature in the network card (using queues) and driver that allows a supporting operating system, such as Windows Server 2012, to dynamically scale up/down the processing of incoming traffic for nonvirtualized workloads across multiple cores. That fact that RSS is for nonvirtualized workloads might make it sound less important, but this is far from the case. RSS enables SMB Multichannel on high-capacity NICs, enabling file services to fully utilize bandwidth for application workloads. This is important for Hyper-V because it provides us with the following:

♦ Faster Cluster Shared Volume (CSV) redirected I/O for metadata operations and storage-path fault tolerance (see Chapter 8)

♦ Support for storing Windows Server 2012 Hyper-V virtual machines on Windows Server 2012 file servers thanks to much faster file services that can match and even beat the speeds of traditional storage mechanisms

Using RSS requires RSS-enabled NICs, and you will see the best results on 10 GbE or faster networking.

PLANNING RSS

Unfortunately, you cannot just turn on a switch to enable RSS. It requires a bit more effort, especially if you have used NIC teaming. Before you start, you should get prepared by following these steps:

1. Check that your NIC(s) supports RSS. Open the properties of the NIC, click Configure, go to the Advanced tab, and browse the various properties, looking for RSS settings. Alternatively, you can run `Get-NetAdapterAdvancedProperty -Name [Networkname]`.

2. Check with your hardware manufacturer for specific guidance on RSS.

3. While you're there, download the latest version of the driver for your NIC(s) from the manufacturer (don't rely on the driver from the Windows installation media) and install it.

4. Document the configuration of any NIC teams that will have RSS enabled.

5. Get the processor details of the host.

6. If you are planning to implement DVMQ, you need to plan it at the same time, because they should not overlap on the processor(s).

The first thing you have to do is to decide how RSS will use cores on the processor. Let's say we have a host with 2×6 core processors, with Hyper-Threading enabled. That gives us 24 logical processors, numbered 0 to 23. RSS (and its sibling DVMQ) works on a per core basis, but we have to identify those cores on a per logical processor basis if Hyper-Threading is enabled. Those processor cores will be numbered 0 (for the first core), 2, 4 … and on until we reach 23.

There are two processor settings that we need to specify when enabling RSS (or DVMQ) for an individual NIC:

◆ `*RssBaseProcNumber` is the first core that RSS on the NIC will use.

◆ `*MaxRssProcessors` configures the maximum number of cores that NIC will use for RSS.

Core 0 (the first core) is the default core for all non-RSS processing, so it should not be configured as the `*RSSBaseProcNumber`. You should always start with core 2 (the second core, because the first core is composed of logical cores 0 and 1) in this example.

With Hyper-Threading turned off or not available, you would have 12 logical processors in our example, and the `*RSSBaseProcNumber` would be set to 1 (the second core).

The next decision is to configure `*MaxRSSProcessors` to indicate the highest number of cores each NIC can use for processing incoming traffic. There are variables to consider when sizing `*MaxRSSProcessors`:

Will Y Be Using DVMQ on Another NIC?   DVMQ and RSS should not share processor cores because it can lead to unexpected results:

◆ No DVMQ: We will allow the RSS-enabled NIC to access all the cores except core 0. There are 12 cores, so `*MaxRSSProcessors` will be set to 11. There will be 11 RSS queues.

◆ DVMQ: We cannot dedicate all the cores to this NIC's RSS. In this case, we will allocate five cores to RSS (`*MaxRSSProcessors` = 5) while reserving the remaining six cores to DVMQ. There will be five RSS queues.

Will There Be More Than One RSS NIC?   This is similar to the scenario with DVMQ. If another independent NIC will also have RSS enabled, you should ensure that both NICs do not share cores. Use a similar method as with the DVMQ scenario.

Will You Be Enabling RSS on a NIC Team?   This scenario requires a lot of planning because of the many ways that a NIC team can function.

RSS uses queues on the NIC. Each incoming stream of traffic is assigned a queue. The way that RSS will use those queues depends on whether your NIC team is configured in Sum-of-Queues mode or in Min-Queues mode—in other words, on how the NIC team should spread the processing workload for the NICs in the team across the cores in the processor(s).

A NIC team that is in Switch-Independent mode with Hyper-V Port load distribution is in Sum-of-Queues mode. This is because each NIC is used for inbound traffic, and it is done in a fashion that is predictable by the NIC team. All other NIC teams are in Min-Queues mode.

If you have a Min-Queues NIC team (which is more likely for RSS because the team will probably use Address Hashing), you should configure each team member to use the same cores. For example, you have a NIC team with two team members in a host with 24 logical processors and Hyper-Threading (12 cores). You want to reserve half of the cores for DVMQ:

◆ Set *RssBaseProcNumber to 2, leaving the default core for non-RSS processing.

◆ Configure *MaxRssProcessors to be 5 for each team member, leaving the remaining six cores to DVMQ. There will be five RSS queues per RSS NIC, and yes, they will share cores.

If you create two teams, both with RSS enabled, then the NICs of team A should not share cores with the NICs of team B.

In the case of a Sum-of-Queues team, you cannot share queues. Each RSS-enabled NIC will require a configuration that specifies a different *RssBaseProcNumber. We are reserving one processor (six cores) for DVMQ in this example. Remember that core 0 is already taken for non-RSS traffic, so we have five cores to play with in the team, with two team members. Therefore, each team member will get two cores, leaving one spare that can be given to DVMQ.

◆ Set *RssBaseProcNumber to 2 on the first NIC, and set *MaxRssProcessors to 2.

◆ Set *RssBaseProcNumber to 6 on the second NIC, and set *MaxRssProcessors to 2.

You'll be glad to hear that we're finished with the mathematics and are going to return to the practical side of things.

ENABLING AND CONFIGURING RSS

To start, you should ensure that the advanced settings of your physical NICs are configured:

◆ Set RSS to enabled.

◆ Configure the maximum number of queues that are required for the NIC.

Then you will edit the Registry to configure RSS for each NIC. You can do this by using PowerShell. The following example sets *RssBaseProcNumber to 2 and *MaxRssProcessors to 5 for a NIC called Ethernet 1.

```
Set-NetAdapterVmq "Ethernet 1" -BaseProcessorNumber 2 -MaxProcessors 5
```

Repeat that cmdlet for each required NIC with the required settings and you will have configured RSS, with no reboots required.

Let's assume you need to configure the two NICs in the Min-Queues example:

```
Set-NetAdatperVmq "Ethernet" -BaseProcessorNumber 2 -MaxProcessors 5
Set-NetAdatperVmq "Ethernet 2" -BaseProcessorNumber 2 -MaxProcessors 5
```

If you want to configure the two NICs in the Sum-of-Queues example, you will run this piece of PowerShell:

```
Set-NetAdatperVmq "Ethernet" –BaseProcessorNumber 2 –MaxProcessors 5
Set-NetAdatperVmq "Ethernet 2" –BaseProcessorNumber 2 –MaxProcessors 5
```

Each NIC that you configured will need to be started, which you can do in Network Connections (disable and enable) or via PowerShell (Disable-NetAdapter and then Enable-NetAdapter).

Dynamic Virtual Machine Queuing

DVMQ does for virtualization traffic passing through a virtual switch what RSS does for networking traffic for nonvirtualization workloads. Virtual NIC traffic is processed by more than one core, enabling much greater performance and scalability.

PLANNING FOR DVMQ

DVMQ uses the same queues on the NIC. Those queues can be either dedicated to RSS or dedicated to DVMQ, but not both. Therefore, a NIC or a NIC team is configured for either RSS or DVMQ.

All of the requirements settings, calculations, and configurations for DVMQ are the same as they are for RSS. We can return to the Min-Queues example that had a host with 24 logical processors and Hyper-Threading (12 cores). The last 6 cores were reserved for DVMQ. A NIC team in Min-Queues mode will be set up with DVMQ. The settings for DVMQ will be as follows:

◆ Set *RssBaseProcNumber to 12, because this is the first core left after RSS consumed the first 6 cores.

◆ Configure *MaxRssProcessors to be 5 for each team member, consuming the remaining cores that are available to RSS.

If we return to the Sum-of-Queues RSS example, we will add a Sum-of-Queues NIC team and enable DVMQ. In the RSS Sum-of-Queues example, we kept the second processor for DVMQ. The first core is 12. There are two NICs, so we will assign 3 cores to each NIC.

◆ Set *RssBaseProcNumber to 12 on the first NIC, and set *MaxRssProcessors to 3.

◆ Set *RssBaseProcNumber to 18 on the second NIC, and configure *MaxRssProcessors to 3.

IMPLEMENTING DVMQ

The implementation instructions for DVMQ are identical to those for RSS, even if the settings in the NIC are labeled as RSS. If you wanted to configure the Sum-of-Queues Registry settings, you could run this PowerShell example:

```
Set-NetAdatperVmq "Ethernet 3" –BaseProcessorNumber 12 –MaxProcessors 3
Set-NetAdatperVmq "Ethernet 4" –BaseProcessorNumber 18 –MaxProcessors 3
```

A virtual NIC must be enabled for DVMQ to take advantage of these settings. This setting, found in the virtual machine settings at Network Adapter ➤ Hardware Acceleration and called Enable Virtual Machine Queue, is on by default. You can clear this box to disable DVMQ for this virtual NIC, or you can run this PowerShell cmdlet:

```
Set-VMNetworkAdapter -VMName I* -VMQWeight 0
```

You can undo this change and re-enable DVMQ for the virtual NIC by setting VMQWeight to a nonzero value of 1 to 100.

You should take an IQ test if you understood the RSS and DVMQ planning process on your first or even second reading. They are some of the most difficult-to-understand configurations that we can implement in Hyper-V. A real-world example at the end of the chapter should help you design a workable solution.

IPsec Task Offload

IPsec is a mechanism that allows you to define a policy to get the operating system to automatically encrypt outbound and decrypt inbound traffic, giving network security to sensitive applications. You can learn more about IPsec at http://technet.microsoft.com/network/bb531150.aspx).

The process of encrypting and decrypting IPsec will impact the processor. The generated load might be sustainable for a single operating system environment, but what will happen to a host's processor if dozens or even hundreds of virtual machines all want to implement IPsec?

IPsec Task Offload is enabled by default in the settings of a virtual NIC. This feature will offload the processing of IPsec to dedicated hardware (if available), thus relieving the host's processor of this load. Check with your hardware manufacturer for support for and capabilities of IPsec Task Offload.

The settings for IPsec Task Offload can be found in the virtual machine settings at Network Adapter ➤ Hardware Acceleration. There are two settings:

◆ Enable IPsec Task Offloading is selected by default.

◆ Maximum Number indicates the maximum number of offloaded security associations, expressed as a number from 1 to 4,096.

If your NIC supports IPsec Task Offload, it will support a limited number of offloaded security associations. To learn more, check with your hardware manufacturer.

You can disable IPsec Task Offload in the virtual machine's virtual NIC settings, or you can use PowerShell to set the -IPsecOffloadMaximumSecurityAssociation to zero:

```
Set-VMNetworkAdapter -VMName "Virtual Machine 2" `
-IPsecOffloadMaximumSecurityAssociation 0
```

You can re-enable the functionality as follows:

```
Set-VMNetworkAdapter -VMName "Virtual Machine 2" `
-IPsecOffloadMaximumSecurityAssociation 512
```

Advanced Networking

Windows Server 2012 is changing how we design networking for servers, and particularly, for Hyper-V. In this section, you are going to look at converged fabrics. You will also look at QoS, which makes converged fabrics possible.

Quality of Service

Although it doesn't create many headlines, QoS is an important feature of Windows Server 2012. Without it, many of the new possibilities that enable flexibility, cost savings, and easier deployment of Hyper-V would just not be possible.

REMEMBERING A WORLD WITHOUT QoS

Why did a clustered Windows Server 2008 R2 Hyper-V host require so many physical NICs? Let's count them, leaving iSCSI aside for a moment:

1. Virtual machines: There would be at least one virtual network (the technology preceding the virtual switch), and each virtual network required one connection to the LAN.

2. Management OS: Although the management OS could share a virtual network's physical NIC, we were always concerned about management traffic affecting virtual workloads, or vice versa.

3. Cluster: A private network between the nodes in the cluster provided a path for the heartbeat, and we usually configure redirected I/O to pass over this network.

4. Live migration: A second private network provided us with bandwidth to move virtual machines within the cluster with zero loss in availability for their workloads.

That is four NICs so far; keep counting. NIC teaming wasn't universal with Windows Server 2008 R2, but if you implemented it, you'd now have eight NICs (two for every function, to make four NIC teams). Many larger deployments would put in an additional backup network or isolate the impact of the backup traffic from the management OS and the services running on the virtual machines. With NIC teaming, you're now adding two more NICs, and you have 10 NICs at this point. And now we can think about iSCSI with its two NICs (using MPIO for iSCSI NICs because NIC teaming is not supported with iSCSI), and you require 12 NICs per host. And we haven't even considered the need to support multiple virtual networks.

THE LIVE MIGRATION NETWORK

The Live Migration network also provided a second path for the cluster heartbeat in case the cluster network had a problem.

Most people deployed 1 GbE NICs. The time it took to put a host into maintenance mode was dependent on how quickly the memory of the virtual machines on that host could be synchronized with other hosts. Imagine an engineer visiting a customer site and being told that it was going to take a weekend to put the 1 TB RAM host into maintenance mode so they could shut it down! This is why the Live Migration NIC became the first network to run at 10 Gbps.

Even with every possible tweak, Windows Server 2008 R2 could never fill a 10 GbE NIC. However, Windows Server 2012 is able to fully utilize these high-bandwidth pipes.

Thanks to the ability to run an unlimited number (depending on your hosts and networking) of simultaneous Live Migrations in Windows Server 2012, you can probably take advantage of even more bandwidth for those 4 TB RAM hosts that you are planning to deploy!

An incredible amount of cabling, documentation, careful implementation (many mistakes were basic networking/cabling errors), and switch ports required yet more spending on hardware, support, and electricity. Did the host hardware even have enough slots for all these quad-port NIC cards? Consider blade servers; they take only so many network expansion cards, and this usually meant buying another pair (or more) of those incredibly expensive blade chassis switches or Virtual Connect type of devices.

Why did we need so many NICs? Couldn't we run these services on fewer NICs? Couldn't larger organizations deploy 10 GbE networking and run everything through just a NIC team?

---

10 GbE HARDWARE FABRICS

Some hardware vendors have been selling 10 GbE fabric solutions that can slice up bandwidth at the hardware layer for years. These solutions are very expensive, have static QoS settings, are inflexible, and lock a customer into a single hardware vendor.

Without expensive hardware solutions, the answer was no; we needed to physically isolate each of these functions in the host. Live Migration needed bandwidth. Services running in virtual machines needed to be available to users, no matter what administrators did to move workloads. Monitoring agents couldn't fail to ping the hosts, or alarms would be set off. Cluster heartbeat needs to be dependable, or we end up with unwanted failover. We physically isolated these functions in the host to guarantee quality of service.

INTRODUCING QOS

QoS has been in Windows Server for some time, offering basic functionality. But we never had a function that could guarantee a minimum level of service to a virtual NIC or a protocol (or an IP port). That is exactly what we are getting with QoS in Windows Server 2012. At its most basic level, we can configure the following rules in QoS:

Bits per Second–Based or Weight-Based   You will choose between implementing QoS by using bps-based or weight-based rules.

The bps-based rules can be quite specific, guaranteeing a very certain amount of bandwidth, which can be useful for some applications. For example, a host company (a public cloud) will usually create rules based on bandwidth that are easy to communicate to customers. However, bps rules can be considered inflexible, especially if workloads are mobile between hosts. Imagine guaranteeing more bandwidth than is possible if two highly guaranteed virtual machines are placed together in a large cloud, where such specific placement rules become unwieldy. Or what if virtual machines have to be moved to a host that cannot offer enough bandwidth?

You get more flexibility with weight-based rules. A weight-based rule is based on a share of bandwidth, with no consideration of the actual speed. For example, a virtual NIC in a virtual machine is guaranteed 50 percent of total bandwidth. On a 10 GbE NIC, that virtual machine is guaranteed 5 Gbps. That virtual machine can move to a different host that has a 1 GbE network. Now the virtual machine is guaranteed 512 Mbps.

While weight-based rules are extremely flexible and are usually going to be the correct choice, bps-based rules do have their uses because of the certainty that they can guarantee.

Minimum Bandwidth   An engineer can guarantee a minimum share of the host's bandwidth to a virtual NIC or a protocol. For example, if you guaranteed 25 percent of bandwidth to the SMB protocol, SMB would always be able to get 25 percent of the total bandwidth. If there was available bandwidth, SMB could consume it if required. However, if SMB is not using the full 25 percent, the idle bandwidth becomes available to other protocols until SMB requires it.

Minimum-bandwidth rules are all about guaranteeing an SLA for a service or function. Because they guarantee a share, they are flexible rules and are the recommended approach to designing QoS. Because flexibility is what we want, you will typically use (but not always) the weight-based approach to creating minimum-bandwidth rules.

Maximum Bandwidth   You can limit the bandwidth consumption of a virtual NIC or protocol with this type of rule. Configuring a virtual machine to not exceed a certain amount of bandwidth can be useful in some circumstances. A hosting company (or public cloud) might limit customers' bandwidth based on how much they are willing to pay. In that scenario, you should note that QoS rules won't understand concepts such as the entity called a customer; QoS rules apply to individual virtual NICs or protocols. Another scenario in which a maximum-bandwidth rule is useful is when some application in a virtual machine goes crazy and wants to consume every bit of bandwidth that it can find. An administrator could temporarily apply a maximum-bandwidth rule to the necessary virtual NIC(s) to limit the problem without disconnecting the virtual machine, fix the problem, and remove the rule.

Maximum-bandwidth rules are all about limiting, and that limits flexibility. There is no concept of guaranteeing a service. There is no burst feature of the minimum rule, whereby a protocol can consume bandwidth if there is no impact on other protocols. And cloud purists might argue that it removes one of the key attributes of a cloud: elasticity.

The focus of Microsoft's effort in Windows Server 2012 was minimum bandwidth. Most of the time, you will implement minimum-bandwidth QoS rules that are based on weight. This is the most flexible solution, because it makes no assumptions about hardware capacity, and it has an elastic nature, whereby virtual NICs or protocols can burst beyond the minimum guarantee.

UNDERSTANDING THE THREE WAYS TO APPLY QoS

There are three ways to apply QoS in Windows Server 2012. How we do it depends on how we design our Hyper-V hosts, and what kind of traffic we want to apply the rules to. Figure 4.18 illustrates how you will decide to apply QoS.

These are the three approaches to applying QoS:

Hyper-V Virtual Switch   If the traffic in question is passing through a virtual switch, you can create QoS rules that are based on virtual NICs rather than on protocols. With this type of rule, you are creating minimum or maximum rules for connections.

Server Networking   This category includes any networking that does not include a virtual NIC and a Hyper-V virtual switch, such as a physical NIC that is used by the management OS, or the NICs used by a file server. The rules are based on protocols rather than on virtual NICs, which can give you great granularity of control. There are two ways to apply QoS when you have physical networking.

FIGURE 4.18
Deciding on a QoS
strategy

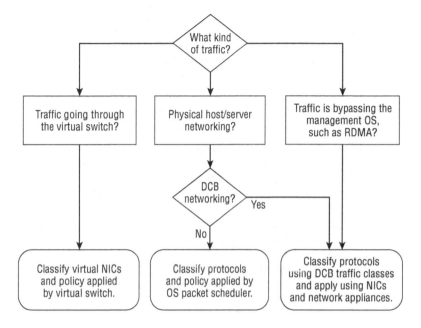

If you have NICs and physical networking (switches and adapters) that support Data Center Bridging (DCB), you can create rules for protocols or IP ports that will be applied by the hardware.

If you do not have end-to-end DCB-capable networking, you can create rules for protocols or IP ports that will be applied by the OS packet scheduler.

DATA CENTER BRIDGING

Data Center Bridging, or DCB (IEEE 802.1), is an extension to Ethernet that allows the classification and prioritization of traffic for lossless transmission. DCB allows you to classify protocols and prioritize them. The QoS rules are applied at the hardware level, therefore not increasing the load on the OS packet scheduler.

You must have end-to-end support, including NICs and networking appliances, to use DCB.

Here's an interesting twist: you can create QoS rules that are based on protocol or IP ports in the guest OS of a Windows Server 2012 virtual machine. QoS will be applied by the OS packet scheduler within the virtual machine, effectively carving up whatever bandwidth the virtual machine's virtual NICs have access to.

Networking That Bypasses the Operating System   Chapter 7 will teach you about something called Remote Direct Memory Access (RDMA). RDMA enables Server Message Block (SMB) Multichannel (powered by RSS) to use 100 percent of bandwidth in very high bandwidth networks without fully utilizing the processor of the server in question. This feature, called SMB Direct, does this by offloading the SMB transfer so that it effectively becomes invisible to the operating system. The throughput of SMB Direct with SMB Multichannel is able to match or exceed that of traditional storage connections. This has made it possible for Microsoft to support storing Windows Server 2012 virtual machines on Windows Server 2012 file shares instead of SAS/iSCSI/Fibre Channel SANs without any drop in performance. In fact, some file server designs will offer performance vs. price that cannot be matched by traditional storage. You should not skip Chapter 7!

High-end Hyper-V deployments that take advantage of SMB 3.0 will use RDMA. We cannot use the OS packet scheduler to apply QoS policies because the traffic is invisible to the management OS. For this reason, we must use DCB to apply QoS rules.

RDMA over Converged Ethernet (RoCE) is a type of high-capacity networking that supports SMB Direct. It is recommended that, if the NIC(s) support it, Priority-based Flow Control (or PFC, IEEE 802.1Qbb) should be enabled for the SMB Direct (RDMA) protocol to ensure that there is no data loss for Hyper-V host storage traffic.

QOS IS NOT JUST FOR HYPER-V

As you can see, only one of the three ways to classify traffic and apply QoS rules is specific to Hyper-V. QoS is useful for Hyper-V host design, but it can also be used outside the cloud in traditional physical servers.

Now you understand how to decide which type of QoS approach to use based on your network requirements. We can summarize as follows:

◆ If the traffic comes from a virtual NIC, create rules for virtual NICs.

◆ You should create rules for protocols or IP ports when the traffic is not coming from a virtual NIC. We'd prefer to do it with DCB, but we can use the OS packet scheduler. That last approach works inside virtual machines too.

◆ Any protocol that the management OS cannot see must use DCB for applying QoS rules.

IMPLEMENTING QOS

This section shows you how to implement each of the three approaches to QoS. There is no way to implement this functionality in the GUI in Windows Server 2012. Every step of the process will be done using PowerShell.

Applying QoS to Virtual NICs

When traffic is passing through a virtual switch, and therefore from a virtual NIC, we create QoS rules that are based on virtual NICs. This is the simplest of the three ways to configure QoS: you have a virtual NIC, and you give it a share of bandwidth.

The first thing we must deal with is the virtual switch, where the QoS rules will be applied. When you create a virtual switch by using PowerShell, you have the option to specify a bandwidth reservation mode (QoS rules guaranteeing a minimum amount of bandwidth) of either weight-based (a share of bandwidth) or absolute (bits per second). The virtual switch has to be one or the other. This does not affect your ability to specify maximum-bandwidth rules of either type. You also must do this at the time you create the virtual switch. If you do not specify an option, the virtual switch will be set to Absolute. The following snippet of PowerShell queries the bandwidth reservation mode of a virtual switch:

```
PS C:\> (Get-VMSwitch "External1").BandwidthReservationMode
Absolute
```

The following example creates a new external virtual switch called `ConvergedNetSwitch` that is linked to a NIC team called `ConvergedNetTeam`. The bandwidth reservation mode is set to weight-based:

```
New-VMSwitch "ConvergedNetSwitch" -MinimumBandwidthMode weight `
-NetAdapterName "ConvergedNetTeam" -AllowManagementOS 0
```

You should perform this configuration on each host that you want to use virtual NIC QoS rules for. For example, maybe a virtual machine was to be assigned an SLA guaranteeing at least 10 percent of bandwidth. In this case, you need to be sure that the weight-based bandwidth reservation mode was configured on the appropriate virtual switch on each host that the virtual machine could be placed on.

We now can create QoS rules for each required virtual NIC. This is a simple operation. The following rule guarantees a virtual machine 10 percent of bandwidth of any virtual switch it is connected to:

```
Set-VMNetworkAdapter -VMName "Virtual Machine 1" -MinimumBandwidthWeight 10
```

You can even specify one particular virtual NIC in a virtual machine. The next example retrieves the first virtual NIC of `Virtual Machine 2`. It then sets an SLA indicating that the virtual NIC will get 20 percent of bandwidth if required, but it will be capped at 1 Gbps. You can see in this example that we are not prevented from using absolute-bps rules to limit bandwidth, even if the switch is set to a weight-based bandwidth reservation mode:

```
Set-VMNetworkAdapter {Get-VMNetworkAdapter -VMName "Virtual `
Machine 2"}[0] -MinimumBandwidthWeight 20 -MaximumBandwidth 1073741824
```

You will see more of this type of rule when you look at the topic of converged fabrics later in the chapter. Here are some important notes on this way of using QoS:

♦ If you assign a virtual NIC a weight of 3 and another virtual NIC a weight of 1, then you have split the bandwidth to 75 percent and 25 percent.

♦ Never assign a total weight of more than 100.

♦ Be conservative when assigning weights to critical workloads such as cluster communications. Although a weight of 1 might be OK on a 10 GbE NIC for cluster communications, Microsoft is recommending that you use a weight of at least 5; the cluster heartbeat is critical in a Hyper-V cluster.

♦ If you are going to assign QoS rules to virtual machines, consider creating classes such as Gold, Silver, and Bronze, with each class having a defined weight. This will make operating and documenting the environment much easier.

♦ At the time of writing this book (just after the release of Windows Server 2012), running `Get -VMNetworkAdapter -VMName *| FL Ba*` will not show you the results of your QoS policies.

Applying QoS to Protocols with the OS Packet Scheduler

We will classify protocols and use the OS packet scheduler to apply QoS for traffic that does not go through a virtual switch in the operating system. This type of rule applies in two scenarios:

◆ Traffic for physical NICs in which we do not have end-to-end support for DCB.

◆ We want to apply QoS inside the guest operating system of a virtual machine, assuming that it is running Windows Server 2012.

The PowerShell cmdlet we will use is `New-NetQosPolicy`. `New-NetQosPolicy` is a very flexible cmdlet, allowing us to create QoS rules. The cmdlet supports built-in protocol classifications or filters shown in Table 4.2.

TABLE 4.2:   Built-in protocol filters for QoS

LABEL	PROTOCOL	MATCHING CRITERIA
`-LiveMigration`	Live Migration	TCP 6600
`-iSCSI`	iSCSI	TCP/UDP 3260
`-SMB`	SMB or file services	TCP/UDP 445
`-NetDirect <Port Number>`	SMB Direct (RDMA)	Match the identified RDMA port
`-NFS`	NFS	TCP/UDP 2049

The cmdlet will allow you to create rules based on source and destination IP details including the following:

◆ Ports or port ranges

◆ Network address

◆ Protocol, such as TCP or UDP

You can even specify the Windows network profile (Domain, Private, or Public), or the priority of QoS rules if there are multiple matches. We could write an entire chapter on this cmdlet alone, so here are a few useful examples:

This first example uses the built-in filter to create a QoS rule to guarantee 30 percent of bandwidth to SMB. The rule is given a priority of 3.

```
New-NetQosPolicy "SMB" –SMB –MinBandwidthWeight 30 –Priority 3
```

Note that –MinBandwidthWeight is short for –MinBandwidthWeightAction, and -Priority is short for -PriorityValue8021Action. You do not need to type in the full names of the flags.

An important protocol to protect is cluster communications; you don't want the cluster heartbeat to not be able to be starved of bandwidth! Notice how this example specifies the destination IP port for cluster communications (3343):

```
New-NetQosPolicy "Cluster" -IPDstPort 3343 –MinBandwidthWeightAction 15 `
–Priority 255
```

The priority of this cluster example is set to the maximum allowable value of 255 (the default is 127 if the priority of the rule is not defined). If we had a scenario in which another rule matched this rule (which is quite unlikely in this case), then this rule would win. The rule with the highest priority always wins. The lowest possible value is 0.

A handy option for `New-NetQosPolicy` is the `-Default` flag. This allows you to create a QoS rule for all protocols not matching a filter in any other rule. The following does this for us:

```
New-NetQosPolicy "EverythingElse" -Default -MinBandwidthWeightAction 15
```

So far, every example applies QoS on a per-server basis using the OS packet scheduler. A handy option is to use a Differentiated Services Code Point (DSCP) value to tag traffic (from 0 to 63) so that the physical network can apply QoS for you. This means that you can stop a single type of traffic from flooding the LAN.

A common source of pain for network administrators is the nightly backup. The next example uses a DSCP flag of 30 to mark backup traffic going to 10.1.20.101. The network administrators can use this flag to identify traffic on the LAN and apply QoS in the network devices to control all backup traffic.

```
New-NetQosPolicy -Name "Backup" -IPDstPrefixMatchCondition `
10.1.20.101/24 -DSCPAction 30
```

Remember that each of these examples can be used on Hyper-V hosts, traditional physical servers, and in virtual machines where the operating system is Windows Server 2012.

Applying QoS to Protocols Using DCB

The final option for QoS rules is to let the hardware do the work. It is the preferred option if you have DCB-capable NICs and network appliances, and it is the required option if you plan on creating QoS rules for SMB Direct (RDMA) to ensure that it has enough bandwidth through a host's NIC(s).

DCB uses priorities to apply QoS policies. You will use the following process to classify protocols and create traffic classes that prioritize the traffic:

1. Install the DCB feature on the server by using Server Manager.

2. Create the required QoS policies by classifying protocols.

3. Create a traffic class that matches each created QoS policy.

4. You should enable PFC if you are using RoCE networking and the NIC(s) support PFC.

5. Enable DCB settings to be applied to the NICs.

6. Specify the NICs that will use DCB.

Enabling the DCB feature can be done in Server Manager or by running the quicker PowerShell alternative:

```
Install-WindowsFeature Data-Center-Bridging
```

Next you will want to create each of your QoS policies. The following example classifies SMB Direct by using `-NetDirectPort 445`. Note how this cmdlet does not specify any minimum or maximum bandwidth settings.

```
New-NetQosPolicy "SMB Direct" -NetDirectPort 445 -Priority 2
```

We specify the bandwidth rule when we create the traffic class for DCB. We should match the name (for consistency) and priority (required) of the QoS classification when we create a DCB traffic class.

```
New-NetQosTrafficClass "SMB Direct" -Priority 2 -Algorithm ETS -Bandwidth 40
```

DCB can work slightly differently as compared to the other examples. We are setting a bandwidth rule of 40 percent, but DCB can use an algorithm to ensure that lesser protocols are not starved. Enhanced Transmission Selection, or ETS (`http://msdn.microsoft.com/library/windows/hardware/hh406697(v=vs.85).aspx`), is an industry standard that ensures lower-priority protocols of a minimum level of bandwidth. The alternative is to specify `Strict` as the algorithm, and that will cause DCB to apply the traffic class with no exceptions.

If we are using RoCE, we should enable PFC for SMB Direct if the NIC(s) support it. This should be done on both ends of the connection, such as a Hyper-V host using SMB storage for virtual machine files, and the file server that is providing that storage. You can enable PFC by running the next example. Once again, the priority will match the SMB Direct QoS policy and DCB traffic class:

```
Enable-NetQosFlowControl -Priority 2
```

The next step is to enable DCB settings to be pushed down to the NICs:

```
Set-NetQosDcbxSetting -Willing $false
```

You then enable DCB on each required NIC:

```
Enable-NetAdapterQos "Ethernet 1"
```

DCB does require a bit more work than the other two ways of implementing QoS. However, it is a hardware function, so it is going to be the most efficient option. And as you will learn in Chapter 7, using SMB Direct will be completely worth the effort.

Using NIC Teaming and QoS

NIC teaming and QoS are compatible features of Windows Server 2012. Classification, tagging, and PFC all work seamlessly. There are some things to watch out for.

Minimum-bandwidth policy for virtual NICs passing through a Hyper-V Port NIC team can be complicated. Remember that virtual NICs are hashed to specific team members (physical NICs) in the team, and they are limited to that team member until a failover is required. The weights of those virtual NICs are used to divide up the bandwidth of a team member. They are not used to divide up the bandwidth of the entire team.

You cannot assign more than the bandwidth of a single team member by using absolute or bps-based rules.

How you configure your NIC team can also affect how DCB behaves, because traffic may not be distributed evenly between the various team members. Review the two modes and two load-distribution methods of NIC teaming from earlier in this chapter to see how this might impact your design.

Understanding the Microsoft Best Practice Design

There is no published best practice on designing QoS from Microsoft. The reason is simple; there are just too many variables in the design process that engineers and consultants will have to work through. Our advice is as follows:

◆ Use the decision process illustrated in Figure 4.18 earlier to decide which type of QoS you need to implement.

◆ Determine how much bandwidth each virtual NIC or protocol requires. One way to do that is to imagine that you can install NICs of any speed and have to always choose the right one for budget reasons, but you could temporarily burst through the limits.

◆ Use the right NIC-team design for your network environment and workload. Ideally, you will be able to define the switch architecture to give you the best results.

◆ Do not enable DCB and the OS packet scheduler QoS rules on the same NICs or networking stack. They are not designed to work together.

Converged Fabrics

We have presented many networking technologies that are new in Windows Server 2012. At times, you might have wondered whether each technology is important. They are, because they led you to this part of the chapter, and possibly one of the most important parts of the book. This is where you learn how to design converged fabrics.

Understanding Converged Fabrics

Fabric is a term that refers to a network. Earlier in the chapter, when we talked about a world without QoS, we listed all the network connections required for building a clustered Hyper-V host. Each one of those connections is referred to as a fabric. We questioned why we needed so many networks. In past versions of Windows Server and Hyper-V, we used physical isolation of those fabrics to guarantee a minimum level of service. However, we now have QoS in Windows Server 2012, which enables us to set a minimum-bandwidth reservation for virtual NICs or for protocols. And this makes it possible for us to converge each fabric into fewer NICs, possibly even as few as one.

The benefits should be immediately obvious. You are going to have fewer NICs. That means less cabling, fewer switch ports, less hardware being purchased, smaller support contracts, and the electricity bill being further reduced. Converged fabrics give us design flexibility too. We can use a NIC or aggregation of NICs (NIC team) and divide it logically to suit the needs of the infrastructure or business.

There are some less obvious benefits too. At this point, you have seen how to script the creation and configuration of all the networking components of Hyper-V. The entire construction of a converged fabric can be scripted. Write it once and reuse it many times; this is going to have huge time-saving and consistency-making rewards, whether you are an operator deploying hundreds of Hyper-V hosts in a public cloud or a field engineer deploying one host at a time for small-business customers.

Another less obvious benefit is that you can make the most of your investments in high-speed networking. Many organizations have started to implement 10 GbE networking. Many others would like to, but there is no way that they could pay to install that many 10 GbE NICs or pay for underutilized switches. Converged fabrics is about making full, but well-controlled, use of bandwidth. An investment in 10 GbE (or faster) networking with converged fabrics will allow more than just the live migration to be faster. Other fabrics can make use of that high-capacity bandwidth while live migration doesn't need it. This is balanced by administrator-defined QoS policies.

Having too many eggs in one basket is always bad. NIC teaming comes to the rescue because we can team two of those high-speed networks to not only achieve failover, but also to take advantage of link aggregation for better sharing of bandwidth.

How much convergence is too much? Or how much convergence is the right amount? Quite honestly, we have to give the classic consultant answer of "it depends" for those questions. You should then look at various factors such as actual bandwidth requirements for each fabric vs. what each NIC or NIC team can provide. We should also consider the hardware enhancements or offloads that we plan to use. For example, you learned earlier in this chapter that RSS and DVMQ can offer greatly improved network performance, but they cannot be enabled on the same NICs.

The days of the traditional physical isolation for every fabric are truly over. Microsoft has given us the tools in Windows Server 2012 to create more-elegant, more-economic, more-flexible, and more-powerful designs.

DESIGNING CONVERGED FABRICS

The beauty of converged fabrics is that there is no one right answer for everyone; the design process is a matter of balancing desired convergence with compatibility and with bandwidth requirements. This section presents designs that we can expect to be commonly deployed over the coming years.

There is no feature in Windows Server 2012 for converged fabrics. There is no control in Server Manager, no option in Network Connections, and no specific PowerShell module. If you have read this chapter from end to end, taking the time to understand each section, you already know what the components are and how to implement converged fabrics. All that remains is to know how to design them.

Using Management OS Virtual NICs

There is a reason that we made a point about virtual NICs in the management OS. You can create a design in which all of the host's fabrics pass through the virtual switch, and on to the NIC or NIC team to reach the physical network, as you can see in Figure 4.19. Pairing this with QoS policies for the virtual NICs will guarantee each virtual NIC a certain amount of bandwidth.

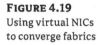

FIGURE 4.19
Using virtual NICs
to converge fabrics

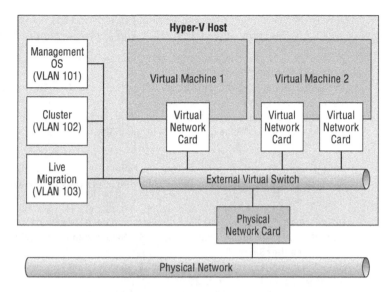

Each management OS virtual NIC is connected to a port on the virtual switch. And each management OS virtual NIC will appear as a connection, with its own protocol configurations, such as IPv4 and/or IPv6 settings. You can even isolate these virtual NICs on the physical network by assigning VLAN IDs to them.

A QoS will be created to assign each management OS virtual NIC a minimum amount of bandwidth. We don't need to use a protocol approach because we're using each virtual NIC for a specific function.

Although you can assign QoS policies to the virtual machine virtual NICs, we're going to try to avoid this unless absolutely necessary. It can become messy. Here's an example why:

1. You assign a weight of 1 to many virtual machines.

2. You use functionality such as Power Optimization or Dynamic Optimization in System Center 2012 Virtual Machine Manager to automatically move virtual machines around a Hyper-V cluster using Live Migration.

3. At night, many idle virtual machines might be squeezed down to a few hosts in a cluster so that idle hosts can be powered down (to reduce power bills).

4. You find yourself assigning a sum weight of well over 100 to all the virtual NICs on the remaining powered-up hosts.

Who really wants to keep track of all those virtual NICs, especially when you might have up to 8,000 virtual machines in a single cloud? Experienced engineers like to manage by exception. We can take this approach with QoS:

1. Assign minimum bandwidth policies to the management OS virtual NICs.

2. Assign a default QoS policy to the virtual switch to reserve bandwidth for all virtual NICs that do not have an explicit QoS policy.

Here is the PowerShell to create a virtual switch and the management OS virtual NICs, assign VLAN IDs to the new virtual NICs, and apply the required QoS policies:

```
write-host "Creating external virtual switch, with no Management OS virtual `
NIC, with weight-based QoS"
#You could substitute the name of a NIC team for the name of the physical `
(NIC Ethernet 2)
New-VMSwitch "ConvergedNetSwitch" -MinimumBandwidthMode weight `
-NetAdapterName "Ethernet 2" -AllowManagementOS 0


write-host "Setting default QoS policy"
Set-VMSwitch "ConvergedNetSwitch" -DefaultFlowMinimumBandwidthWeight 40


write-host "Creating virtual NICs for the Management OS"
Add-VMNetworkAdapter -ManagementOS -Name "ManagementOS" -SwitchName `
"ConvergedNetSwitch"
Set-VMNetworkAdapter -ManagementOS -Name "ManagementOS" `
-MinimumBandwidthWeight 20
Set-VMNetworkAdapterVlan -ManagementOS -VMNetworkAdapterName `
"ManagementOS" -Access -VlanId 101


Add-VMNetworkAdapter -ManagementOS -Name "Cluster" -SwitchName `
"ConvergedNetSwitch"
Set-VMNetworkAdapter -ManagementOS -Name "Cluster" -MinimumBandwidthWeight 10
Set-VMNetworkAdapterVlan -ManagementOS -VMNetworkAdapterName "ManagementOS" `
-Access -VlanId 102


Add-VMNetworkAdapter -ManagementOS -Name "LiveMigration" -SwitchName `
"ConvergedNetSwitch"
Set-VMNetworkAdapter -ManagementOS -Name "LiveMigration" `
-MinimumBandwidthWeight 30
Set-VMNetworkAdapterVlan -ManagementOS -VMNetworkAdapterName `
"LiveMigration" -Access -VlanId 103
```

In a matter of seconds, you have configured a simple converged fabric for a clustered Hyper-V host that uses a type of storage that is not based on iSCSI.

We should do some mathematics before moving forward. A total weight of 100 has been allocated. The percentage of bandwidth allocated to virtual NICs is calculated as follows:

Bandwidth percentage = (allocated weight / sum of weights)

Keep that in mind in case you allocate a total weight of 80 (such as 30, 10, 20, and 20) and you find percentages that look weird when you run the following cmdlet:

```
Get-VMNetworkAdapter -ManagementOS | FL Name, BandwidthPercentage
```

We could take the preceding script one step further by appending the following scripting that configures the IPv4 addresses of the host's new virtual NICs:

```
write-host "Waiting 30 seconds for virtual devices to initialize"
Start-Sleep -s 30


write-host "Configuring IPv4 addresses for the Management OS virtual NICs"
New-NetIPAddress -InterfaceAlias "vEthernet (ManagementOS)" -IPAddress `
10.0.1.31 -PrefixLength 24
Set-DnsClientServerAddress -InterfaceAlias "vEthernet `
(ManagementOS)" -ServerAddresses "10.0.1.11"


New-NetIPAddress -InterfaceAlias "vEthernet (Cluster)" -IPAddress `
192.168.1.31 -PrefixLength "24"


New-NetIPAddress -InterfaceAlias "vEthernet (LiveMigration)" `
-IPAddress 192.168.2.31 -PrefixLength "24"
```

It doesn't take too much imagination to see how quickly host networking could be configured with such a script. All you have to do is change the last octet of each IP address, and you can run it in the next host that you need to ready for production.

A Converged Fabrics Design Process

With so many possible options, you might want to know where to start and how to make decisions. Here is a suggested process:

1. Start with a single NIC in your host design.

2. Decide which kind of storage you want to use. Storage such as SAS and Fibre Channel will have no impact, because they use host bus adapters (HBAs) instead of NICs. Will you need to enable RSS? Will you use RDMA for high-bandwidth SMB 3.0, thus requiring end-to-end support for DCB on the network?

3. Do you want to enable RSS and/or DVMQ? Remember, they cannot share a NIC.

4. How much bandwidth will each connection require? For example, you need at least 1 GbE for live migration in a small-to-medium implementation. Will 1 GbE NICs be enough, or will you need 10 GbE NICs, or faster for SMB storage?

5. Now consider NIC teaming, to add link aggregation and failover.

6. Ensure that whatever approach you are considering for the storage connections will be supported by the storage manufacturer.

A whiteboard, a touch-enabled PC with a stylus, or even just a pen and paper will be tools you need now. We're going to present a few possible converged fabric designs and discuss each one:

Virtualized NICs with NIC Teaming   This design of Figure 4.19 can be modified slightly to use a NIC team for the external virtual switch, as shown in Figure 4.20. An additional management OS virtual NIC has been added to isolate the backup traffic from the host to a specific VLAN.

FIGURE 4.20
Converged fabric
using virtual NICs
and NIC team

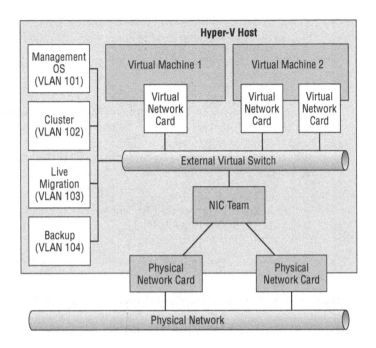

The NIC team will typically be created using Hyper-V Port load distribution because there are many more virtual NICs (including the virtual machines) than there are team members.

The physical makeup of the team members will depend on your requirements and your budget. You could make this solution by using four onboard 1 GbE NICs. But you do have to account for NIC failure in a NIC team; would the bandwidth of three NICs have been enough if you were using a traditional physical NIC fabric design? Maybe this design would be good for a small implementation. Maybe a medium one would do better with an additional quad-port NIC card being added to the team, giving it a total of 8×1 GbE NICs. That's a lot of NICs, and at that point, you might be economically better off putting in 2×10 GbE NICs. Very large hosts (Hyper-V can handle 4 TB RAM in a host) probably want to go bigger than that again.

You could enable DVMQ in this design to enhance the performance of the virtual NICs.

This design is perfect for simple host designs that don't want to leverage too many hardware enhancements or offloads.

Using SMB Storage with SMB Direct and SMB Multichannel   This design (Figure 4.21) is a variation of the previous one, but it adds support for storing virtual machines on a Windows Server 2012 file share and using RSS (SMB Multichannel) and RDMA (SMB Direct).

An additional pair of RDMA-enabled NICs (iWARP, RoCE, or InfiniBand) are installed in the host. The NICs are not NIC teamed; there is no point, because RDMA will bypass the teaming and SMB Multichannel will happily use both NICs simultaneously. The RDMA NICs are placed into the same network as the file server that will store the virtual machines. We do not need to enable QoS for the NICs because the only traffic that should be passing through them is SMB.

You can enable DVMQ on the NICs in the NIC team to improve the performance of virtual-machine networking. SMB Multichannel is going to detect two available paths to the file server and therefore use both storage NICs at the same time. Enabling RSS on those NICs, thanks to their physical isolation, will enable SMB Multichannel to create multiple streams of traffic on each of the two NICs, therefore making full use of the bandwidth.

FIGURE 4.21
Dedicated NICs for
SMB 3.0 storage

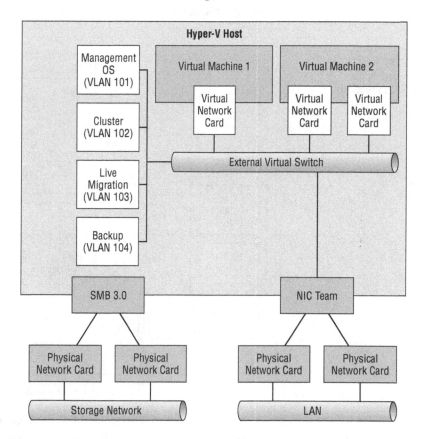

This design can provide a hugely scalable host, depending on the bandwidth provided. SMB 3.0 over InfiniBand has been demonstrated to provide a throughput of around 16 gigabytes (not gigabits) per second with a penalty of just 5 percent CPU utilization (Microsoft TechEd 2012). That is true enterprise storage scalability!

Converged iSCSI Connections Both of the iSCSI connections will be created as Management OS virtual NICs. Each virtual NIC will be in a different VLAN, therefore meeting the requirement of both of them being in unique IP ranges. You can see this design in Figure 4.22. There are three important points to remember with this design. As usual with this style of design, QoS policies will be created for the virtual NICs.

First, you should reserve a minimum amount of bandwidth for each iSCSI virtual NIC that would match what you would use for a physical NIC implementation. Do not starve the storage path.

Second, you should verify that this design will not cause a support issue with your storage manufacturer. The manufacturers often require dedicated switches for iSCSI networking to guarantee maximum storage performance, and this goes against the basic concept of converged fabrics.

Finally, MPIO should be used as usual for the iSCSI connections. If you are using a storage manufacturer's device-specific module (DSM), make sure that this design won't cause a problem for it.

FIGURE 4.22
Converging the iSCSI connections

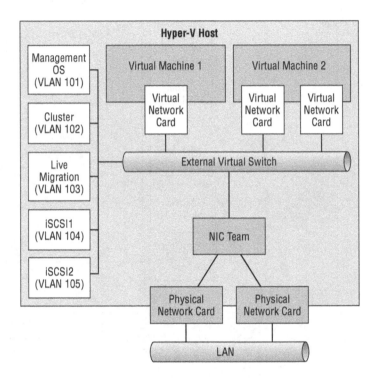

This design is a budget one. Ideally, you will use physical NICs for the iSCSI connections. This is because using nonconverged NICs will allow you to have dedicated switches for the iSCSI fabric, will provide better storage performance, and will have support from those storage manufacturers that require dedicated iSCSI switches.

Physically Isolated iSCSI The supportability of this converged fabric design is maximized by implementing iSCSI using a pair of traditional physical NICs, as shown in Figure 4.23. No QoS needs to be applied to the iSCSI NICs because they are physically isolated.

Enabling SR-IOV SR-IOV-enabled NICs cannot be used in a converged fabric. In this case (Figure 4.24), we are going to abandon the virtual NIC approach for the management OS fabrics.

A pair of SR-IOV-capable NICs are installed in the host. One SR-IOV external virtual switch is created for each of the two NICs. In this example, `Virtual Machine 1` has no network-path fault tolerance because it has just a single virtual NIC. `Virtual Machine 2` does have network-path fault tolerance. It is connected to both virtual switches via two virtual NICs, and a NIC team is created in the guest OS.

FIGURE 4.23
Using physically isolated iSCSI

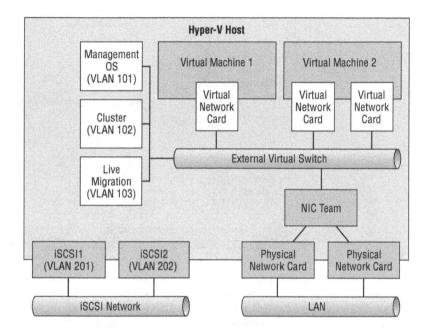

All of the management OS functions are passing through a single team interface on a NIC team, configured with address-hashing load distribution. This algorithm will enable communications to use the bandwidth of the team, within the bounds of QoS. DCB is being used in this example to apply QoS policies on a per-protocol basis, thus negating the need for even virtual isolation. We can further tag the traffic by using DSCP so that network administrators can control traffic at a VLAN level. If DCB NICs were not available, the QoS policies could be enforced by the OS packet scheduler. RSS will also be enabled, if possible, to provide more streams for SMB Multichannel.

The benefit of this design is that it uses fewer VLANs and requires just a single IP address per host for the management OS. Bigger hosts can also be used because the processing of virtual-machine networking is offloaded to SR-IOV rather than being processed by the management OS (virtual switches).

A variation of this design allows you to use RDMA for SMB storage. The NICs in the management OS would not be teamed because RDMA will bypass teaming. DCB would be required for this design, and PFC would be required for RoCE NICs. RSS would be enabled on the management OS NICs for SMB Multichannel.

FIGURE 4.24
Nonconvergence of
SR-IOV NICs

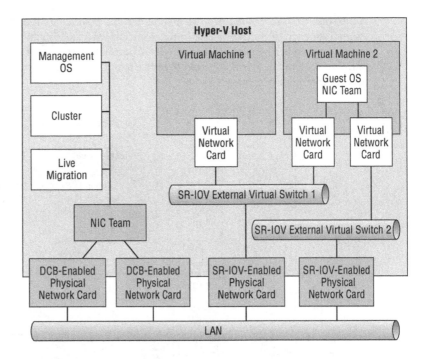

This is just a small sample of the possible converged fabric designs. Using the suggested process will help you find the right design for each project that you do.

With the converged fabric configured on your hosts, you can join them to a domain, install management agents, or start to build Hyper-V clusters.

Once you go converged fabrics, you'll never go back. The flexibility that they provide, the abstraction from physical networks, and the ability to deploy a host configuration in seconds from a reusable script will bring you back every single time.

Real World Solutions

Here are a few examples of how you can use the information in this chapter in the real world.

Implementing RSS and DVMQ

CHALLENGE

You are a consultant starting a cloud project for a customer. The hosts that will be deployed in this cloud have the following specifications:

◆ Two 10 core processors with Hyper-Threading enabled, providing you with a total of 40 logical processors.

◆ Four NICs that will be used to create two NIC teams, one for an external virtual switch (Hyper-V Port and Switch-Independent) and one for host communications (Address Hashing and Switch-Independent). All four NICs support RSS queues, but not SR-IOV.

The project requirements state that you must enable any available hardware acceleration to increase the performance of virtual-machine networking. The hosts will be using SMB storage, and you are also to use any available hardware features to maximize storage bandwidth utilization. How will you accomplish these requirements?

SOLUTION

The presence of RSS queues in all four NICs in the hosts means that you can enable two features:

◆ RSS to provide SMB Multichannel

◆ DVMQ to improve virtual machine networking performance

Figure 4.25 illustrates the design. You will need to enable RSS and DVMQ. The first step is to enable RSS in all four NICs. This feature is used by RSS and DVMQ in Windows. Although they are different features at the OS level, they are using the same queues on the NICs and are incompatible. This requires you to physically isolate NICs that will be used for RSS and for DVMQ, as in the design.

FIGURE 4.25
Converged host networking with RSS and DVMQ

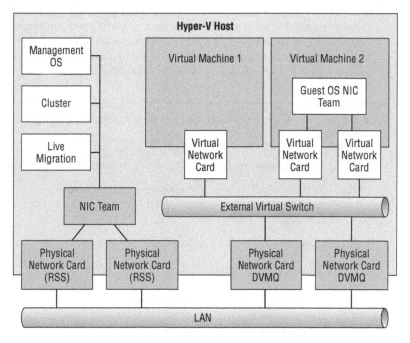

Consult the NIC manufacturer's documentation for specific guidance (if provided). Then enable RSS in the advanced configuration of each NIC's connection in Network Connections.

You will need to calculate two settings, *RssBaseProcNumber and *MaxRssProcessors for RSS and for DVMQ. They will be used to specify the range of cores that

◆ NIC1 can use for RSS

◆ NIC2 can use for RSS

◆ NIC3 can use for DVMQ

◆ NIC4 can use for DVMQ

There are 40 logical processors:

◆ They are numbered 0 to 39.

◆ We can use only cores, not logical processors, for RSS and DVMQ. Therefore, we identify cores by using the number of the first logical processor in that core. They are numbered as 0, 2, 4, 6 and so on, up to 38.

◆ The first core, logical processor 0, is reserved for default (non-RSS and non-DVMQ) network processing.

◆ It is decided to use a roughly 50/50 split between RSS and DVMQ.

The eight remaining logical processors on CPU0 (2–18) will be used by RSS. The logical processors of CPU1 (20–38) will be used by DVMQ.

The settings for the four NICs will depend on whether NIC teaming is in Sum-of-Queues mode or in Min-Queues mode. NIC1 and NIC2 are using Address Hashing so they are in Min-Queues mode. That will mean that the two NICs in this team can share cores. NIC3 and NIC4 are in a Switch-Independent and Hyper-V Port team, so they are in Sum-of-Queues mode. This means that the remaining cores must be split between the two NICs in this team. The settings for the four NICs will therefore be those illustrated in Table 4.3.

TABLE 4.3: RSS and DVMQ settings for scenario host design

	TEAM CONFIGURATION	QUEUES MODE	*RssBaseProcNumber	*MaxRssProcessors
NIC1	Switch-Independent & Address Hashing	Min-Queues	2	9
NIC2	Switch-Independent & Address Hashing	Min-Queues	2	9
NIC3	Switch-Independent & Hyper-V Port	Sum-of-Queues	11	5
NIC4	Switch-Independent & Hyper-V Port	Sum-of-Queues	16	5

You can use PowerShell to deploy these settings to the NICs:

```
Set-NetAdatperVmq "NIC1" -BaseProcessorNumber 2 -MaxProcessors 9
Set-NetAdatperVmq "NIC2" -BaseProcessorNumber 2 -MaxProcessors 9
Set-NetAdatperVmq "NIC3" -BaseProcessorNumber 11 -MaxProcessors 5
Set-NetAdatperVmq "NIC4" -BaseProcessorNumber 16 -MaxProcessors 5
```

The implementation is now complete.

Creating Converged Fabrics with Isolated SMB Storage

CHALLENGE

You have been asked to deploy a cluster of 64 Hyper-V hosts, each having the network configuration that was previously shown in Figure 4.21. The storage NIC team will be in Switch-Dependent LACP mode with Address Hashing for load distribution. The virtual switch NIC team will be in Switch-Independent mode with Hyper-V Port enabled.

The servers that are being used store the PCI names of the NICs. Windows Server 2012 will use these consistent device names and label the network adapters in Network Connections as follows:

◆ Port1

◆ Port2

◆ Port3

◆ Port4

You have been told to complete the following:

1. Use PowerShell to build and configure both NIC teams for all hosts.

2. Configure IPv4 for the storage NIC team.

3. Create the converged fabric for the management OS virtual NICs.

4. Configure the VLAN and IPv4 settings of the management OS virtual NICs.

5. The minimum bandwidth reservations will be 30 for the switch, 5 for Management OS, 5 for Cluster, 40 for Live Migration, and 20 for Backup.

You will write a script that can be quickly modified for each host.

SOLUTION

```
#Set variables for each NIC's IP address
#Modify these values for each host you want to configure

$ManagementOSIPv4 = "10.0.10.1"
$ManagementOSRouter = "10.0.10.254"
$ManagementOSDNS = "10.0.1.51"
```

```
$ClusterIPv4 = "192.168.1.1"
$LiveMigrationIPv4 = "192.168.2.1"
$BackupIPv4 = "10.0.11.1"


$StorageTeamIPv4 = "172.16.1.1"
$StorageTeamRouter = "172.16.1.254"



Write-Host "Creating the NIC teams"
New-NetLBFOTeam -Name "ConvergedNetTeam" -TeamMembers "Port3", "Port4" `
-TeamingMode SwitchIndependent -LoadBalancingAlgorithm HyperVPort -Confirm:$false


New-NetLBFOTeam -Name "StorageTeam" -TeamMembers "Port1", "Port2" `
-TeamingMode LACP -Confirm:$false



write-host "Creating external virtual switch, with no Management OS virtual `
NIC, with weight-based QoS"
New-VMSwitch "ConvergedNetSwitch" -MinimumBandwidthMode weight `
-NetAdapterName "ConvergedNetTeam" -AllowManagementOS 0



write-host "Setting default QoS policy"
Set-VMSwitch "ConvergedNetSwitch" -DefaultFlowMinimumBandwidthWeight 30



write-host "Creating and configuring virtual NIC for the Management OS"
Add-VMNetworkAdapter -ManagementOS -Name "ManagementOS" -SwitchName `
"ConvergedNetSwitch"
Set-VMNetworkAdapter -ManagementOS -Name "ManagementOS" -MinimumBandwidthWeight 5
Set-VMNetworkAdapterVlan -ManagementOS -VMNetworkAdapterName "ManagementOS" `
-Access -VlanId 101



write-host "Creating and configuring virtual NIC for the cluster"
Add-VMNetworkAdapter -ManagementOS -Name "Cluster" -SwitchName `
"ConvergedNetSwitch"
Set-VMNetworkAdapter -ManagementOS -Name "Cluster" -MinimumBandwidthWeight 5
Set-VMNetworkAdapterVlan -ManagementOS -VMNetworkAdapterName "Cluster" `
-Access -VlanId 102
```

```
write-host "Creating and configuring virtual NIC for Live Migration"
Add-VMNetworkAdapter -ManagementOS -Name "LiveMigration" -SwitchName `
"ConvergedNetSwitch"
Set-VMNetworkAdapter -ManagementOS -Name "LiveMigration" `
-MinimumBandwidthWeight 40
Set-VMNetworkAdapterVlan -ManagementOS -VMNetworkAdapterName "LiveMigration" `
-Access -VlanId 103


write-host "Creating and configuring virtual NIC for the backup fabric"
Add-VMNetworkAdapter -ManagementOS -Name "Backup" -SwitchName `
"ConvergedNetSwitch"
Set-VMNetworkAdapter -ManagementOS -Name "Backup" -MinimumBandwidthWeight 20
Set-VMNetworkAdapterVlan -ManagementOS -VMNetworkAdapterName "Backup" `
-Access -VlanId 104


write-host "Waiting 30 seconds for virtual devices to initialize"
Start-Sleep -s 30


write-host "Configuring IPv4 addresses for the Management OS virtual NICs"
New-NetIPAddress -InterfaceAlias "vEthernet (ManagementOS)" -IPAddress `
$ManagementOSIPv4 -PrefixLength 24 -DefaultGateway $ManagementOSRouter `
Set-DnsClientServerAddress -InterfaceAlias "vEthernet (ManagementOS)" `
-ServerAddresses $ManagementOSDNS

New-NetIPAddress -InterfaceAlias "vEthernet (Cluster)" -IPAddress $ClusterIPv4 `
-PrefixLength "24"

New-NetIPAddress -InterfaceAlias "vEthernet (LiveMigration)" -IPAddress `
$LiveMigrationIPv4 -PrefixLength "24"

New-NetIPAddress -InterfaceAlias "vEthernet (Backup)" -IPAddress `
$BackupIPv4 -PrefixLength "24"


write-host "Configuring team interface IPv4 address of the storage steam"
New-NetIPAddress -InterfaceAlias "StorageTeam" -IPAddress `
$StorageTeamIPv4 -PrefixLength "24" -DefaultGateway $StorageTeamRouter
```

Creating Converged Fabrics with DCB and SR-IOV

CHALLENGE

You have been asked to script the creation of a converged fabric design similar to the one previously shown in Figure 4.24. Servers with NIC names that are detectable by Windows Server 2012 are being used. SMB Direct (RDMA over Converged Ethernet with DCB NICs) will be used to minimize the processor impact of SMB Multichannel. Therefore, Port1 and Port2 will not be in a NIC team, as was shown in Figure 4.24.

You are to write a PowerShell script that can be used to configure the networking of hosts using this design. It will configure each NIC's required IPv4 settings, configure QoS over DCB, enable PFC for RDMA, and set up SR-IOV for virtual machine connectivity. The minimum bandwidth reservations should be as follows:

◆ Remote Desktop (TCP 3389): 5 percent

◆ Monitoring (TCP 5723): 5 percent

◆ Cluster communications: 5 percent

◆ Live Migration: 30 percent

◆ Backup (TCP 3148): 20 percent

◆ SMB Direct: 30 percent

Ensure that any low-priority protocol will not be starved of bandwidth by QoS and DCB. You should also enable DSCP tagging (with IDs that will be provided to you) so that network administrators can throttle the total sum of traffic from all hosts in the network.

SOLUTION

```
#Set variables for each NIC's IP address
#Modify these values for each host you want to configure


$Port1IPv4 = "10.0.10.1"
$Port1Router = "10.0.10.254"
$Port1IPv4 = "10.0.11.1"
$Port1Router = "10.0.11.254"



Write-Host "Configuring IPv4 address of Port1"
New-NetIPAddress -InterfaceAlias "Port1" -IPAddress $Port1IPv4 -PrefixLength `
"24" -DefaultGateway $Port1Router



Write-Host "Configuring IPv4 address of Port2"
New-NetIPAddress -InterfaceAlias "Port2" -IPAddress $Port2IPv4 -PrefixLength `
"24" -DefaultGateway $Port2Router
```

```
Write-Host "Installing DCB feature"
Install-WindowsFeature Data-Center-Bridging
write-host "Waiting 10 seconds"
Start-Sleep -s 10


Write-Host "Creating QoS policies"
New-NetQosPolicy "Backup" -IPDstPort 3148 -IPProtocol TCP –Priority 1 `
-DSCPAction 10
New-NetQosPolicy "Remote Desktop" -IPDstPort 3389 -IPProtocol TCP `
-Priority 2 -DSCPAction 11
New-NetQosPolicy "Live Migration" -LiveMigration –Priority 3 -DSCPAction 12
New-NetQosPolicy "Cluster" -IPDstPort 3343 –Priority 4 -DSCPAction 13
New-NetQosPolicy "Monitoring" –IPDstPort 5723 -IPProtocol TCP -Priority `
5 -DSCPAction 14
#You cannot assing a DSCP tag to RDMA traffic
New-NetQosPolicy "SMB Direct" -NetDirectPort 445 –Priority 6


Write-Host "Creating traffic classes"
New-NetQosTrafficClass "Backup" -Priority 1 –Algorithm ETS –Bandwidth 20
New-NetQosTrafficClass "Remote Desktop" -Priority 2 –Algorithm ETS –Bandwidth 5
New-NetQosTrafficClass "Live Migration" -Priority 3 –Algorithm ETS –Bandwidth 30
New-NetQosTrafficClass "Cluster" -Priority 4 –Algorithm ETS –Bandwidth 5
New-NetQosTrafficClass "Monitoring" –Priority 5 –Algorithm ETS –Bandwidth 5
New-NetQosTrafficClass "SMB Direct" –Priority 6 –Algorithm ETS –Bandwidth 30


Write-Host "Enabling PFC for RDMA over Converged Ethernet"
Enable-NetQosFlowControl -Priority 6


Write-Host "Enabling push down of DCB settings"
Set-NetQosDcbxSetting –Willing $false -Confirm:$false


Write-Host "Enabling DCB on NICs"
Enable-NetAdapterQos "Port1"
Enable-NetAdapterQos "Port2"


Write-Host "Creating SR-IOV enabled virtual switches"
New-VMSwitch -Name "ExternalSRIOV1" -EnableIOV $True -NetAdapterName `
"Port3" -AllowManagementOS 0
New-VMSwitch -Name "ExternalSRIOV2" -EnableIOV $True -NetAdapterName `
"Port4" -AllowManagementOS 0
```

Chapter 5

Cloud Computing

Chapter 4, "Networking," introduced you to Windows Server 2012 network architecture and the many features included in the operating system. This chapter takes a deeper dive into the Microsoft extensible virtual switch and the design objectives Microsoft envisioned when architecting Hyper-V and the extensible virtual switch to support public and private clouds.

This Microsoft master plan envisioned a comprehensive and consistent cloud story that would cover both customers and hosters while also providing value-added opportunities for partners.

You will learn how organizations that have a responsibility to protect information can do so—ranging from simply implementing requirements for segregation of duties, to a full isolation of services between the departments of one company or between multiple organizations. The question is whether cloud computing can assist in delivering that protection of intellectual property by aiming for maximum segregation while maintaining a high degree of flexibility.

Windows Server 2012 offers a variety of approaches to supporting this segregation. In this chapter, you will investigate two implementation scenarios: first, the inbox product functionality called Microsoft Network Virtualization, and second, private virtual LANs (PVLANs), which are now also supported by the Hyper-V extensible switch.

Additionally, you will consider what a multi-tenant network really is, and how this concept aligns to cloud computing.

In this chapter, you'll learn about

◆ How virtualization enables isolation through multi-tenancy

◆ The various methods to enable multi-tenancy using Windows Server 2012 Hyper-V

◆ Configuration and use of Microsoft Network Virtualization

◆ PVLANs and how they are implemented

◆ Port Access Controls

◆ Usage Metrics for Cloud Services

Clouds, Tenants, and Segregation

The collapse of Enron in 2001 (which provided the basis for the creation of the Sarbanes-Oxley Act of 2002), organizations such as the Coca-Cola Company and PepsiCo, and cloud providers such as Amazon EC2 and Windows Azure—what do all these have in common? Considering each of these independently or as a group, it is not difficult to see that each has a strong requirement for segregation: the need to ensure that departments within Enron were independently isolated to prevent accounting anomalies; the need to ensure intellectual property such as recipes of two soft drink giants remain confidential; the need to ensure that confidential data hosted on a cloud remains secure, protected, and for appropriate consumption only.

Why? What does this have to do with Microsoft Hyper-V? If Hyper-V is primarily a platform to host virtual machines, what makes any of this relevant?

Today's businesses are continuing to grow their investments in virtualization to reduce their footprints, whether for cost savings, efficiencies, or environmental reasons. We now, more than ever, must have 100 percent confidence that this consolidation of resources, data, and intellectual property continues to remain safe and secure.

How does this become possible? By employing segregation techniques! Consider our consumption of resources on a hosted service such as Salesforce.com as a tenancy. Consider business units within your own organizations as tenants; consider customers utilizing your infrastructure or storing data as tenants.

The Multi-Tenancy Era

Today, as we evolve into a world of virtualization, we begin to share resources. No longer do we continue to purchase dedicated hardware for every business unit or project, but instead we centralize our purchasing to make greater strategic investments in infrastructure, reap far more efficient value for the money, consolidate our footprint, and share our computing power with other departments, customers, and vendors. This is not really a revolutionary step forward, but more of an evolution.

Multi-tenancy as a computer term originates from the 1960s, when companies would rent space and processing power on mainframe computers to reduce their computing expenses. Over the decades, this has continued to evolve, and today services such as Gmail or Office 365 expose functionality to permit multiple users and organizations to securely and independently consume the same service.

We continue to evolve our software architecture so that a single instance running on a server now serves multiple client organizations and consumers (tenants). This is in contrast to the approach of the not-so-distant past, when we would set up separate software and hardware instances and dedicate these for different consumers.

Multi-tenancy architecture is designed to virtually partition data and configuration, so that a client organization works with a customized virtual instance, segregated.

Today this concept of multi-tenancy has become one of the key elements in cloud computing, which in the context of Hyper-V can be quite simply defined as running VMs for multiple tenants securely segregated on the same physical server.

HYPER-V CLOUD

The concept of multi-tenancy and clouds in Hyper-V can be illustrated in its simplest terms by considering a grouping of Hyper-V servers as computing resources that together form the fabric of a cloud. This grouping of resources, or *cloud fabric*, can then be shared among any number of users (subscribers or customers), which become known as *tenants* of the cloud.

The full definition of a cloud is best described in the NIST paper found at the following site:

```
http://csrc.nist.gov/publications/nistpubs/800-145/SP800-145.pdf
```

If you are interested in learning more about Microsoft's technology for hosting your own Microsoft Hyper-V cloud, we highly recommend the book *Microsoft Private Cloud Computing* by Finn, Vredevoort, Lownds, and Flynn (Sybex, 2012).

Although it is an easy concept to grasp, multi-tenancy has been challenging to deliver. If you consider its challenges, this will become perfectly clear to you:

Isolation   Tenant VMs should not see *any* traffic from another tenant VM.

Performance   Tenant VMs should have minimal to no impact on another tenant VM's traffic flow and performance.

Flexibility   Multi-tenancy requires easy and rapid provisioning of additional host capacity to enable changing capacity demands.

Segregation by Isolation

Since Microsoft introduced Hyper-V to the market, organizations have deployed and nurtured large farms of hosts for virtualization. These implementations have been architected to be both scalable and secure while considering the challenges of segregation as data is passed to and from these services.

As time has progressed, the management of these farms has evolved into standardized pooling of resources for storage, computing, and networking, ultimately embraced by a management infrastructure and process portfolio to deliver self-service-enabled clouds for the tenants to consume.

However, through the course of all this evolution, one area that has remained stagnant is the area of network implementations. Although the implementation technologies have evolved in terms of capacity from 1 Gb to teams of 10 Gb and beyond, they have been unable to mature beyond the current standards of virtual LANs (VLANs) and the overheads associated with managing and maintaining this solution.

In this current implementation of segregation, which uses VLANs to achieve network isolation, there still remains a large dependency on the networking teams to configure and enable segmentation across the fabric to support each and every new VLAN required on the cloud. Specifically, enabling VLAN tags on each additional network device involved in the flow of traffic between each host participating in the compute element of the cloud fabric—a process that continues to be prone to error and time-consuming to implement.

Figure 5.1 illustrates a simple fabric scenario demonstrating isolation across three compute hosts, connected by four network switches. In the illustration, the numbers 1, 2, and 3 represent different tenants on this fabric and highlight the number of places where the tenant VLAN tag must be defined to ensure that the virtual machines can successfully communicate while ensuring traffic flow isolation.

FIGURE 5.1

Secure tenant hosting with VLAN isolation

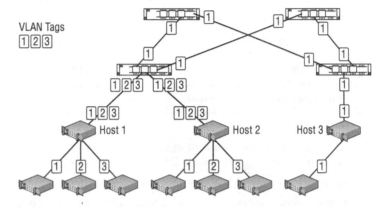

Figure 5.2 extends this scenario, enabling tenant 3 to to place its virtual machines on host 3, thereby illustrating the number of VLAN additions that must be made on the fabric to support this relatively small change to ensure isolated traffic flow is maintained.

FIGURE 5.2

Tenant 3 VLAN isolation to additional hosts

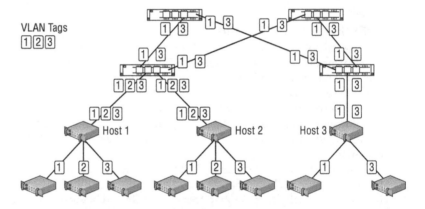

As organizations adapt to implementing cloud solutions within their environments, they have established processes and procedures. These, in turn, have resulted in better forecasting and communication that has enabled a more proactive approach to managing segregation.

Windows Server 2012 Hyper-V set out as part of its original goals to address the requirements for multi-tenancy. These requirements are the focus of the remainder of this chapter. You'll learn about network virtualization, private VLANs (PVLANs), Port Access Controls, and the consumption metering of virtual resources by tenants in your cloud.

Figure 5.3 illustrates a very simplified objective: Hosting multiple tenants on our Hyper-V 2012 cloud fabric, while ensuring that we keep the key concepts of a cloud fabric truly intact.

Additionally, we can consider some of the more complicated objectives we must deliver to our tenants, including, but not limited to

◆ Enabling easy tenant migration to and from a cloud, as well as between clouds

◆ Preserving tenants' network addresses, security, and policies while they are hosted on the cloud

◆ Continuing to deliver a seamless end-user experience

FIGURE 5.3
Multi-tennant
cloud network
isolation

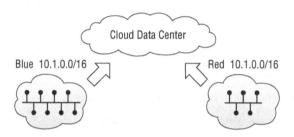

Buckle up, as the real fun is about to unfold!

Microsoft Network Virtualization

In this section, you will look at the architecture and function of the network virtualization solution, along with the two mechanisms available to enable this service. You will also investigate how to go about implementing the network virtualization solution with Windows Server 2012 Hyper-V.

Today we have become comfortable with the concept of virtualization when we think about CPU, memory, and even disks, but the idea of network virtualization is pretty new. We can figure out for ourselves that this obviously extends the concepts we already understand to apply to networks—so, in essence, network virtualization converts physical networks to virtual networks.

Consider for a moment that virtual memory simulates to a VM that it has exclusive ownership of the assigned memory to store data. Extrapolating this concept to virtual networks would simulate that resources such as IP addresses and gateways are dedicated to the virtual environment. In reality, these are also shared with the physical network, just as with our physical memory concept.

With this in mind, the objective would be that virtual machines sharing a virtual network would experience everything the same as if they were just working in a physical, but isolated network.

So why bother? We already have VLANs that are designed just for this job. After all, that's why we call them *virtual* LANs, right? This is nothing new, so why the fuss? Realistically, we have had seamless integration with VLANs in Hyper-V right from the beginning.

VLANs have served us well, but they do have their limitations. For example, we cannot have any more than 4,096 of these defined. This might sound like plenty, but as your clouds take off (excuse the pun), this number starts to quickly become a very real concern. To compound this problem, technology is not always created equal; it is not unusual for some devices to be limited to much lower numbers, with support for just 1,024 VLANs being quite common. Just think for a moment about a network with 4,096 VLANs defined and sharing a number of switches, routers, and VM hosts—the task of configuring and maintaining that number of VLANs would encourage anyone to change professions. The fallout that might result if an error were to occur while creating or editing any of these VLAN definitions could be disastrous.

Okay, so VLANs might have scale issues, but what are the objectives of network virtualization?

◆ Isolate the cloud infrastructure from the physical infrastructure.

◆ Complete segregation of network and cloud administration.

◆ Provide scalability and flexibility to address the limitations of VLANs.

◆ Reduce costs for management and support.

◆ Enable cloud tenants to keep their IP address scheme.

◆ Overlap IP address schemes across clouds with no readdressing.

◆ Have the freedom to place VMs on any host, without concern for networking.

◆ Have minimal performance impact.

◆ Retain the ability to utilize hardware acceleration technologies.

Not a simple set of goals—however, if this were truly possible, then the premise of "Any Service, Any Server, Any Cloud" could finally be realized.

Encapsulated Network Virtualization

We now have the concept sorted: network virtualization provides the capability to run multiple virtual network infrastructures on the same physical network (potentially even with overlapping IP addresses), and each virtual network infrastructure operates as if it is the only virtual network running on the shared network infrastructure.

To make this function, we actually end up with each VM being assigned two IP addresses! The first of these is the IP address visible inside the VM, which we consider the IP address belonging to the cloud-owning tenant; technically, we will refer to this IP address space as the *customer address (CA)*. The second IP address is managed by Hyper-V in Windows Server 2012 and is used to allow network packets to pass over the physical network to other Hyper-V servers; technically, we will refer to this IP address space as the *provider address (PA)*. This approach results in a complete isolation between the IPs utilized by the tenants' virtual machines in the cloud and the physical networks' IP address scheme.

To review, each VM has two IP addresses:

Customer Address The CA is the IP address visible within the virtual machines' network. This address can be assigned by the customer, based on their existing infrastructure. The customer can then pass network traffic within the virtual machine as if it had not been moved to a cloud. Customers can potentially create a VPN from there on premise infrastructure to this cloud space, and simply extend the address space, similar to a stretched VLAN!

Provider Address This IP address, visible on the physical network, is assigned by the fabric administrator (datacenter administrator or hoster) and will be based on the physical network infrastructure. The PA is not presented to the virtual machines and is used exclusively on the physical network to transfer network traffic between Hyper-V and other devices participating in the network virtualization.

Network Virtualization Abstraction

With virtualization of memory, disks, and even CPU, no additional investment in hardware or infrastructure was really necessary. It's exciting that the same is now also true for Hyper-V Network Virtualization, which can be easily deployed into our existing environments.

Because you are now able to assign two IP addresses to each virtual machine, you are actually virtualizing the CA IP address by using the PA IP address when sending networking traffic between Hyper-V hosts. The greatest benefit is that for the physical network, nothing out of the ordinary is occurring, services continue to work untouched, business as usual.

As a bonus, Microsoft has enabled Window Server Hyper-V 2012 to support no less than two abstraction methods: Generic Routing Encapsulation (GRE) and IP Rewrite (NAT).

SYSTEM CENTER VIRTUAL MACHINE MANAGER (SCVMM) 2012 SP1

With the release of SCVMM 2012 SP1, Microsoft has extended the management of their network virtualization stack into the System Center 2012 suite. However in this initial release, only Generic Routing Encapsulation (GRE) is supported, along with PVLANs.

In the majority of environments, GRE should be used for network virtualization, because it provides the highest flexibility and performance. IP Rewrite (NAT) is primarily targeted to provide performance and compatibility in some current high-capacity datacenters but is almost unmanageable in a dynamic environment without any management tools.

NETWORK VIRTUALIZATION STACK

To better understand the isolation of the CAs and PAs, you need to visualize the concept, as shown in Figure 5.4.

FIGURE 5.4
Network
virtualization stack

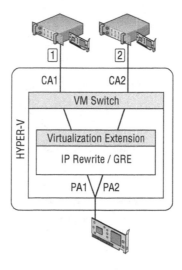

Start by first considering the relationship between the physical and virtual world, and how these are constructed. Let's begin with the virtual machine, which presents a virtual network interface to a virtual port on the virtual switch. The IP address associated with the virtual machine's virtual interface is considered its CA.

Within the virtual switch, packets are processed based on its logic and can be extended through the use of extensions to do much more, as introduced in Chapter 4. The Microsoft Network Virtualization (MS_NETWNV) technology shipped with Windows Server 2012 is in itself an extension module for the Hyper-V virtual switch.

Network interfaces physically installed to the host are bound to the virtual switch and defined as *external* interfaces. These can be trunked (teamed) or stand-alone. After the MS_NETWNV module is enabled on the port of the virtual switch that is connected to these external interfaces, our network virtualization feature is ready for configuration. Once enabled, a special "setting space" is then made available, which we can begin to utilize for storing to hold our new provider (or physical) IP addresses and other configuration details.

These provider addresses are then presented to the physical network through the external network interface. To ensure that network traffic can be routed to other hosts participating in network virtualization, they must be similarly configured, just like any other physical IP address.

Network Virtualization Concept

Now that you have an understanding of where the CAs and PAs exist in our virtual world, you can consider how this concept translates to passing data between virtual machines, especially when they might be hosted on different Hyper-V hosts, and thus need to traverse the physical network.

The simplest analogy is to first consider the CA network packets; these are messages that we place into "envelopes." The PA addresses are then considered the routing address that we place on these "envelopes" for correct delivery.

Let's consider three virtual machines that are hosted on two Hyper-V hosts enabled for network virtualization, and all belonging to the same customer (tenant), as shown in Figure 5.5.

FIGURE 5.5
Network
virtualization
tenant

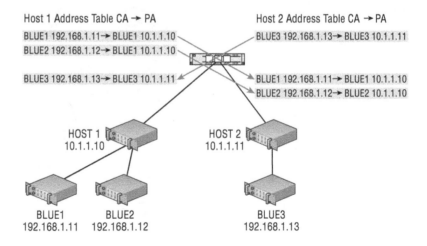

Host 1 Address Table CA → PA

BLUE1 192.168.1.11 → BLUE1 10.1.1.10
BLUE2 192.168.1.12 → BLUE1 10.1.1.10

BLUE3 192.168.1.13 → BLUE3 10.1.1.11

Host 2 Address Table CA → PA

BLUE3 192.168.1.13 → BLUE3 10.1.1.11

BLUE1 192.168.1.11 → BLUE1 10.1.1.10
BLUE2 192.168.1.12 → BLUE2 10.1.1.10

HOST 1
10.1.1.10

HOST 2
10.1.1.11

BLUE1   BLUE2
192.168.1.11   192.168.1.12

BLUE3
192.168.1.13

The first two virtual machines, called BLUE1 and BLUE2, have a local IP address of 192.168.1.11 and 192.168.1.12, respectively, and can communicate with each other as you would expect. BLUE3, which is hosted on HOST2, has a local IP address of 192.168.1.13 and is also capable of communicating with its peers on HOST1.

Unlike our previous conventional VLAN configuration method, these three VMs are utilizing our new network virtualization technology. Therefore, we can immediately consider the local IP addresses we just introduced as being the virtual machines' customer addresses (CAs).

This implies that the virtual machines hosted on the two Hyper-V hosts now need to rely on network virtualization to ensure that they can communicate as expected.

Imagine that data needs to be passed from BLUE1 to BLUE3. This data is handled by our virtual switch, which places the data into an envelope addressed to the host (PA) where BLUE3 is located. The switch marks the address to the attention of BLUE3 and then proceeds to send the data over the physical network to this host.

The receiving host (PA) checks the envelope for the "attention of" message in the address to determine the intended recipient. The host then continues to pass this data to the specified recipient, BLUE3.

Considering this packaging of data contained within the envelopes, we now have essentially a tunnel between the virtual machines on HOST1 and HOST2, with an address book to look up where these virtual machines are currently residing.

CUSTOMER NETWORKS/MULTI-TENANCY

By adding customers to our environment, we can easily extend the concept to address the multi-tenancy scenario.

Let's take our existing hosts and add a new customer to the environment called RED, who also will begin with three virtual machines. To keep the environment nicely balanced, we will place RED1 virtual machine with IP address 192.168.1.11 onto our HOST1, and place both RED2 (192.168.1.12) and RED3 (192.168.1.13) on HOST2, as illustrated in Figure 5.6.

FIGURE 5.6
Network
virtualization
multi-tenant

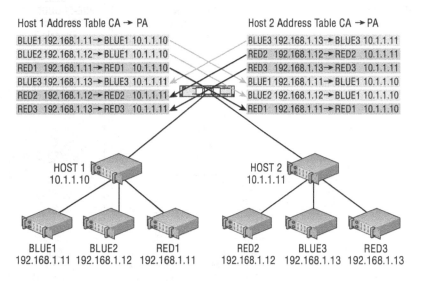

Before we proceed, the first thing to notice is that our new customer RED is employing the same IP addresses that customer BLUE is utilizing. If we do not take any measures, this will immediately result in IP conflicts on our virtual machines and therefore in unhappy customers. However, the Microsoft Network Virtualization feature has yet another interesting capability, which will prevent this impending disaster.

Because our customer (tenant) is the owner of its respective virtual machines deployed to our hosts, it is also quite normal that they may have more than one network (for example, Production and Preproduction), that consists of at least one virtual subnet (for example, DMZ and Core). To address this normal scenario, Microsoft Network Virtualization enables us to segregate these associated virtual subnets through the concept of Routing Domains. Essentially, a routing domain defines a simple relationship between each of the virtual subnets that a tenant may have defined, a domain per say. However, as a bonus, these are called Routing Domains, as the network virtualization stack actually enabled Layer 3 routing between these domains, automatically creating a virtual router! This router cannot be disabled, or even configured, but it is still quite useful for many scenarios. Additionally, here are some points to consider:

◆ Each of these customer networks forms an isolation boundary, enabling the virtual machines within that customer network to communicate with each other. Therefore, virtual subnets in the same customer network must not use overlapping IP address prefixes.

◆ Each customer network has a routing domain that identifies that network. The routing domain ID (RDID) is assigned by the datacenter administrator and stored as a globally unique ID (GUID). This RDID must be unique within a datacenter.

This approach enables customers (tenants) to bring their network topologies to the cloud. Figure 5.7 expands further on our scenario to illustrate BLUE with its Production and Preproduction networks, along with RED's network.

FIGURE 5.7
Virtualized
customer networks
and subnets

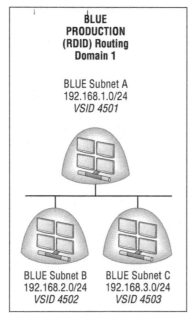

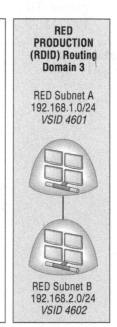

BLUE PRODUCTION (RDID) Routing Domain 1	BLUE PRE-PRODUCTION (RDID) Routing Domain 2	RED PRODUCTION (RDID) Routing Domain 3
BLUE Subnet A 192.168.1.0/24 *VSID 4501*	RED Subnet D 192.168.1.0/24 *VSID 4504*	RED Subnet A 192.168.1.0/24 *VSID 4601*
BLUE Subnet B 192.168.2.0/24 *VSID 4502*	BLUE Subnet C 192.168.3.0/24 *VSID 4503*	RED Subnet E 192.168.2.0/24 *VSID 4505*	RED Subnet B 192.168.2.0/24 *VSID 4602*

As BLUE's Production and Preproduction networks are assigned to different customer networks (RDID), the contained virtual subnets are fully isolated from each other, and therefore IP addresses may overlap!

VIRTUAL SUBNETS

Identical to the concept of physical VLANs, the virtual subnet defines a Layer 3 IP subnet and a Layer 2 broadcast domain boundary and is identified with a unique virtual subnet ID (VSID). When a virtual machine broadcasts a packet, this broadcast is limited to the virtual machines that are attached to switch ports with the same VSID. Each VSID can be associated with a multicast address in the PA. All broadcast traffic for a VSID is sent on this multicast address.

In Figure 5.7, BLUE has three virtual subnets defined: one original subnet with ID 4501, along with two additional subnets assigned the VSID 4502 and 4503. Virtual machines located in BLUE Subnet 1 (4501) can have their packets routed or forwarded by the network virtualization module to virtual machines located in BLUE Subnet 2 (4502) and BLUE Subnet 3 (4503). This routing between the subnets located within the same customer network (RDID) is enabled by default and cannot be disabled. If you wish not to have routing between virtual subnets, you must configure the virtual subnets to a different customer network (RDID).

The routing between these networks is via a default gateway for each virtual subnet, which is transparently implemented by the network virtualization module. The module reserves the first usable IP address in the IP segment for the subnet as the gateway address, and the address must not be assigned to any virtual machines hosted in the virtual segment.

The network virtualization module will check incoming packets from the virtual machine's virtual network adapter and update the VSID of the incoming packet with the VSID of the destination, only if both VSIDs are within the same customer network (RDID). Packets that do not match this criterion will be dropped, ensuring isolation between customer networks.

VIRTUAL SUBNET IDENTIFIER

The virtual subnet identifier (VSID) is universally unique and may be in the range of 4096 to 16,777,214 ($2^{24}-2$).

A VSID of 0 is the default, and it tells the network virtualization module to ignore the traffic (bypass mode).

VSIDs 1–4095 are reserved to use as VLAN tags.

As a virtual subnet ID is applied to a virtual interface on a virtual machine, the VSID will migrate with the virtual machine, and therefore it needs to be assigned only once.

NETWORK VIRTUALIZATION MULTI-TENANCY CONCEPT

If we now take this additional information and update our six virtual machines' virtual interfaces and add their related virtual subnet IDs, we will achieve two objectives:

◆ Assigning a VSID to the virtual interface of the virtual machine will have a similar effect to placing the virtual machine into a virtual network (VLAN).

If we assign customer BLUE the virtual subnet ID of 4501, and customer RED the virtual subnet ID of 4601, and then apply these VSIDs to their respective virtual machines, we would in effect have moved the virtual machines into two different virtual network domains and no longer be experiencing IP conflicts!

♦ Combining our new VSID with the IP address of the virtual machine, and for uniqueness sake, the MAC address of the virtual interface, we now have more than enough details to place on the envelope's address to ensure that we deliver traffic not only to the correct IP address, but also the correct customer.

This essentially addresses a key part of our puzzle: how the virtual network module determines the "shipping addresses" (PAs) corresponding to BLUE and RED CAs.

In summary, you now have a greater understanding of the concepts implemented in the Microsoft Network Virtualization module:

♦ Each virtual machine CA is mapped to a physical host PA.

♦ Virtual machines send data packets in the CA space, and use envelopes when the destination is on a different host.

♦ The CA-PA mappings must contain enough detail to ensure that the envelope is addressed correctly to reach the correct customer and destination address.

ENVELOPES OF DATA

The next challenge is to consider how our envelope is put around the packet, and how the destination hosts can unwrap the packets and deliver to the BLUE and RED destination virtual machines correctly.

Earlier we commented on the point that Microsoft included two address translation mechanisms to implement network virtualization, namely packet encapsulation (GRE) and packet rewrite (NAT). These are the alternate technologies that implement our envelope analogy.

PACKET ENCAPSULATION

The primary IP virtualization mechanism is Generic Routing Encapsulation (GRE). In this implementation, the VM's packet is encapsulated by using CA IP addresses inside another packet using PA IP addresses, along with a copy of the VSID and the virtual machine's sending interface MAC address. This mode of operation is intended for the majority of deployments implementing network virtualization (illustrated in Figure 5.8).

Because of the inclusion of the VSID within the header, we can now identify the customer (tenant) owning the virtual machine on whose behalf data is being processed and not be concerned with any IP address overlap within the CA space.

As we consider this addressing scheme further, we can process all the traffic for our customers and their virtual machines located on our Hyper-V host with just one PA address per host, as we have enough data in the address to correctly identify us. This simplification of PA space usage results in a major boost to scalability by sharing the PA addresses for multiple virtual machines.

FIGURE 5.8
Sample GRE packet

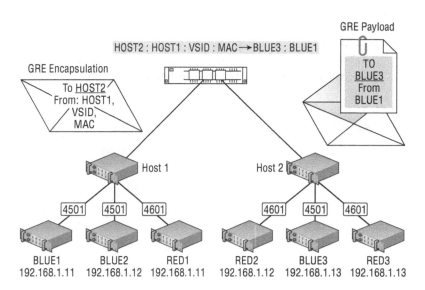

The VSID can also be utilized to potentially implement additional services—for example, per customer (tenant) policies, metering, traffic measurement, and shaping.

Packet encapsulation (GRE) currently has a drawback of no longer supporting the scalability benefits offered from NIC hardware offloads. This is because offloads operate on the packet header, which is now the PA address, and not the CA address. This is relevant for any VMs that require high performance throughput in the 10 Gb bandwidth area. Similarly, datacenter multipath routing ability is also reduced due to the switches utilizing packet headers of the PA when executing its hashing algorithms,completely disabling the switches ability to differenciate between destination VMs.

NETWORK VIRTUALIZATION GENERIC ROUTING PROTOCOL

The Network Virtualization Generic Routing Protocol (NVGRE) is, at the time of this writing, on its second edit as a draft proposal with the IETF. Additional information is available here:

    http://tools.ietf.org/html/draft-sridharan-virtualization-nvgre-01

It is cosponsored by organizations including Intel, Emulex, Broadcom, Arista Networks, Dell, HP, and Microsoft, ensuring that NVGRE will become a standard that quite likely will be embedded into switches, load balancers, firewalls, and routing products. It is even conceivable that in the future, devices such as monitoring and storage will become NVGRE aware, enabling multi-tenancy solutions. (Based on RFC 2784 and 2890)

At the time of this writing, F5 Networks and Cisco are among the first organization to officially announce support, for NVGRE in their BIG-IP and Nexus 1000v products.

PACKET REWRITE

With IP Rewrite, we rewrite the source and destination CA IP addresses in the packet with the appropriate PA addresses as packets leave the host. Similarly, when virtual subnet packets enter the destination host, the PAs are rewritten with appropriate CAs, as shown in Figure 5.9.

FIGURE 5.9

NAT sample packet

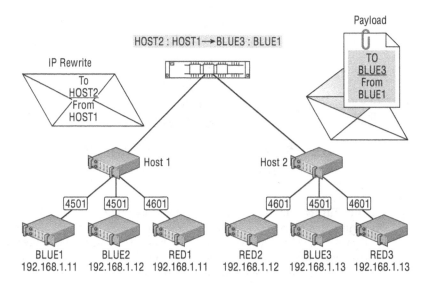

IP Rewrite requires a unique PA for each VM CA in order to isolate VMs from different customers using overlapping IP addresses. IP Rewrite is a NAT technology, therefore it requires a single PA IP for every virtual machine CA. This translates into a requirement for a large PA pool and an equally large lookup table.

The number of IP and MAC addresses that need to be learned by the network infrastructure as a result is substantial. For instance, if every host has an average of 40 VMs, the number of IP and MAC addresses that need to be learned by the network virtualization module for these addresses will be multiplied by the number of hosts participating in network virtualization.

Because the packet format remains unchanged (NAT), network hardware offload technologies such as Large Send Offload (LSO) and Virtual Machine Queue (VMQ), and multipath routing in the switches (for example, ECMP, or equal-cost multi-path routing) now work as expected. These offloads provide significant benefit for network-intensive scenarios in a 10 GbE environment.

Unlike the GRE approach, we are not including the VSID in the packets, removing any of the potential benefits of per tenant operations.

Network Virtualization at Work

Now that you are clear on the benefits and functionality of network virtualization, we can summarize this concept as the ability to move your VMs to the cloud without modifying the VM's network configuration and without worrying about what other systems floating in the clouds may share the same address.

Compared to the original network isolation approach implemented using VLANs, we now have a solution for more-dynamic environments. Tenants may continually change without the requirement to reconfigure the production network fabric every time a tenant is added, changed, or removed. By removing the typical workflow requesting the network engineers to modify the VLANs, we directly improve the overall efficiency of a cloud.

Because tenants can preserve IP addresses when moving to the cloud, those tenants can continue to offer services while keeping their consumers unaware that the VM hosting the service has moved to a new cloud. Previously, this was impossible because, by definition, if you move a VM from one subnet to a different subnet, its IP address must change, which causes a service interruption. Now this is accomplished with network virtualization, as the VM utilizes two IP addresses: the IP address relevant in the context of the datacenter (physical address) can be changed without needing to change the IP address in the VM (customer address). Therefore, the client communicating with our VM via the CA is unaware that the VM has physically moved to a different subnet.

Combined, this enables Microsoft's "Any Service, Any Server, Any Cloud" vision. VMs can now run and live-migrate anywhere in the datacenter without a service interruption— even across subnet boundaries.

Virtual machines are totally unaware that their IP address has been virtualized, with all communication occurring via the CA. Therefore, any supported operating system running within a Hyper-V can be a member of a virtual network. To summarize, the following are just some of the new benefits:

◆ Port ACL rules within the virtual switch isolate traffic.

◆ Network virtualization virtualizes VM IP addresses.

◆ Tenant VMs are unaware of address virtualization.

◆ CA IPs are tenant agnostic and can now overlap.

◆ CA IPs can be any combination of IPv4 or IPv6.

◆ Host (Management OS) traffic is *not* virtualized—only guest traffic.

PAs addresses are managed on the fabric by the administrator, and can be a combination of IPv4 or IPv6, as long as they remain unique on the physical network. The PAs can be abstracted in two methods:

◆ Packet encapsulation (GRE) shares the PA and embeds a virtual subnet ID into the header.

◆ Packet rewrite (NAT) utilizes unique PAs per virtual machine CA.

We have achieved the goal of "Bring Your Own Address" to the cloud.

TRYING NETWORK VIRTUALIZATION

Expanding on our previous examples, we can now invite another customer, GREEN, to join our cloud. This company currently has two systems that they wish to migrate from their environment: a database server called GREEN1 (192.168.1.11) and a web server called GREEN2 (192.168.1.12).

RE-CREATING THE LAB

If you are planning to re-create my basic lab scenario, I am using two Hyper-V hosts: HOST1 and HOST2, both of which are members of the same Active Directory domain. Each host has two network interfaces, which I name Physical Port1 and Physical Port2, respectively.

Utilizing Windows 2012 built-in teaming functions; I have bonded these two interfaces to create *Ethernet Team.*

Next, I added the Hyper-V role to the server, and selected my Ethernet Team to be used for my virtual switch physical external connection.

After the server had completed its required reboots, PowerShell reveals the following network adapter configuration:

```
Get-NetAdapter


Name            InterfaceDescription          ifIndex   Status   MacAddress
----            ----------------              -------   ------   ----------
Physical Port1  Broadcom NetXtreme Gigabit     12        Up       00-15-C5-F5-00-01
Physical Port2  Broadcom NetXtreme Gigabit #2  12        Up       00-15-C5-F5-00-02
Ethernet Team   Microsoft Ethernet Adaptor Mu..  17      Up       00-15-C5-F5-00-01
vEthernet (Mi.. Hyper-V Virtual Ethernet Adap..  26      Up       00-15-C5-F5-00-02
```

With the same configuration on both servers, I now have the basic configuration necessary to begin deploying virtual machines with network connectivity.

As we prepare our environment for our new customer, we make an executive decision to continue to keep the environment balanced, and place GREEN1 on HOST1 (172.16.1.11), and GREEN2 on HOST2 (172.16.1.12).

As a new customer, we also need to assign a VSID for GREEN's systems. This now provides us enough details to determine the address list for all our VMs, which is illustrated in Table 5.1 for IP Encapsulation mode, and in Table 5.2 for IP Rewrite mode.

TABLE 5.1: IP encapsulation table

VM NAME	HOST	VSID	MAC ADDRESS	PA IP	CA IP	GATEWAY
GREEN1	HOST1	4701	00-47-01-00-00-01	172.16.1.101	192.168.1.11	192.168.1.1
GREEN2	HOST2	4701	00-47-01-00-00-02	172.16.1.102	192.168.1.12	192.168.1.1
RED1	HOST1	4601	00-46-01-00-00-01	172.16.1.101	192.168.1.11	192.168.1.1
RED2	HOST2	4601	00-46-01-00-00-02	172.16.1.102	192.168.1.12	192.168.1.1
RED3	HOST2	4601	00-46-01-00-00-03	172.16.1.102	192.168.1.13	192.168.1.1
BLUE1	HOST1	4501	00-45-01-00-00-01	172.16.1.101	192.168.1.11	192.168.1.1
BLUE2	HOST1	4501	00-45-01-00-00-02	172.16.1.101	192.168.1.12	192.168.1.1
BLUE3	HOST2	4501	00-45-01-00-00-03	172.16.1.102	192.168.1.13	192.168.1.1

TABLE 5.2: IP rewrite table

VM NAME	HOST	VSID	MAC ADDRESS	PA IP	CA IP	GATEWAY
GREEN1	HOST1	4701	00-47-01-00-00-01	172.16.1.121	192.168.1.11	192.168.1.1
GREEN2	HOST2	4701	00-47-01-00-00-02	172.16.1.122	192.168.1.12	192.168.1.1
RED1	HOST1	4601	00-46-01-00-00-01	172.16.1.111	192.168.1.11	192.168.1.1
RED2	HOST2	4601	00-46-01-00-00-02	172.16.1.112	192.168.1.12	192.168.1.1
RED3	HOST2	4601	00-46-01-00-00-03	172.16.1.113	192.168.1.13	192.168.1.1
BLUE1	HOST1	4501	00-45-01-00-00-01	172.16.1.101	192.168.1.11	192.168.1.1
BLUE2	HOST1	4501	00-45-01-00-00-02	172.16.1.101	192.168.1.12	192.168.1.1
BLUE3	HOST2	4501	00-45-01-00-00-03	172.16.1.102	192.168.1.13	192.168.1.1

With this information, we can now create a policy (if we recall our envelope analogy, we can consider the policy as an address book) consisting of GREEN's virtual subnet that is used as the CAs, so we can assign their VSID and PAs. We will also need to define the policy for both BLUE and RED.

LAB VIRTUAL MACHINE MAC ASSIGNMENTS

If you are following along in your lab, you should now have your test virtual machines deployed. We can leverage PowerShell to simplify the configuration of our MAC addresses. The following sample assumes you are using the same naming convention; please ensure that you adjust for your lab if necessary:

```
Stop-VM Blue*
(1..3) | % { Set-VMNetworkAdapter -StaticMacAddress "00450100000$_" -VMName blue$_}
(1..3) | % { Get-VMNetworkAdapter -VMName blue$_ }
Start-VM Blue*


Stop-VM Red*
(1..3) | % { Set-VMNetworkAdapter -StaticMacAddress "00460100000$_" -VMName Red$_ }
(1..3) | % { Get-VMNetworkAdapter -VMName red$_ }
Start-VM Red*


Stop-VM Green*
(1..2) | % { Set-VMNetworkAdapter -StaticMacAddress "00470100000$_" -VMName Green$_}
(1..2) | % { Get-VMNetworkAdapter -VMName green$_ }
Start-VM Green*


Get-VMNetworkAdapter -VMName blue*, red*, green* | sort MacAddress
```

It's also polite to point out that if you power up all the virtual machines introduced so far in your lab, you are going to experience IP conflicts. After we configure our virtual machines to assign their respective VSIDs, this issue will be resolved.

These policies will be applied to HOST1 and HOST2, so the Microsoft Virtual Network module will know where to locate services.

Now, let's consider our envelope delivery analogy we visualized a little earlier. This time, we will replace it with a real network virtualization flow, and consider GREEN's web server requesting some data from its associated database server by using encapsulation (GRE):

1. GREEN2, our web server, requests data from the database server, GREEN1, which is physically located on a different host, so we must virtualize the request in order to deliver it.

2. The network virtualization module on HOST2 (172.16.1.102) will look up the policy and determine that it must create a packet with the destination of 172.16.1.101 (PA of GREEN1) and include the VSID of 4701.

3. After the packet is received by 172.16.1.101 (HOST1), the network virtualization module will decapsulate the packet and keep a record of the VSID.

4. The network virtualization module then looks up the policy on the local computer and recognizes that the VSID is for GREEN, finally passing the decapsulated packet up into the VM with the original CA information.

Now, let's do this same example again, but this time we will use IP Rewrite (NAT):

1. GREEN2, our web server, requests data from the database server, GREEN1, which is physically located on a different host, so we must virtualize the request in order to deliver it.

2. The network virtualization module on HOST2 (172.16.2.4) will look up the policy and determine that it must create a packet with the destination of 172.16.1.4 (PA of GREEN1) and replace the CA source (192.168.1.12) and destination (192.168.1.11) addresses with their PA equivalent source (172.16.2.4) and destination (172.16.1.4).

3. After the packet is received by 172.16.1.4 (HOST1), the network virtualization module will again look up the policy and match the source and destination IPs, which it then replaces with their CA equivalents, and will keep a record of the destination IP (PA).

4. The network virtualization module then looks up the policy for the destination IP (PA) and recognizes that the target VM is GREEN1 passing the packet up into the VM.

Enabling MS_NETWNV

We should now be ready to enable the Microsoft Windows Hyper-V Network Virtualization filter on our Hyper-V hosts.

Before we begin this process, we should take a look on our hosts to see both the network interfaces and network filters that are available and whether these are enabled or disabled, per network interface. The simplest way to get this information is by using PowerShell:

```
Get-NetAdapterBinding
```

The resulting table can be pretty long, so a more focused query is called for—just listing the MS_NETWNV filter, which is the short name for the Microsoft Network Virtualization filter extension:

```
Get-NetAdapterBinding -ComponentID "ms_netwnv"
```

Name	DisplayName	ComponentID	Enabled
Physical Port1	Windows Network Virtualization Filter	ms_netwmv	False
Physical Port2	Windows Network Virtualization Filter	ms_netwmv	False
Ethernet Team	Windows Network Virtualization Filter	ms_netwmv	False
vEthernet (Mi.	Windows Network Virtualization Filter	ms_netwmv	False

By default, the Network Virtualization filter is disabled. The Network Virtualization filter is required to be enabled on the physical adapter or LBFO team to which our Hyper-V virtual switch is bound. We can enable the relevant interface change quite simply by using PowerShell and passing on the name of the virtual switch we will be utilizing:

```
$vSwitch = Get-VMSwitch `
-Name "Microsoft Network Adapter Multiplexor Driver - Virtual Switch" `
Enable-NetAdapterBinding -InterfaceDescription `
$vSwitch.NetAdapterInterfaceDescription -ComponentID "ms_netwnv"
```

The first of these two commands creates a reference to our named Hyper-V virtual switch, which we will be using with our virtual machines. We then use the referenced virtual switch to identify the Interface Description of the adapter that it is bound to. This adapter can be either a physical interface, or a LBFO team connected to our physical fabric. This adapter is then enabled for the Microsoft Network Virtualization filter.

Now, if you issue the `Get-NetAdapterBinding` command again, you should see that the filter has been enabled on our selected virtual switch. Remember, we need to enable this on all hosts that will participate in network virtualization.

```
Get-NetAdapterBinding –ComponentID "ms_netwnv"
```

```
Name            DisplayName                               ComponentID   Enabled
----            -----------                               -----------   -------
Physical Port1  Windows Network Virtualization Filter     ms_netwmv     False
Physical Port2  Windows Network Virtualization Filter     ms_netwmv     False
Ethernet Team   Windows Network Virtualization Filter     ms_netwmv     False
vEthernet (Mi.  Windows Network Virtualization Filter     ms_netwmv     True
```

Note: we cannot see this filter from the Hyper-V Manager GUI.

SETTING THE VIRTUAL SUBNET IDENTIFIER

Nothing magical has happened yet, but with the engine primed, we can begin to configure the virtual ports on our virtual switch. The settings defined earlier in Table 5.1 or Table 5.2 present a scenario view of the IP addresses and VSID we will apply to the virtual interfaces of our customer's virtual machines along with the PA we will use depending on our preferred implementation approach of either encapsulation or rewrite.

Currently, after deploying all eight of our virtual machines, we should be experiencing the dreaded IP conflict issues. This conflict arises because all our machines have the default VSID set to zero, which indicates that no virtualization or isolation is currently active.

One of the improved features of the integration components (ICs) is passing richer guest information to the Windows Server Hyper-V host (through the functionality of Key Value Pairs, or KVPs, which are covered in Chapter 3, "Managing Virtual Machines"). We can use PowerShell to query our Hyper-V host to present the information returned by the guest virtual machine. A useful example of this feature is exposing the current guest VM IP address. Using the command `Get-VMNetworkAdapter | Format-List`, we can retrieve lots of additional detail:

```
# Present the Network Adapter details for VM BLUE1
Get-VMNetworkAdapter -VMName BLUE2 | FL
```

```
Name            : Network Adapter
IsLegacy        : False
IsManagementOs  : False
ComputerName    : HOST1
VMName          : BLUE2
VMId            : b0192973-ff36-40af-a80c-27026c0b1f93
SwitchName      : Network Virtualization Switch
```

```
SwitchId                   : 858aaac1-5f46-450c-a90f-5509545f5ac6
Connected                  : True
PoolName                   :
MacAddress                 : 004501000002
DynamicMacAddressEnabled   : False
MacAddressSpoofing         : Off
AllowTeaming               : Off
RouterGuard                : Off
DhcpGuard                  : Off
PortMirroringMode          : None
IeeePriorityTag            : Off
VirtualSubnetId            : 0
BandwidthPercentage        : 0%
MandatoryFeatureId         : {}
MandatoryFeatureName       : {}
Status                     : {Ok}
IPAddresses                : {192.168.1.12, fe80::9d6c:c11d:7b4e:7b58}
```

Among the details reported back, we can see the guest's IP address, along with the static MAC address we assigned to the virtual machines (as per our tables). Also included in this list of settings is the option VirtualSubnetID, which we know is utilized during encapsulation. If this is set to 0, as is currently the case, the Network Virtualization filter we just enabled will ignore this traffic.

Using this published information, we can use PowerShell to quickly report on the key information we are interested in for our virtual machines that are located on the current host. This includes the VM name, interface name, MAC, VSID, and current IP addresses:

```
Get-VMNetworkAdapter -VMName blue*, red*, green* | Select VMName, Name, `
MacAddress, VirtualSubnetID, IPAddresses | ft -AutoSize
```

VMName	Name	MACAddress	VirtualSubnetID	IPAddresses
Blue1	Network Adaptor	0045010001	0	{192.168.1.11,...
Blue2	Network Adaptor	0045010002	0	{192.168.1.12,...
Red1	Network Adaptor	0046010001	0	{192.168.1.11,...
Green1	Network Adaptor	0047010001	0	{192.168.1.11,...

Our first objective is to have our virtual machines configured to three virtual subnets within our cloud. Enabling VSID settings on each virtual machine's virtual interfaces will put this into effect.

The simplest process to set the VirtualSubnetID is to get a reference to each of our virtual machine virtual interfaces with the Get-VMNetworkAdapter command, and pipe the resultant object to the Set-VMNetworkAdapter command, where we can then assign the new VSID. As per our table, we will assign the VSIDs as follows:

◆ BLUE—4501

◆ RED—4601

◆ GREEN—4701

```
Get-VMNetworkAdapter BLUE*  | Set-VMNetworkAdapter -VirtualSubnetId 4501
Get-VMNetworkAdapter RED*   | Set-VMNetworkAdapter -VirtualSubnetId 4601
Get-VMNetworkAdapter GREEN* | Set-VMNetworkAdapter -VirtualSubnetId 4701
```

In some scenarios, your virtual machine may have more than one virtual interface. In that case, we can filter the interfaces that we need to apply the VSID to, using their MAC address. For example, this would work in our sample also:

```
# BLUE VMs have a MAC address starting with 00-45-01
Get-VMNetworkAdapter | where {$_.MACAddress -like "004501*"} | `
Set-VMNetworkAdapter -VirtualSubnetId 4501
# RED VMs have a MAC address starting with 00-46-01
Get-VMNetworkAdapter | where {$_.MACAddress -like "004601*"} | `
Set-VMNetworkAdapter -VirtualSubnetId 4601
# GREEN VMs have a MAC address starting with 00-47-01
Get-VMNetworkAdapter | where {$_.MACAddress -like "004701*"} | `
Set-VMNetworkAdapter -VirtualSubnetId 4701
```

Just to be complete, we should run our PowerShell command again to double check that the virtual interfaces are now configured with our new VSID as we desired:

```
Get-VMNetworkAdapter | Select VMName, Name, MACAddress, VirtualSubnetID, `
IPAddresses
```

VMName	Name	MACAddress	VirtualSubnetID	IPAddresses
Blue1	Network Adaptor	0045010001	4501	{192.168.1.11,...
Blue2	Network Adaptor	0045010002	4501	{192.168.1.12,...
Red1	Network Adaptor	0046010001	4601	{192.168.1.11,...
Green1	Network Adaptor	0047010001	4701	{192.168.1.11,...

At this point, our virtual machines should be isolated to their respective virtual subnets, and therefore we should not see any more IP conflict issues. If we bounce the network interface on the virtual machine, we should see the APIPA IP addresses clear and the assigned IP address now take effect. PowerShell makes this easy also:

```
# Disconnect all our BLUE VMs network from the Virtual Switch
Get-VMNetworkAdapter BLUE* | Disconnect-VMNetworkAdapter
# Reconnect all our BLUE VMs NIC's back to the Virtual Switch
Get-VMNetworkAdapter BLUE* | Connect-VMNetworkAdapter -SwitchName `
"Microsoft Network Adapter Multiplexor Driver - Virtual Switch"
```

Back in our virtual machines, we can run some tests to validate that our VSIDs are functioning. As HOST1 still is home to both BLUE1, RED1, and GREEN1, we should see that they have all stopped complaining of IP conflicts. In addition, HOST1 also is home to the virtual machine BLUE2, which if we try to ping from BLUE1, will reply just as expected.

If we attempt to ping BLUE3 from either BLUE1 or BLUE2, RED2 from RED1, or GREEN2 from GREEN1, or vice versa, of course, these will all fail to reply. Additionally, if we were to migrate BLUE2 to HOST2, the reply from BLUE1 would stop, but the reply from BLUE3 would now function.

Why? Because we now have network virtualization enabled but have not yet addressed the physical network to pass traffic between hosts.

Setting the Provider Address on Our Hosts

We can now begin configuring the PA space on our Hyper-V host.

The provider address must be a routable address between the Hyper-V hosts within our datacenter(s). The IP addresses we utilize for the communications between our hosts can be an address from your existing IP ranges, which are already configured. If you prefer, you can use a dedicated IP range for this task and even elect to utilize a special VLAN for this traffic. Ultimately, the decision will be influenced by your business requirements—for example, if you are going to implement the solution using IP Rewrite, you will need a large pool of IP addresses for the PA space, while GRE requires only a single IP address in the PA space per Hyper-V host.

Because my lab is not very large, I am going to use a specified VLAN and an existing IP range that I configured for my hosts. Referring back to Table 5.1 for GRE encapsulation, we are defining that the PA address of 172.16.1.101 should be assigned to our server "HOST1" (currently also assigned to management IP 172.16.1.11).

While it is not mandatory, to simplify troubleshooting efforts, I strongly recommend that you choose not to use the existing management IP address as your PA address also. Additionally, the IP address(es) you designate on your host for the PA space will not be ping-able locally, but must be reachable from the rest of your hosts.

Previously, we enabled the Network Virtualization filter against the Ethernet adapter (physical or LBFO), which is connected to our fabric. We will be assigning our provider addresses to this same interface. PowerShell again makes the process quite painless, this time creating a reference to our adapter and using this to simplify the assignment of our provider addresses:

```
# Create a reference to our Virtual Switch with network virtualization enabled
$vSwitch = Get-VMSwitch -Name `
"Microsoft Network Adapter Multiplexor Driver - Virtual Switch"
$paAdaptor = Get-NetAdapter -InterfaceDescription `
$vSwitch.NetAdapterInterfaceDescription


# Next, assign a Provider Address to the external network interface
New-NetVirtualizationProviderAddress -InterfaceIndex $paAdaptor.InterfaceIndex `
-ProviderAddress 172.16.1.101 -PrefixLength 24 -VlanID 10
```

Assuming you have not skipped any of the steps so far, our new provider address will now be assigned to the relevant external interface. Of course, if you did skip the step of enabling the Microsoft Network Virtualization filter on your switch, or you enabled the filter on the wrong interface, the command will fail with a general error message.

To check that the new address is active (assuming you have used an IP address from the existing routable subnet you have defined on your Hyper-V servers, as I have in this lab), then from HOST2 you should be able to successfully ping the new PA on HOST1, confirming that the link is functional.

Note that executing the ipconfig.exe utility on HOST1 will not report back the new PA address we have assigned to the host. You need to be careful as you proceed, because any IT engineer working on the host may not be aware of the additional IPs you have enabled and this could start to create a network nightmare. The correct method of checking what provider addresses have been defined on a host is by issuing the following command:

```
Get-NetVirtualizationProviderAddress
```

```
ProviderAddress  : 172.16.1.101
InterfaceIndex   : 18
VlanID           : 10
AddressState     : Preferred
```

As with the previous step of actually enabling the MS_NETNV filter, don't forget to repeat this exercise on the other hosts participating in the network virtualization—for example, HOST2, which is based on Table 5.1 (GRE encapsulation), should be assigned the PA of 172.16.1.102.

Just to stress an earlier point, when you being to validate that your new PA addresses have been correctly assigned, you will quickly learn that these addresses will not reply when pinged from the same host to which they have been assigned. PA addresses, however should reply to pings when tested from other hosts participating in the PA space (for example, HOST1 PA addresses will not reply when pinged from HOST but will should reply when pinged from HOST2).

If your preference is to use IP Rewrite, the process is still the same. However, you will need to repeat `New-NetVirtualizationProviderAddress` for each new provider IP you need to assign to the Hyper-V host, similar to Table 5.2 (NAT). As IP Rewrite is a NAT implementation, you will in essence be assigning a PA address for every virtual machine on the host that must participate in the network virtualization. This will quickly grow to a large number of addresses. Therefore, utilizing a dedicated IP subnet of suitable capacity for the number of virtual machines you plan to host would be an advised approach.

In Table 5.2, I am creating a CA to PA mapping using similar addresses to help create the mapping in the lab. However, in practice you will likely use sequential addresses from a larger pool. Managing the CA / PA mappings is best suited to a tool or utility desiged for the task, for which I would normally suggest Microsoft Virtual Machine Manager. However IP Rewrite functionality is not supported in the current version, which at the time of writing is 2012 SP1.

If you need to check or change the provided address assigned to a host, you can utilize the additional PowerShell commands `Get-NetVirtualizationProviderAddress` and `Set-NetVirtualizationProviderAddress`, respectively.To revoke the address, you can use`Remove-NetVirtualizationProviderAddress`.

DEFINING THE CUSTOMER NETWORK IDENTIFIER

The customer network identifier is defined as a globally unique ID (GUID) for each network that our customers (tenants) have in our cloud. Each VSID will contain one or more customer network identifiers. We will use PowerShell to first generate a new GUID for each of our customers, BLUE, GREEN, and RED:

```
# Format the GUID string properly
$blueGUID  = "{" + [string][system.guid]::newguid() + "}"
$redGUID   = "{" + [string][system.guid]::newguid() + "}"
$greenGUID = "{" + [string][system.guid]::newguid() + "}"
```

In order for the Network Virtualization filter to function correctly for each of our customer networks, we do need to inform the filter of the IP address range that the customer will be using. This will also enable the filter to create the virtual gateway address, which it presents to each of the customer networks (RDID) hosted within the customer's virtual subnet (VSID).

We can define the virtual subnets and their respective CA addresses, which are associated with each of our customer networks, by using the command New-NetVirtualizationCustomer Route:

```
# Associate the BLUE Visual Subnet and CA space with BLUE Production


New-NetVirtualizationCustomerRoute -RoutingDomainID $blueGUID -VirtualSubnetID `
4501 -DestinationPrefix "192.168.1.0/24" -NextHop 0.0.0.0


# Associate the RED Visual Subnet and CA space with RED network


New-NetVirtualizationCustomerRoute -RoutingDomainID $redGUID -VirtualSubnetID `
4601 -DestinationPrefix "192.168.1.0/24" -NextHop 0.0.0.0


# Associate the GREEN Visual Subnet and CA space with GREEN network


New-NetVirtualizationCustomerRoute -RoutingDomainID $greenGUID -VirtualSubnetID `
4701 -DestinationPrefix "192.168.1.0/24" -NextHop 0.0.0.0
```

Again, we must remember to tell the network virtualization module on all the other Hyper-V hosts that are participating in the virtual network about this customer network relationship.

Be careful, though, and do not generate a new GUID for each customer network on every host! If you do, the customers on HOST1 will technically be different from the customers on HOST2, and nothing will appear to work as expected. You have been cautioned!

So, how do you deal with this? PowerShell remoting, of course! The following sample creates a remote session to HOST2. Then we can invoke commands on HOST2, passing over our GUIDs so they are available for us to reference on HOST2:

```
$remote = New-PSSession host2.demo.local
Invoke-Command -Session $remote -ArgumentList $blueGUID, $redGUID, $greenGUID {


    Param($blueGUID, $redGUID, $greenGUID)


    # Associate the BLUE Visual Subnet and CA space with BLUE Production


    New-NetVirtualizationCustomerRoute -RoutingDomainID $blueGUID -VirtualSubnetID `
4501 -DestinationPrefix "192.168.1.0/24" -NextHop 0.0.0.0


    # Associate the RED Visual Subnet and CA space with RED network
```

```
    New-NetVirtualizationCustomerRoute -RoutingDomainID $redGUID -VirtualSubnetID `
4601 -DestinationPrefix "192.168.1.0/24" -NextHop 0.0.0.0


    # Associate the GREEN Visual Subnet and CA space with GREEN network


    New-NetVirtualizationCustomerRoute -RoutingDomainID $greenGUID `
-VirtualSubnetID 4701 -DestinationPrefix "192.168.1.0/24" -NextHop 0.0.0.0


}
```

Of course, if PowerShell remoting is not for you, you can display the GUID that has been created by simply typing the variable name. It will echo its content to the screen, which you can copy and paste to the second host, where you can define the variable from the text string:

```
# On the host where we created the GUID, we can display this by
# just echoing the content of the variable
PS C:\> $redGUID
{01d43d1e-9ec8-4f7b-b7d4-100e1a2f0601}


## On the following hosts, we can use this string to set the string
PS C:\> $redGUID = "{01d43d1e-9ec8-4f7b-b7d4-100e1a2f0601}"
```

DEFINING THE LOOKUP DOMAIN (GRE)

Earlier, we referred to the lookup domain as the address book for our envelopes. We have finally reached the point in the configuration to publish this list. We must take care when we define this list to ensure that the data we are providing to the network virtualization module is accurate, or it will fail to correctly process the packet in the PA space. Think of this as being similar to our analogy of envelopes and addresses, an incorrect address will result in a failed delivery.

Regardless of whether our implementation method has been set to GRE or NAT, the procedure to define this lookup table is almost identical. The only main difference is the translation method we inform the network virtualization module to implement.

Table 5.1 defined the current lookup domain that is accurate for our GRE implementation, based on the current location of our virtual machines. I will use this as the reference to define the lookup domain. The following PowerShell commands add the relevant lookup entries:

```
# Virtual Machines on Host1
New-NetVirtualizationLookupRecord -VMName Blue1  -VirtualSubnetID 4501 `
-CustomerAddress 192.168.1.11 -ProviderAddress 172.16.1.101 -MACAddress `
004501000001 -Rule TranslationMethodEncap -CustomerID $blueGUID


New-NetVirtualizationLookupRecord -VMName Blue2  -VirtualSubnetID 4501 `
-CustomerAddress 192.168.1.12 -ProviderAddress 172.16.1.101 -MACAddress `
004501000002 -Rule TranslationMethodEncap -CustomerID $blueGUID
```

```
New-NetVirtualizationLookupRecord -VMName Red1   -VirtualSubnetID 4601 `
-CustomerAddress 192.168.1.11 -ProviderAddress 172.16.1.101 -MACAddress `
004601000001 -Rule TranslationMethodEncap -CustomerID $redGUID


New-NetVirtualizationLookupRecord -VMName Green1 -VirtualSubnetID 4701 `
-CustomerAddress 192.168.1.11 -ProviderAddress 172.16.1.101 -MACAddress `
004701000001 -Rule TranslationMethodEncap -CustomerID $greenGUID


# Virtual Machines on Host2
New-NetVirtualizationLookupRecord -VMName Blue3  -VirtualSubnetID 4501 `
-CustomerAddress 192.168.1.13 -ProviderAddress 172.16.1.102 -MACAddress `
004501000003 -Rule TranslationMethodEncap -CustomerID $blueGUID


New-NetVirtualizationLookupRecord -VMName Red2   -VirtualSubnetID 4601 `
-CustomerAddress 192.168.1.12 -ProviderAddress 172.16.1.102 -MACAddress `
004601000002 -Rule TranslationMethodEncap -CustomerID $redGUID


New-NetVirtualizationLookupRecord -VMName Red3   -VirtualSubnetID 4601 `
-CustomerAddress 192.168.1.13 -ProviderAddress 172.16.1.102 -MACAddress `
004601000003 -Rule TranslationMethodEncap -CustomerID $redGUID


New-NetVirtualizationLookupRecord -VMName Green2 -VirtualSubnetID 4701 `
-CustomerAddress 192.168.1.12 -ProviderAddress 172.16.1.102 -MACAddress `
004701000002 -Rule TranslationMethodEncap -CustomerID $greenGUID
```

Again, we must remember to educate the network virtualization module on all the other Hyper-V hosts that are participating in the virtual network. For simplicity, the table will be the same command list on each of the hosts. However, if you want to be optimized, you need to include lookup only for virtual machines that are not hosted on the current host.

Recall the caution from earlier regarding our GUIDs, you must be careful not to generate a new GUID for each customer network on every host, and ensure that you use either the remoting trick, or the layman's copy/paste process to ensure that we don't introduce rogue GUIDs!

Congratulations! You should now have your virtual network online! I would like to point out, that during editing of this chapter section, we encountered issues that hampered reaching a successful test of network virtualization in the technical editor's lab. Only later did we realize that we have previously deployed SCVMM 2012 SP1 agents to our Hyper-V hosts for a different testing scenario, which were now kind enough to sneak in while we were not watching and change our CA, PA, and Lookup configurations. So please save yourself some headache and be sure that if you do have your SCVMM 2012 SP1 agents deployed to your lab, that you stop them from running!

DEFINING THE LOOKUP DOMAIN (IP REWRITE)

Repeating the process we just completed in the previous section, we will now re-create the lookup table for our address book, based on the NAT implementation of virtualization, IP Rewrite. The process itself is almost identical, except we will be using a dedicated provider address for each customer address we map.

This, of course, mandates that we must first define a provider address on the relevant host's external interface for each virtual machine to which that host will be a parent. After these are implemented, we can then safely proceed with publishing the lookup table entries.

Table 5.2 defined the current lookup domain, which is accurate for our IP Rewrite implementation, based on the current location of our virtual machines. I will use this as the reference to define the lookup domain. We will start by adding the provider address to our Hyper-V hosts.

On HOST1, this assigns the provider addresses that we have nominated for each of the four virtual machines:

```
$vSwitch = Get-VMSwitch -Name `
"Microsoft Network Adapter Multiplexor Driver - Virtual Switch" `
$paAdaptor = Get-NetAdapter -InterfaceDescription $vSwitch `
.NetAdapterInterfaceDescription


New-NetVirtualizationProviderAddress -InterfaceIndex $paAdaptor.InterfaceIndex `
-ProviderAddress 172.16.1.101 -PrefixLength 24 -VlanID 10 `


New-NetVirtualizationProviderAddress -InterfaceIndex $paAdaptor.InterfaceIndex `
-ProviderAddress 172.16.1.102 -PrefixLength 24 -VlanID 10 `


New-NetVirtualizationProviderAddress -InterfaceIndex $paAdaptor.InterfaceIndex `
-ProviderAddress 172.16.1.111 -PrefixLength 24 -VlanID 10 `


New-NetVirtualizationProviderAddress -InterfaceIndex $paAdaptor.InterfaceIndex `
-ProviderAddress 172.16.1.121 -PrefixLength 24 -VlanID 10 `
```

And on HOST2, a similar set of commands will assign the provider addresses for the remaining four virtual machines:

```
$vSwitch = Get-VMSwitch -Name `
"Microsoft Network Adapter Multiplexor Driver - Virtual Switch" `
$paAdaptor = Get-NetAdapter -InterfaceDescription $vSwitch `
.NetAdapterInterfaceDescription


New-NetVirtualizationProviderAddress -InterfaceIndex $paAdaptor.InterfaceIndex `
-ProviderAddress 172.16.1.103 -PrefixLength 24 -VlanID 10


New-NetVirtualizationProviderAddress -InterfaceIndex $paAdaptor.InterfaceIndex `
-ProviderAddress 172.16.1.112 -PrefixLength 24 -VlanID 10
```

```
New-NetVirtualizationProviderAddress -InterfaceIndex $paAdaptor.InterfaceIndex `
-ProviderAddress 172.16.1.113 -PrefixLength 24 -VlanID 10

New-NetVirtualizationProviderAddress -InterfaceIndex $paAdaptor.InterfaceIndex `
-ProviderAddress 172.16.1.122 -PrefixLength 24 -VlanID 10
```

With our provider addresses in place, we can now proceed to define the lookup table. As in the previous section, we will define the same lookup table on both of our hosts. I am going to continue to use the same customer ID GUIDs, so be sure not to generate new ones!

```
# Virtual Machines on Host1
New-NetVirtualizationLookupRecord -VMName Blue1  -VirtualSubnetID 4501 `
-CustomerAddress 192.168.1.11 -ProviderAddress 172.16.1.101 -MACAddress `
004501000001 -Rule TranslationMethodNat -CustomerID $blueGUID

New-NetVirtualizationLookupRecord -VMName Blue2  -VirtualSubnetID 4501 `
-CustomerAddress 192.168.1.12 -ProviderAddress 172.16.1.102 -MACAddress `
004501000002 -Rule TranslationMethodNat -CustomerID $blueGUID

New-NetVirtualizationLookupRecord -VMName Red1   -VirtualSubnetID 4601 `
-CustomerAddress 192.168.1.11 -ProviderAddress 172.16.1.111 -MACAddress `
004601000001 -Rule TranslationMethodNat -CustomerID $redGUID

New-NetVirtualizationLookupRecord -VMName Green1 -VirtualSubnetID 4701 `
-CustomerAddress 192.168.1.11 -ProviderAddress 172.16.1.121 -MACAddress `
004701000001 -Rule TranslationMethodNat -CustomerID $greenGUID

# Virtual Machines on Host2
New-NetVirtualizationLookupRecord -VMName Blue3  -VirtualSubnetID 4501 `
-CustomerAddress 192.168.1.13 -ProviderAddress 172.16.1.103 -MACAddress `
004501000003 -Rule TranslationMethodNat -CustomerID $blueGUID

New-NetVirtualizationLookupRecord -VMName Red2   -VirtualSubnetID 4601 `
-CustomerAddress 192.168.1.12 -ProviderAddress 172.16.1.112 -MACAddress `
004601000002 -Rule TranslationMethodNat -CustomerID $redGUID

New-NetVirtualizationLookupRecord -VMName Red3   -VirtualSubnetID 4601 `
-CustomerAddress 192.168.1.13 -ProviderAddress 172.16.1.113 -MACAddress `
004601000003 -Rule TranslationMethodNat -CustomerID $redGUID

New-NetVirtualizationLookupRecord -VMName Green2 -VirtualSubnetID 4701 `
-CustomerAddress 192.168.1.12 -ProviderAddress 172.16.1.122 -MACAddress `
004701000002 -Rule TranslationMethodNat -CustomerID $greenGUID
```

Looking closer at the commands we just used to define the lookup table, there are only two differences from the same command set we used while defining the GRE table. The first of these should by now be quite obvious: -ProviderAddress this time is using a unique address for each -CustomerAddress, creating our 1:1 NAT relationship, or the CA address that will be rewritten with the PA address.

The second change is a little more trivial: the -Rule we are using for the Lookup process, which now reads as TranslationMethodNAT, instructs the network virtualization driver that we are utilizing IP Rewrite functionality. Referring to the previous section, the rule that we were using was TranslationMethodEncap to identify that we are enabling GRE (encapsulation) for this rule.

VERIFYING NETWORK VIRTUALIZATION

We have successfully configured our network virtualization and demonstrated the power of this fantastic new technology with our BLUE, RED, and GREEN tenants/customers. Each of these vendors can now successfully connect with other virtual machines owned by the customer, regardless of which host it currently resides on, thanks to the lookup records we created (our address book).

However, one thing we must consider for a moment is that throughout all the demonstrations we have so far completed, none of the virtual machines has moved to alternate hosts. We know that in the real world, this will never be the case, and we can expect lots of movement.

Just as in real life, when we move to a new house, we must inform our friends so they can update their address books and inform the post office so it can be sure to route our messages appropriately. With network virtualization, this scenario stands true also.

Each time we move a virtual machine from one host to another, we will need to update the lookup tables with the changes that have just occurred, removing the old entry and depositing a new address record on each host to represent the change.

We can use PowerShell to view the lookup domain as it's currently defined on the active host:

```
Get-NetVirtualizationLookupRecord | select VMName, CustomerAddress, CustomerID, `
macaddress, Provideraddress, rule
```

As an example, let's assume that virtual machine RED2 is moved from HOST2 to HOST1. What we will immediately experience is that this virtual machine will have issues connecting back to RED3, which is still on HOST2. This is due to the lookup domain no longer being current, so we must manually adjust for this change, to get virtualization working again.

To fix this, on each host we will need to remove the old lookup record for this virtual machine and replace it with a new current record. In this example, as listed in Table 5.3, the VM is now on HOST1. To use its provider address 172.16.1.101 for GRE, use the following:

```
# RED2
Remove-NetVirtualizationLookupRecord -CustomerAddress 192.168.1.12 -VMName RED2


New-NetVirtualizationLookupRecord -VMName Green2 -VirtualSubnetID 4701 `
-CustomerAddress 192.168.1.12 -ProviderAddress 172.16.1.122 -MACAddress `
004701000002 -Rule TranslationMethodNat -CustomerID $greenGUID
```

TABLE 5.3: IP encapsulation table update

VM NAME	HOST	VSID	MAC ADDRESS	PA IP	CA IP	GATEWAY
GREEN1	HOST1	4701	00-47-01-00-00-01	172.16.1.101	192.168.1.11	192.168.1.1
GREEN2	HOST2	4701	00-47-01-00-00-02	172.16.1.102	192.168.1.12	192.168.1.1
RED1	HOST1	4601	00-46-01-00-00-01	172.16.1.101	192.168.1.11	192.168.1.1
RED2	HOST1	4601	00-46-01-00-00-02	172.16.1.101	192.168.1.12	192.168.1.1
RED3	HOST2	4601	00-46-01-00-00-03	172.16.1.102	192.168.1.13	192.168.1.1
BLUE1	HOST1	4501	00-45-01-00-00-01	172.16.1.101	192.168.1.11	192.168.1.1
BLUE2	HOST1	4501	00-45-01-00-00-02	172.16.1.101	192.168.1.12	192.168.1.1
BLUE3	HOST2	4501	00-45-01-00-00-03	172.16.1.102	192.168.1.13	192.168.1.1

Of course, if you are using the IP Rewrite functionality, the command needs to be adjusted a little. As Table 5.4 suggests, there are actually no changes required for the PA itself. However, we will remove the provider address from the old host and assign it to the new host, after which we don't need to make any more changes. Because of our one-to-one relationship, the lookup table will still be correct!

TABLE 5.4: IP rewrite table update

VM NAME	HOST	VSID	MAC ADDRESS	PA IP	CA IP	GATEWAY
GREEN1	HOST1	4701	00-47-01-00-00-01	172.16.1.121	192.168.1.11	192.168.1.1
GREEN2	HOST2	4701	00-47-01-00-00-02	172.16.1.122	192.168.1.12	192.168.1.1
RED1	HOST1	4601	00-46-01-00-00-01	172.16.1.111	192.168.1.11	192.168.1.1
RED2	HOST1	4601	00-46-01-00-00-02	172.16.1.112	192.168.1.12	192.168.1.1
RED3	HOST2	4601	00-46-01-00-00-03	172.16..113	192.168.1.13	192.168.1.1
BLUE1	HOST1	4501	00-45-01-00-00-01	172.16.1.101	192.168.1.11	192.168.1.1
BLUE2	HOST1	4501	00-45-01-00-00-02	172.16.1.102	192.168.1.12	192.168.1.1
BLUE3	HOST2	4501	00-45-01-00-00-03	172.16.1.103	192.168.1.13	192.168.1.1

Start on the old host (HOST2) and remove the PA:

```
#Host2
Remove-NetVirtualizationProviderAddress -ProviderAddress 172.16.1.112
```

Now, on the new host (Host1), we can use our existing experience and add the PA for the virtual machine on its new home:

```
#Host1
$vSwitch = Get-VMSwitch -Name `
"Microsoft Network Adapter Multiplexor Driver - Virtual Switch" `
$paAdaptor = Get-NetAdapter -InterfaceDescription `
$vSwitch.NetAdapterInterfaceDescription


New-NetVirtualizationProviderAddress -InterfaceIndex $paAdaptor.InterfaceIndex `
-ProviderAddress 172.16.1.112 -PrefixLength 24 -VlanID 10
```

And that is it! You now have the knowledge to embrace network virtualization and implement it with either encapsulation or rewrite.

One final note about these VM moves: speed in keeping the lookup records up-to-date is essential. The moment a virtual machine migrates to a new host, that VM is essentially missing until the address book is updated on each of the hosts with the new information. To facilitate this ever-changing environmental issue, Microsoft System Center Virtual Machine Manager 2012 SP1 has new features to manage this process at scale.

DEFINING PROVIDER ADDRESS VLANS AND ROUTES

In more-sophisticated environments, your Hyper-V hosts that are participating in network virtualization are quite likely to be deployed in different subnets within your datacenter, or possibly in different datacenters, which you might not even be hosting.

In these cases, we still need to ensure that the PAs can be routed between these hosts. This will not be much of a challenge if you are using the same IP subnet and VLANs, as these will likely already route. However, if you are using dedicated IP subnets or VLANs, you will need to define gateways for the PA space to utilize.

You can defining VLANs specifically for the PA we have already encountered in our examples, simply by providing the switch –VLAN when utilizing the PowerShell command New-NetVirtualizationProviderAddress, as in this example:

```
New-NetVirtualizationProviderAddress -InterfaceIndex $paAdaptor.InterfaceIndex `
-ProviderAddress 172.16.1.101 -PrefixLength 24 –VlanID 10
```

Configuring our Hyper-V hosts to route our PA addresses is also quite simple. PowerShell offers a command specifically for the task: New-NetVirtualizationProviderRoute. This command again references the interface (physical or LBFO team) that is connected to our datacenter and used by our selected virtual switch. We simply provide it a routing network and gateway. In the following example, we are setting 172.16.1.1 as the default gateway for our PA space on the current host:

```
New-NetVirtualizationProviderRoute -InterfaceIndex $paAdaptor.InterfaceIndex `
-DestinationPrefix "0.0.0.0/0" -NextHop "172.16.1.1"
```

USING MULTIPLE VIRTUAL SUBNETS PER ROUTING DOMAIN

Earlier in the chapter we introduced the idea of multiple subnets per routing domain. The sample we presented in Figure 5.7 illustrated RED with two subnets, A and B, which could represent, for example, a trusted and DMZ network.

One of the features of the Microsoft Network Virtualization filter is automatic routing, enabling virtual machines within the same routing domain, but hosted on different virtual subnets. This feature is enabled by default and defined by the customer route, using the PowerShell command New-NetVirtualizationCustomerRoute. The -DestinationPrefix switch defines the IP range for the subnet, with the first address of the subnet reserved as the automatic virtual router function. This reserved address should not be used for any virtual machines in the subnet, regardless of whether you plan to utilize this feature or not.

```
# Associate the RED Visual Subnet and CA space with RED network


New-NetVirtualizationCustomerRoute -RoutingDomainID $redGUID -VirtualSubnetID `
4601 -DestinationPrefix "192.168.1.0/24" -NextHop 0.0.0.0 -Metric 255
```

In order to use this feature, we must define a second subnet in the routing domain. As part of this definition, we will assign a new virtual subnet ID to the routing domain (RDID), along with the IP subnet that will be utilized.

```
# Create a second Associate the RED Visual Subnet and CA space with RED network


New-NetVirtualizationCustomerRoute -RoutingDomainID $redGUID -VirtualSubnetID `
4602 -DestinationPrefix "192.168.2.0/24" -NextHop 0.0.0.0 -Metric 255
```

To test out this functionality, deploy a new virtual machine (for example, RED4) and assign it a new unique MAC address. Set the VSID to the new ID we just defined (for example, 4602). Set the VM's IP address from the new scope (192.168.2.0/24) and its gateway to the first IP in the scope (192.168.2.1). Now you should be able to ping or traceroute from this new VM RED4 to any of the other RED VMs on the same host.

For VMs belonging to the same customer on other hosts, remember to publish the lookup records for this new virtual machine and any added additional PA entries if you are using IP Rewrite.

Network Virtualization Gateways

On its own, this new network virtualization feature enabled with our Hyper-V extensible switch offers some very sophisticated and scalable options for our new private clouds. After you begin to utilize this new technology, you will quickly start to consider some additional requirements to extend the reach of our virtual machines hosted within the virtual networks to the physical network.

Enterprises will want to use existing services and technologies already implemented in their environment—for example, load balancers, firewalls, and so forth. All of these must be routed or bridged between their physical address space and the virtual machines' virtual address space.

Traffic traversing between these networks can be compared to traffic flowing between our on-premise networks and the public Internet, or services requiring some form of gateway technology:

◆ Routing gateways

◆ VPN gateways

ROUTING GATEWAYS

Primarily of interest with connecting private clouds hosted on-premise, the routing gateways simply route traffic between the virtualized network and the physical network.

VPN GATEWAYS

Offering greater flexibility of usage options, VPN gateways are suitable for use both on and off premise, including hosted clouds. The VPN gateway creates a tunnel from the virtual machine address space back to your physical network address space.

SUMMARY

The inbox network virtualization platform that Microsoft has delivered with Windows Server 2012 is an amazing solution to a problem that has challenged many private cloud implementations as they begin to mature and scale. Offering flexibility that previously was not possible, this solution offers customization and scalability suitable for the average organization to the largest of hosters, while also ensuing the new crafted protocols are adopted as a recognized standard.

At the time of this writing, F5 and other third parties have already announced support for NVGRE in their upcoming products, confirming the industry's support for this new technology.

It is clear from our examples in this section, however, that successful deployment of this solution will require management tools for efficient implementation and maintenance. These will be either in-house tools and utilities built on top of the existing API, or Microsoft's own System Center Virtual Machine Manager 2012 SP1.

PVLANs

We must first think about local area networks (LANs) and virtual LANS (VLANs) before we can begin considering private VLANs (PVLANs). To form a VLAN, we partition a physical network so that distinct broadcast domains are created. To physically replicate the function of a VLAN, you would require a separate isolated network per LAN, cabled back to the devices participating in the specific LAN.

VLANs are typically implemented on switch or router devices. However, simpler, less-expensive devices support only a subset of the VLAN implementation features. These may be implemented in the devices firmware as a form of partitioning at the port level on the device. In these scenarios, spanning VLANs to additional devices would require running dedicated cabling for each VLAN to each target device.

As we move into the enterprise-class hardware, more-sophisticated devices have the ability to mark Ethernet packets through tagging (802.1q), so that a single port or group of ports may be used to transport data for multiple LANs (or VLANs). This port configuration is commonly referred to as a *trunk*.

Physical LANs and VLANs share the same attributes. However, VLANs permit easier grouping of members through software configuration instead of physically relocating devices or connections.

PVLANs allow splitting this VLAN domain into multiple isolated broadcast *subdomains*, introducing sub-VLANs inside a VLAN. One of the characteristics of VLANs is their inability to communicate directly with each other—they require a Layer 3 device to forward packets between separate broadcast domains (for example, a router). This same restriction applies to PVLANS, because the subdomains are still isolated at Layer 2.

As we host our virtual machines in different VLANs, these typically map to different IP subnets. When we split a VLAN by using PVLANs, hosts in different PVLANs will normally still belong to the same IP subnet. However, they may still require a Layer 3 router to communicate with each other (for example, by using Local Proxy ARP). In turn, the router may either permit or forbid communications between sub-VLANs by using access control lists. Commonly, these configurations arise in multi-tenant environments yet provide a good level of isolation.

PROXY ARP

Address Resolution Protocol (ARP) is utilized by network devices to query other devices on the network to which traffic should be passed. Proxy Address Resolution Protocol is an extension to this process, whereby a device on the local network answers the ARP queries for a network address that is not on that network.

In order to function, the Proxy ARP device will be aware of the location of the destination device. In the query reply, the Proxy ARP sends its own MAC address as the answer, effectively instructing the querying device to, "send it to me, and I'll pass it on to the relevant destination."

Private VLAN is an extension to the VLAN standard, and is already available in several vendors' physical switches. It adds a further segmentation of the logical broadcast domain to create private groups. It is highly recommended that you check the feature sets of your physical switch devices to validate their implementation of PVLANs before proceeding to production deployment of the technology. PVLAN traffic between Windows 2012 Hyper-V hosts will require this functionality to ensure successful implementation.

Private means that the hosts in the same PVLAN are not able to be seen by the others, except the selected ones in the promiscuous PVLAN.

PROMISCUOUS MODE

Promiscuous mode is a mode of operation for a computer's wired or wireless network interface controller (NIC) that causes the controller to pass all traffic it receives to the central processing unit (CPU) rather than passing only the packets that the controller is intended to receive.

This mode would normally be considered as a solution for packet sniffing or for bridged networking with hardware virtualization.

Understanding PVLAN Structure

Prior to configuring PVLANs, we will start with an introduction to help you understand the main concepts and terms that you will encounter for this technology and how they relate to each other.

PRIMARY

The original VLAN that is being divided into smaller groups is called the *primary*, and all the secondary PVLANs exist only inside the primary.

Figure 5.10 illustrates the relationship of the primary and secondary LANs in a PVLAN configuration.

FIGURE 5.10
PVLAN segment relationships

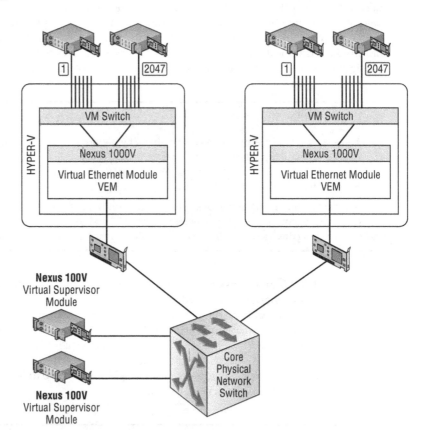

SECONDARY

The *secondary* PVLANs exist only inside the primary. Each secondary PVLAN has a specific VLAN ID associated with it, with packet passing tagged with an ID similar to regular VLANs.

The switch then associates a special PVLAN behavior of Isolated, Community, or Promiscuous, depending on the definition for the VLAN ID found in each packet.

Depending on the type of VLAN involved, hosts may not be able to communicate with each other, even if they belong to the same group. To help understand the behavior of each of these types of secondary VLANs, we can again refer to the traffic arrows in Figure 5.10 as we describe each in turn.

PROMISCUOUS

Any node that is attached to a port (network interface) in a *promiscuous* secondary PVLAN may send to and receive packets from any other node located in any other secondary VLAN associated with the same primary VLAN. Routers are typically attached to promiscuous ports.

This port type is allowed to send and receive Layer 2 frames from any other port on the PVLAN.

Traffic from the promiscuous secondary VLAN is restricted to its associated primary VLAN only. Therefore, if other secondary VLANs with the same secondary ID exist, which is associated with a different primary VLAN, these are treated as two isolated and independent VLANs.

COMMUNITY

A node attached to a port in a *community* secondary PVLAN may send to and receive packets from other ports in the same secondary PVLAN. In addition, nodes hosted in the community are permitted to send packets to and receive packets from a promiscuous VLAN that is a member of the same primary VLAN.

ISOLATED

A node attached to a port in an *isolated* secondary PVLAN may send packets to and receive packets only from the promiscuous PVLAN in the same primary VLAN—that is, these are isolated ports.

Compared to the community VLAN, nodes hosted in the isolated VLAN do *not* have the ability to communicate with each other. You commonly see this implementation when deploying systems that need to be isolated from each other, with the exception of the nodes hosted in the promiscuous VLAN. Only one isolated secondary can be defined within the PVLAN.

Understanding How PVLANs Work

To understand how all this relates to multi-tenancy and clouds, consider a sample scenario environment utilizing PVLAN technology to isolate participating virtual machines.

First, let's summarize what you have learned so far:

◆ A promiscuous VLAN transports packets from hosts or a router to all hosts in isolated or community VLANs.

◆ An isolated VLAN transports packets only from the isolated hosts to the promiscuous VLAN (normally where the router is hosted).

◆ A community VLAN allows bidirectional packet exchange within the VLAN. In addition, a community VLAN may forward packets to a promiscuous VLAN.

Our sample environment, illustrated in Figure 5.11, depicts a simple Hyper-V implementation built out as follows:

Hyper-V host, which we are configuring with PVLAN support

Switch, connected to our Hyper-V hosts as a physical gateway

Shared services "cloud," a promiscuous VLAN hosting shared services (for example, DNS and DHCP servers)

Special isolated "cloud," an isolated VLAN for single-node tenants (YELLOW)

Orange "cloud," the first community VLAN for our ORANGE tenant

Purple "cloud," the second community VLAN for our PURPLE tenant

FIGURE 5.11
PVLAN scenario
environment

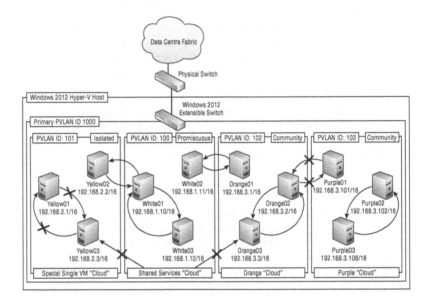

Our Hyper-V host is connected to an external physical switch to enable the facility of sharing PVLAN information with other Hyper-V hosts that may be located within our environment, and to act as a gateway to the router. This physical switch should be aware of PVLAN packets and should be configured to match the primary and secondary VLAN IDs that it may need to process.

Configuring the physical switch PVLAN is outside the scope of this book, as each hardware vendor will utilize different command sets to define and enable its services.

While utilizing PVLANs, we typically will utilize a single large Layer 3 subnet for all the virtual machines associated with the primary VLAN. This approach permits us to host, for example, a shared DHCP and DNS server in the promiscuous VLAN, which can safely address each node in the environment and simplifies the definition of segments and gateways for our tenants.

In our Shared Services Cloud, in Figure 5.11, we are presenting three virtual machines labeled WHITE01, WHITE02, and WHITE03, which can be easily configured to offer common services to all our tenants. To facilitate this functionality, the Shared Services Cloud is labeled as a secondary VLAN with ID 100 and identified to be implemented as a promiscuous VLAN.

The Special Single VM Cloud also hosts a number of virtual machines, this time identified as YELLOW01, YELLOW02, and YELLOW03. However, their secondary VLAN is to be configured as a secondary isolated VLAN with ID 101. As per the rules of an isolated VLAN, none of the YELLOW nodes will have the ability to communicate with each other, or for that matter, with any other node (ORANGE or PURPLE) in the primary VLAN, with the exception of the WHITE nodes.

The remaining two clouds in the environment are for our ORANGE and PURPLE tenants, both of which are hosted in community secondary VLANs, with the IDs of 102 and 103, respectively. As with the previous VLANs, communication rules apply here also. This time, nodes in ORANGE can communicate with each other and WHITE only, while nodes hosted in PURPLE can again communicate with each other and WHITE only.

The help illustrate out scenario, Table 5.5 narrates the configuration details of the nodes illustrated in Figure 5.11, Including thier associated PVLAN modes, IDs and IP addresses. All the participating nodes although members of the same Layer 3 IPv4 subnet, are isolated at Layer 2 via the functionality of PVLANs.

TABLE 5.5:   PVLAN Configuration Matrix

VM NAME	CLOUD	MODE	PRIMARY VLAN ID	SECONDARY VLAN ID	IP ADDRESS
WHITE01	Shared Services	Promiscuous	1000	100	192.168.1.10/16
WHITE02	Shared Services	Promiscuous	1000	100	192.168.1.11/16
WHITE03	Shared Services	Promiscuous	1000	100	192.168.1.12/16
ORANGE01	Orange	Community	1000	102	192.168.3.1/16
ORANGE02	Orange	Community	1000	102	192.168.3.2/16
ORANGE03	Orange	Community	1000	102	192.168.3.2/16
PURPLE01	Purple	Community	1000	103	192.168.3.101/16
PURPLE02	Purple	Community	1000	103	192.168.3.102/16
PURPLE03	Purple	Community	1000	103	192.168.3.103/16
YELLOW01	Special Singles	Isolated	1000	101	192.168.2.1/16
YELLOW02	Special Singles	Isolated	1000	101	192.168.2.2/16
YELLOW03	Special Singles	Isolated	1000	101	192.168.2.3/16

Now you have a clear picture of the multi-tenancy rules achieved through the use of PVLAN technology. However, prior to progressing to the fun part of implementing this configuration, let's take a moment to reflect on the traffic flow over the network layer, as this is still critical to understand:

◆ VMs should not see *any* traffic from another tenant VM.

◆ Standard 802.1Q tagging indicates that there is no encapsulation of a PVLAN inside a VLAN. Everything is done with one tag per packet.

◆ Traffic between virtual machines on the same PVLAN but on different Hyper-V hosts passes through the physical switch. Therefore, the physical switch must be trunked, PVLAN aware, and configured appropriately to allow the secondary PVLAN's traffic to reach its destination.

◆ No Double Encapsulation indicates that the packets are tagged according to the switch port configuration (EST mode), or they may arrive already tagged if the port is configured as a trunk (VST mode).

◆ Switch software determines which port the packet will be forwarded to, based on both the packets VLAN tag and the defined PVLAN tables.

◆ Ethernet MAC address learning and forwarding procedures remain the same, as broadcast/multicast flooding procedures within boundaries of primary/secondary VLANs.

If we proceeded to implement a PVLAN on physical network switches, as depicted in our sample (Figure 5.11), it is important to remember that we would actually be required to configure our PVLAN-specific settings on any switch participating in the environment. (This manual configuration requirement may not be true if your network switches support and are enabled for VTPv3. Refer to your hardware support for additional details.)

VIRTUAL TUNNEL PROTOCOL

Consider a switch as a Virtual Tunnel Protocol (VTP) server that sends an advertisement every 5 minutes or whenever a change is made in the VLAN database.

The advertisement contains the name of our VLANs, VLAN ID, switch ports participating in the VLANs, and a revision number. Switches containing an older revision of the database would then automatically update to the latest version on receipt.

VTP is a Cisco proprietary protocol, with the latest generation switches including support for VTPv3, which enables switches to update each other regarding PVLAN membership. This is not possible with VTPv2, as it has no TLVs to carry PVLAN information.

Configuring Private VLANs

Similar to our experience in the previous section of this chapter focusing on network virtualization, the Windows 2012 extensible switch has built-in support for PVLAN technology. However, this feature is also not accessible from the graphical user interface. Instead, we will again rely on PowerShell to configure and manage the feature.

The key commands that we utilize to manage this feature are `Get-VMNetworkAdapterVlan` and `Set-VMNetworkAdapterVlan`.

Prior to commencing with the configuration of any VLAN, we should first check the existing VLAN settings for our virtual machine by using the `Get-VMNetworkAdaptorVlan` command, providing the name of the virtual machine we are interested in:

```
PS> Get-VMNetworkAdapterVlan -VMName WHITE01


VMName    VMNetworkAdapterName   Mode     VlanList
------    --------------------   ----     --------
WHITE01   Network Adapter        Access   10
```

The results of our preceding sample illustrate that WHITE01 had previously been configured to use a tagged connection on VLAN10. Therefore, for this scenario, we will reset the VLAN configuration for the WHITE01 virtual machine back to the default, which turns off tagging and places the VM in the default VLAN:

```
PS> Set-VMNetworkAdapterVlan –VMName WHITE01 –Access –VlanID 0
```

Or, you might prefer to go to true defaults with the following command:

```
PS> Set-VMNetworkAdapterVlan –VMName WHITE01 –Untagged
```

To be confident that the configuration for our test is going to work, we should repeat the preceding procedure on each of the virtual machines we will be working with.

If you attempt to make any of these VLAN changes while the virtual machine is powered on, you will be presented with an error reminding you that you cannot perform the actions while the virtual machine is in this state. To successfully apply the setting, you must ensure that the virtual machine is first powered off.

DEFINE THE PROMISCUOUS VLANS

Now, with the basic concepts covered and the virtual machines all checked, we are ready to begin configuring our VLANs to represent the plan we are illustrating back in Figure 5.11.

The initial VLAN we will focus on is the promiscuous VLAN, or the shared services cloud in the scenario, which is hosting our DHCP, DNS, and other services that will be utilized by the rest of the virtual machines in our clouds.

Our first operation is to configure the virtual interface of our WHITE virtual machines, setting these into Trunk mode. By default, the normal mode of operation for a virtual interface is called Access mode, whereby the interface is configured to participate in a single VLAN. In contrast, Trunk mode enables the interface to process multiple VLAN tags. For PVLAN operation, this is important, as the virtual machine will communicate with members of its primary VLAN, and potentially the associated secondary VLANs.

PowerShell simplifies the process of defining the primary or native VLAN ID, along with any of the secondary VLANs that are to be permitted to communicate with our virtual machines through the use of a single command:

```
PS> Set-VMNetworkAdapterVlan -VMName WHITE01 -Trunk -NativeVlanId 1000 `
-AllowedVlanIdList "100,101,102,103"
PS> Set-VMNetworkAdapterVlan -VMName WHITE02 -Trunk -NativeVlanId 1000 `
-AllowedVlanIdList "100,101,102,103"
PS> Set-VMNetworkAdapterVlan -VMName WHITE03 -Trunk -NativeVlanId 1000 `
-AllowedVlanIdList "100,101,102,103"
```

With the interface now in the correct mode, and with both our native and associated VLANs identified, we are going to inform the interface that it will be participating not just in normal VLAN trunking, but instead in the more-sophisticated PVLAN configuration.

The command we are going to use for this is surprisingly the same as the one we previously used. However, this time we are going to provide a slight change in the parameters. The syntax for enabling PVLAN services is to identify the VLAN ID of our primary VLAN, augmented with the list of secondary VLANs to be associated with it. Finally, we must indicate which PVLAN mode we should enable the virtual interface for—in this case, promiscuous.

```
PS> Set-VMNetworkAdapterVlan -VMName WHITE01 -Promiscuous -PrimaryVlanId 1000 `
-SecondaryVlanIdList 100-103
PS> Set-VMNetworkAdapterVlan -VMName WHITE02 -Promiscuous -PrimaryVlanId 1000 `
-SecondaryVlanIdList 100-103
PS> Set-VMNetworkAdapterVlan -VMName WHITE03 -Promiscuous -PrimaryVlanId 1000 `
-SecondaryVlanIdList 100-103
```

Before we proceed to configuring the virtual interfaces for the remaining nodes, we should take a moment to check that our desired interface settings have indeed been applied. Using the PowerShell command Get-VMNetworkAdapterVlan that we utilized a little earlier, we can quickly check to ensure that our desired settings have been applied:

```
PS> Get-VMNetworkAdapterVlan -VMName WHITE01 | format-list
```

```
VMName              : WHITE01
AdapterName         : Network Adapter
OperationMode       : Private
PrivateVlanMode     : Promiscuous
PrimaryVlanId       : 1000
SecondaryVlanIdList : 100-103
```

DEFINE THE COMMUNITY VLANS

Referring back to our sample environment in Figure 5.11, we will next focus on our ORANGE and PURPLE clouds, both of which are similar. Again, the virtual machines hosted within these two clouds will each be configured by using the same methodology as we utilized for our promiscuous node.

Starting with the ORANGE virtual machines, we will set the virtual interface into PVLAN Community mode and define the primary VLAN that these are members of, before finally setting the secondary ID that we assigned to ORANGE (which was 102).

```
PS> Set-VMNetworkAdapterVlan -VMName ORANGE01 -Community -PrimaryVlanId 1000 `
-SecondaryVlanIdList 102
PS> Set-VMNetworkAdapterVlan -VMName ORANGE02 -Community -PrimaryVlanId 1000 `
-SecondaryVlanIdList 102
PS> Set-VMNetworkAdapterVlan -VMName ORANGE03 -Community -PrimaryVlanId 1000 `
-SecondaryVlanIdList 102
```

Now, simply repeat the same process for all our PURPLE virtual machines, this time setting the secondary ID to its assigned value of 103:

```
PS> Set-VMNetworkAdapterVlan -VMName PURPLE* -Community -PrimaryVlanId 1000 `
-SecondaryVlanIdList 103
```

DEFINE THE ISOLATED VLANS

The final secondary VLAN that we need to configure is the isolated VLAN, which in our scenario environment is called Special Single VM Cloud and hosts our YELLOW virtual machines, with a secondary ID of 101.

Again, repeating exactly the same process as for our community virtual machines, we will configure the virtual machines' virtual network interfaces this time in Isolated mode:

```
PS> Set-VMNetworkAdapterVlan -VMName YELLOW* -Isolated -PrimaryVlanId 1000 `
-SecondaryVlanIdList 101
```

ISOLATED VLAN

You can create only a single isolated VLAN per primary VLAN.

VERIFY PVLAN FUNCTIONS

With the configuration now implemented, we can refer to our sample environment and validate that the PVLAN functionality is behaving as we expect. This permits us to experience the benefits of using PVLAN technologies as a potential technology for multi-tenancy with our clouds.

We will begin in Orange Cloud, which is defined as a Community. Working from the virtual machine ORANGE01 (192.168.3.1), we should now be able to ping ORANGE02 (192.168.3.2) and ORANGE03 (192.168.3.3). Additionally, we should be able to ping WHITE01 (192.168.1.10), WHITE02 (192.168.1.11), and WHITE03 (192.168.1.12) in the Shared Services Cloud (promiscuous VLAN), but nowhere else.

Moving over to PURPLE Cloud in our scenario, the experience should be exactly the same. This time working from PURPLE01 (192.168.3.101), we should have the ability to communicate with PURPLE02 (192.168.3.102) and PURPLE03 (192.168.3.103) and additionally WHITE01, WHITE02, and WHITE03—but should have no access to any of the other VMs in the environment.

In the Special Single VM Cloud, we should be able to connect with only WHITE01, WHITE02, and WHITE03 in the Shared Services Cloud, but regardless of which node we test from—for example, YELLOW01 (192.168.2.1)—we will be unable to ping any other node in this cloud, including YELLOW02 (192.168.2.2) and YELLOW03 (192.168.2.3), or nodes in either ORANGE or PURPLE.

Finally, if we connect to a node in the Shared Services Cloud—for example, WHITE03 (192.168.1.3)—we should be unable to communicate to any node within the primary VLAN, including WHITE, YELLOW, ORANGE, and PURPLE.

USE MULTIPLE VIRTUAL NETWORK INTERFACES

In the preceding scenario, one assumption we held during the configuration process is that each virtual machine has only one virtual network interface. Additionally, if our virtual machines were configured with multiple virtual interfaces, each of these would have been configured exactly the same, as the commands we issued focused on the virtual machine, instead of specific virtual interfaces.

In some cases, our virtual machines may be configured with more than a single virtual network interface, and our requirements may be to just configure a specific interface for virtual networking. As an example, I have added a second virtual interface to WHITE01. By using the PowerShell command `Get-VMNetworkAdapter`, we can now see that the name of the virtual network interface is unfortunately not unique. However, we do know that the MAC address should always be unique.

```
PS> Get-VMNetworkAdapter -VMName WHITE01


Name              VMName   SwitchName   MacAddress    IPAddresses
----              ------   ----------   ----------    -----------
Network Adapter   WHITE01  Microso...   00155DE67404  {192.168.1.1, fe80:...
Network Adapter   WHITE01  Microso...   00155DE67405  {192.168.1.32, fe80:...
```

Using the MAC address as a filter, we can then modify our PowerShell command into three stages, so that we set only the desired interface into Promiscuous mode.

In the following example, first we utilize the `Get-VMNetworkAdaptor` command to list all the virtual network interfaces for the selected virtual machine. Next we take the results we just retrieved and filter for the network interface with the matching MAC access we plan to configure, and finally we execute the `Set-VMVirtualNetworkVLAN` command on the matching interface, setting just it into Promiscuous mode.

```
PS> Get-VMNetworkAdapter –VMName WHITE01 | where {$_.MACAddress -like `
"00155DE67404"} | Set-VMNetworkAdapterVlan -Promiscuous -PrimaryVlanId 1000 `
-SecondaryVlanIdList 100-103
```

Because this process is a little less trivial than the default assumption, we should check that the desired interface on the virtual machine is the only one that we altered, again using PowerShell:

```
PS> Get-VMNetworkAdapterVlan -VMName WHITE01
```

```
VMName   VMNetworkAdapterName Mode      VlanList
------   -------------------- ----      --------
WHITE01  Network Adapter      Untagged
WHITE01  Network Adapter      Promiscuous 1000,100-103
```

The results of the preceding command quickly validate that our more-complex command has indeed had the desired effect: setting just one of our virtual interfaces into PVLAN Promiscuous mode, while retaining the default untagged settings on the other interface.

Summary

As we continue to uncover the flexibility and features that Microsoft has added to the new extensible switch, it is ever clearer that a lot of foundational work has to be completed to facilitate the requirements of security with tenancy within clouds.

However, foundation work is what this is, and as we reflect back on the new concepts we have just learned, and how to implement PVLAN solutions, it is quite obvious that we must pay close attention to the components of the fabric on which we will be constructing our new cloud services. In this scenario, the focus points directly to the network itself, and the requirement for that infrastructure to also be PVLAN aware.

Additionally, just as you learned in the previous section on network virtualization, a management tool is going to be necessary if we are to grow this out to any type of production scale, so that we can maintain control, and simplify deployment, while also addressing the concepts of the cloud, especially self-service.

One approach that will revolutionize implementation practices is the use of extensions that third parties are currently preparing for the extensible switch. The upcoming Cisco Nexus 1000V, for example, promises to keep the network configuration, including PVLANs, in the hands of the network engineers, while allowing the Hyper-V and cloud administrators to focus on the technologies they know best.

Port Access Control Lists

An *access control list (ACL)* is simply a set of filters that enable you to control packet flow as you permit or deny their access in or out of a system. Historically, ACLs have been utilized by the systems administrator to protect the operating system via a local firewall feature, and by the network administrator to filter traffic and provide extra security for their networks, generally applied on routers and switches.

The primary reason for configuring ACLs is to provide security in your environment, by using this powerful method to control traffic flow in quite a granular fashion.

How ACLs Work

We all know the phrase, "If you are not on the list, you are not getting in." In reality, we see this in effect as people line up to enter a location through a door that is protected. The protection at the door refers to a list that someone checks to see whether your name matches a name on the list, to determine whether to permit or deny your entry.

In a simple analogy, we can consider the protection as the filter, while the list is the access control list.

This filtering device or service uses a set of rules to determine whether to permit or deny traffic based on certain criteria, including source or destination IP addresses, source port or destination port, or the protocol of the packet. These rules are collectively called access control lists, or ACLs.

Extensible Switch Packet Filter

Among all the features packed into the extensible switch that we have already examined, Microsoft has also seen fit to include an implementation of a packet filter. This filter is again implemented at the port or virtual interface level, ensuring that any access control list configurations applied will of course remain with the virtual machine, even when moved to alternative hosts. These port Access Control List, or port ACL, rules can specify whether a packet is allowed or denied on the way into or out of the VM.

The ACLs have the following elements:

Local and/or Remote MAC and/or IP address   Packets can be matched to either the IP address of the source machine or the destination IP address. The IP address can be declared as either IPv4 or IPv6, and can be as granular as a single host address (for example, 192.168.3.2 or 2001:770:1bc:0:edge:b00b:2001:2222) or a subnet (for example, 192.168.3/25 or 2001:770:1bc:0::1/64). Additionally, the IP address can be defined as a wildcard—for example, 0.0.0.0/0 for all IPv4 addresses, ::/0 for all IPv6 addresses, or ANY for all IPv4 and IPv6 addresses.

Similarly, packets can be matched to the MAC address of the source or destination machine, declared in the normal format of 00-11-22-33-44-55-66 or by using ANY to match all MAC addresses.

Direction   An important consideration when filtering traffic is to determine which direction the traffic is flowing. For example, we may want to allow users to RDP to our virtual machine, but we might not want these users to create another RDP session from the virtual machine to another destination. In this scenario, we would want to Allow RDP traffic Inbound, but Deny RDP traffic Outbound. Of course, we may not want RDP traffic to travel to or from the virtual machine, in which case we would want to Block RDP traffic in Both directions. Valid directions for the ACL, therefore, are Inbound, Outbound, or Both.

Action   You need to determine what action the filter should take on the packet it if is matched to any of the previous policies. The obvious two are, of course, Allow and Deny. However, a third action is available, called Meter, which can be utilized to measure the number of matching packets that pass through the filter.

You can configure multiple port ACLs for a Hyper-V switch port. During operations, the port ACL whose rules match the incoming or outgoing packet is used to determine whether the packet is allowed or denied.

It's important to point out that the port ACLs work at the address level (IP or MAC) and not at the port or protocol level. Therefore out of the box, this feature is unsuitable to implement our RDP scenario described in the "Direction" sub-section at the required TCP 3389 port granularity. If your filtering requires this extra level of granularity, you should look at one of the third-party extension vendors—for example, the Cisco Nexus 1000v and 5nine Security Manager.

Configuring Port ACL

At this point, it will not be a surprise that the management and configuration of the extensible switch port ACL feature is through the PowerShell interface.

The key commands that we utilize to manage this feature are `Get-VMNetworkAdapterAcl` and `Add-VMNetworkAdapterAcl`.

Using the command `Get-VMNetworkAdaptorAcl` and providing the name of the virtual machine you are interested in, a default set of four ACLs will be presented, two of these for inbound traffic, one for IPv4, and the other for IPv6, with the same repeated for outbound traffic. The action for all four of these is defined as Meter. However, the metered traffic may be blank if virtual machine metering is not enabled; additional information on metering can be found in the next section of the chapter.

```
PS> Get-VMNetworkAdapterAcl -VMName WHITE01



VMName: WHITE01
VMId: 7bdf1c8b-c40d-4771-8b53-df5f309c4c85
AdapterName: Network Adapter
AdapterId: Microsoft:7BDF1C8B-C40D-4771-8B53-DF5F309C4C85\68A681A3-0A01-...


Direction    Address                              Action
---------    -------                              ------
Inbound      Remote ::/0                          Meter (6 Mbytes)
Inbound      Remote 0.0.0.0/0                      Meter (19 Mbytes)
Outbound     Remote 0.0.0.0/0                      Meter (1 Mbytes)
Outbound     Remote ::/0                          Meter (2 Mbytes)
```

Adding an ACL to our machine is also very easy. You use the command `Add-VMNetworkAdapterAcl` along with the elements we introduced earlier:

```
Add-VMNetworkAdapterAcl -VMName WHITE01 –RemoteIPAddress All `
–Direction Both –Action Deny
Add-VMNetworkAdapterAcl -VMName WHITE01 –RemoteIPAddress 192.168.1.3 `
–Direction Both –Action Allow
```

In the preceding example, the first command instructs the filter to deny all traffic inbound and outbound from the virtual machine to be denied, or dropped, resulting in the virtual machine being isolated. The second command punches a hole in the deny list, this time allowing the virtual machine to communicate with a single other system, with the IP address of 192.168.1.3.

Cleaning up any access control roles is also quite easy. Repeating the same parameters as we utilized while adding the rule, we will use the `Remove-VMNetworkAdapterAcl` command:

```
Remove-VMNetworkAdapterAcl -VMName WHITE01 –RemoteIPAddress All `
–Direction Both –Action Deny
Remove-VMNetworkAdapterAcl -VMName WHITE01 –RemoteIPAddress 192.168.1.3 `
–Direction Both –Action Allow
```

ADVANCED USAGE SCENARIO

An advanced usage for the port ACL filters is to protect against a man-in-the-middle attack on the local network, better known as *ARP spoofing*.

The scenario for the attack exists when a potential attacker associates a MAC address with the real address of an existing machine on the network, sending fake Address Resolution Protocol (ARP) responses to asking machines. This enables the attacker to capture data packets that were actually destined for the real machine, whose address we are faking.

If we consider a simple cloud solution utilizing a shared subnet, hosting multiple tenant virtual machines for short term, low security deployments ARP spoofing could be a potential concern. In this configuration each virtual machine is assigned a dedicated IP address, for example GREY01 is assigned the address 192.168.1.33 and MAGENTA01 is assigned 192.168.1.66 by the cloud administrator.

Using Port ACL's we can ensure that each virtual machine can only communicate using its assigned IP address, dropping any packets which are sourced or sent.

```
Add-VMNetworkAdapterAcl -VMName GREY01 -RemoteIPAddress All -Direction Both `
  -Action Deny
Add-VMNetworkAdapterAcl -VMName GREY01 -RemoteIPAddress 192.168.1.32 `
  -Direction Both -Action Allow
```

Similarly, we can apply rules on the node MAGENTA01 to protect it also:

```
Add-VMNetworkAdapterAcl -VMName MAGENTA01 -RemoteIPAddress All -Direction Both `
  -Action Deny
Add-VMNetworkAdapterAcl -VMName MAGENTA01 -RemoteIPAddress 192.168.1.66 `
  -Direction Both -Action Allow
```

To test this functionality, connect to the virtual machine GREY01 and ping virtual machine MAGENTA01, assuming everything is working, this should reply successfully.

Next, change the IP address assigned to GREY01 to another ip in the same subnet, for example 192.168.44. Repeat the ping test to virtual machine MAGENTA01 again, however this time, these will fail to reply due to our port ACL dropping what it considers spoofed addresses, disabling communications.

These ACL's can be further hardned, but also adding rules to filter based on the Virtual Network Interfaces MAC address is so desired to secure the evnironment further.

DHCP Guard

A special ACL that can be flagged per virtual machine is available, called DHCP Guard. This flag specifies whether to drop DHCP packets from our virtual machines, which might be claiming to be a DHCP server.

When this flag is set to On, the filter will deny outbound DHCP messages. This feature is useful in our cloud environments, where a tenant may enable a DHCP server on the virtual machine, which could result in some unpleasant side effects.

```
PS> Set-VMNetworkAdapter -VMName YELLOW03 -DhcpGuard On
```

The flag can be set to Off, permitting the DHCP offers to be broadcast, if the DHCP is trustworthy:

```
PS> Set-VMNetworkAdapter -VMName YELLOW03 –DhcpGuard Off
```

Of course, PowerShell is also useful when running a quick audit on the status of the DHCP Guard setting:

```
PS> Get-VMNetworkAdapter * | Select VMName, DhcpGuard


VMName     DhcpGuard
------     ---------
WHITE01    On
WHITE02    On
WHITE03    On
YELLOW01   Off
YELLOW02   On
YELLOW03   Off
```

As you can tell, DHCP Guard is similar to Port ACL, except that instead of blocking IP or MAC addresses, we are blocking specific packet types, a feature that Port ACL does not offer itself.

Router Advertisement Guard

Generally, as we work with IPv4 address space, we regularly manage our address space using DHCP. A side effect of this approach is that we are regularly subject to attacks via rogue DHCP servers. In response, the extensible switch has a feature called DHCP Guard to protect from these attacks. You learned about DHCP Guard in the preceding section.

As networks switch to IPv6, DHCP will become less used, with many organizations deciding not to even implement DHCPv6. Instead, router advertisements may be used to help systems discover the network and to configure themselves. But just like DHCP, router advertisements (RA) may be spoofed. To protect your network from rogue RAs, the extensible switch implements a feature called Router Guard, or RA-Guard, as it is more commonly known. This feature is similar to DHCP snooping.

Simply described, Router Guard will allow the forwarding of IPv6 or IPv4 router announcements only if the virtual interface is not configured to block or drop packets.

When Router Guard is enabled, the Virtual NIC will discard the following egress packets from the VM

◆ ICMPv4 Type 5 (Redirect message)

◆ ICMPv4 Type 9 (Router advertisement)

◆ ICMPv6 Type 134 (Redirect message)

◆ ICMPv6 Type 137 (Router advertisement)

Using PowerShell, we can turn on the Router Guard filter to deny outbound router announcement messages.

```
PS> Set-VMNetworkAdapter -VMName YELLOW02 -RouterGuard On
```

The flag can be set to Off, permitting the router announcement offers to be broadcast, if the node is trustworthy.

```
PS> Set-VMNetworkAdapter -VMName YELLOW02 -RouterGuard Off
```

Of course, PowerShell is also useful when running a quick audit on the status of the DHCP Guard setting:

```
PS> Get-VMNetworkAdapter * | select VMName, RouterGuard


VMName     RouterGuard
------     -----------
WHITE01    On
WHITE02    On
WHITE03    On
YELLOW01   On
YELLOW02   Off
YELLOW03   On
```

When you enable DHCP/Router Guard the Hyper-V switch will discard the following egress packets from the VM. (Actually more accurately the NIC discards the packets, not the switch.)

◆ ICMPv4 Type 5 (Redirect message)

◆ ICMPv4 Type 9 (Router Advertisement)

◆ ICMPv6 Type 134 (Router Advertisement)

◆ ICMPv6 Type 137 (Redirect message)

Hyper-V Virtual Machine Metrics

Hosting virtual machines on our Hyper-V servers consumes important resources, which must be paid for. There are many ideas about how to recover the initial investment in infrastructure and ongoing running costs, a topic better addressed in a different context.

Every virtual machine exposes different load characteristics based on the function and its workload, resulting in a random utilization of our valuable resources. In Windows 2012, Microsoft has enabled us to measure the utilization of these resources so we can use more accurate information in calculating the costs associated with the virtual machines.

This functionally is not enabled by default on our Hyper-V servers, but once active, the following metrics are monitored per virtual machine:

◆ Average CPU usage (MHz)

◆ Average physical memory usage (MB)

- Minimum physical memory usage

- Maximum physical memory usage

- Maximum amount of disk space usage

- Per adapter, total incoming network traffic (MB)

- Per adapter, total outgoing network traffic (MB)

It's important to note that after resource metering is enabled and our virtual machines move between different Hyper-V hosts, the usage data remains with the virtual machine.

ENABLE RESOURCE METERING

Initially, resource metering is not enabled for our virtual machines. However, this can be easily changed with a simple PowerShell command. The command `Enable-VMResourceMetering` takes just one parameter, which is the name of the virtual machine:

```
Enable-VMResourceMetering -VMName <Virtual Machine Name>
```

Normally, you will likely want to enable resource metering for all your virtual machines, which can simply be achieved with the following command:

```
Enable-VMResourceMetering *
```

RESET RESOURCE METERING

The counters for resource metering are cumulative. Therefore, depending on your usage scenario, you might need to reset the counters at various times—for example, daily, weekly, or monthly, depending on your reporting requirements.

PowerShell offers a command to reset the metering data:

```
Reset-VMResourceMetering -VMName <Virtual Machine Name>
```

DISABLE RESOURCE METERING

Disabling resource metering also can be accomplished using PowerShell. When this command is issued against a virtual machine, any current counter values will also be reset:

```
Disable-VMResourceMetering -VMName <Virtual Machine Name>
```

QUERY RESOURCE METERING

After the data collection is active, you will want to check the utilization of the virtual machine at different intervals, depending on your metering usage scenarios. For example, you might generate a daily report before resting the counters for the next day's work or create a comparison report for a metric at a point in time for all the virtual machines on your host.

Regardless of the objective, a single PowerShell command will return all the collected data for nodes that we are monitoring:

```
PS> Measure-VM *
```

```
VMName    AvgCPU(MHz)  AvgRAM(M)  MaxRAM(M)  MinRAM(M)  TotalDisk(M)  NetworkIn(M)
------    -----------  ---------  ---------  ---------  ------------  -----------
WHITE01   27           864        864        864        40960         70
WHITE02   0            0          0          0          0             0
WHITE03   129          1759       1759       1759       46080         75
YELLOW01  13           1822       1822       1822       306176        10
YELLOW02  92           4096       4096       4096       301056        5
YELLOW03  339          1697       1697       1697       40960         68
```

Sorting through this list can be quite a challenge. However, the built-in grid view feature of PowerShell functions extremely well here, offering filtering and sorting:

```
Measure-VM –VMName * | Select * | Out-GridView
```

In the preceding sample, I have chosen to pipe the output of `Measure-VM` to select all properties before sending the results to `Out-GridView` for rendering. Normally, while working from the console, the default output from `Measure-VM` offers only a subset of the metrics collected, however when working in the grid view, it is much easier to work with the full data set.

Real World Solutions

CHALLENGE

A line-of-business multi-tier application has stopped functioning correctly, with one of the nodes involved in the tiers appearing to have stopped network communications.

As the application has been deployed to our cloud, all the nodes involved in the tiers are virtual, thus rendering it impossible to have our networking team set a switch port into monitor mode without seeing all the traffic for each virtual machine hosted on the host. This is far too much data to consume and process, and as a result, this is a last-resort option only.

The Windows Server 2012 Hyper-V extensible switch presents new options to address this scenario.

SOLUTION

Start by creating a new virtual machine on your Hyper-V host with a single network interface. This node should then be configured with your favorite Windows Server 2012 Hyper-V-supported operating system deployed to it, along with a copy of Wireshark that can be downloaded from the following site: `www.wireshark.org/download.html`.

Launch Wireshark. On the Capture pane, select the sole listed network adapter, which should start with the name Microsoft Corporation: \Device\NPF. Then click Start. The view will change, and packet capture will begin to scroll on the screen.

Back on the Hyper-V console of your hosting server, open the properties of your WireShark virtual machine. On the Hardware list, expand the Network Adapter to present the section called Advanced Features. Selecting this option will render a new properties page. Locate the section titled Port Mirroring, and set the Mirroring mode for the Wireshark machine to Destination.

While still in the Hyper-V console, select the VM that is illustrating the problem, and open its properties dialog. As before on the Hardware list, expand the Network Adapter to present the section called Advanced Features. On the properties page, locate the section titled Port Mirroring, and set the Mirroring mode for this machine to Source.

The Wireshark virtual machine can now capture the traffic that is mirrored from the source machine. Decoding this capture will still be a task for the engineers with networking experience, however as a visualization administrator, the only requirement you have to focus on, is to ensure that both the source and destination virtual machines must be located on the same Hyper-V host.

CHALLENGE

As we deploy additional VM Hosts and VMs to our environment, tracking their utilization becomes an ever-increasing challenge. Hyper-V 2012 has been extended with new metering functionality which vastly simplifies our options to report on utilization, however out of the box generating reports from this data, requires some skill and time to configure and prepare.

As we deploy additional VM Hosts, and VMs to our environment, tracking their utilization becomes an ever increasing challenge. Hyper-V 2012 has been extended with new metering functionality that vastly simplifies our options to report on utilization, however out-of-the box, generating reports from this data requires both skill and time to configure and prepare.

We could create a set of scripts that would, at a scheduled interval, export the current metrics for each of our virtual machines, which could then be parsed to create a set of reports, updated at our defined interval.

SOLUTION

Leveraging the Open Source world, well respected and fellow MVP Yusuf Ozturk has addressed our scripting challenge and released packaged solution called PoSHStats (located at http://poshstats.net). The package is designed to be installed on your Hyper-V host, or a member of a Hyper-V cluster, gathering metrics from both your Hosts and VMs, to be presented in using a lightweight web server, which has also been created in PowerShell, as Microsoft has recommend against installing the IIS role on your Hyper-V servers.

Once downloaded and installed, PoSHStats is started from the Powershell interface with the following command:

```
Start-PoSHStats -Hostname localhost -port 8080
```

During the first execution, the script will prepare to store and capture the metric from your VMs and also verify if it should enable metric collection on all your VMs. Once the script has completed, the new light web server will be listening for your browser connection at the port you specified; in the above example, this would be `http://localhost:8080/`, which will render a web page similar to Figure 5.12.

FIGURE 5.12
PoSHStats
VM Metrics

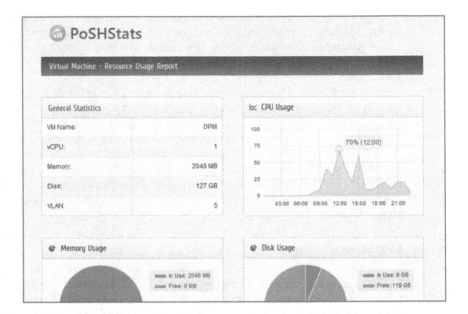

PoSHStats gathers data hourly, and presents details for CPU, Memory, Disk, and Network usage in Hourly, Daily, Weekly, and Monthly views, along with the options to copy, export, or print the reports for further analysis.

Part 3

Storage and High Availibility

## Chapter 6

Microsoft iSCSI Software Target

The Microsoft iSCSI Software Target has a long history at Microsoft. Originally developed by String Bean Software as WinTarget before Microsoft acquired the company in 2006, for the last few years it has been available as part of Windows Storage Server. MSDN and TechNet subscribers have also been able to use it for development and testing, but without production support when they're not using a Windows Storage Server SKU. However, since April 2011, Microsoft iSCSI Software Target version 3.3 has been made available to everyone as a free download, and it includes production support on a regular server running at least Windows Server 2008 R2.

Now with Windows Server 2012, downloads of an additional component are no longer required as Microsoft has included the iSCSI target server as part of the operating system. This means a full storage area network (SAN) can be built to provide block storage remotely to applications running on other servers without additional licensing costs.

In this chapter, you'll learn about

- ◆ Using the Microsoft iSCSI Software Target
- ◆ Installing and configuring the iSCSI target server as well as the iSCSI Initiator from Microsoft
- ◆ Leveraging some of the new features
- ◆ Creating new iSCSI virtual disks and targets
- ◆ Connecting an iSCSI Initiator
- ◆ Migrating older versions of Microsoft iSCSI Software Target to Windows Server 2012

Introducing the Microsoft iSCSI Software Target

For those not familiar with the Microsoft iSCSI Software Target, it allows a Windows Server to share block-level storage for other remote servers that uses this storage for their applications. The iSCSI protocol is the most widespread mechanism available to provide block-level storage access over a generic Ethernet (TCP/IP) network. In other words, The Microsoft iSCSI Software Target is a component that provides centralized, software-based and hardware-independent iSCSI disk subsystems in SANs.

The Microsoft iSCSI Solution

An iSCSI storage array consists of two components: the target and the initiator. The server that holds the storage is called the *iSCSI target*. Servers such as Hyper-V connect to the iSCSI target server by using an iSCSI initiator. Figure 6.1 shows how these two components interact.

FIGURE 6.1
iSCSI architecture
overview

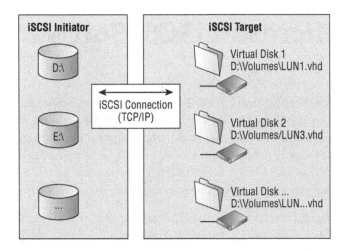

The Microsoft iSCSI solution consists of various objects, which are explained in Table 6.1.

TABLE 6.1: Components used in a Microsoft iSCSI solution

Component	Function
iSCSI target server	Storage provider and name of the installed server role
iSCSI target	Connectable instance containing one or multiple virtual disks
iSCSI virtual disk	VHD image, which is assigned to one iSCSI target and represents the hard disk used by an application
VHD	Virtual hard disk (. vhd file format) used by the iSCSI virtual disk
iSCSI initiator	Client (application, operating system) that consumes the storage

THE iSCSI TARGET SERVER

An iSCSI target server allows remote computers to make a connection to virtual disks created locally. They are also referred as *iSCSI LUNs*. These virtual disks are stored on the storage server by using the VHD file format (.vhd). The iSCSI target keeps track of all concurrent connections in terms of who can access what. These connections are initiated by using an iSCSI initiator.

Access to an iSCSI target is granted (or not) based on the information of the remote computers. Therefore, the iSCSI initiator's computer name, IP address, MAC address, or iSCSI qualified name (IQN) could be used. Multiple initiators—remote computers—can connect to the same iSCSI target at the same time.

THE iSCSI INITIATOR

The iSCSI Initiator enables a remote computer to connect to the just explained iSCSI target. Microsoft iSCSI Initiator is installed natively on Windows Server 2012, Windows Server 2008 R2, Windows Server 2008, Windows 7, and Windows Vista. On these operating systems, no installation steps are required. For previous versions of Windows, Microsoft provides a downloadable version of the iSCSI initiator component:

```
http://go.microsoft.com/fwlink/?LinkID=44352
```

What you have to keep in mind is that using a so-called software iSCSI initiator leverages only a standard network adapter, the caveat being that all the processing for the iSCSI communication is performed by the server itself—your Hyper-V host, which affects processor resources, and to a lesser extent, memory resources. If this causes a serious performance problem, a hardware iSCSI initiator, a so-called host bus adapter (HBA), should be considered. Such an HBA would then take all the overhead associated with the iSCSI connection and minimize the resource use on the Hyper-V host.

By being compliant with the iSCSI protocol that is outlined in RFC 3720, any iSCSI initiators, including third-party vendors, could interoperate with the iSCSI target implementation. This of course includes Microsoft iSCSI Initiator.

As mentioned before, the definition of which initiator could access which target is configured on the iSCSI target, by using the IQN, for example. As the IQN is typically long, the iSCSI target server wizard will be able to resolve the computer name to the IQN if the computer is a member of a Windows Server 2012 domain. If the initiator is running a previous Windows OS, the initiator IQN can be found by typing a simple `iscsicli` command in the command window, as shown in Figure 6.2, or by simply opening Microsoft iSCSI Initiator:

1. In Server Manager, choose Tools ➤ iSCSI Initiator.

2. If you launch iSCSI Initiator, the first time it responds with a pop-up message, asking to start the service. Click Yes to automatically start the service when Windows starts. Note that when you click No, the Initiator Name is not populated.

3. Click the Configuration and verify the information populated in the Initiator Name.

FIGURE 6.2
iSCSI Initiator IQN

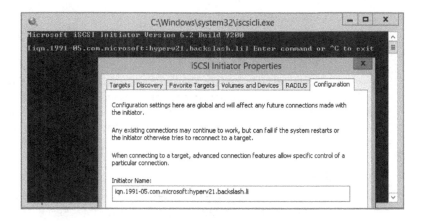

FIGURE 6.2
iSCSI Initiator IQN

Changes in Windows Server 2012

Although the Microsoft iSCSI Software Target has been around for a while, Windows Server 2012 adds several improvements, including the following, which are explained further in this section:

◆   Integration in Windows Server

◆   Support for 4K sector drives

◆   Continuous availability improvements

◆   New server management user experience

◆   Improvements to Windows PowerShell

◆   Best Practice Analyzer

◆   New Windows Server 2012 cluster role

SUPPORT FOR 4K SECTOR DRIVES

The data storage industry will be transitioning the physical format of hard disk drives from 512-byte sectors to 4,096-byte sectors in the near future. There are a couple of reasons for this increase: drive size and reliability. This transition causes incompatibility issues with existing software, including operating systems and applications. More information about using large-sector drives with Windows is available from the following KB article:

`http://support.microsoft.com/kb/2510009/en-us`

Older, 512-byte-sector drives require quite a bit of space just to store the error-correcting code (ECC) for each sector. The ECC section contains codes that are used to repair and recover data that might be damaged during the reading or writing process.

The legacy sector format contains a Gap section, a Sync section, an Address Mark section, a Data section, and an ECC section (see Figure 6.3).

FIGURE 6.3
Legacy sector layout
on hard drive media

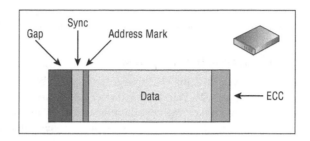

As drive manufacturers are increasing the amount of data that can be stuffed into an area, which is called the *areal density*, the signal-to-noise ratio (SNR) is adversely affected. The lower the ratio, the more drive space must be given up to ECC. At a certain point, any gain made in areal density is almost lost to additional ECC.

Going forward to drives with 4K sectors, the ECC used for a single sector is significantly less than it would be for eight 512-byte sectors. In other words, the less space used for ECC, the more space can be used to store real data.

What does this mean to the Microsoft iSCSI Software Target? The iSCSI target server in Windows Server 2012 stores the virtual disk file (.vhd) on disk drives and needs to be aware of the underlining 4K disk drives, as well as make sure that data is aligned to the 4K standard. However, the iSCSI target server always exposes the virtual disk as a 512-byte drive. This means for the remote computers the iSCSI LUN is still recognized as a standard 512-byte-sector emulation drive (512e). It's only a 4K sector drive under the hood, but it emulates a 512-byte sector drive by presenting two sector sizes to the OS.

WHAT ABOUT VHD AND VHDX?

Virtual disks have been mentioned a few times already. Both Hyper-V and the iSCSI target server are using the same VHD format to store their data. This means that a VHD image from the iSCSI target can be attached to a Hyper-V virtual machine, and the guest operating system would be able to read the data from this virtual disk. But, as always, there are some aspects to consider: see Table 6.2.

TABLE 6.2:   VHD compatibility matrix

CREATED BY	HYPER-V	ISCSI TARGET
iSCSI target (up to 2 TB)	Compatible	Compatible
iSCSI target (up to 16 TB)	Not supported	Compatible
Hyper-V (VHD format)	Compatible	Compatible
Hyper-V (VHDX format)	Compatible	Not supported

With VHDX in Windows Server 2012, a new format for virtual hard disks was made available to address the technological demands by increasing storage capacity, protecting data, and ensuring quality performance on large-sector disks. However, VHDX is not supported by the iSCSI target server and works only with Windows Server 2012 Hyper-V.

CONTINUOUS AVAILABILITY IMPROVEMENTS

In Windows Server 2012, the iSCSI target server can be built as a highly available solution through integration with Windows Failover Clustering.

The implementation of high availability for an iSCSI target in previous versions of Windows Server suffered from design limitations when implemented as a continuously available solution. Effectively, these limitations did not make it really scalable. The main limitations have to do with the cluster-resource design and mapping of cluster concepts to iSCSI-specific concepts. Every iSCSI target had its own cluster resource for every target group—and there could be quite a few when serving different hosts or clusters. Having many cluster groups also increases the time a planned failover would require. All this makes the management very complex.

In Windows Server 2012, only one cluster resource is created for the iSCSI target server directly. This change addresses the named limitations and brings scalability and key reliability metrics in the range for the definition of continuous availability.

Design and Architecture

The iSCSI target server in Windows Server 2012 can be used for different scenarios without the need for adding additional hardware to provide block-level storage to application servers. Block-level storage, like the iSCSI target server, presents itself to servers by using the industry-standard Fibre Channel (FC) and iSCSI protocol. In theory, iSCSI can take advantage of the existing Ethernet network, which means no additional hardware is needed. For best performance, it is highly recommended to separate the storage traffic from any other network traffic. Therefore, the Microsoft iSCSI Software Target was very common for test lab and demo environments—for example, to enable failover cluster scenarios with Hyper-V. Now with the enhancements in its own availability and new management options added in Windows Server 2012, the use of this component is expected to change.

The Microsoft iSCSI Software Target is a perfect solution for operating systems and/or applications that do require block-level storage—for example:

- Microsoft Exchange Server

- A server that needs to boot from a SAN functionality

- Hyper-V before Windows Server 2012

Microsoft's Windows Server 2008 R2 Hyper-V product required block-level storage for placing the virtual machines and did not support Server Message Block (SMB) in the past—even though this protocol is very common in the Windows world. But with Windows Server 2012, Hyper-V finally also includes support for SMB3 file-level storage.

WINDOWS SERVER EDITION

To build a solution leveraging the iSCSI target server, Windows Server 2012 or Windows Storage Server 2012 could be used. Unlike in previous versions, there is no technical difference between Windows Server and Windows Storage Server—there are no special features or performance optimizations. The only differences are licensing and usage terms. However, even Windows Storage

Server is not specially optimized for storage scenarios, it comes with an excellent economics for a shared storage solution by leveraging industry-standard hardware.

Windows Storage Server 2012 offers greatly enhanced capabilities and benefits when compared to previous versions:

- High performance and reliable file storage

- Flexible, cost-effective options for shared storage

- Continuous availability for enterprise-class operations

Windows Storage Server 2012 is the platform used by OEM partners for their network-attached storage (NAS) appliances. These partners can use this operating system edition and integrate it in their storage system. Windows Storage Server (WSS) is available in two SKUs, the Workgroup and Standard edition. The main differences between the two editions are outlined in Table 6.3.

TABLE 6.3:   Windows Storage Server editions

WSS WORKGROUP EDITION	WSS STANDARD EDITION
50 connections	No license limit
Single processor socket	Multiple processor sockets
Up to 32 GB of memory	No license limit
6 disks (no external SAS)	No license limit
	Failover Clustering
	Hyper-V incl. 2 instances
	Deduplication
	BranchCache

As mentioned earlier, there are no technical differences between Windows Storage Server (Standard edition) and Windows Server (Standard/Datacenter edition). Either can be used as the iSCSI target server for Hyper-V.

AVAILABILITY

As you will see later in this chapter, the iSCSI target server is typically installed and configured in less than an hour. There is one important thing to consider: having a Hyper-V cluster relying on a stand-alone iSCSI target server is not high availability. Even though it looks like a decent cluster from a Hyper-V perspective, and the Cluster Validator does not tell you there's anything wrong, it is actually the iSCSI target where you will have the single point of failure (SPOF). This means that if you need a highly available Hyper-V environment, you have to look at it from an end-to-end perspective and include the computer, network, and storage pattern.

CORE INSTALLATION MODE

The Microsoft iSCSI Software Target does fully support Server Core. However, the iSCSI Target does not have any optimization for the Server Core installation mode specifically.

Again here, consider an intermediate state where you start using a Server with a GUI installation and you can use the graphical tools to configure the server. Whenever the configuration is finished you can remove the GUI at any time. See Chapter 2 for additional details on how to uninstall/install the GUI.

WINDOWS NIC TEAMING VS. MPIO

The Microsoft support policy for NIC teaming on the iSCSI network adapter has been very clear for a long time: Don't use iSCSI and NIC teaming in the same path. Of course there have been good reasons why this is not supported, one of which was the difficulty of troubleshooting networking problems when combining Microsoft iSCSI Initiator and a 3rd party NIC teaming solution. The solution for a redundant network connection was to use the Microsoft "Multipath I/O" (MPIO) component, which allows multiple paths to a storage platform.

Moving forward to a converged network where some blade servers might have only two network adapters, this statement needs to change. And with Windows Server 2012 and the introduction of load balancing and failover (LBFO) this has changed! LBFO now can be used together with Microsoft iSCSI Target Server and this design would be fully supported by Microsoft. Please note, the support statement for a 3rd party NIC Teaming solution does not change.

Looking at the details, how would a converged network have to be setup? Since NIC Teaming provides bandwidth aggregation capabilities in the presence of multiple TCP streams, iSCSI Initiators should consider using MPIO to improve bandwidth utilization.

Therefore create two virtual NICs using the method described in Chapter 2 or Chapter 4 using PowerShell:

```
Add-VMNetworkAdapter -ManagementOS -Name "iSCSI01" -SwitchName "External Public"
```

To ensure each source gets the appropriate amount, use Quality of Service (QOS) to reserve the iSCSI bandwidth. It's recommended to use weights rather than absolute bandwidth settings, for example:

```
Set-VMNetworkAdapter -ManagementOS -Name "iSCSI01" -MinimumBandwidthWeight "5"
```

Repeat this to create the second vNIC and then enable MPIO for these two network adapters. The preferred teaming mode for Hyper-V hosts running iSCSI initiators is Switch Independent teaming mode, with Hyper-V Port load distribution.

For the iSCSI target server itself, the preferred teaming mode is Switch Dependent, which is based on Link Aggregation Control Protocol (LACP), with Address Hash based load distribution. Alternatively, you can simply use MPIO on the iSCSI initiator.

KNOWING THE LIMITS

Because it's free, the Microsoft iSCSI Software Target Server is a very good deployment option for small to medium implementations and also for test environments in general. Scaling it up suits some medium-sized environments. Therefore, it's important to understand not only the strengths, but also the weaknesses, of the storage solution. What might be missing when going into medium-sized environments, compared to other software-based iSCSI targets?

◆ Write-back caching in memory or flash disks

◆ Synchronous replication of data

◆ Online (and offline) deduplication of data

◆ Support for ODX

Even though a few points are addressed in Windows Server 2012 as features in other components of the operating system, such as deduplication or ODX, they are not integrated into the iSCSI target server.

Building the iSCSI Target

The iSCSI target server in Windows Server 2012 has two designs:

◆ Stand-alone with local storage and no high availability

◆ Clustered with shared storage that is either SAS, iSCSI, or has Fibre Channel attached

This section also covers the transformation of a stand-alone iSCSI target to the clustered design, how an iSCSI target has to get configured, and how iSCSI initiators can get connected.

Installing a Stand-Alone iSCSI Target

The iSCSI Target is a role of Windows Server, meaning the first requirement is to have a freshly installed operating system. A stand-alone iSCSI target architecture is mainly considered for small deployments with local storage and no high availability requirements, as Figure 6.4 illustrates.

FIGURE 6.4
Stand-alone iSCSI
target server

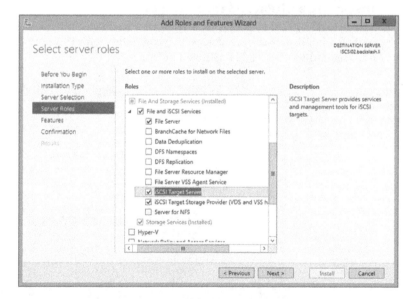

The installation and configuration of Windows Server is straightforward. You may want to create an updated version of the installation checklist described in Chapter 2.

As soon as the system is ready, the iSCSI target server can be installed by using Server Manager. The Add Roles And Features Wizard simplifies the installation process and takes care of all role dependencies:

1. In Server Manager, choose Manage ➢ Add Roles And Features.

2. On the Before You Begin page, verify the Destination Server and then click Next.

3. On the Installation Type page, select Role-Based Or Feature-Based Installation and then click Next.

4. On the Server Selection page, select the server from the Server Pool and then click Next.

5. Now you can select iSCI Target Server And ISCSI Target Storage Provider (VDS And VSS Hardware Providers) when required from the Server Roles page and click Next.

6. The File Server role is automatically selected as it's a requirement for the iSCSI target server. Click Next to proceed.

7. No features have to be selected for the stand-alone deployment. Click Next.

8. On the Confirmation page, click Install. No reboot is required.

As mentioned, as part of the installation, the File Server role is added to the server automatically. Verify whether the installation was finished successfully by checking Server Manager again.

As an alternative: For the iSCSI target, Windows PowerShell can be leveraged to install and configure the iSCSI target server role. The following is a ready-to-fire PowerShell command that will work on both Server Core and Server with a GUI installation:

```
Install-WindowsFeature -Name FS-iSCSITarget-Server
```

Installing a Clustered iSCSI Target

The clustered iSCSI target server architecture leverages Windows Failover Clustering to offer high availability. Therefore, at least two computers with Windows Server 2012 and shared storage are required, which is illustrated in Figure 6.5.

FIGURE 6.5
Clustered iSCSI
target server

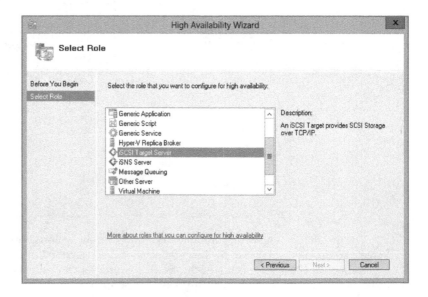

Compared to the stand-alone deployment, at least two hosts are required for the installation with access to shared storage, which can be either SAS or Fibre Channel. Again, creating an updated version of the installation checklist described in Chapter 2 might be helpful before proceeding with the installation.

The iSCSI target server can be installed by using the Server Manager to launch the Add Roles And Features Wizard:

1. On the first iSCSI target server, open Server Manager. In Server Manager, choose Manage ➤ Add Roles And Features.

2. On the Before You Begin page, verify the Destination Server and then click Next.

3. On the Installation Type page, select Role-Based Or Feature-Based Installation. Click Next.

4. From the Server Selection page, select the server from the Server Pool and then click Next.

5. Now you can select iSCSI Target Server And ISCSI Target Storage Provider (VDS And VSS Hardware Providers) when required from the Server Roles page and click Next.

6. The File Server role is automatically selected as it's a requirement for the iSCSI target server. Click Next to proceed.

7. Select Failover Clustering from the Features section and confirm the pop-up with Add Features to add the management tools. Click Next.

8. On the Confirmation page, click Install. No reboot is required.

9. Repeat steps 1–8 for the second iSCSI target server.

As the next step, the iSCSI target server will be configured for high availability:

1. On one of the iSCSI target servers, open Failover Cluster Manager.

2. Select Roles and start the Configure Role Wizard. Click Next.

3. Enter the Name and IP Address for the Client Access Point. Click Next.

4. Select (and assign) the Cluster Disks. Click Next.

5. Read the Confirmation page and then click Next.

Finally, the cluster resource is created. The iSCSI target is now highly available, acting as a two-node failover cluster. Just one note: There is no option in Failover Cluster Manager to start the iSCSI target. This has to be done in Server Manager.

Transforming a Stand-Alone to a Clustered iSCSI Target

As described earlier, the iSCSI target server can be operated in two modes: stand-alone or clustered. Unfortunately, a transition from stand-alone to cluster mode is not supported, because the iSCSI target server stores its configuration differently in these two modes and there is no built-in migration capability.

When using the clustered mode for iSCSI target server, all related information is stored in the cluster configuration. In contrast, in the stand-alone mode, all information is stored locally.

If, for example, a stand-alone iSCSI target is converted to cluster mode, all configuration would be lost after the next service restart, as the cluster configuration would be empty. In this case, the iSCSI target settings should be saved before and restored again after the iSCSI target has switched successfully to cluster mode. Having just a short I/O delay during failover, it's a failover with almost zero downtime.

Configuring the iSCSI Target

After the iSCSI target server role has been successfully enabled, Server Manager shows an iSCSI page under File And Storage Services, as shown in Figure 6.6.

FIGURE 6.6

Server Manager iSCSI target server

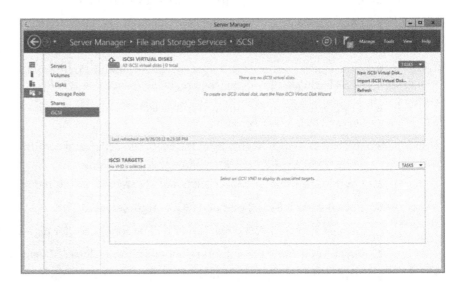

After the installation, no virtual disks have been configured. Follow these steps for the configuration:

1. In Server Manager, click File And Storage Services.

2. In the Navigation section, click iSCSI.

3. Under Tasks, select New iSCSI Virtual Disk. The New iSCSI Virtual Disk Wizard starts.

4. Verify the Server. Select the Volume or choose Type A Custom Path if you don't want to use `<volume>:\iSCSIVirtualDisks` by default. Click Next.

5. By default, the wizard prepopulates the path by using the `<volume>:\iSCSIVirtualDisks` folder. Define the Name of the new virtual disk and then click Next.

6. Specify the virtual disk Size in megabytes, gigabytes, or terabytes. Click Next.

7. Because no iSCSI Target exists, the wizard automatically selects New iSCSI Target. Click Next.

8. Define the Name of the new iSCSI Target and add a description (which is optional). Click Next.

9. The Access Servers page allows you to specify the iSCSI initiators, which can access the virtual disk. Click Add.

10. This wizard will resolve the computer name to its IQN if the initiators' operating system is Windows Server 2012. Click OK and then click Next.

11. On the Enable Authentication tab, CHAP can be configured as an authentication mechanism to secure access to the iSCSI target. This step is optional. Click Next.

12. Review the settings on the Confirmation page. Click Create to finish the configuration.

After the job(s) has been completed, the overview page shows the newly created virtual disk, including all details as illustrated in Figure 6.7.

FIGURE 6.7
Server Manager
iSCSI details

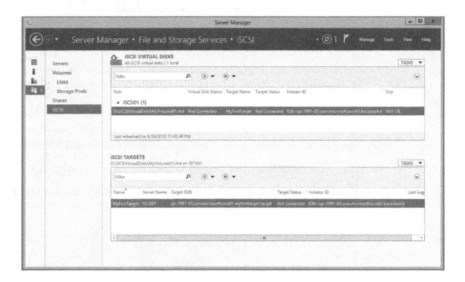

The iSCSI virtual disks are now also shown under the Volumes page. When selecting the appropriate volume, you have the option to jump to the iSCSI overview for further details or management.

NOTE The Server Manager user interface allows you to manage multiple servers from one console, for example, to create virtual disks on any server managed by this instance on a remote server.

The same configuration can also be done easily using PowerShell. First, a new virtual disk has to be created:

```
New-IscsiVirtualDisk -Path D:\iSCSIVirtualDisks\MyVolume01.vhd -Size 50GB
```

Second, the iSCSI target is created:

```
New-IscsiServerTarget -TargetName MyFirstTarget -InitiatorIds "IQN:iqn.1991- `
05.com.microsoft:MyVM.contoso.com"
```

And finally, the virtual disk is assigned to the iSCSI target:

```
Add-IscsiVirtualDiskTargetMapping MyFirstTarget `
D:\iSCSIVirtualDisks\MyVolume01.vhd
```

Connecting the Initiator

After the iSCSI target has been created and the iSCSI virtual disk(s) is assigned, the defined iSCSI initiators are ready to log on. Because the initiator and target are on different machines (typically, at least), the iSCSI target server IP address or hostname needs to be specified:

1. In Server Manager, choose Tools ➤ iSCSI Initiator.

2. If you launch iSCSI Initiator, the first time it also asks for permission to start the service. Click Yes to automatically start this service when Windows starts.

3. In the Discovery tab, click Discover Portal.

4. Add the IP Address or DNS Name of the iSCSI target server and click OK. Change the port only if you don't use the default TCP 3260.

5. All discovered targets are displayed in the box. Select the target you need and click Connect. This launches the Connect To Target pop-up.

6. The advanced settings allow you to specify dedicated network adapters to be used for iSCSI traffic. By default, any adapter/IP can be used for iSCSI connections.

7. The CHAP Log On or IPsec settings also can be configured in this screen, if required to access the iSCSI target. Click OK to proceed.

8. Select Enabled Multi-path to leverage Multipath I/O (MPIO). Click OK.

9. When successfully logged on, the target will show Connected. Click OK to close the menu.

This can also be done using PowerShell. First, the iSCSI Initiator service needs to be started and configured for automatic startup:

```
Start-Service msiscsi
Set-Service msiscsi -StartupType "Automatic"
```

Then the iSCSI target server must be specified:

```
New-IscsiTargetPortal -TargetPortalAddress "MyiSCSIPortal"
```

And then the connection can be established:

```
Get-IscsiTarget | Connect-IscsiTarget
```

If only one target should be connected, you need to provide the node address. This can be found by running the following:

```
Get-IscsiTarget | Format-Table -Property NodeAddress
```

You register the address by running this command:

```
Connect-IscsiTarget -NodeAddress "iqn.1991-05.com.microsoft:MyiSCSIPortal.
contoso.com-myfirsttarget-target"
```

The target has to be registered as a favorite target, so it will automatically reconnect after a host reboot. The SessionIdentifier should be available as an output from the Connect-IscsiTarget or Get-IscsiSession command:

```
Register-IscsiSession -SessionIdentifier "fffffa83020e9430-4000013700000004"
```

NOTE Because the iSCSI Initiator service is not started by default, the PowerShell cmdlets do not function. The service needs to be started before running the commands.

At this stage, the new disk is listed and available in the disk management console. This disk just needs to be formatted and will then be ready for the first use. You can learn how to use PowerShell to initialize and format the disk in the "PowerShell" section later in this chapter.

Managing the iSCSI Target Server

The iSCSI target server in Windows Server 2012 can be managed by using the user interface through Server Manager, as seen in earlier chapters, or PowerShell cmdlets. This section also walks through the Best Practice Analyzer (BPA) and the options with System Center. With System Center 2012 Virtual Machine Manager, storage arrays also can be managed using an SMI-S provider.

Storage Providers

Windows Server 2012 has two features related to the iSCSI target server:

◆ Volume Shadow Copy Service (VSS)

◆ Virtual Disk Service (VDS)

VSS is a framework that allows a volume backup to be performed while the application continues with I/Os. VSS coordinates among the backup application (requester), applications such as Hyper-V (writer), and the storage system such as the iSCSI target (provider) to complete the application-consistent snapshot.

The iSCSI target VSS hardware provider communicates with the iSCSI target server during the VSS snapshot process, thus ensuring that the snapshot is application consistent.

The VDS manages a wide range of storage configurations. In the context of an iSCSI target, it allows storage management applications to manage iSCSI target servers. In previous versions of Windows Server, the Storage Manager for SANs could be used for storage management tasks. In Windows Server 2012, this console snap-in was removed and replaced by Server Manager, PowerShell/WMI, and Storage Management Initiative Specification (SMI-S). Such an SMI-S provider for the iSCSI target will be made available together with System Center 2012 SP1, which is covered in the next section.

These storage providers are typically installed on a different server than the one running iSCSI target server—for example, a virtual guest cluster running Exchange Server. If this guest is not running Windows Server 2012, you will need to download and install the down-level storage providers:

```
www.microsoft.com/en-us/download/details.aspx?id=34759
```

iSCSI Target SMI-S Provider

In Windows Server 2012, the management of the storage device, the iSCSI Software Target, can be done using a SMI-S provider. An SMI-S provider is a software component for a particular storage product. It implements an HTTP/HTTPS server, parses XML requests, and knows how to control those specific devices that usually have their own unique management interfaces.

With the release of SP1 for System Center 2012 Virtual Machine Manager (VMM), the iSCSI target server becomes its own SMI-S provider. The provider follows an *embedded* provider model, which means the component is installed directly on the iSCSI target server. Figure 6.8 shows how the components interact. The SMI-S provider manages the iSCSI target server by using the iSCSI target WMI provider.

FIGURE 6.8
SMI-S architecture

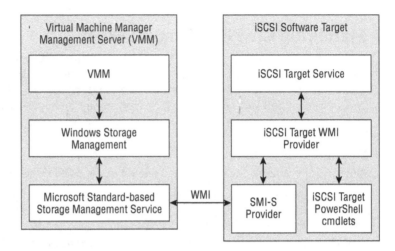

Microsoft has published an interesting blog article, "Introduction to SMI-S," with additional information on SMI-S. You can access the article here:

`http://blogs.technet.com/b/filecab/archive/2012/06/25/introduction-to-smi-s.aspx`

As mentioned before, the iSCSI target server role service must first be installed before the provider can be installed, which means the provider will be installed directly on the iSCSI target server. Therefore, make sure this service role is installed before starting the installation. Also make sure Microsoft KB 276147 is installed on this host to improve the performance of the discovery later on.

To start the installation of the SMI-S provider, locate the installation binaries `iSCSI TargetSMISProvider.msi` under one of the following locations:

- SCVMM installation media: `\amd64\Setup\msi\iSCSITargetProv\`
- SCVMM installation directory: `C:\Program Files\Microsoft System Center 2012\ Virtual Machine Manager\setup\msi\iSCSITargetProv\`

Follow these instructions to install the SMI-S provider on one of the iSCSI target server(s):

1. From the VMM installation media, navigate to `\amd64\Setup\msi\iSCSITargetProv\` and execute.
2. Read the Welcome Page and then click Next.
3. Accept the License Terms. Click Next.
4. Click the Install button to start the installation process.
5. Click the Finish button to close the window.

Finally, the iSCSI Software Target SMI-S provider can be presented to VMM by running the following PowerShell cmdlets on the VMM management server.

First we need to create a RunAs account to authenticate against the iSCSI target server:

```
$RunAsCredentials = Get-Credential


$RunAsAccount = New-SCRunAsAccount -Name "<iSCSITargetAdmin>" `
-Credential $RunAsCredentials
```

The SMI-S provider then can be added as follows:

```
Add-SCStorageProvider -Name "Microsoft iSCSI Target Provider" `
-RunAsAccount $RunAsAccount -ComputerName "<iSCSITargetComputer>" `
–AddSmisWmiProvider
```

The Microsoft iSCSI Software Target will then be available in VMM for further management, as illustrated in Figure 6.9.

FIGURE 6.9
iSCSI target
server in VMM

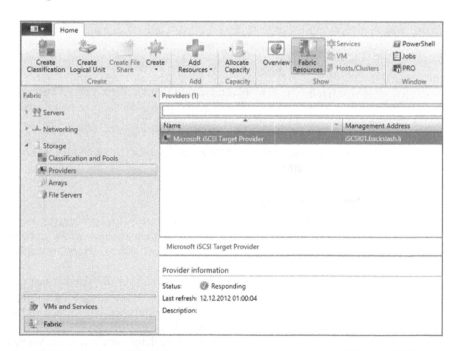

To provision LUNs by using SCVMM, only two more steps are required. In the SCVMM admin console, perform the following steps:

1. In the Fabric view, navigate to Arrays.

2. Open the Properties of the newly added iSCSI target server.

3. Under the Storage Pools tab, select the appropriate storage pools, assign a Classification, and Click OK (see Figure 6.10).

FIGURE 6.10
Storage pools in
SCVMM

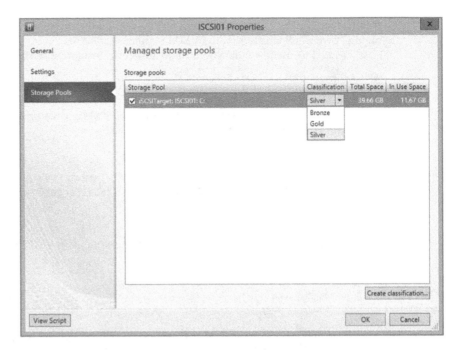

VMM can now create LUNs and assign them to the Hyper-V hosts. Additional information on how SCVMM discovers, classifies, and provisions remote storage can be found on TechNet:

```
http://technet.microsoft.com/en-us/library/gg610600.aspx
```

Note that this version of the SMI-S provider for the iSCSI target server supports only the integration with SCVMM.

Best Practice Analyzer

Microsoft defines guidelines, *recommended practices*, for configuring Windows Server 2012 that are considered as ideal under normal circumstances. So, wouldn't it be great to adopt these best practices and incorporate them into the product to give administrators instant feedback on their configuration? Nothing simpler than that...

Windows Server includes a Best Practice Analyzer (BPA), which can be used by an administrator to check whether a server role runs with the recommended configuration by Microsoft. Deviations from this recommended practice, even critical ones, are highlighted for further investigation—note that not all findings are necessarily problematic, as BPA matches the live configuration against a rule set it receives and updates regularly from Microsoft Update. Running the BPA regularly is a good idea to gain an understanding of how close the configuration is to Microsoft's recommendation—and to understand how and why deviations in your own configuration happen. Findings marked as critical can then be evaluated and resolved, minimizing the risk of configurations that result in poor performance or reliability, security risks, or data loss.

A best practice scan can be started in Server Manager for the whole File Services role, including the iSCSI target:

1. In Server Manager, click Local Server.

2. Scroll down to Best Practice Analyzer.

3. Under Tasks, select Start BPA Scan. The scan starts.

The results will be displayed in the same view with a related problem statement and description.

Alternatively, you can use PowerShell to scan a specific model—for example, the iSCSI Target BPA model. To get an overview of all available modules, just use the following cmdlet:

```
Get-BpaModel | Format-Table -Property Id
```

The best practice scan is started using the Invoke- cmdlet:

```
Invoke-BpaModel -ModelId Microsoft/Windows/FileServices
```

PowerShell

As the iSCSI target management user interface focuses on the presentation of enabling end-to-end scenarios, the underlying cmdlets provide the logic for management tasks that the user interface relies on. The PowerShell capabilities used in the previous version of Windows Server have been expanded for the 2012 release to include the following features:

♦ Disk snapshot management

♦ Differencing disk management

♦ Server global setting management

♦ Additional filters

The metadata for the iSCSI target server PowerShell modules are stored in `MicrosoftiSCSITarget.psd1`.

NOTE   PowerShell scripts that have been developed using the previous release are not guaranteed to work with Windows Server 2012. Although cmdlet names remain valid, required parameters and their input format might have changed. We suggest explicit testing of existing scripts prior to production use with Windows Server 2012.

To get a list of the new available iSCSI Initiator cmdlets, you can use the `Get-Command -Module iSCSI` command in PowerShell. For the iSCSI target, the command would be `Get -Command -Module IscsiTarget`. You can always get detailed help within PowerShell, including a list of parameters for a specific cmdlet, by using `Get-Help`. For instance, if you want help creating a new iSCSI target portal, you can obtain help by using the following PowerShell command: `Get-Help New-IscsiTargetPortal`.

Windows PowerShell 3 also introduces a new cmdlet called `Show-Command`, which opens a graphical user interface leveraging the Windows PowerShell ISE. This capability makes it easy to understand available parameters and cmdlet syntax. The syntax of New-IscsiTargetPortal, for example, can be displayed by typing **Show-Command New-IscsiTargetPortal** in a PowerShell console, which opens the dialog box shown in Figure 6.11.

FIGURE 6.11
PowerShell
Show-Command

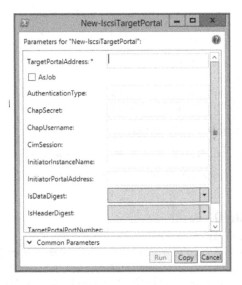

Quite a few cmdlets have already been shown at the beginning of this chapter. Did you know that you also could use PowerShell to configure the provide disk? Have a look at this example:

1. Check whether the new disk is available from the operating system:

```
Get-Disk
```

2. You should see a new disk with the friendly name MSFT Virtual HD SCSI Disk Device and an operational status of Offline. You now can bring the disk online by using the appropriate number:

```
Set-Disk -Number 1 -IsOffline 0
```

3. The status of the disk changes to Online. In the next step, you have to make it writeable:

```
Set-Disk -Number 1 -IsReadOnly 0
```

4. Then you can initialize it (MBR or GPT partition style):

```
Initialize-Disk -Number 1 -PartitionStyle MBR
```

5. Finally, you can create a new partition on this disk by using the maximum size, for example:

```
New-Partition -DiskNumber 1 -UseMaximumSize
```

6. To avoid pop-ups from Windows Explorer, you can skip to assigning a drive letter by using -AssignDriveLetter:$False. This step, however, is optional.

7. Finally, you can format the volume and assign a drive letter:

```
Get-Partition –DiskNumber 1 | Format-Volume
```

8. If you need to assign a drive letter, you can just run the following command. Note that Cluster Shared Volumes (CSV) or Cluster Quorum disks do not require a drive letter.

```
Get-Partition –DiskNumber 1 | Add-PartitionAccessPath -AccessPath D:
```

9. Of course, the very well-known diskpart.exe can still be used and would be the preferred tool for previous Windows Server releases.

Migrating

What if you have already used Microsoft iSCSI Software Target 3.3 and you are planning an in-place upgrade to Windows Server 2012? There are a few things to consider before proceeding. This final section covers the migration from previous versions of Microsoft iSCSI Software Target to Windows Server 2012.

Migration to Windows Server 2012

As mentioned, a few things need to be considered before proceeding and upgrading an iSCSI target to Windows Server 2012. Otherwise, the target or the VDS/CSS providers may not be functional after the upgrade.

In short, the safest method is to uninstall the iSCSI target server before the upgrade and then enable the role after upgrade to Windows Server 2012. In Windows Server 2012, the iSCSI target server as well as the iSCSI Target Storage Provider (VDS and VSS) are available as built-in sub-features of the File And Storage Services role.

In Windows Server 2008 or Windows Server 2008 R2, the DCOM Remote Protocol was used by the iSCSI target. For an application server connecting to Windows Server 2012 iSCSI targets, this causes problems, as now WMI interfaces are in the provider to communicate with the iSCSI target.

Microsoft has released a hotfix, KB 2652137, that addresses this problem.

VHD Conversion

When talking about iSCSI target migration, the discussion is probably related more to the data (the VHDs) than to the migration of the iSCSI target configuration. So what needs to be considered when you migrate from Windows Server 2008 R2 iSCSI Software Target 3.3 to Windows Server 2012?

The easiest approach is to copy the (fixed) VHDs to the new iSCSI target server and then import them:

1. In Server Manager, click File And Storage Services.

2. In the Navigation section, click iSCSI.

3. Under Tasks, select Import iSCSI Virtual Disk. The Import iSCSI Virtual Disk Wizard starts.

4. Browse to locate the old virtual disk file. Click Next to proceed.

5. Select an Existing iSCSI target to assign the virtual disk. Alternatively, create a New iSCSI target. Click Next.

6. Review the settings on the Confirmation page. Click Import to start the import.

For fixed VHDs, the new iSCSI target server will automatically fix any alignment issues.

In case you used differencing VHDs in Windows Server 2008 R2, these virtual disks would have to be converted by using the following cmdlet to align the metadata:

```
Convert-IscsiVirtualDisk -Path \\MyOldiSCSIPortal \VHDs\MyOldVolume.vhd `
- DestinationPath D:\iSCSIVirtualDisks\MyVolume02.vhd
```

If you don't convert the VHD, the import will fail. A conversion is performed only when the source VHD is a different VHD and/or not supporting a 4K drive.

Chapter 7

Using File Servers

Storage costs within an IT project are always a large component in terms of capital expenditures (CapEx). In a server application such as Microsoft Exchange, SQL Server, or even a Hyper-V workload, three main storage solutions are typically supported: direct-attached storage (DAS), iSCSI storage, and Fibre Channel storage. Each storage option presents issues involving data availability, CapEx, and data mobility that need to be addressed, especially when planning your overall storage architecture.

With DAS, the issue is one of high availability. DAS is not highly available by nature, although it is reasonably inexpensive to purchase and has a good overall level of performance. If a server with DAS fails, the associated storage on that server is no longer accessible.

Storage area network (SAN) technologies such as iSCSI or Fibre Channel, but in particular Fibre Channel, have a high acquisition cost, as well as high ongoing operational expenditures (OpEx). However, unlike DAS, both iSCSI and Fibre Channel SANs support Windows Failover Clustering. Specialized skilled resources are required to manage these SANs. In addition, storage manufacturers often use hardware-specific tools that are highly configurable, and so these skills don't easily transfer from one storage manufacturer to another.

Customers may have concerns about data mobility with DAS- and SAN-based storage; they may also be concerned about their ability to easily move databases or virtual machines between independent (nonclustered) servers for DAS, or between different clusters when using a SAN.

With Windows Server 2012, Microsoft introduces an additional storage option, with support for Scale-Out File Servers (SOFS) and Server Message Block 3.0 (SMB 3.0). Applications such as SQL Server and Hyper-V workloads can take advantage of this new storage option and store databases and log files or virtual machine files (including VHDs, configuration, and snapshot files) in a shared folder.

In this chapter, you'll learn about

- ◆ The improvements Microsoft has made to the File Server role in Windows Server 2012

- ◆ How to implement Hyper-V or SQL Server over SMB 3.0 and take advantage of SOFS

Introducing Scale-Out File Servers

Scale-Out File Servers (SOFS) represent a big step beyond the traditional file server we have come to know and love in previous versions of the Windows operating system. In fact, in Windows Server 2012, the File Server role is in vogue again. SOFS provide continuously available file services, which means that system administrators can easily extend the number of SOFS to respond to the increased demands being placed upon them by simply bringing additional file servers online.

SOFS are built on top of Microsoft's well-proven, enterprise-class, high-availability technology: Windows Failover Clustering. In Windows Server 2012, Windows Failover Clustering is designed to provide continuous availability to scale file-based server storage for enterprise applications such as SQL Server and virtualized workloads running on top of Hyper-V. SOFS is also dependent on the Server Message Block 3.0 (SMB 3.0) protocol, which provides the kind of solid and reliable performance that we have come to expect with enterprise-class storage. The main advantages of SOFS and SMB 3.0 in Windows Server 2012 are as follows:

Reduced CapEx Costs   You can start as small as a two-node cluster and scale up to support up to eight nodes.

Reduced OpEx Costs   Specialized storage expertise is not needed.

Ease of Provisioning and Management   It is much easier to manage a file share than it is a SAN.

No Specialized Storage Networking Hardware   You get to leverage your existing investment in converged networking.

Increased Flexibility   You can dynamically relocate SQL Server databases and virtual machines.

In essence, SOFS and SMB 3.0 enable you to implement a scalable storage platform that can address the storage challenges within organizations of all sizes, starting from a basic architecture (as shown in Figure 7.1). SOFS, along with SMB 3.0, provide a significant opportunity to organizations looking to drive down the cost of Windows storage, while still providing continuous high availability.

FIGURE 7.1
Basic example of
file-based storage

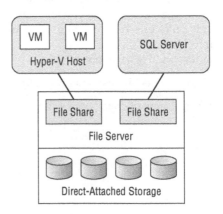

Limitations in Availability and Performance with Windows Server 2008 R2

So why couldn't all of these advantages be realized with Windows Server 2008 R2 today? A file server running Windows Server 2008 R2 has limitations when used as a storage platform. These limitations affect both availability and performance. The main limitations in Windows Server 2008 R2 are listed here:

◆ Failover of file shares in Windows Failover Clustering in Windows Server 2008 R2 is not a transparent operation. When a file share is moved or is failed over to a surviving node, any open file handles that the operating system had temporarily assigned do not survive. The net result is that a SQL Server database would lose access to its database files or a virtual machine would lose access to its virtual hard disks (VHDs), configuration files, or snapshots.

◆ SMB 2 throughput is constrained for network interface controllers (NICs) enabled for high-speed receive-side scaling (RSS). The SMB 2 client has affinity to a single core, and this can limit SMB 2 performance.

◆ SMB 2 communications (as implemented in Windows Server 2008 and Windows Server 2008 R2) was constrained to a single NIC and would leverage only the throughput of that one NIC. Although you could install multiple NICs into your Windows file server, SMB 2 would not take advantage of these multiple NICs.

◆ SMB 2 had a high CPU cost. With high-speed networking, there is an associated cost in terms of core CPU usage, not only to process requests but also in terms of the associated TCP/IP traffic. This is especially true when compared to DAS or when using an iSCSI or Fibre Channel SAN.

◆ Up until this point, file servers had been traditionally used to store office documents and had not been optimized for use by SQL Server (in terms of database storage) or Hyper-V (in terms of VHDs, configuration files, or snapshots). Take, for example, a SQL Server database running an online transaction processing (OLTP) workload. Typically, this kind of work-load carries out small, random, read/write I/O, and SMB 2 was never optimized for this kind of data I/O pattern.

THE VERSIONS OF SMB

Different versions of the Windows operating system have used SMB. In fact, going back to Windows NT 4, SMB was first introduced as Common Internet File System (CIFS). The various iterations of SMB are listed here:

◆ SMB 1.0 was first introduced in Windows 2000 and superseded CIFS.

◆ SMB 2.0 was introduced with Windows Vista/Windows Server 2008.

◆ SMB 2.1 was introduced with Windows 7/Windows Server 2008 R2.

◆ SMB 3.0 was introduced with Windows 8/Windows Server 2012.

Technical Overview of the Key Changes

SOFS, as previously mentioned, takes advantage of new features that are included in Windows Failover Clustering in Windows Server 2012 as well as improvements that have been made to the SMB protocol. Specifically, the following new features and improvements exist in terms of Windows Failover Clustering:

◆ Scale-Out File Server Resource type

◆ Distributed Network Name (DNN)

◆ Scale-Out File Server High Availability role

◆ Windows Server 2012 Cluster Shared Volumes (CSV)

The New SMB 3.0 functionality, which is enabled by default in Windows Server 2012, provides several new capabilities that enable continuous availability of file server–based storage, supporting application data storage, such as SQL Server and Hyper-V based workloads. Specifically, the following are new features and improvements to SMB 3.0:

◆ SMB 3.0 Transport Failover

◆ SMB 3.0 Multichannel

◆ SMB 3.0 Direct

◆ SMB 3.0 Encryption

◆ SMB 3.0 Performance Optimizations

◆ SMB 3.0 Management via Windows PowerShell

WINDOWS SERVER 2012 WINDOWS FAILOVER CLUSTERING FEATURE CHANGES

Windows Server 2012 introduces changes to Windows Failover Clustering, which includes many improvements associated with SOFS. The following are some of the key changes.

Scale-Out File Server Resource Type

A new cluster resource type called the Scale-Out File Server Resource supports SOFS. There are two modes implemented in a Windows failover cluster when providing highly available file services:

◆ The traditional file server resource

◆ The scale-out file server resource

A Windows failover cluster can implement both of these modes at the same time, in the same cluster. Unlike SOFS, when a traditional File Server resource comes online, no File Server resource clones are brought online on any other nodes in the cluster. The SOFS Resource is responsible for the following:

◆ Adding, removing, and modifying shares associated with the resource (these reside on the CSV LUNs)

◆ Storing file share information in the cluster database

- Distributing and applying share information across all nodes in the cluster

- Monitoring the state/health of all CSV LUNs

- Providing standard Windows Failover Clustering resource-specific controls

- Ensuring that a SOFS clone is started on all nodes in the cluster and is listed as Possible Owners for the SOFS Group

Distributed Network Name

In Windows Failover Clustering, the cluster service runs in the context of a local system account. This account is given all the rights needed on the local machine for the cluster to function properly. Because the local system account is different for each node within the cluster, the common identity for the cluster is the computer object that is created in Active Directory when the cluster is formed. This computer object is referred to as the Cluster Name Object (CNO) and equates to the Network Name resource that resides in the Cluster Core Resource Group on each cluster. The CNO is the security context for the cluster and is used for all interactions that require security.

Kerberos is enabled by default on all Network Name resources that are created in a Windows failover cluster. The CNO is the security context for the entire cluster and is used to create all other computer objects corresponding to Network Name resources created on a cluster as part of creating a Client Access Point (CAP). These computer objects are referred to as Virtual Computer Objects (VCOs). The CNO is an owner of that computer object and is listed in the Security tab for the VCO in Active Directory.

When accessing highly available roles provided by Windows Failover Clustering, clients connect using the CAP. The CAP consists of a network name resource (NetBIOS name) and one or more IP Address resources (either IPv4 or IPv6). The CAP is registered in DNS and WINS, assuming that the cluster nodes are configured to register with DNS and WINS in the first place, and more important, that these services accept dynamic registrations.

A highly available role within Windows Failover Clustering can also include other resource types, depending on the services being provided. For example, a highly available traditional File Server would include a CAP, a File Server Resource, and a Physical Disk resource. When the highly available File Server is configured using the High Availability Wizard, all the correct resource dependencies are set within the cluster. For a Client Access Point, the Network Name resource depends on the IP Address resource. This means the IP Address resource must come online first, before the Network Name resource is brought online.

A CAP in a traditional File Server can be online on only a single node in the cluster at any one time. This means that when clients are making a connection, only the node hosting the CAP will be providing that specific highly available role to the clients connecting to it. None of the other nodes in the cluster will have access to those resources as long as those resources continue to remain online on the current owner.

SOFS use a different method for servicing applications that use shares hosted in a Windows failover cluster. This group consists of a DNN and a SOFS resource. Unlike the File Server Resource Group, no IP Address or Storage type resources are present in this new resource group.

The SOFS Resource Group comes online on only one node in the Windows failover cluster. This node is considered the leading node. All nodes in the cluster will host clones of this resource group, and the clones are under the control of the leading node. The leading node sequences the startup and shutdown of the clones and tracks their state on the other nodes in the cluster. The

SOFS group should never go offline as long as at least one of the clones is functioning on a node in the cluster. The leading node function can move to any node in the cluster, in the event that the cluster service unexpectedly terminates on the current owner.

Moving the ownership of the leading node to another node in the cluster has no impact on file share availability. However, if a cluster administrator intentionally takes the SOFS group offline, the leading node will shut down all of the clones and the group will be marked as offline. In addition, all scale-out file shares will be torn down.

Although the Scale-Out File Server Group does not show any dependencies for an IP Address resource, the DNN actually depends on the IP addresses of each node in the Windows failover cluster. The DNN resource registers with DNS by using the IP addresses of each node in the cluster for each NIC configured in the cluster to accept client connections. It will also create the appropriate VCO in Active Directory to support Kerberos functionality. The DNN resource is also responsible for tracking the nodes in the cluster and updating DNS when the following occurs:

◆ A node is added or evicted from the cluster.

◆ A specific IP address is added or removed to a public cluster network (a network enabled for Client Access).

◆ Refresh of the DNS records occurs. (The default is every 24 hours or whenever the DNN resource comes online in the cluster.)

Scale-Out File Server High-Availability Role

With the introduction of SOFS in Windows Server 2012, there are now a couple of options available when configuring a highly available File Server in Windows Failover Clustering. Using the High Availability Wizard, shown in Figure 7.2, the File Server role is initially listed as a File Server. Only by continuing through the configuration do the two modes actually reveal themselves.

FIGURE 7.2
High Availability
Wizard

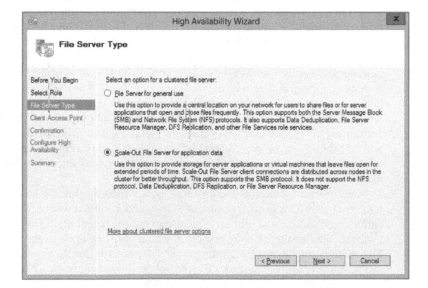

Depending on the configuration choice made, the High Availability Wizard will determine what additional information is required to complete the configuration. For example, the File Server For General Use will require you to configure your storage options. A SOFS does not require this, as it is assumed the CSV LUN will be used for storing application data.

It is also important to note the restrictions imposed upon you when configuring a SOFS. SOFS do not support Network File System (NFS) or certain role services, such as File Server Resource Manager (FSRM) and Distributed File System Replication (DFSR).

Cluster Shared Volumes

Cluster Shared Volumes (CSV) is a distributed access file system feature that was originally optimized for the Hyper-V role in Windows 2008 R2. CSV was designed to allow virtual machines and their disk resources to reside on any node within the cluster. CSV enabled multiple nodes to concurrently access a single shared volume, providing complete transparency with respect to cluster node ownership of virtual machines and client access during failover using Live Migration.

Windows Server 2012 CSV has been extended to support SOFS. Implementing SOFS requires all application data shares to be hosted on a Windows Server 2012 CSV LUN. This is the only way SMB clients are able to gain access to all shares configured in the context of the Scale-Out File Server Resource (provided access controls are properly configured to allow this to happen) from any node in the cluster.

In Windows Server 2012, CSV has been improved: the primary focus was to expand the Windows roles that supported CSV plus improve the backup and restore process on those CSV volumes. The Windows Server 2012 CSV improvements include the following:

◆ The CSV namespace is now enabled by default as a core Failover Clustering feature, making it easier to add storage to it.

◆ The CSV File System (CSVFS) that mounts on top of Windows Server 2012 CSV volumes provides the following:

◆ Local file semantics to clustered applications (SQL, Hyper-V).

◆ Support for NTFS features (except transactions—that is, TxF). Windows Server 2012 CSV still requires an NTFS partition.

◆ Direct I/O for file data access, including sparse files.

SPARSE FILES

Sparse files are files that may have regions in the file without allocated space on a CSV.

◆ Redirected I/O for metadata operations to the Coordinator node.

◆ Synchronized data and metadata access to files, providing end-to-end data consistency guarantees.

◆ Fault tolerance for both data and metadata access.

◆ Opportunistic locking (oplocks) for applications accessing CSV files (such as SMB/SRV), enabling remote caching of CSVFS file data.

> **OPPORTUNISTIC LOCKING**
>
> Opportunistic locks, or *oplocks*, were originally introduced into the file system to provide network file sharing clients the ability to cache data and at the same time provide a mechanism to ensure data consistency when multiple clients read from or write to the same stream.

- Use of oplocks to ensure data consistency when a file is being accessed simultaneously by multiple CSVFS instances.

- Ability to do concurrent remote distributed snapshots (backup) without I/O redirection or moving volumes between cluster nodes.

- Improved virtual machine creation.

- Improved file copy performance.

- Multi-subnet support (that is, multisite clusters implemented using routed networks).

- Integration with SMB Multichannel and SMB Direct, which allows for streaming CSV traffic across multiple network adapters in the cluster and for leveraging network adapters with RDMA. This provides improved I/O performance when a volume is in redirected mode.

- Better integration with third-party filter drivers (antivirus, continuous data protection, backup, and data replication applications).

- Support for BitLocker encryption of CSV volumes.

WINDOWS SERVER 2012 SMB FEATURE CHANGES

Windows Server 2012 introduces changes to Server Message Block (SMB) that include many improvements associated with SOFS. The following are some of the key changes.

SMB 3.0 Transparent Failover

SMB 3.0 transparent failover enables you to perform both hardware and software maintenance (planned maintenance) to nodes in a traditional file server cluster by moving highly available file shares between nodes within the cluster without interrupting the server applications that are storing data on these file shares.

For SOFS, clients simply reconnect to another node within the cluster without interruption of service. Failover is a transparent operation to the application; any errors within the application are not apparent, and there is simply a short delay in network I/O while the automatic reconnection occurs. SMB 3.0 transparent failover has the following requirements:

- A Windows failover cluster that contains at least two nodes running Windows Server 2012.

- The Windows failover cluster must pass the cluster validation tests using either the validation wizard or the appropriate PowerShell cmdlets.

- On all SOFS cluster nodes, the File Server for Scale-Out Application Data must be installed. This role provides the persistent store and enables the file server to resume file handles after a failover. It also provides a witness service that helps clients more quickly reconnect to a surviving node after unplanned failure.

- File shares need to be enabled for continuous availability (although this property is enabled by default).

- Both the server hosting the application (in this instance, either the SQL server or Hyper-V server) and the server hosting the continuously available enabled file share must be running Windows Server 2012.

SMB 3.0 Multichannel

SMB 3.0 Multichannel enables the aggregation of network bandwidth and network fault tolerance, when multiple network paths are available between an SMB 3.0 client and server. This enables server applications to take full advantage of the available bandwidth and be resilient to network failures. SMB 3.0 Multichannel is enabled by default and there is no real need to disable it, unless you are carrying out some form of performance testing or you have a complex network environment. To verify that SMB Multichannel is enabled from the server side, use the PowerShell command `Get-SmbServerConfiguration | Select EnableMultichannel`. On the client side, use `Get-SmbClientConfiguration | Select EnableMultichannel`.

SMB 3.0 Multichannel can be disabled from the server side via the PowerShell command `Set-SmbServerConfiguration -EnableMultichannel $false`. From the client side, use `Set-SmbClientConfiguration -EnableMultichannel $false`. SMB 3.0 Multichannel has the following requirements:

- Two servers running Windows Server 2012 are required. No extra roles or features need to be installed or configured because SMB 3.0 Multichannel is enabled by default.

- The following network configurations are recommended, as shown in Figure 7.3:

  - Although not optimal, a single 10 GbE NIC. Each of the two servers is configured with a single 10 GbE NIC.

  - Dual 1 GbE NICs. Each of the two servers is configured with two 1 GbE NICs, with each card using a different subnet.

  - Dual 1 GbE NICs in a team. Each of the two servers is configured with two 1 GbE NICs in a load balancing and failover (LBFO) team. Communication occurs across the teamed interface.

  - Dual 10 GbE NICs. Each of the two servers is configured with two 10 GbE NICs, with each card using a different subnet.

  - Dual 10 GbE NICs in a team. Each of the two servers is configured with two 10 GbE NICs in an LBFO team. Communications occurs across the teamed interface.

  - Dual InfiniBand NICs. Each of the two servers is configured with two InfiniBand NICs, with each card using a different subnet.

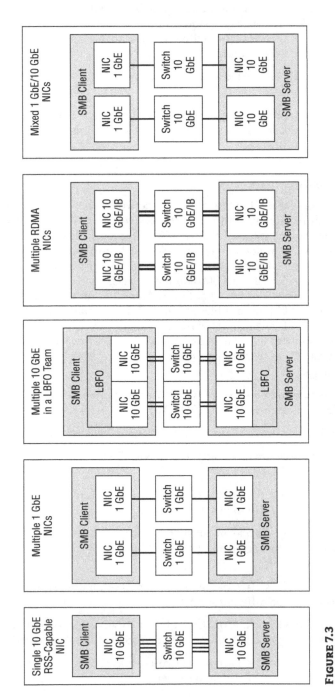

FIGURE 7.3

Sample Multichannel configuration options

Equally multiport NICs (dual- or quad-port adapters) can be used with SMB 3.0 Multichannel, because these adapters show up in Windows as multiple individual NICs. However, this type of adapter does not offer a high-enough level of network fault tolerance, and so the preceding examples aim to avoid the use of multiport NICs.

NIC TEAMING

While the use of NIC teaming provides a level of fault tolerance, SMB without Multichannel creates only one TCP/IP connection per team, leading to limitations in the number of CPU cores utilized, and potentially restricting the ability to fully utilize the entire bandwidth of the team.

However, NIC teaming continues to offer failover capability, which works faster than using SMB Multichannel by itself. NIC teaming is also a recommended option because it offers failover capabilities to other workloads, such as a traditional highly available file server that does not rely on the enhancements in SOFS and therefore cannot benefit from the transparent failover capabilities of SMB 3.0 Multichannel. There is one exception to this, and that is when you are using RDMA NICs (R-NICs). When teaming R-NICs, the team itself is reported in Windows as non-RDMA capable. If you intend to use R-NICs, do not team them.

In Windows Server 2012, SMB 3.0 Multichannel is initiated after an SMB read or SMB write is issued within a session. To verify that multiple connections are in use, you can execute the following PowerShell command from the SMB Client Get-SmbConnectionNetworkInterface, or you can use Windows Performance Monitor.

SMB Multichannel Constraints

SMB Multichannel Constraints allows you to control the SMB Multichannel behavior in more-complex networking environments. For example, if you have six NICs in your server and you want the SMB client to use only two of those NICs, you can accomplish this kind of configuration by using Windows PowerShell and the cmdlet SmbMultichannelConstraint. If you wanted to use the first two adapters in your server, and the Interface Index for those adapters was 12 and 13, you would use the following PowerShell command:

```
New-SmbMultichannelConstraint -ServerName HOST1 -InterfaceIndex 12, 13
```

INTERFACE INDEX

The interface index specifies the network adapter interface index number for a given adapter and is determined by using the Get-NetAdapter PowerShell cmdlet.

SMB 3.0 Multichannel Constraints have the following configuration requirements:

◆ Is configured on the SMB 3.0 Client and is persisted within the Registry.

◆ Multichannel Constraints are configured on a per server basis. You can configure different sets of interfaces for each server if required.

- ◆ You list the network interfaces that you want to use, and not the interfaces you want to exclude.

- ◆ For servers not specified, the default SMB Multichannel behavior continues to apply.

SMB 3.0 Direct

SMB 3.0 Direct or SMB 3.0 over RDMA (as shown in Figure 7.4) enables support for a special type of NIC: an R-NIC that has remote direct memory access (RDMA) functionality and can operate at full speed, with little latency, while using minimal core CPU. For server applications such as SQL Server or Hyper-V workloads, SMB 3.0 Direct allows the remote file server to have a similar performance characteristic to locally attached storage. SMB 3.0 Direct has the following requirements:

- ◆ Two servers running Windows Server 2012 are required. No extra roles or features need to be installed, as SMB 3.0 Direct is enabled by default.

- ◆ NICs that support RDMA. Currently these R-NICs come in three types:

  - ◆ iWARP

  - ◆ InfiniBand

  - ◆ RDMA over Converged Ethernet (RoCE)

For further details on iWARP, InfiniBand, or RoCE, take a look at the following links:

```
http://blogs.technet.com/b/josebda/archive/2012/07/31/deploying-windows-server-
2012-with-smb-direct-smb-over-rdma-and-the-intel-neteffect-ne020-card-using-iwarp-
step-by-step.aspx
```

```
http://blogs.technet.com/b/josebda/archive/2012/07/31/deploying-windows-server-
2012-with-smb-direct-smb-over-rdma-and-the-mellanox-connectx-2-connectx-3-using-
infiniband-step-by-step.aspx
```

```
http://blogs.technet.com/b/josebda/archive/2012/07/31/deploying-windows-server-
2012-with-smb-direct-smb-over-rdma-and-the-mellanox-connectx-3-using-10gbe-40gbe-
roce-step-by-step.aspx
```

FIGURE 7.4
SMB Direct
(SMB over RDMA)

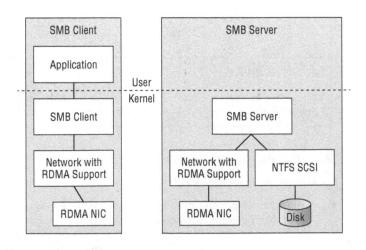

The main advantages of SMB 3.0 Direct or SMB 3.0 over RDMA include the following:

◆ Minimal core CPU utilization for remote file server processing

◆ Low-latency networking with the ability to leverage high-speed R-NICs

◆ The ability to provide a Fibre Channel–equivalent solution at a much cheaper cost

◆ SMB 3.0 Direct provides all the management benefits of SMB-based file storage:

   ◆ SMB-based file storage is easy to provision and manage.

   ◆ SMB 3.0 Direct can leverage converged networking (see Chapter 4, "Networking," for more information on converged networking).

   ◆ No application or administrative changes are required to benefit from SMB 3.0 Direct.

SMB 3.0 Encryption

SMB 3.0 encryption enables end-to-end encryption of SMB data to protect network communications from eavesdropping when communication occurs over an untrusted network, while the data is in flight. SMB encryption can be configured either per file share or for the entire server without the need for a certificate authority infrastructure, and it uses AES-128 in CCM mode.

SMB 3.0 encryption adds no cost overhead and removes the need to configure IPsec or the use of specialized encryption hardware and WAN accelerators.

SMB 3.0 Performance Optimizations

With SMB 3.0 performance optimizations, both the SMB 3.0 client and the SMB 3.0 server have been optimized for small, random read/write I/O. This type of data pattern is common in server applications such as SQL Server OLTP. In addition, the large maximum transmission unit (MTU 9000) is turned on by default and uses a 1-MB SMB message size, which significantly enhances performance in large sequential transfers, such as in a SQL Server enterprise data warehouse, SQL database backup and restore jobs, or for deploying or copying Hyper-V virtual hard disks.

SMB 3.0 Management via Windows PowerShell

You can view and manage the capabilities of SMB 3.0 not only from the user interface but by also using Windows PowerShell. The PowerShell management in SMB 3.0 allows system administrators to manage SMB 3.0 end to end from the command line.

Installing and Configuring Scale-Out File Servers

Before you can install and configure SOFS, you need to make several deployment decisions, as well as understand the prerequisites:

◆ You will need to decide the number of nodes within your SOFS cluster (this is from two to eight nodes).

◆ Determine what kind of converged network you will have in place to support your SOFS cluster.

◆ Determine what kind of storage you will have in place to support your SOFS cluster (Storage Spaces or SAN based).

◆ Before you can implement SOFS, you will need to install features that are included in the File and Storage Services role and the Failover Clustering feature.

◆ You will need to ensure that the cluster passes validation, create your Windows failover cluster, configure networking, and add storage (one of more CSV LUNs).

STORAGE SPACES

Storage Spaces is a new virtualization capability within Windows Server 2012 aimed at reducing the cost associated with highly available storage for hosted, virtualized, and cloud-based deployments. Storage Spaces is based on a storage-pooling model, whereby storage pools can be created from affordable commodity-based hardware, depending on your storage needs. A storage space is then carved out of the storage pool and presented as a virtual disk to Windows.

Complying with Installation Prerequisites

SOFS requires the File Server role and the Failover Clustering feature to be installed on each node that will be a part of the SOFS. The File Server role and the Failover Clustering feature can be installed independently of each other, or at the same time, using either Server Manager or the appropriate PowerShell command.

INSTALLING ROLES AND FEATURES

Use the following procedure to install the File Server role and the Failover Clustering feature using Server Manager:

1. Open the Server Manager dashboard and click Manage at the top-right of the screen, as shown in Figure 7.5. Then click Add Roles And Features. The Add Roles And Features Wizard appears.

2. On the Before You Begin page, click Next. On the Select Installation Type page, click Role-Based or Feature-Based Installation, and then click Next.

3. On the Select Destination Server page, select the appropriate server, and then click Next. (By default, the local server appears in the Server Pool.)

4. On the Select Server Roles page, expand File And Storage Services, expand File Services, and then select the File Server check box. Click Next.

5. On the Select Features page, select the Failover Clustering check box, and then click Next.

6. On the Add Features That Are Required For Failover Clustering page, click Add Features.

7. On the Confirm Installation Selections page, click Install. Verify that the installation succeeds, and click Close.

FIGURE 7.5
Server Manager
dashboard

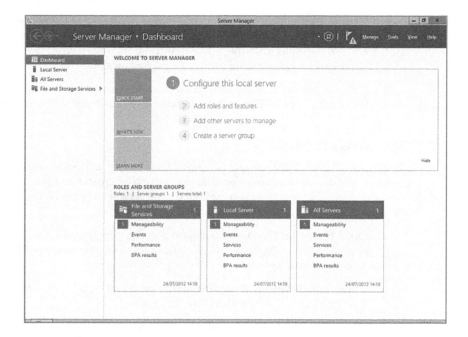

To install the prerequisite roles and features by using PowerShell, run the following Windows Server Manager PowerShell command:

```
Add-WindowsFeature –name File-Services,Failover-Clustering `
-IncludeManagementTools
```

VERIFYING A SUCCESSFUL INSTALLATION

Verify the successful installation of the prerequisite roles and features by running the following Windows Server Manager PowerShell command:

```
Get-WindowsFeature | Where {$_.installed}
```

Configuring Failover Clustering

The next task on the road to implementing SOFS is to implement Windows Failover Clustering. The cluster will provide support for a highly available SMB file share that can then be used by applications such as SQL Server and for workloads running on Hyper-V. Before you can install and configure Windows Failover Clustering, consider the following:

◆ You will need to run the cluster validation process and ensure that it completes, without reporting any failures.

◆ After the successful creation of your multi-node cluster, you will need to verify that the Core Cluster Resources group and any shared storage have come online.

◆ If the shared storage was added prior to the cluster being formed, all the LUNs except for the Witness Disk will have automatically been added to the Available Storage Group and will be brought online. SOFS requires the storage to be a CSV LUN, and the CSV namespace is now enabled by default in Windows Server 2012.

◆ If the storage is added after the cluster has been formed or the check box Add All Available Storage To The Cluster was not selected, then the storage will need to be added manually.

VALIDATING A CLUSTER

Cluster validation is a process that is designed to identify any potential hardware, software, or general configuration issues prior to configuring your cluster and placing that cluster into production. After the validation is complete, you can create the cluster. Use the following procedure to validate your cluster:

1. Open the Server Manager dashboard and click Tools at the top-right of the screen, as shown earlier in Figure 7.5. Then click Failover Cluster Manager. The Failover Cluster Manager MMC appears.

2. Under the Management heading, in the center pane, click the Validate Configuration link. The Validate A Configuration Wizard appears.

3. On the Before You Begin page, click Next. On the Select Servers Or A Cluster page, enter the names of the servers you want to validate in an FQDN format—such as, for example, **FS1.DEMO.INTERNAL**. Then click Next.

4. On the Testing Options page, ensure that the Run All Tests (Recommended) option is selected, and then click Next.

5. On the Confirmation page, click Next. On the Summary page, ensure that the Create The Cluster Now Using The Validated Nodes check box is deselected, and then click Finish.

To validate the hardware, software, and general configuration of your Windows Failover Cluster by using PowerShell, run the following Windows Failover Cluster PowerShell command:

```
Test-Cluster -Node fs1.demo.internal, fs2.demo.internal
```

Make sure to separate each node of the cluster with a comma.

CREATING A CLUSTER

After installing the required roles and features to support SOFS and validating your configuration, the next step is to create a new cluster. Creating a cluster can be accomplished either with the Failover Cluster Manager MMC or the appropriate PowerShell cmdlet. Use the following procedure to create your cluster:

1. Open the Server Manager dashboard and click Tools at the top-right of the screen. Then click Failover Cluster Manager. The Failover Cluster Manager MMC appears.

2. Under the Management heading, in the center pane, click the Create Cluster link. The Create Cluster Wizard appears.

3. On the Before You Begin page, click Next. On the Select Servers page, enter the names of the servers you want to join the cluster, in a FQDN format, such as **FS1.DEMO.INTERNAL**, and click Next.

4. On the Access Point For Administering The Cluster page, in the Cluster Name box, type the name of your cluster.

Additionally, if DHCP-assigned addresses are not being used on the NICs associated with the cluster, you will have to provide static IP address information.

USING DHCP-ASSIGNED IP ADDRESSES

Since Windows Server 2008 Failover Clustering, the capability has existed for cluster IP address resources to obtain their addressing from DHCP as well as via static entries. If the cluster nodes themselves are configured to obtain their IP addresses from DHCP, the default behavior will be to obtain an IP address automatically for all cluster IP address resources. If the cluster node has statically assigned IP addresses, the cluster IP address resources will have to be configured with static IP addresses. Cluster IP address resource IP assignment follows the configuration of the physical node and each specific interface on the node.

---

5. Deselect any networks that will not be used to administer the cluster. In the Address field, enter an IP address to be associated with the cluster and then click Next, as shown in Figure 7.6.

FIGURE 7.6
Access point
for administering
the cluster

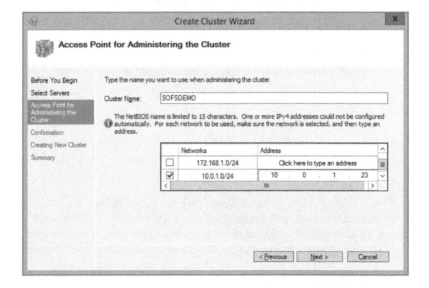

6. On the Confirmation page, click Next. On the Summary page, click Finish.

To create your Windows Failover Cluster by using PowerShell, run the following Windows Failover Cluster PowerShell command:

```
New-Cluster -Name SOFSDEMO -Node FS1.DEMO.INTERNAL,FS2.DEMO.INTERNAL -NoStorage `
-StaticAddress 10.0.1.23
```

CONFIGURING NETWORKING

Communication between SOFS cluster nodes is critical for smooth operation. Therefore, it is important to configure the networks that you will use for SOFS cluster communication and ensure that they are configured in the most optimal way for your environment.

At least two of the cluster networks must be configured to support heartbeat communication between the SOFS cluster nodes, and this will avoid any single points of failure. To do so, configure the roles of these networks as Allow Cluster Network Communications On This Network. Typically, one of these networks should be a private interconnect dedicated to internal communication. However, if you have only two physical NICs, rather than two LBFO pairs, these two NICs should be enabled for both cluster use and client access.

Additionally, each SOFS cluster network must fail independently of all other cluster networks. This means that two cluster networks must not have a component in common that could cause a common simultaneous failure, such as the use of a multiport (dual- or quad-port) network adapter. To attach a node to two separate SOFS cluster networks, you would need to ensure that independent NICs are used.

To eliminate possible communication issues, remove all unnecessary network traffic from the NIC that is set to Internal Cluster communications only (this adapter is also known as the *heartbeat* or *private network adapter*) and consider the following:

◆ Remove NetBIOS from the NIC.

◆ Do not register in DNS.

◆ Specify the proper cluster communication priority order.

◆ Set the proper adapter binding order.

◆ Define the proper network adapter speed and mode.

◆ Configure TCP/IP correctly.

ADDING STORAGE

After going through the process of creating your cluster, the next step is to add storage to Cluster Shared Volumes. SOFS requires the storage to be a CSV LUN, with the benefit here being that the CSV LUN can be accessed by more than one node at a time. You can add a CSV LUN by using Failover Cluster Manager. Use the following procedure to add your storage to the cluster:

1. Open the Server Manager dashboard and click Tools at the top-right of the screen. Then click Failover Cluster Manager. The Failover Cluster Manager MMC appears.

2. Expand the Storage node in the left pane, click the Disks node, right-click the disk that you want to add to Cluster Shared Volumes within the center pane, and then click Add To Cluster Shared Volumes. Repeat this process for each disk you would like to add to the SOFS cluster.

To add available storage to Cluster Shared Volumes by using PowerShell, run the following Windows Failover Cluster PowerShell command (note that "`Cluster Disk 2`" represents the disk number that you want to add and may differ in your setup):

```
Add-ClusterSharedVolume "Cluster Disk 2"
```

Configuring Scale-Out File Services

SOFS requires that you configure the File Server role, as well as create a continuously available file share, on your CSV LUN. Use the following procedure to configure SOFS and add your continuously available file share to your cluster:

1. Open the Server Manager dashboard and click Tools. Then click Failover Cluster Manager. The Failover Cluster Manager MMC appears.

2. Right-click the Roles node and click Configure Role. The High Availability Wizard appears.

3. On the Before You Begin page, click Next. On the Select Role page, click File Server and then click Next.

4. On the File Server Type page, select the Scale-Out File Server For Application Data option and then click Next.

5. On the Client Access Point page, in the Name box, type the DNN that will be used to access Scale-Out File Server (note that the DNN is limited to a maximum of 15 characters). Then click Next.

6. On the Confirmation page, confirm your settings and then click Next. On the Summary page, click Finish.

To configure the File Server role by using PowerShell, run the following Windows Failover Cluster PowerShell command:

```
Add-ClusterScaleOutFileServerRole -Name SOFS -Cluster SOFSDEMO
```

When complete, the SOFS Role should be online on one of the nodes within your cluster. The group will contain a DNN and the SOFS resource (see Figure 7.7).

FIGURE 7.7
SOFS role
dependency list

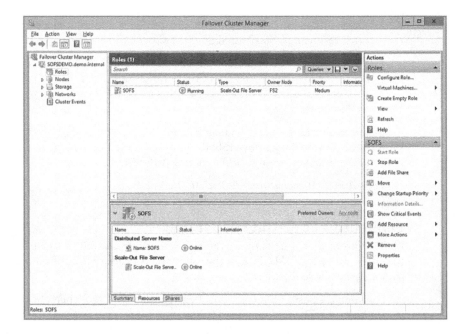

Configuring a Continuously Available File Share

After going through the process of configuring your SOFS role, the next step is to add a continuously available file share to the CSV LUN. Use the following procedure to add your continuously available file share to your cluster:

1. Open the Server Manager dashboard and click Tools. Then click Failover Cluster Manager. The Failover Cluster Manager MMC appears.

2. Expand the Roles node in the left pane, right-click the SOFS resource within the center pane, and then click Add File Share.

   Alternatively, shared folders can be created by using the PowerShell command New-SmbShare or directly with Windows Explorer.

3. On the Select The Profile For This Share Page, click SMB Share – Applications, as shown in Figure 7.8. Then click Next.

4. On the Select The Server And Path For This Share page, select the Cluster Shared Volume to host this share and then click Next.

5. On the Specify Share Name page, in the Share Name box, type a share name, such as **SOFSSHARE**, and then click Next.

6. On the Configure Share Settings page, ensure that the Enable Continuous Availability check box is selected, optionally select Encrypt Data Access, and then click Next.

7. On the Specify Permissions To Control Access page, click Customize Permissions, grant the following permissions, and then click Next.

FIGURE 7.8
Selecting a
Profile in the
New Share Wizard

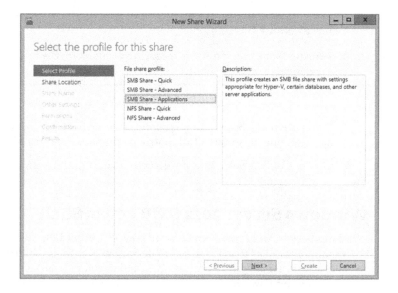

If you are using this Scale-Out File Server file share for Hyper-V, then all Hyper-V computer accounts, the SYSTEM account, and all Hyper-V administrators, must be granted full control on the share and the file system (see Figure 7.9). If the Hyper-V server is part of a Windows Failover Cluster, the CNO must also be granted full control on the share and the file system.

FIGURE 7.9
Advanced security
settings—stand-
alone host

> **CLUSTER NAME OBJECT**
>
> The Cluster Name Object (CNO) is the security context for the cluster and is used for all interactions requiring a security context.

If you are using Scale-Out File Server on Microsoft SQL Server, the SQL Server service account must be granted full control on the share and the file system.

8. On the Confirm selections page, click Create. On the View results page, click Close.

Windows Server 2012 SMB PowerShell

Windows Server 2012 provides a series of PowerShell cmdlets and WMI objects to manage the SMB shares as well as to manage access permissions to those shares. These new PowerShell cmdlets are aimed at both IT professionals and developers alike.

The following PowerShell cmdlets are available for SMB share management:

◆ `Get-SmbShare`

◆ `New-SmbShare`

◆ `Set-SmbShare`

◆ `Remove-SmbShare`

The following PowerShell cmdlets are available for SMB share access permission management:

◆ `Get-SmbShareAccess`

◆ `Grant-SmbShareAccess`

◆ `Revoke-SmbShareAccess`

◆ `Block-SmbShareAccess`

◆ `Unblock-SmbShareAccess`

The SMB cmdlets are packaged up nicely into two modules called `SmbShare` and `SmbWitness`. They can be loaded by using the PowerShell command `Get-Module -ListAvailable Smb* | Import-Module`. However, if you simply start using the cmdlets from within PowerShell, the related modules will automatically be loaded for you.

To get a list of the available SMB PowerShell cmdlets, use the PowerShell command `Get-Command -Module SMB* | Select Name`.

> **GETTING HELP**
>
> You can get help within PowerShell, including a list of parameters for a specific cmdlet, by using the `Get-Help` cmdlet. For instance, if you want help creating a new SMB share, you can use the PowerShell command `Get-Help New-SmbShare -Detailed`.

The following are some common use cases for leveraging the SMB PowerShell cmdlets:

◆ Managing SMB shares: New, Get, Set, Remove

◆ Managing SMB share permissions: Get, Grant, Revoke, Block, Unblock

The following are some common operational tasks that you might carry out when managing SMB file shares:

◆ Create a new file share: New-SmbShare -Name ShareName -Path C:\FolderLocation

◆ Get a list of existing file shares: Get-SmbShare

◆ Change the configuration of an existing share: Set-SmbShare -Name ShareName -Description " Hyper-V share"

◆ Remove a file share: Remove-SmbShare -Name ShareName

The following are some common operational tasks that you might carry out when managing SMB share permissions:

◆ Add permissions for a user when creating a file share: New-SmbShare -Name ShareName -Path C:\FolderLocation -FullAccess UserName

◆ Grant permissions for a user after the file share is already created: Grant-SmbShareAccess -Name ShareName -AccountName UserName -AccessRight Full

◆ Get a list of permissions for a file share: Get-SmbShareAccess -Name ShareName

◆ Revoke permissions for a user: Revoke-SmbShareAccess -Name ShareName -AccountName UserName

◆ Block a specific user from a file share: Block-SmbShareAccess -Name ShareName -AccountName UserName

◆ Unblock a specific user from a file share: Unblock-SmbShareAccess -Name ShareName -AccountName UserName

Windows Server 2012 Hyper-V over SMB 3.0

Windows Server 2012 Hyper-V introduces support for SMB 3.0 remote file storage as an additional storage option. Windows Server 2012 Hyper-V can now store virtual machine files in a file share, using the SMB 3.0 protocol. The main advantages of being able to use a remote file share are as follows:

◆ An SMB 3.0 remote file share provides ease of provisioning and management of your Hyper-V storage.

◆ SMB 3.0 remote file share provides an increased level of flexibility in terms of your Hyper-V storage.

◆ With an SMB 3.0 remote file share, you can leverage your existing investment in your converged networking.

◆ SMB 3.0 provides options for reducing both your CapEx and OpEx costs associated with your Hyper-V storage.

Windows server 2012 Hyper over SMB 3.0 has the following requirements:

◆ One or more servers configured with the Hyper role

◆ One or more servers configured with the File Services role

◆ A common Active Directory infrastructure (although this Active Directory infrastructure does not need to run Windows Server 2012)

Some Real-World Examples

Although it is not practical to explain every possible Windows Server 2012 Hyper-V over SMB 3.0 configuration, this section presents a few examples. These examples show an increased level of complexity, starting from a basic configuration with no fault tolerance whatsoever, all the way to a configuration that is entirely clustered.

CONFIGURATION EXAMPLES 1 AND 2

Configuration example 1 shows one or more stand-alone Windows Server 2012 Hyper-V servers, connecting to a stand-alone file server, which has numerous internal SATA drives available in a non-RAID disk design. The main problem with this configuration example is that there are three points of failure:

◆ The storage is not fault tolerant.

◆ The file server is not continuously available.

◆ The virtual machines are not highly available.

Configuration example 2 shows one or more stand-alone Windows Server 2012 Hyper-V servers, connecting to a stand-alone file server, which has numerous internal SATA drives available in a fault-tolerant disk design, using a mirrored storage space. While the disk subsystem is now fault tolerant, there are still a couple of points of failure with this example:

◆ The file server is not continuously available.

◆ The virtual machines are not highly available.

Figure 7.10 illustrates these first two examples.

FIGURE 7.10
Real-world
examples 1 and 2

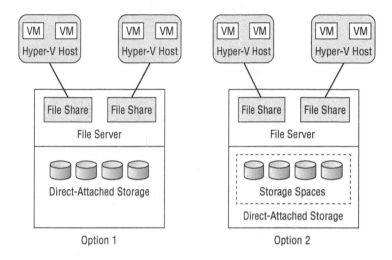

CONFIGURATION EXAMPLES 3, 4, AND 5

Configuration example 3 shows one or more stand-alone Windows Server 2012 Hyper-V servers, connecting to a SOFS cluster. While the storage is now fully fault tolerant, there is still one point of failure with this example:

◆   The virtual machines are not highly available.

Configuration example 4 shows two or more Windows Server 2012 Hyper-V servers in a failover cluster, connecting to a stand-alone file server, which has numerous internal SATA drives available in a fault-tolerant disk design. While the disk subsystem is now fault tolerant and the virtual machines are highly available, there is still one point of failure with this configuration example:

◆   The file server is not continuously available.

Configuration example 5 shows two or more Windows Server 2012 Hyper-V servers in a failover cluster, connecting to a SOFS cluster, which has a number of shared SAS drives available in a fault-tolerant disk design. In this configuration, the storage subsystem could be either an iSCSI or Fibre Channel storage array. In this configuration, the following is achieved:

◆   The storage is fault tolerant.

◆   The file server is continuously available.

◆   The virtual machines are highly available.

Figure 7.11 illustrates examples 3, 4, and 5.

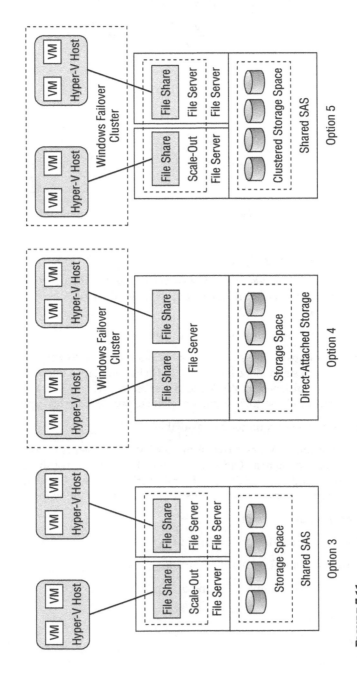

FIGURE 7.11
Real-world examples 3, 4, and 5

Configuring Windows Server 2012 Hyper-V to Use Scale-Out File Server Cluster

Now that you have managed to configure your SOFS, the next step is to configure a virtual machine to use the continuously available file share. You can create a virtual machine by using either the Hyper-V Manager MMC or Windows PowerShell. When you are prompted or when you need to specify the virtual machine location, enter the name of the CAP that is configured in the failover cluster for Scale-Out File Server.

Use the following procedure to configure a virtual machine to use the continuously available file share:

1. On one of the SOFS nodes, open the PowerShell command prompt and validate that the continuously available share has the appropriate permissions configured by using the PowerShell cmdlets `Get-Acl` and `Get-SmbShareAccess`.

   To verify that your continuously available share has the appropriate permissions configured, run the following Windows Security and SMB PowerShell commands (see Figure 7.12):

   ```
   Get-Acl C:\ClusterStorage\Volume1\Shares\SOFSSHARE | Select *
   ```

   These will return the appropriate file system permissions. The following will return the appropriate share-level permissions:

   ```
   Get-SmbShareAccess SOFSSHARE
   ```

FIGURE 7.12
Determining
the appropriate
permissions

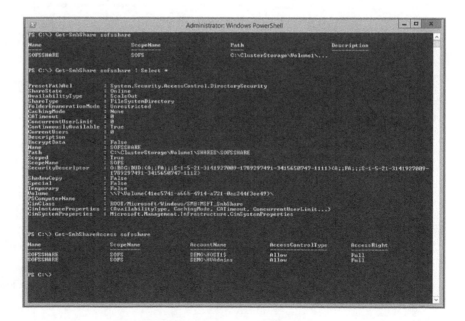

2. On one of the Hyper-V servers, open the Server Manager dashboard and click Tools. Then click Hyper-V Manager. The Hyper-V Manager MMC appears.

3. Right-click the Hyper-V server, point to New, and then click Virtual Machine.

4. On the Before You Begin page, click Next. On the Specify Name And Location page, in the Name box, type a name for the virtual machine, as shown in Figure 7.13. Select the Store The Virtual Machine In A Different Location check box. In the Location box, type the CAP that is configured in the failover cluster for Scale-Out File Server using a UNC format, such as **\\SOFS\SOFSSHARE**, and then click Next.

5. On the Assign Memory page, type the desired amount of memory in the Startup memory box, such as **1024**, and then click Next.

6. On the Configure Networking page, in the Connection box, choose the appropriate network for your environment, and then click Next.

7. On the Connect Virtual Hard Disk page, shown in Figure 7.14, create a virtual hard disk and ensure that the set location is configured to redirect to the CAP that is configured in the failover cluster for SOFS, such as **\\SOFS\SOFSSHARE\VMTEST\Virtual Hard Disk**. Then click Next.

FIGURE 7.13
Specifying name and location

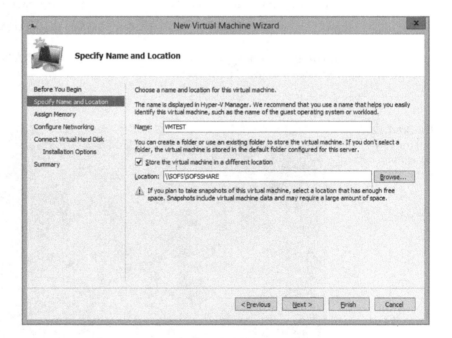

8. On the Installation Options page, select the appropriate option to install an operating system and then click Next.

9. On the Completing The New Virtual Machine Wizard page, click Finish.

FIGURE 7.14
Creating a VHD

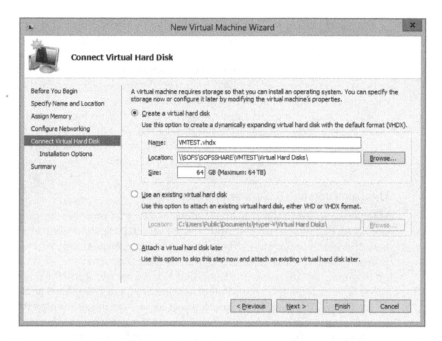

Alternatively, a new virtual machine can be created by using the PowerShell commands New-VHD and New-VM. To create a new virtual machine by using PowerShell, run the following Hyper-V PowerShell command:

```
New-VHD -Path "\\SOFS\SOFSSHARE\VMTEST\Virtual Hard Disk\VMTEST.VHDX" -SizeBytes `
64GB -Dynamic
New-VM -Name VMTEST -Path \\SOFS\SOFSSHARE\ -VHDPath "\\SOFS\SOFSSHARE\VMTEST\ `
Virtual Hard Disk\VMTEST.VHDX" -Memory 1GB -SwitchName External
```

To verify that the virtual machine is using the SOFS share using Windows PowerShell, from the Hyper-V server, execute the following PowerShell command:

```
Get-VM VMTEST | Select *
```

Configuring SQL Server to Use Scale-Out File Server Cluster

Typically, when you think about implementing SQL Server and you look at the storage architectures that organizations tend to implement, these architectures fall into one of two categories:

◆ DAS

◆ SAN based

DAS is the norm for smaller customer deployments. Typically, you get very good performance, at a great cost point, but DAS creates a fragmented storage architecture. Effectively, you can't leverage this storage from other servers within your environment—and for certain customers such as hosters, that might be OK. For larger deployments, customers implement a SAN. This gets around the issue of having a fragmented storage architecture, because you can get access to the storage from other servers, but this comes at a cost.

You end up with a dedicated network (which is often Fibre Channel, but in some cases can be iSCSI) that provides access to the storage. There is no doubt that by implementing a SAN, you can increase the availability and utilization of your overall storage investment. However, under Windows Server 2012, there is now a new option: SOFS.

Understanding SQL Server Prerequisites

SQL Server is one of the only applications to date that provides support for SOFS as a storage solution. Both SQL Server 2008 R2 and SQL Server 2012 are supported. However, SQL Server 2008 R2 is supported in only a stand-alone configuration (nonclustered), whereas SQL Server 2012 is supported in both a stand-alone configuration and in a cluster.

Because you are using this Scale-Out File Server file share for SQL server, the SQL service account, which needs to run under the context of a domain-level account, and all appropriate SQL administrators, must be granted full control on the share plus the file system. If the SQL server is part of a Windows Failover Cluster, then much as in the case of Hyper-V, the CNO must also be granted full control on the share and the file system.

Running SQL Server Setup

There are several ways to install SQL Server. The most popular method is via the SQL Server Installation Wizard, which is based on Windows Installer. It provides a single installation routine to install the following SQL Server components:

- Database Engine
- Analysis Services
- Reporting Services
- Integration Services
- Master Data Services
- Data Quality Services
- Management tools
- Connectivity components

You can install each component individually or select a combination. Use the following procedure to install SQL Server 2012 and configure both the data and log files to use a SOFS continuously available file share:

1. On your SQL Server, insert the SQL Server installation media into your DVD drive. If this is a virtual machine from the Media menu, select DVD Drive, select Insert Disk, and point to your SQL Server 2012 ISO file.

2. Navigate to the DVD drive. From the root, double-click `setup.exe`. The Installation Wizard runs the SQL Server Installation Center. To start a new installation of SQL Server, click Installation in the left pane, and then click New SQL Server stand-alone installation or add features to an existing installation.

3. The Setup Support Rules run a discovery operation on your server. To continue, click OK. Alternatively, you can view the details on the screen by clicking the Show Details button, or as an HTML report by clicking the View Detailed Report link.

4. On the Product Key page, select an option to indicate whether you are installing a free evaluation edition of SQL Server, or a production version that has a PID key. Then click Next.

5. On the License Terms page, review the license agreement and, if you agree, select the I Accept The License Terms check box, and then click Next. Optionally, to help improve SQL Server, you can also enable the Send Feature Usage Data To Microsoft option.

6. On the Product Updates page, the latest available SQL Server product updates are displayed via Windows Update. If you don't want to include the updates, clear the Include SQL Server Product Updates check box and click Next. If no product updates are discovered, SQL Server Setup does not display this page and advances automatically to the Install Setup Files page.

7. On the Setup Support Rules page, take note of any warnings of failures before setup can continue and either rectify them and click the Re-run button or click Next.

8. On the Setup Role page, select SQL Server Feature Installation, and then click Next to continue to the Feature Selection page.

9. On the Feature Selection page, select only the Database Engine Services and the Management Tools. Accept the default directory options and click Next.

10. On the Installation Rules page, click Next. On the Instance Configuration Page, click Next. On the Disk Space Requirements page, click Next.

11. On the Server Configuration page for both the SQL Server Agent and the SQL Server database engine, specify the service account that has the appropriate permissions to the SOFS continuously available file share. As shown in Figure 7.15, enter a valid password, set the Startup Type for both of these services to Automatic, and click Next.

12. On the Database Engine Configuration page, shown in Figure 7.16, click the Add Current User button and then click the Data Directories tab. In the Data Root Directory, specify the path to the SOFS continuously available file share, such as **\\SOFS\SQLDATA**, and click Next. You will be prompted to confirm that the right permissions have been assigned on the share. Simply click Yes.

13. On the Error Reporting page, click Next. On the Installation Configuration Rules page, click Next. On the Ready To Install page, click Install. On the Installation Complete page, click Close.

FIGURE 7.15
Service account
configuration

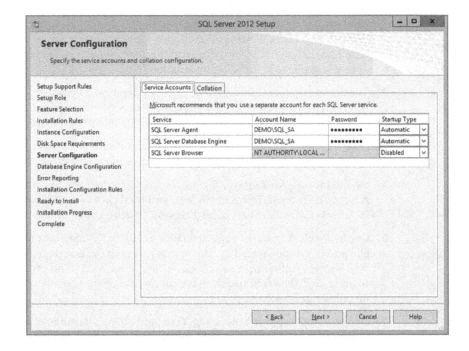

FIGURE 7.16
Database engine
configuration

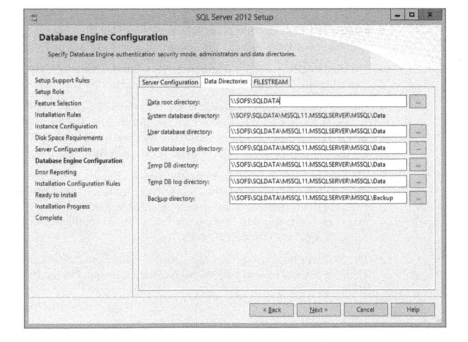

Troubleshooting Scale-Out File Servers

Troubleshooting requires a logical and often systematic search for the source of the problem, so that ultimately the problem can be resolved, and the product or component that was failing can be brought back online and be considered in an operational state once again.

Various techniques can be used to troubleshoot issues encountered when implementing and managing SOFS in support of application data. The following are meant to provide assistance when troubleshooting problems as they are encountered.

Using Troubleshooting Tools

Troubleshooting tools for SOFS can be divided into the following components:

- Windows Failover Clustering
- Hyper-V
- File services
- SMB 3.0
- SQL Server

WINDOWS FAILOVER CLUSTERING

The primary troubleshooting tools for Windows Failover Clustering are the cluster log, the Windows system event log, and the logs located under `Applications and Service Logs\ Microsoft\Windows`. Depending on how complex the problem is, additional tracing can be enabled, but this would require contacting Microsoft Product Support and speaking to a customer support engineer. When working with Microsoft support engineers, additional data can be gathered by running custom diagnostic tools that collect and upload data directly to Microsoft for further analysis.

The Windows Failover Clustering Diagnostic log can be generated by using the Failover Cluster PowerShell cmdlet `Get-ClusterLog`. The log that is generated is placed in the `%systemroot%\ cluster\reports` directory. The following logs are also applicable to Windows Failover Clustering:

- FailoverClustering
  - Diagnostic
  - Operational
  - Performance-CSV
- FailoverClustering-Client
  - Diagnostic
- FailoverClustering-CsvFlt
  - Diagnostic
- FailoverClustering-CsvFs
  - Diagnostic

- FailoverClustering-Manager

  - Admin

  - Diagnostic

- FailoverClustering-WMIProvider

  - Admin

  - Diagnostic

WINDOWS SERVER 2012 HYPER-V

The primary troubleshooting tools for Windows Server 2012 Hyper-V are the Windows system event log and the logs located under Applications and Service Logs\Microsoft\Windows. Again, depending on how complex the problem is, additional tracing can be enabled when contacting Microsoft Product Support. The following logs are applicable to Windows Server 2012 Hyper-V:

- Hyper-V-Config

  - Admin

  - Analytic

  - Operational

- Hyper-V Hypervisor

  - Admin

  - Analytic

  - Operational

- Hyper-V-Integration

  - Admin

  - Debug

- Hyper-V-SynthFC

  - Admin

  - Debug

- Hyper-V-SynthNic

  - Admin

  - Debug

- Hyper-V-SynthStor

  - Admin

  - Analytic

- ◆ Debug
- ◆ Operational
- ◆ Hyper-V-VID
  - ◆ Admin
  - ◆ Analytic
- ◆ Hyper-V-VMMS
  - ◆ Admin
  - ◆ Analytic
  - ◆ Networking
  - ◆ Operational
  - ◆ Storage
- ◆ Hyper-V-Worker
  - ◆ Admin
  - ◆ Analytic
  - ◆ VDev-Analytic

FILE SERVICES

The primary troubleshooting tools for File Services are the Windows system event log and the logs located under `Applications and Service Logs\Microsoft\Windows`. Again, depending on how complex the problem is, additional tracing can be enabled when contacting Microsoft Product Support. The following logs are applicable to File Services:

- ◆ FileServices-ServerManager-EventProvider
  - ◆ Admin
  - ◆ Debug
  - ◆ Operational

SMB 3.0

The primary troubleshooting tools for SMB 3.0 are the Windows system event log and the logs located under `Applications and Service Logs\Microsoft\Windows`, especially the logs located under `Remotefs-Smb`. Again, depending on the complexity of the problem, additional tracing can be enabled when contacting Microsoft Product Support. The following logs are applicable to SMB 3.0:

- ◆ Remotefs-Smb
  - ◆ Operational

- ◆ HelperClassDiagnostic
- ◆ ObjectStateDiagnostic
- ◆ XPerfAnalytic
- ◆ SMBDirect
    - ◆ Admin
    - ◆ Debug
- ◆ SMBWitnessClient
    - ◆ WintnessClientAdmin
- ◆ SMBWitnessService
    - ◆ WitnessServiceAdmin

SQL SERVER

The primary troubleshooting tools for SQL Server are the SQL Server error logs, the Windows system event log, and the logs located under Applications and Service Logs\Microsoft\SQL Server. The SQL Server error logs, which are located in the %Program Files%\Microsoft SQL Server\Mssql\Log\Errorlog directory, can be viewed by using SQL Server Management Studio. Again, depending on the complexity of the problem, additional tracing can be enabled when contacting Microsoft Product Support.

Troubleshooting Client Network Connectivity Issues

If SMB 3.0 clients are having problems connecting to the Scale-Out File Server, consider executing the following steps:

1. Inspect the Windows system event log for any errors related to network connectivity.

2. Open a command prompt and execute an nslookup test to determine whether the SOFS CAP can be resolved. If name resolution is not working, check your DNS server for the proper registration records.

3. Open a command prompt and execute a basic ping connectivity test. Consider pinging your Default Gateway, the SOFS cluster nodes, and the SOFS CAP to determine whether the client is able to make contact.

4. If either of the tests in step 2 or step 3 fails, take a network trace while executing those tests to help isolate any connectivity issue. A local network trace can be obtained by executing the command Netsh trace start capture=yes. When you have repeated the issue, stop the trace by executing the command Netsh trace stop. The trace information will be stored in the user's profile folder, under c:\Users\<user_name>\AppData\Local\Temp\NetTraces. The trace data can be opened and examined in Microsoft's Network Monitor utility.

5. If all network connectivity tests pass, on the SOFS cluster, open the Failover Cluster Manager and select the SOFS Role. In the details pane, with the role selected, click the Shares tab at the bottom and review the file share information, ensuring that all configured shares are displayed.

Troubleshooting Access Denied Issues

If SMB 3.0 clients are receiving Access Denied messages when attempting to connect to SOFS, execute the following steps:

1. Open the Failover Cluster Manager MMC.

2. Locate the Scale-Out File Server role. With the role highlighted, click the Share tab at the bottom of the page and verify that all file shares are available.

3. If the file share is available that a client is receiving an Access Denied error for, double-click the file share and click Permissions.

4. Click the Customize Permissions button. The Advanced Security Settings for the share are displayed. Review the permissions and ensure that they are correct.

5. Click the Effective Access tab and click either Select A User or Select A Device to review the effective permissions. The PowerShell cmdlet `Get-SMBShareAccess` can also be used to obtain information about file share permissions.

Troubleshooting Cluster Resource Issues

Use the following troubleshooting steps to resolve problems associated with Windows Failover Cluster:

1. Identify the issue by either inspecting the Failover Cluster Manager MMC and looking for failures, or by inspecting the Windows system log for any events sourced by Failover Clustering.

2. Determine whether the issue is isolated to a specific node in the cluster or is occurring on all nodes.

3. Generate the cluster log by using the `Get-ClusterLog` PowerShell cmdlet to run the command `GetClusterLog -Cluster SOFS -Node FS1 -TimeSpan 120 -Destination c:\dump -UseLocalTime`.

4. Compare events in the Windows system log, the cluster log, and any other appropriate log.

Real World Solutions

CHALLENGE

A large-sized company wants to implement Windows Server 2012 Hyper-V to consolidate a number of unmanaged tier 2 and tier 3 SQL server databases, since these databases have become business critical. One of the deployment blockers that is stopping this company from carrying out such a SQL consolidation exercise is the fact that their existing storage area network (SAN) does not currently offer support for Windows Server 2012. However, there are alternative storage options available that could be leveraged outside of Fibre Channel.

The CEO of the company has made it clear that it would be difficult to fund the replacement of this SAN within the first half of the year, due to unforeseen budgetary constraints. The CIO of the company is pushing the IT department to come up with innovative ways of being able to better support these business critical databases and is pushing for the use of shared SAS as an alternative storage architecture.

SOLUTION

The solution would be to implement SOFS in combination with Storage Spaces to provide a resilient storage solution on shared SAS. This allows the company to implement Windows Server 2012 Hyper-V and enables the protection of business critical workloads without having to fund a replacement Fibre Channel SAN.

CHALLENGE

The company is satisfied that they can leverage SOFS as an alternative storage option for their business critical tier 2 and tier 3 SQL databases. They now want to be able to verify the SMB configuration. How could this be accomplished?

SOLUTION

The solution would be to leverage the following PowerShell cmdlets to verify SMB Multichannel is enabled and to confirm the NICs are being properly recognized by SMB.

On the SMB client, run the following PowerShell cmdlets:

```
Get-SmbClientConfiguration | Select EnableMultichannel
Get-SmbClientNetworkInterface
```

On the SMB server, run the following PowerShell cmdlets:

```
Get-SmbServerConfiguration | Select EnableMultichannel
Get-SmbServerNetworkInterface
```

Chapter 8

Building Hyper-V Clusters

The definition of a *cluster* is a group of servers and associated shared storage that work together and can be accessed as a single system. The individual nodes of the cluster act together to distribute the workloads running on the cluster and to provide for the automatic recovery from failure of one or more components within the cluster. Hyper-V itself has no clustering capability and relies on close integration with Windows Failover Clustering to provide such services.

In this chapter, you'll learn about

- The basics of Failover Clustering
- Configuring Cluster Shared Volumes
- Integrating BitLocker into a failover cluster
- Implementing Cluster-Aware Updating
- Making a virtual machine highly available
- Configuring the various availability scenarios

Introduction to Building Hyper-V Clusters

As previously mentioned, a cluster is a group of appropriately configured servers and shared storage, certified for Windows Server 2012, that work together and can be accessed as a single system. When you look at the anatomy of a cluster, as shown in Figure 8.1, it is typically made up of several components:

- Servers that are connected to multiple networks, either via a single NIC or an LBFO team of NICs
- Servers that are connected to some form of shared storage (that is, shared SAS, iSCSI, or Fibre Channel), either via a single path to the storage array or via multipath

FIGURE 8.1
Hyper-V cluster

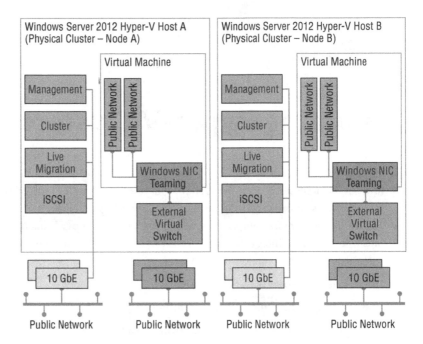

Maintaining reliability, redundancy, and connectivity among the nodes within the cluster is extremely important to the success of its operation. This is no different if the cluster is located within a single location or across multiple locations, that is, a multi-site cluster. The general requirements are as follows:

◆ Two or more independent networks must connect the nodes in a cluster in order to avoid a single point of failure—that is, the networks must be able to fail independently of one another. Cluster configurations using a single network are not recommended as a best practice and will result in a warning during the cluster validation process.

◆ Each cluster network must be configured as a single IP subnet whose subnet number is distinct from those of other cluster networks.

◆ It is recommend to configure the entire set of network adapters used to attach nodes to the cluster network in an identical fashion: the same speed, duplex mode, flow control, media type, and hardware offloads should be configured.

◆ The storage array must support SCSI-3 SPC3-compliant SCSI commands for persistent reservation and release. The cluster validation process will test for this, and noncompliant arrays will result in errors.

◆ All host bus adapters (HBAs) must use the Storport/miniport driver model provided by Microsoft in order to be listed in the Windows Server Catalog.

◆ All multipath solutions must be MPIO based to be listed in the Windows Server Catalog. Additional multipath software, such as the storage vendor's MPIO, is required to ensure that the host gets a single view of the devices across multiple HBAs.

MULTIPATH I/O

Multipath I/O provides redundant failover and load-balancing support for multipath disk devices, which may be disks or logical units. The goal of the MPIO is to ensure correct operation of a disk device that can be reached via more than one storage path. When the OS determines that there are multiple storage paths to a disk device, it uses the multipath drivers to correctly initialize, and then uses one or more of the available physical paths, depending on the MPIO load-balancing algorithm.

Active Directory Integration

Active Directory integration is key to the success of running and operating a reliable cluster. Nodes within a cluster are required to be members of the same Active Directory domain. It is recommended that the cluster CNO and cluster node machine names be placed in their own Organizational Units (OUs) within Active Directory. The main reason for utilizing a dedicated OU is to ensure that Group Policies and any operating system hardening via security templates don't have an undesirable effect on the reliability of the cluster.

Failover Clustering Installation

The installation procedure for Failover Clustering is not that much different from that of Windows Server 2008/R2. Failover Clustering is considered a *feature* in Windows Server 2012, much as it was in Windows Server 2008 R2. Failover Cluster consists of the following components:

◆ Failover Clustering feature

◆ Failover Cluster Management tools (These include the Failover Cluster Manager and the Cluster-Aware Updating UI.)

◆ Failover cluster modules for PowerShell

◆ Failover Cluster Automation Server (This is the deprecated COM programmatic interface MSClus.)

◆ Failover cluster command interface (This is the deprecated cluster.exe command-line tool.)

The Failover Clustering feature can be installed by using either Server Manager or the command line. Use the following procedure to install Failover Clustering in Windows Server 2012:

1. Open the Server Manager dashboard, click Manage, and then click Add Roles And Features.

2. In the Add Roles And Features Wizard, on the Before You Begin page, click Next.

3. On the Select Installation Type page, select Role-Based or Feature-Based Installation and then click Next.

4. On the Select Destination Server page, click Next.

5. On the Select Server Roles page, click Next.

6. On the Select Features page, click Failover Clustering and then click Next.

7. Click Add Features.

8. On the Select Features page, click Next.

9. On the Confirm Installation Selections page, click Install.

10. On the Results page, click Close.

To enable the Failover Clustering feature by using Windows PowerShell, run the following Server Manager PowerShell command:

```
Install-WindowsFeature -Name Failover-Clustering -IncludeManagementTools
```

Performing Validation

Windows Server 2008 introduced the concept of cluster validation prior to forming a cluster within the Failover Cluster Manager console. Validation ensures that your chosen hardware will function as required. This is not really a new concept, and in fact, Windows Server 2003 included cluster validation via an out-of-band tool called ClusPrep.

ClusPrep would complete a system inventory and run a series of focused tests on the servers that were targeted to be nodes within the failover cluster, the only difference being that ClusPrep was a separately downloaded tool. Windows Server 2012 has expanded on the cluster validation process by not only updating some of the existing tests but also by adding tests (see Table 8.1 for further information).

TABLE 8.1: Cluster validation tests

TEST CATEGORY	TESTS
Cluster Configuration	List Cluster Core Groups
	List Cluster Network Information
	List Cluster Resources
	List Cluster Volumes
	List Clustered Roles (new to Windows Server 2012)
	Validate Quorum Configuration
	Validate Resource Status
	Validate Service Principal Name
	Validate Volume Consistency
Inventory Storage	List Fibre Channel Host Bus Adapters
	List iSCSI Host Bus Adapters
	List SAS Host Bus Adapters

TABLE 8.1: Cluster validation tests *(continued)*

TEST CATEGORY	TESTS
Inventory System	List BIOS Information
	List Environment Variables
	List Memory Information
	List Operating System Information
	List Plug and Play Devices
	List Running Processes
	List Services Information
	List Software Updates
	List System Drivers
	List System Information
	List Unsigned Drivers
Network	List Network Binding Order
	Validate Cluster Network Configuration
	Validate IP Configuration
	Validate Network Communications
	Validate Windows Firewall Configuration
Storage	List Disks
	List Potential Cluster Disks
	Validate CSV Network Bindings
	Validate CSV Settings (new to Windows Server 2012)
	Validate Disk Access Latency
	Validate Disk Arbitration
	Validate Disk Failover
	Validate File System
	Validate Microsoft MPIO-Based Disks
	Validate Multiple Arbitration
	Validate SCSI Device Vital Product Data (VPD)
	Validate SCSI-3 Persistent Reservation
	Validate Simultaneous Failover
	Validate Storage Spaces Persistent Reservation (new to Windows Server 2012)

TABLE 8.1: Cluster validation tests *(continued)*

TEST CATEGORY	TESTS
System Configuration	Validate Active Directory Configuration
	Validate All Drivers Signed
	Validate Memory Dump Settings
	Validate Operating System Edition (new to Windows Server 2012)
	Validate Operating System Installation Option
	Validate Operating System Version (new to Windows Server 2012)
	Validate Required Services
	Validate Same Processor Architecture
	Validate Service Pack Levels
	Validate Software Update Levels
Hyper-V (new to Windows Server 2012 if the role is installed)	List Hyper-V Virtual Machine Information
	List Information About Servers Running Hyper-V
	Validate Compatibility of Virtual Fibre Channel SANs for Hyper-V
	Validate Firewall Rules for Hyper-V Replica Are Enabled
	Validate Hyper-V Integration Services Version
	Validate Hyper-V Memory Resource Pool Compatibility
	Validate Hyper-V Network Resource Pool and Virtual Switch Compatibility
	Validate Hyper-V Processor Pool Compatibility
	Validate Hyper-V Role Installed
	Validate Hyper-V Storage Resource Pool Compatibility
	Validate Hyper-V Virtual Machine Network Configuration
	Validate Hyper-V Virtual Machine Storage Configuration
	Validate Matching Processor Manufacturers
	Validate Network Listeners Are Running
	Validate Replica Server Settings

Validation can be performed either before or after forming a cluster. Microsoft recommends that you complete the initial validation process before forming a cluster. This is required to obtain support from Microsoft Support. In addition, all hardware components in the solution must be certified for Windows Server 2012. See http://technet.microsoft.com/en-en/

library/jj134244 for further information. When making changes to your cluster, Microsoft also recommends that you rerun the validation process to ensure conformity and again ensure that you can obtain support.

The validation process ensures network connectivity between the nodes and connectivity to, and the functionality of, the shared storage. The minimum number of nodes required to run all tests is two. Attempting to run the test with one node will result in many of the critical storage tests not being executed.

The cluster validation process itself is also a great troubleshooting tool that can be used on an already operational cluster. When executing the cluster validation process, a smaller subset of the validation tests can be selected to assist in diagnosing a particular issue.

Running Cluster Validation

Use the following procedure to validate your failover cluster in Windows Server 2012:

1. Launch Server Manager. In the navigation pane, click Dashboard, click Tools, and then click Failover Cluster Manager.

2. In Failover Cluster Manager, in the Actions pane, click Validate Configuration to launch the Validate A Configuration Wizard.

3. On the Before You Begin page, click Next.

4. On the Select Servers Or A Cluster page, in the Enter Name field, type the FQDN of your targeted cluster nodes (for example, **host1.demo.internal).** Use semicolons to add nodes, as shown in Figure 8.2, and click Next.

5. On the Testing Options page, click Run All Tests (Recommended) and then click Next.

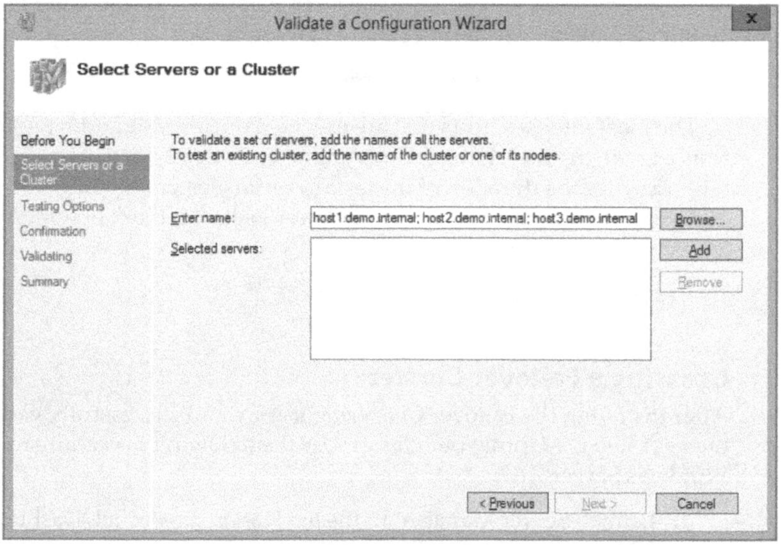

FIGURE 8.2
Select servers
or a cluster

6. On the Confirmation page, review the test list and then click Next. (Note that tests may take up to 10 minutes to complete.)

7. On the Summary page, deselect the Create The Cluster Now Using The Validated Nodes check box, and then click View Report. (If the check box is selected, the Create Cluster Wizard will launch automatically using the validated nodes.)

8. If required, correct any errors found during the validation process and then revalidate the configuration. Otherwise, close the report and click Finish.

To run cluster validation using PowerShell, run the following Windows Failover Clustering PowerShell command:

```
Test-Cluster -Node host1,host2,host3
```

The following categories of tests, listed in Table 8.1, are run during the cluster validation process:

◆ Cluster Configuration gathers and displays information about the cluster.

◆ Inventory gathers and displays information about the nodes.

◆ Network verifies the network settings and connectivity to the nodes.

◆ Storage verifies that the storage is configured properly and supports Failover Clustering.

◆ System Configuration compares the software configuration of the different nodes.

◆ Hyper-V Configuration, if the role is installed, gathers and displays information about the Hyper-V capabilities of the nodes.

To rerun cluster validation on an already formed cluster using PowerShell, run the following Windows Failover Clustering PowerShell command:

```
Test-Cluster -Cluster Cluster01
```

The most intensive tests that are executed during validation are the storage tests. If storage tests are run against storage that is online and already in use by the cluster, a production outage will occur for the duration of the test. To rerun cluster validation on an already formed cluster and exclude a specific disk by using PowerShell, run the following Windows Failover Clustering PowerShell command:

```
Test-Cluster -Disk "Cluster Disk 2"
```

Creating a Failover Cluster

After installing the Failover Clustering feature and successfully validating your configuration, the next step is to form your cluster. Use the following procedure to form your failover cluster in Windows Server 2012:

1. Launch Server Manager. In the navigation pane, click Dashboard, click Tools, and then click Failover Cluster Manager.

2. In Failover Cluster Manager, in the Actions pane, click Create Cluster to launch the Create Cluster Wizard.

3. On the Before You Begin page, click Next.

4. On the Select Servers page, in the Enter Name field, type the FQDN of your targeted cluster nodes (for example, **host1.demo.internal**). Use semicolons to add any nodes and then click Next (see Figure 8.2 previously).

5. On the Access Point For Administering The Cluster page, in the Cluster Name box, type **Cluster01.**

6. In the Networks section, deselect any inappropriate networks; these might be networks that are internal networks used for internal cluster communications and not production facing. With the remaining network selected, type an IP address in your network range, such as **10.0.1.23**, as shown in Figure 8.3, and then click Next.

FIGURE 8.3
Access point for administering the cluster

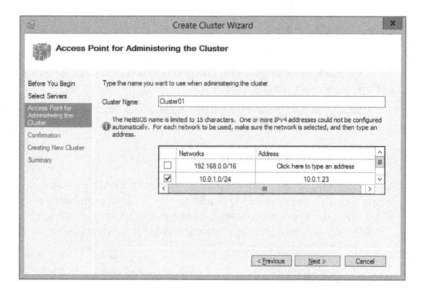

7. On the Confirmation page, deselect the Add All Eligible Storage To The Cluster check box, as shown in Figure 8.4. Review the cluster information and then click Next.

8. On the Summary page, click Finish. In Failover Cluster Manager, in the navigation pane, expand the cluster if necessary, and click Nodes. Verify that the status of Host1, Host2, and Host3 is Up.

FIGURE 8.4

Confirmation page

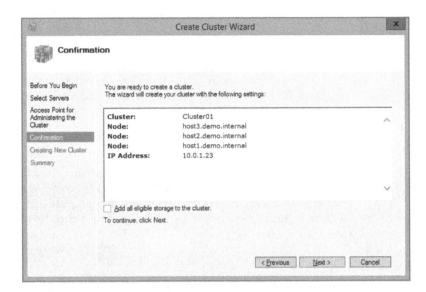

To create a cluster by using PowerShell, run the following Windows Failover Clustering PowerShell command:

```
New-Cluster -Name Cluster01 -Node Host1,Host2,Host3 -StaticAddress 10.0.1.23 `
-NoStorage
```

Adding Disks

After installing the Failover Clustering feature, validating the targeted cluster nodes, and creating a cluster, the next step is to add storage. This storage needs to be provisioned to the cluster by using the appropriate storage management tools. Storage is typically added to the cluster for additional services and applications. Use the following procedure to add disks to your failover cluster in Windows Server 2012:

1. Launch Server Manager. In the navigation pane, click Dashboard, click Tools, and then click Failover Cluster Manager.

2. In Failover Cluster Manager, in the navigation pane, expand the cluster if necessary and click Storage. Right-click Disks and select Add Disk.

3. In the Add Disk To A Cluster interface, select the appropriate available disks and click OK.

4. Verify the status of the added disks (for example, Cluster Disk 1 is Online and assigned to a current Owner Node). Note that at this stage, these disks start out as Physical Disk Resources and not a Cluster Shared Volume.

To add an available disk to the cluster by using PowerShell, run the following Windows Failover Clustering PowerShell command:

```
Add-ClusterDisk "Cluster Disk 2"
```

To get a list of available disks, consider using the following Windows Failover Clustering PowerShell command:

```
Get-ClusterAvailableDisk | fl Name
```

Configuring Network Prioritization

Like Windows Server 2008 R2, Windows Server 2012 automatically prioritizes the failover cluster private communications between nodes on the networks configured for cluster use. The communication between cluster nodes uses little bandwidth. Therefore, typically there is no need to prioritize which network the cluster uses.

To achieve prioritization in Windows Server 2012, a cluster property for each cluster-enabled network is implemented. Each network is given a Metric value, which is automatically weighted by the cluster.

Any network that has a default gateway defined is considered a public network and has a value of 10,000 or more. Any network without a default gateway is considered a private interconnect and given a value between 1,000 and 10,000. The Metric value represents a cost. The lower the value, the more likely this network path will be used for private cluster communications including redirected I/O of Cluster Shared Volumes (CSV).

The network used for Live Migration is also initially defined by the Metric setting, although it can be changed in the properties of a virtual machine resource.

VIEWING NETWORK PRIORITY

It is possible to manually specify a network to be used for CSV traffic by setting it to the lowest Metric value, using a number below 1,000. If a network becomes unavailable or is marked as failed, the cluster's private communication traffic, including CSV network traffic, will automatically switch to an available network with the next lowest Metric value.

If a network with a lower Metric value becomes available, the private communications will be automatically moved to that network. The ability to switch networks dynamically allows the cluster to always use the most preferred network without requiring reboots as the Metric values may be manually reset or new networks may be commissioned.

To view the current cluster-enabled network's Metric settings by using PowerShell, run the following Windows Failover Clustering PowerShell command:

```
Get-ClusterNetwork | FT Name, State, Metric, AutoMetric, Role
```

The networks are assigned Metric values in an arbitrary order determined by the cluster service. There is no weight given for the actual bandwidth capacity or network speed to initially define the network Metric value.

CONFIGURING NETWORK PRIORITY

There is no user interface for configuring the network priority, and so this property must be manually configured by using PowerShell to set the Metric property. This provides a greater degree of control to administrators who prefer to designate a specific network for CSV and cluster communications rather than allowing the cluster itself to automatically determine the networks.

To set the current cluster-enabled network's `Metric` settings by using PowerShell, run the following Windows Failover Clustering PowerShell command:

```
Get-ClusterNetwork "Cluster Network 1" | %{$_.Metric=600}
```

To reset a manually configured cluster network back to the default setting, set the `AutoMetric` property back to True by running the following Windows Failover Clustering PowerShell command:

```
Get-ClusterNetwork "Cluster Network 1" | %{$_.AutoMetric="True"}
```

Refer to Chapter 4, "Networking," for further details on converged fabric designs and some real-world networking solutions.

Cluster Shared Volumes

Cluster Shared Volumes (CSV) was originally introduced in Windows Server 2008 R2, and at that time, it was used to simply share storage configurations for Hyper-V Failover Clustering. Effectively, CSV eliminated the need to use drive-letter identifiers on volumes and removed the need for one logical disk per virtual machine in the cluster.

From its original implementation in Windows NT, Failover Clustering has always used a shared nothing storage architecture. This means that each disk was owned by a single node within the cluster, and only that node could perform direct I/O to that specific disk. This model also meant that the smallest unit of failover for clustering was at the logical disk level, not at a volume level. This meant that storage administrators were required to create individual LUNs for each clustered resource group to achieve an independent failover capability for each resource group.

CSV breaks these restrictions and enables multiple nodes within the cluster to concurrently access a single shared volume, while providing complete transparency with respect to cluster node ownership.

With CSV, one of the nodes in the cluster is responsible for synchronizing access to files on the shared volume. This is the node that currently owns the cluster's physical disk resource associated with that LUN, and it is referred to as the *coordinator node*. Each LUN has its own coordinator, and all nodes within the cluster are equal and could therefore also be a coordinator node. When a virtual machine is deployed and running on a CSV volume, almost all of the hypervisor's access to the virtual hard disk is disk I/O, and the coordinator node is not involved. This enables virtual machines to have fast, direct access to the disk.

An exception occurs when redirected mode kicks in. Metadata changes have to be controlled and managed through the coordinator node. Invariably these changes occur on any node within the cluster, and as a result are redirected over the network to the coordinator node.

Cluster Shared Volumes Compatibility

CSV is compatible with any block-level attached storage, which includes Fibre Channel, iSCSI, and Serial Attached SCSI (SAS). CSV utilizes the Windows NTFS file system on basic disks, leveraging either Master Boot Record (MBR) or GUID Partition Table (GPT) format disks with no additional hardware or software requirements.

CSV is designed for single shared LUNs or multi-site clusters, where nodes in the same cluster reside in different network subnets. CSV disk resources can be extended and placed in maintenance mode, just like any clustered physical disk resource, and can take advantage of new SMB3 features such as multichannel and RDMA. (See Chapter 7, "Using File Servers," for further information on SMB3.)

Prerequisites

The following prerequisites must be in place to support CSV in a Windows failover cluster:

◆ Only NTFS partitions can be used in the CSV namespace.

◆ Client for Microsoft Networks and File and Printer Sharing need to be enabled for Cluster Shared Volumes.

There have been several improvements to CSV in Windows Server 2012. Some of the key changes are as follows:

◆ The CSV namespace is now enabled by default and identifies itself as CSVFS so applications can discover that they are running on CSV.

◆ Support for CSV is no longer limited to Hyper-V. CSV now provides support for the File Server role, Scale-Out File Server, and SQL Server 2012. (See Chapter 7 for further details.)

◆ CSV now uses standard mount points (no longer as a reparse point as in R2).

◆ Improved backup and restore of CSV volumes including support for parallel and incremental backup. (See Chapter 10, "Backup and Recovery," for further details.)

◆ Better integration of file system minifilter drivers with antivirus software.

◆ CSV scales up to 64 nodes in a Windows Server 2012 failover cluster.

◆ CSV leverages the advanced storage and networking technologies in Windows Server 2012:

- ◆ RDMA (remote direct memory access)
- ◆ LBFO (load balancing and failover)
- ◆ SMB Multichannel
- ◆ Virtual Fibre Channel
- ◆ Storage Spaces

◆ CSV integrates with the new/improved file system in Windows Server 2012:

- ◆ CHKDSK
- ◆ ODX (Offloaded Data Transfer)
- ◆ Defrag

◆ Support for opportunistic locking (Oplocks) for applications accessing CSV files, enabling remote caching of CSV file system data.

◆ Multiple subnet support.

- Better VM creation and copy experience, because a copy can be performed from any node with the same high performance.

- BitLocker support.

- Direct I/O for more scenarios.

- Support for memory-mapped files.

Enabling Cluster Shared Volumes

Adding a cluster disk to the CSV namespace is a simple operation. Use the following procedure to enable CSV support in Windows Server 2012 Failover Clustering:

1. Launch Windows Failover Manager, expand the Cluster node, click the Storage node, and then click the Disks node.

2. Select a physical disk resource in the Disks view. Right-click and choose Add To Cluster Shared Volume.

To verify information about the CSV by using PowerShell, run the following Windows Failover Manager PowerShell command:

```
Get-ClusterSharedVolume "Cluster Disk Name" | fl *
```

CSV Namespace

CSV provides a single, consistent namespace across all the nodes in a Windows failover cluster. Files have the same name and path regardless of which node those files are viewed from. CSV volumes are exposed as directories and subdirectories under the %SystemDrive%\ClusterStorage directory. This also enables CSV to scale to large numbers of volumes, without the limitation of running out of drive-letter identifiers. Each node in the cluster maps the identical namespace to each shared volume:

```
C:\ClusterStorage\Volume1\
C:\ClusterStorage\Volume2\
```

In Windows Server 2008 R2, CSV volumes were reparse points. In Windows Server 2012, CSV volumes are standard mount points. Reparse points are no longer supported in CSV V2.

CSV Resiliency

CSV implements a mechanism called *redirected mode*, whereby I/O can be rerouted based on connection availability. In the event of a network failure, all I/O is dynamically redirected over an alternate network with no data loss. If the subsequent network connections fail after a retry, the failure is reported back to the application as any disk I/O failure would be.

A CSV volume in redirected mode indicates that all I/O to that volume, from the perspective of that particular node in the cluster, is being redirected over the CSV network to another node in the cluster that still has direct access to the storage supporting the CSV volume. This is, for all intents and purposes, a recovery mode. This functionality prevents the loss of all connectivity to storage. Instead, all storage-related I/O is redirected over the CSV network.

Redirected mode prevents a total loss of connectivity, thereby allowing virtual machines to continue functioning. This provides the cluster administrator with an opportunity to pro-actively evaluate the situation and potentially evacuate virtual machines to other nodes in the cluster that are not experiencing storage connectivity issues. There are four main reasons that a CSV volume may be in redirected mode:

◆ The CSV volume is intentionally placed into redirected mode.

◆ There is a storage connectivity failure for a node, and in this case, all I/O is redirected over a network designated for CSV traffic.

◆ When metadata updates occur—for example, during snapshot creation.

◆ An incompatible filter driver is installed on the node.

WHEN DO METADATA UPDATES OCCUR?

Metadata updates can occur with CSV during the following scenarios:

◆ Virtual machine creation or deletion

◆ Virtual machine power on/off

◆ When live-migrating a virtual machine

◆ When storage migrating a virtual machine

◆ During snapshot creation

◆ Extending a dynamic virtual hard disk

◆ Renaming a virtual hard disk

Keep in mind, however, that metadata updates are small transactions that happen infrequently for virtual machines and that CSV server-side synchronization allows for these updates to occur in parallel and nondisruptively.

CSV Optimizations

CSV Block Caching is a feature that allows you to allocate system memory (RAM) as a write-through cache. The CSV Block Cache provides caching of read-only unbuffered I/O. CSV Block Caching can improve the performance for applications such as Hyper-V, which conducts unbuffered I/O when accessing a VHD file. Unbuffered I/Os are operations that are not cached by the Windows Cache Manager. What CSV Block Cache delivers is caching that can boost the performance of read requests, with write-through for no caching of write requests.

CSV Block Caching has tremendous value for pooled virtual machines in virtual desktop scenarios, using differencing disks based off a master copy of a parent virtual hard disk. Two configuration parameters allow you to control the CSV Block Cache:

◆ CsvEnableBlockCache

◆ SharedVolumeBlockCacheSizeInMB

CsvEnableBlockCache

CsvEnableBlockCache is a property of the cluster's physical disk resource and thus allows you to enable CSV Block Caching on a per disk basis. This gives you the flexibility to configure a cache for read-intensive virtual machines running on specific disks, while allowing you to disable and prevent random I/O on other disks from purging the cache. The default setting is 0 for disabled. Setting the value to 1 enables CSV Block Cache on that disk.

To enable CSV Block caching by using PowerShell, run the following Windows Failover Cluster PowerShell command:

```
Get-ClusterSharedVolume "Cluster Disk 1" | Set-ClusterParameter `
CsvEnableBlockCache  1
```

SharedVolumeBlockCacheSizeInMB

SharedVolumeBlockCacheSizeInMB is a property of the cluster that allows you to define how much memory (in megabytes) you wish to reserve for the CSV Block Cache on each node in the cluster. If a value of 512 is defined, then 512 MB of system memory will be reserved on each node in the failover cluster. Configuring a value of 0 disables CSV Block Caching.

To configure a shared volume block cache by using PowerShell, run the following Windows Failover Cluster PowerShell command:

```
(Get-Cluster).SharedVolumeBlockCacheSizeInMB = 512
```

SHARED VOLUME BLOCK CACHE

Microsoft recommends a default value of 512 MB. No system downtime is required to modify this value. However, an additional consideration that may need to be taken into account is how this might impact Hyper-V and the Root Memory Reserve. To allow Hyper-V to automatically recalculate the Root Memory Reserve, the system will require a reboot.

CSV Best Practices

Consider the following best practices when implementing CSV in a Windows failover cluster:

- Defragment virtual hard disks before placing them on CSV storage.
- Distribute logical disk ownership across the nodes in the cluster.
- Route non-Hyper-V I/O through the CSV owner (coordinator node).
    - Distribute logical disk ownership to prevent any cluster hot spots.
    - Implement at least one CSV volume per host to provide the best balance.

BitLocker

BitLocker Drive Encryption is a data-protection feature of the Windows operating system that was first introduced in the Windows Server 2008 time frame. Subsequent operating system releases from Microsoft have continued to expand and improve not only the security but the functionality offered by BitLocker, allowing the operating system to provide BitLocker protection in various scenarios to more drives and devices.

BitLocker addresses the threat of data theft or exposure from lost, stolen, or inappropriately decommissioned disks. With Windows Server 2012, BitLocker has increased in functionality and now provides support for Cluster Shared Volumes. There are two methods for using BitLocker in a Windows failover cluster:

- Enable BitLocker on data volumes before these data volumes are added to the cluster. In this scenario, the data volume in question can either be an empty data volume or can contain data.

- Enable BitLocker on a data volume that is already in use within the cluster. In this scenario, the data volume can be a standard clustered disk or a Cluster Shared Volume.

Prerequisites

The following prerequisites must be in place to support CSV in a Windows failover cluster:

- Windows Server 2012 Failover Clustering must be installed and configured in each node that will form part of the cluster.

- A Windows Server 2012 domain controller must be reachable from all nodes of the cluster.

- BitLocker Drive Encryption must be installed on all nodes in the cluster.

- The following Group Policy needs to be configured: `BitLocker Drive Encryption\Fixed Data Drives\Choose how bitlocker-protected fixed drivers can be recovered`.

Installing BitLocker

Use the following procedure to install BitLocker in Windows Server 2012 Failover Clustering:

1. Launch Server Manager. In the navigation pane, click Dashboard and then click Add Roles And Features.

2. In the Add Roles And Features Wizard, on the Before You Begin page, click Next.

3. On the Select Installation Type page, select Role-Based or Feature-Based Installation and then click Next.

4. On the Select Destination Server page, click Next.

5. On the Select Server Roles page, click Next.

6. On the Select Features page, click BitLocker Drive Encryption and then click Next.

7. Click Add Features.

8. On the Select Features page, click Next.

9. On the Confirm Installation Selections page, click Install.

10. On the Results page, click Close.

To enable BitLocker Drive Encryption by using PowerShell, run the following Windows Server Manager PowerShell command:

```
Install-WindowsFeature BitLocker -IncludeAllSubFeature -IncludeManagementTools `
-Restart
```

Configuring BitLocker on Cluster Shared Volumes

When configuring BitLocker on volumes that you plan to add to the cluster, the volume will need to be enabled for BitLocker before it can be added to the cluster storage pool. If the volume has already been added to a cluster and online, the disk will need to be put into maintenance mode.

Windows PowerShell or the manage-bde command-line tool are the preferred options when it comes to managing BitLocker on a Cluster Shared Volume in Windows Server 2012 and Failover Clustering. Their use is highly recommended over the use of the BitLocker control panel applet, and this is because Cluster Shared Volumes are volume mount points within the operating system and so do not require the use of a drive-letter identifier. The BitLocker control panel applet isn't able to manage a volume when a drive-letter identifier isn't present. Furthermore, the Active Directory–based protector is required for standard clustered disks or Cluster Shared Volumes, and this functionality is not available in the BitLocker control panel applet.

VOLUME MOUNT POINTS

Volume mount points are specialized NTFS file system objects that are used to mount and provide an entry point to other volumes. An example of this is the Clustered Shared Volume namespace %SystemDrive%\ClusterStorage directory. This technique enables Clustered Shared Volumes to scale to a large number of volumes, without the limitation of running out of drive-letter identifiers.

USING ACTIVE DIRECTORY BITLOCKER PROTECTOR

The Active Directory BitLocker protector uses a domain security identifier (SID) and can be bound to a user account, machine account, or a group. When an unlock request is made for a protected volume, the BitLocker service interrupts the request and uses the BitLocker protect /unprotect APIs to unlock or deny such a request. For the cluster service to self-manage BitLocker-enabled volumes, an administrator must add the Cluster Name Object (CNO), which is the Active Directory identity associated with the cluster network name, as a BitLocker protector to the target volume. BitLocker will unlock protected volumes in the following order:

1. Clear key

This is when a computer's integrity verification has been disabled, the BitLocker volume master key (the key used to actually encrypt the volume) is freely accessible, and no authentication is necessary.

2. Driver-based auto unlock key

3. Registry-based auto unlock key

AUTO UNLOCK KEY

An auto unlock configures BitLocker to automatically unlock mounted data volumes during startup, without requiring any human interaction.

---

4. Active Directory–based protector

CLUSTER NAME OBJECT

The Cluster Name Object (CNO) is the security context for the cluster and is used for all interactions that require a security context.

ENABLING BITLOCKER BEFORE ADDING DISKS TO A CLUSTER

The main advantage of encrypting a volume prior to adding it to a cluster is that the volume is not required to be in maintenance mode, and thus the disk resource does not need to be suspended to complete the operation.

Use the following procedure to enable BitLocker on a volume before adding that volume to the cluster:

1. Install the BitLocker Drive Encryption feature.

2. Ensure that the volume is formatted with NTFS and has a drive letter assigned to it.

3. Enable BitLocker on the volume by using your choice of protector.

To use PowerShell to enable BitLocker Drive Encryption on a volume before it is added to the cluster, run the following BitLocker PowerShell command (see Figure 8.5):

```
Enable-BitLocker G: -PasswordProtector
```

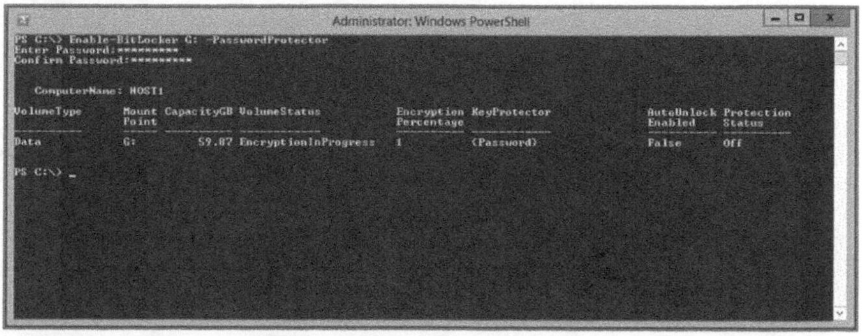

FIGURE 8.5
Enabling BitLocker password protector

4. Identify the name of the cluster.

   To identify the name of the cluster by using PowerShell, run the following Failover Cluster PowerShell command:

   ```
   Get-Cluster
   ```

5. Add an Active Directory SID–based protector to the volume by using the cluster name.

   To use PowerShell to add an Active Directory SID–based protector, run the following BitLocker PowerShell command (see Figure 8.6):

   ```
   Add-BitLockerKeyProtector G: -ADAccountOrGroupProtector -ADAccountOrGroup `
   CLUSTER01$
   ```

FIGURE 8.6
Enabling BitLocker AD account or group protector

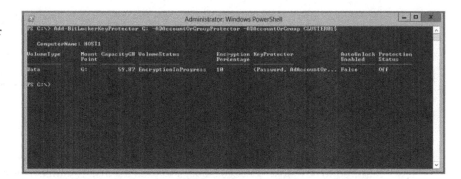

6. Add the volume to the cluster. In Windows Failover Manager, expand the Cluster node, click the Storage node, right-click the Disks node, and select Add Disk.

7. Enable a recovery password protector.

   To generate a recovery password by using PowerShell, run the following BitLocker PowerShell command:

   ```
   Enable-BitLocker G: -RecoveryPasswordProtector
   ```

RECOVERY PASSWORD PROTECTOR

The creation of a recovery password and the backing up of that recovery password to Active Directory is an important step that provides a mechanism to restore access to a BitLocker-protected drive in the event that the drive cannot be unlocked normally. An Active Directory administrator can obtain the recovery password and use it to unlock and access the drive.

It is essential that you capture and secure the password protector for future use!

To use PowerShell to back up the recovery password to Active Directory, run the following BitLocker PowerShell command:

```
$protectorId = (Get-BitLockerVolume <drive or CSV mount point>).Keyprotector | `
Where-Object {$_.KeyProtectorType -eq "RecoveryPassword"}
Backup-BitLockerKeyProtector G: -KeyProtectorId $protectorId.KeyProtectorId
```

DISABLING BITLOCKER

To disable BitLocker, simply run the following BitLocker PowerShell command (see Figure 8.7):

```
Disable-BitLocker G:
```

FIGURE 8.7
Disabling
BitLocker

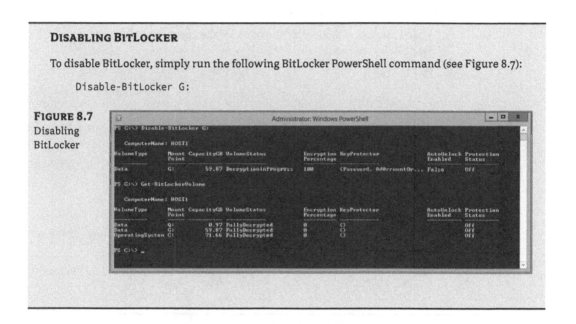

ENABLING BITLOCKER ON A CLUSTER SHARED VOLUME

When the cluster already owns a disk resource, the disk needs to be placed into maintenance mode before BitLocker can be enabled. Use the following procedure to enable BitLocker on a volume that has already been added to the cluster:

1. Install the BitLocker Drive Encryption feature.

2. Check the status of the cluster disk.

   To use PowerShell to check the status of the cluster disk, run the following BitLocker PowerShell command:

   ```
   Get-ClusterResource "Cluster Disk 1"
   ```

3. Put the physical disk resource into maintenance mode.

   To use PowerShell to put the physical disk resource into maintenance mode, run the following BitLocker PowerShell command:

   ```
   Get-ClusterResource "Cluster Disk 1" | Suspend-ClusterResource
   ```

4. Enable BitLocker on the volume, using your choice of protector.

   To use PowerShell to enable BitLocker Drive Encryption on a volume before it is added to the cluster, run the following BitLocker PowerShell command:

   ```
   Enable-BitLocker G:\ClusterStorage\Volume1 -PasswordProtector
   ```

5. Identify the name of the cluster.

   To use PowerShell to identify the name of the cluster, run the following Failover Cluster PowerShell command:

   ```
   Get-Cluster
   ```

6. Add an Active Directory SID–based protector to the volume, using the cluster name.

   To use PowerShell to add an Active Directory SID–based protector, run the following BitLocker PowerShell command:

   ```
   Add-BitLockerKeyProtector G:\ClusterStorage\Volume1 -ADAccoutOrGroupProtector `
   -ADAccountOrGroup CLUSTER01$
   ```

7. Enable a recovery password protector.

   To use PowerShell to generate a recovery password, run the following BitLocker PowerShell command:

   ```
   Enable-BitLocker G:\ClusterStorage\Volume1 -RecoveryPasswordProtector
   ```

RECOVERY PASSWORD PROTECTOR

The creation of a recovery password and the backing up of that recovery password to Active Directory is an important step that provides a mechanism to restore access to a BitLocker-protected drive in the event that the drive cannot be unlocked normally. An Active Directory administrator can obtain the recovery password and use it to unlock and access the drive.

It is essential that you capture and secure the password protector for future use!

To use PowerShell to back up the recovery password to Active Directory, run the following BitLocker PowerShell command:

```
$protectorId = (Get-BitLockerVolume <drive or CSV mount point>).Keyprotector | `
Where-Object {$_.KeyProtectorType -eq "RecoveryPassword"}
Backup-BitLockerKeyProtector G:\ClusterStorage\Volume1 -KeyProtectorId `
$protectorId.KeyProtectorId
```

During the encryption process, a cluster shared volume will be placed into redirected mode until BitLocker builds its metadata and watermark on all data present on the encrypted volume.

The duration of redirected mode is directly proportional to the size of the volume, the actual amount of stored data plus the size of the data on disk, and the BitLocker encryption mode picked:

◆ Used Disk Space Only

◆ Full

BitLocker Encryption Mode: Used Disk Space Only

Used Disk Space Only allows for a much quicker encryption approach by encrypting only used blocks on the targeted volume.

Disabling BitLocker

To use PowerShell to disable BitLocker Drive Encryption, run the following Windows BitLocker PowerShell command:

```
Disable-BitLocker G:\ClusterStorage\Volume1
```

Enabling Used Disk Space Only Encryption

Used Disk Space Only encryption means that only the portion of the drive that contains data will be encrypted. Unused space will remain unencrypted. This causes the encryption process to be much faster, especially for new disks. When BitLocker is enabled with this method, as data is added to the drive, the portion of the drive used will be encrypted, and this is the recommend option for thinly provisioned storage such as virtual hard disks.

To use PowerShell to encrypt a volume with Used Disk Space Only encryption, run the following BitLocker PowerShell command:

```
Enable-BitLocker G: -PasswordProtector -UsedSpaceOnly
```

Cluster-Aware Updating

In Windows Server 2008 R2, update management of a failover cluster was a very laborious and often a manual task, which often used a series of disparate tools and technologies that didn't necessarily understand the criticality of the workload running on the Windows failover cluster. Patching a cluster required a high level of coordination between the datacenter administrators and the line-of-business application owners, and this would typically involve several groups within an organization. Further, updating the cluster required multiple manual steps, with associated failover and failback rules needing to be applied, all during what was a very small maintenance window. This made the process error prone and thus increased the risk of unplanned service outages.

Cluster-Aware Updating (CAU) is a reliable, automated, and integrated update management feature that allows cluster administrators to patch clustered servers with minimal or no loss in availability during the update process. CAU is designed to reduce service outages and to eliminate the need for manual update management.

CAU is a cross-cluster automation solution. The entire end-to-end update management process is automated and is not subject to human error. However, CAU is compatible only with Windows Server 2012 failover clusters and the clustered roles supported on Windows Server 2012.

The computer running the CAU process is called an *update coordinator*. The CAU update coordinator automates the cluster-updating process while running on a node within the cluster, on a Windows Server 2012 machine outside the cluster, or a Windows 8 client, when installed with the appropriate Remote Server Administration Toolkit. When hosting the CAU update coordinator on a node within the cluster, this is referred to as a *self-updating cluster*. There are several benefits to a self-updating cluster:

◆ A self-updating cluster doesn't require a separate instance of Windows Server 2012 or Windows 8 to drive the cluster update process.

◆ A self-updating cluster can be configured to update the cluster on a user-defined schedule.

◆ The CAU orchestrator becomes fault tolerant itself, because it is running on the cluster and functions like any clustered workload.

CAU works seamlessly with the existing Windows Update Agent (WUA) and your Windows Server Update Services (WSUS) infrastructure, using the inbox Windows Update plug-in to download and install important Microsoft updates. CAU also comes with a hotfix plug-in that is used to download and install Microsoft hotfixes that have been prestaged on an internal file server. This hotfix plug-in can be customized to install even non-Microsoft updates such as BIOS updates from hardware manufacturers or third-party device drivers. The CAU process functions in the following way:

1. Scans for and downloads applicable updates to each node within the cluster

2. Verifies that the cluster has quorum before commencing the updating process

3. Executes any optional pre-update scripts as required

4. Moves clustered workloads off each cluster node in turn by placing the node into maintenance mode

5. Installs updates on the node that is currently in maintenance mode and reboots, if necessary

6. Scans for any additional updates and repeats step 5 until there are no further applicable updates

7. Brings the node out of maintenance mode and moves the clustered workloads back to the patched node

8. Executes any optional post-update scripts as required

9. Generates Updating Run reports and stores them on each cluster node at `%SystemRoot%\Cluster\Reports`

CAU selects the order of the nodes to update based on the level of activity. The node or nodes hosting the least number of roles is updated first.

MAINTENANCE MODE

Taking a cluster node out of service for planned maintenance is a common administrative task. You might carry out this task to install a hotfix, install a service pack, or carry out a hardware-related task. With maintenance mode (referred to as *node drain* in Failover Cluster Manager), you can automate moving workloads off a cluster node. The following occurs when you initiate maintenance mode:

1. The cluster node is put in a paused state. This prevents other workloads hosted on other nodes within the cluster from moving to the node.

2. The virtual machines currently owned by the cluster node are sorted according to their priority order (High, Medium, Low, and No Auto Start).

3. The virtual machines are then distributed via either Live Migration (for High- and Medium-priority virtual machines) or Quick Migration (for Low-priority virtual machines) to the other active nodes in the cluster in priority order.

4. When all the virtual machines are moved off the cluster node, the operation is complete.

Prerequisites

The following prerequisites must be in place to support CAU in a Windows failover cluster:

◆ The cluster nodes are running Windows Server 2012 and have the Failover Clustering feature installed.

◆ The cluster name can be resolved on the network by using DNS.

◆ A sufficient number of nodes within the cluster, using the correct quorum model, can remain available during the update process so that quorum is maintained.

◆ The cluster nodes are on a network that is reachable by the update coordinator.

◆ The CAU update coordinator running on either Windows Server 2012 outside the failover cluster being updated or on a Windows 8 client must have the Failover Clustering tools installed.

◆ If using internal update management servers (for example, WSUS servers), WSUS distribution points must be correctly identified, with approved updates for the cluster nodes, and those cluster nodes must not be configured to automatically install updates. It is, however, recommended to configure Windows Update on each cluster node to automatically download the updates.

Installing and Configuring CAU

CAU functionality is automatically installed on each node of the cluster as part of the Failover Clustering feature, and CAU tools are installed with the Failover Cluster Feature Administration tools. Failover Clustering management tools may also be installed on any Windows Server 2012 system, even if it is not a member of the cluster, or on a Windows 8 client as part of RSAT. Figure 8.8 provides an overview of the architecture.

FIGURE 8.8
CAU architecture

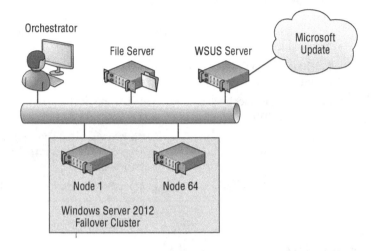

Orchestrator

File Server

WSUS Server

Microsoft Update

Node 1

Node 64

Windows Server 2012
Failover Cluster

INSTALLING THE CAU UPDATE COORDINATOR

The Failover Cluster Manager can also be installed as part of the RSAT. This is the preferred option when installing on a member server that will not be part of the actual failover cluster. To install the Failover Cluster Management interface, use the following procedure:

1. Launch Server Manager. In the navigation pane, click Dashboard, and then click Add Roles And Features.

2. In the Add Roles And Features Wizard, on the Before You Begin page, click Next.

3. On the Select Installation Type page, select Role-Based or Feature-Based installation and then click Next.

4. On the Select Destination Server page, click Next.

5. On the Select Server Roles page, click Next.

6. On the Select Features page, expand Remote Server Administration Tools, expand Feature Administration Tools, select Failover Clustering Tools, and then click Next.

7. On the Confirm Installation Selections page, click Install.

8. On the Results page, click Close.

To use PowerShell to install the Failover Clustering tools, run the following Windows Server Manager PowerShell command:

```
Add-WindowsFeature -name RSAT-Clustering
```

VERIFYING THE INSTALLATION

To verify that the CAU Windows PowerShell cmdlets are properly installed, run the following Windows Server Manager PowerShell command:

```
Import-Module ClusterAwareUpdating
```

CONFIGURING A FILE SERVER TO HOST HOTFIXES

Use the following procedure to configure a file server to automate patching of Windows Server 2012 failover clusters, using the default hotfix plug-in:

1. Verify the File Server Remote Management (SMB-In) firewall rule is enabled by running the following Windows Firewall PowerShell command (see Figure 8.9):

```
Get-NetFirewallRule -Displayname "File Server Remote Management (SMB-In)"
```

FIGURE 8.9
Get-NetFireWall-
Rule output

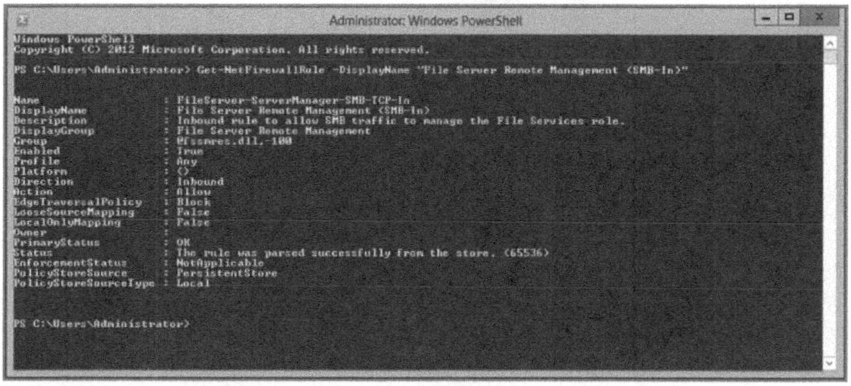

2. Prepare the directory structure on the file server that will host the hotfixes. On an appropriate disk on the file server, create a folder called **Hotfixes**.

3. Under the Hotfixes folder, create another folder called **Root**.

4. Under the Root folder, create the following folders: **CAUHotfix_All**, **Host1**, **Host2**, and **Host3**. (Add folders for each additional node in the cluster as appropriate.)

5. Copy the DefaultHotfixConfig.xml file to the Root folder. This file is located under the %SystemRoot%\System32\Windows PowerShell\v1.0\Modules\ClusterAwareUpdating folder.

6. Create a new SMB share called **Hotfixes** with a path to the Hotfixes folder created in step 2 by using the following Windows File Server PowerShell command:

```
New-SmbShare -Path C:\Hotfixes -Name Hotfixes
```

7. Set the correct NTFS permissions on the Root folder, as shown in Figure 8.10. The required NTFS permissions include Full Control for Local Administrators, SYSTEM, CREATOR OWNER, and TrustedInstaller.

FIGURE 8.10
NTFS permissions

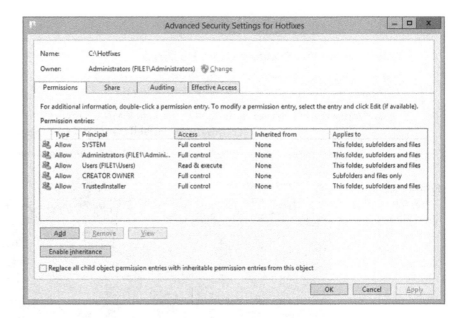

The local Users group requires Read permissions unless the hotfix is an executable file, in which case the local Users group will also require Execute. Use the following PowerShell command to display the assigned permissions (see Figure 8.11):

```
Get-Acl -Path C:\Hotfixes\Root | fl AccessToString
```

FIGURE 8.11
Get-ACL output

SETTING PERMISSIONS ON THE ROOT FOLDER

Any other accounts or groups than those listed in Figure 8.11 with Full Control and that can write or modify access to the Root folder will result in an error during a CAU run.

---

8. Configure SMB Data Security by using either SMB Signing or SMB Encryption. SMB Encryption is supported only on Windows Server 2012 and is the easier of the two to configure. Run the following Windows SMB PowerShell command to configure SMB Encryption:

```
Set-SmbShare -Name Hotfixes -EncryptData $True -Force
```

9. Copy your required Windows Server 2012 hotfixes to the CAUHotfix_All folder.

10. Launch Server Manager. In the navigation pane, click Dashboard, click Tools, and then click Cluster-Aware Updating.

11. In the Cluster-Aware Updating UI, connect to the failover cluster that will be patched and click Connect.

12. In the Cluster-Aware Updating UI, under Cluster Actions, click Preview Updates for this cluster.

13. Under Select Plug-in, choose Microsoft.HotfixPlugin, as shown in Figure 8.12. In the Plug-In Arguments input field, enter **HotfixRootFolderPath = \\file1\Hotfixes\ Root** and **HotfixConfigFileName = DefaultHotfixConfig.xml**. Then click the Generate Update Preview List button.

FIGURE 8.12
Selecting a plug-in

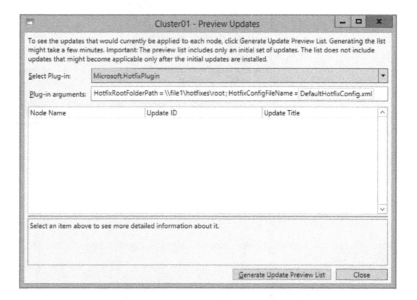

CONFIGURING CLUSTER NODES FOR PATCHING

One of the easiest ways to determine whether the cluster nodes are configured for patching is to run the Cluster-Aware Updating Best Practice Analyzer. This will ensure that the cluster is configured correctly to support the patching process. Use the following procedure to configure the cluster nodes for patching:

1. On each cluster node, run the following PowerShell commands to enable the required Remote Shutdown firewall rules:

   ```
   Enable-NetFirewallRule -Displayname "Inbound Rule for Remote Shutdown (TCP-In)"
   ```

   and

   ```
   Enable-NetFirewallRule -Displayname "Inbound Rule for Remote Shutdown (RPC-EP- `
   In)"
   ```

2. On your file server, in Server Manager, choose Tools ➢ Cluster-Aware Updating to open the Cluster-Aware Updating UI.

3. Connect to the cluster Cluster01, if not already connected. Under Cluster Actions, click the Analyze Cluster Updating Readiness option.

4. Verify that all the tests pass without error (see Figure 8.13). Implement any remedial actions to fix any errors.

FIGURE 8.13
Cluster updating readiness results

PATCHING THE CLUSTER

Now that you have configured a file server to host your hotfixes and ensured that the cluster nodes themselves are configured to allow the actual patching to run, the final step is to patch the failover cluster. Use the following procedure to do so:

1. On the file server, launch Server Manager. In the navigation pane, click Dashboard, click Tools, and then click Cluster-Aware Updating to open the Cluster-Aware Updating UI.

2. In the Cluster-Aware Updating UI, connect to the failover cluster that will be patched, Cluster01.

3. In Cluster Actions, click Apply Updates to this cluster to start the Cluster-Aware Updating Wizard.

4. Review the Getting Started screen and click Next.

5. On the Advanced Options screen (see Figure 8.14), make selections as needed. For CauPluginName, choose Microsoft.HotfixPlugin from the drop-down list. In the CauPluginArguments box, enter **HotfixRootFolderPath = \\file1\hotfixes\root**. Click Next.

FIGURE 8.14
Advanced options

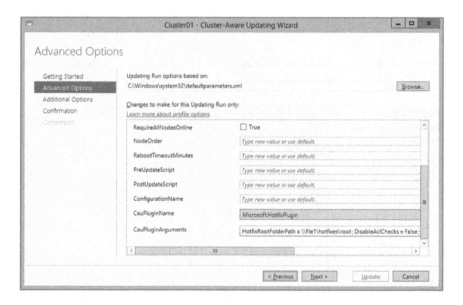

6. On the Additional Options screen, shown in Figure 8.15, verify the path to the `DefaultHotfixConfig.xml` file on the file server. Select the SMB Encryption check box. Either select the Access Check box, or not, and then click Next.

7. On the Confirmation screen, verify all the information and click Update.

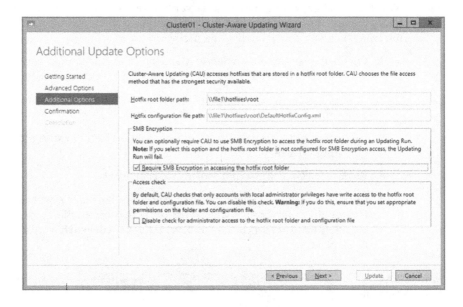

FIGURE 8.15
Additional update
options

8. Close the wizard. Monitor the update running in the Cluster-Aware Updating UI
(see Figure 8.16).

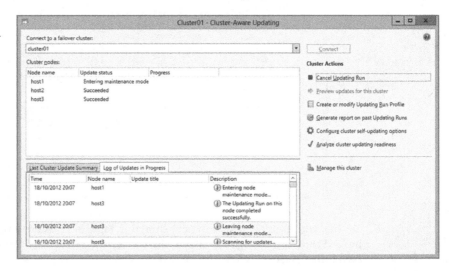

FIGURE 8.16
Monitoring Cluster-
Aware Updating

9. After the update completes and all nodes in the cluster reflect a status of Succeeded in the
UI (Last Run Status column), in the Cluster Actions list, click Generate Report On Past
Updating Runs.

10. Modify the Start and End dates to reflect today's date. Then click Generate Report. The report reflects which updates were applied to each node.

11. In the report screen, with a report selected, click Export Report. Save the report as an HTML file to a location of your choice.

12. Close the Generating Update Report screen. Locate the exported file and open it in Internet Explorer to view the results.

CONFIGURING CLUSTER SELF-UPDATING

The alternative to manually patching your cluster is to enable Cluster Self-Updating. Use the following procedure to enable this feature on your failover cluster:

1. On one of the nodes of your cluster, such as, for example, Host1, launch Server Manager. In the navigation pane, click Dashboard, click Tools, and then click Cluster-Aware Updating to open the Cluster-Aware Updating UI.

2. In the Cluster-Aware Updating UI, connect to the failover cluster that will be patched, Cluster01.

3. Under Cluster Actions, click Configure Cluster Self-Updating Actions. The Configure Self-Updating Options Wizard appears.

4. Review the Getting Started screen and click Next.

5. In the Add CAU Clustered Role With Self-Updating Enabled page (see Figure 8.17), select the check box labeled Add The CAU Clustered Role, With Self-Updating Mode Enabled, To This Cluster. If a Computer Object was pre-staged in AD, select the appropriate check box. Click Next.

FIGURE 8.17
Enabling self-updating by adding the CAU role

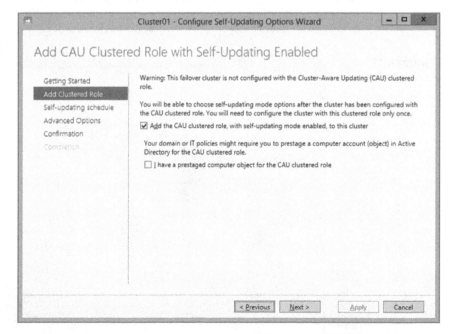

6. On the Self-Updating Schedule screen, shown in Figure 8.18, make appropriate selections in terms of frequency and schedule. Click Next.

FIGURE 8.18
Specifying a schedule

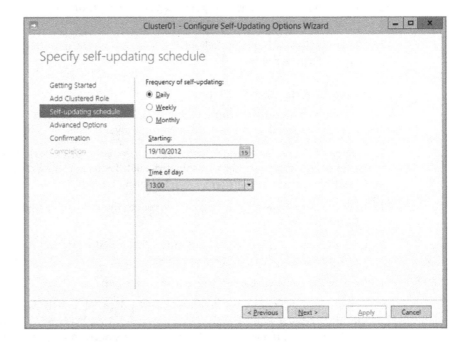

7. On the Advanced Options screen, shown in Figure 8.19, for the CAUPluginName, choose Microsoft.HotfixPlugin from the list. As a minimum, under CauPluginArguments enter **HotfixRootFolderPath = \\file1\Hotfixes\Root** and click Next.

FIGURE 8.19
Advanced options

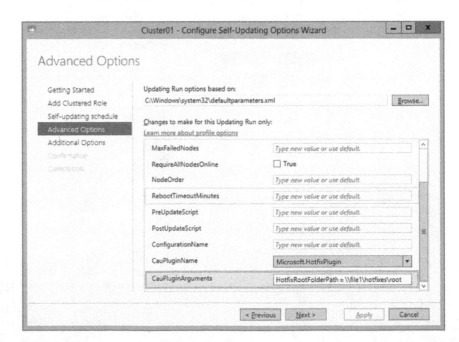

8. On the Additional Options screen, shown in Figure 8.20, select the Require SMB Encryption In Accessing The Hotfix Root Folder check box. If desired, also select Disable Check For Administrator Access To The Hotfix Root Folder And Configuration File. Click Next. Review the information in the Completion page and click Close.

FIGURE 8.20
Additional update options

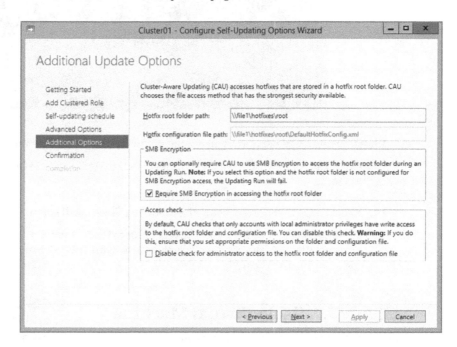

9. To determine the cluster node that is hosting the CAU role, run the following PowerShell command from one of the nodes of your cluster:

```
Get-CauClusterRole
```

10. Examine the output of the command and notice the ResourceGroupName entry that includes the name of one of the nodes of the cluster. This indicates the node in the cluster that is currently hosting the role (note that this role is not visible in the Failover Cluster Manager).

11. On the cluster node that is hosting the CAU role, open a PowerShell command window and run the following PowerShell command, as shown in Figure 8.21:

```
Invoke-CauScan -CauPluginArguments (@{ "HotfixRootFolderPath" = "\\ `
file1\hotfixes\root"}) -CauPluginName @("Microsoft.HotfixPlugin")
```

12. To apply updates to the failover cluster, run the following PowerShell command:

```
Invoke-CauRun -Force -CauPluginName @("Microsoft.HotfixPlugin") `
-MaxRetriesPerNode 3 -CauPluginArguments @{ "HotfixRootFolderPath" = "\\ `
file1\hotfixes\root"; "DisableAclChecks" = "False"; "HotfixConfigFileName" `
= "DefaultHotfixConfig.xml"; "RequireSmbEncryption" = "True"} `
-EnableFirewallRules;
```

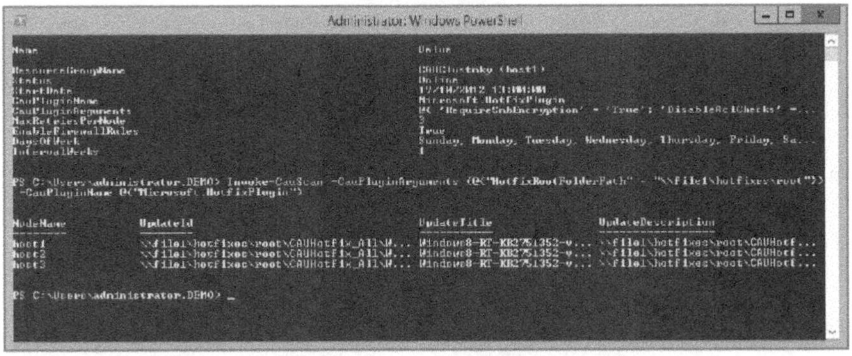

FIGURE 8.21
Output from
Invoke-CauScan

13. Generate a CAU Report by using the following PowerShell command:

```
Get-CauReport  -ClusterName Cluster01 -Detailed -StartDate 18/10/2012 -EndDate `
20/10/12
```

14. Export a CAU Report by using the following PowerShell command:

```
Get-CauReport -ClusterName Cluster1 -Detailed -Last | Export-CauReport `
-Format HTML -Path 'C:\dump\Cluster1_latest.html' -Timezone ([system. `
timezoneinfo]::local)
```

Highly Available Virtual Machine

Since Windows Server 2008, Failover Clustering has supported the concept of a highly available virtual machine. Windows Server 2012 improves on the integration between Failover Clustering and Hyper-V by adding capabilities. One of the biggest improvements that Failover Clustering has made in the Windows Server 2012 time frame is the increase in scale. Windows Server 2012 supports 64 nodes in a cluster, a maximum of 8,000 virtual machines per cluster, and has a limit per node of 1,024 virtual machines.

Implementing a Highly Available Virtual Machine

Implementing a highly available virtual machine requires that you perform your specific configuration tasks through Failover Cluster Manager. Use the following procedure to create a new highly available Windows Server 2012 server:

1. On one of the nodes of your cluster (for example, Host1), launch Server Manager. In the navigation pane, click Dashboard, click Tools, and then click Failover Cluster Manager.

2. In Failover Cluster Manager, in the navigation pane, expand the cluster and then click Roles.

3. In the Actions pane, click Virtual Machines and then choose New Virtual Machine.

4. In the New Virtual Machine Wizard dialog box, select the Host1 node. Click OK.

5. On the Before You Begin page, click Next.

6. On the Specify Name And Location page, in the Name box, type **Demo-HAVM1**. Select the Store The Virtual Machine In A Different Location check box and then click Browse.

7. In the Select Folder dialog box, navigate to C:\ClusterStorage\Volume1 and then click Select Folder.

8. On the Specify Name And Location page, click Next.

9. On the Assign Memory page, click Use Dynamic Memory For This Virtual Machine and then click Next.

10. On the Configure Networking page, in the Connection list, select Production and then click Next.

11. On the Connect Virtual Hard Disk page, choose Install An Operating System Later and then click Next.

12. On the Completing The New Virtual Machine Wizard page, click Finish.

13. On the Summary page, click Finish. The process should complete successfully, and there is a report available for viewing if required. Click Finish.

14. Repeat steps 3 through 13 to create a non–highly available virtual machine named Demo-VM1.

Examining the Virtual Machine Role

To configure and administer services and applications, you use Failover Cluster Manager. There are multiple property sheets for each resource. In addition, the settings available on each tab can vary based on the resource type. Use the following procedure to review the Role property pages of a virtual machine:

1. On one of the nodes of your cluster, such as Host1, launch the Server Manager. In the navigation pane, click Dashboard, click Tools, and then click Failover Cluster Manager.

2. In Failover Cluster Manager, in the navigation pane, expand the cluster. Click Roles.

3. Right-click the virtual machine Demo-HAVM1 and click Properties.

ROLE PROPERTY PAGES

The Role property pages for a highly available virtual machine are similar to the property pages for other roles supported by Failover Clustering (see Figure 8.22). One of the more important settings with respect to the virtual machine role is the Priority setting on the General tab.

FIGURE 8.22
Role property pages

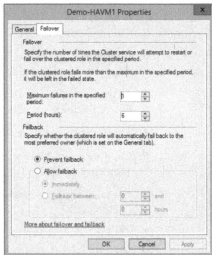

The Role Priority settings are Low, Medium, High, and No Auto Start. The Role property settings are used to determine which roles have priorities over others. The Priority setting indicates which workloads have priority over others when the cluster first starts and when the virtual machines are live-migrated. When the cluster first starts, all High-priority roles are brought online first, then the Medium-priority roles, and then finally the Low-priority roles, until the resource limits of the cluster are reached.

When a node's resource limit is reached, roles are distributed to other nodes in the cluster. When the cluster service is placing virtual workloads on the cluster nodes when the cluster starts, the following logic is used:

◆ Place a virtualized workload on the same node it was running on before the cluster was restarted.

◆ Place a virtual workload on a node in the cluster that is part of the Preferred Owners list for the resource group.

◆ If a node that hosted virtual workloads before the cluster was restarted is no longer part of the cluster, the cluster will place those workloads on other nodes in the cluster based on available resources on the nodes.

If virtual machine workloads cannot be brought online, the cluster continues to poll all the nodes in the cluster every 5 minutes to determine whether any resources are available so it can bring additional workloads online. When cluster resources become available, the virtual workloads are brought online.

VIRTUAL MACHINE ROLE OPTIONS

Many of the virtual machine options (listed in Table 8.2) are duplicates of those available in Hyper-V Manager. Use the following procedure to review the virtual machine role options:

1. On one of the nodes of your cluster, such as Host1, launch Server Manager. In the navigation pane, click Dashboard, click Tools, and then click Failover Cluster Manager.

2. In Failover Cluster Manager, in the navigation pane, expand the cluster. Click Roles.

3. Right-click the virtual machine Demo-HAVM1.

TABLE 8.2: Virtual machine role options

OPTION	DESCRIPTION
Connect	Connects to the virtual machine, and the virtual machine Connection interface is displayed.
Start	Starts the virtual machine if it is not started.
Save	Saves the virtual machine state.
Shutdown	Shuts down a running virtual machine.
Turn Off	Turns off the virtual machine without taking advantage of a graceful shutdown using the Operating System Shutdown integration service. Using this could result in guest operating system corruption.
Settings	Displays the settings for the virtual machine. Most settings cannot be changed while the virtual machine is running.
Manage	Opens Hyper-V Manager with a focus on the virtual machine.
Replication	Allows the virtual machine to be enabled for replication using the Hyper-V Replica functionality, which is part of the Hyper-V role.
Move	Allows the virtual machine to be migrated using either Live or Quick Migration. Alternatively, it allows only the virtual machine storage to be migrated.
Cancel Live Migration	Cancels an in-progress Live Migration.
Change Startup Priority	Allows the priority for the role to be changed. Options are High, Medium, Low, and No Auto Start.
Information Details	If an error or warning is associated with the role, selecting Information Details provides more-detailed information about the alert.
Add Storage	Adds cluster storage to the role.

TABLE 8.2: Virtual machine role options *(continued)*

OPTION	DESCRIPTION
Add Resource	Adds additional cluster resources to the role.
More Actions	Show Critical Events
	Show Dependency Report
	Configure Monitoring
	Start Role
	Stop Role
	Delete Saved State
	Pause
	Resume
	Reset
Remove	Removes the role from the cluster.
Properties	Displays Role property pages.
Help	Provides help that is context specific.

VIRTUAL MACHINE RESOURCE OPTIONS

The Virtual Machine Resource properties page presents five tabs that provide additional configuration options for the resource. Most of the tabs are generic and are similar across cluster resources. The Settings tab, however, provides unique configuration options that are specific to a virtual machine resource.

The Settings tab allows an administrator to choose a cluster-controlled offline action and to set health monitoring for the virtual machine (for more information on health monitoring, see Chapter 9, "Virtual SAN Storage and Guest Clustering"). Two settings are associated with virtual machine health monitoring, and both are enabled by default:

◆ The Enable Heartbeat Monitoring For The Virtual Machine setting allows the cluster service to tap into the Heartbeat integration service running in the virtual machine so it can react if the heartbeat stops.

◆ The Enable Automatic Recovery For Application Health Monitoring setting allows an administrator to configure application health monitoring.

With health monitoring enabled, the cluster service will execute recovery actions. These include restarting the virtual machine on the current owning node or shutting down the virtual machine, moving it to another node in the cluster, and restarting it.

Virtual Machine Mobility

In Windows Server 2008 R2, Microsoft supported the ability to both quick-migrate and live-migrate virtual machines within a failover cluster. In Windows Server 2012, not only have Quick Migration and Live Migration been enhanced, but now additional mobility scenarios are supported:

◆   Storage Migration

◆   Hyper-V Replica

One of the main enhancements in Windows Server 2012 Hyper-V is the capability to do more than one Quick or Live Migration simultaneously between the same pair of cluster nodes. In fact, the number of simultaneous Live Migrations is configurable in the Hyper-V Server Settings. However, if left unconfigured, the default setting will carry out only two simultaneous Live Migrations.

When the maximum number of Quick or Live Migrations is in progress, all remaining migration requests are queued. It should be noted that Live Migration is not restricted to failover clusters. Virtual machines can be migrated between stand-alone Windows Server 2012 Hyper-V servers or between a stand-alone Windows Server 2012 Hyper-V server and a Windows Server 2012 Hyper-V failover cluster. The only real restriction is the ability to live-migrate a highly available virtual machine. As you would expect, a highly available virtual machine can't be live-migrated outside the Windows Server 2012 Hyper-V failover cluster, and this is because it is configured for high availability. To be able to live-migrate such a virtual machine, it must first be removed from the cluster. Then it can be live-migrated to another Windows Server 2012 Hyper-V server by using the Move action in Hyper-V Manager.

Live Migration of a virtual machine between two stand-alone servers running Windows Server 2012 Hyper-V, which uses local storage for the virtual machine, can also be accomplished. In this case, the virtual machine's storage is mirrored to the destination server over the network, and then the virtual machine is migrated, while it continues to run and provide services. Live Migration of a virtual machine outside a cluster involves the following steps:

1. Throughout the majority of the move operation, disk reads and writes go to the source virtual hard disk.

2. While reads and writes occur on the source virtual hard disk, the disk contents are copied over the network to the new destination.

3. After the initial disk copy is complete, disk writes are mirrored to both the source and destination virtual hard disks while outstanding disk changes are replicated.

4. After the source and destination virtual hard disks are completely synchronized, the virtual machine Live Migration is initiated, following the same process that is used for Live Migration with shared storage.

5. After the Live Migration is complete, and the virtual machine is successfully running on the destination server, the files on the source server are deleted.

Live-Migrating Virtual Machines

Use the following procedure to configure the number of Live Migrations to ensure that a minimum of five can be performed simultaneously:

1. On one of the nodes of your cluster, such as Host1, launch Windows PowerShell.

2. Run the following PowerShell command:

```
Get-ClusterNode | ForEach-Object {Invoke-command -Computername $_.name `
-scriptblock {Set-VMHost -MaximumVirtualMachineMigrations 5}}
```

3. Optionally, you can verify that this configuration has been applied for each host by using Hyper-V Manager and Hyper-V Settings.

4. Ensure that there are sufficient virtual machines running using Failover Cluster Manager.

5. Initiate simultaneous Live Migration of all highly available virtual machines by selecting all highly available virtual machines. Then, in the Actions pane, click Move, then click Live Migration, and then click Best Possible Node.

   If the highly available virtual machines were all owned by Host1, you will see a status of Live Migrating for five of the virtual machines, and a status of Live Migration Queued for any remaining virtual machines.

Using Live Storage Migration

In addition to live-migrating virtual machines between Windows Server 2012 Hyper-V servers, Windows Server 2012 also enables you to live-migrate just the virtual machine storage without system downtime. You can move the storage while the virtual machine remains running. You can perform this task by using the Move Wizard in Hyper-V Manager or by using the new Windows Server 2012 Hyper-V PowerShell commands.

In the most common scenario leveraging Live Storage Migration, an organization needs to upgrade the physical storage device that is hosting the source virtual machine and its associated virtual hard disk. You also may want to move virtual machine storage between physical storage devices at runtime to take advantage of new, lower-cost storage supported in Windows Server 2012 Hyper V, such as Server Message Block version 3 (SMB3). For more details on SMB3, refer to Chapter 7. Live Storage Migration involves the following steps:

1. At the beginning of the move operation, disk reads and writes go to the source virtual hard disk.

2. While reads and writes occur on the source virtual hard disk, the disk contents are copied to the new destination virtual hard disk.

3. After the initial disk copy is complete, disk writes are mirrored to both the source and destination virtual hard disks, while outstanding disk changes are replicated. After the Live Migration is complete, and the virtual machine is successfully running on the destination server, the files on the source server are deleted.

4. After the source and destination virtual hard disks are completely synchronized, the virtual machine switches over to using the destination virtual hard disk, and the source virtual hard disk is deleted.

SETTING UP SHARED STORAGE

Use the following procedure to configure shared storage to support Live Storage Migration:

1. On one of the nodes of your cluster, such as Host2, launch Windows PowerShell.

2. Use the following PowerShell command to create a shared folder and set the correct share and NTFS permissions:

```
MD '<LOCAL_DRIVE_PATH>\VM-Store'


New-SmbShare -Name VM-Store -Path "<LOCAL_DRIVE_PATH>\VM-Store"' -FullAccess `
demo\administrator, demo\host1$, demo\host2$, demo\host3$


(Get-SmbShare -Name VM-Store).PresetPathAcl | Set-Acl
```

INITIATING LIVE STORAGE MIGRATION

Use the following procedure to initiate a Live Storage Migration between different storage repositories:

1. Log on to Host. In Server Manager, choose Tools ➤ Hyper-V Manager.

2. In Hyper-V Manager, in the Actions pane, in the Demo-VM1, click Start. Before proceeding any further, ensure that the virtual machine starts successfully.

3. In Hyper-V Manager, in the Virtual Machines list, select Demo-VM1. In the Actions pane, click Move.

4. In the Move Machine Wizard, on the Before You Begin page, click Next.

5. On the Choose Move Type page, select Move The Virtual Machine's Storage. Then click Next.

6. On the Choose Options For Moving Storage page, leave the default Move All Of The Virtual Machine's Data To A Single Location option selected, and click Next.

7. On the Choose A New Location For Virtual Machine page, in the Folder box, type **\\Host2\VM-Store\Demo-VM1**, click Next, and then click Finish.

8. Monitor the Storage Migration in Hyper-V Manager until the migration completes.

9. When the migration completes, check the virtual machine Settings to verify the new location for the storage.

To initiate Live Storage Migration by using PowerShell, run the following Hyper-V PowerShell command:

```
Move-VMStorage -VMName Demo-VM1 -DestinationStoragePath "\\Host2\VM-Store\ `
Demo-VM1"
```

Finally, Windows Failover Clustering supports Windows Server 2012 Hyper-V Replica. This topic is discussed in further detail in Chapter 12, "Hyper-V Replica."

Real World Solutions

CHALLENGE

A medium-sized company wants to implement Windows Server 2012 Failover Clustering so that they can create a series of highly available virtual machines. The IT Director has specified a couple of requirements but one of the main requirements is that when the failover cluster first starts or when virtual machines are live migrated, specific workloads running on the cluster should have priority over other workloads on the cluster. For example, the IT Director is mandating that Active Directory Domain Controllers should have a high priority over other virtual machines when the Failover Cluster is started.

SOLUTION

The solution when implementing a highly available virtual machine would be to configure the Role Priority settings and specify a High value for Active Directory Domain Controllers. The Role Property settings would then determine that these virtual machines have priority over others virtual machines running on the same cluster and start these virtual machines first.

CHALLENGE

The company is satisfied that they can prioritize which virtual machines have priority. They would now like to set up and configure live storage migration, so they can move just the storage related elements, while the virtual machines remain in an online state. The use of storage migration is important to this company, as they have plans to upgrade the physical storage device currently used in the near future.

SOLUTION

The solution would be to test and validate Live Storage Migration. Live Storage Migration can be initiated by using either Hyper-V Manager or via Windows PowerShell, by running the following command:

```
Move-VMStorage -VMName Demo-VM1 -DestinationStoragePath "\\Host2\VM-Store\ `
Demo-VM1"
```

Chapter 9

Virtual SAN Storage and Guest Clustering

Virtual Fibre Channel, a new feature to Windows Server 2012 Hyper-V, provides the capability to present a virtual host bus adapter (HBA) inside a virtual machine. The benefit is that the virtual machine then has direct access to the Fibre Channel Storage Area Network (SAN) fabric. Virtual Fibre Channel also provides new capabilities in terms of an additional shared storage architecture for Windows Server 2012 Hyper-V and guest clustering. Previously, iSCSI was the only storage option available when implementing guest clustering. Virtual Fibre Channel also serves as an alternative hardware-based I/O path to the virtual hard disk. Now physical workloads that may have previously leveraged Fibre Channel storage for specific I/O requirements can be virtualized.

In this chapter, you'll learn about

◆ Virtual SAN storage

◆ N_Port ID Virtualization

◆ Configuration of Virtual Fibre Channel

◆ Guest clustering

◆ Virtual machine monitoring

Introduction to Virtual SAN Storage

Until the advent of Windows Server 2012 and Virtual Fibre Channel, one barrier stood in the way of migrating some of your existing workloads into the cloud, and that was the ability to access a Fibre Channel storage array from within a virtual machine. If you had a high-performance workload (for example, a Microsoft SQL Server Parallel Data Warehouse or an online transaction processing workload), you could pretty much guarantee that it was configured to use a Fibre Channel SAN, thus barring it from being a good candidate for cloud computing. As a result, you would have deferred from performing such a migration.

Virtual Fibre Channel removes this deployment blocking issue by providing Fibre Channel ports within the guest operating system of the virtual machine. This allows a server application such as Microsoft SQL Server running within a virtual machine to connect directly to logical unit numbers (LUNs) on a Fibre Channel SAN. The support for Virtual Fibre Channel within a virtual machine includes support for many features related to Windows Server 2012, such as virtual SANs, live migration, multipath I/O (MPIO), and Offloaded Data Transfer (ODX).

OFFLOADED DATA TRANSFER

ODX works as a complementary feature on Fibre Channel SANs. This new capability in Windows Server 2012 increases the value of Fibre Channel technology when deployed on compatible storage arrays. ODX enables direct data transfers within or between compatible storage devices without transferring the data to the host server, and instead uses token passing between the storage array and the virtual machine.

Enabling ODX functionality on a compatible storage array requires assigning ODX-capable Fibre Channel LUNs to the virtual machine's virtual Fibre Channel HBA.

Overview of Virtual Fibre Channel

Virtual Fibre Channel provides supported virtual machines instantiated on Windows Server 2012 Hyper-V with direct access to a SAN by using a standard World Wide Name (WWN) associated with a virtual machine. Windows Server 2012 Hyper-V can now leverage the Fibre Channel SAN to virtualize workloads that require direct access to SAN LUNs. Having access to a Fibre Channel SAN allows you to implement new storage scenarios, such as running the Windows Failover Clustering feature inside the guest operating system of a virtual machine connected to shared Fibre Channel storage.

WORLD WIDE NAME

A World Wide Name (WWN) is a unique identifier that is assigned to a hardware manufacturer by the Institute of Electrical and Electronic Engineers (IEEE) and is hard-coded into a Fibre Channel device. WWNs are important when setting up SANs. Each device has to be registered with the SAN by its WWN before the SAN will recognize it.

Virtual Fibre Channel presents an alternate hardware-based I/O path to the virtual hard disk. This allows you to use the advanced functionality offered by your storage vendor's SAN directly from within the Windows Server 2012 Hyper-V virtual machine. You can now use Windows Server 2012 Hyper-V to offload storage functionality (for example, taking a snapshot of a LUN on the SAN) by using a hardware Volume Shadow Copy Service (VSS) provider. The new Virtual Fibre Channel adapter supports up to four virtual HBAs assigned to each virtual machine. Separate WWNs are assigned to each virtual HBA, and N_Port ID Virtualization (NPIV) is used to register virtual machine ports on the host.

REQUIREMENTS

The Virtual Fibre Channel feature in Windows Server 2012 Hyper-V has the following hardware and software requirements:

◆ An installation of Windows Server 2012 with the Hyper-V role enabled.

◆ A server with a minimum of one or more Fibre Channel HBAs that also has an updated HBA driver that supports Virtual Fibre Channel.

UPDATED HBA DRIVERS

Updated HBA drivers are updated drivers that are downloaded from either the hardware vendor or the original equipment manufacturer (OEM) and can typically be found on the hardware vendor's or the OEM's website. To determine whether your hardware supports Virtual Fibre Channel, you should contact your hardware vendor or OEM.

◆ An NPIV-enabled SAN.

◆ Virtual machines configured to use a Virtual Fibre Channel adapter, and these virtual machines are limited to Windows Server 2008, Windows Server 2008 R2, or Windows Server 2012 as the guest operating system.

◆ Storage accessed through a Virtual Fibre Channel supports devices that are presented as logical units.

N _ PORT ID VIRTUALIZATION

NPIV is an extension to the Fibre Channel industry standard (ANSI T11) that is supported across numerous hardware vendors or OEMs, HBAs, and SANs. NPIV delivers significant advantages when running multiple virtual machines and managing those workloads across multiple physical Windows Server 2012 Hyper-V servers. System administrators now have the ability to control access to LUNs on a per virtual machine basis.

In a Windows Server 2012 Hyper-V environment, NPIV allows each virtual machine to have a unique Fibre Channel WWN, thus enabling multiple virtual machines to share a single physical HBA and switch port. By providing a unique virtual HBA port, system administrators can implement SAN best practices, such as zoning for individual virtual machines. System administrators can also take advantage of SAN-based management tools, simplifying migration of virtual machines and their storage resources. NPIV has the following benefits:

◆ Maintaining a smaller hardware footprint reduces the number of points of failure, thus resulting in improved availability and storage network uptime.

◆ Less hardware, with easily transferable interconnects, and virtual machine–level zoning, contributes to simplified SAN and Windows Server 2012 Hyper-V management.

◆ NPIV allows the SAN best practices that are available with physical servers to be maintained within cloud computing.

◆ NPIV provides for more granular security by restricting LUN access to individual virtual machines.

> **ZONING**
>
> Zoning is the process of segmenting the switched fabric. Zoning can be used to create a barrier between environments. Only members of the same zone can communicate within that zone, and all other attempts from outside that zone are rejected. Zoning can be implemented in one of two ways.
>
> Hardware zoning is based on the physical fabric port number. The members of a zone are physical ports on the fabric switch. Hardware zoning is less flexible because devices have to be connected to a specific port.
>
> Software zoning is implemented by the fabric operating systems within the fabric switches. When using software zoning, the members of the zone can be defined by using their WWN and World Wide Port Name (WWPN). A WWPN is a unique 64-bit identifier that is assigned to a Fibre Channel node port, also called an N_port.

There are a few requirements within the storage infrastructure in terms of software and hardware to enable NPIV:

HBAs   NPIV needs to be supported on the HBAs connected to the SAN switches.

Ensure that the number of NPIV ports on the HBA is sufficient (some lower-end HBAs have considerably fewer than 255 NPIV ports).

SAN Switches   NPIV needs to be supported and enabled on the SAN switches.

SAN Switch Ports   NPIV may need to be enabled on the actual port, and sufficient logins per port need to be configured.

Storage   NPIV is completely transparent to storage arrays, and so no specific support for NPIV is required.

VIRTUAL SANS

Windows Server 2012 Hyper-V allows you to define one or more virtual SANs to support scenarios in which a single Windows Server 2012 Hyper-V host is connected to different SANs via multiple Fibre Channel ports. A virtual SAN defines a named group or set of physical Fibre Channel ports that are connected to the same physical SAN. For example, assume that a Windows Server 2012 Hyper-V host is connected to two SANs, a production SAN and a development SAN. The Windows Server 2012 Hyper-V host is connected to each SAN through two physical Fibre Channel ports. In this example, you might configure two virtual SANs, one named Production_SAN that has the two physical Fibre Channel ports connected to the production SAN, and one named Development_SAN that has two physical Fibre Channel ports connected to the development SAN.

You can configure as many as four virtual Fibre Channel adapters on a virtual machine and associate each virtual Fibre Channel adapter with a virtual SAN. Each virtual Fibre Channel adapter connects with two WWN addresses to support live migration, and these WWNs can be set either automatically or manually.

LIVE MIGRATION

The use of Virtual Fibre Channel and the allocation of WWNs have an influence on live migration. Let's face it—when you live-migrate a virtual machine, you will still want to maintain Fibre Channel connectivity.

LIVE MIGRATION

Live migration allows you to transparently move running virtual machines from one Windows Server 2012 host to another host without perceived downtime or dropping client network connections. To learn more about live migration, see Chapter 3, "Managing Virtual Machines."

To support live migration of virtual machines across Windows Server 2012 Hyper-V hosts and maintain Fibre Channel connectivity, two WWNs are configured for each virtual Fibre Channel adapter. As shown in Figure 9.1, these WWNs are indicated as Address set A and Address set B.

FIGURE 9.1
Virtual Fibre
Channel WWNs

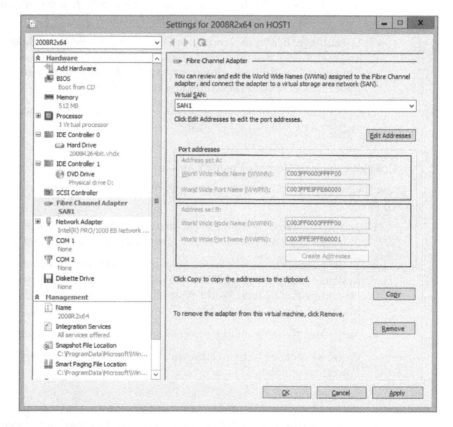

Windows Server 2012 Hyper-V automatically alternates between the set A and set B WWN addresses during a live migration. This ensures that all LUNs are available on the destination host before the migration and that no downtime occurs during the migration.

USE OF MULTIPATH I/O

Windows Server 2012 Hyper-V can leverage multipath I/O (MPIO) functionality to ensure continuous connectivity to Fibre Channel storage from within a virtual machine. MPIO is a

Microsoft framework designed to mitigate the effects of HBA failure by providing an alternate data path between storage devices and the Windows operating system. You can use MPIO functionality with Fibre Channel in the following ways:

- Use MPIO for Windows Server 2012 Hyper-V host access. Install multiple Fibre Channel ports on the host, preferably across multiple Fibre Channel HBAs, and use MPIO to provide highly available connectivity to the LUNs accessible by the host.

  - Consult your hardware vendors or OEM for specific guidance on setting up any MPIO-specific load-balancing policies.

- Configure multiple virtual Fibre Channel adapters inside a virtual machine, and use a separate copy of MPIO within the guest operating system of the virtual machine to connect to the LUNs that the virtual machine can access. This configuration can coexist with Windows Server 2012 Hyper-V host MPIO setup.

- Use different hardware vendors' or OEMs' device-specific modules (DSMs) for the host and each virtual machine. This approach allows live migration of the virtual machine configuration, including the configuration of DSM, connectivity between hosts, and compatibility with existing server configurations and DSMs.

  - Consult your hardware vendors or OEM for specific guidance on recommended policies for configuring the DSM.

CONFIGURATION OF VIRTUAL FIBRE CHANNEL

Use the following procedure to configure a Virtual Fibre Channel in Windows Server 2012 Hyper-V:

1. Launch the Hyper-V Manager console and in the Actions pane, click Virtual SAN Manager. With the New Fibre Channel SAN selected, click the Create button.

2. In the Name field, enter a name for your Virtual SAN (for example, SAN1). In the list of available HBAs (these are HBAs available within your Windows Server 2012 Hyper-V host, identified by their World Wide Node Name [WWNN]) select the appropriate HBA. Then click Create Virtual SAN.

3. Verify that the correct HBA has been selected and click OK, as shown in Figure 9.2.

   To get a list of one or more HBAs by using Windows PowerShell, run the following PowerShell cmdlet:

   ```
   Get-InitiatorPort
   ```

   However, this includes iSCSI, Serial Attached SCSI (SAS), and Fibre Channel initiators, and there is no distinction between Fibre Channel and Fibre Channel over Ethernet. An alternative approach would be to use the Windows Management Instrumentation (WMI) Hyper-V provider:

   ```
   Get-WmiObject -n Root\Virtualization\V2 Msvm_ExternalFcPort | ft WWPN, WWNN, `
   IsHyperVCapable
   ```

   The benefit here is the use of the `IsHyperVCapable` property.

FIGURE 9.2
Virtual SAN
Manager

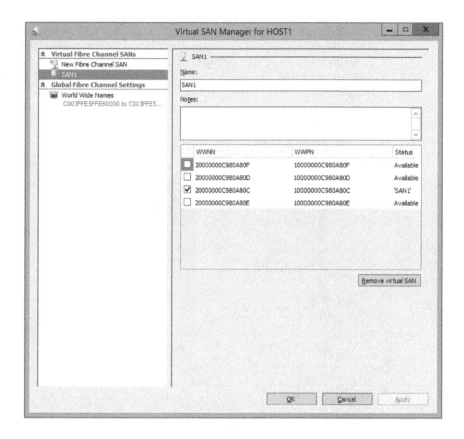

To create a new virtual SAN by using Windows PowerShell, run the following PowerShell cmdlet:

```
New-VMSan –Name SAN1 –Note "Initial production SAN" –WorldWideNodeName `
20000000C980A80C –WorldWidePortName 10000000C980A80C.
```

A simple way to combine these two Windows PowerShell commands would result in the following:

```
$initiatorports = Get-InitiatorPort | new-vmsan -Name San1 -HostBusAdapter `
$initiatorports[0]
```

4. Under Global Fibre Channel Settings, click World Wide Names. Here you can set (if required) the WWPN address parameters, minimum and maximum, and you can set the WWNN that will be used for the Windows Server 2012 Hyper-V ports. After you have verified these values, click OK.

   Next you can choose to either create a new virtual machine or modify an existing virtual machine, to add support for Virtual Fibre Channel. (In this example, we are going to modify an existing virtual machine.)

5. In the list of Virtual Machines, select the appropriate virtual machine (note that this virtual machine needs to be powered off). In the Actions pane, click Settings. In the Add Hardware section, select Fibre Channel Adapter (as shown in Figure 9.3) and click Add. (Remember that you can have up to four Virtual Fibre Channel adapters per virtual machine.)

FIGURE 9.3
Adding a Fibre Channel adapter

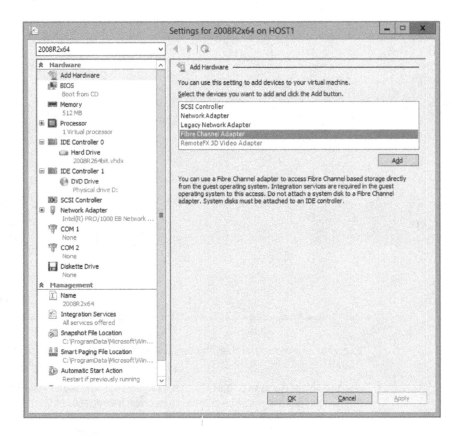

6. In the Hardware section of the virtual machine, select Fibre Channel Adapter—Not Connected. In the Virtual SAN drop-down menu, select SAN1, as shown in Figure 9.4. Now when this virtual machine is started, an NPIV port will be created on the selected physical HBAs associated with SAN1 and will use the automatically generated WWNN values. To edit these values, click the Edit Addresses button and configure any specific port addresses. Otherwise, click OK.

7. To verify that the Virtual Fibre Channel adapter has been added, start the selected virtual machine, log in with an account that has appropriate permissions, and type **Computer Management** (for Windows Server 2012) or **COMPMGMT.MSC** (for Windows 2008 R2 or below). Select Device Manager and then select Storage Controllers, as shown in Figure 9.5. Note that you have the Microsoft Hyper-V Virtual Channel HBA available.

FIGURE 9.4
Connecting the
adapter to the
virtual SAN

FIGURE 9.5
Device Manager—
Microsoft Hyper-V
Virtual Channel HBA

Guest Clustering

Guest clustering, while maybe not a well-known industry term, is the process of implementing Windows Failover Cluster across a series of virtual machines, which may or may not be hosted on a physical Windows Server 2012 Hyper-V cluster.

Guest clustering isn't exactly a new concept either. In fact, you could implement guest clustering in Windows Server 2008. However, prior to Windows Server 2012, the only supported storage solution for guest clustering was iSCSI. Now with Windows Server 2012 Hyper-V, you can use Virtual Fibre Channel and Fibre Channel storage in your guest cluster. The usage of guest clustering also features in Microsoft Private Cloud Fast Track Reference Architecture, providing a highly available SQL server. A typical guest cluster setup includes the following:

- Preparing your virtual machines
- Configuring your virtual networking
- Configuring your shared storage
- Installing Windows Failover Clustering
- Validating your guest cluster

You can set up guest clustering in several configurations, depending on your environment.

Guest Clustering on a Single Host

A guest cluster on a single host consists of two or more virtual machines running on the same Hyper-V host, as shown in Figure 9.6. The virtual machines are connected to the same series of networks and storage, either iSCSI or Fibre Channel. This configuration protects against failures within the virtual machine and at the application level but does not offer any protection against hardware failure. This kind of solution is ideal for test and development environments but offers limited value within a production environment.

FIGURE 9.6
Guest clustering on a single host

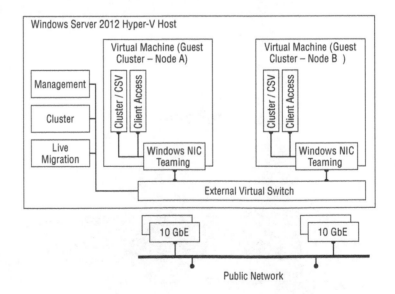

Guest Clustering across Physical Hosts

A guest cluster split across physical hosts, as shown in Figure 9.7, consists of two or more virtual machines running across a number of physical hosts. This kind of guest cluster protects against failures within the virtual machine, at the application level, and offers protection against hardware failures. The virtual machines, as in the previous example, are connected to the same series of networks and storage, either iSCSI or Fibre Channel. Guest clustering across physical hosts can offer significant cost savings and provides a platform for consolidating physical clusters.

FIGURE 9.7
Guest clustering across physical hosts

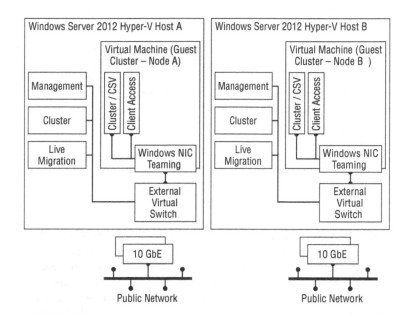

CREATING AFFINITY RULES

It is recommended that the nodes of a guest cluster should reside on different physical Windows Server 2012 Hyper-V hosts to achieve the highest levels of system availability. If a Windows Server 2012 Hyper-V host were to fail, having virtual machines from the same guest cluster distributed across multiple Windows Server 2012 Hyper-V hosts would enable the workload to recover quickly or always remain available in a setup with SQL Server AlwaysOn Availability Groups. To accomplish this, configure the cluster group property `AntiAffinityClassName`. The Windows Server 2012 Hyper-V host cluster will attempt to keep virtual machines with a consistent string value (such as the virtual machine name) off the same host. `AntiAffinityClassName` can be configured by Windows PowerShell. Use the following Windows PowerShell cmdlet to configure `AntiAffinityClassName`:

```
Get-ClusterGroup *SQLVM* | %{$_.AntiAffinityClassNames = "Microsoft SQL Virtual `
Server"}
```

Note that you no longer need to use `CLUSTER.EXE` since Windows PowerShell has replaced its functionality. However, if you still want to use it, you can enable it by using the Add Roles And Features in Server Manager to include Failover Cluster Command Interface, as it is now a subset of the Failover Clustering tools.

HEARTBEAT THRESHOLDS

It may be necessary to increase the cluster heartbeat thresholds of a guest cluster (see Table 9.1) when the virtual machine node is being moved to a new Windows Server 2012 Hyper-V host, via live (storage) migration. Increasing the thresholds will keep Windows Failover Clustering from assuming the virtual machine node is down and incorrectly taking recovery actions. The heartbeat thresholds can be modified by increasing the SameSubnetThreshold and SameSubnetDelay cluster common properties. The correct values for these settings can be derived only from testing in customer-specific scenarios. Use the following Windows PowerShell commands to configure SameSubnetThreshold and SameSubnetDelay properties, respectively:

```
$cluster = Get-Cluster; $cluster.SameSubnetThreshold = <value> and $cluster = `
Get-Cluster; $cluster.SameSubnetDelay = <value>
```

TABLE 9.1:   Heartbeat thresholds

DESCRIPTION	DEFAULT	MINIMUM	MAXIMUM
SameSubnetThreshold	5	3	10
SameSubnetDelay	1,000 milliseconds	250 milliseconds	2,000 milliseconds

Guest Clustering across Physical Hosts and Virtual Machines

A guest cluster split across both physical hosts and virtual machines (as shown in Figure 9.8) offers a solution for an environment in which the workload has a small hardware resource requirement. This kind of solution is ideal for simple disaster recovery environments. Install and configure your physical hosts to correspond to a virtual machine running on a standby host. In the case of a hardware failure with one of the physical hosts, the associated virtual machine running on the standby server can take over.

FIGURE 9.8
Guest clustering across physical hosts and virtual machines

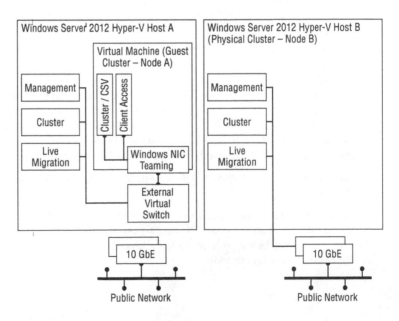

Creating a Guest-Based Cluster

Setting up a guest-based cluster involves a similar level of preparation to building out a physical cluster. Virtual machine nodes, instead of physical cluster nodes, need to be provisioned. Networking needs to be in place, only here we are talking about virtual networks. And finally, shared storage needs to be presented to all the virtual machine nodes within the cluster (with one exception, and this is when an asymmetric storage configuration is implemented.

ASYMMETRIC STORAGE CONFIGURATION

In an asymmetric storage configuration, not all nodes in the cluster see all the storage associated with the cluster. The storage is visible to only a subset of nodes in the cluster. Windows Failover Clustering recognizes an Asymmetric Storage architecture and is able to accommodate a disk witness in this configuration setup. The cluster service will ensure that the Core Cluster Group, which contains the disk witness resource, comes online only on the nodes that have connectivity to the shared storage. This type of configuration is mostly used in multisite clusters (also known as geo-clustering).

Virtual Machine Preparation

The first step in building out your guest-based cluster is to prepare your virtual machine nodes. A minimum of two nodes are required, but these virtual machine nodes don't have to be running Windows Server 2012. In fact, as mentioned earlier, they can have any of the following operating systems, if Integration Services has been updated:

- Windows Server 2008

- Windows Server 2008 R2

- Windows Server 2012

Virtual machines can be created by either using the Hyper-V Manager Microsoft Management Console (MMC) or the Hyper-V PowerShell module. Creating a virtual machine in Hyper-V Manager MMC using the New Virtual Machine Wizard is the same as it was in Windows Server 2008 R2 SP1 or below. Use the following procedure to create a virtual machine in Windows Server 2012 Hyper-V:

1. Launch the Hyper-V Manager and in the Actions pane, click New and then Virtual Machine.

2. The New Virtual Machine Wizard starts. Review the Before You Begin page and click Next.

3. The Specify Name And Location page appears. Enter a name for the virtual machine (for example, VMCLNODE01) and choose to store the virtual machine in a different location from the default location configured on your Windows Server 2012 Hyper-V server. Consider entering a UNC path here, if using an SMB 3.0 file share on a remote file server, and click Next. (For more details on SMB 3.0 and how to set up an SMB 3.0 file share, see Chapter 7, "Using File Servers.")

4. The Assign Memory page appears. Unless you have specific memory requirements, consider allocating 2 GB of startup memory (the default assigned startup memory is 512 MB). Optionally, choose to use dynamic memory by selecting the Use Dynamic Memory For This Virtual Machine check box. Click Next.

5. The Configure Networking page appears. Ensure that the connection value is set to Not Connected and click Next.

6. The Connect Virtual Hard Disk page appears. Choose the Create A Virtual Hard Disk option and specify a size in gigabytes, such as 40 GB for your virtual machine's hard disk (note this is a suggested size) and click Next.

7. The Installation Options page appears; click Install An Operating System Later and click Next.

8. The Completing The New Virtual Machine Wizard page appears. Click Finish to create your virtual machine.

9. Repeat steps 1 through 8 to create a second virtual machine node within your guest cluster.

To configure a virtual machine by using Windows PowerShell, run the following PowerShell cmdlet:

```
New-VM -Name VMCLNODE01 -MemoryStartupBytes 2GB -NewVHDPath \\CAFS\VMSTORE\ `
VMCLNODE01.VHDX -NewVHDSizeBytes 40GB
```

The next step in building out your guest cluster is to prepare your virtual networking. Create two virtual network switches in the Hyper-V Manager. One will serve as the production-facing network (external network switch) and the other one will be for cluster communication (this may be either an internal or external virtual switch, and this choice is dependent on whether your guest cluster is limited to a single host or you have implemented guest clustering across physical hosts).

1. Launch the Hyper-V Manager and in the Actions pane, click Virtual Switch Manager.

2. In Virtual Switch Manager, click Create Virtual Switch. In the Name field, enter a name that reflects the usage of this virtual switch (for example, Production01). In the Connection Type field ensure that External Network is selected, and from the drop-down menu select the appropriate network adapter. Deselect Allow Management Operating System To Share The Network Adapter and click OK.

3. Repeat step 2 to create a second virtual switch for your guest cluster on your initial physical host. If clustering across physical hosts, then repeat the creation of both virtual switches on the second physical host.

To configure a virtual switch by using Windows PowerShell, run the following PowerShell cmdlet:

```
New-VMSwitch "Production01" –NetAdapterName "Production Net" -AllowManagementOS `
$false
```

To be able to determine the `NetAdapterName`, you can use the following Windows PowerShell command:

```
Get-NetAdapter
```

If you need to rename your network adapter prior to creating a virtual switch, then you can run the following PowerShell cmdlet:

```
Rename-NetAdapter
```

Finally, the last step in building out your guest cluster is to present your shared storage to each node. This can be achieved by leveraging Virtual Fibre Channel and Virtual SANs.

Virtual Machine Monitoring

Windows clusters are designed to provide high availability for the workloads running on the cluster. There are resource monitors in place that report the status of the resource group to the cluster service, and these resource monitors allow the cluster service to query the resource status and take actions in case interruptions to proper functioning occur. However, resource monitors don't offer the capability to monitor specific applications running inside the virtual machine.

In previous versions of Windows Failover Clustering (Windows Server 2008 R2 or below), there was no native capability to monitor specific applications running inside a virtual machine either. For example, for a print server running on Windows Server 2012 Hyper-V, it is critical that the Print Spooler service continue to function properly. There are mechanisms built into the operating system via Service Control Manager (SCM) that allow the end user to set a number of recovery actions, as shown in Figure 9.9.

FIGURE 9.9
Print spooler
recovery options

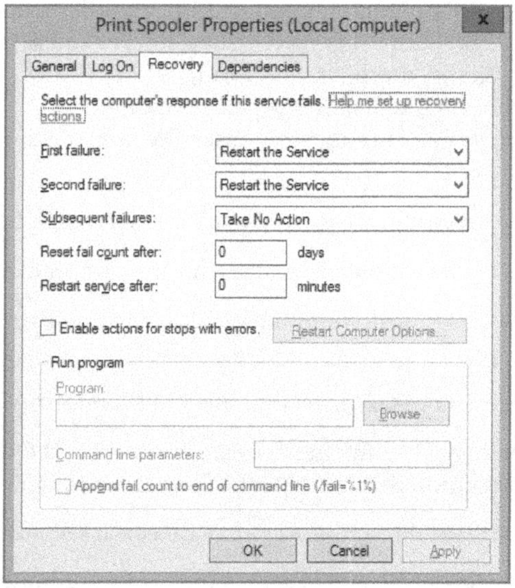

SERVICE CONTROL MANAGER

Service Control Manager (SCM) is a special system process that starts, stops, and interacts with service processes running on the Windows platform. It is located in `%SystemRoot%\System32\` as the executable `SERVICES.EXE`. Service processes interact with SCM via a Windows application programming interface (API), and this same API is used internally by Windows management tools such as the MMC snap-in `SERVICES.MSC` and the command-line Service Control utility `SC.EXE` to manage service processes.

There are cluster-aware applications such as SQL Server that have the capability to monitor critical SQL services. This is accomplished by writing cluster-aware resource DLLs so that failures of these critical services will result in the cluster taking actions to remediate the situation. In a private cloud environment, the only choice you had if you wanted to monitor the application (outside of implementing something such as System Center Operations Manager) was to implement guest clustering. Here, guest clustering would provide the monitoring inherent in the cluster service, with the cluster itself running as a virtualized workload on either a Windows Server 2008 R2 Hyper-V stand-alone server or as part of a Windows Server 2008 R2 Hyper-V cluster.

Windows Failover Clustering in Windows Server 2012 provides application health detection inside a virtual machine, where the cluster service running in the host takes remedial action. This is totally independent of a guest clustering configuration. The only requirement is that the host and guest must be running Windows Server 2012 as the operating system, and Windows Server 2012 Hyper-V Integration Services must be installed in the virtual machine (this is installed by default). Other virtual machines running other operating systems that have Windows Server 2012 Integration Services installed can signal an application-critical state, but the cluster will not take any action. Other applications—for example, System Center Operations Manager 2012—can trigger a critical state and cause the cluster to take recovery action. However, virtual machine monitoring is very flexible and can monitor both services and events without the need to deploy a separate solution.

The sequence of events when a service fails inside a virtual machine that is being monitored is as follows:

1. The service process fails inside the virtual machine.

2. The Service Control Manager in the virtual machine registers a 7034 event.

3. The task scheduler in the virtual machine launches a custom task (which is a custom script).

4. The custom task calls into the VM Monitoring COM API.

5. The heart-beating mechanism running in the virtual machine by way of Hyper-V Integration Services sets the `GuestInCritical` state property in WMI.

6. The virtual machine resource detects a secondary failure when `IsAlive` is called.

7. The cluster service executes the configured failure-handling policies.

8. The virtual machine is forcibly shut down.

9. The virtual machine is then either brought back online (restarted) on the current node in the cluster, or moved to another node in the cluster and restarted.

The recovery actions that are available include the following:

◆ Application-level recovery in the virtual machine, whereby SCM restarts the service

◆ Virtual machine–level recovery, whereby the cluster service reboots the virtual machine

◆ Node-level recovery, whereby the cluster service moves the virtual machine to another node in the cluster

The following requirements must be met in order for virtual machine monitoring to work correctly:

◆ The virtual machine must be running Windows Server 2012.

◆ The cluster administrator must be a member of the local administrators group in the virtual machine.

◆ The virtual machine and the Windows Server 2012 Hyper-V node must be in the same Active Directory domain, or a trust must exist between the respective domains. As a minimum, this is a one-way trust and the domain where the virtual machine resides needs to trust the domain where the Hyper-V node resides.

◆ The virtual machine–monitoring firewall exception must be enabled in the virtual machine.

◆ The recovery settings for the service being monitored in the virtual machine must be configured correctly.

Configuring Virtual Machine Monitoring

Use the following procedure to prepare for virtual machine monitoring by enabling print and document services within a virtual machine. Note that you will start by configuring virtual machine monitoring for a print server so that you can see how service failures can trigger automatic recovery actions:

1. Launch Server Manager from within the virtual machine. In the navigation pane, click Dashboard, and then click Add Roles And Features.

2. In the Add Roles And Features Wizard, on the Before You Begin page, click Next.

3. On the Select Installation Type page, select Role-Based or Feature-Based installation, and click Next.

4. On the Select Destination Server Selection page, click Next.

5. On the Select Server Roles page, select Print And Document Services.

6. In the Add Roles And Features Wizard, click Add Features.

7. On the Select Server Roles page, click Next.

8. On the Select Features page, click Next.

9. On the Print And Document Services page, click Next.

10. On the Select Role Services page, click Next.

11. On the Confirmation Installation Selections page, click Install.

12. On the Results page, click Close.

Use the following procedure to configure virtual machine monitoring in Windows Server 2012:

1. Launch Server Manager from within the virtual machine. In the navigation pane, click Local Server.

2. Click the hyperlink to the right of Windows Firewall to open the Windows Firewall Control Panel applet.

3. In Windows Firewall, in the left pane, click Allow An App Or Feature Through Windows Firewall.

4. In the Allowed Apps And Features control panel applet, scroll down to Virtual Machine Monitoring and then select the Domain, Private, and Public check boxes. Click OK, as shown in Figure 9.10.

To enable the Virtual Machine Monitoring firewall rule by using Windows PowerShell, run the following PowerShell cmdlet:

```
Set-NetFirewallRule -DisplayGroup "Virtual Machine Monitoring" -Enabled True
```

FIGURE 9.10
Windows Firewall allowed apps

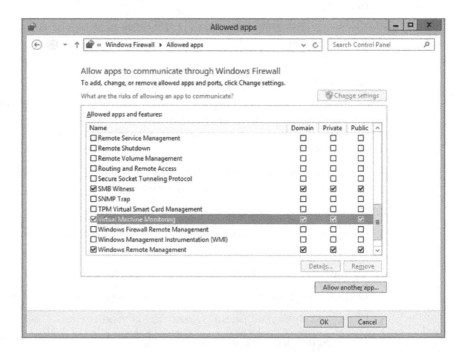

5. Close the Windows Firewall Control Panel applet and switch to the Hyper-V host.

6. Launch Failover Cluster Manager, expand the cluster node, and click Roles.

7. In the Roles node, select the appropriate virtual machine (for example, `WinSvr2012`). In the lower pane, click the Resources tab and then right-click Virtual Machine WinSvr2012. Click Properties.

8. In the Virtual Machine WinSvr2012 Properties dialog box, click the Settings tab, shown in Figure 9.11. Note the default settings for actions when the virtual machine is taken offline or stopped. Verify that the Heartbeat settings are both selected and then click OK.

FIGURE 9.11
Virtual machine heartbeat settings

9. In Failover Cluster Manager, in the Roles node, right-click WinSvr2012 and click More Actions, and then click Configure Monitoring.

10. In the Select Services dialog box, shown in Figure 9.12, select Print Spooler and then click OK.

As an alternative, to configure the service you want to monitor by using Windows PowerShell, run the following cmdlet:

```
Add-ClusterVMMonitoredItem –VirtualMachine WinSvr2012 -Service spooler
```

Use the following procedure to verify that the service you want to monitor is being monitored, by running the following PowerShell cmdlet:

```
Get-ClusterVMMonitoredItem - VM WinSvr2012 | fl *
```

FIGURE 9.12
Select services to
monitor.

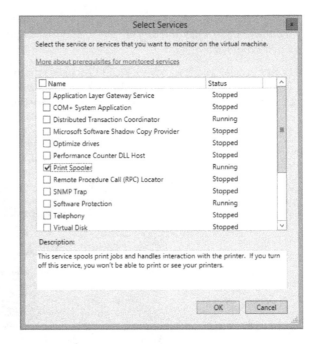

11. Verify that the lower pane of Failover Cluster Manager, in the Summary tab, now displays Print Spooler listed next to Monitored Services when WinSvr2012 is selected.

Use the following procedure to test virtual machine monitoring in Windows Server 2012 Hyper-V:

1. From within the virtual machine WinSvr2012, right-click the taskbar and click Task Manager.

2. In Task Manager, click More Details. On the Details tab, right-click the Print Spooler process SPOOLSV.EXE and then click End Process Tree.

3. In the Task Manager dialog box, click End Process Tree. This simulates a spooler failure.

4. Repeat steps 2 and 3 at least two times. You need to do this three times in total as the Service Control Manager will restart the Print Spooler process the first two times, and virtual machine monitoring will not take action until the third simulated spooler failure. After the third "failure," the process is restarted.

5. Switch to your Windows Server 2012 Hyper-V node where your virtual machine WinSvr2012 is executing. In Failover Cluster Manager, ensure that WinSvr2012 is selected in the Roles list.

6. After a few moments, Failover Cluster Manager will display Running (Application in VM Critical) as the virtual machine status in the lower pane; the WinSvr2012 virtual machine will then restart automatically.

7. Switch to Server Manager. In the menu bar, click Tools and then click Event Viewer. In Event Viewer, expand Windows Logs and then click System. Locate an Event ID 1250 indicating a critical state notification, as shown in Figure 9.13.

FIGURE 9.13
Event 1250 Failover Clustering

8. Switch to the console of virtual machine WinSvr2012. Log in using domain credentials and repeat the steps in Step 2 above to terminate the Print Spooler process three more times. Note that this must be completed within 15 minutes of when you performed the original step. Failover Cluster Manager will indicate that the application in the virtual machine is critical and another Event ID 1250 is logged in the system event log.

9. Switch to your Windows Server 2012 Hyper-V node where your virtual machine WinSvr2012 is executing. In Failover Cluster Manager, ensure that WinSvr2012 is selected in the Roles list. After a few moments, Failover Cluster Manager will display Running (Application in VM Critical) as the virtual machine status in the lower pane. The WinSvr2012 virtual machine will shut down and then should fail over, based on the cluster configuration.

10. In Failover Cluster Manager, in the Roles list, verify that WinSvr2012 is now running on another node in your cluster.

Real World Solutions

CHALLENGE

A large-sized company wants to consolidate a number of two-node file and print server clusters it has deployed and has decided to standardize on Windows Server 2012 Hyper-V as the operating system of choice to achieve this goal. One of the deployment blockers that stopped this company from carrying out such a consolidation exercise in the past is the fact that it had standardized on storage area networks (SANs) that are based on Fibre Channel. A Systems Engineer has been assigned to carry out the task of configuring N_Port ID Virtualization and needs to draw up a list of the prerequisites in order to configure NPIV within his/her environment.

SOLUTION

The solution would be to use Virtual Fibre Channel in Windows Server 2012 Hyper-V. This solution protects the investment the company has made in Fibre Channel, enables the systems engineer to virtualize workloads that use direct access to Fibre Channel storage, and allows guest clusters to connect to shared storage over Fibre Channel in the future:

◆ HBAs

◆ NPIV needs to be supported on the HBAs connected to the SAN switches.

◆ Ensure that the number of NPIV ports on the HBA is sufficient (some lower- end HBAs have considerably less than 255 NPIV ports).

◆ SAN Switches

◆ NPIV needs to be supported and enabled on the SAN switches.

◆ SAN Switch Ports

◆ NPIV may need to be enabled on the actually port, and sufficient logins per port need to be configured.

◆ Storage

◆ NPIV is completely transparent to storage arrays, and so no specific support for NPIV is required.

CHALLENGE

The company is satisfied that they can consolidate a number of two-node file and print server clusters using Virtual Fibre Channel and now wants to be able enable application health detection inside a virtual machine for the Spooler service. How could this be accomplished?

SOLUTION

The solution would be to implement Virtual Machine Monitoring, which can monitor services and events inside the virtual machine from the Windows Server 2012 Hyper-V Failover Cluster. You can enable Virtual Machine Monitoring by using the following PowerShell example:

```
Add-ClusterVMMoniotoredItem -VirtualMachine WinSvr2012 -Service spooler
```

Part 4

Advanced Hyper-V

## Chapter 10

Backup and Recovery

One of the most important tasks in the IT industry is ensuring that the data and services of a business are safe. Computers, storage, and networking are complex; no matter how many redundancies we install, something can break, and without a working backup—from which we can restore data successfully—we can lose critical information and line-of-business applications. Those are the days that administrators have nightmares about!

Hyper-V in Windows Server 2008 and Windows Server 2008 R2 aimed to simplify how we do backup. Unfortunately, it is fair to say that backup with Cluster Shared Volumes was difficult to engineer well without understanding and designing for the complexities of redirected I/O. Many learned this lesson too late.

The folks at Microsoft invested a lot of effort into Windows Server 2012 Hyper-V, Failover Clustering, storage, and backup to improve our experience. Design has been simplified. The new storage options of using Server Message Block (SMB) 3.0 file shares and the Scale-Out File Server are accounted for. And yes, you can start to use the built-in Windows Server Backup for backing up Hyper-V virtual machines in Windows Server 2012.

In this chapter, you'll learn about

◆ The improvements of backup in Windows Server 2012 Hyper-V

◆ How backup works in Windows Server 2012 with the various storage options

◆ Using Windows Server Backup to back up and restore virtual machines

How Backup Works with Hyper-V

What is a virtual machine? From the perspective of a storage system, it's normally just a few files. That's one of the nice things about virtualization: virtual machines are just files, and files are easy to back up *and* restore. Backing up a physical server isn't so bad, but it sure is stressful when you get a call at 2 a.m. on a Saturday to do a bare-metal restoration to a different set of hardware. Not so with virtual machines; they are abstracted from the underlying hardware. A virtual machine restoration is much like restoring a few files—although it requires just a little bit more than that, as you are about to learn.

Volume Shadow Copy Service Framework

Microsoft introduced the Volume Shadow Copy Service (VSS) framework to enable consistent backups of open files. Initially it was used to dependably back up open files, such as those on a file server. But soon after, Microsoft added VSS support for databases such as SQL Server and Exchange to enable their databases and log files to be consistently backed up.

Consistency is critical; you cannot have a safe backup if the database file is backed up at one point, the log file then commits and flushes, and then the log file is backed up. If you were to restore this database and log file, the database would be missing the data that was committed after the backup, and the database would be inconsistent.

Not only does VSS allow open files to be backed up, but it also briefly places VSS-compatible services into a quiescent state. Placing a virtual machine into a quiescent state is a process whereby buffers are flushed and writes are briefly paused. This brief pause allows a consistent VSS snapshot to be created of the volume in question, containing the data that is to be backed up. The snapshot is maintained long enough for the backup application to perform the backup from the snapshot.

SNAPSHOT! WHAT SNAPSHOT?

Snapshot is a term that is overused in the world of virtualization. There are three types of snapshots in Hyper-V:

HYPER-V SNAPSHOT

Also known as a *checkpoint*, a Hyper-V snapshot captures the state of a virtual machine at a certain point in time by using AVHD files. An administrator can create this snapshot, perform some work on a virtual machine (such as doing a demo or testing an application), and then apply the snapshot to return the virtual machine to that point in time. Hyper-V snapshots are not a form of backup. A backup stores a historical copy of the virtual machine on some out-of-band remote storage. That's not what a Hyper-V snapshot is; it maintains a constantly growing AVHD file in the same location as the virtual machine in question. Keeping this kind of snapshot also reduces the performance of a virtual machine. Lose the virtual machine, and you lose the Hyper-V snapshot. There are some unfortunate stories of Hyper-V snapshots being misused in this manner, and they never end well—except for the consultant who is called in to rescue a client and is charging by the hour.

VSS SNAPSHOT

VSS creates a snapshot, or a shadow copy, of a storage volume by using spare space within the targeted volume. This allows two important things to happen. First, open files can be backed up. Second, when combined with a brief pause of VSS-compatible services, it enables the data of those services to be backed up consistently. This chapter focuses on VSS snapshots.

STORAGE AREA NETWORK SNAPSHOT

A storage area network (SAN) may have the ability to create snapshots of a LUN by using additional storage on the SAN. This feature can be built in or can require additional licensing to be purchased from the SAN vendor. With the supporting software from the SAN manufacturer, SAN snapshot functionality can be used by VSS to create volume snapshots more rapidly than Windows Server can do it. This is particularly useful when dealing with large volumes because the snapshot process is much quicker than a snapshot performed by VSS alone.

Several components are involved in the creation of a consistent VSS backup, as seen in Figure 10.1:

Requestor The Requestor initiates a VSS-enabled backup operation. This is usually a backup agent, such as Windows Server Backup, System Center Data Protection Manager (DPM), or others.

Volume Shadow Copy Service   The Requestor invokes VSS, which in turn enumerates the Writers and starts the VSS snapshot-creation process.

Writers   Every VSS-compatible service has a Writer. This includes SQL Server, Exchange, and Hyper-V. The Requestor can communicate with a Writer to discover which files, and therefore which volumes, must be backed up for a particular service, such as a virtual machine.

Writers also interface with the services in question. They arrange to briefly pause the services, putting them into a quiescent state, so that a snapshot of the service's files can be created. This can include actions such as flushing caches and committing open transactions before flushing the file system buffer. The maximum length of this pause is 60 seconds. The Writer will inform the VSS framework, which is orchestrating the backup, after the targeted volumes are in a quiescent state.

Providers   The Provider, started by the VSS framework now that the volume is in a quiescent state, is responsible for creating a snapshot for each volume that contains files to be backed up. If files included in the backup span more than one volume, the Provider will synchronize the creation of snapshots of the volumes to ensure consistency. The Provider has up to 10 seconds to create the snapshot. The pause that was initiated by the Writers is ended after the Provider has created the snapshot. The Provider will return the location of the snapshot to the Requestor. The Requestor will perform the backup from the snapshot, and the snapshot will then be removed.

FIGURE 10.1
The components
of VSS

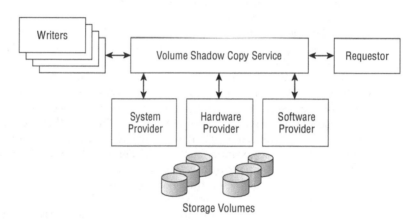

VSS can use three types of Providers:

System Provider   This is built into Windows and will create a VSS snapshot of a volume by using free space within the volume for a backup.

Hardware Provider   Some SANs support the creation of a SAN snapshot of a LUN for the purposes of VSS. This solution requires that the SAN manufacturer support the creation of Cluster Shared Volume (CSV) snapshots for Windows Server 2012 Hyper-V. Be sure of this; many have experienced problems when they incorrectly assumed they had support for creating SAN snapshots of Windows Server 2008 R2 CSVs. If you have this support, and if your SAN has the feature turned on or licensed, then you can install Hardware Providers on each host connected to the SAN; check with your SAN manufacturer for instructions.

Windows will automatically favor the Hardware Provider over the Software Provider. Maybe you are having issues with a Hardware Provider and need to force Windows to use the System Provider. You can force this override by setting `UseMicrosoftProvider` (REG_ DWORD) in the Registry at `HKLM\System\CurrentControlSet\Control\BackupRestore`.

Software Provider   A Software Provider provides the same functionality as a Hardware Provider, but for software-based storage. The difference is that the hardware solution uses hardware to create and manage snapshots, whereas the Software Provider solution must use software.

You will now look at how VSS can be used to perform different kinds of backup of virtual workloads on Hyper-V.

Virtual Machine Backup Strategies

There are a number of strategies you can take with backup and Windows Server 2012 Hyper-V. There is no one right strategy. One will be right for company A. Company B might go in another direction. And company C might choose to use bits of one strategy and bits of another. Here are some of your options:

STORAGE-LEVEL BACKUP

With this type of backup, your solution backs up virtual machines, as they are running, using VSS at the host or storage level, just as if it were backing up a database on a SQL server. The Requestor, or the backup agent, is installed on all of your Hyper-V hosts in the management OS. It will be responsible for backing up the running virtual machines. There is no need to install a backup agent in the virtual machines' guest operating systems.

The Hyper-V VSS Writer identifies the volumes that targeted virtual machines are stored on. The VSS Provider uses this information to create snapshots of those volumes. To maintain consistency, the Hyper-V VSS Writer is used. It not only places the virtual machines into a safe quiescent state but also uses any VSS writers found within the virtual machine to place services running within the virtual machine into a consistent quiescent state. This means that sensitive-to-backup applications such as SQL Server or Exchange can be safely backed up with this method. Note that clearing the check box for Backup (Volume Snapshot) in the Integration Services section of a virtual machine's settings will disable this default behavior.

The benefit of this approach is that backing up a virtual machine becomes simple: you just target the virtual machine in your backup application. Restoration is an administrator's dream come true; if you lose a virtual machine, you just restore it. The backup application restores the files for you. Some backup products will even register the virtual machine in Hyper-V for you. It doesn't matter if you backed up the virtual machine on a Dell host and are restoring it on an HP cluster. The hardware is abstracted, thanks to virtualization. Compare that to trying to do a bare-metal restoration of a physical server.

Storage-level backup works only with virtual hard disks (VHD or VHDX).

In the past, it was recommended that you do a storage-level backup on an infrequent basis, such as once per week or once per month. This was for two reasons. In a cluster with CSVs, backup caused redirected I/O to occur across the network designated for cluster communications (the network with the lowest network metric). That's no longer a problem in Windows Server 2012, thanks to a new distributed snapshot system.

The other reason was that this type of backup was always a full one, not incremental, when the virtual machines were on a Hyper-V cluster. This was wasteful; a typical virtual machine would have a relatively tiny amount of growth every day, but everything had to be backed up, transmitted over the network, and archived. That would consume a lot of space on the disk-to-disk backup storage or tape library. Windows Server 2012 does a lot to alleviate this problem by adding the ability to do incremental backup of running virtual machines. This means that if your backup solution can support it, you can take just the changes from the backup application.

Many Hyper-V backup solutions favor this style of backup, particularly solutions that are designed for small and medium enterprises (SMEs). And many solutions, including System Center DPM, include the ability to mount a backed-up virtual hard disk and restore individual files from it.

Two kinds of virtual machine will have issues with storage-level backups. Linux does not support VSS. The storage-level backup requires virtual machines with a Linux guest OS to pause for the host volume snapshot. This is not a problem if in-virtual machine backup is used with virtual machines with Linux guest operating systems. They are simply backed up as if they were physical machines but still retain the other benefits and flexibility of virtualization.

The Hyper-V Writer enables you to protect virtual machine files in a volume. Pass-through disks are not files in a volume; they are a volume. That means that pass-through disks cannot be protected with this simple backup and restoration strategy. This is another reason to use VHDX files instead of pass-through disks.

In summary, the ability of a storage-level backup to restore a virtual machine with its complex workload and data via just a few mouse clicks is attractive. But there are downsides:

◆ Protecting an entire virtual machine requires more space than just protecting the business data in the virtual machine.

◆ The dependency on the Hyper-V VSS Writer precludes protection of Linux gusts and pass-through disks.

In-Virtual Machine Backup

With this method, you are doing the same kind of backup that you would do with a physical server. The Requestor, or the backup agent, is installed into each and every guest operating system. The backup administrator then has to select every individual file that will be backed up, as opposed to selecting the virtual machine with the storage-level backup type. The backup administrator will also have to protect the system state if they want to protect against losing the entire virtual machine in the case of corruption or accidental deletion.

The benefit of this approach is that it is very granular; the backup administrator, depending on the organization's policy, can pick as many or as few files/services to protect as desired. A few will choose to back up the system state and the entire file system—doing a storage-level backup would be more efficient! Most who choose the in-virtual machine backup will protect the changing data such as file shares or databases. That strategy can greatly reduce the size of a backup. Selective targeting will prove attractive to those who are concerned with the storage requirements for protecting an entire virtual machine; and you'll probably have lots of virtual machines!

Historically, the in-virtual machine backup was considered more efficient than the storage-level backup. Only the changing data was protected, probably incrementally, at the block rather than the file level, as opposed to an entire virtual hard disk being protected every time.

Although storage-level backup can safely restore individual files, sometimes that is not granular enough. What if you want to do a brick-level backup of your Exchange or SharePoint databases that enables you to restore individual files or emails? For that, you will need an in-virtual machine backup using an agent that understands these services, such as DPM.

In-virtual machine backup will also be attractive to administrators of Linux virtual machines and virtual machines that use pass-through disks. This is because the Requestor, or backup agent, is installed in the guest OS and treats the guest's volumes as if they were physical, whether they are (pass-through disk) or not (VHD/X-attached Linux guest).

If you have backed up the system state and the entire file system, you can do a bare-metal restoration within a blank or template virtual machine. If you have backed up just the changing business data, you need to create a new virtual machine, install the necessary software, apply hotfixes and security updates, and then restore the data. This will be slow, but it consumes very little space.

Also consider that restoring a virtual machine from a storage-level backup restores one or a few large files (the virtual hard disks) and a few XML files. Restoring from an in-virtual machine backup restores thousands of small files, each of which must be found, have metadata queried, be confirmed as restored, and so on; restoring fewer, larger files will be much quicker. To summarize in-virtual machine backups,

◆ You can protect just the data that you want to protect.

◆ Applications can be backed up and restored at an object level, such as SharePoint-stored files or Exchange emails.

◆ File systems for which the Hyper-V VSS Writer cannot create snapshots can be protected, such as Linux guests and pass-through disks.

No Backup

As odd and as unsafe as this might sound, some organizations choose not to do backups. Sometimes there are too many virtual machines and too much data to protect. This is truly a rare situation; how many businesses can dispense with backups that are required for protection or regulatory compliance reasons? Those few organizations that do fit in this tiny niche might choose to rely on selective disaster-recovery replication (see Chapter 11, "Disaster Recovery") instead of a normal backup archive.

A Hybrid Backup Strategy

There are positives and negatives with both the in-virtual machine and the storage-level backup strategies. It is possible to use both approaches to create a single strategy:

◆ Perform an infrequent storage-level backup on Hyper-V VSS Writer-compatible virtual machines.

◆ Perform a more frequent in-virtual machine backup for Hyper-V VSS Writer-compatible guests, targeting the changing business data.

◆ Perform an infrequent in-virtual machine backup for non-Hyper-V VSS Writer-compatible guests, protecting the system state and the entire file system.

◆ Do not protect low-priority virtual machines that are used for testing.

If you find that you need to do a restoration, your plan will depend on what has been lost:

Files from a Windows Virtual Machine File Share   The files could be restored from the in-virtual machine backup.

A Lost Linux Virtual Machine   A bare-metal restoration would have to be done from the in-virtual machine backup.

A Lost Windows Virtual Machine   Assuming it uses only VHD or VHDX storage, the virtual machine could be simply restored from the storage-level backup.

A Lost Pass-through Disk   The files and folders would be restored from the in-virtual machine backup.

Choosing a Backup Strategy

Which is the right backup strategy for your virtual machines? We hate to say it, but unfortunately this is a case for the consultant's answer: it depends. In this section, you will look at a few examples. Bear in mind that these are examples and not rules:

A Public Cloud   In the hosting world, every cent spent on infrastructure, administration, and support must be passed on to the customer. Each customization to the backup strategy adds cost. If customer A has one policy and customer B has another, then it becomes more expensive to implement a self-service solution and more time-consuming to manage the infrastructure. In a highly competitive world, in which every company with an Internet connection appears to be launching a public-cloud service, offering a low-cost service is critical. Typically, a public-cloud customer is trying to save money. The base service that the customer subscribes to must be economical, to compete not only with other hosting companies, but also with private-cloud alternatives.

In the world of a public cloud, one might choose to extend the pay-for-what-you-consume model into the backup strategy. A simple solution might be to enable self-service in-virtual machine backup and restore. With this approach, customers can choose what data they want to protect and therefore limit the cost of backup. Customers can be completely empowered to select files/folders for backup and be able to restore those files/folders depending on the backup solution that is implemented.

Remember that the backup data is now leaving the confines of your security boundary, and it could be leaving the country. The data may even be entering the legal reach of another country just by being stored in a data center owned by a native of that country (for instance, under the U.S. Patriot Act). How will this impact your security and regulatory requirements?

A Small/Medium Enterprise   Windows Server 2012 might be referred to as a *cloud operating system* by Microsoft, and they might believe that everyone is implementing private clouds, but not everyone is big enough to justify the complexities and costs of a cloud infrastructure. Implementing a private cloud requires a number of integrated management systems, and this alone could be bigger than the business system's infrastructure.

A small/medium enterprise (SME) might have a small or even an outsourced IT department. SMEs want something that is not complex and that can be used by entry-level IT staff. In this case, a storage-level backup solution could be implemented. Restoring a virtual machine is easy, as is restoring a file. The only need for additional complexity is if the business needs granular restorations for applications such as Exchange or SharePoint—but Microsoft would argue that this SME should be using Office 365 for mail and collaboration services anyway!

A Private Cloud   Although IT has little involvement with day-to-day operations of the virtual machines, there will likely be a requirement for regulatory compliance to ensure protection of business data. Administrators will never really know what's happening inside virtual machines; end users could be installing MySQL, SQL Server, IIS, Tomcat, or anything else that serves the business's needs. That's why a private cloud was deployed in the first place. In order to provide a base level of adequate protection, the IT department can choose to protect all virtual machines with a storage-level backup strategy, maybe performing the backups once per night. The new incremental backup support for Hyper-V virtual machines in Windows Server 2012 will minimize the consumption of required archive space.

Bear in mind that organizations that are big enough to have a private cloud are probably likely to have a mixture of Windows Server and Linux guests. It might be unpopular to have Linux guests pausing while their host volume has a snapshot created by the Hyper-V VSS Writer. You would either live with this, or engineer your automation systems to place virtual machines onto dedicated CSVs and deal with the Linux guests by using a different backup strategy.

The self-service nature of the private cloud will require that you empower end users (usually application administrators, testers, or developers) to back up and restore files for themselves. This would mean that you adopt a hybrid backup strategy rather than just doing storage-level backups. The private-cloud infrastructure—System Center 2012, for example—could enable end users to install the protection agent (VSS Requestor), configure backups, and restore files without the involvement of the IT department. However, the storage-level backup is always there as a fallback point just in case the users screw things up!

These are just examples. The backup strategy that an organization chooses to implement will usually be dictated by the board of directors or the CIO, and an engineer or consultant will interpret that to create a solution. There are options for all situations, and no one size will fit all.

Improvements in Windows Server 2012 Hyper-V Backup

Windows Server 2008 R2 backup was a hot topic of discussion. If implemented correctly, it made life much easier for administrators. If implemented incorrectly, it was a nightmare. Microsoft listened to the feedback and gave us what we wanted in Windows Server 2012.

Incremental Backup

We already mentioned that in previous versions of Hyper-V, a storage-level backup would perform a full backup of a highly available virtual machine every single time. It did not matter if little or no change occurred in the virtual machine's virtual hard disks (see Figure 10.2). Every single storage-level backup would result in every single byte of the VHDs being transmitted over the network and stored. That meant there was a bigger impact on the infrastructure (possibly forcing the implementation of a dedicated backup network) and a longer backup window.

A result of this was that even though a company might have been happy with just a storage-level strategy as their regular backup, they often had to resort to a hybrid approach to reduce their storage costs and reduce the size of their backup window.

Windows Server 2012 introduces incremental backup for VHD or VHDX files undergoing a storage-level backup. Compare Figure 10.2 with and without incremental backup. In this example, a few hundred megabytes might change each day in a database stored on the 100 GB virtual hard disk. Before Windows Server 2012, a twice-daily nonincremental backup would back up 200 GB of VHD (the entire VHD twice). With enough of those virtual machines, a company might choose to implement an alternative backup strategy. Thanks to incremental backup in Windows Server 2012, the twice-daily backup now will transmit and store only the changes, making the entire process more efficient and more cost-effective, and making the simpler storage-level backup more attractive.

FIGURE 10.2
Incremental virtual
hard disk backup

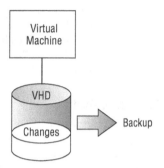

Incremental virtual machine backup might not sound like an exciting new feature at first, but an organization with even just a hundred virtual machines could save quite a bit every day, and that makes it important—and backup administrators are probably excited!

Windows Server Backup

Windows Server Backup (WSB) is the backup tool that is built into Windows Server. It is not an enterprise backup solution; it can back up only files and services that are on the local server. If you need to back up something over the network, you should look at something such as DPM.

BACKUP PRODUCTS FOR WINDOWS SERVER 2012 HYPER-V

In the past, some backup product manufacturers have stated that they supported Hyper-V, but their customers soon found that "support" and "worked well with" were two very different things.

You really should verify that the backup tool that you are planning to use supports Windows Server 2012 Hyper-V, Hyper-V Server 2012, Hyper-V clusters, CSVs, backup of virtual machines on SMB 3.0 file shares or Scale-Out File Servers, VHDX files, in-virtual machine backup of Linux guests, and so forth, depending on your implementation. There is nothing like a proof-of-concept or a trial license to verify that the product will meet your requirements before you commit financially.

Note that System Center 2012 DPM requires Service Pack 1 to support Windows Server 2012 and Hyper-V Server 2012. DPM also adds support for incremental virtual machine backups.

Although WSB is not an enterprise backup solution, it is valuable for SMEs, test labs, and even for consultants providing a proof-of-concept for enterprise customers.

In previous versions, WSB wasn't able to work with Hyper-V without some Registry hacking to register the Hyper-V VSS Writer. See http://support.microsoft.com/kb/958662 if you'd like to learn more about that. Even with that change, you were limited to backing up running virtual machines that were stored on internal storage or direct-attached storage (DAS); you could not protect virtual machines on a CSV by using WSB.

The story has changed with Windows Server 2012. WSB now works with the Hyper-V VSS Writer without any Registry edits. It also can protect running virtual machines that are stored on DAS or on a CSV. Virtual machines running on any host in the cluster, stored on CSVs, can be protected from a single node. That opens up a much larger audience for WSB than ever before.

WSB uses VHDX files as its backup medium. The VHDX files can be stored on a local volume on the host, on an external drive, or on a file share. Because WSB uses VHDX files as the backup media, the maximum size of the job is 64 TB.

You will look at using WSB later in this chapter.

Distributed CSV Snapshots

If you want to bring chills to the spine of a Windows Server 2008 R2 consultant, say these two words: *CSV backup*. Backing up virtual machines on an internal disk or direct-attached storage is nice and simple. It would take quite a while to discuss how CSV backup worked in Windows Server 2008 R2. There was redirected I/O for the snapshot creation, and for the backup if using the System VSS Provider. Each host might take the CSV Coordinator role of the CSV to create its own snapshot of the CSV that was identified by the Hyper-V VSS Writer. This could cause complications with some Hardware VSS Providers. And as mentioned before, there was no incremental backup of highly available virtual machines. CSV needed to improve a lot in Windows Server 2012 and, thankfully, it did.

A new CSV backup architecture, which is depicted in Figure 10.3, is introduced in Windows Server 2012. In the figure, you can see that there is a cluster. Virtual machines are stored on a single CSV, and they are spread across all the nodes in the cluster. The new backup process runs as follows:

1. The backup server connects to a host, shown as the backup node. That causes the Requestor to start VSS to create a snapshot of the volume.

2. The Hyper-V Writer on the backup node inventories the files of the locally hosted virtual machines that are to be backed up.

3. A new element, called the CSV Writer, will coordinate with the other nodes in the cluster by interacting with their Hyper-V Writers.

4. Each Hyper-V Writer on each of the other nodes will return the file locations of their virtual machines to the backup node's CSV Writer.

5. Another new element, named the CSV Provider, can synchronize the snapshot between the backup node and the other nodes in the cluster. It works with the Hyper-V Writer on the local (backup) node and the other nodes in the cluster. This allows a synchronized placement of virtual machines in a quiescent state.

6. After the virtual machines are in a quiescent state, one of the VSS Providers (with any existing Hardware Provider normally being preferred) on the backup node will create a snapshot of the CSV LUN.

7. After the snapshot is created, the Hyper-V Writer can release the virtual machines from quiescence.

8. Now the Requestor is presented with the snapshot location so that it can back up the virtual machines.

FIGURE 10.3
Distributed CSV snapshot with direct I/O

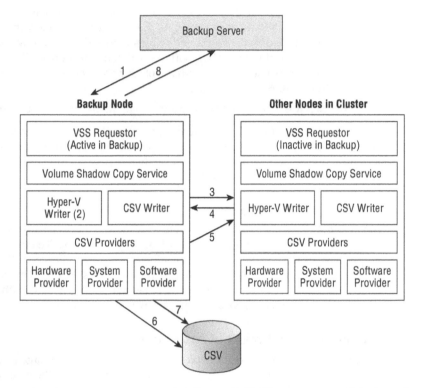

You will notice that there was no mention of redirected I/O! This is just one of the huge benefits of the Windows Server 2012 CSV backup solution:

Direct I/O for Backup Redirected I/O for backup is a thing of the past. The long-term benefits of this are numerous. You can now plan an active/active multi-site cluster without stressing about redirected I/O traffic over the WAN. A true self-service cloud can be built with Hyper-V without worrying about virtual machine placement. And now, consultants don't have to waste time explaining to their customers that they need to design their backup policies before they architect their CSVs. More important, it means that the storage performance hit that would have been caused by backup-induced redirected I/O has been eliminated.

CSV Coordinator Does Not Move during Backup A single snapshot is being created for each CSV (in Windows Server 2012), as opposed to one being created by each host that was running virtual machines (in Windows Server 2008 R2). That will simplify the entire process, thus making it more stable. It should eliminate creating unwanted complications for the Hardware VSS Provider that used to result in orphaned CSVs in the SAN and a problem called disk signature collisions (`http://blogs.msdn.com/b/clustering/archive/2011/05/30/10169759.aspx`).

Parallel Backups   In Windows Server 2008 R2, best practice was to stagger your backups very carefully. In Windows Server 2012, multiple backups can be performed per CSV or per node at once.

Improved Interoperability   The new architecture means that the backup application does not need to be CSV-aware. However, in the real world, any backup solution that you use should be certified by the vendor as being supported for Windows Server 2012 Hyper-V and CSV. It's one thing for Microsoft to say that the backup application should work, but it's another thing completely to call Microsoft Support and ask them to explain why "Honest Bob's Backup 2008" isn't working!

Faster Backups   The entire backup job is faster thanks to a single distributed snapshot per CSV.

You do not need to configure anything to make Windows Server 2012 perform this new, efficient distributed backup of CSVs; it just works out of the box. Understanding the new architecture will help you understand how exactly this new solution offers the preceding benefits of CSV backup in Windows Server 2012.

VSS for SMB File Shares

In Chapter 7, "Using File Servers," you learned how Windows Server 2012 offers a new storage option for application workloads such as Hyper-V. SMB 3.0 enables Windows Server 2012 Hyper-V hosts to store their virtual machines on Windows Server 2012 file servers and, preferably, continuously available file shares on Scale-Out File Servers. This means that nonclustered and clustered hosts can store their virtual machine files on a UNC path instead of a local drive or a CSV. And that means we also need a way to back them up.

UNDERSTANDING VSS FOR SMB FILE SHARES

System and Hardware Providers have no connections to the storage if the virtual machines are placed on a file share instead of on a disk that is connected to the host. They cannot create a snapshot for the Requestor to use for its backup.

Microsoft added a new mechanism called VSS for SMB File Shares in Windows Server 2012 Hyper-V to deal with this situation, as you can see in Figure 10.4. If you do store virtual machines on a file server and perform a storage-level backup on your hosts, the process will work as follows:

1. The Requestor initiates a backup on behalf of the backup server, starting the VSS process.

2. VSS instructs the Hyper-V Writer to gather metadata information about the virtual machines and their storage locations. If any file shares are identified as storing targeted virtual machines, this will trigger the rest of the file server snapshot process for those file shares.

3. The Hyper-V Writer places the virtual machines into a quiescent state.

4. VSS now sends a snapshot request to the File Share Shadow Copy Provider, a new VSS element that enables integration with an SMB 3.0 file server.

5. This snapshot request is relayed to the File Share Shadow Copy Agent on the file server that was identified by the Hyper-V Writer on the host.

6. The File Share Shadow Copy Agent requests the local VSS to create a writerless snapshot. It can be writerless because the files in question (the virtual machines) have been placed into a quiescent state by the Hyper-V Writer on the host.

7. The appropriate provider (Hardware or System) is chosen by VSS, and a snapshot is created for each required file share.

8. Any file share snapshot is presented as a Shadow Copy Share, a special kind of hidden share that contains the snapshot. The Shadow Copy Share will be named something such as `\\<FileServerName>\<ShareName>@{GUID}`.

9. The Volume Shadow Copy Agent on the file server informs the Volume Shadow Copy Provider on the host of the location of the snapshot(s). The Hyper-V Writer can now release the pause.

10. The Requestor is informed of the location of the snapshot(s).

11. The Requestor relays the location of the snapshot(s) to the backup server.

12. The backup server backs up the required virtual machine files from the Shadow Copy Share(s) on the file server. The snapshot and the Shadow Copy Share should be released and destroyed after the backup.

FIGURE 10.4
VSS backup with
SMB 3.0 storage

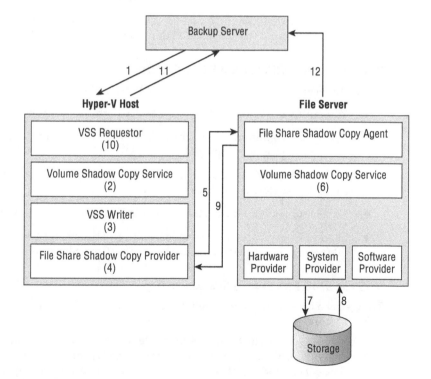

CONFIGURING VSS FOR SMB FILE SHARES

The following are infrastructure requirements for VSS for SMB File Shares:

◆ The Hyper-V host (the application server) and the file server must both be running Windows Server 2012.

◆ Both the Hyper-V host and the file server must be joined to the same Active Directory domain.

◆ The File Server VSS Agent Service role service must be running on the file server. (Instructions follow this list.)

◆ The backup agent (Requestor) must be running with an account that has Backup Operator and Administrator rights on both the Hyper-V host and the file server. Check with your backup software vendor for instructions on how to configure this.

◆ The virtual machine file shares must permit at least read access to the account that the backup agent is running as.

You do not need to install or configure anything on the hosts to set up the Volume Shadow Copy Provider. You do need to install the File Server VSS Agent on the file server(s) to have a Volume Shadow Copy Agent. You can do this in Server Manager or use this PowerShell cmdlet to perform the installation:

```
Add-WindowsFeature File-Services,FS-VSS-Agent
```

After you have configured the backup configuration, the entire VSS for SMB File Shares process takes place behind the curtain. You don't need to get involved with it in any way.

RESTRICTIONS ON VSS FOR SMB FILE SHARES

There are several restrictions on the usage of VSS for SMB File Shares:

◆ You cannot use Windows Server Backup to perform this type of backup.

◆ A loopback configuration, in which a host's virtual machines are stored on a file share on the same host, is not supported.

◆ You cannot use VSS for SMB File Shares to back up virtual machines where the guest application is also storing data on a file share.

◆ Data mount points beneath the root of the file share are not supported.

◆ Shadow Copy Shares do not support failover; a backup will fail if the node in the Scale-Out File Server cluster that is hosting the Shadow Copy Share fails.

VSS FOR SMB FILE SHARES SCENARIOS

Things get a little more complicated if you have multiple file servers or multiple hosts in the infrastructure:

Multiple Hyper-V Hosts and a Single File Server If you have multiple nonclustered Hyper-V hosts, all using a single file server, each Hyper-V host must be backed up in turn. The File Server VSS Agent Service can perform a snapshot for only one host at a time.

Even though host A and host B may use a single file share, only the virtual machines of host A will be backed up by a backup job that is running on host A.

Multiple Hyper-V Hosts and Multiple File Servers   In this scenario, there are multiple nonclustered Hyper-V hosts and multiple nonclustered file servers, with virtual machines and virtual hard disks scattered across the file servers.

VSS for File Shares will have no problems backing up virtual machines on a single host that are spread across multiple file servers. VSS will not even have problems with a virtual machine that has virtual hard disks stored on numerous file servers. The Shadow Copy Shares will be created by each file server and returned back to the Volume Shadow Copy Provider on the host that is being backed up.

As with the previous example, you must back up virtual machines one host at a time, because the File Server VSS Agent Service cannot handle simultaneous VSS requests from multiple hosts.

Multiple Hyper-V Hosts and a Scale-Out File Server   In this case, many nonclustered Hyper-V hosts share a single Scale-Out File Server (SOFS). The Volume Shadow Copy Provider on the host being backed up will be informed of the SOFS node name that it is working with when it partners with the Volume Shadow Copy Agent. The SOFS node will perform the snapshot.

SOFS shares are stored on CSVs; this makes it possible for the SOFS to be active/active and to have transparent failover (in conjunction with cluster and SMB client witness processes). The VSS Provider on the active SOFS node will perform the snapshot and create the Shadow Copy Share. The Shadow Copy Share is not shared by the SOFS; it is shared by the SOFS node that performs the snapshot. If this SOFS node goes offline, the Shadow Copy Share goes offline, because it does not support failover.

ADMINISTRATION AND TROUBLESHOOTING FOR VSS FOR SMB FILE SHARES

There can be a lot of moving pieces in VSS for SMB File Shares. There is a network, which could have issues, and there is more latency than VSS would normally encounter.

Event Logs   You can start your troubleshooting process by checking the following logs for information, warnings, or errors:

- `Microsoft-Windows-FileShareShadowCopyProvider`
- `Microsoft-Windows-FileShareShadowCopyAgent`

Long-Running Snapshots   By default, VSS will abort the creation of a snapshot if it takes longer than 30 minutes. This ensures that applications not caused unwanted delays by the unexpectedly long snapshot. You can configure `LongWriterOperationTimeoutInSeconds`, a Registry value in `HKLM\SYSTEM\CurrentControlSet\Services\fssagent\Settings`, to extend this time if you require more than 30 minutes to create a snapshot.

Scale-Out File Server   You may find that you need to extend the time-out for long-running snapshots on an SOFS as well. There is a cluster property called `SharedVolumeVss-WriterOperationTimeout` that has a default value of 1,800 seconds, with a minimum of 60 seconds and a maximum of 7,200 seconds.

It is expected that you tune this value for your environment. You should check the logs for the time taken for `PrepareForSnapshot` and `PostSnapshot` calls. You then configure `SharedVolumeVssWriterOperationTimeout` to allow enough time for the longest one of those two calls.

Security   The communications across the network between the Volume Shadow Copy Provider and the Volume Shadow Copy Agent are signed and mutually authenticated—a benefit of being in the same Active Directory domain.

The traffic is not encrypted by default. You can configure encryption in Local Computer Policy or Group Policy by using Administrator Templates ➤ System ➤ File Share Shadow Copy Provider.

Using IP Addresses Instead of Names Although using computer names or fully qualified domain names is the preferred option for specifying UNC paths, you can use IPv4 or IPv6 addresses if the situation demands it:

- IPv4—for example, \\10.4.5.6\VMShare1

- Global IPv6 and its literal format

- Site-local IPv6 format (which starts with FEC0)

- IPv6 tunnel address and its literal format

IPv6 link-local addresses (which start with FE80) are not supported.

For the small or medium business, the SMB 3.0 file server can provide an economical alternative to a SAN. For the enterprise, the SMB 3.0 file server can offer immensely fast SSD-based storage with 40 or 56 Gbps connectivity (with additional link aggregation) at a fraction of the cost of the traditional SAN solution for creating IOPS. There may be a little more work to tune backups of a file server, but the benefits of the storage solution far outweigh the small amount of engineering.

Using Windows Server Backup

There are a huge number of backup solutions for Hyper-V. Some of them work only with stand-alone hosts, some work with clusters, and some work *well* with clusters and work well when virtual machines move around a cluster. Some solutions are economical, and others are expensive enterprise products. And there is WSB, which is built into Windows Server 2012 and supports backing up virtual machines on stand-alone hosts and clustered hosts with CSVs. This section discusses how to use WSB to protect your virtual workloads.

BACKUP AND VIRTUAL MACHINE MOBILITY

Storage-Level backup typically works as follows:

1. Virtual machines are running on known hosts or clusters.

2. A backup job is created to backup virtual machines according to some schedule.

3. The backup job runs and expects to find those virtual machines on the previously known hosts or clusters.

Windows Server 2012 Hyper-V gives us Live Migration that allows virtual machines to move between hosts and clusters. For example, a management system might be able to load balance virtual machines across non-clustered hosts that share common SMB 3.0 storage. Those hosts aren't unified under a single Active Directory identity, as you would expect a cluster to be. That means that a backup job might not know where to find those virtual machines. This means that you need to consider

- Finding a backup solution that understands this mobility and tracks virtual machines as they move around the data center

- Using simple protection policies that back up all virtual machines on a host or CSV at the same time

- Not using these new Live Migration features if your backup solution is not fully aware of the flexibility in Windows Server 2012 Hyper-V

Installing Windows Server Backup

WSB is not installed on a server by default; it is a feature that must be enabled. There are two ways you can enable WSB.

The first way is to use Server Manager:

1. Launch Server Manager.

2. Open the Manage menu and choose Add Roles And Features.

3. Skip through the Add Roles And Features Wizard until you reach the Select Features screen.

4. Select the check box for Windows Server Backup (see Figure 10.5).

5. Complete the wizard.

FIGURE 10.5
The Add Roles And
Features Wizard

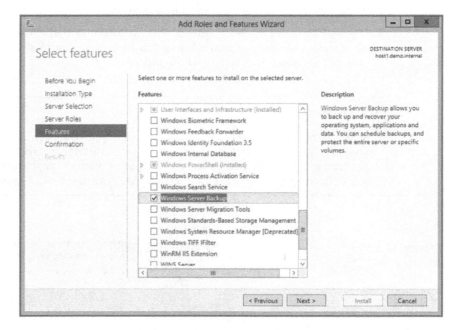

You can also install Windows Server Backup by using the following PowerShell cmdlet:

```
Install-WindowsFeature Windows-Server-Backup
```

WSB can protect only local workloads; it cannot protect remote servers or virtual machines. You will need to enable it in the management OS of every host that has virtual machines that you want to back up. You will need to use an alternative product, such as System Center DPM, if you want centralized protection of virtual machines and data.

Protecting Nonclustered Hyper-V Hosts

First you will look at the simplest scenario: how to back up and restore virtual machines that are running on a nonclustered Hyper-V host.

BACKING UP VIRTUAL MACHINES ON A NONCLUSTERED HOST

Typically, you will want to create a scheduled backup. Follow these instructions to create an automated backup to protect your virtual machines:

1. Launch Windows Server Backup and browse to Local Backup. Note that Windows Online Backup (where you can back up to Windows Azure storage in the cloud) does not currently support Hyper-V.

2. In the Actions pane, click Backup Schedule.

3. In the Select Backup Configuration screen, choose to create a Custom backup. There is little need to protect the management OS of the host itself; you can probably rebuild a host more quickly than you can do a bare-metal restoration. We're more interested in backing up the virtual machines and their workloads/data.

4. Click Add Items to open the Select Items screen.

5. Figure 10.6 shows the Select Items screen. Select the virtual machines that you would like to automatically protect with this scheduled job. Note that Host Component has also been selected to protect the Hyper-V configuration.

HOST COMPONENT

The host component protects parts of the host configuration, such as the virtual switches, resource pools, and Windows Authorization Manager. Microsoft has shared very little information on the topic at the time of writing this book. It seems that the host component is intended to enable you to build a new host to replace a lost one and quickly restore the configuration of Hyper-V.

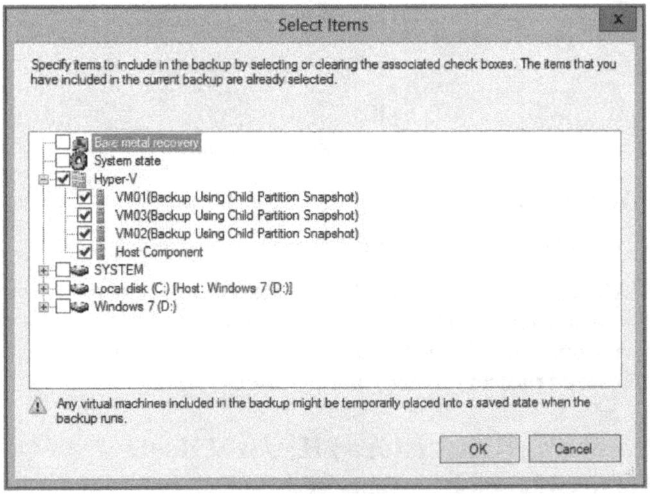

FIGURE 10.6
Selecting
Hyper-V
components to
back up

6. Back in the Select Items For Backup screen, click the Advanced Settings button. In the VSS tab, you have two options. Select VSS Full Backup if WSB is the only backup tool that you will be using on this host. This will clear the backup history of each file. Otherwise, you should choose VSS Copy Backup. This option will retain application log files for other backup tools to use.

7. The Specify Backup Time screen allows you to schedule the backup job. By default, it will run once per day. You can change this to be more frequent—the Available Time selection is in 30-minute intervals, from 00:00 until 23:30. Be aware that a backup will mean that VSS will have to place virtual machines and their applications into a quiescent state. It may also cause a lot of data transfer over the network, so choose your schedule wisely; you don't have to create a backup every 30 minutes just because you can!

8. You can choose your backup media for the scheduled job in the Specify Destination Type screen. Your choices are as follows:

   Back Up to a Hard Disk Dedicated for Backups This is the recommended option in the GUI and is suitable for a small business. Typically, this hard disk would be a LUN, a DAS, or even a removable disk such as a USB drive. It is used just for backup. In the event of a host failure, you could connect this disk (assuming that it is portable) to a new host and restore the virtual machines. WSB will maintain the data on the disk for you. Although it is not a very scalable solution, you could use removable media and transport them offsite for a budget offsite backup storage solution. Note that you must have attached the disk before you start the Backup Schedule Wizard or it won't be detected. The disk will be erased, and a new volume will be created for the backup target.

   Back Up to a Volume This option is the simplest of the three, but it is not a great one. WSB will use a local volume for the backup. This can be useful if you do not have any other choice and you must do a backup for short-term reasons. Bear in mind that if you lose the server, you will also lose the backup. Note that the screen warns you that the performance of the disk may drop by up to 200 percent during the backup job!

   Back Up to a Shared Network Folder The third option gives you both a remote storage location, giving you some security, and the ability to use a file server that has lots of disk space. Unfortunately, there is a cost; backing up to a shared folder means that WSB will retain only one backup. The previous backup data will be erased. There is a way to script your way around this problem, as you will see later in the chapter. The WSB backup job will be a scheduled task that runs with a user account. Make sure that this account has Change rights on the share, Modify rights on the folder, and is a member of either Backup Operators or Administrators on the host that you are backing up. The wizard will later ask you to provide the username and password for this account.

9. The next screen will ask you to specify your storage location, and the wizard will change depending on the type of location that you will choose.

You can create the same scheduled backup job by using PowerShell. This script will back up to a disk every day at 1 p.m. and 9 p.m. Make sure you pay attention to the warnings that are embedded as comments in the script, such as the following:

```
#Plug in just 1 external drive before running this script
$Policy = New-WBPolicy
```

```
$VMs = Get-WBVirtualMachine
Add-WBVirtualMachine -Policy $Policy -VirtualMachine $VMs


$ExternalDisk = Get-WBDisk | Where-Object {$_.Properties -Like "*External*"}
#Run Get-WB-Disk manually to verify which index in the $Disks array is the
 desired disk
$BackupLocation = New-WBBackupTarget -Disk $ExternalDisk -Label "Backup Drive"
Add-WBBackupTarget -Policy $Policy -Target $BackupLocation

Set-WBVssBackupOptions -Policy $Policy -VSSFullBackup
Set-WBSchedule -Policy $Policy -Schedule 13:00,23:00
#Add -Force to following to disable confirmation prompt to format disk: at your
 own risk
#Verify that it is OK to format this disk before continuing
Set-WBPolicy -Policy $Policy
```

This script will do the following:

1. Create a policy template.

2. Query the host for all the virtual machines and the Hyper-V component.

3. Add all the virtual machines and the Hyper-V component to the policy.

4. Find the plugged-in external disk.

5. Set the external disk as the backup target.

6. Configure the advanced backup options.

7. Set the schedule of the backup.

8. Save the policy.

You should now see the Scheduled Backup details in the central pane in WSB under Local Backup. It should match your schedule. You should also see when the next backup will be (under Next Backup).

A new scheduled task is created when you complete the wizard. You can find it in Task Scheduler (in Administrative Tools) under Task Scheduler Library ➢ Microsoft ➢ Windows ➢ Backup, as seen in Figure 10.7.

If you do open the properties of the task, you'll learn a little about how WSB does its work. The task will execute wbadmin.exe from the \Windows\System32 folder. Wbadmin.exe is instructed to start backup and is given a GUID with the -templateid flag. The GUID identifies the backup policy. The policy describes the backup job: what it backs up, how it backs up, and where it backs up to.

Note that a restriction of WSB is that you can have only one stored policy at a time. That means that you can have only one scheduled WSB backup job on a server. You should use an alternative backup solution if you need multiple backup policies per server.

FIGURE 10.7
The scheduled backup job in Task Scheduler

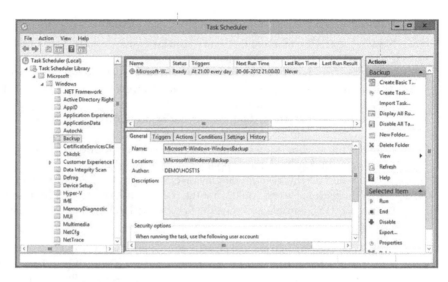

You can modify an existing backup schedule. To do it in the GUI, open the WSB console and click the Backup Schedule action to modify the backup. You can also do this via PowerShell. This example modifies the schedule of the job:

```
#The Editable flag allows the policy to be changed
$Policy = Get-WBPolicy -Editable
Set-WBSchedule -Policy $Policy -Schedule 9:00,13:00,18:00
Set-WBPolicy -Policy $Policy
```

If you need to, you can also perform an on-demand backup by clicking the Backup Once action in the WSB console. This opens the Backup Options wizard. You have two options:

◆ Schedule Backup Options: WSB will run an existing scheduled backup immediately.

◆ Different Options: You can create a custom backup by selecting the virtual machines you want to back up and where you want to back them up to.

You can do something similar to the above with PowerShell:

```
$Policy = Get-WBPolicy
Start-WBBackup -Policy $Policy
```

You can monitor the execution of and troubleshoot backup jobs in a few ways:

Messages This area in the central pane of the WSB console shows the history of your jobs. You can double-click an entry to see more information.

Event Viewer You can find more information in Applications And Services ➤ Microsoft ➤ Windows ➤ Backup.

RESTORING VIRTUAL MACHINES ON A NONCLUSTERED HOST

Now we reach the moment that every administrator dreads: "Can I reliably restore a lost virtual machine?" There is only one way to be sure that you can, and that is to test, test, and test again. No backup can be trusted by the business unless it is tested on a regular basis. If you are really lucky, that is the only time you will have to restore a virtual machine. But in reality, you will need to know how to do a restore.

In this demonstration, the three virtual machines that were backed up by the scheduled and on-demand backup jobs have been stopped, removed from the Hyper-V Manager, and deleted from the file system. Now you will see how easy it is to restore these virtual machines, their guest operating system, their applications, and their data.

You could do this restoration via PowerShell—but really, would you want to? A restoration is one of those times when you'll want the reassurance of the GUI. To restore the virtual machines, launch the WSB console and start the Recover action in Local Backup. This opens the Recovery Wizard:

1. The Getting Started screen asks you where the backup is stored. Is it on This Server or is it A Backup Stored On Another Location? If you choose This Server, the WSB policy will be queried for the backup location. Choosing A Backup Stored On Another Location allows you to restore from somewhere not listed in the WSB policy.

2. After you have found the backup location, you will have to choose which backup you want to restore from. Figure 10.8 shows the Select Backup Date screen, which lists each backup job on the media.

FIGURE 10.8
Choose a backup to restore from.

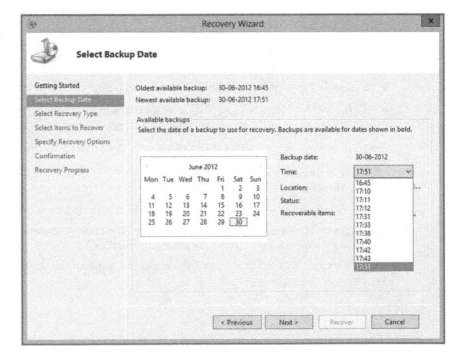

3. The Select Recovery Type screen asks what kind of data you want to restore from the backup. In this example, we backed up virtual machines on a nonclustered host, so we should select the Hyper-V option.

4. You can browse through the selected backup to choose what you want to restore. You can see that each virtual machine has been selected in Figure 10.9.

5. The Specify Recovery Options screen allows you to do one of three things. You can recover virtual machines to their original location, recover them to a different location, or copy the files from the backup without recovering the virtual machine to Hyper-V.

FIGURE 10.9
Choose virtual machines to restore.

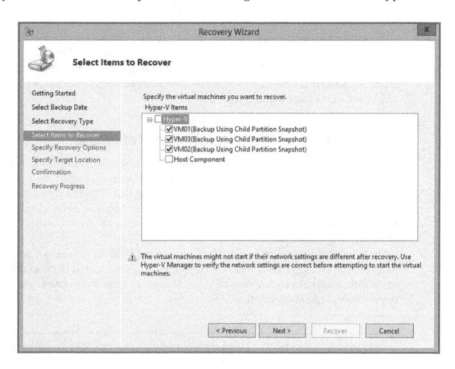

If you choose one of the two recover options, the virtual machines will then be restored and registered in Hyper-V. You can see the virtual machines are there, off in a saved state, if you open Hyper-V Manager. You can start the virtual machines if you are sure everything is OK.

Protecting Hyper-V Clusters

The ability to use WSB to back up and restore VMs on a cluster and CSV is new in Windows Server 2012. WSB should not be of interest to medium or large enterprises. One could argue that if you have a Hyper-V cluster, you fall into this category. Many organizations have small Hyper-V clusters, and the licensing costs for enterprise backup solutions are prohibitive.

Unlike an enterprise backup solution, WSB can run on only the local host, and it can see and back up locally running virtual machines. If you tried to create a backup policy to protect all of your virtual machines from a clustered node, the Select Items screen (Figure 10.6) would show only the virtual machines that were running on that clustered node.

With some lab time, you might experiment with backing up your virtual machines by selecting the CSV that the virtual machines are stored on, instead of selecting the Hyper-V virtual machines. That will give you mixed results.

Imagine that you have two hosts, Host1 and Host2. Virtual machine VM01 is running on Host1, and VM02 is running on Host2. You now run a backup of the CSV from Host1. You will get an application-consistent backup of VM01. But you will not get that with VM02; it will instead have a crash-consistent backup without the application consistency.

If you want to use WSB on a Hyper-V cluster, you will have to run a backup job on each host in the cluster. Each WSB backup job will protect the virtual machines running on the local host.

If you followed the nonclustered host example, you saw how we created a backup policy and selected virtual machines. This might work for a once-off backup, but it is not practical for a scheduled backup. Virtual machines will move around the cluster, and the policy will be outdated soon after creation. But there is another way, as you'll see when you look at some real-world solutions later in the chapter.

The Impact of Backup on the Network

How big will an incremental backup be on your hosts or clusters, and how often will you perform that backup? Will there be gigabytes or terabytes of data flying across the network to your backup servers? If you have a huge farm, can you live with the management OS network being congested with this traffic? Remember that this is the same network connection that is used for RDP, for remote management, for monitoring, and so on. Are you still OK with massive amounts of data going across that network?

In Windows Server 2008 and Windows Server 2008 R2, it was not unusual to see an additional network card or NIC team being added for a dedicated backup network in *very large* installations, where backup traffic would cause a problem. Instructions on how to set this up depend on the backup solution.

SYSTEM CENTER 2012 DATA PROTECTION MANAGER BACKUP NETWORK ADDRESS

System Center DPM has a concept called the Backup Network Address, which keeps backup traffic from traversing the primary production network. You can learn more about the Backup Network Address by reading the Operations Guide for System Center 2012 DPM at www.microsoft.com/download/details.aspx?id=2969.

As usual, Windows Server 2012 gives us options if we do need to control the impact of backup traffic on the network:

Quality of Service   You can use quality of service, or QoS (see Chapter 4, "Networking"), to manage the bandwidth utilization of the management OS NIC or NIC team. A certain amount could be guaranteed to remote management, monitoring, and backup, with the ability for each category to burst beyond its guaranteed amount if there is idle bandwidth.

This option could be used where a share of the management OS NIC or NIC team bandwidth will suffice for backup traffic.

Converged Fabric If hosts have been built by using one or more converged fabrics, an additional management OS virtual NIC could be created and bound to a physical network VLAN that is dedicated to backup traffic (see Chapter 4 for more information). Once again, QoS rules would be applied to manage the bandwidth of the NIC team that is used by the converged fabric.

You might use the converged fabric approach if you find that the management OS VLAN on the physical network is becoming congested by the cumulative backup traffic from all of the hosts and impacting management/monitoring functions. This approach continues to assume that a share of the NIC or NIC team is sufficient, but it isolates the backup traffic to a dedicated VLAN after the traffic reaches the physical switch port.

Physically Isolated Backup Network Using this technique, a dedicated physical NIC or NIC team is placed into each host and connected to a dedicated backup network. It might be the simplest concept of all the approaches, but it comes with a steep cost: additional network cards, cabling, switch ports, hardware support, and electricity. That all adds up over a three-year period, and that's why very large datacenters balance scale-up with scale-out, trying to find the economic/performance sweet spot.

If you have immensely dense hosts, and a share of a NIC team (which can have up to 32 NICs as team members) will be insufficient for backup traffic, then you will want to use this physically isolated backup network technique. In another scenario, you might need to physically isolate the network switches due to load, and this requires additional NICs in the hosts.

Real World Solutions

Here are a few problems and solutions that you might encounter when using Windows Server 2012 Hyper-V.

Using WSB to Back up a Hyper-V Host and Retain Backup Data

Challenge

You have deployed a Windows Server 2012 Hyper-V and a number of virtual machines. You need to use WSB to back up the virtual machines to a file share and retain backup data for seven days. How can this be done?

Solution

The following script will create a temporary backup policy to back up all of the virtual machines on the local host to a file share. The script will then start to manage the backup data. It will detect what day of the week it is. If it finds an existing backup from the previous week, it will erase it. Then it will take the current backup data and store it in a subfolder named after the day of the week. This will retain seven days of data on the file share.

```
#Build up the path to store this host's backup
```

```
$HostName = Get-Content Env:ComputerName
$Share = "\\FileSvr1\Backups\$HostName"

Write-Output "Creating backup policy..."

#Create a new backup policy that will be used but won't be saved
$Policy = New-WBPolicy
$VMs = Get-WBVirtualMachine
Add-WBVirtualMachine -Policy $Policy -VirtualMachine $VMs

#Configure the policy to use the file share
$BackupLocation = New-WBBackupTarget -NetworkPath $Share
Add-WBBackupTarget -Policy $Policy -Target $backupLocation

Set-WBVssBackupOptions -Policy $Policy -VssFullBackup

#Start the backup
Write-Output "Starting backup..."
Start-WBBackup -Policy $Policy

#Maintain 7 days backup retention
Write-Output "Moving backup files to day-of-week folder..."
$Day = (Get-Date).DayOfWeek

If  (Test-Path "$Share\$Day")
#Remove any backup data from same day of last week
{
    Remove-Item $Share\$Day\* -Recurse
}
Else
#Create a new folder for today's backup
{
    New-Item -Type Directory "$Share\$Day"
}

#Move today's backup to the folder for today's backup
Move-Item "$Share\WindowsImageBackup" "$Share\$Day\" -Force
Write-Output "Backup completed!"
```

Save the script as C:\Scripts\CSVBackup.PS1. Then create a scheduled task on the host that will do the following:

◆　Run whether a user is logged on or not

- Run with the highest privileges and be configured for Windows Server 2012

- Be triggered to run at the time of your choosing every day

- Execute C:\Windows\System32\WindowsPowerShell\V1.0\PowerShell.EXE with "C:\ Scripts\CSVBackup.PS1" as an additional argument.

- Run as a user account that has Change rights on the share and Modify rights on the share folder, and is a member of either the Backup Operators or Administrators groups on the host in question

You can monitor this task by using Scheduled Tasks and the Get-WBJob cmdlet while the Start-WBBackup cmdlet in the script is running.

Other ways to extend this solution are as follows:

- Tweak the folder preservation algorithm to conserve a month or even a year of data.

- Use a file-replication solution such as Distributed File System Replication (DFS-R) to replicate the backup data to a remote location.

Performing Automated WSB Backup of a Hyper-V Cluster

CHALLENGE

The company is satisfied that the previous backup solution for the Hyper-V host works, but now you must deploy a small Hyper-V cluster. There is no budget for an enterprise backup solution until next year. Can you use WSB to perform an application-consistent backup of the virtual machines on the cluster, while retaining the backup data for seven days?

SOLUTION

You will need to run a backup on each host in the cluster to have an application-consistent backup. You can use the script in the previous challenge to do this; it backs up all of the virtual machines on the local host and manages the backup data for seven days.

The script can be stored in the backup file share as \\FileSrv1\Backup\Scripts\ HVC1Bacup.PS1.

Now you need to run this script on every host in the cluster at the same time. A Clustered Scheduled Task can be used to run the backup script from every host. The following snippet of PowerShell will create the task:

```
$Action = New-ScheduledTaskAction -Execute "C:\Windows\System32\ `
WindowsPowerShell\V1.0\PowerShell.EXE" -Argument `
"\\FileSrv1\Backup\Scripts\HVC1Bacup.PS1 -NoExit"
$Trigger = New-ScheduledTaskTrigger -At 21:00 -Daily
Register-ClusteredScheduledTask -Cluster Demo-HVC1 -TaskName ClusterDailyBackup `
-TaskType ClusterWide -Action $Action -Trigger $Trigger
```

Note that the Clustered Scheduled Task (see Chapter 8, "Building Hyper-V Clusters") will run as System on all of the hosts in the cluster, instead of Demo\Backup as in the previous examples in this chapter. That's because it is not supported to run Clustered Scheduled Tasks as a user. That means you should do the following:

1. Create a domain security group (HVC1-Hosts, for example), add the hosts to this group, and reboot each host in turn (using the cluster pause/resume feature) to inherit this new membership.

2. Grant the security group Change rights on the share and Modify rights on the share folder.

The final step is to test this solution, as you should with any backup engineering, to ensure that it works without negatively impacting your production systems, and that you are able to restore your backups reliably.

## Chapter 11

Disaster Recovery

An organization has a responsibility to its shareholders, employees, partners, and customers to be able to survive a disaster. It is one thing for people to be able to return to work after the disaster, but will they have the tools, processes, and information that enable them to *work*?

Countless headline-making disasters have reminded us of the importance of implementing a business continuity plan that makes it possible for IT to recover the systems and data that enable the business. Virtualization has, in theory, made disaster recovery (DR) replication easier because we can deal with simple files rather than a wide variety of applications. Unfortunately, the complexities and costs of the offsite replication mechanisms still prove to be a challenge. And that remains true for enterprises, medium businesses, and especially small businesses, for which this challenge has the greatest impact on the community.

You will look at numerous ways that a business can enable DR for Windows Server 2012 Hyper-V, starting with the most basic offsite backup and moving on to complex multi-site clusters.

In this chapter, you'll learn about

◆ How virtualization makes DR easier

◆ The various methods to enable DR when using Windows Server 2012 Hyper-V

◆ Designing a multi-site Hyper-V cluster

Introducing Disaster Recovery

The destruction of the twin towers in the September 11, 2001, terrorist attacks, the hurricane along the Louisiana/Mississippi Gulf Coast, the floods in Eastern Australia, and the tsunamis that have hit Asia all made huge headlines. Countless lives were lost. Families were destroyed.

It's difficult to see past the personal tragedies of these events. But many businesses, government departments, and nongovernmental organizations (NGOs) were impacted too. Each of these organizations has a responsibility to their shareholders and communities to survive these disasters and resume operations as soon as possible. A stock exchange needs zero or near-zero downtime. A hospital's systems need to stay operating so that patients can be treated and tracked. Members of the community need their employers to resume operations so they can earn money to continue to care for their families. NGOs need to be active as soon as possible to care for the most vulnerable in society.

What makes business operations possible? Is it a building? If all a business needed to survive was a building with furniture, life would be easy—but this is not the case. Is it the people and their skills/knowledge? To a certain extent, yes, but these factors are very limited in this digital information age. It is the data, the processes, and the communications systems that enable people to work, use their experience, and make decisions that really make the business what it is. The IT infrastructure and applications exist to enable and empower the employees of the organization. Without IT, most businesses cease to exist as meaningful entities.

> ### HIGH AVAILABILITY VS. DISASTER RECOVERY
>
> The concepts of high availability (HA) and disaster recovery (DR) are similar, but they serve different purposes.
>
> HA provides us with physical server fault tolerance. In the case of Hyper-V, a failover cluster of Hyper-V hosts enables virtual machines to automatically relocate to another host in a cluster if the original host has a hardware or management OS failure. This is primarily a local tolerance of individual hosts inside a single site.
>
> DR is bigger. It enables an organization to suffer the loss of a building in a campus or the loss of a complete site, and still to continue to operate by using replicas of the workloads and data in a fault-tolerant DR site. This is an inter-site solution rather than a local solution.
>
> There is a fuzzy space between these two concepts because their difference is subtle: fault tolerance inside of a site vs. fault tolerance of sites. The differences are further clouded because we can use Windows Server Failover Clustering to enable automated DR across a multi-site cluster.

The Evolution of Disaster Recovery

The events of September 11, 2001, drove home the point that every business requires a business continuity plan (BCP) to survive a fire, a natural disaster, an industrial leak, an extended infrastructural issue, or a terrorist attack. Systems and data must be replicated to a remote location, preferably local enough that people can get to it, but far enough away that it is not affected by the disaster. For example, the DR site should not be on the same flood plain or power grid as the production site.

It is this DR replication that proves to be the challenging issue. The methods being used have evolved greatly over the years.

Over the past decade, most mid-sized and large enterprises have investigated the possibility of implementing a BCP. In the early days, workload-specific replication and failover mechanisms were required. BCP testing usually proved that these methods were fragile. One almost had to walk softly past the server racks to ensure that they stayed running.

A lot of mainstream products have developed reliable and elegant replication capabilities over recent years. Active Directory is designed to be fault tolerant thanks to replication and the multi-master nature of domain controllers; all that might be required is that the Flexible Single Master Operations (FSMO) roles be seized if the production site is completely lost. Exchange Server now includes Database Availability Groups (DAGs). SQL Server 2012 introduced a similar technology called AlwaysOn Availability Groups.

Per-workload replication mechanisms rely on a lot of engineering that is very specific. Maybe some services such as SQL Server and Exchange Server handle this well, but most businesses have many more applications that either have no built-in replication model or require a lot of money to be paid to vendors for a replication license.

This complexity led some to question whether the actual risk of a disaster was worth the effort that was required to implement and maintain the DR systems.

DISASTER RECOVERY AND THE CLOUD

There is no doubt that we have entered the cloud era. Windows Server 2012 is a *cloud operating system* for building public clouds (multi-tenant service providers) and private clouds (dedicated to a single business). One of the traits of a cloud is self-service, the ability for users to deploy resources for themselves via a portal with no interaction with those people who maintain the cloud fabric. In the case of Hyper-V, that means developers, testers, and application administrators will deploy virtual machines to host the IT-based services that enable business operations.

If you are an engineer or administrator in a medium-sized to large enterprise, ask yourself this: when do you find out that your application management colleagues have deployed a new SQL server? Unfortunately, the answer usually is this: when they ask you to restore a backup that doesn't exist because you never knew that SQL Server was installed. So what happens to per-workload DR replication engineering in a true cloud, where you have no involvement with virtual machine or service deployment? Can you trust the developers to implement a DR plan? Are these developers the same people who assume that you can read their minds? This might sound a bit inflammatory, but engineers who design for the worst-case scenario are the ones who implement reliable systems, and DR engineering is all about dependable systems.

Automation is essential. Assumptions and human interaction with the systems must be eliminated in the cloud. To put it quite bluntly: remove the meat (humans) from the machine.

Virtualization Simplifies DR

Per-workload replication requires intimate knowledge of each set of data or application that was to be replicated, and a specific replication and failover system for that workload. The beauty of virtualization is that it is an abstraction mechanism. Virtual machines, their operating systems, their software, and their data (as long as you use virtual hard disks) are not tied to the hardware. Virtual machines are just files, and those files can be replicated as easily as files in a share (from the perspective of IT pros, but there is really more to it than that).

What this basically means is that we can enable replication of a file system or a LUN, and any virtual machine in that volume will be replicated to a destination site. In the event of a disaster, those virtual machines can be failed over and powered up in the DR site. Any new virtual machine that appears on a replicated LUN will automatically be replicated, and this is something that is suitable for a cloud; engineers don't need to be engaged to enable DR replication, and human effort is saved for other project and quality assurance tasks.

The replication mechanisms used depend on the size of the organization and the type of storage being used. An enterprise may use SAN-to-SAN replication. A medium-sized business might use meshed storage, in which a SAN is made of fault-tolerant appliances that span two sites. A smaller organization might use a software-based SAN to replicate virtual machines or a host-based replication to replicate virtual machines from a host in the production site to a host in the DR site.

With some investment in the virtual machine replication system, the business gets a more reliable failover mechanism. That reliability is evident during day-to-day operations because only a single replication mechanism likely exists for the entire cloud compute cluster, working at a very low level. The reliability should also be evident when the BCP is invoked; virtual machines can be failed over by using a single mechanism (maybe even orchestrated using PowerShell or System Center Orchestrator), which could even feature 100 percent automation of that failover.

AUTOMATED FAILOVER OR NOT?

To automate the failover of virtual machines or not, that's the million-dollar question! Actually, that could be a billion-dollar question for some enterprises.

Failing virtual machines over from the production site to a DR site is a big deal. If some sort of infrastructure fault leads to a split-brain scenario (that is, the production site and DR site each think they should be active), some serious issues could arise when that fault goes away. For example, some users could have been storing data in the production site, while others were using the DR site. How do you merge this? All sorts of clever mechanisms can be put in place to create third-party witnesses, but even the most detailed designs can fail, as headlines of datacenters failing can prove. Fortunately, common infrastructure issues happen way more frequently than genuine disasters. Unfortunately, this means that false alerts can cost a lot of money when you have to undo unwanted automated failovers.

One approach is to design your BCP so that a senior person must decide whether a human element should be involved in invoking the plan. Some organizations, such as a stock market, cannot tolerate any downtime. Every second down can cost millions, if not billions, of dollars, so they must have complete automation.

Other organizations might be able to tolerate a few minutes or a few hours of downtime. In that case, a quick meeting or phone conference by senior decision makers (with informed input from IT) can be enough to decide that the trigger is pulled, and a failover is started. At that point, an authorized person might need only to start a PowerShell script or System Center Orchestrator run book, which then invokes the BCP and automates all the necessary failover steps. That business rapidly responds to the disaster, gets systems back online quickly, and eliminates the risks of a false alert.

Replication of virtual machines rather than of individual workloads is often the preferred way of enabling DR, particularly in the case of cloud computing Infrastructure as a Service (IaaS). That's the topic of the next section.

DR Architecture for Windows Server 2012 Hyper-V

In this section, you will look at the high-level architecture of how to build a DR solution by using Windows Server 2012 Hyper-V. Please remember that the exact mechanisms and detailed designs vary wildly depending on the specific server, storage, and replication product(s) that you use. If you are planning to use storage to replicate virtual machines, your storage manufacturer will be dictating most of the design.

DR Requirements

There are many ways to replicate virtual machines from one site to another for the purposes of disaster recovery. They run from the very economical to the very expensive, from simple-to-implement to requiring great skill in engineering, and from completely automated and rapidly invoked to time-consuming to recover. Choosing the right option requires understanding the requirements of the business. Remember, these are not IT-dictated requirements; you will need guidance from the directors of the organization in question. Of course, you also need to be aware of the technical limitations of each replication solution. Some requirements are as follows:

Recovery Time Objective   The recovery time objective (RTO) is the amount of time that is allowed for essential business operations to be restored, according to the BCP. This is dictated by various factors, including these:

- Level of automation for invoking the failover

- Complexity of the failover

- The need to fail over systems in a particular order

- The availability of a copy of the data at the right location

The business will usually state how long the RTO should be, and then IT must engineer systems to meet the requirement.

Achieving a low RTO is very achievable with virtualization because you are just replicating files, and virtual machines are quick to power up, especially if this is orchestrated.

Recovery Point Objective   A business's recovery point objective (RPO) defines how much data (measured in time) the business can afford to lose. This could range from 0 seconds to days, depending on how critical the data is to the business.

Much like trying to go from a 99.9 percent uptime to a 99.99 percent uptime, shaving minutes or seconds from an RPO costs exponentially more as you try to aim for zero. The infrastructure and networking required for 0 seconds may cost millions of dollars to own and operate when compared to using solutions that you may already own for a 10-minute RPO.

Budget   It is not unusual for an engineer or a consultant to hear that the business or client wants an RTO of 0 seconds and an RPO of no data being lost. The systems and the data are far too important for any loss of service or data. That's when your client must be introduced to a stranger called reality. RTO and RPO of 0 seconds are possible—if you can afford the required systems and networking.

A balancing act must be performed between the risks of a disaster happening, the costs of implementing a DR solution, and the costs of not having a DR solution in the event of the disaster.

If your boss or customer asks for a 0-second solution, carefully explain how you can offer a 0-second solution (business people hate it when IT pros say no "all of the time"), but only if they can pay the bills. Then offer more-affordable options with a more realistic business-driven negotiated RPO and RTO.

Before you look at specific solutions, you need to understand the two basic methods of getting data from one site to another.

Synchronous and Asynchronous Replication

Every method of replicating data (such as virtual machines) from a production site to a DR site falls into one of two categories: synchronous or asynchronous. This has a direct impact on the RPO of the solution.

Synchronous replication, shown in Figure 11.1, works as follows. Note that this is a generalized example, and specific systems may work slightly differently, but the concept remains the same:

1. The host in the production site writes (on behalf of a virtual machine) to the local storage. An acknowledgement is not immediately sent from the storage to the production host at this time as would normally happen.

2. The production storage replicates the modified data to the DR storage.

3. The DR storage acknowledges that the replicated change has been committed in the DR site.

4. The production storage acknowledges that the modification has been committed. This acknowledgement can happen only if both the array controllers of the production and DR storage have been able to commit the write.

FIGURE 11.1
Synchronous
replication

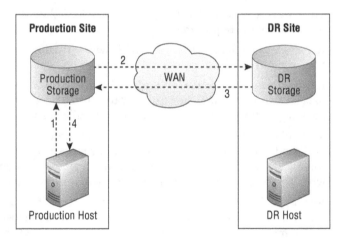

Synchronous replication offers zero or near-zero data loss, or RPO. If something is written in site A, it is guaranteed to also be written in site B. This comes at a great cost; the link between the production and DR sites must be of a very high quality, with the following characteristics, so as not to impact the write performance of the storage:

◆   High bandwidth, offering high throughput

◆   Low latency, meaning high speed and short distances between the sites

Very often, you need multi-gigabit links with 2 milliseconds or lower latency, depending on the solution. This sort of link can be expensive, assuming that it is even available in the area, meaning that a small percentage of organizations will use it.

Keep in mind that this requirement for very low latency (usually dictated by the storage manufacturer) will restrict how far away the DR site can be. The need for distance between sites to avoid disasters may prevent synchronous replication.

Figure 11.2 shows asynchronous replication in action. Once again, this is a high-level illustration. Many types of replication can fall under the category of asynchronous replication, and they may not use replication LUNs as shown in this figure. However, the high-level concept remains the same:

1. The production host writes some new data to the production storage.

2. The production storage commits the write and acknowledges this to the host immediately. The storage does not wait for replication to occur for this acknowledgment.

3 Replication of the new data happens. This could be continuous, it could be interval based, or it could happen only during a scheduled window of time.

4. The replication mechanism acknowledges that the changed files or blocks of storage have been replicated to the DR site.

FIGURE 11.2
Asynchronous replication

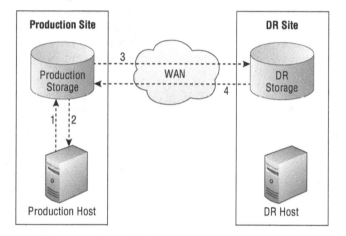

Although asynchronous replication still requires sufficient bandwidth to replicate the data in the required time frame (the rate of replication must be faster than the rate of change), there is little or no impact on the write performance of the Hyper-V host in the production site. That means you don't need the same low-latency links (such as under 2 milliseconds) and that sites can be farther apart—for example, an office in Wellington, New Zealand could replicate to a datacenter in Dublin, Ireland if there was sufficient bandwidth.

Asynchronous replication can offer an RPO of maybe a few seconds to a few days depending on the solution being used. While this offers more geographic latitude and more-economical DR solutions, this can rule out asynchronous solutions for the few organizations that really do have a genuine requirement for a 0-second RPO.

Armed with this information, you are now ready to look at architectures and solutions for enabling DR replication of virtual machines hosted on Windows Server 2012 Hyper-V.

DR Architectures

There are a number of architectures that a business can deploy for enabling DR with Hyper-V. The one you choose will depend on the storage you use, your desired RPO and RTO, the amount of automation you want to have in failover, and of course, your budget.

REPLICATION BETWEEN NONCLUSTERED HOSTS

A small business may run two or more virtual machines on a nonclustered host. Just because the business is small doesn't mean that it doesn't have a need or responsibility for a DR plan.

The Great Big Hyper-V Survey of 2011 (`www.greatbighypervsurvey.com`) found that one-third of organizations used only nonclustered hosts. Another third of organizations had a mixture of clustered and nonclustered hosts. It is also known that hosting companies (public cloud) like nonclustered hosts because of the lower costs (DAS instead of SAN and no need for host fault tolerance). These organizations need the ability to replicate their nonclustered hosts, possibly to another nonclustered host.

A common example of this particular requirement is a small hotel chain, in which each hotel runs a single Hyper-V host with a number of virtual machines for managing that hotel's operations. In this case, a solution could be engineered whereby each hotel would replicate to another neighboring hotel, as shown in Figure 11.3. This mutual DR site solution is not unusual in small to medium enterprises. If two sites each require a Hyper-V host and a DR site, then each site's host would be given additional capacity and be configured to replicate.

FIGURE 11.3
Nonclustered hosts replicating in a hotel chain

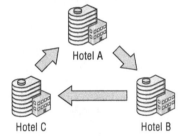

Hotel A

Hotel C   Hotel B

The costs of DR are minimized by using the already existing remote location and by simply adding RAM, storage, or CPUs to existing host hardware. There might be minimal or even no additional Windows Server licensing costs if the original licensing was Windows Server 2012 Datacenter with its unlimited virtualization rights.

MULTI-SITE CLUSTER

In Chapter 8, "Building Hyper-V Clusters," you learned how to build a cluster within a site. A cluster can also be built to span more than one site. With this design, shown in Figure 11.4, if the hosts in the production site fail to communicate their availability to the DR site hosts via a heartbeat, the virtual machines will fail over to the hosts in the DR site. Combining this with synchronous replication will give you an RPO of 0. With the automated failover of a cluster, you get a simple invocation plan, and the RTO is the time it takes for virtual machines to fail over and boot. This can make the multi-site cluster a very attractive option.

A cluster requires shared storage such as a SAN, a file server, or a Scale-Out File Server. In a multi-site cluster (sometimes called a *geo-cluster*, a *metro-cluster*, or a *stretch cluster*), as you can see in Figure 11.4, there are replicating SANs between the production site and the DR site. Many SANs will require expensive extensions to enable this functionality. The SAN replication copies the virtual machines to the DR site. The independent SAN in the DR site allows the virtual machines to fail over even if the SAN in the production site is lost. This aspect of the design changes depending on the DR replication solution and the model and manufacturer of the SAN.

FIGURE 11.4
A multi-site cluster

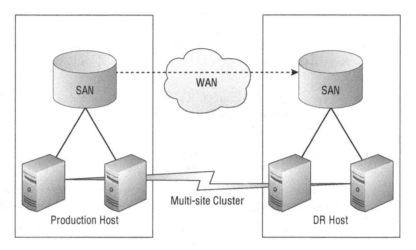

Traditionally, a multi-site cluster is designed to have active/passive sites. All of the virtual machines will normally run on hosts in the production site. There will be sufficient host capacity in the production site to deal with normal host maintenance or the occasional failure, without failing virtual machines to the DR site.

In an interesting variation of the multi-site cluster, both of the sites are active. Virtual machines are running in both sites. Ideally, virtual machines that provide services to site A are running in site A, and virtual machines that provide services to site B are running in site B. This was a nightmare scenario in Windows Server 2008 R2 Hyper-V, thanks to redirected I/O during backup. Although that issue has gone away, we still have some backup considerations:

◆ What host in the multi-site cluster will the backup server connect to, and will there be cross-WAN backup traffic?

◆ Will agents in virtual machines be backed up across the replication link? The active/active multi-site cluster requires much more consideration, and make sure you do not deploy one while incorrectly thinking that there is just a single site.

REPLICATION BETWEEN CLUSTERS

An alternative to the multi-site cluster is to create two Hyper-V clusters, whereby the virtual machines are replicated from the cluster in the production site to the cluster in the DR site. Each cluster has completely independent storage, and can be very different. For example, one site might be using a high-end Fibre Channel SAN, and the other site might be using a lower-cost Scale-Out File Server.

Usually the replication uses a host-based solution instead of hardware-driven SAN replication. This makes it more flexible and allows heterogeneous Hyper-V clusters that can span security boundaries. For example, an HP-based Hyper-V cluster with NetApp storage in a customer site could replicate to a Dell Hyper-V cluster with EMC storage in a hosting company's site, assuming that the replication software supported this security model.

MIXING CLUSTERED AND NONCLUSTERED HOSTS

The concept of mixing clustered and nonclustered hosts is an extension of the architect where one cluster replicates to another cluster, whereby the host-based replication now supports heterogeneous host architectures rather than just heterogeneous storage. There are several reasons that you would want to be able to replicate from a Hyper-V cluster to nonclustered hosts, and vice versa:

◆ A service provider could sell space on a DR cloud, and that cloud is made up of economical nonclustered hosts. The solution must be open to customers who own Hyper-V hosts, clustered or not.

◆ Alternatively, the service provider could offer a higher-value DR cloud with very high levels of uptime into which businesses with clustered and nonclustered hosts can replicate.

◆ A business has the option of implementing a budget DR solution without shared storage while using a Hyper-V cluster with higher-quality hosts and storage in the production site.

Once again, we are looking at using host-based storage for this hardware- and storage-agnostic solution with great flexibility.

You have seen how the Hyper-V hosts can be architected, and now you must look at how virtual machines will be replicated from the production site to the DR site.

DR Replication Solutions

This section presents each DR option for Hyper-V at a high level, without using any vendor specifics. You will learn how they work, and what their impacts will be in terms of RTO, RPO, and budget. Each solution may have dozens of variations from the many manufacturers in the world. This text cannot cover every unique feature and requirement but will help you understand the mechanisms, merits, and problems of each type of solution, giving you a starting point for talking to vendors about the products that they offer.

DISTRIBUTED FILE SYSTEM REPLICATION

You cannot replicate virtual machines with Distributed File System Replication (DFSR). DFSR replicates files when their write file handles are closed. Unless you plan to shut down virtual machines for 8 hours a day, this rules out this file server replication solution. And the same applies to XCopy and Robocopy. Chapter 12, "Hyper-V Replica," shows you how to replicate virtual machines by using a solution that is built right into Windows Server 2012 Hyper-V at no extra cost.

SAN-to-SAN Replication

You can use SAN-to-SAN replication to create a multisite cluster. With this type of solution, which is normally a licensed feature of the most expensive SAN products, a SAN administrator can enable replication of LUNs in a SAN (usually) to an identical model of SAN in the DR site. The replication can be synchronous or asynchronous depending on the model of the SAN.

There is a chance that some SAN-to-SAN replication solutions will not support replicating CSVs if you want to create a multi-site Hyper-V cluster. If you have one of these SANs and you want to replicate highly available virtual machines in a multi-site Hyper-V cluster, you have two choices:

♦ You can use the SAN's replication mechanism but will have to create an individual LUN for every virtual machine. This is a pretty dreadful solution that will require an incredible amount of automation and attention to detail. It is not at all cloud-friendly because of the amount of human effort that will be required, thus limiting the effectiveness or even the possibility of self-service virtual machine or service deployment. If running a cloud and using SAN-based replication are your goals, you need a different SAN that can support the replication of CSV.

♦ Alternatively, you can continue to use the SAN for its storage and backup features, and use a host-based replication solution instead to replicate virtual machines that are stored on CSVs.

Be sure you have verified the functionality of the SAN and decided this strategy before you purchase a SAN or replication licensing.

In theory, it is possible to use SAN-to-SAN replication to copy virtual machines from a Hyper-V cluster in the production site to a Hyper-V cluster in the DR site. However, the DR site cluster would have no awareness of virtual machine creation, deletion, or modification on the storage. The virtual machines would have to be imported into the Hyper-V cluster. Maybe that is something that the SAN manufacturer can offer or that you could script by using PowerShell?

SAN-to-SAN replication is a feature of the highest range of SANs, the ones that offer huge scalability, performance, and that the hardware vendors claim are cloud storage platforms. All of this can be true; just be sure that you have a solution for CSV replication before you make a commitment.

Meshed SAN Storage

A new type of iSCSI SAN has become very popular over the last three years that is based on using appliances instead of the traditional controllers and disk trays. Each appliance looks like a server filled with disks; it runs a special storage operating system, and the appliances can be stacked to create a single SAN.

A possible architecture with this meshed storage is a variation on the SAN-to-SAN replication method to build a multi-site cluster. Meshed SAN storage is more economical than the SANs used in SAN-to-SAN replication, and it normally supports the replication of CSV because it is a multi-master storage system.

You can see an example of the more common types of these solutions in Figure 11.5. This particular SAN, which has proven to be a very popular DR solution for Hyper-V, uses several appliances spread between the production site and the DR site. Any LUN created on the appliances in the production site is also created and updated by using synchronous replication in the DR site.

This design features near-zero RTO and zero RPO. An iSCSI mesh connects every host to every SAN appliance, and this is used to create synchronous replication with zero data loss in the event of a disaster. If connectivity with the hosts in the production site is lost, the multi-site cluster will cause virtual machines to fail over from the hosts in the production site to the hosts in the DR site where they will boot up. The price of the solution in Figure 11.5 includes requiring a multi-gigabit WAN link with less than 2 milliseconds' latency between the two sites. It also supports a very restricted number of hosts and CSVs. Each host has two connections to each appliance, including those in the other site, and this consumes a lot of SCSI-3 reservations.

FIGURE 11.5
Mesh SAN storage with synchronous replication

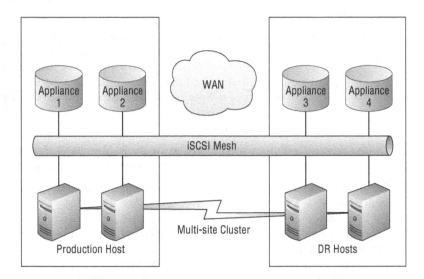

There are several SAN mesh solutions similar to this one. Each has designs and features that are unique to the manufacturer. While this one features synchronous replication, others may provide asynchronous replication or both. The design of the entire multi-site cluster will be dictated by the manufacturer and could include the following specifics:

◆ What networking offloads to use (or not use) on iSCSI network cards and how to configure them.

◆ Whether to use dedicated switches for the SAN and how to configure them (memory consumption by jumbo frames is an issue).

◆ The version of DSM/MPIO to use for iSCSI path fault tolerance.

◆ Any requirements and configuration of the WAN connection.

◆ Whether or not a third site is required where a virtual SAN appliance is placed to provide quorum to this SAN "cluster." This third site may require independent links to the production site and the DR site to avoid a split-brain scenario if the DR replication link (SAN heartbeat) fails.

The major benefit of the SAN mesh is that it is a fire-and-forget solution. You could choose to replicate all LUNs by default, and therefore everything is protected by default in the DR site. Alternatively, you could choose to replicate some LUNs. This would limit the amount of replication traffic and reduce the amount of storage required in the DR site SAN.

DISKS ARE NOT CHEAP!

Every once in a while, you might hear a speaker in a podcast or on a stage saying that disks are cheap. It's then that you can tell that this presenter rarely purchases anything of value with their own budget. You might be able to buy a terabyte of USB 2.0 disk for under $100, but try doing that for a server or a SAN, and it will cost many times more.

This is why you might consider not replicating every virtual machine by default. For example, if the budget is limited, you might replicate only production systems, leaving out the development and test versions of virtual machines from the policy. An interesting approach to this is to run these systems of "lesser" importance in the DR site instead of the production site so they don't have to be replicated, but they will be available after a disaster.

SAN-based replication is a one policy per LUN system. If you want to replicate some virtual machines but not others, you need at least two LUNs. That's just a very simple and small example. An enterprise with thousands of virtual machines could have many LUNs, some not replicating, some that are. And even those LUNs that are replicating might have different policies. You should consider the following if this is the case:

◆ You will have to architect the self-service of a cloud to enable the end user to choose and switch between replication policies. This will dictate where virtual machines are placed.

◆ You will not be able to just enable/disable or switch replication policies. Instead you will be using Storage Live Migration to relocate virtual machines to different LUNs in the SAN with zero service downtime. Offloaded Data Transfer (ODX, if supported by the SAN) will speed this up with Windows Server 2012 Hyper-V hosts.

While SAN mesh storage can provide a superb architecture, it does have scalability limitations. This can be fine for a mid-sized enterprise multi-site cluster that has tight control over the number of CSVs that are deployed, disks that are required, and dense hosts (which also offer the best cost of ownership over the life of the hardware) that are used. But this is not a solution for a large enterprise or a large public cloud because of the (relatively) limited clustered storage scalability.

SOFTWARE-SAN REPLICATION

Small and medium enterprises (SMEs) often cannot afford a hardware SAN, so they purchase a software SAN simulator that turns an economical storage server into an iSCSI SAN. While Windows Server does include the iSCSI target to offer this same basic functionality, these third-party solutions can sometimes offer other features, such as these:

◆ The ability to create a SAN mesh solution by using this software running on storage servers instead of dedicated appliances

◆ A VSS provider to improve the performance of storage-level backups

◆ The ability to replicate LUNs from one site to another by using asynchronous replication

It is this latter feature that draws the attention of SMEs to this type of solution, which is sold at a fraction of the cost of even the most basic SAS-attached SAN without any replication mechanism.

You must be careful of one particular aspect of these solutions. Consider the following scenario:

◆ A volume containing virtual machines is being replicated from the production site to the DR site.

◆ There might be no software VSS provider for the SAN, so the system VSS provider creates a VSS snapshot within the volume every time a storage-level backup is performed.

In this case, the SAN can start replicating the data in the VSS snapshot every time a backup job runs. This can be quite a shock for an SME that has a modest connection to the DR site. Ideally, you will have a solution that does have a VSS provider and that creates the snapshot outside of the LUN being backed up so that the snapshot can be excluded from replication.

We have now looked at three kinds of SAN-based replication. They can offer an amazing DR solution with low RPO, low RTO, complete automation, and a simple BCP when used in a multi-site cluster. But there are some drawbacks:

◆ SANs with SAN replication licensing can be prohibitively expensive for some.

◆ An enterprise can find it challenging to provide a central DR site if each branch office is buying a different model or manufacturer of SAN. The complexity and variety of skills can make centralization impossible.

◆ The networking can be very complex.

◆ SAN-based replication does imply a level of trust between the sites. What if a service provider wants to offer a hosted DR service? Should they buy matching SANs and hire the required skills for every client?

The SME, the service provider, and the enterprise might like something that is storage and host agnostic.

Host-Based Replication

Each of the solutions so far assumes that you have bought a SAN that includes or can include (at a price) replication. What solution can you use for DR replication if you are using one of the following storage systems?

◆ Standalone hosts with DAS.

◆ An SMB 3.0 solution such as a file server or Scale-Out File Server.

◆ A low-end SAN with no built-in replication.

◆ A high-end SAN that won't support CSV in a multi-site cluster.

◆ The storage in the production and in the DR site are completely different and have no common replication systems.

◆ There is no trust between the storage in the production and the storage in the DR site—for example, a customer and a service provider.

You can use a host-based replication solution to replicate the virtual machines of your choosing from one host or cluster in the production site to another site or cluster in the DR site. Typically (but not always), this is an asynchronous-based replication product that costs several thousand dollars per host. Microsoft has included the ability to support third-party filter drivers in Windows Server 2012 CSVs so that these volumes can be replicated by host-based products, assuming that the manufacturers support CSV replication.

For a business, this can often be the only realistic way to get virtual machines replicated to the DR site with a reasonable RPO and RTO at a fraction of the cost of SAN-based solutions. Unfortunately, the following factors are also true:

◆ The problems that some third-party replication solutions can cause can be greater than the risk of a disaster. Make sure you evaluate and test as much as you can and do lots of market research before you commit to purchase.

◆ The solutions may not be all that flexible. For example, they might not be able to replicate from nonclustered host to cluster or vice versa.

◆ These products cost several thousand dollars per host, and even this can put the solution out of reach of an SME.

Windows Server 2012 Hyper-V includes a new feature called Hyper-V Replica. With no additional license cost, Hyper-V Replica offers the following:

◆ A solution that was designed for small businesses with commercial broadband, but can be used by enterprises

◆ Asynchronous interval-based inter-site change-only replication of selected virtual hard disks from selected virtual machines

◆ Storage type abstraction

◆ The ability to replicate between nonclustered hosts, clusters, and between nonclustered hosts and clusters

◆ Replication inside a company (Kerberos authentication) and to a service provider (X.509 v3 certificate authentication)

◆ IP address injection for use in the DR site

◆ The ability to do test failovers, planned failovers, and unplanned failovers of virtual machines

◆ The ability to invoke a past version of a virtual machine to keep inter-virtual machine consistency

◆ Support for VSS if using applications that require data consistency

You will return to the subject of Hyper-V Replica in the next chapter. It is being referred to as a killer feature because it is quite powerful and is included in Windows Server 2012 for free with unlimited usage rights. Because it has a small RTO and RPO and is included for free in Windows Server 2012, you can expect to see lots of organizations, from SMEs to enterprises, adopting Hyper-V Replica.

OFFSITE BACKUP

Having an offsite backup is normally considered good practice. It gives a business an offsite archive of machines and data, with the ability to restore information from a week ago, a month ago, a year ago, or even longer. For some businesses, this is not a choice but a requirement of the law. Some SMEs decided to kill two birds with one stone: they could not afford SAN-based replication or host-based replication, so they decided to replicate their backup to another site. This other site could be a public cloud (hosting company), a service provider, or another office in the company. In the event of a disaster, the company would restore the lost virtual machines from backup.

The solution offers abstractions from host and storage architecture. But it does have a very long RPO and RTO. While a backup solution (such as System Center Data Protection Manager) might be able to synchronize many times per day, it might create only one or two restoration points per day; it is from these times that a virtual machine is restored. If a virtual machine's restoration point is at midnight, there would be a 12-hour RPO if the virtual machine was restored at midday the following day. The RTO would also be quite long; how long does it take to restore all of your virtual machines from backup? Ideally, this is a disk-disk backup with a disk replica in the DR site. But if you're talking about tapes being sent offsite, the RPO could be never if the disaster prevents the courier from getting to your DR site.

The emergence of Hyper-V Replica, a free host-based replication solution, does not eradicate the need for offsite backup. Replication and backup do two very different things. Replication creates an instant or near-instant copy of the virtual machine in a remote location. If data is corrupted (maybe via a malware attack or database corruption) in the primary site, it is corrupted in the secondary site. Backup will retain archives of data going back days, weeks, or potentially longer if there is sufficient storage.

You might introduce Hyper-V Replica as the new mechanism for DR because of the lower RTO and RPO, but your replicated backup still will have a role in the DR site. The requirement for an archive that you can restore from does not disappear when you invoke the BCP. You will still have people deleting files, systems corrupting databases, and maybe even still have a legal requirement to be able to restore aged files.

Virtual Machine Connectivity

How will you configure the networking of your virtual machines if they can fail over to another site, possibly one with a different collection of subnets, as shown in Figure 11.6? Do you measure RTO based on how long it takes to get your services back online in the DR site, or do you measure it based on how long it takes to get your services available to all of your clients? The business cares about service, not servers, and that is why RTO measures the time that it takes to get your applications back online for users.

The solutions vary—from basic to complex, from free to costly add-ons, from easy-to-manage to complex, and from quick to very slow.

Keep this in mind: your virtual machines will be booting up in the DR site after failing over. That means that they will register their IP addresses and start with an empty DNS cache. But what about clients in other locations who accessed the services provided before the disaster?

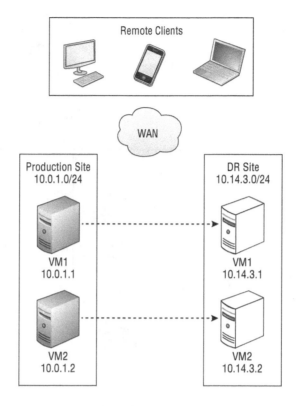

FIGURE 11.6
Virtual machines
failing over to
another site and
subnet

DHCP FOR THE VIRTUAL MACHINES

A free solution that you could use is to configure the IP stacks of the virtual machines to use DHCP-allocated IP addresses (Figure 11.7). A DHCP server in the production site would allocate IP addresses to virtual machines that are suitable for the production-site networks. An alternative DHCP server in the DR site would allocate IP addresses to virtual machines that are suitable for the DR site. This would allow virtual machines to be automatically re-addressed for the network as soon as they come online in either site. Remember that service availability, and therefore RTO, will be subject to DNS record time-to-live (TTL) lengths.

It would not be realistic to use any random IP address from the DHCP pool(s); network policies and firewall rules, and even some applications will need some level of IP address predictability. You could configure each virtual machine's IP stack to use a reserved DHCP address. This would have to be done on the DHCP servers in the production site and in the DR site.

There are some points to consider:

◆   By default, Hyper-V virtual machines have dynamic MAC addresses. DHCP reservations require static IP addresses, so you will have to configure each virtual network card to use a static MAC.

◆   Your DHCP servers just became mission critical. You absolutely must ensure that the DHCP reservations are being backed up. You also might want to give some thought to clustering your DHCP services.

FIGURE 11.7
Assigning DHCP
addresses to virtual
machines

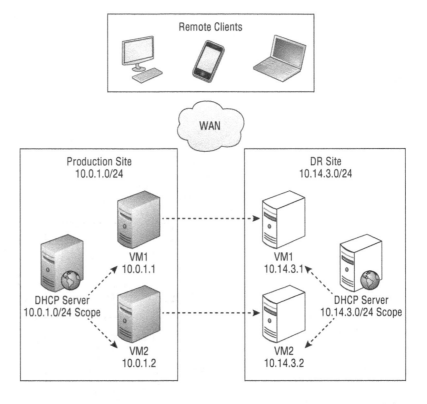

Would you really want to have DHCP running as a virtual machine that is being failed over? If so, make sure it is given a High failover priority and that all virtual machines depending on DHCP are either Medium or Low. This will ensure that the DHCP virtual machine will power up before the others. This does restrict the number of possible High virtual machines; using a physical DHCP server/cluster would be better, but this increases the cost of ownership, which is counterintuitive for an "economy" solution. You could do a lot of mouse-powered engineering to configure the MAC address of your virtual machines in the properties of each virtual machine's virtual network cards in Hyper-V Manager. It would be quicker to use PowerShell:

```
Set-VMNetworkAdapter VM1 -StaticMacAddress "001DD8B71C00"
```

If you have System Center 2012 Virtual Machine Manager (with Service Pack 1), you could use the Static MAC address pool feature to do this configuration for you and set each virtual machines' network card(s) and virtual machine template to use static MAC addresses by default.

You can create each DHCP reservation one at a time by using the DHCP console, or you can bulk-create the DHCP reservations by using PowerShell:

```
Add-DhcpServerv4Reservation -ComputerName VM1 -ScopeId 10.14.3.0 -IPAddress `
10.14.3.1 -ClientId 00-1D-D8-B7-1C-00 -Name VM1 -Description "Reservation for VM1"
```

Many engineers and consultants *hate* using DHCP, even with reservations, to address servers. It is a risk, and it adds one more moving part to the invocation of a BCP.

There is no doubt that using DHCP reservations is an economic way to allocate IP addresses to a large number of virtual machines when they power up in the DR site. It is also very flexible, allowing virtual machines to move between networks or clouds that are owned by different organizations, such as cloud DR service providers and their many customers' networks.

STRETCHED VLANs

Changing the IP addresses of a machine that provides a network service is disruptive. Consider this scenario:

1. A client wants to access a web service running on VM1. It will perform a forward DNS lookup, retrieving an A (IPv4) or AAAA (IPv6) record to convert the DNS name of VM1 into an IP address. In this case, an A record resolving VM1 to 10.0.1.1 is retrieved.

2. The client, and any involved intermediary DNS server, will cache the DNS resolution of 10.0.1.1 for VM1. The time that it is retained in cache is determined by the TTL for the record. An A record has a default TTL of 20 minutes on a Windows Server 2012 DNS server.

3. The client starts to use the web service on VM1.

4. For whatever reason, the IP address of VM1 changes from 10.0.1.1 to 10.14.3.1. VM1 registers this change with its assigned DNS server.

5. The client continues to attempt to connect to 10.0.1.1 for the web service on VM1. That's because the name resolution is still cached. Any DNS clients of the intermediary DNS servers continue to be told that VM1 can be found at 10.0.1.1, even though it is at 10.14.3.1.

6. Eventually the TTL will expire, and the affected clients and intermediary DNS servers will perform a fresh query. Active Directory–enabled DNS servers will update their records via Active Directory replication. And some 20 or more minutes later, everything can reconnect to the web service on VM1.

That is the experience with changing just the IP address of a single virtual machine. Imagine this happening to dozens, hundreds, or thousands of virtual machines and the many clients that are accessing them. You might have designed and deployed a multi-site Hyper-V cluster that enables virtual machines to fail over and start up in just a matter of minutes, but you could have clients that cannot access these services for a relatively long time. For some applications that queue up transactions (such as SMTP/POP3 email at an email hosting company), this could have a compound result that creates the effects of a distributed denial-of-service (DDoS) attack when the clients are able to resume operations when they all try to push through their workloads at once.

The DHCP reservation method for allocating IP addresses that was just discussed would be subject to this. Even though the virtual machines might be running and their services could be reached by their new IP addresses, just about every client will fail to connect to the services until their cached DNS records' TTLs have expired. If we were being conservative, we would have to say that the DNS record TTL has to be counted as a part of the RTO, possibly extending it from 5 minutes to 25 minutes or longer.

One solution might be to reduce the TTL of the DNS records to a time such as 5 minutes. You would have to be careful of doing this in large enterprises because it would create a much greater load on the DNS servers, which are usually domain controllers. You would have to manually configure existing TTL records or do this via a script, careful to avoid any that should not be modified. The default TTL can be modified by using the instructions found at `http://support.microsoft.com/kb/297510`. This would not be an option for public clouds, where the DNS records could be anywhere on the planet, with whatever registrar that the customer is using to host the zone.

It is for this reason that an organization will prefer to keep the IP addresses the same when a virtual machine fails over from the production site to the DR site. Normally a subnet or VLAN is restricted within a physical site. But it is possible for network administrators to stretch VLANs across sites so that subnets can exist in the production site and the DR site at the same time, as illustrated in Figure 11.8. Stretching the VLANs means that virtual machines can be configured with static IP addresses, as normal, and they will continue to communicate in the DR site with the same IP address.

NOTE   Some organizations might want to consider assigning DHCP addresses to virtual machines even if they have stretched VLANs. For example, a highly available virtual desktop infrastructure (VDI) solution would use DHCP addresses rather than static ones. A new feature in Windows Server 2012, called DHCP Failover, allows you to create active/active and active/passive DHCP "clusters" with a replicated DHCP database. A DHCP server in the production site could replicate and work in cooperation with a DHCP server in the DR site, allocating addresses to the shared VLANs.

This is a common database, so it is suitable only when the production and DR sites have a common address space, such as stretched VLANs.

You can learn more about DHCP Failover at `http://blogs.technet.com/b/teamdhcp/archive/2012/06/28/ensuring-high-availability-of-dhcp-using-windows-server-2012-dhcp-failover.aspx`

One consideration about stretched VLANs: you can do it only between two infrastructures that you own. In other words, you can stretch VLANs between two networks or private clouds that your organization owns. A service provider that is selling a public-cloud DR solution could stretch VLANs from each client site to the hosted multi-tenant cloud.

The benefits of stretched VLANs are as follows:

◆   Each virtual machine requires just a single IP address.

◆   There is no disruption to normal IP address allocation or DNS operations.

◆   The RTO does not need to include the length of time of the DNS records' TTL.

◆   Stretching VLANs also simplifies the implementation of multi-site clusters.

◆   Stretched VLANs is a set-it-and-forget-it solution that is cloud friendly. A virtual machine's cloud-allocated IP address is effective across all sites in the cloud.

FIGURE 11.8
Stretched VLANs

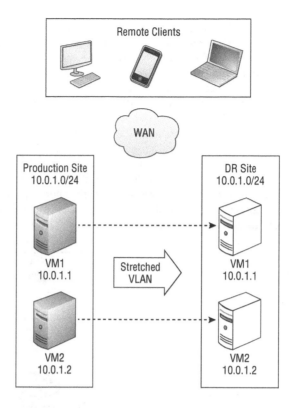

NETWORK APPLIANCE QUORUM TIME-OUTS

Your network engineers may have to create a kind of cluster for their network devices when they stretch the server VLANs of the production site into the DR site. This network cluster will have its own heartbeat and failover mechanism. Make sure that the design won't impact your Hyper-V farm. In some situations, the network devices might pause operations until they reach quorum, and this could actually pause the entire network itself. This could break a Hyper-V cluster in the site because it cannot make quorum itself because of a lack of connectivity with the local hosts.

NETWORK ABSTRACTION DEVICES

In rare circumstances, an organization cannot stretch VLANs across datacenters. DHCP reservations must be used, but the RTO requirements are too low to allow for a 5-minute DNS record TTL. A large enterprise or telecommunications company solution is to use network abstraction devices, as shown in Figure 11.9.

Each datacenter has its own set of VLANs and DHCP servers. Every virtual network card in every virtual machine has a reserved DHCP address in the production datacenter and the DR datacenter.

A device or devices reside on the WAN between the production and DR datacenters. This abstraction solution integrates with and heartbeats with network devices in the production and DR datacenters. A policy is configured in the abstraction solution to map a virtual IP address (VIP) for each virtual machine to the reserved IP address(es) for that virtual machine. For example, VM1 is 10.0.1.1 in the production datacenter, and it is 10.14.3.1 in the DR datacenter. A policy is created for it to map the VIP of 10.100.1.1 to both of those IP addresses. The DNS record for VM1 resolves to the VIP of 10.100.1.1. That means that no matter what IP address DHCP gives to VM1, it is always known to clients as 10.100.1.1, and they can always connect to it as that.

During normal operations, a remote client on the WAN will try to connect to VM1. DNS resolves the name as 10.100.1.1. When traffic is routed to this address, the network abstraction solution intercepts the traffic and reroutes it to 10.0.1.1. In the event of a disaster, the abstraction solution will detect a failure and start to reroute traffic to the alternative IP address of VM1, 10.14.3.1. Meanwhile, VM1 will fail over to the DR site, power up, and be allocated the DR site address of 10.14.3.1. Clients will continue to resolve VM1 and 10.100.1.1, and 10.100.1.1 will be routed to 10.14.3.1.

FIGURE 11.9
Using a device to abstract the production and DR VLANs

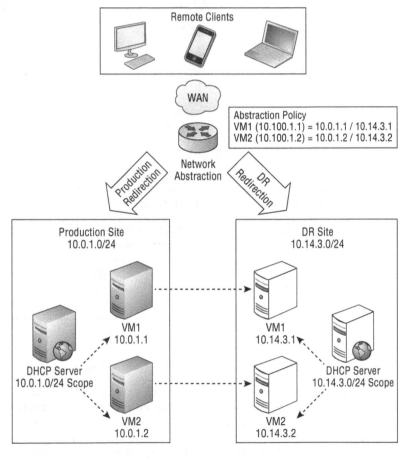

This is a solution for the large enterprise or a telecom company. The abstraction solution lives on the WAN, between the remote clients and the fault-tolerant data centers. A number of high-end appliances will be involved in this solution, and they are not the sort of thing that will fit into the budget of an SME. There are some questions you have to ask yourself when considering a solution such as this if you are building a large farm or a self-service powered cloud:

◆ Do you have to create/delete a VIP policy for each DHCP address or can you have a more static policy?

◆ Can you get the abstraction solution to register the DNS records or must they be created manually?

◆ How automated (scripting/orchestration) can the VIP/DNS configuration be made? This is important in a true cloud, where IT is the last to know about frequently new/removed virtual machines, IP address allocation, or services.

WINDOWS SERVER 2012 HYPER-V NETWORK VIRTUALIZATION

The network abstraction solution should have sounded familiar. You learned about a new cloud feature called Network Virtualization in in Chapter 5, "Cloud Computing."

Thanks to Network Virtualization, a virtual machine can move from the production site to a DR site without having to change its static IP address. The DR site will have a completely different physical IP address, but the virtualization of the network communications offered by Hyper-V will hide this from clients and the virtual machines themselves.

Figure 11.10 shows how VM1 can move from the production site to the DR site without the need to change the IP address and without the need to use stretched VLANs.

FIGURE 11.10
Network Virtualization enabling static IP failover without stretched VLANs

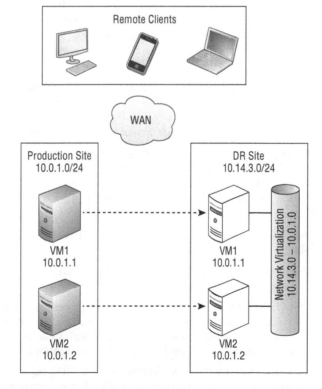

Network Virtualization will be of great interest to those designing DR solutions for Windows Server 2012 Hyper-V in situations where a business cannot stretch VLANs between the production and DR site. This could be the enterprise that was looking at a network abstraction device solution. This could be a business that has a network issue that prevents stretched VLANs. It could also be a situation where a hosting company is selling a hosted multi-tenant (public cloud) DR to many customers.

WHERE DO THE CLIENTS FAIL OVER TO?

For a large enterprise, client devices such as PCs are usually in an office that is remote from the production datacenter, so they fall out of scope for the Hyper-V engineer. But it is different in small businesses, and maybe even medium-sized enterprises, as the production site probably consists of a normal office building with a computer room where the Hyper-V compute cluster is located. In this case, we have to consider how clients are going to access the services that are being failed over to the DR site. What point is there in having a BCP for the services that are running in the virtual machines when there are no PCs for the end users to use those services on?

The traditional solution was for this company to use a specialist DR data center. A number of rooms would be filled with office furniture, phones, PCs, and printers. These rooms were either dedicated to a client of the datacenter or made available on a first-come, first-served basis. Either way, the rooms were typically full of old PCs that were normally turned off, with either no current image or no image at all. Getting these PCs powered up and configured/updated was another thing for IT to do during the invocation of the BCP. In some cases, these rooms were available only on a first-come, first-served basis. If a widespread disaster occurred, only the first few customers of the DR site would get a suite for their users to work in.

There are a few approaches to solving this problem. This is one of the scenarios where Remote Desktop Services (RDS) offers something that a PC cannot. RDS Session Hosts (formerly known as Terminal Servers) and/or VDI (hosted on Hyper-V hosts) can be deployed in one of two ways:

Use Highly Available RDS Virtual Machine for Production   The virtual machines running the RDS services would fail over to the DR site and can be accessed by employees remotely via the RDS Gateway. The benefit is that this brings a current working environment online very quickly, but at the cost of running RDS all of the time.

Deploy RDS in the DR Site during BCP Invocation   Either the IT department or a DR cloud-hosting company could turn on or deploy RDS services as a part of the DR invocation (which could be scripted or orchestrated). This would allow the business to use normal PCs, laptops, and tablets as client devices during normal production and avoid the additional licensing costs and restrictions of RDS until they are required.

There are a few ways for users to access the RDS Gateway and the business services that lie behind it:

Work from Home   Users could be told to go home and connect to a URL to access the RDS Gateway.

Rent Office Space   A preselected set of key employees and directors (documented in the BCP) would travel to rented office space, such as a hotel meeting room, and use laptops or PCs that could be purchased from a local retail store. Armed with just a URL, they could access the RDS Gateway and securely use applications and information.

Use Cloud Service Provider Terminals   A DR cloud-hosting company could have one or more rooms available to customers with office furniture and dumb terminals. Instead of deploying/maintaining an operating system, the terminals can be powered up and configured to access the RDS Gateway securely with just a minimum amount of work.

Other solutions might include the following:

Windows-To-Go and Direct Access   A new feature of Windows 8 Enterprise is the ability to install the operating system in a USB 3.0 stick. End users could be given these and told to boot up their PCs (at home, in a rented office, in a DR site suite, and so on), assuming that they have USB 3.0 ports. The stick is installed with all the usual end user applications and configured with Direct Access to give a seamless, and always on, secure tunnel into the corporate network and the DR site. A nice new feature of Direct Access in Windows 8 and Windows Server 2012 is the ability to define multiple Direct Access servers. This means that users could use this solution to dial into the production system normally, and then fail over to a Direct Access server in the DR site without any human intervention.

Traditional PC Suite with System Center Configuration Manager   Maybe the company already has an investment in a PC suite or an existing contract with a service provider. If so, System Center Configuration Manager (ConfigMgr) could be used to rapidly provision PCs. The ConfigMgr site server would be a fault tolerant virtual machine that is failed over to the DR site. ConfigMgr would already have updated operating system images with the standard office applications and knowledge of deployment policies for users. An administrator, even help desk staff, could run around to each PC in the suite, power it up, and start an OS deployment task sequence. This would automate the complete deployment and configuration of the PC. Any outstanding applications could be installed by the end users from the Application Catalog by self-service, without much or even any administrator intervention. See *Mastering System Center 2012 Configuration Manager* (Sybex, 2012) for more information on how to do this work.

Mobile Devices and Windows Intune   It's only a matter of time before the IT press start telling us that "this is the year of bring-your-own-device (BYOD)." BYOD means that employees buy their own mobile devices, such as laptops, tablets, and smartphones, for use at work. Microsoft's solution for managing these devices is Windows Intune, which can be used to deploy policy and company apps on the devices. During a disaster, end users will likely have these personal devices with them. If so, the devices will continue to work as normal. If not, users can get new ones, and Windows Intune can configure them over the Internet.

These are just some examples of how to let business users have access to services running the DR site after a disaster. Many options exist, and the number is only increasing, thanks to the explosion in mobile computing and the evolution of remote working.

We'll end this subject with some thoughts for your BCP author to ponder.

Have you considered whether there will be Internet access to the DR site after the emergency? Past disasters have shown us that the telecommunications industry is put under huge stress as friends and family try to make contact and stay in touch. While remote access solutions are economical, they are subject to these stresses. In this situation, traditional PC suites at a DR site are best.

Have you assumed that people can get to the DR site? Will the emergency prevent travel? It became impossible to escape the confines of New Orleans before Hurricane Katrina because of traffic congestion. Routes in and out of Manhattan Island were sealed off after the 9/11 attacks.

Maybe one solution for connecting end users to the services in the DR site is not the right way to go. And sadly, we should not write our BCP to depend on any one person. There might be victims in the emergency, and some may understandably prioritize the safety of their families over their employer's business.

Finally, the plan should be documented, communicated, and tested. It should include as much automation as you consider reasonable, and should assume that things will go wrong and that the day will be the worst of everyone's lives.

Implementation of a Hyper-V Multi-site Cluster

At a high level, creating a multi-site Hyper-V cluster looks like it is going to be just like creating a normal Hyper-V cluster (see Chapter 8). For the most part, it is, with one teeny, tiny exception: there's a limited-bandwidth, (relatively) high-latency link connecting the two sites that the clustered Hyper-V hosts are spread between. You saw examples of this earlier, in Figure 11.4 and Figure 11.5.

How you create the cluster depends greatly on various factors, including the following:

◆ What storage are you using?

◆ How will you configure the cluster to calculate quorum? What happens to the cluster islands if the site link fails?

◆ What sort of link exists between the two sites? Is there enough bandwidth for replication and cluster communications? How latent is the link?

To be honest, the storage manufacturer is going to dictate a lot of the cluster design—probably including terms for the bandwidth and latency. You will design and deploy the replicating SANs in the two sites according to this guidance. The manufacturer may even have instructions for the storage connections of the hosts. Yes, this has turned into a storage engineering project because in a multi-site cluster, the storage is more important than ever; and it already started out as being a keystone in the virtualization project.

After that is done, you will create the Hyper-V Cluster. Everything you read in Chapter 8 still applies, but there are some sides to the engineering that are specific to multi-site clusters, and that's where this section offers you help.

Replication Link Networking

High reliability, relatively low latency, and bandwidth that is sufficient for the needs of cluster communications and SAN replication is required for a multi-site cluster. Consider these factors for your bandwidth:

SAN Replication Your SAN manufacturer will give you some guidance on minimums for bandwidth, but the truth is that you need to perform an assessment to determine the rate of data change. Only with empirical data will you be able to accurately determine average bandwidth requirements and safely estimate peak-usage requirements. The SAN manufacturer will be quite firm about maximum latency times for synchronous replication.

Virtual Machine Migration If you are running an active/active multi-site cluster with virtual machines active in both sites, you need to consider the needs of Live Migration during normal operations. It requires at least 1 Gbps of bandwidth, and more in very dense hosts. In the case of an accidental failover of virtual machines to a DR site, you will need to get virtual machines back to the production site; that's the risk of automated failover! You could use Quick Migration, whereby virtual machines are put into a saved state, fail over, and are woken up again. This requires just 100 Mbps of bandwidth, but it does mean that virtual machines are offline. It will cause a huge spike in SAN replication traffic as the virtual machines save their state to disk.

Cluster Communications   The cluster communications link is used for redirected I/O. In Windows Server 2012, this is initiated when SAN connections fail, or during extremely brief metadata operations such as a virtual machine starting. The more important role of the cluster communication link is the cluster heartbeat. This requires only 100 Mbps of bandwidth. But more important, it requires a high level of service, which we will return to later.

REMINDER: VLANs

We dealt with the question of VLANs earlier in this chapter. The simplest design for the cluster engineer is to use stretched VLANs. Note that Windows Server 2012 CSV supports a Hyper-V cluster residing in different VLANs in the production and DR sites.

Another important question is whether you have a dedicated or multipurpose link for DR replication:

Dedicated Link   This is the ideal scenario, because it guarantees that production and DR communications cannot interfere with each other. But it is an ideal; many organizations will not be able to afford multiple links, so they need an alternative.

Multipurpose Link   After you have sufficient bandwidth in place between the production and DR sites, you can use traffic shaping or quality of service (QoS) to control what bandwidth is allocated to particular VLANs or protocols. You should not use Windows Server 2012 QoS for this because it cannot control traffic shaping for other machines or appliances on a shared link.

Multi-site Cluster Quorum

You might remember that quorum comes into play when a cluster becomes fragmented. The cluster uses quorum to decide which of the two fragments should remain online. In a single-site cluster, this is a minor risk. But it is a genuine risk in a multi-site cluster.

The thing that keeps the multi-site cluster (hosts in two sites) acting as a unit is the WAN link. How reliable are WAN links normally? You might put in dual WAN links. But what happens if there's a power outage outside your control? What happens if work on a building or road tears up the ground where both ISPs are running their cable? And unfortunately, it seems that every datacenter has a single point of failure, even those designed to withstand just about anything.

File Share Witness

Using a witness disk for quorum just won't be reliable in a multi-site Hyper-V cluster. That is why Microsoft has historically recommended using a File Share Witness for quorum. The File Share Witness is actually just a file share. Where do you create the file share?

Create the File Share in the Primary Site?   This is not a bad idea if you are truly dealing with an active/passive site scenario in which the DR site truly is on standby. If the WAN link fails, the primary site will remain active, and the DR site will remain offline because it does not have quorum. However, if a disaster occurs, you will have to force quorum manually in the DR site to bring the hosts online, because they have no access to the file share witness.

Create the File Share in the Secondary Site? In a word: no. Although your DR site will have quorum and come online automatically when the primary site disappears, this will also happen when the cross-WAN cluster heartbeat fails for more mundane reasons such as an ISP router failure. The result would be quite painful.

Create the File Share in a Third Site? This option is shown in Figure 11.11. The File Share Witness is created in a third site. This third site has independent network connections to both the production and the DR site. The risk of a single WAN link failing will not cause disruption to quorum. For example, if the DR replication link fails, we still have quorum because both the production and DR sites have an independent networking path to the File Share Witness.

The third site could be a head office, a branch office, another datacenter, or even a virtual machine hosted on a public cloud, such as Microsoft's Windows Azure Virtual Machines, with a site-to-site VPN connection to secure communications.

FIGURE 11.11
A File Share Witness running in a third, independently networked site

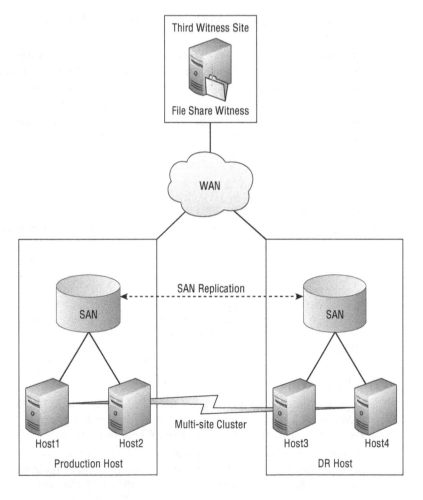

A good practice is to create a file share that is named after the cluster's Client Access Point (CAP—the name of the cluster) in question. The Active Directory computer object for the cluster/CAP should be given read/write permissions to the share and to the folder in the file system.

Configure the cluster quorum to use the File Share Witness after the cluster is created:

1. Right-click the cluster in Failover Cluster Manager, and choose More Actions ➢ Configure Cluster Quorum Settings.

2. In the Configure Cluster Quorum Wizard, select the option to Add Or Change The Quorum Witness.

3. In the Select Quorum Witness screen, choose Configure A File Share Witness.

4. In the Configure File Share Witness screen, browse to the cluster's witness file share or type in the UNC path.

5. Complete the wizard, and the cluster will switch to the new quorum model.

You should test and stress the cluster repeatedly to ensure that you get predictable results during host, link, and site failure. You should not assume that everything will work perfectly; in this type of environment, assumption is the first step to unemployment.

WHAT SORT OF MACHINE WILL HAVE THE FILE SHARE WITNESS?

As you can imagine, the file share that is used as the File Share Witness is quite important, because without it, this multi-site cluster cannot decide quorum. You could use a file share on a normal file server (which could be a virtual machine in the witness site), but you will lose quorum if that file server is offline and if the production site is offline too. Ideally, you will use a highly available file share. This could be hosted on a file share cluster (physical or virtual) or even on a Scale-Out File Server in the witness site.

The File Share Witness absolutely should not be hosted on the multi-site cluster that uses it for quorum, either directly as a highly available file share, or in a virtual machine that is hosted on the same cluster.

QUORUM VOTING RIGHTS

Microsoft has historically advised that when we build a multi-site cluster, we use the File Share Witness in a third site. This can add complexity and cost to the infrastructure:

◆ You need a third site for the witness, and that might involve paying for virtual machine hosting in a public cloud if you don't have one.

◆ The production and DR sites need independent networking paths to the witness site.

◆ Ideally, the File Share Witness needs to be clustered. Does this cluster need to be a multi-site cluster too? Where do you locate the File Share Witness for the File Share Witness cluster?

We have an alternative way to disable the multi-site Hyper-V cluster hosts from forming quorum without using a File Share Witness. The quorum vote that is normally assigned to nodes in the cluster can be manipulated. By disabling a node's or nodes' right to vote, we can dispense with the need for the File Share Witness at all. Figure 11.12 depicts an example of a quorum vote being disabled.

FIGURE 11.12
Using disabled quorum votes to maintain quorum in a multi-site cluster

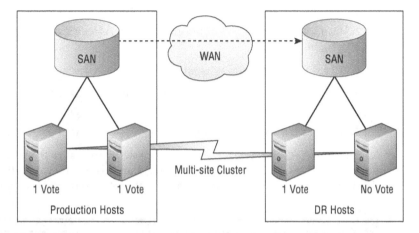

We can configure the ability of cluster nodes (hosts) to vote for quorum by doing the following:

1. Open Failover Cluster Manager, right-click the cluster, and choose More Actions ➤ Configure Cluster Quorum Settings to open the Configure Cluster Quorum Wizard.

2. Choose Advanced Quorum Configuration And Witness Selection.

3. Use the option of Select Nodes in the Select Voting Configuration screen. Select the check boxes for the nodes that will have quorum voting rights, and clear the boxes for the nodes that should not be allowed to vote (shown in Figure 11.13).

4. In Configure Quorum Management, clear the check box for Allow Cluster To Dynamically Manage The Assignment Of Node Votes, even though it is normally recommended to use this setting.

5. Select Do Not Configure A Quorum Witness. We no longer need a witness with this architecture.

6. Finish the wizard.

You can do this in PowerShell by running the following:

```
(Get-ClusterNode Host2).NodeWeight = 0
```

The NodeWeight is 0 if the node has no vote, and the NodeWeight is 1 if the node does have a vote.

FIGURE 11.13
Disabling cluster
node voting rights

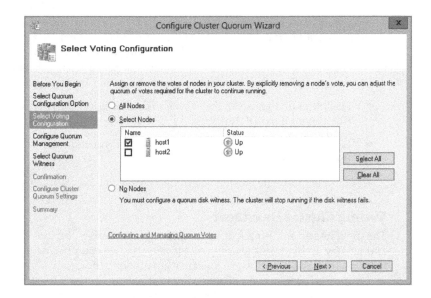

DYNAMIC MANAGEMENT OF NODE VOTES

We disabled the Allow Cluster To Dynamically Manage The Assignment Of Node Votes setting even though it was recommended. It will alter the voting weight of nodes in the multi-site cluster. This allows less than half of the surviving cluster nodes to form quorum. Although this might be useful in a single-site cluster, it could be dangerous in a multi-site cluster because a split-brain scenario could occur if the production-DR sites' WAN link failed. Both islands of the cluster would independently calculate quorum and cause a split-brain situation to occur with all of our virtual machines becoming active in both sites.

Using the example that was previously shown in Figure 11.12, we could disable the voting rights of one node in the DR site. This results in the following:

Even Number of Hosts   We can have an even number of hosts in the active and passive sites, with an even total number of nodes in the cluster. That means we don't have to purchase/deploy/maintain additional hosts just to maintain quorum, thus reducing the cost of ownership of the multi-site cluster.

No Witness Required   The DR site has been manipulated so that less than half of the hosts in the multi-site Hyper-V cluster are voting. Therefore, they cannot form quorum and failover virtual machines if the DR link fails. This allows us to dispense with the File Share Witness.

No DR Quorum or Automated Failover   Note that the DR site hosts cannot automatically fail over virtual machines because they do not have quorum. You will have to force quorum to enable you to fail over the virtual machines.

How many votes should you disable in the DR site? That depends on your architecture. You could disable all of the nodes in the DR site from voting. There is a risk with this; what happens if a number of voting hosts in the production site (V) is less than half the size of the total number of hosts in the cluster (C), because of maintenance or normal host failure? If V < (C/2), you don't have enough hosts left to form quorum. There is a balancing act:

◆ Disable enough hosts in the DR site so that they don't have enough to form quorum by themselves if the DR link fails.

◆ Leave enough hosts with voting rights so that you can survive host maintenance/failure in the production site.

In a simple multi-site cluster, you might disable one host's vote in the DR site.

Tuning Cluster Heartbeat

The most important thing for cluster communications is not bandwidth; it is quality of service and latency. Using traffic shaping on the network, we can provide the cluster communications network (heartbeat, and so on) a reliable amount of bandwidth.

Latency is important for cluster communications. The heartbeat between the nodes in the cluster tests to see whether neighboring nodes are responsive. The heartbeats work as follows by default:

Same VLAN or Subnet   Two cluster settings define heartbeat failure between hosts in the same subnet or VLAN. The first is a value called SameSubnetDelay. This value, in milliseconds, is 1,000 (1 second) by default and controls how often a heartbeat is sent. The second value is SameSubnetThreshold. The threshold defines how many missed heartbeats in a row indicate a host failure and it is set to 5 by default. Imagine you have HostA in one subnet and HostB in the *same* subnet. If HostA misses five heartbeats in a row over 5 seconds, HostB will consider it offline.

Multiple Subnet Multi-site Cluster   Two more settings configure heartbeat for hosts in different subnets. CrossSubnetDelay is similar to SameSubnetDelay. It is a milliseconds value and is configured to be 1 second by default. CrossSubnetThreshold determines how many heartbeats in a row must be missed before a host is seen as offline. Now imagine you have HostA in one subnet and HostB in a *different* subnet. If HostA misses five heartbeats in a row over 5 seconds, HostB will consider it offline.

The cluster heartbeat is sensitive to latency. By stretching a cluster across multiple sites, we have introduced latency, and this can create false-positives, where nodes may appear offline because the default heartbeat settings are too strict. We can alter the heartbeat settings to compensate for the increase in latency. Configuring the cluster heartbeat is

◆ Done in PowerShell

◆ A cluster-wide operation, not a per-host one

DEALING WITH NETWORK PROBLEMS

If your network has stability problems (not latency), tweaking the heartbeat settings will only temporarily mask the issues. Fix the underlying issue before it does cause problems.

You can see the value of a setting by running `Get-Cluster` to query the cluster and adding the heartbeat setting as an attribute of the query:

```
(Get-Cluster).SameSubnetDelay
```

That gives you one value at a time. If you want to see the values for the same subnet, you could run this example that uses a wildcard:

```
Get-Cluster | Fl SameSubnet*
```

You can also see all the heartbeat settings at once by specifying multiple values with wildcards:

```
Get-Cluster | Fl *SubnetDelay, *SubnetThreshold
```

The following example shows how you can set any one of the four heartbeat settings. It will configure the delay for multiple subnet multi-site clusters to be 5 seconds, extending the heartbeat time-out to be five times the original value:

```
(Get-Cluster).CrossSubnetDelay = 5000
```

How do you decide on the configuration of these settings?

◆ Quite simply, do not change the default values if you do not need to. Start by testing and stressing a new cluster to see what (if any) problems may occur. You might unearth infrastructure issues that need to be dealt with by the responsible engineers. You should adjust the heartbeat settings only if you have genuine latency issues that are causing false-positive failovers.

◆ If you find a latency issue impacting a stretched VLAN multi-site cluster, determine the nature of the issue and tune the same-subnet heartbeat settings. Adjusting the cross-subnet settings will do nothing for this cluster.

◆ If you find a latency issue impacting a multiple VLAN multi-site cluster, determine the nature of the issue and tune the cross-subnet heartbeat settings. Do not tune the same-subnet settings in this scenario, because they will not impact the cross-WAN heartbeat.

Preferred Owners (Hosts)

What is a cluster? It is a compute cluster, a pool of compute power that is managed as a unit. In a cloud, services are deployed to a compute cluster and that's normally that—you don't care what host the virtual machines (that make up the services) are running on. In fact, the cloud may be using features such as Dynamic Optimization to load-balance the host workloads, or Power Optimization to power down hosts (both features of System Center 2012 Virtual Machine Manager). The cloud could also be using Live Migration to consolidate and balance the virtual machines across the cluster in ways that appear random to us humans outside the "black box" that is the cloud. Hyper-V cluster administration features such as Cluster Aware Updating do something similar, sending virtual machines around the cluster so that management OS patching can be orchestrated and even automated.

This would be *bad* if left uncontrolled on a multi-site Hyper-V cluster. This single cluster spread across two sites has no concept of active site or passive site. By default, each virtual machine sees a pool of hosts, and it can run on any of them. That means that not long after you deploy virtual machines in the production site of a multi-site cluster, they can start Live Migrating or failing over to the DR site. But there is something you can do to limit this.

Each resource group, such as a virtual machine, in a cluster has a Preferred Owners setting. This setting instructs the cluster to attempt to fail over the configured virtual machine to the preferred nodes (hosts) first, and to use the nonpreferred hosts if there is no alternative. You could configure the Preferred Owners setting for each virtual machine.

In an active/passive multi-site cluster, the preferred owners would be the hosts in the production site. In the event of a host failure, the virtual machines will fail over to hosts with capacity in the production site. If you lose the production site, the virtual machines will fail over to the DR site.

In the case of an active/active multi-site cluster, the virtual machines in site A would prefer the hosts in site A, and the virtual machines in site B would prefer the hosts in site B.

You can also order the preferred ownership (hosting) of a virtual machine if you want to.

You can configure Preferred Owners in two ways. The first is to use Failover Clustering Manager:

1. Navigate into Roles, right-click a virtual machine, and choose Properties.

2. The Properties screen shown in Figure 11.14 appears. Select the check boxes for the hosts that are in the site that the virtual machine should normally be running in.

3. Clear the check boxes that should not be preferred hosts for this virtual machine.

4. You can order the preferred ownership of the virtual machine, ranging from most preferred to least preferred, by selecting a host and using the Up and Down buttons.

5. Click OK.

You might also take this opportunity to configure the failover priority (the Priority setting) while in this window. This subject was covered in Chapter 8; you can order the bootup of virtual machines after failover by using one of three buckets: high, medium, or low.

FIGURE 11.14
Configuring preferred owners for a virtual machine

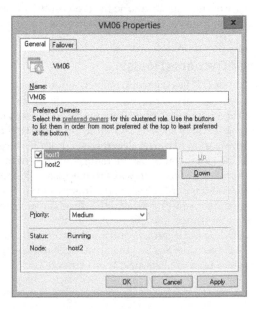

If you use Failover Clustering Manager only to manage the Hyper-V cluster and the virtual machines, this is a very good solution. However, an organization that is big enough to afford a multi-site cluster will probably put in a management system or a cloud such as System Center. If that's the case, there is some bad news. System Center 2012 Virtual Machine Manager pays no attention to the Preferred Owners setting when it performs Intelligent Placement during operations such as Dynamic Optimization (virtual workload balancing). That means it will start sending your virtual machines all over the cluster, turning your active/passive multi-site cluster into an active/active multi-site cluster. That will have implications on bandwidth, application performance, and possibly more.

Summarizing Multi-site Clusters

A multi-site cluster will create a hugely scalable DR solution. It is very much a storage salesperson's dream come true because it requires expensive storage, twice the normal amount of that storage, and maybe even additional licensing/hardware to enable synchronous replication. Your account manager in the ISP is also going to have a good day when you ask about networking for this solution.

You will end up with a fire-and-forget architecture, where virtual machines that are placed in site A will automatically appear in site B. That sounds like it is the ideal way to do DR for a cloud. It can give you completely automated failover of virtual machines after a disaster, having services back online within minutes, without waiting for any human intervention.

But there are complications. Management systems will see both sites in the cluster as a single compute cluster, placing virtual machines on the "best possible" host. And let's be honest: creating a stretched cluster creates a lot of moving parts that can drive up the cost of the cloud to unreasonable levels, way beyond the real risk of a disaster. Fortunately, Windows Server 2012 Hyper-V includes an alternative that you can consider.

Real World Solutions

Here are a number of possible solutions for real world problems that you might encounter.

Designing Hybrid DR

CHALLENGE

A customer has traditionally purchased servers and storage from a manufacturer called ABC for their Hyper-V cluster. They have a limited budget to do the following:

◆ Replace Windows Server 2008 R2 Hyper-V with Windows Server 2012 Hyper-V.

◆ Implement a new DR site.

After the purchasing process has completed, they have decided to acquire new server and storage hardware from manufacturer XYZ. How will you do the following?

◆ Upgrade the customer to a Windows Server 2012 Hyper-V cluster.

◆ Deploy their DR site by using storage from ABC and XYZ.

◆ Do this with a minimum of downtime.

SOLUTION

This will be a multi-phase project. The first consideration is that you cannot upgrade a cluster from one version of Windows Server to another; a side-by-side migration is required.

The first phase of the project will be to deploy the new hardware from XYZ in the production site beside the ABC hardware, and to build a new Hyper-V cluster on it. Test the new XYZ cluster to ensure that the build is stable.

Phase 2 of the project will be to migrate virtual machines from the old hardware to the new hardware. There are two ways to approach this:

Cluster Migration Wizard   Connect the XYZ cluster to the ABC SAN. You can then run the Cluster Migration Wizard to migrate the SAN LUNs and ABC virtual machines to the new XYZ cluster. Upgrade the virtual machine integration components, and then use Storage Live Migration to move the virtual machines' storage to the XYZ SAN. Finally, you can remove the old SAN from the XYZ cluster.

Export/Import   Using the Cluster Migration Wizard will require additional host bus adapters (HBAs) to connect to the old SAN, and this will drive up the cost. You could do a gradual export of virtual machines from the ABC cluster and import them to the XYZ cluster. Using System Center 2012 will speed up this process.

Phase 3 of the project will be to relocate the ABC cluster to the DR site and rebuild it with Windows Server 2012.

In phase 4, you will enable Hyper-V Replica and start to replicate virtual machines to the ABC cluster in the DR site.

The older hardware is providing the DR site infrastructure as an economical solution. The project is now complete, and the infrastructure is handed over to the administrators. Regular testing of the DR site should be conducted, using the test failover feature of HVR to verify that replication is successful and that the infrastructure is still functioning correctly.

Designing Hosted Disaster Recovery

CHALLENGE

You are employed by a company that is building a public cloud. The company wants to sell a multi-tenant virtual DR solution. It must be as economical as possible, must support heterogeneous hardware, and must offer as short an RTO as possible. How will you design this solution? Consider the following:

◆ Clustered or nonclustered hosts

◆ Storage

◆ Replication

◆ IP address allocation

◆ How to fail over lots of virtual machines in an ordered fashion

SOLUTION

The requirements state that the solution should be as economical as possible. This factor will reduce the cost of the solution for the customer and has an impact on two of the considerations:

Clustered or Nonclustered Hosts A feature of a virtualization cluster is additional host capacity to enable highly virtual machines to fail over from one host to another. The requirements did not stress high availability, but they did stress economy. By going with nonclustered hosts, we can remove the additional host capacity, and the associated hardware, licensing, rack space, networking, power, and maintenance costs. This in turn reduces the cost that must be passed on to the customer and makes the virtual DR offering more attractive to customers that have a lower budget for their BCP.

Storage Shared storage, such as a SAN, is the most expensive storage available. The hosting company could use internal disk or DAS for the nonclustered hosts. Shared-Nothing Live Migration could be used to move virtual machines from one host to another if preventative maintenance was required. Another economical storage option would be to use SMB 3.0 file shares. This would cost more than DAS, but it would allow Live Migration without the need to move storage, thus reducing the time to move workloads around the datacenter.

A hosted virtual DR site cannot assume that customers have specific models of server or storage; this rules out SAN-based replication. Host-based replication must be used, but this also cannot depend on any third-party products, for the following reasons:

◆ They add cost.

◆ Customers may have different preferences.

Hyper-V Replica is built into Windows Server 2012 and can be used to replicate Hyper-V virtual machines at no extra cost. It is designed to use SSL for secure replication to service providers and is the perfect way to offer a hosted virtual DR solution.

Although Hyper-V Replica does have IP address injection during failover of virtual machines, the best solution in a hosted virtual DR site is to use Windows Server 2012 Network Virtualization. This can be defined by policy (using System Center 2012) by the DR site administrators. It is also more scalable and automatable than IP address injection.

There are ways to invoke the DR plan and fail over lots of virtual machines in a specific order:

◆ PowerShell scripts can be written to order the failover of virtual machines.

◆ System Center 2012 can be used to orchestrate the failover of virtual machines in the required order.

## Chapter 12

Hyper-V Replica

The virtualization world was rocked when Microsoft announced Hyper-V Replica (HVR) at the Worldwide Partner Conference in 2011. Not only was it the very first feature of Windows Server 2012 that was announced, but it offered something that nothing else did: host-based replication in the hypervisor at no extra cost. This means that a Hyper-V customer can use Hyper-V Replica to replicate running virtual machines using the free Hyper-V Server 2012, and Hyper-V on Standard and Datacenter editions of Windows Server 2012. HVR was designed to abstract hardware and to work on commercial broadband. These factors alone made it attractive to a number of audiences. Now you will read why Hyper-V was declared a killer feature.

In this chapter, you'll learn about

◆   What the Hyper-V Replica feature provides

◆   How Hyper-V Replica works

◆   How to use Hyper-V Replica

DISASTER RECOVERY IS NOT HIGH AVAILABILITY

Hyper-V Replica is designed for site-to-site DR asynchronous replication, where one site has a slightly older copy of the virtual machines. It is not intended to be an alternative to a cluster inside a single site. Microsoft knew very early on that many would confuse this, implement Hyper-V Replica in ways it was not intended to be used, and have unexpected results. That's why Microsoft is very clear on this: do not use Hyper-V Replica as an alternative to a cluster. If you need highly available virtual machines in a site, you deploy a Hyper-V cluster.

Introducing Hyper-V Replica

Hyper-V Replica is a host-based virtual machine replication solution that is built into all editions of Windows Server 2012 Hyper-V, including the free Hyper-V Server 2012. Hyper-V Replica does not require any special licensing; it is free and there to be used if you choose to. It will replicate running virtual machines from one site to another, and allow you to perform planned, unplanned, and test failovers of those virtual machines. This section introduces you to Hyper-V Replica.

How Hyper-V Replica Works

Understanding how HVR works will help you decide whether it is suitable for your design, and how to correctly configure it. Figure 12.1 illustrates a simple HVR scenario from a high level.

FIGURE 12.1
An illustration of
Hyper-V Replica

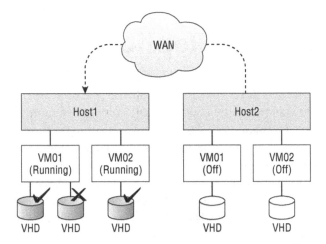

1. Host2 is configured to enable inward replication. The replication is authenticated either by Active Directory or X.509 v3 certificates.

2. In the production site, you enable replication for individual virtual machines on Host1. Virtual hard disks can be excluded. This gives the BCP some level of granularity over what is replicated, conserving replication bandwidth and DR host/storage capacity.

3. The virtual machines are synchronized (the initial copy) to Host2 in the DR site. This process creates a complete copy of each virtual machine, and there are different methods for dealing with bandwidth limitations. After the synchronization is complete, asynchronous replication begins.

4. Hyper-V tracks the block-level changes of each virtual hard disk to a Hyper-V Replica Log (HRL) for that virtual hard disk.

5. Every 5 minutes, Hyper-V will swap out the active HRL for a new HRL. The old HRL is replayed across the WAN to host Host2 in reverse order, eliminating the redundant replication of a block that has changed more than once during the last 5 minutes. The transmitted data is compressed by default.

6. The virtual machines are duplicated on Host2, where they are kept in a powered-down state.

7. A preconfigured number (up to 15) of historical hourly snapshots of a virtual machine can be maintained on the replica host. This snapshot can be application consistent.

8. Administrators can perform a planned or an unplanned failover to start the virtual machines on Host2; there is no automated failover. A test failover can also be conducted on Host2 to test the BCP without impacting the production virtual machines and the

offline replicas. The failover can be done with the current state of the replica or by using one of the optional historical copies.

9. After recovering from a disaster, administrators can reverse replication and fail the virtual machines back to the original production site.

That's a high-level view of what is going on when you use HVR. There is much more detail, as you will soon see.

Target Markets for Hyper-V Replica

You might think, "Oh, here we go! Another solution for the Fortune 1000s," but HVR really was designed for various markets:

The Small Business It is safe to say that the multi-site cluster is well outside the budget of small organizations, and software solutions are usually expensive too. HVR is free, so that checks an important box for the SME. HVR was also designed to work with commercial broadband, with all the problems that it has. HVR does not perform automated failover, so an ISP outage will not cause a split-brain scenario. HVR also uses asynchronous replication, which is suitable for cheaper, latent connections. HVR enables us to be very selective with what is being replicated, and that can conserve bandwidth.

The Mid-Sized Enterprise Organizations of this size sometimes want to deploy a DR site in another office that they have on the other side of a campus or in another city. Sometimes they want those sites to provide mutual DR, where site A is the DR site for site B, and vice versa. These sites might have very different hosts and storage. HVR doesn't care; it will happily replicate from one Windows Server 2012 Hyper-V host to another, including Hyper-V Server 2012.

The Large Enterprise HVR wasn't originally designed for large enterprises, but Microsoft quickly discovered that there was demand for the new feature. Although large enterprises might be happy with SAN replication for the central datacenters, branch offices continue to be a problem. Supporting SAN-based replication from the branch office to central datacenters is impossible for several reasons. Some branch offices have purchasing autonomy; they're buying all kinds of storage. That means the datacenter must buy matching heterogeneous storage, which complicates purchasing and requires acquiring more staff for the necessary skills. Synchronous replication requires low-latency links, which is impossible if the branch office is halfway across the continent. And some branch offices just aren't big enough for SANs, so that rules out that kind of replication. A hypervisor that is built into the operating system licensing and that includes host-based, hardware-agnostic replication is just what the large enterprise needs to solve these problems.

You might question the suitability of HVR in the large enterprise if HVR was in fact designed to meet the needs of the SME. However, HVR scales out (with some planning), and with System Center or even PowerShell, provides very high levels of automation.

SME IT Service Provider Most SMEs have a single site. These businesses often rely entirely on their IT service providers for anything beyond basic IT skills. These consultants usually have intimate knowledge of their customers' environments, and applications are in the best position to offer custom-engineered hosted DR service to the customer. With HVR, the service provider can build a central Hyper-V server and replicate numerous customers over the

Internet by using SSL authentication for secure access. After the service is proven, central Hyper-V infrastructure can be scaled out to include more customers.

Hosting Companies   In Chapter 5, "Cloud Computing," you read how to build a multi-tenant cloud by using Windows Server 2012 and Hyper-V. Hosting companies can use these techniques, in combination with Hyper-V Replica, to build and sell Disaster Recovery as a Service (DRaaS). Businesses can use self-service to turn on their DR site in the cloud. They then can configure Hyper-V Replica, possibly even using a tool (provided by the hosting company) that will do the engineering work for them.

Hyper-V Replica Requirements

The requirements for Hyper-V Replica are short and sweet. The source and replica hosts must be running one of the following:

◆ Windows Server 2012 Standard/Datacenter Hyper-V

◆ Hyper-V Server 2012

The source and replica hosts must be able to mutually authenticate for security reasons, so they must do one of the following:

◆ Be in the same Active Directory forest

◆ Import mutually trusting X.509 v3 certificates

The virtual machine's operating system is irrelevant to replication, so you can use any working guest OS, but remember that you have to stick to the supported guest OS list if you expect to get help from Microsoft.

To get application-consistent historical replicas of a virtual machine, you will need current Hyper-V Integration Components (Services) to be installed in the guest operating system of that virtual machine. Volume Shadow Copy Service (VSS) is used to create a snapshot that will provide application consistency. That means you need a supported version of Windows as the guest OS for this feature.

Bandwidth Requirements

In the ideal situation, a dedicated link exists between the production and DR sites. This will allow replication to use all available bandwidth without interfering with production systems.

BANDWIDTH VS. LATENCY

Bandwidth and latency are two different things. Latency is a measure, in milliseconds, of how fast a packet travels from the source to the destination. It is important for synchronous replication and cluster heartbeats. Bandwidth measures, in bits per second, how much traffic we can send through a network connection at once. The bigger the pipe, the bigger the packet and the data section of the packet can be.

The link can be slow or latent. HVR uses asynchronous replication, so you can replicate virtual machines between points on opposite ends of the planet.

The million-dollar question is: how much bandwidth is required? The amount of bandwidth will dictate whether virtual machines can be replicated, and how many. The answer is one of those consultant classics: it depends. Every site, even every virtual machine, will be different. Here is one method that is being recommended to *estimate* the requirements:

1. Determine the amount of data being backed up every day (X) and the time frame during which most of that data is being created.

2. Calculate the number of 5-minute windows in the time frame (Y). Divide X by Y to estimate the amount of data that is created every 5 minutes.

3. Use that to determine how much upload bandwidth will be required in the production site, and how much download bandwidth will be required in the DR site.

Here is an example of how to use this method to calculate the bandwidth requirements for Hyper-V Replica: say a company works between 09:00 and 18:00. There are 108 5-minute windows in that time frame. An analysis of the incremental backups has shown that an average of 20 GB of new data is created every day. That means that each 5-minute window needs to be able to replicate an *average* (allow for spikes) of 189.63 MB of data. You might round this up to 200 MB. The replication link must provide sufficient bandwidth for this transfer rate to ensure that the data logged in an HRL (5-minute window) is replicated before the next HRL is lined up for replication.

Make sure you leave some room for error, because this is an estimate. You should also consult with the directors of the organization to find out whether they are planning substantial growth. It would be a shame if you locked yourself into one kind of network connection that wasn't scalable, only to find you needed to add another contract a few months later, making the original one redundant.

What Can You Replicate Between?

HVR does not care what kind of storage your virtual machines are stored on. It takes advantage of the abstraction that virtualization gives us and it just works with virtual machines and virtual hard disks. That means you can replicate virtual machines between any kinds of storage that are supported by your Windows Server 2012 Hyper-V host.

WHAT VIRTUAL MACHINE STORAGE IS SUPPORTED BY HYPER-V REPLICA?

Hyper-V Replica logs the modifications to blocks in virtual hard disks. This includes both VHD and VHDX. Pass-through disks cannot be replicated by using HVR. This is one of many reasons to stop deploying pass-through disks and switch to VHDX with its 64 TB scalability.

You might use passthrough disks as the shared storage of a guest cluster (a cluster created using virtual machines). You will not be able to replicate this shared storage using HVR. You should consider using virtualized storage if you need to replicate a guest cluster.

HVR checks another important box: you can replicate between hosts in the scenarios shown in Table 12.1.

TABLE 12.1: Hyper-V replication between hosts

SOURCE HOST TYPE	DESTINATION HOST TYPE
Nonclustered host	Nonclustered host
Hyper-V cluster	Hyper-V cluster
Nonclustered host	Hyper-V cluster
Hyper-V cluster	Nonclustered host

Replication can be set up between the following:

◆ One source host/cluster and a single replica host/cluster

◆ Many source hosts/clusters to a single replica host/cluster

In fact, because replication policies are configured per virtual machine, you can replicate VM01 from Host1 to Host2 and VM02 from Host1 to Host3, getting a 1-to-N solution. If you are so inclined, you could design a very complicated N-to-M solution.

The only limitations are as follows:

◆ You cannot replicate virtual machines from one host to another host *in the same* cluster. That makes a lot of sense, considering that a cluster has "single shared storage," even if that shared storage is replicated from one site to another.

◆ You can replicate a virtual machine to only a single destination (host or cluster).

AFTER THE DISASTER

It is quite a success story when a business is able to use a DR site to recover from a disaster. The DR site is a short-term solution. It is usually a smaller location, sufficient for skeleton-crew operations, and there might be an additional cost to occupying that site. The BCP should have been written with a long-term view, planning not only to get to the DR site but also how to get from the DR site back to a production site.

Eventually, the insurance company will pay for the damage done, and the company can start making its way back to the old site or to a new site. After an infrastructure is in place, Hyper-V Replica can be used to reverse replication and perform a smooth, planned failover to the new infrastructure.

The likelihood is that whatever infrastructure was purchased originally for the production and the DR site will no longer be what is sold by the manufacturers. Although this could be a huge issue for other architectures, such as a multi-site cluster, the hardware abstraction of HVR will not care about this and will continue to function as required.

HVR gives you a lot of flexibility. For example, an SME might want to deploy a cluster with a Scale-Out File Server in its production site, but save on costs by deploying nonclustered hosts with DAS in its DR site. A hosting company can purchase economical nonclustered hosts without having to consider what hardware their customers (whom they have almost no human interaction with) are using.

At this point, you should have an understanding of what HVR can do. You will now start to look at how to use HVR so you can learn more about what it can do.

Enabling Hyper-V Replica between Nonclustered Hosts

In the simplest HVR scenario, you replicate between two nonclustered hosts in the same Active Directory forest. This section demonstrates and explains this scenario: Host1 is going to replicate three virtual machines (VM01, VM02, and VM03) to Host2, in another site, via a secure site-to-site VPN link.

By default, a Hyper-V host is configured to block (Windows Firewall) and reject (authentication) attempts to replicate virtual machines to it. You must enable any hosts in the DR site to accept replication attempts from other hosts.

The first step in enabling inward replication on Host2 is to enable Hyper-V Replica in the host settings:

1. Verify that both Host1 and Host2 can resolve each other's names in DNS.

2. Launch Hyper-V Manager, right-click the host, and select Hyper-V Settings. You will see the screen shown in Figure 12.2.

FIGURE 12.2
Enable Hyper-V Replica on a nonclustered host.

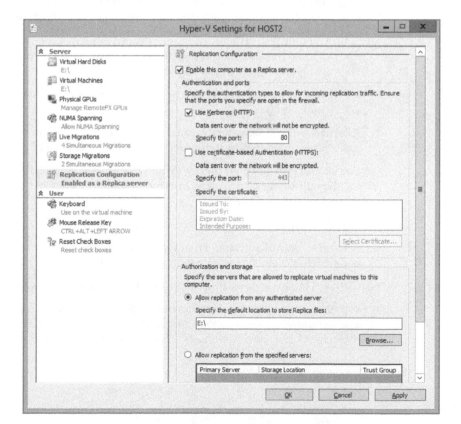

3. Select the Enable This Computer As A Replica Server check box.

There are two authentication types in HVR to mutually authenticate the source and replica hosts. If you are replicating between two hosts in the same Active Directory forest, and over a secure link, you should choose the Use Kerberos (HTTP) option. By default, this will replicate over port TCP 80. You can change this to another TCP port.

You would select the option to Use Certificate-Based Authentication (HTTPS) if you needed to replicate virtual machines in one of these situations:

◆ Between hosts that are not in the same Active Directory forest

◆ Over an insecure link

Using HTTPS will require an X.509 v3 certificate to perform the mutual authentication instead of Kerberos.

4. In this case, we are replicating between hosts in the same forest over a secure link, so select the Use Kerberos (HTTP) check box under Authentication And Ports, and leave the Specify The Port option set to 80.

You can configure if and how source hosts are authenticated under Authorization And Storage. You can configure a one-size-fits-all policy that accepts replication from all hosts that can authorize via Kerberos or via certificate trust. This would store the replica virtual machines on a single location on the replica host. This simple approach could be appropriate if both of these statements are true:

◆ You have complete control over the entire IT infrastructure, and no one can create a rogue Hyper-V host in your network.

◆ There will be a simple storage policy that uses just a single volume to store all replica virtual machines.

Alternatively, policies can be created to allow replication from only specified hosts. Each policy can use a different storage location on the replica host for each source host.

You should not store your replica virtual machines on the C: drive. You don't want to accidentally fill the C: drive and break your management OS. Use a dedicated volume for storing your virtual machines.

In this example, we will have a one-size-fits-all policy.

5. Select the Allow Replication From Any Authenticated Server radio button. Specify the path where the replica virtual machines will be stored—the E: drive, for example.

6. Click OK to save your settings and close the Hyper-V Settings dialog box.

A pop-up dialog box appears, shown in Figure 12.3, informing you that you must configure the firewall to allow inbound replication. This applies to any firewalls you have on the network and the replica hosts' Windows Firewall, which is turned on by default.

FIGURE 12.3
A reminder for you
to configure the
firewall for inbound
replication

Windows Firewall has two inbound rules (see Figure 12.4), and you must enable at least one of them, depending on the authentication that you have just configured:

◆ Hyper-V Replica HTTP Listener (TCP-In): Enable this rule if the replica host is using Kerberos/HTTP authentication.

◆ Hyper-V Replica HTTPS Listener (TCP-In): Turn this rule on if the replica host will use SSL/HTTPS authentication.

Note that the rules are configured to use the default ports for HTTP and HTTPS. You will need to create new rules if you used custom ports.

FIGURE 12.4
The two Hyper-V
Replica Windows
Firewall rules.

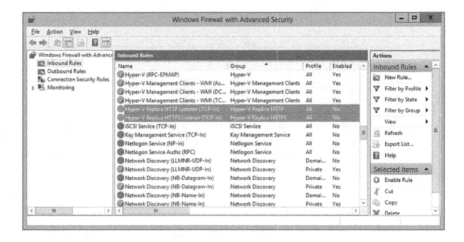

7. To enable the required rule for this example, open Windows Firewall on Host2. Right-click the Hyper-V Replica HTTP Listener (TCP-In) rule and select Enable.

Don't forget to configure any network firewalls to also allow the required ports (HTTP or HTTPS) from the source hosts to the replica hosts.

You can use Telnet to help you verify end-to-end communications on the source host.

8. Log in to Host1 and run the following at the command prompt:

```
Telnet Host2 80
```

The Command Prompt screen should quickly turn blank if a connection is formed. There is a connectivity issue if Telnet appears to time out and you can resolve the hostname for Host2 via DNS from Host1.

Host2 is now configured to accept replicas from all authorized Hyper-V hosts, using Kerberos (encapsulated in HTTP), and to store the replicas on the root of the E: drive.

The next step is to configure replication. You can enable inbound replication on the replica host by using PowerShell instead of the Hyper-V Manager:

```
Set-VMReplicationServer -ReplicationEnabled $True -AllowedAuthenticationType `
Kerberos -ReplicationAllowedFromAnyServer $True -DefaultStorageLocation E:\
```

The syntax is as follows:

◆ `ReplicationEnabled`: `$True` will enable replication, and `$False` will disable replication to this host.

◆ `AllowedAuthenticationType`: This will configure the type of authentication. The values can be `Kerberos`, `Certificate`, or `CertificateAndKerberos`.

◆ `ReplicationAllowedFromAnyServer`: Once again, we use `$True` or `$False` to enable or disable replication from any authenticated server.

◆ `DefaultStorageLocation`: Configure where the replica virtual machines will be stored if we allow replication from any authenticated server.

FIND ALL OF THE HYPER-V REPLICA POWERSHELL CMDLETS

You can quickly find all of the PowerShell cmdlets for Hyper-V Replica by running the following two commands:

```
get-command -Module hyper-v | where {$_.Name -like "*replication*"}
get-command -Module hyper-v | where {$_.Name -like "*failover*"}
```

The next line of PowerShell will configure the Windows Firewall for Kerberos/HTTP authentication:

```
Enable-NetFirewallRule -DisplayName "Hyper-V Replica HTTP Listener (TCP-In)"
```

You can disable the firewall rule by using the same parameters with the `Disable -NetFirewallRule` PowerShell cmdlet.

Imagine how quickly you could configure 10 or 100 hosts for HVR with a script that contains just two lines of PowerShell!

Enabling Virtual Machine Replication

Virtual machine replication is enabled on a per-machine and per-virtual hard disk basis. In this section, you are going to replicate three virtual machines from Host1 to Host2, each using a different method to perform the initial copy.

Understanding Copy Methods

HVR must copy the entire virtual hard disks that are selected for replication before the more efficient change-only block-level replication can begin. By using this approach, the replica is ready for failover, be it planned, unplanned, or a test. There are three ways to send the initial replica of virtual machines from the source host to the replica host:

Send Initial Copy over the Network   If you choose this option, by default, HVR will copy the virtual machine to the replica server over the replication network. This copy method is the simplest, but also the least usable in environments with limited upload bandwidth from the production or source site. An organization with a dedicated replication link with ample bandwidth might like this option because it is simple to use.

There is a suboption to delay the initial copy until a specific date and time. You could use this to delay the copy until the evening, when there is less demand on the Internet connection.

An organization that has a bandwidth bottleneck on its replication link should choose one of the other two options.

The major benefit of this solution is that it is simple; you do not need to mess with backups or removable media, and there is no physical presence required in the DR site.

Send Initial Copy by Using External Media   This option creates an online export of a virtual machine to a location of your choice, such as a USB drive. The removable media can then be transported to the DR site where the virtual machine is imported. This method would be used when a company has a number of virtual machines to copy and it could take days or weeks to complete. Obviously, this is a good method for the SME, but it could also be a good solution for a larger enterprise with *many* terabytes of data to synchronize. It is expected that this will be a widely adopted approach for sending the initial replica.

The removable media should be encrypted. Company applications, data, passwords, and other sensitive information are leaving the secure confines of the computer room or data-center and are traveling by road/air to a remote location. Any lost or stolen information could cause a lot of trouble for the organization, especially if the data contains employee or customer information. Windows Server 2012 includes BitLocker To Go, which can be used to secure removable media with AES disk encryption. You could use alternative encryption products for removable media.

Note that this method might be impossible in some situations for procedural reasons. For example, a virtual DR site might be hosted in a very secure datacenter that will not accept removable media for security reasons.

Use an Existing Virtual Machine on the Replica Server as the Initial Copy   Microsoft warns us to be careful with this option because it will be very easy to get wrong.

Many organizations have replicated, and will continue to replicate, their backups to a DR site. For example, they might back up to a DPM server in the production site, and it replicates the backup data and the metadata to a replica DPM server in the DR site.

If the backup data is already in the DR site, it would be possible to restore the virtual machines from the backup and use that as the initial seed for synchronization. When HVR is enabled for the virtual machine, a fix-up is done to synchronize the restored virtual machine in the DR site with the active virtual machine in the production site.

This method will reduce the amount of synchronization traffic, but the removable media option still has a much lesser impact on the replication link.

You must be very careful with this method. If you want to synchronize VM3, you must restore VM3 from backup. You *should not* restore VM1, because it is similar to VM3. You *should not* restore a virtual machine template that VM3 was based on. You will have corruption if you do not restore VM3 to synchronize VM3.

Replicating a Virtual Machine with Network Copy

In this section, you will replicate VM01 by using a copy over the network. You will then repeat the process, skipping the repeated steps, to replicate VM02 and VM03 by using the alternative copy methods. Follow these steps:

1. Log in to Host1, open Hyper-V Manager, select VM01, right-click, and select Enable Replication. The Enable Replication Wizard opens.

2. In Specify Replica Server, enter the name of the server that you want to replicate to. Use the verified fully qualified domain name (FQDN) of the replica host if it is not in the same domain.

3. HVR will verify the configuration for a few moments, before proceeding to the Specify Connection Parameters screen, shown in Figure 12.5. The replica host, Host2, is configured for HTTP, so we will choose the default Authentication Type of Use Kerberos Authentication (HTTP).

FIGURE 12.5
Specify connection parameters for HTTP.

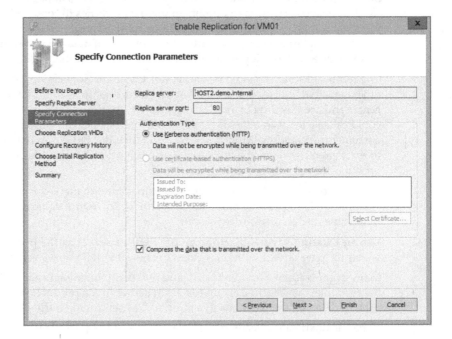

At the bottom of the Specify Connection Parameters screen is an option to Compress The Data That Is Transmitted Over The Network. Normally this will be left enabled to reduce the amount of bandwidth required for the replication of this virtual machine.

You would want to disable HVR compression in one circumstance: if you have network traffic de-duplication/acceleration appliances (such as those sold by Riverbed Technology or Citrix), they can have a greater impact on bandwidth reduction if HVR compression is turned off. That will allow the appliances to optimize the traffic by using de-duplication from multiple hosts over a longer time frame.

This screen is also where you would configure a certificate that mutually trusts the certificate on the replica host if you were using HTTPS authentication. We will cover that option later in the chapter.

4. You can choose which virtual hard disks you want to replicate in the Choose Replication VHDs screen, shown in Figure 12.6.

FIGURE 12.6
Choose the VHDs to replicate.

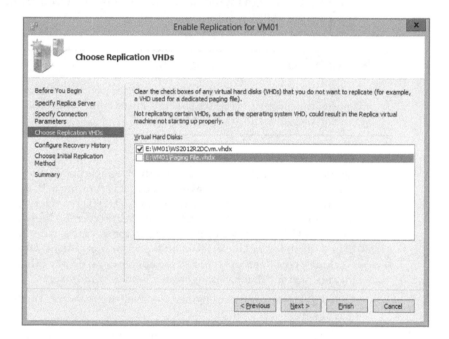

Microsoft has a few useful suggestions for this screen to help reduce the amount of replication traffic and to reduce the space required in the DR site when it is not active (most of the time, if you remember that you should test from time to time):

Isolate Paging Files   The paging file is constantly changing. That means a paging file in a replicated VHD is constantly causing blocks of that VHD to be logged in a HRL and replayed to the DR site. You can start a virtual machine and its applications without a guest OS paging file *if* the virtual machine can acquire enough memory from the host. The virtual machine might not have optimal performance, but it will function. You could add a VHD to the virtual machine (using the IDE controller), and configure a paging file (requiring a reboot) afterward if the virtual machine was to stay operational in the DR site for a sustained length of time.

Most organizations would be willing to accept this temporary drop in performance of their virtual workloads if it gave them a reliable and cost-effective DR solution. In this case, the VHD that is used for the paging file would not be selected for replication.

Note that you will need to reconfigure (requiring a reboot) existing virtual machines if they use the default location (%systemroot%) for the paging file before you configure the HVR policy.

This approach could work in a true self-service cloud if the template virtual machines could be deployed with the paging file placed on an alternative drive. However, there is a risk that the users of the virtual machine will see a disk that they can store data on, and that data won't be replicated. The only way to prevent that would be to make the drive just big enough for the paging file, and prevent it from being extended through the cloud's service catalog portal.

PAGING FILE AND CRASH DUMPS

Up to Windows Server 2003/R2 and Windows XP, the paging file had to be on the %systemroot% volume for the operating system to be able to create crash dump files. This is not a requirement in Windows Server 2008 R2/Vista and newer.

Replicate Only Data Drives   An alternative suggestion is to replicate only data drives. An example might be a virtual machine that is running SQL Server. The first VHD (C:) contains the operating system. The second VHD (D:) contains the SQL Server database files, and the third VHD (E:) contains the SQL Server log files. In this example, you could configure HVR to replicate just the D: and the E: VHDs. After invocation, you would have to deploy template VHDs with the operating systems, attach them to the virtual machines, boot them up, reinstall the applications, do any other customizations/updating, reattach any databases, re-create file shares, and so on.

This option creates a very engineering-intensive recovery. The BCP would have to allow maybe several days' RTO.

This is not a cloud-friendly option either, because the user will have administrative rights, and you can almost guarantee that they will store important business data on the C: drive, no matter what policies are communicated.

Realistically, although this option will reduce the amount of synchronized data, it provides little improvement over the isolated paging file option.

You might want to keep your VHD selection as simple as possible if you want non-complex automation and a quick RTO with no dependency on engineering effort after the disaster. If that is the case, select all of the VHDs, assuming that you do have the required bandwidth.

5. The Configure Recovery History screen, shown in Figure 12.7, allows you to specify whether Hyper-V recovery points (which are Hyper-V snapshots) of the replicated virtual machines should be retained on the replica host. And if you do enable this feature, you can set the number of snapshots that should be retained. The default is Only The Latest Recovery Point, which will retain no historical snapshots in the DR site.

In this example, the Additional Recovery Points option is enabled and the maximum of 15 snapshots will be retained. Note that it will require an estimated *additional* 12.9 GB of space on the replica server's storage.

Using this feature means that an administrator can choose which one of the snapshots to use when performing a failover. For instance, say a disaster affected some virtual machines 2 hours ago, and some 1 hour ago, and some were not affected at all. An administrator could bring back all the virtual machines by using a snapshot from 3 hours ago to get as close to a consistent set of data as possible.

Maintaining Additional Recovery Points will incur a cost in terms of IOPS and storage space in the DR site. This is covered in detail later in this chapter.

6. Still in the Configure Recovery History screen (see Figure 12.7), the Replicate Incremental VSS Copy Every option has been set to every 2 hours.

FIGURE 12.7
Configure the
recovery history.

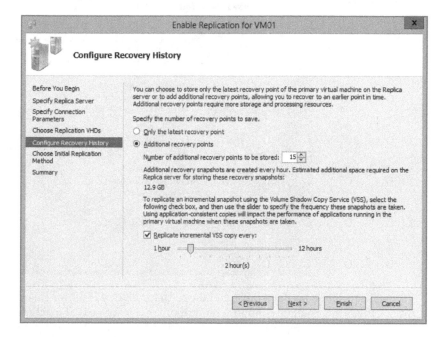

If you have a need for application consistency (SQL Server, Exchange Server, and so on) for the additional recovery points, you should choose the option to replicate incremental VSS copies.

This will use VSS to put the virtual machine and its VSS-compatible guest applications into a quiescent state (see Chapter 10, "Backup and Recovery" to learn more about Hyper-V and VSS). Doing this too often might cause performance issues for the virtual machine's workload. That is why we have an option to create an application-consistent snapshot by using a sliding scale, from every hour to every 12 hours. You can move this slider to strike a balance between getting more application-consistent historical snapshots and better application performance.

In our example, we are keeping 15 snapshots of the virtual machine's replicated VHDs. By replicating a VSS copy every 2 hours, every second one of those snapshots will actually be a VSS snapshot.

7. The next step in the wizard is to choose how the initial copy of the virtual machine will be done (see Figure 12.8). In this example, choose Send Initial Copy Over The Network. With this option, you can see that Start Replication Immediately is selected by default; the synchronization will start after you complete the wizard and the HVR connection to Host2 is successful. You can choose the alternative Start Replication On option to delay the synchronization until a desired date and time. This uses the usual Microsoft date/time selection tools.

FIGURE 12.8
The Choose Initial Replication Method screen

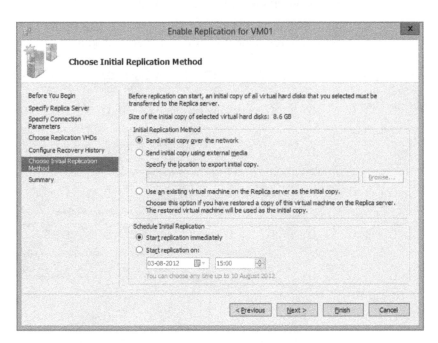

That completes the wizard and the configuration of HVR for this virtual machine.

If you are going to configure replication for a lot of virtual machines, you might want to use PowerShell for a rapid and consistent configuration. The following cmdlet will configure VM01 to replicate exactly as was just shown in the GUI:

```
Enable-VMReplication -VMName VM01 -ReplicaServerName "host2.demo.internal" `
-ReplicaServerPort 80 -AuthenticationType Kerberos -RecoveryHistory 15 `
-VSSSnapshotFrequency 2 -ExcludedVhdPath "E:\VM01\Paging File.vhdx"
```

You can change the replication configuration of a virtual machine by using Set-VMReplication. The initial copy will not begin until you instruct it to

```
Start-VMInitialReplication -VMName VM01
```

You could have added –InitialReplicationStartTime "08/08/2014 08:08 AM" to the Set-VMReplication cmdlet to set up the initial copy to automatically start at a later date and time.

During the copy, the following will happen:

1. HVR will create a snapshot of VM01 on Host1, called `VM01 - Initial Replica` with a date/time stamp in the title.

2. Now HVR is free to copy the desired VHD to Host2, because VM01 is locking the snapshot's AVHD instead.

3. The snapshot is merged (live) back into the original VHD(s) after the copy is complete.

4. Over on Host2, the virtual machine appears. It is powered off and has a snapshot called `VM01 - Initial Replica` with a date/time stamp. If we were to fail over, we could choose this snapshot as the point in time to return to. Up to 15 snapshots will be retained for this virtual machine on Host2.

At this point, the virtual machine will start the replication process by using the HRL.

The way that the virtual machine is stored on the replica host, Host2, will look quite unfamiliar. On the E: drive is a folder called *Hyper-V Replica*. It has four subfolders:

Planned Virtual Machines stores any virtual machine that you do a planned failover for.

Snapshots stores the snapshots that are the historical copies of the virtual machines.

Virtual Hard Disks stores the replicated VHDs.

Virtual Machines stores the XML files for the virtual machines.

Each of those folders has a subfolder that is named after the GUID of VM01 (as it is on Host2): 553EF368-C19A-4005-B725-CE9E2F589801, with the exception of snapshots that have their own GUID. Those subfolders are where the files for VM01 are stored, with one exception; the XML for the virtual machine (named after the GUID) is stored in the root of the Virtual Machines subfolder.

Although this approach to folder placement and naming might be unfriendly to us humans, it offers a big advantage. HVR can do N-to-1 replication. Another host, Host3, could be added and it could replicate another virtual machine, also called VM01. HVR will accept this and use the GUID for VM01 instead of the virtual machine name for the folder. This makes the folder structure of HVR very scalable and suitable for the large enterprise (distributed management with centralized DR) for service providers (multi-tenant DR).

USING ALTERNATIVE FOLDER NAMES ON THE REPLICA HOST

You might not want to use the default GUID approach because you have a virtual machine naming standard and are not creating a multi-tenant DR site. In that case, have a look at this blog post by Rahul Razdan of Microsoft:

```
http://blogs.technet.com/b/virtualization/archive/2012/07/20/hvr-powershell-
series-don-t-want-replica-folder-names-as-guids.aspx
```

In the post, you will see how to use a PowerShell script to enable inbound replication to a folder structure that is based on virtual machine names instead of GUIDs.

Replicating a Virtual Machine with Removable Media

The process for replicating a virtual machine by using removable media for the initial copy starts just as it would with a network copy. This exercise demonstrates the removable media copy method with a virtual machine called VM02:

1. Launch the Enable Replication Wizard on Host1, select VM02, and configure replication for the virtual machine until you reach the Choose Initial Replication Method screen, shown in Figure 12.9. There, things change.

FIGURE 12.9
Using external media for the initial copy

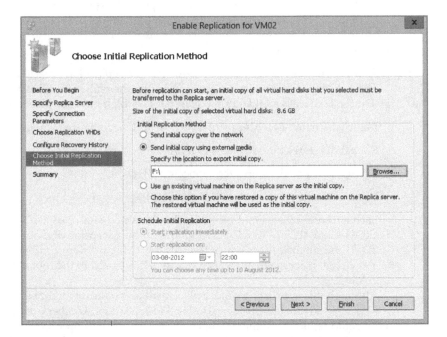

2. Plug a removable media device, such as a USB drive, into the host that the virtual machine is hosted on (Host1). Do not plug the drive into your local machine if you are doing this work remotely, because it won't be accessible to the host. This disk really should be encrypted.

3. Type in or browse to the path of the drive (optionally with a subfolder) that will be used to transport the virtual machine.

4. Complete the wizard.

   If you opened up Hyper-V Manager on Host1, you would see that VM02 has a status of Sending Initial Replica. The send is to the USB drive; no VHD data is being sent to Host2. No replication will take place until you have imported the virtual machine on Host2.

   A folder is created on the root of the USB drive, named after the virtual machine with a GUID to make it unique. In this example, the folder was called VM02_42A162A6-1F01-4211-9A0E-EB69B4FFED96. The virtual machine files are exported into this folder. This export process may take some time because you are using slow, removable media, especially if you are configuring a number of virtual machines at once.

5. Monitor the status of the virtual machine in Hyper-V Manager or by using PowerShell (Get-VM -VM VM02) to see when the export is finished. You cannot proceed until it has.

6. Transport the USB drive to Host2 and plug it in. If the drive is encrypted, make it usable. For example, enter the secure password when prompted.

7. Log in to Host2. A copy of VM02 is present, but it is not synchronized. Right-click the virtual machine for which you want to complete the copy and choose Replication ➢ Import Initial Replica. The Import Initial Replication dialog box appears.

8. Either type or browse to the folder that contains the exported copy of the virtual machine and then click Complete Initial Replication.

SETTING UP BITLOCKER TO GO

It is strongly recommended that you encrypt any removable media that is used for transporting virtual machine files, such as a Hyper-V initial copy. BitLocker To Go is the AES-based removable media encryption that was introduced in Windows 7 Enterprise/Ultimate and Windows Server 2008 R2. It is also in Windows 8 Pro/Enterprise and Windows Server 2012. Being built-in, secure, and free makes it a viable solution. BitLocker To Go will require you to enable the BitLocker feature in Server Manager if you are using Windows Server. You can configure a drive for BitLocker To Go as follows:

1. Plug the removable media, such as a USB drive, into a physical machine with a supporting operating system.

2. Open File Explorer, right-click the USB drive, and select Turn On BitLocker.

3. There are two ways to unlock the drive for usage. You can use a smart card, but the best option in this scenario is to use a password. The disk might be sent by courier to a remote site. Physically sending the key to unlock the disk (password or smart card) would not be smart. A password can be shared securely via some electronic means.

4. A recovery key enables the disk to be accessed if the password is lost. You can save it to file or print it. Restrict access to this key and store it securely.

5. You have two ways to encrypt. If this is a new disk, the most suitable (and quickest-to-deploy) way is to encrypt new data as it is added to disk. If the disk already contains data, you need to use the slower approach that encrypts the entire disk.

6. Monitor the BitLocker Drive Encryption dialog box to see when the disk is encrypted and ready to use.

7. When you plug the encrypted disk into a machine, it will remain locked (visible by a locked padlock icon) and inaccessible until you unlock it with a password (the padlock icon unlocks too).

Now you have a USB drive that is encrypted using BitLocker To Go.

USING RAID-ENABLED REMOVABLE MEDIA

If you are transporting a very large amount of data, paying a lot to get it transported, or facing time pressures, you might want to use removable media that has disk fault tolerance (RAID). It would be a shame to use a nontolerant drive, have it arrive in the DR site, and find that the disk is dead or the data is corrupted, only to have to repeat the entire costly and time-consuming process. If you are facing time pressures, keep in mind that a RAID-5 disk is going to be much slower than a RAID 1/10 disk during the export process.

The status of the virtual machine changes to Import Initial Replica with a progress report expressed as a percentage. The process is complete after the import is done.

At the time of writing this book, we were unable to find or re-create a way of duplicating this synchronization method by using PowerShell.

Replicating a Virtual Machine with Offsite Recovery

The process for replicating a virtual machine by using media virtual machine recovery (from backup) for the initial copy starts just as it would with a network copy. We are going to demonstrate the offsite recovery from backup synchronization with a virtual machine called VM03.

There are some important considerations when you do the initial replication by restoring the virtual machine from backup.

The first step is to restore the virtual machine on the replica server. If you want to see how to do this using Windows Server Backup, check out Chapter 10. Your restore tool will restore the virtual machine, but the folder structure of Hyper-V Replica might be alien to it if the virtual machine was not originally stored in the same way on the source host. That means if you are a service provider who intends to offer a multi-tenant virtual DR site, this method won't work for you; this method probably wasn't suitable anyway, because there is no guarantee that you will have the same backup software as the many customers you are intending to sign up to the service.

This synchronization method starts differently than the others. You will start in the DR site and restore the virtual machine(s) that you want to synchronize, ensuring that their GUIDs match—that is, if you are replicating VM03, you will restore a backup of VM03 in the DR site:

1. Restore the virtual machine VM03 to the replica host, Host2.

2. Launch the Enable Replication Wizard on Host1, select VM03, and configure replication for the virtual machine until you reach the Choose Initial Replication Method screen (shown earlier in Figure 12.9).

3. Choose Use An Existing Virtual Machine On The Replica Server As The Initial Copy and finish the wizard.

The virtual machine on the source host has probably been active and stored changes since the backup was done. HVR will perform a fix-up of the replica virtual machine over the network before replication will commence. Therefore, it makes sense to use a very recent backup for the restore process. Even with a very recent backup, this synchronization could take some time to complete for virtual machines with large VHDs, but it will be quicker than using the default option to send the initial copy over the network.

Using Authentication with Certificates

So far, you have looked at using the HTTP option for mutually authenticating the source and replica hosts. Now you will look at the HTTPS alternative, which is recommended for replicating over nontrusted networks (for encryption) and for hosts that are not in the same Active Directory forest.

Understanding Certificate Requirements

Both the source and replica hosts must have certificates that are mutually trusted. In other words, they must both trust the same parent or come from the same certificate authority (CA).

In an enterprise deployment, Windows Active Directory Certificate Services could be used. The CA certificate(s) can be deployed via Group Policy, thus ensuring that any issued certificates from that CA or CAs would be trusted by both the source and the replica hosts.

CERTIFICATE SERVICES

Certificate services, CAs, and certificates are a much bigger topic of conversation than we can include here. We strongly recommend that you do some additional research on this topic if you need to do HTTPS authentication. Microsoft maintains a site for Active Directory Certificate Services at `http://technet.microsoft.com/windowsserver/dd448615.aspx`.

A service provider would have to do one of the following:

Maintain an Untrusted CA A small service provider could set up a CA service and issue certificates from it. The root CA cert and the certs for the Hyper-V hosts would have to be installed on their hosts to get trust. This applies to the hosts in the service provider's site and the customers' sites.

Maintain a Trusted CA A very large service provider may already have the ability to issue certs that are trusted by default through the default certificate trust list in Windows Server. This service provider can just issue the computer certificates for the Hyper-V hosts in both sites.

Purchase CA certificates If you want simplicity and rapid deployment, you can purchase certificates for the Hyper-V hosts in both sites from an online CA that is on the Windows certificate trust list.

The requirements of an individual certificate that is being requested are as follows:

Enhanced Key Usage This field in the certificate must be set up for both Client and Server authentication. This dictates the acceptable usage of the cert.

The Subject Field The certificate is bound to the name of the machine that is documented in the Subject field. This field must be set to the FQDN of the host. For example, it might be set to `host3.lab.internal` for a machine with that FQDN. Wildcards are supported, such as `*.lab.internal`.

We cover clusters later in the chapter.

Certificate Trust There must be a chain of trust for the certificate to a root CA that is present in the Trusted Root Certification Authorities store for the host in question. This should be a common trust on the source and replica hosts.

> **READ MORE ABOUT CUSTOM CERTIFICATE REQUESTS**
>
> Praveen Vijayaraghavan of Microsoft has written a series of blog posts on Hyper-V Replica. One of them discusses how to create a custom certificate request for Hyper-V Replica certificates that you can send to a CA. You can find this article at http://blogs.technet.com/b/virtualization/archive/2012/07/02/requesting-certificates-for-hyper-v-replica-from-cas.aspx.

Enabling Hyper-V Replica with HTTPS

The process for enabling the replica host (Host2) in the DR site to use HTTPS authentication is as follows:

1. Log in to the replica host. Import the certificate for Host2 into the Personal store for the local computer by using the Certificates snap-in in MMC. Note the details of the certificate and verify the root CA trust.

2. Enable replication on the host (Hyper-V Settings in Hyper-V Manager). Select HTTPS in the Authentication And Ports section. Click Select Certificate and choose the certificate that you just imported.

3. Continue with the process of enabling HVR, including configuring Authentication And Storage.

4. Enable the Hyper-V Replica HTTP Listener (TCP-In) rule in the Windows Firewall.

You can also perform this configuration by using PowerShell. The first step is to import the certificate. The first line of code will set the destination as the local computer's Personal store. The path to that store is `Cert:\LocalMachine\My`:

```
Set-Location -Path Cert:\LocalMachine\My
```

Then you can import the certificate:

```
Import-Certificate -Filepath "C:\Host2.Cert"
```

Identify the thumbprint of the certificate. You can do this in PowerShell by running the following:

```
Dir Cert:\\LocalMachine\My
```

Now you can enable HVR with HTTPS authentication on Host2 by using the identified certificate thumbprint:

```
Set-VMReplicationServer -ReplicationEnabled $True -AllowedAuthenticationType `
Certificate -ReplicationAllowedFromAnyServer $True -CertificateThumbprint `
" 2AB3F96C2C25AEFDB6E1175E26F6D277D19F4A69" -DefaultStorageLocation "E:" `
-CertificateAuthenticationPort 443
```

The next line of PowerShell will configure the Windows Firewall for Kerberos/HTTP authentication:

```
Enable-NetFirewallRule -DisplayName "Hyper-V Replica HTTPS Listener (TCP-In)"
```

Note that you can have both HTTP and HTTPS authentication enabled at the same time by merging this and the earlier examples of `Set-VMReplicationServer` and setting `-AllowedAuthenticationType` to `CertificateAndKerberos`.

Replicating Virtual Machines via HTTPS

The following is a set of instructions for replicating VM04 from Host1 to Host2 by using HTTPS.

On the source host, Host1, you will need to import the certificate for Host1 into the local computer's Personal certificate store. The steps (GUI and PowerShell) are the same as they were for the replica host.

1. In Hyper-V Manager, you will enable replication of the virtual machine as before. Choose HTTPS instead of HTTP in the Specify Connection Parameters screen.

2. Click Select Certificate to select the host's certificate that you just imported.

3. Complete the wizard.

Alternatively, you can use PowerShell to configure the virtual machine replication:

```
Set-VMReplication -VMName VM04 -ReplicaServerName "host2.demo.internal" `
-ReplicaServerPort 80 -AuthenticationType Certificate -CertificateThumbprint `
"2AB3F96C2C25AEFDB6E1175E26F6D277D19F4A70" -RecoveryHistory 15 `
-VSSSnapshotFrequency 2 -ExcludedVhdPath "E:\VM01\Paging File.vhdx"
```

Using Advanced Authorization and Storage

HVR has the ability to create rules to store replica virtual machines in the DR site in different locations based on the name of the source virtual machine. The isolated locations might be different folders, different volumes, or even different classes of storage. Examples of why you might do this include the following:

- You are running a multi-tenant DR cloud and need to isolate customers.

- The SAN has a feature that you want to use on some virtual machines but not on others.

- It has been decided to offer customers a choice of different tiers of storage/price plans.

This exercise will show how to create HVR Authorization And Storage policies on Host2 (a hosting company) for Host1 (Customer X) and Host3 (Customer Y) to Host3.

1. Log in to Host2 and create folders called CustomerX and CustomerY to store the replica virtual machines for those customers.

2. Enable HVR and configure the authorization type (HTTP or HTTPS).

3. Choose the Allow Replication From The Specified Servers option in Authorization And Storage.

   You will create a policy for each source host.

4. Click Add to create a new policy called an *authorization entry*. This opens the dialog box shown in Figure 12.10. Complete the fields.

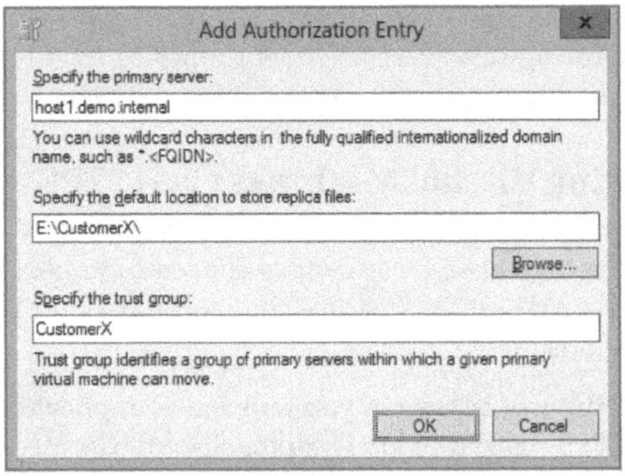

FIGURE 12.10
The Add
Authorization
Entry dialog box

There are three settings in an authorization entry:

Specify The Primary Server   This is the FQDN of the source host that will be associated with the authorization entry. You can use a wildcard to include many servers from a single domain.

Specify The Default Location To Store Replica Files   Any replica virtual machine from the source host will be stored in this folder.

Specify The Trust Group   This is a label, and it can be used in a query to logically group a number of authorization entries. For example, a hosting company might want to invoice customers based on resources consumed. A customer might have numerous authorization entries. Grouping them together will enable easier invoicing.

You can repeat the steps for each additional source host. The final result for this exercise will look like Figure 12.11.

You can change an existing authorization entry by selecting it and clicking the Modify button. You can change the storage path and the trust group name. Changing the storage path will not move existing replicas; it will change only the location for new replicas from the source server.

A medium/large enterprise or a hosting company won't want to use Hyper-V Manager to create many authorization entries; PowerShell will be a better alternative for them.

HVR will have to be enabled on Host2 by using the Allow Replication From The Specified Servers option:

```
Set-VMReplicationServer -ReplicationEnabled $True -AllowedAuthenticationType `
Kerberos -ReplicationAllowedFromAnyServer $False
```

The following command will add an authorization entry for all hosts in the lab.internal domain (using a wildcard), storing their replica virtual machines at E:\Lab:

You can change the settings of authorization entries by using Set -VMReplicationAuthorizationEntry and can delete them by using Remove- VMReplicationAuthorizationEntry. Get-VMReplicationAuthorizationEntry allows you to query the policies. The following example shows how the trust group can be used to filter the query.

```
PS C:\> Get-VMReplicationAuthorizationEntry -TrustGroup "Lab"


AllowedPS        StorageLoc        TrustGroup
---------        ----------        ----------
*.lab.external E:\Lab External\ Lab
*.lab.internal E:\Lab Internal\ Lab
```

FIGURE 12.11
Authorization entries for multiple customers

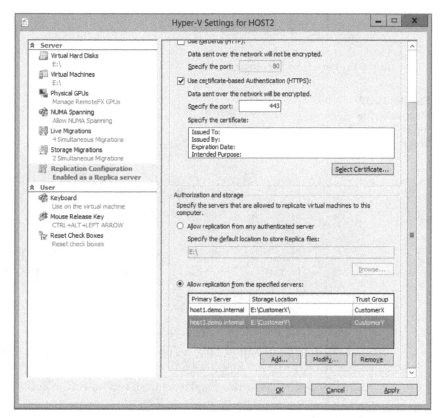

Using Hyper-V Replica with Clusters

A cluster of Hyper-V hosts is a logical unit of virtualization. A virtual machine hosted on a cluster can be on any node in the cluster. Management systems or humans can move that virtual machine around the hosts in the cluster at any moment with no service downtime. This means that if we want to replicate virtual machines to a cluster, we will need something to simplify setup and to deal with that movement.

Understanding the Hyper-V Replica Broker

We can create a highly available role on a cluster called a Hyper-V Replica Broker to deal with the multi-host nature of the cluster. This role has a Client Access Point (CAP) with an associated Active Directory computer account, DNS name, and an IP address. We use the CAP's FQDN instead of the host names when we replicate to or from a cluster. Figure 12.12 illustrates two examples of how the CAP is used to replicate clusters.

The HVC1-Prod cluster has an HVR Broker called HVC1-Prod-HVR. The DR site cluster, HVC1-DR, also has an HVR Broker, called HVC1-DR-HVR. The HVC1-DR-HVR broker is configured to allow inward replication from the production cluster. The individual members of the production cluster are not specified; instead, the HVC1-Prod-HVR broker is specified as being authorized to replicate. In the production site, each required virtual machine is configured to replicate to the DR cluster's broker, HVC1-Prod-HVR. A third has a nonclustered host called Host5 that replicates to the DR cluster too. Its virtual machines are also configured to replicate to the broker of the DR cluster.

FIGURE 12.12
Illustrating the
Hyper-V Replica
Broker

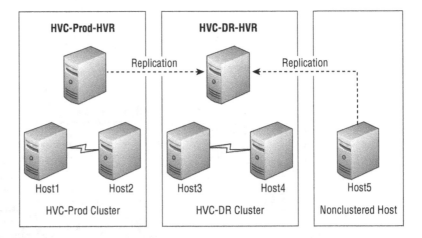

The HVR Broker does the following for us:

Simplified Administration It gives us a single CAP instead of a collection of hosts to authorize on the replica host/cluster or to target on the source virtual machines.

Node Placement When a virtual machine is replicated to a cluster, the broker decides on which host to place the replica virtual machine. The source host then replicates to the assigned replica host.

Automated High Availability The broker makes the new replica highly available.

Track Virtual Machine Placement If a virtual machine moves to a different host, the source host will lose the HVR connection. It contacts the replica cluster's broker and is directed to the new host of the virtual machine.

HYPER-V REPLICA, CLUSTERS, AND CERTIFICATES

When we talked about certificates, we said that the Subject field must be set to the FQDN of the host. In the case of a cluster, the Subject field should be set to the FQDN of the Hyper-V Replica Broker's CAP.

The certificate should be imported into the computer's Personal certificate store on each host in the cluster.

Creating the Hyper-V Replica Broker

In this demonstration, we are going to configure the cluster, HVC1, to have a HVR Broker. HVC1 has hosts as members called Host1 and Host2.

1. Open Failover Cluster Manager to manage the HVC1 cluster. Click the Configure Role action to launch the High Availability Wizard.

2. Choose Hyper-V Replica Broker in the Select Role screen.

3. Configure the Client Access Point as shown in Figure 12.13. The broker's CAP will require a computer name and IP address.

FIGURE 12.13
Configure the broker's Client Access Point.

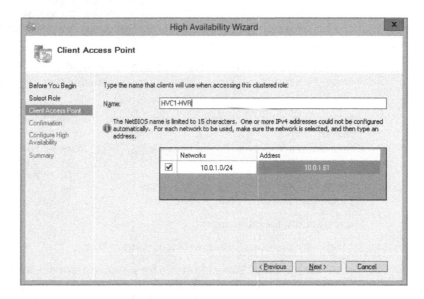

4. Complete the wizard and verify in Roles that the new broker is there and running.

You can create a HVR Broker by using PowerShell, but it does require quite a bit of code:

```
#Configure Broker CAP name and IP Address
$BrokerName = "HVC1-HVR"
$BrokerIPAddress = "192.168.1.69"


#Configure the resource group names as if the wizard created them
$BrokerResourceName = "Virtual Machine Replication Broker"
$TempBrokerGroupName = $BrokerName + "Group"


#Create a new Hyper-V Group using WMI with a temporary name to group all of the
  HVR Broker resources
```

```
([wmiclass]"root\MSCluster:MSCluster_ResourceGroup"). `
CreateGroup($TempBrokerGroupName, 115)
#Create the HVR Broker
Add-ClusterResource -Name $BrokerResourceName -Group $TempBrokerGroupName `
-ResourceType "Virtual Machine Replication Broker"

#Create the HVR Broker CAP
Add-ClusterServerRole -Name $BrokerName -StaticAddress $BrokerIPAddress

#Move the HVR Broker CAP to the cluster resource group and create the dependency
Move-ClusterResource -name $BrokerName  -Group $TempBrokerGroupName
Add-ClusterResourceDependency  $BrokerResourceName $BrokerName

#Remove the old cluster group that was created with the HVR Broker CAP
Remove-ClusterGroup -name  $BrokerName -RemoveResources -Force

#Rename the HVR Broker resource group from the temp name to the name of the
 broker
Get-ClusterGroup $TempBrokerGroupName | %{ $_.Name = $BrokerName }

#Start the HVR Broker resource Group
Start-ClusterGroup -Name $BrokerName
```

The script does the following:

1. It creates a resource group with a temporary name.

   A WMI command is used to create the resource group because the alternative of Add-ClusterGroup does not create the same type of group (the 115 code) as the wizard. A temporary name is used because the HVR Broker will be created in another resource group with the name we do want to use.

2. The HVR Broker is created and added into the resource group.

3. A role (CAP) is created with the HVR Broker name and IP address. This is created in a resource group with the name of the HVR Broker.

4. The CAP resource is moved into the original resource group.

5. Now we can delete the empty resource group, freeing up the resource group name that we want to use.

6. The original resource group with the temporary name is renamed to the name of the HVR Broker.

7. The HVR Broker resource group (and the Broker) is started.

With a running Hyper-V Replica broker, this cluster is now able to replicate highly available virtual machines to other hosts or clusters just by permitting the broker's CAP.

TROUBLESHOOTING THE HYPER-V REPLICA BROKER'S CAP

The CAP requires a computer object in Active Directory. This will be created in the same OU as the cluster. This act requires that the cluster's CAP computer object has sufficient rights to create computer objects in this Active Directory OU. The broker cannot start without this computer account. You should also verify that the IP address of the CAP is unique on the network.

More troubleshooting information can be found by expanding the broker's resources in Failover Cluster Manager, right-clicking the Server Name object of the broker, and selecting Show Critical Events.

You can change the settings of the broker's CAP. Open Failover Cluster Manager, click the role of the broker, navigate into Resources (bottom pane), and expand the Server Name object. You can edit the properties of either the Server Name object or the IP Address object.

Allowing Replication from a Cluster

We are going to permit the hosts in the HVC1 cluster to replicate to a nonclustered host called Host3. On Host3, you can add an authorization entry for the cluster's broker (HVC1-HVR, in this case) to the host settings, as shown in Figure 12.14. A single entry is created that specifies the FQDN of the HVR broker. No entries are required for the hosts in the HVC1 cluster.

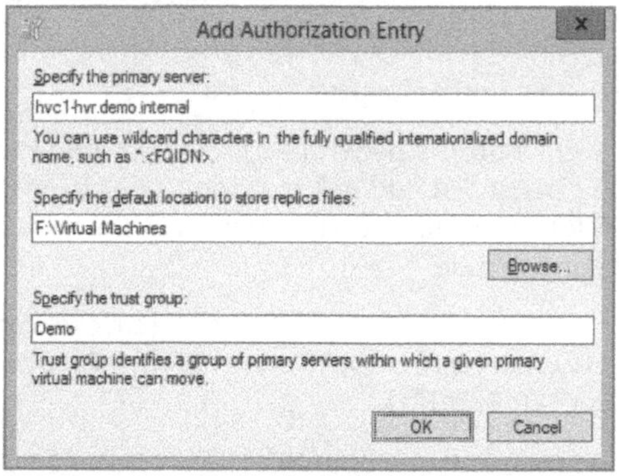

FIGURE 12.14
Permitting a
Hyper-V Replica
Broker to replicate
to another host

Enabling replication of a highly available virtual machine on a cluster can be done from either the Hyper-V Manager (as before) or from Failover Cluster Manager. Right-click the virtual machine in Roles and choose Replication ➤ Enable Replication.

You will use the same PowerShell cmdlets `Enable-VMReplication` and `Start-VMInitialReplication` that you used on nonclustered hosts to enable replication of a virtual machine from a cluster. Run the cmdlets from the host that is running the virtual machine.

FIREWALL APPLIANCES

If you are replicating to or from a Hyper-V cluster, you must open up some holes in any firewall appliances that are in the way. You are probably using certificates and HTTPS authentication, so allow network communications for the Hyper-V Replica Broker and all of the hosts in the cluster.

You can do an end-to-end test of connectivity from the source hosts to the destination hosts by using PowerShell:

```
Test-VMReplicationConnection -ReplicaServerName host3 -AuthenticationType `
Kerberos -ReplicaServerPort 80
```

Allowing Replication to a Cluster

With a nonclustered host, we enabled inward replication, configured authentication, and set up authorization and storage policies in the Host Settings window. A cluster can have up to 64 nodes, and that would require a lot of work to configure consistently. Luckily, with a cluster, we have to enable HVR only on the broker:

1. Open Failover Cluster Manager, manage the cluster in question, navigate into roles, right-click the HVR Broker, and choose Replication Settings.

2. A Hyper-V Replica Broker Configuration window appears. It is identical to Replication Configuration in the Hyper-V Settings of a nonclustered host. Configure it as you normally would.

3. When creating authorization entries, ensure that you choose CSV volumes in `C:\ClusterStorage` for the storage of replica virtual machines.

4. Enable the Windows Firewall to accept incoming HTTP and/or HTTPS replication on *every* host in the cluster.

PowerShell definitely helps speed up the configuration of a Hyper-V cluster for inward HVR traffic. You can use `Set-VMReplicationServer` from any one of the cluster members to enable inward HVR traffic. Then you can configure the Windows Firewall on all cluster members with this single line of code:

```
Get-ClusterNode | ForEach-Object  {Invoke-Command -ComputerName $_.Name `
-ScriptBlock {Enable-NetFirewallRule -DisplayName "Hyper-V Replica HTTPS `
Listener (TCP-In)"}}
```

Now you can configure source hosts to replicate virtual machines to this cluster, HVC1, by targeting the HVR Broker, HVC1-HVR.

Exploring Hyper-V Replica in Greater Detail

So far we have talked about Hyper-V Replica functionality at a higher level. This section provides more detail so you can better understand and troubleshoot HVR.

Hyper-V Replica Logging and Swapping

HVR is quite tolerant of the brief outage that occurs; it isn't going to alert you unless 20 percent or more of replications fail during the default Monitoring Interval of 12 hours (more on this later in the chapter). To understand how HVR deals with replication failure, you need to dig a little deeper into the replication process.

Each VHD (or VHDX) that is being replicated has a HRL file that is kept in the same folder as the VHD. Changed blocks are logged in this file. HVR will attempt to do the following every 5 minutes:

◆ Swap out the HRL file

◆ Create a new HRL file

◆ Replay the HRL file for the last period to the replica host in reverse order, with compression turned on by default

Resynchronization

HVR is normally going to be tolerant of a replication outage; it will hold onto the HRL file until it can communicate with the replica host and then swap out and replay the HRL file. While waiting for that to happen, the HRL file continues to grow.

Microsoft has determined that it no longer makes sense to maintain a HRL file after the HRL for a VHD is 50 percent of the size of the VHD. At this point, it would be quicker to perform what is called a resynchronization; think of it as a fix-up of the differences over the network. The virtual machine goes into a Resync State and suspends replication until after the resynchronization has completed.

You can see if and how this resynchronization is configured, on a per virtual machine basis, by running the following PowerShell:

```
PS C:\ > Get-VMReplication -VMName VM01 | fl AutoResync*


AutoResynchronizeEnabled       : True
AutoResynchronizeIntervalStart : 18:30:00
AutoResynchronizeIntervalEnd   : 06:00:00
```

You can see that resynchronization is turned on by default. You can also see that resynchronization is set to happen only during a limited time window of 18:30 until 06:00. This is typically when people aren't working and the replication link might have the least contention, but that isn't a universal rule. You can modify this behavior on the source host by using PowerShell:

```
Set-VMReplication -VMName * -AutoResynchronizeEnabled $True `
-AutoResynchronizeIntervalStart "00:00:00" -AutoResynchronizeIntervalEnd `
"08:00:00"
```

Those same parameters are also available in `Enable-VMReplication` so you can set up the resynchronization of a virtual machine when you first enable HVR for it.

The Performance Impact of Hyper-V Replica

There is a performance cost for enabling HVR on your virtual machines. On the source host where HRL files are being created, the following are affected:

CPU and Memory Host-based replication will consume host resources. There will be less than a 3 percent hit on the processor and 50 MB of RAM per replicating virtual machine.

Storage Space You will require additional storage space for the HRL files. The amount of space required can be discovered during the assessment. You should have calculated what the rate of change is over a 5-minute window to determine network requirements. This will roughly be the same for the HRL files. Be conservative; leave a little more space to allow for blocks being overwritten and for spikes in activity.

IOPS for HRL File Every write to a VHD is also being recorded to a HRL file in the same volume. Microsoft estimates that the total IOPS will be 1.5 times the normal amount without HVR being enabled. It should go without saying that this is very important for medium to large enterprise deployments.

DO YOU NEED A SAN?

Before Windows Server 2012, you couldn't talk about a Windows Failover Cluster without talking about the SAN you were going to use. A SAN gave us multi-host connectivity, SAN-based replication, scalability, and IOPS performance.

Windows Server 2012 supports using SMB 3.0 file server and Scale-Out File Servers (SOFS). Microsoft and their storage partners have demonstrated how they can get some amazing performance numbers out of these solutions. These numbers were demonstrated by Microsoft at the TechEd Europe conference in June 2012:

◆ Over 1,000,000 IOPS from a Hyper-V virtual machine

◆ Nearly 16 giga*bytes* (not giga*bits*) per second transfer rate

If we can get this performance, the stability, and the required scalability, then you have to wonder about the following:

◆ Does a SAN offer anything that SMB 3.0 can't?

◆ Why don't you use HVR to replicate Hyper-V virtual machines from one SMB 3.0 storage system in the production site to another in the DR site without worrying too much about IOPS?

There is also an impact on the replica hosts in the DR site:

Disk Space It is estimated that each recovery point that is maintained (with a limit of 15) will consume 10 percent of the disk space of the original VHD.

IOPS for HRL Replay HRL replay will cause IOPS to increase 0.6 times the original IOPS of the VHD being replicated.

IOPS for Recovery Point Maintenance   The maintenance of recovery points on the replica host has a much higher impact on IOPS, which will increase three to five times to receive, apply, and merge recovery points. Would it be better to replicate your backup data than to create lots of recovery points? A backup might have 2+ weeks of restoration points, whereas you can keep a maximum of only 15 hours of recovery points.

As you can see, a replica host has quite a lot of storage processing to do. This will be an important factor when you monitor the health and performance of HVR. Microsoft strongly recommends that replica hosts should not be used for production workloads. In reality, smaller businesses have to keep costs down and might need to consider mixing the workloads. If this is the case for you, we strongly recommend that you perform a thorough assessment (use the free Microsoft Assessment and Planning Toolkit) to see whether the planned hardware will meet the needs of the production and replica workloads.

Managing Hyper-V Replica

If you use Hyper-V Replica, it will be a critical resource for you. You can observe and manage replication health as well as monitor the network utilization of the replication traffic.

Monitoring Replication

You can quickly observe the health of a virtual machine in Hyper-V Manager and Failover Cluster Manager. In Hyper-V Manager, you can select a virtual machine and observe the health of replication in the Replication tab in the bottom-middle pane (see Figure 12.15).

FIGURE 12.15
Observing the replication status of a virtual machine

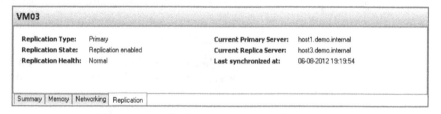

You can do something similar in Failover Cluster Manager. Select the virtual machine, select the Summary tab in the bottom-middle pane, and scroll down to see the Replication data that is there. PowerShell can also give you the health of HVR for a replicating virtual machine:

```
PS C:\ > Get-VM VM03 | FL Replication*


ReplicationState  : Replicating
ReplicationHealth : Normal
ReplicationMode   : Primary
```

THE HYPER-V REPLICA MONITORING INTERVAL

This is the time window used when calculating the health of replication. It is set to 12 hours (starting at 08:00) by default, and can range from 1 hour to 7 days. You can view the Monitoring Interval by running the following:

```
Get-VMReplicationServer | Select MonitoringInterval, MonitoringStartTime
```

You can change the Monitoring Interval to suit your needs:

```
Set-VMReplicationServer -MonitoringInterval "08:00:00" -MonitoringStartTime `
"00:00:00"
```

Microsoft recommends keeping the Monitoring Interval reasonably long. This is to avoid brief glitches creating noisy alarms that could be safely dealt with by Hyper-V Replica, without us having to intervene. However, a short Monitoring Interval could be a useful investigation tool when troubleshooting a larger problem; remember to reset it back afterward.

A more detailed report of replication can be created in either Hyper-V Manager or Failover Cluster Manager by right-clicking a replicating virtual machine and choosing Replication ➤ View Replication Health. This opens the Replication Health window shown in Figure 12.16. Replication Health has four possible values:

Not Enabled   HVR is not enabled for this virtual machine.

Normal   The health state of normal indicates a healthy state if the following are true:

- Less than 20 percent of replication attempts have been missed; HVR expects the ups and downs of commercial broadband.

- The average latency is less than 5 minutes. That's important because HVR wants to replicate the HRL every 5 minutes, and a replication should be completed in that 5-minute window.

- The last historical copy (if enabled) was also created less than an hour ago; HVR tries to create one (if enabled) every hour.

Warning   A virtual machine has a warning state if any of the following happen:

- Twenty percent or more of replications have been missed during the current monitoring interval. This indicates problems with the replica host (is it running or is it overloaded with IOPS?) or the link to the replica host. There is no alert if less than 20 percent of replications have been missed during the current monitoring interval; it is assumed that Hyper-V replica is dealing with and overcoming issues that can be common with commercial broadband.

- One hour or more has passed since the last send replica was successfully sent or received.

- The initial copy or synchronization has not completed.

♦ Failover has been started, but reverse replication has not been started.

♦ The source virtual machine's replication is paused.

Critical The health of the virtual machine's replication goes into a critical state if the following occur:

♦ The source host is unable to send HVR traffic to the replica host.

♦ Replication is suspended on the replica host, indicating that a service provider has suspended the service. You would normally suspend replication in a private cloud on the source host.

There are a few nice features in this window. You can reset the statistics, which will be useful if you want to get numbers for a small time window. You can also click Save As to save the information from this dialog box as a CSV file.

FIGURE 12.16
Viewing Replication Health for a virtual machine

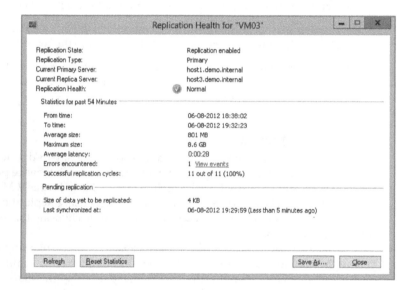

If any errors are reported in Replication Health, you can click a hyperlink that opens Event Viewer and brings you straight to Applications And Services Logs ➢ Microsoft ➢ Windows ➢ Hyper-V VMMS, which is where you'll find all logged events for the Virtual Machine Management Service, including those for HVR.

PowerShell can also dig up a lot of information on the health of HVR. `Get-VMReplication` can report back the replication configuration of all virtual machines. If you want in-depth information on all virtual machines, try running the following line of code; it is like getting the Replication Health (previous) plus the configuration for all virtual machines in one easy step on either the source or replica hosts:

```
Measure-VMReplication * | fl *
```

You can use this query to get the health of a replica host:

```
Get-VMReplicationServer | FL *
```

Performance Monitor has the following Hyper-V Replica VM counters that you can select on a per-VM or all-VM basis:

Average Replication Latency indicates the average replication latency in seconds.

Average Replication Size indicates the average replication size in bytes.

Compression Efficiency indicates the compression efficiency of HVR.

Last Replication Size indicates the last replication size in bytes.

Network Bytes Recv indicates total replication bytes received for the virtual machine since the VMMS was started.

Network Bytes Sent indicates total replication bytes sent for the virtual machine since the VMMS was started.

Replication Count indicates the replication count since the VMMS was started.

Replication Latency indicates the last replication latency, calculated by measuring the number of seconds it takes for the changes to be applied to the replica since they were snapped.

Resynchronized Bytes indicates the total bytes sent and received by HVR for the virtual machine during the resynchronize operation since the VMMS was started. High numbers can indicate replication link issues.

Managing Replication

There are some things that you might want to do during day-to-day administration of HVR.

If you are planning on having an extended outage or maintenance period, you can proactively suspend replication of virtual machines. You can do this in Hyper-V Manager or Failover Cluster Manager by right-clicking the virtual machine and choosing Replication ➤ Pause Replication on either the source or replica host. You can reverse this by choosing the Resume Replication option from the same menu.

Suspend-VMReplication can be used to pause replication of a single virtual machine. But you might want to pause replication for all replicating virtual machines if you are doing some planned maintenance. You can run this command on either the source or the replica host:

```
Get-VMReplication | Where {$_.State -Like "*Replica*"} | Suspend-VMReplication
```

You can resume replication by running this:

```
Get-VMReplication | Where {$_.State -Like "Suspended"} | Resume-VMReplication
```

You can also resume replication in the GUI by right-clicking the virtual machine and choosing Replication ➤ Resume Replication.

Microsoft kept two things in mind when designing the process for disabling replication and deleting virtual machines (source and replica):

Accidental Deletion   Deleting a virtual machine on the source host will not delete it on the replica host, or vice versa. This protects the virtual machine from accidental deletion.

The Service Provider Model   You can disable replication on either the source or the replica host. This means that a disgruntled customer can stop their service without any cooperation from the service provider. Also, the service provider can cut off a customer who fails to pay their bills. You should note that neither the source nor replica is deleted by disabling replication.

You can disable replication in the GUI by right-clicking the virtual machine and choosing Replication ➤ Remove Replication. You should do this on both the source and the destination host; no signal is sent from the source host to the replica host, or vice versa, to mirror this action. You can also use PowerShell to disable HVR for one or more virtual machines:

```
Remove-VMReplication -VMName *
```

When you disable replication, you will probably want to delete the replica virtual machine. Remember to delete it from both of these:

◆   The replica host it was running on

◆   The cluster, if the replica virtual machine was highly available

Setting Up Failover Networking

There are two aspects to networking when you are working with HVR:

◆   What IP address will a replica virtual machine use when it is active in the DR site?

◆   Should a replica virtual machine be on an isolated network when conducting a test failover?

Failover TCP/IP

How are you going to get the virtual machines onto the network when the virtual machines fail over to the DR site? It is unlikely that you have stretched VLANs when dealing with host-based replication such as HVR. And stretched VLANs will be impossible for the hosted service provider, when everyone is probably using one of the common private IP ranges such as 192.168.1.0/24.

We have two options with Windows Server 2012 Hyper-V. We mentioned Network Virtualization earlier in the chapter. This would be a good option for a DR in the cloud run by a very large service provider. An administrator (or an orchestrator) in the service provider's datacenter can set up a policy in advance for each customer to abstract their IP networks during failover.

HVR has another way that is nice and simple to set up for the small to medium enterprise. There is a feature in the network settings of a Hyper-V virtual machine called Failover TCP/IP. You can see the Failover TCP/IP settings in Figure 12.17.

These settings allow you to preconfigure IPv4 and/or IPv6 addresses for the virtual machine. This is done on the source virtual machine in the production site. HVR will use these settings to update the virtual machine when it is failed over to the DR site. The assumption here is that the administrator in the production site knows what the IP addresses should be. This approach is not as suitable for the service provider as Network Virtualization.

You might have a lot of virtual machines to prepare with Failover TCP/IP settings, so a PowerShell script could be written to run the following line of code:

```
Set-VMNetworkAdapterFailoverConfiguration -VMName VM06 -VMNetworkAdapterName `
"Network Adapter" -IPv4Address "129.228.17.11" -IPv4SubnetMask "255.255.255.0" `
-IPv4DefaultGateway "129.228.17.254" -IPv4PreferredDNSServer "129.228.17.11" `
-IPv4AlternateDNSServer "129.228.17.12"
```

FIGURE 12.17
Failover TCP/IP

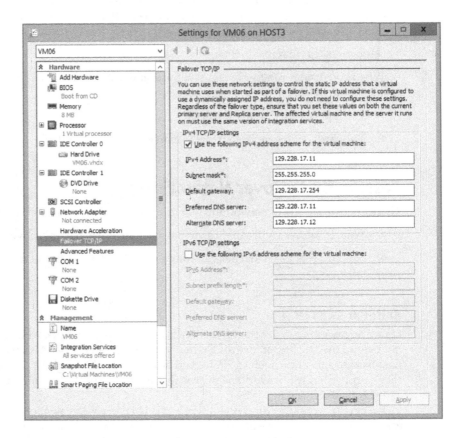

Test Failover Virtual Switch

A BCP should be regularly tested. This not only tests the response of the infrastructure and applications, but also gives the humans an opportunity to practice and become familiar with the processes. The more practice, the better; the day you invoke the BCP will be your worst day in work—if you are still around, that is. That might sound morbid, but it's realistic. So give more people an opportunity to be involved in a test run. And do lots of test runs.

The historical problem with a test run of the BCP is that you have to bring everything online to really test the BCP. That was always a challenge before virtualization, because we couldn't bring up copies of production systems in the DR site while they were running in the production site. Did you really want either to have split-brain or to shut down production systems? HVR deals with this by enabling us to configure a test failover virtual switch connection for each virtual network card. You configure this in the replica virtual machine settings; this makes sense because the production site administrator might not have any knowledge of the replica site network, and it also gives the replica site administrators plenty of flexibility.

If you want to change a few virtual machines, you can use the GUI to edit the properties of the virtual machine (see Figure 12.18). Expand the Network Adapter in question and click Test Failover. There you can expand the Virtual Switch drop-down box and select the virtual switch of choice.

FIGURE 12.18
Configure the Test Failover virtual switch.

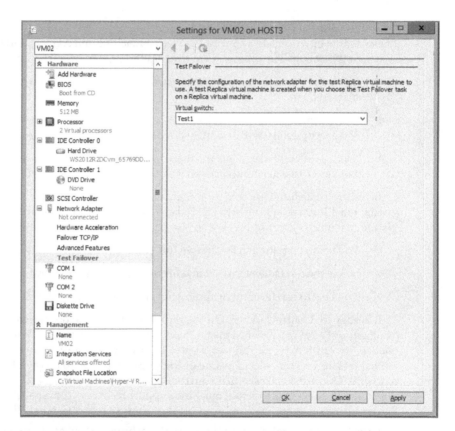

If you are automating this or want to configure lots of virtual machines at once, you will want to use PowerShell:

```
Set-VMNetworkAdapter -VMName VM02 -TestReplicaSwitchName Test1
```

Remember to set this for each virtual network adapter in the virtual machine. After you have done this, the virtual machine will be connected to the test failover virtual switch when you conduct a test failover.

Failing Over Virtual Machines

There are three ways to fail over virtual machines from the production site to the DR site when using HVR:

◆ A test failover

◆ A planned failover

◆ An unplanned failover

Performing a Test Failover

The test failover will create a copy of the virtual machine and connect it to the test failover virtual switch (if it is set up). The process for setting up the copy of the virtual machine is quite clever:

◆ A clone of the virtual machine is created. You can choose a recovery point if you have enabled them.

◆ A differential VHD is created, using the replica virtual machine's storage as the parent. The parent storage will be a snapshot AVHD file if you chose a recovery point.

◆ Using a differential disk means that a minimum amount of space is consumed by the test failover virtual machine and that it can be very quickly deployed.

Be careful: The test failover virtual machine is created in the same volume as the replica virtual machine. Yes, a differential VHD will consume very little space, but it will grow if the virtual machine is left running. We advise you to follow these guidelines:

◆ Don't plan on testing in an already full volume.

◆ Delete the test failover virtual machines as quickly as possible.

◆ Don't try to get clever by swapping out parent VHD or AVHD files.

It is easy to do a test failover. On the replica host, you can do it from either Hyper-V Manager or Failover Cluster Manager. Select the replica virtual machine, right-click, and choose Replication ➢ Test Failover. Figure 12.19 shows the Test Failover dialog box that appears. Here you can select any one of the recovery points that is available for the virtual machine. This effectively sends the virtual machine back in time. Please make sure that any guest applications in the virtual machine support recovery from snapshots! You can see in Figure 12.18 how there are three kinds of these hourly recovery points that you can choose from:

Latest Recovery Point A replica virtual machine will always have one of these; it is the latest version of the replica virtual machine from the most recent HRL replay.

Standard Recovery Point This is a normal recovery point without VSS.

Application-Consistent Recovery Point If you enable it, these VSS-made recovery points will appear in the list, replacing the Standard Recovery Point. The frequency depends on how you configured HVR for the virtual machine.

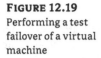

FIGURE 12.19
Performing a test failover of a virtual machine

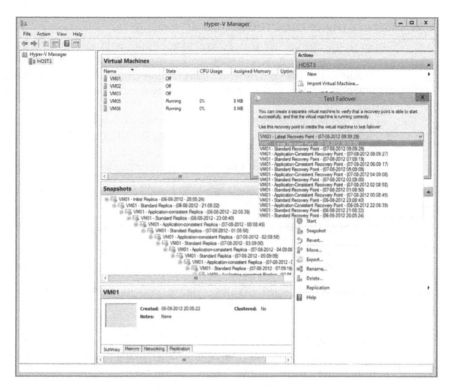

You can run `Start-VMFailover -VMName VM01 -AsTest` to perform a test failover by using PowerShell. If you are using a replica cluster, you should know that `Start-VMFailover` does not make the test failover virtual machine highly available. The following code will pick a historical snapshot of a virtual machine, perform a test failover, and make the virtual machine highly available:

```
$VM = "VM01"
$snapshots = Get-VMSnapshot -VMName $VM -SnapshotType Replica
Start-VMFailover -VMName $VM -AsTest $snapshots[0] -Force
Add-ClusterVirtualMachineRole -Cluster "hvc1" -VMName "$VM"
```

The SnapshotType parameter of `Get-VMSnapshot` also accepts the value of `AppConsistentReplica` to retrieve the VSS-created application-consistent replicas of the virtual machine.

You should end the test failover as soon as possible after the test of the BCP has been completed. You can do this in the GUI by selecting the *original* replica virtual machine, right-clicking, and choosing Replication ➢ Stop Test Failover. This removes the test failover copy of the replica virtual machine. You can also do this in PowerShell (make sure you remove the virtual machine from a cluster first!):

```
Stop-VMFailover -VMName VM05
```

Returning to the Production Site

Earlier in the chapter, we warned you to not limit the BCP to invoking the DR site. You also need a plan to recover the business from the DR site. Maybe the chemical leak has been cleaned up; maybe the insurance company has paid for new premises and equipment. It will be better for the business to resume full operations once again in a dedicated facility. How are you going to do that?

HVR has the ability to reverse replication from the replica hosts to the production hosts after you have failed over your virtual machines to the DR site. This will replicate changes, just as you originally did to the production site.

Here are the requirements for reversing replication:

◆   The production site hosts must be enabled for replication and must authenticate the replica site hosts.

◆   You must enable the relevant HVR listener rule (HTTP or HTTPS) in the Windows Firewall.

◆   You will need to set up rules in any network appliances to allow HVR traffic from the DR site hosts to the production site hosts, including any HVR Brokers.

We will look at the activity of manually reversing replication when we talk about unplanned failovers.

Performing a Planned Failover

A planned failover is a proactive action. When using this method, you know in advance that you want the following to happen:

1. You will shut down a virtual machine(s) in the production site and start a planned failover.

2. A prerequisite check will run to verify that the virtual machine is turned off and that replication can be successfully reversed. Note that a planned failover will not commence if both prerequisites are not met.

3. HVR will flush the last rights to the HRL file(s).

4. The HRL files will be pushed out to the replica host and applied. This, in combination with the source virtual machine being off and the HRL being flushed, means that there is zero data loss during a planned failover (zero RPO).

5. Replication will be reversed. This is a planned failover, and HVR assumes that you will want to fail virtual machines back.

6. The replica virtual machine(s) will be automatically powered up on the replica host, automatically injecting any failover TCP/IP settings.

There is some downtime for the virtual machine when you do a planned failover. However, it will have a much smaller impact on the WAN than a Shared Nothing Live Migration from the production hosts to the replica hosts. A planned failover will be useful in a few circumstances:

Disaster Warning   Some disasters, such as a hurricane or extended power outage, come with several days of notice. You can perform a smooth transition to the DR site without any of the panic that will happen when the disaster hits. The entire process could be automated by using PowerShell or an orchestration tool.

Lost Access to Production Site　A disaster has hit that prevents access to the production site, but the virtual machines are still running. You can do a planned failover of the virtual machines to the DR site for performance or access reasons.

Preventative Maintenance　Maybe you are going to swap out your SAN or your hosts? What if the datacenter is undergoing a massive power maintenance project? Usually this requires a considerable amount of planning to minimize the inevitable disruption to services. You can temporarily move your virtual machines to a DR site and replicate them back when the maintenance is complete.

Mandatory DR Site Utilization　Some organizations might have a requirement to really test DR sites by running production systems in that site for a certain amount of time every year. A planned failover will enable the switch over and switch back to be as smooth as possible.

Switch Sites　An unintended way you could use an HVR planned failover is to relocate virtual machines from one site to another. An SME could move virtual machines to a new office. A service provider could use a planned failover as a way to smoothly transition customers from their private cloud to a public cloud.

You can run a planned failover on the source hosts by using Hyper-V Manager or Failover Cluster Manager:

1. Verify that the source host/cluster can accept replication from the replica host/cluster (authorization and firewalls).

2. Shut down the virtual machine.

3. Select the virtual machine, right-click, and choose Replication ➤ Planned Failover. The Planned Failover dialog box opens (Figure 12.20), showing what actions it will do to the virtual machine.

4. Click Fail Over to start the process. The HRL files are flushed, replicated, and applied, and the virtual machine is powered up on the replica host for you.

FIGURE 12.20
Performing a
planned failover

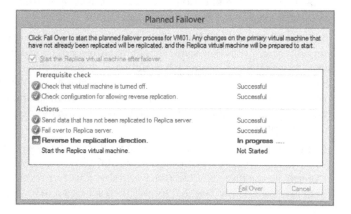

You can do a planned failover by using PowerShell. There are two scripts that you will need to run. The first is run on the original host to prepare the planned failover:

```
$VM = "VM01"
Stop-VM $VM -Force
Start-VMFailover -VMName $VM -Prepare -Confirm:$false
```

You will need to follow this up on the replica host with another script to complete the failover. During this time, the virtual machine is locked in a prepared state for a planned failover, which can be cancelled. This follow-up script is to be run on the replica host to fail over the virtual machine:

```
$VM = "VM01"
Start-VMFailover -VMName $VM -Confirm:$false
Set-VMReplication -reverse -VMName $VM
Start-VM $VM
```

Note that you could use the code from the test failover example to use a historical copy of the virtual machine.

Performing an Unplanned Failover

An unplanned failover is done in response to an unexpected emergency such as a catastrophic datacenter failure, a flood, or an earthquake that causes you to lose the production site. You cannot do an unplanned failover of a powered-up replicating virtual machine. An unplanned failover is intended to be one that assumes that the production site is a lost cause and can fail over independently of the production site hosts. You can do an unplanned failover by shutting down the production site virtual machine.

You should ask yourself a few questions when deciding how to fail over the virtual machines in response to the disaster:

All Virtual Machines Are Still Running   If all of your virtual machines are still running, you should do a planned failover. This smooth transition will not lose any data.

All Virtual Machines Are Unavailable   In this case, you should do an unplanned failover. If you choose the last recovery point, you will lose only data since that recovery point (the most recent HRL replication). If everything was operating normally before the disaster, you should lose less than 5 minutes of data (RPO).

Virtual Machines in Mixed State   The world, and disasters, are rarely binary. After a disaster, you might find that some virtual machines are running and the rest have failed. Those failed virtual machines may have failed at different times. If there is a cross-application consistency concern, you can reset all virtual machines to a similar point in time. Shut down the running virtual machines. Then perform an unplanned failover on the replica host/cluster, choosing a common recovery point (or as common as you can, because they are all independently captured).

Data Corruption   Have you been hit by the latest piece of malware? Did it just activate and destroy your virtual machines or data? If so, you can try to do an unplanned failover. Determine the nature of the attack and find a fix to prevent or remove the malware (your data is gone!). Try to test that fix and then set up an automated deployment of it in the DR site. Power down the production site virtual machines, and do an unplanned failover to a recovery point before the malware attack. You should prevent it from reoccurring if your fix and the deployment mechanism are working.

An unplanned failover is one of those scenarios where having a replica of your backup data in the DR site can help you restore applications to a known consistent state if HVR doesn't help. To simulate an unplanned failover, you can do the following:

1. Turn off the virtual machine in the production site.

2. Log in to the replica host, right-click the virtual machine, and choose Replication ➤ Failover.

3. The Failover dialog box appears, enabling you to select either the Latest Recovery Point or any available historical recovery point. The virtual machine powers up on the replica host.

Any additional recovery points are retained as normal Hyper-V snapshots. This means that you can apply any one of those snapshots to jump around the recovery points.

You can use PowerShell to do an unplanned failover:

```
$VM = "VM02"
Start-VMFailover -VMName $VM -Confirm:$false
Start-VM $VM
```

Remember that you could use the code from the test failover example to use a historical copy of the virtual machine.

You can reverse replication from the DR site in one of two circumstances:

◆ The production site comes back online with the original equipment.

◆ You deploy a new infrastructure to replace the original equipment/site.

You can reverse replication by right-clicking the virtual machine and choosing Replication ➤ Reverse Replication. The process assumes that a long time has passed since the unplanned failover was done. Therefore, you're going to be walked through the whole enable replication process, specifying replica host/cluster, authentication, recovery points, and the initial copy/synchronization. This gives you some flexibility in case you have had to replace the infrastructure or have a huge amount of data to synchronize over limited bandwidth.

Summarizing Hyper-V Replica

Anyone using Windows Server 2012 is entitled to free and unlimited usage of Hyper-V Replica. This very powerful DR solution is just a few mouse clicks or a PowerShell script away. It offers functionality for all scales of enterprise and the flexibility of using nonclustered and/or clustered hosts. Try it, and you'll see why the market started calling HVR a killer feature a year before Windows Server 2012 Hyper-V was made generally available.

Real World Solutions

Here are some examples of how you can use Hyper-V Replica to solve problems that you might encounter.

Enabling Replication for Lots of Virtual Machines

CHALLENGE

The company you are working for has completed an upgrade from Windows Server 2008 R2 to Windows Server 2012 and has converted a large number of virtual machines from VMware vSphere. This has been done so that the company can use Hyper-V Replica as a DR solution. There are 300 virtual machines to configure. You need to complete the following:

◆ Document the DR plan for the virtual machines.

◆ Enable HVR by using the network for the initial data copy.

◆ Do this as quickly as possible, while trying to limit the impact on the network.

SOLUTION

You can rule out using the GUI if there are 300 virtual machines to configure. The best solution is to use Microsoft Excel to document the required configuration for each virtual machine and save the document as a CSV file. There will be one line per virtual machine. The CSV file can then be read in, one line at a time, to configure HVR for each virtual machine. A time delay can be built into the script to slow down the process.

Create a CSV file that looks like the following example. It will serve two purposes. First, it will document the DR plan for each virtual machine. Second, it will be used by a PowerShell script to enable Hyper-V Replica.

```
VM,ReplicaHost,Port,Authentication,History,VSSFreq
VM01,host3.demo.internal,80,Kerberos,0,0
VM02,host3.demo.internal,80,Kerberos,15,2
VM03,host3.demo.internal,80,Kerberos,7,3
```

Note that if History is 0, there will be no recovery points, and if VSSFreq is 0, application-consistent snapshots will not be created. The following script will read this CSV file and implement HVR for you:

```
#Configure sleep timer
$SleepInSeconds = 300


Import-CSV C:\Scripts\Replica.csv | foreach {
#Will there be recovery points?
if ($_.History -eq 0)
    {
    #No recovery points
    Enable-VMReplication -VMName $_.VM -ReplicaServerName $_.ReplicaHost `
-ReplicaServerPort $_.Port -AuthenticationType $_.Authentication
    }
```

```
else
{
    #Will VSS be used?
    if ($_.History -eq 0)
        {
        #No VSS
        Enable-VMReplication -VMName $_.VM -ReplicaServerName $_.ReplicaHost `
-ReplicaServerPort $_.Port -AuthenticationType $_.Authentication `
-RecoveryHistory $_.History
        }
    else
        {
        #VSS
        Enable-VMReplication -VMName $_.VM -ReplicaServerName $_.ReplicaHost `
-ReplicaServerPort $_.Port -AuthenticationType $_.Authentication `
-RecoveryHistory $_.History -VSSSnapshotFrequency $_.VSSFreq
        }
}

Start-VMInitialReplication -VMName $_.VM


Write-Host "$_.VM :: Replication configured"
Write-Host "Sleeping for $SleepInSeconds seconds"


Start-Sleep -s $SleepInSeconds
}
```

THIS SCRIPT IS A STARTING POINT

You could take this script and extend it to do much more for you, such as configuring failover TCP/IP settings for IPv4 and IPv6, or excluding VHDs from replication.

Running a Planned Failover

CHALLENGE

You have 300 virtual machines running in your production site. There is news of a hurricane bringing floods that will affect the area. You need to invoke your DR plan as quickly as possible so that the following can occur:

◆ Employees can evacuate with their families.

◆ The company will still be operational in the DR site, which is a safe, remote location.

How will you do this work as quickly as possible?

SOLUTION

There are two parts to the planned failover. The first part is to initiate the planned failover on the production hosts. The following script will find each replicating source virtual machine, power it down, and initiate a planned failover. The script should be run on each host in the production site:

```
Get-VM | Where {$_.ReplicationMode -eq "Primary"} | ForEach-Object {


Stop-VM $_.Name -Force
Start-VMFailover -VMName $_.Name -Prepare -Confirm:$false


}
Write-Host "First half of planned failover is complete. Please continue in `
DR site"
```

The second part of the process has to be run on each host in the DR site. This script will complete the failover, reverse replication, and start up every replica virtual machine found on the host:

```
Get-VM | Where {$_.ReplicationMode -eq "Replica"} | ForEach-Object {


Start-VMFailover -VMName $_.Name -Confirm:$false
Set-VMReplication -reverse -VMName $_.Name
Start-VM $_.Name
}
Write-Host "Planned failover and replication reverse is complete."
```

ORDER VIRTUAL MACHINE FAILOVER

This is a simple example of a failover that might suffice for many sites. You might need to order the startup of virtual machines in the DR site. One way you could do this is to use the Notes attribute of each virtual machine, using a system such as the High/Medium/Low failover priority of Failover Clustering. You could order the startup of virtual machines based on this value.

A service provider probably wouldn't want to start every virtual machine and might have a pre-written script to find and start each of a customer's virtual machines in a specific order.

Another option might be to create a comma separated values (CSV) file that lists the name of each virtual machine in the order in which it must be started. This file could be available to the replica hosts. The DR site script would import that file and perform Start-VMFailover, Set-VMReplication, and Start-VM for each virtual machine in the desired failover order.

```
Import-CSV C:\Scripts\OrderedFailover.csv | foreach {
Start-VMFailover -VMName $_.VM -Confirm:$false
Set-VMReplication -reverse -VMName $_.VM
Start-VM $_.VM
}
Write-Host "Planned ordered failover and replication reverse is complete."
```

Scripting an Ordered Unplanned Failover

CHALLENGE

You have been asked to create a solution that will orchestrate the unplanned failover of virtual machines in the DR site using a PowerShell script. The script must start up each virtual machine in order and record if the virtual machine was able to successfully start up within a predetermined amount of time. This time out will vary from one virtual machine to another. There could be large number of virtual machines running on several hosts.

SOLUTION

This solution is going to use a PowerShell script. The script will

1. Read a CSV file. This file will record each virtual machine in the order it is to be started, what host it can be found on, and the time that the script will wait for the virtual machine to start.

2. Attempt to start the virtual machine if it is found to be in a healthy state.

3. Verify that the virtual machine starts up within the timeout by checking that the guest OS integration components respond to a heartbeat check from the host's management OS.

The following is an example CSV file, saved as C:\Scripts\Failover.txt:

```
Host,VM,Timeout
Host2,VM01,10
Host2,VM02,60
Host2,VM03,10
```

This is the script:

```
Function Check-VM ($CheckHost, $CheckVM, [int]$CheckTimeout)
{


#Set this variable so it works in the following while loop
$TheVM = $CheckVM


Write-Output "Checking $TheVM Now"
Write-Output "Timeout is $CheckTimeout seconds"


#Configure a time out
$LoopTimeout = new-timespan -Seconds $CheckTimeout
$SW = [Diagnostics.StopWatch]::StartNew()


#Keep checking the VM while the time out hasn't expired
While ($SW.elapsed -lt $LoopTimeout){

    #Check the VM's integration component heartbeat
    $HeartBeat = Get-VMIntegrationService -ComputerName $CheckHost -VMName `
$TheVM -Name Heartbeat -ErrorAction Continue
```

```
        If ($HeartBeat.PrimaryStatusDescription -Eq "OK")
            {
            Write-Output "$TheVM is running"
            #The VM is running so we can break out of the loop
            Break
            }
        Else
            {
            Write-Output "Waiting on $TheVM ... "
            #The VM is not yet running so sleep 5 seconds before checking again
            sleep 5
            }

    }


    #The script only gets here if the time out has expired
    if ($HeartBeat.PrimaryStatusDescription -Ne "OK")
        {
        If ((Get-VM $TheVM -ComputerName Host2).State -EQ "Running") `
    { Stop-VM -ComputerName $CheckHost $TheVM -Force }
        #The VM is not responding to the integration heartbeat so we time out and
         stop the VM
        write-output "$TheVM Timed out"
        }


    #End of function
    }


    #The unplanned failover script starts here
    cls


    #Define the comma seperated values (CSV) file
    $CSVFile = "C:\Scripts\Failover.txt"


    #In this script, there are 3 columns in the CSV file:
    # - Host: The name of the host/cluster that the VM replica is on
    # - VM: The name of the virtual machine being failed over
    # - Timeout: How long (in seconds) should the script wait for the VM to be online


    Import-CSV $CSVFile | ForEach {
        $FailHost = $_.Host
        $FailVM = $_.VM
        $FailTimeout = $_.TimeOut
```

```
    If ((Get-VM -ComputerName $FailHost $FailVM).ReplicationMode -EQ "Replica")
        {
        Write-Output "Failing over $FailVM on $FailHost now"
        Start-VMFailover -ComputerName $FailHost -VMName $FailVM -Confirm:$false
        Start-VM -ComputerName $FailHost -VMName $FailVM
        Check-VM $FailHost $FailVM $FailTimeout
        }
    else
        {
        Write-Output "$FailVM on $FailHost is not ready for failover"
        }
}
```

This script could be made more powerful by adding some functionality such as the following:

◆ Performing further health checks on the virtual machine before attempting to start it up

◆ Adding virtual machine dependencies into the CSV, and verifying that those other virtual machines are running before starting the dependent virtual machine

◆ Recording all activity in a log file for easy troubleshooting

◆ Using a PowerShell workflow to start up several virtual machines at once to reduce the RTO

## Chapter 13

Using Hyper-V for Virtual Desktop Infrastructure

Everyone is talking about mobility and the new, flexible, modern work style—but what technology is used behind the scenes? One very famous solution is the virtual desktop infrastructure, or VDI. In a Microsoft world, VDI is based on Remote Desktop Services (RDS), previously known as Terminal Services. RDS provides technologies that enable users to access Windows-based programs installed on a Remote Desktop Session Host (RD Session Host) server. These technologies also enable users to access the full Windows desktop, assign virtual machines to users, or have RDS dynamically assign an available virtual machine to a user upon connection.

This chapter does not focus on all aspects of VDI (this topic could fill almost another book), but it does provide a good overview of how Hyper-V fits perfectly in these scenarios.

In this chapter, you'll learn about

◆   Changes in Remote Desktop Services

◆   How to build a basic VDI environment

◆   How to leverage Hyper-V

Using Virtual Desktops, the Modern Work Style

Windows Server 2012 RDS offers options to provide users access to resources that are available in the datacenter. RDS can host either session-based desktops, pooled virtual machines, or personal virtual machines. Administrators have the flexibility to deploy the right type of desktop for their users.

What Is VDI?

VDI can mean different things to different people. One of the easier ways of explaining VDI is that it allows users to seamlessly access their Windows environment, from anywhere, anytime, from any device. Although many people understand the differences between session and desktop virtualization, some still do mix up the scenarios for which each VDI is used. Because there are two types of virtual desktops, pooled and personal:

With *pooled virtual machine collections,* the administrator can choose to deploy VDI through virtual machine pools. In this model, all users in the virtual machine pool share a single master image. The changes that each user makes during a session are stored in a virtual hard disk that will be discarded as soon as the user logs off. The main advantage of this model is having only a single image to manage, which reduces storage requirements and simplifies management, thereby reducing deployment costs.

On the other hand, *personal virtual machine collections* are based on a master virtual machine. Windows Server 2012 automates the rollout process by copying the master image for each instance of the personal virtual machine. After the initial rollout is completed, the administrator can maintain virtual machines as if they were physical machines and manage them by using WSUS, System Center Configuration Manager, and Virtual Machine Manager.

To complete the picture, what about *session virtualization deployments*? RDS session virtualization, formerly known as Terminal Services, is a proven and mature centralized desktop infrastructure that many organizations deploy instead of VDI to increase user density on the host and therefore reduce costs. Windows Server 2012 makes it easier to deploy this architecture by offering a session virtualization deployment scenario.

Table 13.1 compares the options for client virtualization, including session hosts, also known as terminal servers.

TABLE 13.1:   Client virtualization comparison

	SESSION	**POOLED VM**	**PERSONAL VM**
Personalization	Medium	Medium	High
Application compatibility	Medium	High	High
Image management	High	Medium	Low
Cost-effectiveness	High	Medium	Low

Generally, session virtualization is the obvious choice because it is less expensive than virtual desktops and can support more users on the same physical server with sessions than with virtual machines. However, VDI is a very good choice when session virtualization is not an option—for instance, when the application is not supported in a shared session, or the application or user requires local administrative privileges.

The Benefits of Using Hyper-V for VDI

Because the hypervisor is a core component of a virtual desktop infrastructure, choosing the right hypervisor seems to be key. And it's certainly not a big surprise that this book recommends Hyper-V as the best option for this scenario. But what are the real facts and figures that make Hyper-V the preferred choice for VDI?

With Windows Server 2008 R2 Service Pack 1 (SP1), two major features were introduced to support the VDI story: Dynamic Memory and RemoteFX.

Dynamic Memory lets you pool available physical memory on the host and dynamically allocate that memory to virtual machines based on workload needs. By enabling more-efficient use of physical memory resources, Dynamic Memory allows more virtual machines to be running simultaneously on a virtualization host without noticeable performance impact. This is important for the VDI scenario because it means fewer hypervisor-capable servers are needed in the datacenter for hosting large numbers of virtual desktops. Details on Dynamic Memory are discussed in Chapter 3, "Managing Virtual Machines."

Microsoft RemoteFX is a feature of the RDS server role. RemoteFX lets you provide users with a rich user experience when accessing virtual desktops from a broad range of end-point devices. For example, using RemoteFX in a VDI environment, users can work remotely in a Windows Aero desktop environment, watch full-motion video, enjoy Silverlight animations, and even run 3D applications from any end-point device.

Changes in Windows Server 2012

While RDS has been around for a while, the VDI scenario was introduced with Windows Server 2008 R2. Several improvements have been made in Windows Server 2012, including the following:

- Automated single-image management
- Unified central experience
- Less-expensive storage
- User profile disk
- CSV Block Cache
- Smart Paging

The topics CSV Block Cache and Smart Paging will be addressed in a later section of this chapter.

AUTOMATED SINGLE-IMAGE MANAGEMENT

Single-image management allows using a master, or golden, virtual machine to take advantage of automated ways to deploy and manage pooled virtual desktops with a template. A golden master is created (once) and maintained by the administrator. This image then can be easily deployed to hundreds of users at a time by duplicating. Its hardware configuration and software content will be used for all automatically created virtual machines in this virtual desktop collection.

An administrator no longer needs to manually duplicate and create virtual machines to be part of a VDI deployment or use other, more complex software to manage the automatic creation of virtual machines.

UNIFIED CENTRAL EXPERIENCE

Windows Server 2012 introduces the Remote Desktop Management Service and user interface, designed to not only simplify administrative tasks but also provide a centralized management solution for all RDS role services and scenarios. It allows administrators to deploy a virtual desktop infrastructure quickly from one single console.

Instead of using separate administrative tools for each role service installed, RDMS provides a single user interface that displays an overview of all the servers in an RDS deployment as well as providing a management interface for every server in the deployment.

LESS-EXPENSIVE STORAGE

In Windows Server 2012, a new feature called the Scale-Out File Server cluster role was introduced. With this role, all file shares are online on all nodes simultaneously. File shares associated with this type of clustered file server are called *scale-out file shares*. This is sometimes referred to as *active/active*. VDI in Windows Server 2012 supports using Scale-Out File Server clusters to store server application data and SMB3. If both file server high availability and scalability are important to you, we highly encourage you to check out the new Scale-Out File Server feature in Windows Server 2012 failover cluster services, and take full advantage of it for your Windows Server 2012 VDI deployment!

Chapter 7, "Using File Servers," provides more details on what such a solution would look like.

USER PROFILE DISK

With previous versions of Windows, preserving the user state of a virtual machine was accomplished by using roaming profiles and folder redirection. Although this solution does preserve the user state, using these technologies still has several disadvantages. To name just the top three:

◆ Loading roaming profiles over the network can increase logon time.

◆ Data loss can occur when using roaming profiles outside VDI.

◆ Some applications still do write outside the user profile.

In Windows Server 2012, user and application data can be stored in a single VHDX file that is stored on a network share. This user profile disk can reduce the cost and complexity of the management for user profile related data while also solving the problem of application data that is not written to the user profile.

Design and Architecture

This section describes the components used in a virtual desktop infrastructure design based on pure Microsoft technologies. It's probably better to take a few more minutes to think about your environment and the deployment before you insert the DVD (or ISO image) and start with the installation.

WINDOWS SERVER EDITION

For a dedicated VDI host environment, Microsoft Hyper-V Server 2012 is a good virtualization platform and available without additional cost. For a mixed-host environment that also includes virtualized server workloads, Windows Server 2012 would be the better choice because of the virtual guest rights. Depending on the environment, the RDS components could be placed on a separate virtualization host/cluster. Additional information can be found in Chapter 2, "Deploying Hyper-V Hosts."

Be aware that the client virtual desktops are not covered by the Windows Server Datacenter edition use rights. Also make sure which client access licenses (CALs) and VDA licenses are required to access the virtual desktops.

RDS ROLES

RDS allows remote users to gain access to their corporate desktops or applications running either as sessions on a Remote Desktop Session Host (RD Session Host) server, or virtual machines on a Remote Desktop Virtualization Host (RD Virtualization Host) server, by using a remoting protocol from various end-point devices.

This section describes the role services required to deploy a virtual desktop environment. The implementation aspects of each feature—with detailed information about data formats and how data flows into and out of each component—are also discussed where applicable.

The architecture of the following RDS role services and features are discussed:

◆ RD Management Service (RDMS)

◆ RD Connection Broker (RDCB)

◆ RD Web Access (RDWA)

◆ RD Virtualization Host (RDVH)

◆ RD Gateway (RDGW)

◆ RD Licensing

RD Management Service

Windows Server 2012 introduces the RD Management Service and user interface (UI) designed to not only simplify remote desktop administrative tasks but also to provide a centralized management solution for all RDS role services and scenarios. Instead of using separate administrative tools for each role service installed, as in the previous version of Windows, RD Management Service provides a single user interface that displays an overview of all the servers in an RDS deployment as well as providing a management interface for every server in the deployment.

When creating an RDS deployment in Windows Server 2012, an administrator will run the RDS-based deployment wizard from Server Manager. During the process of creating a deployment, a server must be chosen to host the RD Connection Broker role service. This server becomes the RD Management Server for the deployment. A single RD Management Service server can manage multiple collection types.

RD Connection Broker

The RD Connection Broker is used to provide desktop connections to users. It supports load balancing and reconnecting to existing sessions on virtual desktops. The RD Connection Broker functions as the centralized management solution for Windows Server 2012 remote desktop deployments. Virtual machine–based desktop deployments are managed by the RD Management Service user interface. As detailed in the RDMS section, every remote desktop deployment in Windows Server 2012 will have at least one RD Connection Broker server that functions as the RD Management Server. Prior to Windows Server 2012, Connection Broker was not a required component of an RDS deployment.

The process for deploying a highly available RD Connection Broker has changed significantly in Windows Server 2012. A wizard has been added to the RD Management Service that will guide an administrator through the process of creating an active/active RD Connection Broker deployment. With an active/active RD Connection Broker configured for high availability, the RDS deployment will continue to function normally. Administrators can still manage collections even if one of the Connection Broker nodes stops functioning. A Microsoft SQL Server would be required for this scenario.

NOTE   When working with Windows PowerShell, the RD Connection Broker with the RD Management Service is always required to perform an operation.

RD Web Access

RD Web Access enables users to access RemoteApp and Desktop Connection through the Start screen on a computer that is running Windows 8 or through a web browser. If a user connects to a virtual desktop, a remote desktop connection is made to a virtual machine that is running on an RD Virtualization Host server. To configure which virtual desktops will be available through RemoteApp and Desktop Connection, an administrator must install the RD Connection Broker role service on a computer that is running Windows Server 2012, and then use the RD Management Service, the Server Manager plug-in, to configure a virtual machine–based desktop collection.

RD Web Access does not run as a service on Windows Server 2012 and instead depends on Internet Information Services (IIS) to host the web page. When RD Web Access is installed, IIS is installed as a required component and the RD Web Access site is installed and configured automatically.

NOTE   RD Web Access provides customization options for the RD Web Access interface, including the ability to control default RD Gateway server settings and redirection settings. These settings are controlled by editing the web.config file located in %SYSTEMROOT%\Web\RDWeb\Pages.

RD Virtualization Host

RD Virtualization Host is the role that interacts with Hyper-V to provide virtual machines that can be used for personal or pooled virtual desktop pools.

An administrator can make personal virtual desktops or virtual desktop pools available to users by using either RemoteApp and Desktop Connection or RD Web Access. These virtual desktops are virtual machines hosted on a machine that is running Windows Server 2012 with Hyper-V and RD Virtualization Host installed.

RD Gateway

RD Gateway is used to allow access to a remote desktop environment from the Internet by managed and unmanaged client machines. The server chosen for the RD Gateway role service should have a network interface on the public network and is often deployed on an edge network in a demilitarized zone (DMZ). Gateway and Web Access role services could also be deployed on the same server.

The RD Gateway role service is not a requirement for an RDS deployment; it's an optional feature.

RD Licensing

Saving the best for last, RD Licensing is required to manage the RDS CALs that are required for each device or user to connect to an RD Session Host server.

RDS can be installed and evaluated for a 120-day grace period without the need for a RD license server. After the grace period expires, however, a RD license server must be installed and activated before users will be allowed to connect to an RDS deployment of either the session-based desktop or virtual machine–based desktop types.

NOTE Small deployments can host both the RD Session Host and the RD Licensing role service on the same machine. For larger deployments, it is recommended that the RD Licensing role service be installed on a separate computer from the RD Session Host role service.

RemoteFX

An important requirement for a successful virtual desktop infrastructure is a positive user experience and user acceptance. However, one big difference users will notice very quickly is that graphics are displayed differently when compared to the way they are displayed on a full desktop computer, for example, when a user uses Bing or Google Maps, or wants to watch movies, or needs to run any other graphic-intense application. This, of course, could negatively affect the user experience. The challenge for administrators is to be able to deliver a local-like user experience to a wide variety of end-point devices over varying network conditions.

In Windows Server 2008 R2 SP1, Microsoft introduced RemoteFX, which enables the delivery of a full Windows user experience to a range of remote client devices including rich clients, thin clients, and ultrathin clients. RemoteFX delivers a rich user experience for VDI by providing a 3D virtual adapter, intelligent codecs, and the ability to redirect USB devices in virtual machines.

Windows Server 2012 builds on this platform to enable a far richer and easier experience on all types of networks and all types of devices:

◆ RemoteFX for WAN to maintain a consistent user experience over highly variable connections

◆ RemoteFX Adaptive Graphics to provide a full Windows Aero and 3D user experience over WANs

◆ RemoteFX USB redirection to support the RD Session Host role service and allow all standard USB devices to appear only within each user's individual remote session

◆ RemoteFX Media Remoting to provide a smooth multimedia experience over variable or unreliable networks

◆ RemoteFX Multitouch, which allows users to use touch-enabled and gesture-enabled applications in remote desktop environments

◆ RemoteFX vGPU, which enables virtual machines to utilize a GPU in the host server to deliver a more robust experience and enable use of 3D or video-intensive applications in a remote session

Server and Client Requirements

Before deploying RDS virtual machine–based desktops with RemoteFX, verify that the server hardware that will host these virtual machines meets the minimum system requirements.

To determine whether the server hardware meets the minimum system requirements, do the following:

1. Open a command prompt or Windows PowerShell.

2. Run `msinfo32.exe`.

3. Go to the System Summary page.

4. Verify that the hardware reported is supporting the following:

   ◆ Second Level Address Translation extensions

   ◆ Virtualization

When implementing RemoteFX, consider the following:

◆ Ensure that the Hyper-Threading technology is enabled in the BIOS of the RD Virtualization Host.

◆ Configure the proper amount of memory:

   ◆ x86-based machines must have at least 1 GB of RAM.

   ◆ x64-based machines must have at least 2 GB of RAM.

◆ The RemoteFX server and the RemoteFX-enabled virtual desktop must meet the RemoteFX hardware requirements. As the requirements have not changed since Windows Server 2008 R2 SP1, see this link for additional information:

   `http://go.microsoft.com/fwlink/?LinkId=191918`

How to now bring this all together? Figure 13.1 shows how the previously explained roles are linked and work together.

NOTE   Microsoft has released a hotfix, KB 2770440, that addresses a problem with poor graphics performance in the virtual machines when using AMD processors. Always make sure to check if there are other updates required for Hyper-V or RemoteFX to support new hardware components. `http://support.microsoft.com/kb/2770440/en-us`

FIGURE 13.1
VDI overview

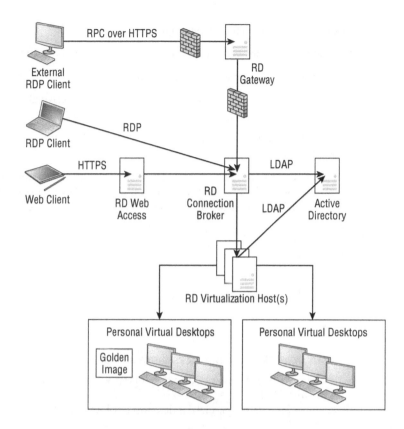

Building a Microsoft VDI Environment

Deploying RD Virtualization Host servers along with Connection Broker and Web Access role services to allow users to access a virtualized desktop is also known as a virtual machine–based desktop deployment.

The administrator has to choose the virtual machine–based deployment option in Server Manager as the installation mode for RDS.

Installing Remote Desktop Services

Installation of all RDS roles and scenarios are performed by using Server Manager. The new interface included with Windows Server 2012 provides both local and remote server management and uses a series of plug-ins to manage specific server functions, role services, and deployment types.

PREPARE SERVER MANAGER

Choose one machine to run the console and perform the installation of the required components. But before Server Manager can remotely manage and install the needed role services, each server that will be part of the RDS deployment has to first be added to the server pool in Server Manager. There is no import/export functionality, so this all needs to be done manually.

To add a server to the Server Manager, do the following:

1. Open Server Manager and click All Servers in the navigation pane.

2. From the menu, choose Manage ➢ Add Servers.

3. Add each server to the list either by searching in Active Directory, looking up the name in DNS, or importing a file with the server names.

4. Add the machines that have been found by clicking the arrow button and then click OK to proceed.

Server Manager will query each machine that was added to the pool and provide the IP Address, Manageability Status, and Activation Status. Before proceeding to RDS installation, make sure each server is listed as Online by Server Manager (see Figure 13.2).

FIGURE 13.2
Server Manager's
All Servers view

RUN THE REMOTE DESKTOP SERVICES INSTALLATION

Now that servers have been added to the Server Manager server pool, the system is ready to execute the installation.

To start the installation of virtual desktop deployment, do the following:

1. In Server Manager, click All Servers in the navigation pane, as shown in Figure 13.2.

FIGURE 13.3
Server Manager
RDS Servers

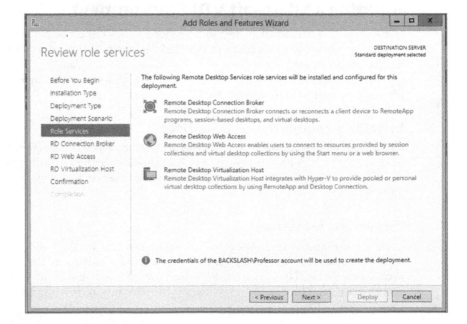

2. Click Manage in the menu bar of Server Manager and then select Add Roles And Features.

3. On the Before You Begin page, verify the information and then click Next.

4. Select Remote Desktop Services Installation as the installation type and then click Next.

5. On the Deployment Type screen, select Standard Deployment and then click Next.

6. On the Deployment Scenario screen, select virtual machine–based desktop deployment and then click Next.

7. Server Manager displays a summary of the role services that are associated with the selected workload that must be installed. For a virtual machine–based desktop deployment, the required server roles are RD Connection Broker, RD Web Access Server, and at least one RD Virtualization Host server, as shown in Figure 13.3.

8. On the RD Connection Broker screen, select the server on which to install the RD Connection Broker role and then click Next.

9. On the RD Web Access screen, select the server on which to install the RD Web Access role and then click Next.

10. Finally, select the machine on which to install the RD Virtualization Host role and then click Next. This server must meet the minimum hardware requirements for Hyper-V, and a compatibility check will be run on this server to make sure it will support the installation of Hyper-V and the RD Virtualization Host role services.

11. Server Manager displays a summary of the selections made by using the wizard. To install the role services to each machine and create the deployment, click Deploy. The next screen will show you an overview of the installation status of each role, as shown in Figure 13.4.

FIGURE 13.4
Server Manager
RDS installation

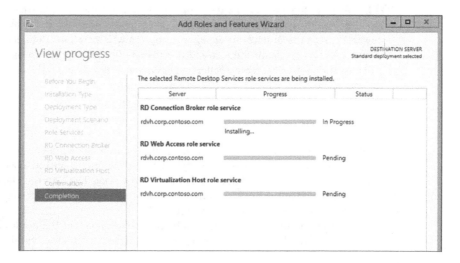

12. After the deployment has finished installation, click the close button in the Server Manager.

Server Manager will display the status of the role service installation on each machine in the deployment, and if selected, reboot each machine if the role installation requires a reboot. When installing Hyper-V role services, the server will need to be restarted. In this case, the option Restart The Destination Server Automatically If Required needs to be selected before the Deploy button becomes active.

Server Manager will reboot each machine if the role installation requires a reboot. When installing Hyper-V role services, the server will need to be restarted. In this case, the option Restart The Destination Server Automatically If Required needs to be selected before the Deploy button becomes active.

The progress bar for each server installation displays a status indicator that shows the current state of installation for each server. The following list describes each status indicator:

Installing The role service is currently being installed.

In Progress The server installation and configuration is in progress.

Pending The role service is pending the completion of the role service that is currently in the installing state.

Configuration Pending The installation has completed, but configuration is pending a reboot.

Restarting The server is currently restarting after a role service was installed.

Configuring The role service is installed and is being configured.

Succeeded The scenario-based deployment has finished installing and configuring all role services on the machine.

Failed The installation or configuration of the server failed. The reason is displayed in the status window.

NOTE A Quick Start deployment can be used when all role services are deployed on a single machine and the goal is to create a virtual machine–based desktop deployment as quickly as possible. Using the Quick Start deployment option will install RD Connection Broker and RD Web Access on a single machine. In addition to installing all required role services, Quick Start will also automatically create a collection of virtual desktops and publish the collection to the RD Web page.

VERIFY THE INSTALLATION

To verify installation of the required role services, either close and reopen Server Manager or refresh the view by using the refresh arrows. Server Manager will discover the newly installed role services on each server that is part of the server pool. The Remote Desktop node should now become active at the bottom in the Server Manager navigation. It displays an overview page for the RDS deployment, as shown in Figure 13.5.

The Deployment Overview shows each server that is part of the deployment. These servers are also listed in the Deployment Servers view, which displays the installed role services.

FIGURE 13.5

Server Manager
RDS overview

PERFORM FURTHER CONFIGURATION

Even though the RDS roles are installed and running, a few more steps are required before the first virtual machine can be deployed. Creating and managing a VDI deployment is accomplished by using a series of steps:

1. Configuring global settings

2. Deploying certificates

3. Configuring the OU that the virtual machines will be deployed to

4. Building a template virtual machine (golden image)

5. Creating a collection

6. Configuring collection properties and settings

7. Managing user connections

Settings that apply to every RDS server in a deployment, such as licensing settings, are configured using the Deployment Properties user interface in RD Management Service. From this interface, an administrator can configure settings for RD Gateway, RD Licensing, digital certificates, and Active Directory.

NOTE   As explained earlier, this part of the book is very basic, because its main focus is Hyper-V. Consider a book focusing on Remote Desktop Services to fill the gap. TechNet is a great resource covering more of the details on RDS.

Installing RD Virtualization Hosts

Earlier in this chapter, the standard deployment of an RDS installation was described. A remote desktop role can also be installed separately on each server. This might be done for existing Hyper-V hosts.

To install the RD Virtualization Host by using the role-based installation method, do the following:

1. In Server Manager, click Local Servers in the navigation pane.

2. From the Server Manager menu, choose Manage ➤ Add Roles And Features.

3. On the Before You Begin page, verify the information and then click Next.

4. Select Role-Based or Feature-Based Installation as the installation type and then click Next.

5. On the Server Selection page, verify the Destination Server and then click Next.

6. Select the Remote Desktop Services check box and then click Next.

7. Bypass the Features page by clicking Next, and then click Next again on the Remote Desktop Services page.

8. Select the Remote Desktop Virtualization Host check box and then click Next.

9. On the Confirmation page, select Restart The Destination Server Automatically If Required and then click Install.

NOTE   After the server restarts, you must log on with the same user account that started the installation to allow Server Manager to finish the installation.

Using CSV Block Cache

CSV v2 provides a new feature called CSV Block Cache. CSV Block Cache is a second-layer cache used to hold blocks to limit the number of read I/O. Hyper-V I/O leverages unbuffered I/O that is not cached by the Windows Cache Manager, resulting in no caching of I/O by Windows. This is addressed by the new CSV Block Cache in Windows Server 2012 providing a read-only cache.

It's primarily VDI scenarios that will profit from CSV block caching. Think about the I/Os created during VM boot storms, VHD provisioning, and differencing VHDs. CSV Block Cache will deliver the most value in scenarios where VMs are used primarily for read requests and are less write intensive—scenarios such as pooled VDI VMs.

Twenty percent of the total physical memory of a Hyper-V host can be allocated for a CSV write-through cache, which will be consumed from nonpaged pool memory. 512 MB is expected as the recommend default value if enabled. Two configuration settings are available for CSV Block Cache:

CsvEnableBlockCache This disk property enables caching to the CSV volumes. This setting is enabled via Windows PowerShell by using the following cmdlet:

```
Get-ClusterResource <cluster disk name> | Set-ClusterParameter `
CsvEnableBlockCache 1
```

SharedVolumeBlockCacheSizeInMB This cluster property can be used to set the size of the cache. This property is cluster wide and can be adjusted without downtime. This setting is enabled via the following PowerShell cmdlet:

```
(Get-Cluster).SharedVolumeBlockCacheSizeInMB = 512
```

A value of 0 indicates that the feature is disabled or will be disabled. This can be used for `CsvEnableBlockCache` as well as for `SharedVolumeBlockCacheSizeInMB`.

USING SMART PAGING

Windows Server 2012 also introduces a feature called Smart Paging for robust restarting of VMs. Although minimum memory increases VM consolidation numbers, it also brings a challenge. If a VM has a smaller amount of memory than its startup memory and it is restarted, Hyper-V needs additional memory to restart the VM. Because of host memory pressure, Hyper-V might not always have additional memory available. This can cause sporadic VM restart failures, which could (should) be avoided by always having enough physical memory available—which is expensive—or leveraging Smart Paging in Windows Server 2012. Smart Paging is used to bridge the memory gap between minimum memory and startup memory and let VMs restart more reliably.

This memory management method uses disk resources as additional, temporary memory when more memory is required to restart a VM. This approach has advantages and drawbacks. It provides a reliable way to keep the VM running when there is no available physical memory. However, it can degrade VM performance because disk access speeds are much slower than memory access speeds. Smart Paging can lead to lower costs, especially in environments that have many idle or low-load virtual machines, such as pooled VDI environments.

INSTALLING REMOTEFX

RemoteFX is installed by default when the RD Virtualization Host role service is installed. The GPU will now be listed in the Hyper-V Settings under Physical GPUs—of course, only if a compatible GPU is available. If multiple GPUs are installed in that host, the administrator can enable or disable the GPU for use with RemoteFX by using the GPU drop-down list and check box (see Figure 13.6).

FIGURE 13.6
RemoteFX GPU

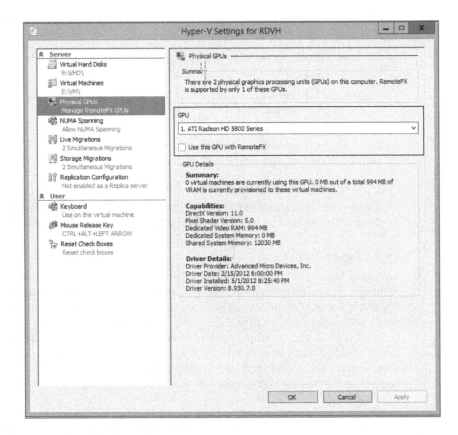

Deploying Virtual Guests

When building a new VDI environment, Hyper-V and RDS are basically used only to provide a client VM to the service consumer—for example, a user from the business. This section describes how such an initial guest template could be built for a VDI collection.

BUILDING A TEMPLATE VIRTUAL MACHINE

Before creating a collection of virtual machines, a single template virtual machine (golden image) must be created on the RD Virtualization Host server. This template virtual machine will then be cloned to create additional virtual machines for a pooled collection.

To create a template virtual machine, do the following:

1. In Server Manager, click Tools ➤ Hyper-V Manager. Verify that the desired host is added to the console.

2. Create a virtual machine and install Windows 7 SP1 or 8 by using the preferred staging method.

   A. Add the virtual machine to the domain.

> **B.** Install all applications required by the users.
>
> **C.** Configure the virtual machine with any additional required settings before running SYSPREP.

3. If the RD Virtualization Host has been configured for RemoteFX, and the virtual machine is to be used for graphic-intense scenarios, add the RemoteFX 3D Adapter to the virtual machine.

4. Run the following command to generalize the virtual machine and prepare it for duplication:

```
sysprep.exe /generalize /oobe /shutdown /mode:vm
```

As soon as the SYSPREP process has been completed, the virtual machine will be shut down. The template virtual machine is now ready to be used as the golden image.

You probably noticed the /mode:vm option for sysprep.exe and wonder what this is used for. This could be used for VMs where the hardware remains the same for the deployment. After the VM restarts, the VM can boot to OOBE, but this means the hypervisor needs to have the same hardware profile to avoid unexpected issues.

Please note: This VM mode is new for Windows 8, and running this mode outside a VM is not supported.

NOTE RD Management Service will check the status of the template virtual machine to make sure it has been generalized using Sysprep.exe and it is shut down.

CREATING A COLLECTION

Virtual desktop collections are created and managed differently by RD Management Service based on the collection type. Table 13.2 shows the capabilities available with each collection type.

TABLE 13.2: Collection types

	PERSONAL VIRTUAL DESKTOP COLLECTION		POOLED VIRTUAL DESKTOP COLLECTION	
	Managed	*Unmanaged*	*Managed*	*Unmanaged*
New virtual machine creation based on template	✔	✔		
Re-create virtual machines based on template	✔			

TABLE 13.2: Collection types *(continued)*

	PERSONAL VIRTUAL DESKTOP COLLECTION		POOLED VIRTUAL DESKTOP COLLECTION	
	Managed	*Unmanaged*	*Managed*	*Unmanaged*
Store user settings on a user profile disk	✔		✔	
Permanent user assignment to the virtual desktop		✔		✔
Administrative access on the virtual desktop		✔		✔

To create a pooled virtual desktop collection, do the following:

1. In Server Manager, click Remote Desktop Services in the navigation pane.

2. Click Collections. In the Collections tile, click Tasks ➤ Create A Virtual Desktop Collection.

3. On the Before You Begin page, verify the information and then click Next.

4. Specify the Name and an optional description for the collection and then click Next.

5. Specify the Collection Type by selecting Pooled Virtual Desktop Collection, as shown in Figure 13.7. Select the Automatically Create And Manage Virtual Desktops check box to create a collection that is managed by RD Management Service.

6. On the Specify The Virtual Desktop Template page, select the template virtual machine to be used for the collection and then click Next.

7. On the Specify The Virtual Desktop Settings page, select the option Provide Unattended Installation Settings to have the wizard generate an answer file for the virtual machine, or select Use An Existing Sysprep Answer File if you wish to use an answer file that has been created manually. The recommended setting is the default setting to have the wizard create an answer file. Click Next.

8. Specify the unattended settings that will be used to configure each virtual machine on its initial startup and then click Next.

9. Specify the users and collection size. The number of users should be greater than or equal to the expected number of simultaneous users. By default, Domain Users of the selected domain will be given access to this collection, but additional groups can be added or removed on this page. Specify the prefix name for each virtual machine and then click Next.

10. Select the RD Virtualization Host servers that the virtual machines will be deployed to and then click Next.

11. Select the storage used for the virtual machines. Specify a local storage path, SMB share storage location, or Cluster Shared Volume. Click Next.

12. To configure user profile disks for the deployment, select the Enable User Profile Disks check box. Specify the path to the user disks in the location box, and optionally adjust the maximum size.

13. Confirm all of the previously selected settings and then click Create to create the deployment.

FIGURE 13.7
Create Collection
Wizard

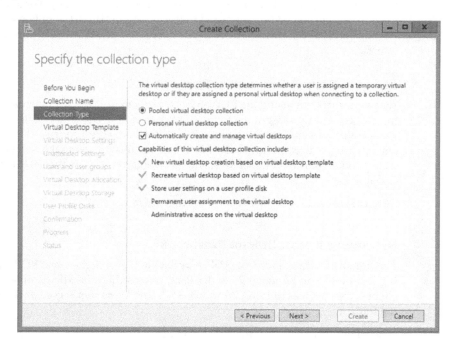

After the reference virtual machine template has been exported, RD Management Service will create the collection in the RD Management Service UI. To access the status of the collection creation, right-click the collection and select Details.

NOTE   Ensure that selected RD Virtualization Hosts have Full Control permissions on the selected share and that the logged-on user currently running the wizard has administrative privileges on the server hosting the share.

Connecting to the VDI Environment

After a collection has been created and virtual desktops have been added to this collection, users will be able to connect to the virtual desktops by logging on to the RDWeb page or by subscribing to the RemoteApp and Desktop Connections feed.

ACCESSING THE **RDWEB** PAGE

The RDWeb portal is used to allow connections to virtual machine–based desktop deployments. It can be accessed using the following URL:

```
https://<fqdn of RDWEB Server>/RDWeb
```

After installation of the RD Web Access role service, the website will be configured to use an automatically generated self-signed certificate. This certificate is used for SSL connections to the website and can also be used to sign virtual machine–based desktop collections.

Because client machines do not trust a self-signed certificate by default, the certificate would have to be imported into the trusted root certificate's store of the client machines that are accessing the website without needing to bypass the certificate warning. For a production deployment, the RDWeb site should be configured to use a domain trusted or public trusted certificate. To configure the certificate used by RD Web Access, use the RDMS Certificate Management user interface.

USING THE DESKTOP CONNECTIONS FEED

As an alternative to using the RDWeb page, users may also access virtual machine–based desktop workspaces by subscribing to the RDWeb feed. The Desktop Connections feed contains the same collections that are available in RDWeb and are accessed from the Start menu of the client machine. A user can manually connect to the feed by using the RemoteApp and Desktop Connections user interface, or an administrator can configure the default connection URL with Group Policy:

```
https://<fqdn of rdweb server>/Rdweb/feed
```

UPDATING TO REMOTE DESKTOP PROTOCOL 8

The Remote Desktop Protocol (RDP) 8 update will enable the latest RDP enhancements (including RemoteFX) on Windows 7 Service Pack 1. According the Microsoft Support KB 2592687, the client access devices running Windows 7 SP1 and Windows Server 2008 R2 SP1 will benefit from the following:

◆ Remote Desktop Connection 8 client

◆ Dynamic in-session USB redirection

◆ Reconnect for RemoteApp and Desktop Connections

◆ Improved single sign-on experience for RD Web Access

◆ Support for RemoteFX media redirection APIs for VoIP applications

◆ Support for nested sessions

For remote computers running Windows 7 SP1, the update adds the following capabilities:

◆ RemoteFX for WAN

◆ RemoteFX network auto-detect

- ◆ RemoteFX adaptive graphics

- ◆ RemoteFX USB redirection for non-RemoteFX vGPU virtual desktops

- ◆ Support for nested sessions

- ◆ Performance counters for monitoring the user experience

You can find installation and downloading instructions at Microsoft Support KB 2592687:

`http://support.microsoft.com/kb/2592687/en-us`

NOTE RDP 8 cannot be enabled for remote computers that are running Windows Server 2008 R2 SP1. In addition, this update will not be made available to Windows XP. The latest version for Windows XP is the Remote Desktop Connection 7 update.

What about non-Windows? At the time writing this chapter Microsoft hasn't released nor disclosed anything about providing an updated RDP client for non-Windows products. Therefore a third-party application would be required. An interesting choice would be iTAP. Why? iTAP supports NLA (Network Level Authentication), RD Gateway, RemoteFX, and much more that is required for this scenario.

`http://itap-mobile.com/`

Real World Solutions

In this chapter you found some tips and tricks for challenges you might encounter when installing a new Windows Server 2012 Virtual Desktop Environment using Remote Desktop Services.

CHALLENGE

Even though Windows 7 and 8 are more common and great operating systems, there are still customers using Windows XP as a client operating system. What would that mean to the solution?

SOLUTION

Of course the situation is not optimal as Windows XP SP3 is already in extended support, which ends at April 8, 2014. In this case always make sure you install the latest Remote Desktop Connection Client, at this time 7.0 for XP. Also configure the Credential Security Support Provider (CredSSP) as documented in KB 951608:

`http://support.microsoft.com/kb/951608/en-us`

If the clients are not joined to the domain, or connecting from the Internet you might have to disable the Network Level Authentication (NLA) on the Remote Desktop Virtualization Hosts - on your Hyper-V Hosts.

Another interesting solution would be the Windows Thin PC, which is available to customer with Software Assurance (from their Enterprise Agreement). These customers can download this from the Microsoft Volume Licensing site. What you have to be aware of is that there is no update for Windows 8 available at the time writing this book. But you can install the latest RDP 8 client to the Thin PC.

CHALLENGE

In a Remote Desktop environment the different parameter for time or disconnection limits is a critical configuration aspect for every Virtual Desktop Infrastructure. But where can you find them in Windows Server 2012?

SOLUTION

As the MMC we know from Windows Server 2008 R2 no longer exists, the different limit must be configured through policies. Best of course is to have one central group policy for configuring the Remote Desktop Virtualization Hosts.

The required configuration for Remote Desktop Services can be found under the following path: `Computer Configuration\Administrative Templates\Windows Components\Remote Desktop Services\Remote Desktop Session Host\Session Time Limits`

When you consider using RemoteFX, keep in mind that some environments do require additional configuration. These policies can be found under: `Computer Configuration\Administrative Templates\Windows Components\Remote Desktop Services\Remote Desktop Session Host\Remote Session Environment`

CHALLENGE

Where is the information stored when you use a standalone Remote Desktop Connection Broker? And what happens when you install Highly Available Connection Broker later on?

SOLUTION

During the installation of the Remote Desktop Connection Broker, the Windows Internal Database is used. This stores its database at the following path `C:\Windows\rdcbdb`. By using the SQL Server Management Studio (even the Express Edition) you can open this database and check the configuration. Simple connect to "`\\.\pipe\Microsoft##WID\tsql\query`" using Windows Authentication.

The Microsoft SQL Server Management Studio Express Edition can be downloaded from the Microsoft Download Center:

`www.microsoft.com/en-gb/download/details.aspx?id=22985`

Index

Note to the Reader: Throughout this index **boldfaced** page numbers indicate primary discussions of a topic. *Italicized* page numbers indicate illustrations.